BIOGRAPHICAL MEMOIRS
OF FELLOWS
OF THE ROYAL SOCIETY

VOLUME 62

BIOGRAPHICAL MEMOIRS
OF FELLOWS
OF THE ROYAL SOCIETY

2016
VOLUME 62

Published by the Royal Society
6–9 Carlton House Terrace
London SW1Y 5AG

Published December 2016

Editor: Professor Malcolm Longair

Commissioning editor: Helen Eaton
Production editor: Kelly Mulroue
Fellowship records and archives: Keith Moore
Picture curator: Katherine Marshall
Typeset by Perfect Page, London, and by
Nova Techset Private Limited, Bengaluru and Chennai, India
Printed by Henry Ling Limited, The Dorset Press, Dorchester

The Royal Society makes all reasonable efforts to obtain necessary permissions for the use of images that are copyright material. If you are the copyright owner of any images reproduced within any volume of *Biographical Memoirs* (or its forerunner, *Obituary Notices*) and are uncertain as to whether we hold your up-to-date contact information, please contact The Librarian, Library and Information Services of the Royal Society (email: library@royalsociety.org).

ISBN: 978-1-78252-219-5
ISSN: 0080-4606

CONTENTS

EDITORIAL

By Malcolm Longair* CBE FRS FRSE

Welcome to volume 62 of *Biographical Memoirs of Fellows of the Royal Society*, the 2016 edition. It is a particular honour to take over as Editor-in-Chief of *Biographical Memoirs* since I have long valued the excellent biographies written by our colleagues to celebrate the lives of Fellows of the Society. I have had the experience of writing three memoirs and so fully appreciate the effort needed to create a lasting memorial to those commemorated.

My enthusiasm for *Biographical Memoirs* has been greatly enhanced over the past few years while I was writing my recent book, *Maxwell's enduring legacy: a scientific history of the Cavendish Laboratory*. I used *Biographical Memoirs* every day as a splendid resource for understanding the achievements and personalities of so many distinguished scientists. There are several features of the essays that make them especially valuable. Most important is the fact that they are written by scientists for scientists and so they concentrate strongly and authoritatively upon the content of the science and the scientific achievement. Furthermore, the recommended length of about 20 printed pages is sufficient to gain a good appreciation of the key contributions of those commemorated. There are references to comprehensive bibliographies for those who wish to delve more deeply. As one of my colleagues put it to me, *Biographical Memoirs* preserves the DNA of the Royal Society. In my dealings with other Fellows of the Society, they all comment upon the fact that *Biographical Memoirs* is particularly enjoyed and appreciated by them. The challenge is to continue and enhance what is already a most valuable and inspiring publication.

My first pleasant duty is to pay fulsome tribute to Trevor Stuart, my predecessor as Editor-in-Chief, for his outstanding editorship over the past few years. The publication has flourished under his editorship, and his advice and help to me, as I have begun to get on top of the job, have been most valuable. Much of the initiative for commissioning the essays in this volume is thanks to Trevor.

One of the first issues that the editorial team and I have tackled has been the size and composition of the Editorial Board: Trevor and I agreed that there would be significant advantages in considerably expanding its membership. The two main reasons were the need to obtain expert advice across the enormous range of disciplines in which Fellows have been engaged and to relieve the amount of work which the (previous) nine members of the Board had to deal with. We are delighted that we received a very positive response to our invitations to join the Editorial Board, with the result that it now comprises the 27 members listed on page iv. We are most grateful to all these colleagues for offering their services in tasks that primarily involve suggesting authors for memoirs and refereeing the draft memoirs.

* msl1000@cam.ac.uk

http://dx.doi.org/10.1098/rsbm.2016.0023

The second major task has been catching up with the backlog of memoirs that have yet to be commissioned for deceased Fellows. Our aim is to be as comprehensive as possible and we have embarked upon a campaign to commission memoirs, some of which extend back to Fellows who died in the early 2000s. The Editorial Board has been very supportive of this initiative and we are making progress. We are very appreciative of the suggestions that we receive for potential authors from the families, the Fellowship and other colleagues. Although writing a memoir is a significant task and not to be taken on lightly, in my experience many authors regard it as a duty to honour a deceased Fellow, who will often have been a colleague, supervisor or close friend. We urge any interested readers not to be over-modest in proposing their own names as authors—the committed author is always a joy to work with.

Over the next year or so, we will be developing ideas about how we can enhance the value of the memoirs. Every effort is made to ensure that the science is accessible to the general reader, and behind each of them is a human story revealing the huge diversity of backgrounds, education, family circumstances and so on that fostered the subsequent achievement. These should be more widely known as providing a true picture of the research scientist and the way in which new understandings come about. We will greatly value all thoughts about how this aim can be achieved.

Memoirs are published on the *Biographical Memoirs* website as they are ready, before collection into the annual printed volume, so please look out for new essays throughout the year.

BIOGRAPHICAL MEMOIRS 2016

There are 27 memoirs in the 2016 print edition of *Biographical Memoirs*, spanning a huge range of the sciences. The following notes are intended to act as a guide to the different disciplines represented, with a brief summary of the achievement, largely taken from the memoirs' synopses. These memoirs, and those in previous volumes, can be accessed on the Royal Society's website (http://rsbm.royalsocietypublishing.org).

Mathematics

John McLeod was a brilliant solver of problems in mathematical analysis, primarily differential equations. He was noted for his contributions to applied analysis, particularly to the theory of partial differential equations with applications to practical problems. He was internationally recognized as the leading British authority on the practical applications of functional analysis, including the analysis of nonlinear equations arising in applications to mechanics, physics and biology.

Physics

Richard Dalitz was a theoretical physicist whose principal contributions were intimately connected to some of the major breakthroughs of twentieth-century particle and nuclear physics. His formulation of the 'τ–θ' puzzle led to the discovery that parity is not a symmetry of nature—the first of the assumed space-time symmetries to fail. The 'Dalitz plot' and 'Dalitz pairs' are now part of the vocabulary of particle physics.

Leslie Morley's research focused on modelling structural behaviour, with particular emphasis on plates and shells. He developed the Morley shell equation, which has been acknowledged as the simplest equation consistent with first-order shell theory. As the finite element method rose to prominence he developed elements for both plates and shells in both the linear and nonlinear regimes.

Ronald Newman was one of the most versatile semiconductor physicists of his generation and is distinguished for his work in several different areas, most notably epitaxial growth and the behaviour of impurities and dopants in a range of device-related materials, mainly silicon and gallium arsenide. His most significant contributions came from the application of local vibrational-mode spectroscopy to studies of the segregation and diffusion of oxygen and hydrogen in silicon.

Astronomy and meteorology

Sir Bernard Lovell was one of the pioneers of radio astronomy in the UK. Building on his wartime experience in radar, he created the Jodrell Bank Radio Observatory of the University of Manchester. His major achievement was the construction of the 250 ft (Lovell) radio telescope, which was the largest single-dish telescope in the world at the time and which pioneered many aspects of radio astronomy.

Sir John Mason will be remembered for establishing cloud microphysics as a coherent discipline and for building the Meteorological Office into an international centre of excellence on the international stage. His research was notable for carrying out laboratory experiments of direct relevance to the nucleation of ice crystals and the electrification of clouds.

Metallurgy and materials science

Brian Eyre was an outstanding metallurgist who played a leading role in the development of nuclear engineering materials. His experiments on irradiated metals enabled a theoretical understanding of the mechanisms of radiation damage, and in particular the formation of voids and void swelling in structural steels. He was instrumental in transforming the UK Atomic Energy Authority from an organization whose mission was to develop nuclear power generating systems into the privatized AEA Technology.

George Gray was a renowned materials chemist, internationally distinguished for his research into liquid crystals and their applications in flat-panel displays. His seminal invention of the liquid-crystalline cyanobiphenyls underpinned the creation of the modern electronic displays industry, which began with digital watches and has continued through to smart and three-dimensional televisions.

Raymond Smallman was one of Britain's leading physical metallurgists. Based at the University of Birmingham, he made important contributions, often using electron microscopy, to the understanding of crystal defects and deformation behaviour in metals, alloys, intermetallic compounds and ceramics.

Engineering

Sir John Horlock was one of the outstanding engineers of his generation. His expertise was in the thermodynamics and fluid mechanics of turbines and compressors, as used for jet engines and for power generation. In Cambridge he founded the Whittle Laboratory, which became one of the world's leading centres for turbomachinery research.

Kenneth Johnson was renowned for the insightful analysis of meticulous experiments in contact mechanics. His major publications included topics in fraction and wear, rheology and lubrication, rolling contact and adhesion. Important applications included the prediction of corrugations and cracks in railway lines. He was gratified that his ideas in adhesion were used by others to explain the climbing behaviours of insects and other small animals with soft feet.

Chemistry

Alan Carrington was an outstanding physical chemist who made important contributions to molecular spectroscopy. He pioneered the fields of electron paramagnetic resonance spectroscopy of doped single crystals, solutions of organic radicals, and especially the high-resolution spectroscopy of gaseous free radicals and ions.

Michael Lappert was one of the giants of twentieth-century organometallic chemistry. His research, carried out over six decades, had a profound and influential effect on the field, and his contributions covered almost every block of the Periodic Table. He had a lifelong interest in amides, including those of carbon, and especially electron-rich olefins, which remarkably were the ready source of numerous transition-metal carbene complexes.

Lord Jack Lewis helped to pioneer the development of modern inorganic chemistry. He was one of the small group of scientists who led the expansion of inorganic chemistry from its renaissance through the syntheses and study of new transition-metal and organometallic complexes. Their characterization was accomplished through the perceptive application of the newly available physical techniques of spectroscopy, magnetism, mass spectrometry and X-ray diffraction. He was created a life peer in 1989.

Benton Rabinovitch was one of the pioneers of chemical dynamics. His brilliant experiments performed during his four decades at the University of Washington in Seattle provided most of our early quantitative measurements of the efficiency with which energy is transferred between molecules in gas-phase molecule–molecule collisions and in collisions of molecules with solid surfaces.

Biochemistry

Sir John Cornforth was a pioneer in the detailed chemistry used by living systems to construct the organic substances that they contain. From his teenage years he was handicapped by profound deafness, yet he overcame this to reach the highest pinnacles of scientific achievement, including the 1975 Nobel Prize in Chemistry.

Ephraim Katchalski-Katzir was a leading researcher in the development of polyamino acids, which allowed new insights into the reactions and behaviour of proteins. His work developed pathways into the exploration and investigation of antigenicity. He was President of Israel between 1973 and 1978.

Robert Williams was a pioneer in advancing our understanding of the roles of chemical elements, especially the metals, in biology and in biological evolution. He studied the thermodynamic stabilities of transition-metal complexes with organic ligands, their redox properties, magnetism and colour, to understand their biological function. He developed high-field nuclear magnetic resonance to study the mobility and dynamics of many protein structures, leading to a deeper understanding of protein function.

Ecology and agriculture

Michael Elliott was the leader of work at what is now known as Rothamsted Research that invented and subsequently commercially developed the pyrethroids, a new class of insecticides. He made probably the greatest individual contribution to the control of insect pests that not only constrain global food production but also affect the health of humans and livestock.

Lloyd Evans was a leading plant scientist who published extensively on the regulation of flowering and on crop production. His significant achievements included the identification of a gibberellin plant hormone as a flowering regulator in the grass *Lolium temulentum*, the discovery of a synthetic gibberellin growth retardant that blocked endogenous gibberellin synthesis, and the discovery of a novel biological flowering clock in *Pharbitis nil* with a 12 h period.

John Lund absorbed the different traditions in systematic and physiological ecology from successive contacts with two leading authorities and combined them to good effect in his main work on the ecology of freshwater planktonic algae. With his wife, Hilda, they extended her mycological work to epidemics of chytrid parasitism in planktonic population dynamics.

Microbiology and genetics

Sir Howard Dalton was an outstanding microbiologist who devoted himself to the elucidation of the process of methane oxidation by bacteria that use this relatively inert gas as their sole source of carbon and energy. He discovered two completely novel multicomponent monooxygenase enzymes responsible for the initial oxidation of methane to methanol.

Paul Polani is rightly considered one of the most influential founders of modern medical genetics. Contrary to expectations, he showed that sex determination in humans did not follow the *Drosophila*-based model. He also discovered that Down syndrome is sometimes caused by chromosomal translocations that, if inherited from unaffected carriers, may cause familial clustering of the disease.

John Postgate was one of the foremost microbiologists of his generation. He is most famous for his lifelong research on sulfate-reducing bacteria and nitrogen fixation and for his seminal contributions to understanding the survival and death of bacteria. His other great love was jazz: he was an amateur cornet player of note, the leader of several jazz groups and a highly knowledgeable writer, reviewer and author of two books on the subject.

Neuroscience

Paul Fatt made discoveries that are fundamental to our understanding of synaptic transmission in the nervous system. His work with Bernard Katz demonstrated for the first time that neurotransmitters are released in small packets, or 'quanta'. His work with John Eccles and Katz provided an understanding of the mechanism underlying synaptic inhibition, and his work with Bernard Ginsborg identified voltage-gated calcium currents for the first time.

David Hubel was one of the great neuroscientists of the twentieth century. His experiments revolutionized our understanding of the brain mechanisms underlying vision. In collaboration with Torsten Wiesel he revealed the beautifully ordered activity of single neurons in the visual cortex, how innate and learned factors shape its development, and how these neurons might be assembled to ultimately produce vision. He shared the 1981 Nobel Prize in Physiology or Medicine with Wiesel and Roger Sperry.

Medicine

Donald Metcalf was one of Australia's most distinguished medical researchers and is acknowledged internationally as the father of the modern field of haemopoietic growth factors. He defined the hierarchy of haemopoietic progenitor cells, purified and cloned the major molecular regulators of their growth and maturation, determined their mechanisms of action and participated in their development for clinical use in patients with cancer.

ACKNOWLEDGEMENTS

First and foremost, we are enormously indebted to the authors of the 27 memoirs in this volume for their outstanding work in producing biographies of lasting value. In my opinion they are all well up to the standards of the best biographies in the series and will be widely enjoyed and appreciated.

I am also personally indebted to the publications and editorial team at the Royal Society, whose names and roles are listed on page iv. Their enormous help has made my task of understanding my new role all the easier.

Special thanks are due to Bruce Goatly, who has overseen the copy-editing and typesetting of the memoirs for almost 20 years. He retires from this role after the publication of this volume, and new arrangements will be put in place for the future online and printed versions of *Biographical Memoirs*. We wish him a long, happy and busy 'retirement'.

AUTHOR PROFILE

Malcolm Longair

Malcolm Longair CBE FRS FRSE is Jacksonian Professor Emeritus of Natural Philosophy and Director of Development, Cavendish Laboratory, University of Cambridge. He has held many highly respected positions within the fields of physics and astronomy. He was appointed the ninth Astronomer Royal of Scotland in 1980, as well as the Regius Professor of Astronomy, University of Edinburgh, and the director of the Royal Observatory, Edinburgh. He was head of the Cavendish Laboratory from 1997 to 2005. He has served on and chaired many international committees, boards and panels, working with both NASA and the European Space Agency (ESA). He has chaired numerous committees for specific science projects, including the Planck and Euclid missions of ESA.

His main research interests are in high-energy astrophysics, astrophysical cosmology and the history of physics and astrophysics. His book *Maxwell's enduring legacy: a scientific history of the Cavendish Laboratory* was published in July 2016.

ALAN CARRINGTON CBE

6 January 1934 — 31 August 2013

Biogr. Mems Fell. R. Soc. **62**, 7–17 (2016)

ALAN CARRINGTON CBE

6 January 1934 — 31 August 2013

Elected FRS 1971

By A. D. Buckingham[1] CBE FRS and R. J. Saykally[2]

[1]*Department of Chemistry, Cambridge University, Cambridge CB2 1EW, UK*
[2]*Department of Chemistry, University of California, Berkeley, California 94720, USA*

Alan Carrington was an outstanding physical chemist who made important contributions to molecular spectroscopy. During his distinguished career in the universities of Southampton, Cambridge and Oxford he was a pioneer in the fields of electron paramagnetic resonance spectroscopy of doped single crystals, solutions of organic radicals, and especially the high-resolution spectroscopy of gaseous free-radicals and ions. He wrote three books and was an excellent teacher and lecturer. His honours included the Davy Medal, the Faraday Medal of the Royal Society of Chemistry, and election as a Foreign Associate of the National Academy of Sciences.

Early life and education

Alan Carrington was born in the winter of 1934 in Greenwich, a historic town on the Thames east of London. He was the only child of Albert and Constance Carrington. Albert came from the Yorkshire/Derbyshire area and was an orphan at the age of three years. He had little education but could read and write; he was working in a coal mine at the age of 13 years. He served throughout World War II as a soldier, was evacuated with the British Expeditionary Force from the beaches of Dunkirk in June 1940 and then joined the Eighth Army in North Africa. He studied and became expert in postage stamps, budgerigars or whatever caught his interest, a trait that would be reflected in his son.

Alan's mother, Constance Carrington (*née* Nelson), was one of six children who grew up in east London. Her education was basic but she had an unshakeable faith in the value of education. She worked in a zip factory and was an expert knitter, winning several prizes. Alan and his mother did not see Albert for five years during the war. His childhood, like that of

http://dx.doi.org/10.1098/rsbm.2015.0024

Figure 1. The first XI of Colfe's School in 1952. Alan is seated in the captain's chair in the middle of the front row.

many of his contemporaries, was dominated by the harsh realities of war. He was evacuated with thousands of other children from London during the Blitz; his good fortune was to live with his mother for five years with a loving family, the Cliftons, in Godmanchester, west of Cambridge. The Cliftons had a son of similar age to Alan. He attended a small primary school and was taught by two teachers, evacuees from London, Miss Harbord and Miss Thornton. Miss Harbord was the headmistress and told Constance that 'Alan definitely has a brain!' On Sundays he and his mother attended St Mary's Church and he was much taken with the organ; his lifelong interest in music began in Godmanchester, as did his love of fishing and of the English countryside. At the end of the war in 1945 Alan took the '11-plus' exam and passed, so he could proceed to a grammar school. He and his mother returned to London.

He started at Colfe's Grammar School, a boys' school, in the autumn of 1945 in temporary buildings in Lewisham, a suburb in southeast London, a six-mile train journey from home in New Eltham, near Greenwich. Colfe's was founded in 1652 and its original buildings had been destroyed in 1944 by a 'doodlebug' (V1 flying bomb). His academic performance was 'middle of the road', his best subjects being history and geography. His mathematics teacher, Mr Birnberg, was superb but Alan found the subject difficult. His O-level examination performance was respectable and Alan wanted to continue into the sixth form. His mother was supportive but his father was unsympathetic. Mr Birnberg came to the family home, argued with Alan's father and won, so Alan stayed on at Colfe's and took chemistry, physics and mathematics at A-level. His results were good enough to take him on to the next stage of his education. He was active in sport at Colfe's, became a member of the first rugby XV and was captain of the first cricket XI in his final year (figure 1). He was a batsman and wicketkeeper. He continued to enjoy sport in his later life.

Out of school, Alan's most important interest was undoubtedly music. He joined the choir of Holy Trinity Church in Eltham and came under the influence of Bob Stainton, who was the organist and choir master and a much respected friend. That friendship was to last for a decade. He and Alan would play piano duets in the Carrington home and Alan learnt much about organ playing. He succeeded in playing, for the cost of £1 per hour, the organ of the Royal Albert Hall in London.

SOUTHAMPTON UNIVERSITY, 1952–59

Alan was determined to go on to university and applied to Southampton to read for an honours degree in chemistry. He sat a scholarship examination and was awarded an Exhibition that contributed £50 per year to his income. A State Scholarship provided all university fees and an annual maintenance grant. He left home in September 1952 and moved into South Stoneham House, a university hall of residence and a former stately home with the river Itchen running through the grounds. The hall held about 70 male students, and the university had just over 800 students. Southampton University obtained its Royal Charter in 1952, so Alan was part of its first intake of students.

The head of the Chemistry Department, and Alan's first tutor, was Professor N. K. Adam FRS, a distinguished surface chemist. At the end of his first term, Alan was top of the examination list—his first such success. His interests in chemistry leant towards the small-molecule physics end of the subject. His affection for quantum theory was stimulated by the lectures and book of Dr Edward Cartmell and Dr Gerry Fowles. Throughout his undergraduate career he came top, or nearly top, in the examinations in chemistry and in his subsidiary subjects, mathematics and physics. His final examinations were taken in June 1955 and Alan was surprisingly placed on the border of a first-class and upper-second-class degree. The external examiner, Professor F. S. (later Lord) Dainton (FRS 1957), conducted an oral examination that did not embrace Alan's strengths; he was awarded an upper-second-class degree, much to the surprise and disappointment of the staff of the Chemistry Department. He was nevertheless awarded the department's premier research studentship, enabling him to continue in the department as a research student.

Alan joined the research group of Dr M. C. R. Symons (FRS 1985), a young lecturer in the Department of Chemistry who was collaborating with Dr D. J. E. Ingram, a lecturer in the Electronics Department and a pioneer in the field of electron paramagnetic resonance (EPR) spectroscopy, the technique that would raise Alan to the apex of physical chemistry when he applied it to highly reactive gas-phase free radicals. Alan set about seeking to understand the intense colour of transition-metal oxyions as in potassium permanganate and potassium manganate. The latter, which is obtained from the former by reduction in an alkaline solution, is a deep emerald-green colour; its MnO_4^{2-} anion has an unpaired electron and so could be studied with EPR. Alan succeeded in growing single crystals of potassium chromate (K_2CrO_4) containing 1% of the magnetic potassium manganate (K_2MnO_4). Commercial EPR apparatus was still a long way off and Alan was excited to work with apparatus that was entirely home-built. The manganate anion exhibits fast spin–lattice relaxation, so it was necessary to cool the sample to very low temperatures to obtain a spectrum; this was achieved, with some danger, with liquid hydrogen. Alan's first two scientific papers were published in *Journal of the Chemical Society* in 1956 (1, 2)*. Dr Ingram and Dr D. Schonland, a lecturer in the Mathematics Department, were vital contributors to the second paper. The research showed

* Numbers in this form refer to the bibliography at the end of the text.

that the intense colour of potassium permanganate is due to a charge-transfer transition in which an electron moves from an orbital delocalized over the four O atoms to a degenerate orbital localized on the Mn atom.

After just two years of research at Southampton, Alan went to the University of Minnesota to oversee the laboratory of Dr John Wertz, who was in Oxford on sabbatical leave. The laboratory contained excellent nuclear magnetic resonance and EPR spectrometers, both home-built, and Alan was let loose on them for a year. The Wertz laboratory was where he began his independent career by studying the EPR spectra of aromatic ions in solution (3). He was fascinated by proton hyperfine structure in organic free radicals, an interest that remained with him throughout his career. After a year in Minneapolis, Alan returned to Southampton to finish his PhD thesis, entitled 'The electronic structure, spectra and properties of transition metal oxyanions'. Alan wrote to Professor Christopher Longuet-Higgins FRS in Cambridge enquiring whether he could spend a year in the Theoretical Chemistry Group in Cambridge and was delighted to be offered a postdoctoral fellowship funded by General Electric.

In his second postgraduate year in Southampton, Alan joined the University Operatic Society, accompanying singers on the piano. In 1956 the opera was Gilbert and Sullivan's *Patience* and the leading role was sung by Hilary Taylor from Bristol, an undergraduate in the English Department. Alan fell in love with her at once and they began a relationship that was to last for the remainder of Alan's life. They were married in the Priory Church of St James in Horsefair, Bristol, a Grade I listed building, on 7 November 1959.

CAMBRIDGE, 1959–67

Alan moved to Cambridge in August 1959. He joined Christopher Longuet-Higgins, Frank Boys (FRS 1972), John Griffith, Leslie Orgel (FRS 1962), Andrew McLachlan (FRS 1989) and John Murrell (FRS 1991) in the Theoretical Chemistry Group in the Department of Organic and Inorganic Chemistry of Cambridge University (John Pople FRS, Nobel laureate 1999, had left the Group in 1958 for the National Physical Laboratory). The department head was Sir Alexander (later Lord) Todd FRS (PRS 1975–80; Nobel laureate 1957), and Professor Harry Eméleus FRS was the Professor of Inorganic Chemistry. The department moved to a new building in Lensfield Road in 1958 and shared the building with the Department of Physical Chemistry, whose head was Professor R. G. W. Norrish FRS (Nobel laureate 1967). Alan knew of Andrew McLachlan, for Andrew worked with Martyn Symons in Southampton in 1957–58; it was their interaction in Cambridge that convinced Alan that he needed to know more theory.

Christopher Longuet-Higgins had decided that some experimental work would not be out of place in the Theoretical Chemistry Group, so he and Alan submitted a joint application for funds to purchase a Varian EPR spectrometer. While waiting for the result and then for the equipment, Alan wrote a review article on the EPR spectra of transition-metal ions (4). Christopher's influence on Alan was profound. He hugely admired Christopher's talents as a theoretician and as a musician. When the spectrometer arrived, Alan continued his work on aromatic radicals and radical ions. His research students included Jorge dos Santos Veiga (who later became Vice-Rector of Coimbra University in Portugal), Jim Bolton, Ray Golding, Peter Todd and Ian (I. C. P.) Smith (who became Director of the National Research Council Molecular Biophysics Laboratory in Winnipeg, Canada). Among the discoveries made during this work was the hyperfine line-width alternation in the durosemiquinone cation, which turned out to be due to intramolecular motion causing isomerization between *cis* and *trans* forms (5, 6). Another novel result was the observation of free-radical partial alignment in a nematic liquid crystal, work carried out with Geoffrey Luckhurst (7).

In 1960 Alan was appointed to the university position of Assistant in Research (and later an Assistant Director of Research) and he was elected to a Research Fellowship (and later to a teaching Fellowship) in Downing College. In the next few years he was awarded the Harrison Memorial Prize, the Meldola Medal and Prize, and the Marlow Medal. Overseas trips were becoming a regular part of Alan's life, as were invitations to lecture at British universities.

The arrival in 1964 of Don Levy from Berkeley as a postdoctoral fellow and Terry Miller from the University of Kansas as a research student provided the impetus for experimental work on small free radicals in the gas phase. The first system studied was a mixture of chlorine and oxygen flowing through the resonant cavity in a quartz tube; the researchers were immediately rewarded with a beautiful spectrum of the ClO radical (8). This was soon followed by other diatomic radicals (10). Thus began a Carrington legend, which would be augmented—in Southampton—by the arrival of John Brown (FRS 2003) and Brian Howard.

In 1966 Alan had the opportunity to spend a few months with Jim Hyde at Varian Associates in California. Together they developed a new microwave cavity that had particularly large entrance and exit holes. It greatly enhanced the gas-phase work and proved to be valuable for studying much larger solid-state samples. It formed the basis of Varian's later electron–nuclear double resonance (ENDOR) cavity.

Alan and Hilary's three children were born in Cambridge: Sarah in 1962, Rebecca in 1964 and Simon in 1966. All three became successful musicians. Music figured hugely in both Alan's and Hilary's lives in Cambridge. They were members of the Cambridge University Musical Society choir and Hilary was much in demand as a soloist in college concerts. Alan enjoyed his teaching duties, and his popular final-undergraduate-year course on magnetic resonance led to the publication, with Andrew McLachlan, of his first book, *Introduction to magnetic resonance* (9). Alan's research in Cambridge and Southampton on the intricacies of the interactions in open-shell molecules led to his second book, *Microwave spectroscopy of free radicals* (14).

SOUTHAMPTON, 1967–84

Alan was appointed to a new Professorship of Chemistry at his alma mater, the University of Southampton, in 1965 but did not take up the chair until 1967. He was able to take his laboratory equipment with him and it was installed successfully in the old Assembly Hall with much help from Terry Miller and Brian Howard. John Brown rejoined the group as an ICI Postdoctoral Fellow in 1968 and became a lecturer and Reader before moving to Oxford in 1983.

Alan's research continued to prosper in Southampton. High-resolution electron resonance studies were extended to triatomic radicals such as NCO, which provides an interesting example of the Renner effect, where electronic degeneracy of the linear structure leads to a coupling of the motion of the electrons and nuclei, something that is absent in the Born–Oppenheimer approximation (11). The first spectrum of a nonlinear triatomic radical, HCO, with fine and hyperfine structure was reported (12, 13). Alan's attention was turning towards the spectroscopic study of gaseous ions: in 1977 he and Peter Sarre published a paper on the spectrum of CO^+ (15) and in 1978 on the sub-Doppler laser spectroscopy of molecular ions in ion beams (16). Rich vibrational spectra of the simple diatomic, HD^+ (17), and of the simplest triatomic, H_3^+ (18), were obtained, posing a significant challenge for theoretical chemists.

Recognition of Alan's distinction came with the Royal Society of Chemistry's Award in Structural Chemistry and the Tilden Lectureship and Medal, and in 1971 with his election to the Fellowship of the Royal Society at the very young age of 37 years. In 1976 Alan was appointed to the first Senior Fellowship of the Science Research Council, a five-year position that enabled the holder to concentrate on research. Among the members of his group were Juliet Buttenshaw, Peter Sarre and Tim Softley.

In 1979 Alan was appointed to a Royal Society Research Professorship, which gave him the freedom to concentrate on research, rather than on administrative matters in the university. He was to hold this prestigious position until his retirement 20 years later.

OXFORD, 1984–87

After 17 years as Professor of Chemistry at Southampton, Alan was thinking about a move; Oxford was attractive because two of his former research students, John Brown and Brian Howard, were members of staff in the Physical Chemistry Laboratory (PCL), and the head of that Laboratory, Sir John Rowlinson FRS, made it clear that Alan would be welcome in the PCL. The Royal Society agreed that his Research Professorship could be transferred. The move to a laboratory on the second floor went smoothly and Alan found the department exhilarating. He was appointed to a Fellowship at Jesus College and lived there in a small room from Mondays to Fridays. Although he was very happy in the college, living in Oxford during the week and in Chandler's Ford near Southampton at the weekend was far from ideal. Hilary had been appointed Lending Librarian at Fareham Public Library in 1984 and the prospect of finding a similar position in or near Oxford was not good.

Alan was thinking about some new experiments aimed at obtaining the electronic spectrum of the hydrogen molecule ion, H_2^+—the simplest molecule. Apparatus was designed and built but the early experiments were not successful.

Two major honours were awarded to Alan while at Oxford: he was elected a Foreign Honorary Member of the American Academy of Arts and Sciences in 1987, and in 1985 he received the Faraday Medal of the Royal Society of Chemistry—the Society's premier award in physical chemistry, made every third year.

The difficulties coming from living five days per week away from his family finally persuaded Alan to return to Southampton, so after three years in the PCL he went through the complicated process of transferring his equipment back to the Assembly Hall in Southampton, a move that was facilitated by two students, Christine Montgomery and Iain McNab, who continued their research in Southampton.

RETURN TO SOUTHAMPTON, 1987–99

The new experiments on the hydrogen molecule ion that had been designed in Oxford had immediate success in Southampton. It was a beautiful result: a single-line spectrum arising from an electronic transition in the heavy-hydrogen molecular ion D_2^+ (19). Characteristically eschewing the routine, Alan turned his ion spectroscopy studies towards the precise measurement of ion-beam spectra of highly excited electronic states of HD^+, excited vibrational states of the simplest polyatomic molecule H_3^+, and ultrahigh-resolution spectra of other simple ions (20). Electric-field dissociation was used to state-select the very weakly bound near-dissociation levels of molecular ions (21). These experiments presented a daunting challenge to theorists, requiring the abandonment of the usual simplifying assumptions in the Born–Oppenheimer approximation. Alan judged his work on the hydrogen molecular ion and on similar molecular systems to be the best of his scientific career, and it continued until his retirement in 1999. The microwave experiments were extended to heavier ions such as He...Ar^+ (22) and He...H_2^+ (23).

In 1992 Alan was awarded the Davy Medal of the Royal Society, and in 1994, much to his and Hilary's delight, he was elected a Foreign Associate of the US National Academy of Sciences. In 1997 he became President of the Faraday Division of the Royal Society of Chemistry. At his first Faraday Discussion, he broke with tradition by replacing the President's customary speech at the conference dinner by Hilary's songs, with Alan at the piano! He was also heavily and successfully involved in the birth of the European journal *Physical Chemistry Chemical Physics* (known as PCCP) from a union of *Faraday Transactions* of the Royal Society of Chemistry and *Berichte der Bunsen Gesellschaft für Physikalische Chemie*. The journal has thrived and is now jointly owned by 14 European chemical societies and published by the Royal Society of Chemistry.

In 1999 Alan was appointed a Commander of the Order of the British Empire and in 2000 he was elected to an Honorary Fellowship at Downing College, Cambridge.

To mark Alan's 65th birthday and his impending retirement, his friends and colleagues in Southampton and Oxford organized a conference and social event in January 1999 in St John's College, Oxford. It was attended by more than 100 people from many parts of the world. Alan gave the first lecture, and his family and friends contributed much beautiful music.

RETIREMENT

Alan retired from his Royal Society Research Professorship and from his chair at the University of Southampton at the age of 65 years on 30 September 2000. He and his colleague John Brown were writing a book entitled *Rotational spectroscopy of diatomic molecules* (25). The writing was well underway before retirement and continued from his home in Chandler's Ford, aided by the award of a Leverhulme Senior Fellowship, which provided the means to attend conferences overseas. The book took five years to write and was published by Cambridge University Press in 2003. It has 1013 pages and 11 chapters that develop the theory behind the energy levels of diatomic molecules and summarize the many experimental methods of studying the high-resolution spectra of these molecules in the gaseous state.

Alan's retirement was enriched especially by music, but also by a love of the English countryside and of boats, including the building of intricate models of classic sailing ships, including *Victory* and *Cutty Sark*. Alan and Hilary would often visit Beaulieu, where *Victory* was built. He was a heavy smoker for much of his life but succeeded in giving up the habit in 2000. His health remained good until 2011 when he was treated for pancreatic cancer. He died in Winchester Hospital, surrounded by his family.

ACKNOWLEDGEMENTS

We have drawn heavily upon Alan's article in *Annual Review of Physical Chemistry* (24) and from his unpublished autobiography. We are grateful to Hilary Carrington, Professor Brian Howard and Dr Andrew McLachlan for many helpful comments, and to Mrs J. Cardnell, Head of Careers & Librarian, Colfe's School, for information about Alan at school and for providing the photograph in figure 1.

The frontispiece photograph was taken in 1977 by Godfrey Argent and is reproduced with permission.

BIBLIOGRAPHY

The following publications are those referred to directly in the text. A full bibliography is available as electronic supplementary material at http://dx.doi.org/10.1098/rsbm.2015.0024 or via http://rsbm.royalsocietypublishing.org.

(1) 1956 (With M. C. R. Symons) Structure and reactivity of the oxyanions of transition metals. Part I. The manganese oxyanions. *J. Chem. Soc.*, 3373–3380.

(2)   (With D. J. E. Ingram, D. Schonland & M. C. R. Symons) Structure and reactivity of the oxyanions of transition metals. Part II. Investigations of electron spin resonance. *J. Chem. Soc.*, 4710–4715.

(3) 1959 (With F. Dravnieks & M. C. R. Symons) Unstable intermediates. Part IV. Electron spin resonance studies of univalent aromatic hydrocarbon ions. *J. Chem. Soc.*, 947–952.

(4) 1960 (With H. C. Longuet-Higgins) Electron resonance in crystalline transition-metal compounds. *Q. Rev. Chem. Soc.* **14**, 427–452.

(5) 1962 (With J. R. Bolton) Line width alternation in the electron spin resonance spectrum of the durosemiquinone cation. *Mol. Phys.* **5**, 161–167.

(6)   Theory of line width alternation in certain electron resonance spectra. *Mol. Phys.* **5**, 425–431.

(7) 1964 (With G. R. Luckhurst) The electron resonance spectra of free radicals dissolved in liquid crystals. *Mol. Phys.* **8**, 401–402.

(8) 1966 (With D. H. Levy) Electron resonance studies of free radicals in the gas phase. Detection of ClO, BrO and NS. *J. Chem. Phys.* **44**, 1298–1299.

(9) 1967 (With A. D. McLachlan) *Introduction to magnetic resonance*. New York: Harper & Row.

(10) 1970 (With P. N. Dyer & D. H. Levy) Gas phase electron resonance spectra of BrO and IO. *J. Chem. Phys.* **52**, 309–314.

(11) 1971 (With A. R. Fabris, B. J. Howard & N. J. D. Lucas) Electron resonance studies of the Renner effect. Gaseous NCO in its $^2\Pi_{3/2}$ ($n = 1$), $^2\Delta_{5/2}$ ($n = 2$) and $^2\Phi_{7/2}$ ($n = 3$) vibronic states. *Mol. Phys.* **20**, 961–980.

(12) 1973 (With I. C. Bowater & J. M. Brown) Microwave spectroscopy of non-linear free radicals. I. General theory and application to the Zeeman effect in HCO. *Proc. R. Soc. Lond.* A **333**, 265–288.

(13)   (With P. S. H. Bolman, J. M. Brown & G. J. Lycett) Microwave spectroscopy of non-linear free radicals. II. Zeeman effect studies of DCO. *Proc. R. Soc. Lond.* A **335**, 113–126.

(14) 1974 *Microwave spectroscopy of free radicals*. London: Academic Press.

(15) 1977 (With P. J. Sarre) Electronic absorption spectrum of CO^+ in an ion beam. *Mol. Phys.* **33**, 1495–1497.

(16) 1978 (With P. J. Sarre) Sub-Doppler laser spectroscopy of molecular ions in ion beams. *J. Physique* **40**, 54–56.

(17) 1982 (With J. Buttenshaw & R. A. Kennedy) Vibration–rotation spectroscopy of the HD^+ ion. *J. Mol. Spectrosc.* **80**, 47–69.

(18) 1984 (With R. A. Kennedy) Infrared predissociation spectrum of the H_3^+ ion. *J. Chem. Phys.* **81**, 91–112.

(19) 1988 (With I. R. McNab & C. A. Montgomerie) Observation of the $2p\sigma_u - 1s\sigma_g$ electronic spectrum of D_2^+. *Phys. Rev. Lett.* **61**, 1573–1575.

(20)   (With I. R. McNab & C. A. Montgomerie) Spectroscopy of the hydrogen molecular ion at its dissociation limit. *Phil. Trans. R. Soc. Lond.* A **324**, 275–287.

(21)   (With I. R. McNab & C. A. Montgomerie) Laser excitation and electric field dissociation spectroscopy of the HD^+ ion. *Chem. Phys. Lett.* **151**, 258–262.

(22) 1995 (With J. M. Hutson, M. M. Law, C. A. Leach, A. J. Marr, A. M. Shaw & M. R. Viant) Microwave spectroscopy and interaction potential of the long-range He...Ar^+ ion. *J. Chem. Phys.* **102**, 2379–2403.

(23) 1996 (With D. I. Gammie, A. M. Shaw, S. M. Taylor & J. M. Hutson) Observation of a microwave spectrum of the long-range He...H_2^+ complex. *Chem. Phys. Lett.* **260**, 395–405.

(24) 2001 A free radical. *Annu. Rev. Phys. Chem.* **52**, 1–13.

(25) 2003 (With J. M. Brown) *Rotational spectroscopy of diatomic molecules*. Cambridge University Press.

SIR JOHN WARCUP CORNFORTH AC CBE

7 September 1917 — 8 December 2013

Biogr. Mems Fell. R. Soc. **62**, 19–57 (2016)

SIR JOHN WARCUP CORNFORTH AC CBE

7 September 1917 — 8 December 2013

Elected FRS 1953

By Sir Alan R. Battersby[1],* FRS and Douglas W. Young[2],‡ FRSE

[1]*Department of Chemistry, University of Cambridge, Lensfield Road, Cambridge CB2 1EW, UK*

[2]*Department of Chemistry, University of Sussex, Falmer, Brighton BN1 9QJ, UK*

Sir John Cornforth was a pioneer in discovering the detailed chemistry used by living systems to construct the organic substances they contain. From his teenage years, he was handicapped by profound deafness yet he overcame this to reach the highest pinnacles of scientific achievement. His work was carried out in several different research centres, both academic and medical, and he was a leading figure in all.

The authors of this memoir decided at the outset that we should cover his personal biography and his scientific work in largely separate sections. We have endeavoured in this way to give a clear and full account of his life.

PERSONAL BIOGRAPHY (A.R.B.)

Life and career

John Warcup Cornforth, always known as Kappa to his friends, was born in Sydney, Australia, on 7 September 1917. His father, John William Warcup Cornforth, was born in Bristol of Yorkshire stock; he had read Classics at Oxford before travelling to Australia, where he met and later married Kappa's mother Hilda (*née* Eipper). She was a nurse and a native Australian, the grand-daughter of Christoph Eipper, a German minister who was a pioneering missionary in Australia. Hilda's mother came from an Irish line, and Kappa enjoyed referring to this mixture in the origins of his parents and grandparents. There were four children in the Cornforth family; he had an older sister, a younger brother and a younger sister. When Kappa was about six or seven years old (figure 1) the family moved to Armidale in the northern tablelands of New South Wales. Armidale was then a country town of about 5000 inhabitants.

* arb1005@cam.ac.uk; ‡ d.w.young@sussex.ac.uk

http://dx.doi.org/10.1098/rsbm.2015.0016

Figure 1. John Cornforth as a boy. (Copyright © Philippa Cornforth.)

It was here that he had his primary schooling and the first year of secondary education while his father for some time taught classics in a private school, clearly of high standing as it was a member of the 'Great Public Schools of NSW'. However, his father was also involved in several other activities, including the setting up of a mortgage company. Unfortunately, the outcome was poor and the family suffered from financial insecurity. Nevertheless, Kappa won the inaugural Dangar Scholarship in 1928 for study at Armidale High School. The family moved back to Sydney after about five years away and Kappa entered Sydney Boys High School where he received a very good education. He enjoyed this period and he studied at high school for six years. He was well ahead of his years when he entered Sydney University at the age of 16 years.

However, this was the time when his hearing loss, first noticed at the age of around 10 years as a small problem, became very serious. The cause was otosclerosis, which was passed through his mother's line and also affected other members of the family, but less severely than Kappa. He was soon to be totally deaf. He had to decide on the direction of his future career; his father had favoured entry into law but thoughts on these lines had to be abandoned. However, he had already developed a love for chemistry, strongly encouraged by a fine young chemistry teacher at the High School, Leonard Basser. Further, this seemed to him to offer a career in which deafness might not be an insuperable handicap.

He realized that his deafness meant he would have to learn all the chemistry he needed by himself from textbooks and practical manuals and later, at the university, from the original literature. One can see his logical mind then at work in that he decided that, to do this self-learning, he must strengthen his mental powers in every way he could. So he took up astronomy and later, together with a friend at Oxford, built a telescope from a piece of steel pipe and an 8-inch parabolic mirror that they ground by hand. He became adept at chess (about which more later) and he learned German from a dictionary. He enjoyed saying that he was not good at German grammar but that he had a huge vocabulary! He later learned French also and had a first-class command of it. As a practical part of his training process, and surely also because it was fun, he set up his own laboratory in the family laundry. He built his own weighing balance there, using the lids of two shoe-polish tins. The book he used most at this stage was *Practical organic chemistry* by J. B. Cohen, which gave instructions for both chemical and biochemical preparations. The latter awakened his interest in biochemistry to carry forward alongside his love for chemistry.

He was able to enter the University of Sydney at the remarkably young age of 16 years to study chemistry and he was strongly attracted to organic chemistry, especially to the study of natural substances and processes. The seed from which his love for this area of science came was his bush walks as a boy in the Blue Mountains, which were within reach of Sydney. There he saw the huge variety of plants and trees producing a plethora of colours, scents, gums, structural materials and so on. He became enthralled by all he saw but also intensely curious about them; thus was shaped the rest of his scientific career. To Kappa, work in science starts with curiosity, the asking of questions and then designing experiments to try to answer them. He also often said 'You never stop learning.'

His undergraduate studies show the scale of the handicap that he had to overcome. Because he could not hear any of the lectures, he found out from the lecturers and from his fellow students what topics were being covered. He then used textbooks and also read the original literature to gain an outstandingly detailed and deep grasp of each topic. Much of the original literature at that time was in German, so his earlier decision to learn that language was well rewarded. As he read the textbooks and occasionally some of the original literature, he realized that they contained errors; that gave him a thrill because he felt he could set things right. Throughout his later career, he relied exclusively on the primary literature and he had an immense and detailed knowledge of that literature. He began to realize that science is a continuous process of discovery and correction and could see himself as a part of that process. Kappa enjoyed spotting errors, not only in science but also in any human activity, and he loved to be able to provide the correction. As a result, he was in demand from his colleagues and from editors to look at the papers that they had drafted or received, and he was amazingly good at picking out any flaws.

He graduated from Sydney in 1937 with first-class honours and was awarded a university medal; he then moved on to study for a master's degree. One of his early original papers described work on the constituents of Australian plants such as the caustic vine (*Sarcostemma australe*). He greatly enjoyed doing practical work at the bench, such as the extraction of natural substances from the caustic vine followed by their purification by skilful manipulation. At that time a researcher had to be adept at handling materials to make any progress, and being able to crystallize and recrystallize compounds was of key importance. Kappa was a master of all aspects of practical experiments. For example, he was able later in his career, when the amount of material he could obtain was minute, to crystallize and recrystallize a tiny sample in a melting-point tube. This is a 'vessel' holding so small a volume that one drop of liquid would more than half fill it! He carried out experiments at the bench all his life. He also found the companionship of working in the laboratory with others helped to overcome to some extent the loneliness he often felt as a result of his deafness.

Another skill he developed at this time was as a glassblower. For a chemist, this involves less 'blowing', more the joining together of heated glass, usually glass tubing and flasks.

Figure 2. At Cape Town en route for Oxford. (Copyright © Philippa Cornforth.)

Kappa used a gas blowtorch to heat the glass and, characteristically, his was home-made from an old Bunsen burner. He earned quite a reputation as a glassblower and was often asked by fellow students to repair their broken glassware; this was to have far-reaching consequences, as will be seen later.

It was during the university period of his life that he acquired the nickname 'Kappa', which arose because he scratched this Greek letter onto his glassware to stop fellow students from 'borrowing' it to add to their set. Apparently, he would have liked to have used the equivalent for the letter C but the Greek alphabet does not have one, so he used Kappa as the best near alternative. One rarely heard anyone in the chemical community speak of John Cornforth, it was always Kappa Cornforth.

It was not possible in the late 1930s in Australia go beyond a master's degree, so study for a doctorate required travelling abroad. Kappa's outstanding achievements thus far led to the award of an 1851 Exhibition Scholarship for doctoral study at Oxford. Only two of these highly prized scholarships were awarded each year in Australia, and the second one was won by another organic chemist, Rita Harradence. She was one year ahead of Kappa at Sydney University and she, too, opted to study at Oxford. Their research supervisor was to be Sir Robert Robinson FRS (PRS 1945–50), who had been Professor of Organic Chemistry at the University of Sydney from 1913 to 1915. Fittingly, the laboratory in which Kappa and Rita had done their work for the master's degree had been designed by Robinson.

During her time at the university, Rita broke the glass sidearm off her Claisen flask, then a precious item of equipment. Her friends knew of Kappa's reputation as a glassblower and advised her to see whether he would repair her flask. By then he had been able to obtain a proper blowtorch, and he gladly made the repair. This seems to have been the first real contact between Rita and Kappa.

World War II broke out as they were travelling by boat to England and as a result they were diverted around South Africa. By the time they reached Cape Town (figure 2) they had to decide whether to continue to a Britain at war or return to Australia, far from the conflict.

Figure 3. At the Dyson Perrins Laboratory in the 1940s. (Copyright © Philippa Cornforth.)

They opted to continue the journey to Oxford. The diversion caused a substantial delay, so that the whole journey took eleven weeks rather than the usual five. On arrival in Oxford they were both brought into the effort, guided by Robinson, aimed at the synthesis of steroids. These are vital substances in our bodies, examples being cholesterol and the sex hormones such as testosterone. They worked in the Dyson Perrins laboratory, and figure 3 shows Kappa there with some of his colleagues. (The laboratory coats are interesting.) Their contributions to the synthetic programme were rewarded by the award to both of the DPhil degree after only two years; normally a longer period of research is needed. Rita and Kappa became engaged during the preparation of their theses and they were married in 1941 before the formal award of their doctorates.

After the research on steroids, the focus switched to various problems connected with the war effort, one being studies of antimalarial materials. But this was, in a way, a 'starter' as they then became members of the team working on the structure of the newly isolated antibiotic penicillin. It was clear from the properties of penicillin that it could have a massive effect on the war by saving the lives of war casualties. Initially only small quantities of penicillin were available, so great efforts were made to improve its preparation and to determine its structure. The crucially important contributions that Kappa made to the latter research are described in the scientific section of this memoir; he also helped to write *The chemistry of penicillin* (1949), which records the international effort that was focused on this antibiotic. Rita and Kappa's first child, Brenda, was born (in 1943) during the penicillin period, and over the years the family expanded further with the arrival of John (1946) and Philippa (1948). When Brenda was born, they received strong support from Dorothy Hodgkin (FRS 1947) (who like Kappa was later awarded the Nobel Prize); they became close friends of Dorothy and remained so for life.

For recreation, Rita and Kappa joined a group of friends who made cycle rides into the countryside, not only around Oxford but also far afield, for example to Scotland. They camped under a strung-up tarpaulin just as they had in the Blue Mountains of Australia. Another Australian chemist, Arthur J. Birch (FRS 1958), was one of this group.

Figure 4. Kappa at Milstead.

After the war they moved, in 1946, with the support of Robert Robinson, from Oxford to join the scientific staff at the National Institute for Medical Research, which was located first in Hampstead and later at Mill Hill. There, Kappa and Rita returned to the synthetic work on steroids, still in collaboration with Robinson. This long association of Kappa with Robert Robinson led to a close friendship that lasted until Robinson's death in 1975. In a typical observation Kappa said, 'The nature of our friendship was a continuous sequence of differences of opinion. Robert was an argumentative person and I have known the same thing to have been said of myself.' In about 1950 the family bought a modest house, 22 Shakespeare Road in Mill Hill, a short bus ride from the Institute. They had no car, so everyone took a bus or walked to school or to the shops. Rita juggled with the many tasks of coping with three children, her deaf husband and her scientific work while having no extended family in the UK to give help.

Kappa and Rita worked at the National Institute for 16 years and he spoke of this period as the best years of his life. He particularly appreciated the spirit within the Institute, where there was cooperation and cross-fertilization across the various divisions. This environment led him to say that scientific advances are the product of an ambience created by many people, not just those who have the best ideas. In particular, he interacted fruitfully with several biological scientists; one such interaction, with George Popják (FRS 1961), developed into a long-running collaboration on the biosynthesis of cholesterol. This involved uncovering the detailed chemical steps used by living systems to construct this important molecule. The collaboration with Popják developed into a strong, close friendship that extended to the whole family. Kappa undoubtedly felt it keenly when Popják left (see below) for the USA.

Kappa was elected a Fellow of the Royal Society in 1953, during his time at the Institute and at the remarkably young age of 35 years.

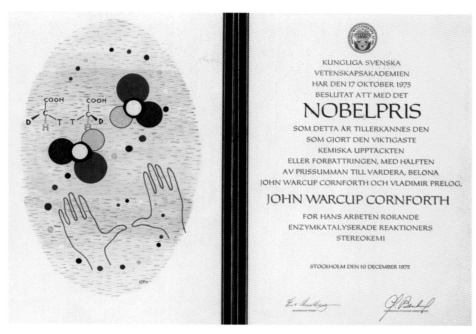

Figure 5. The Nobel Citation with the two non-mirror image structures.
(Artist: Tage Hedqvist. Copyright © The Nobel Foundation, 1975.)

He was approached in the early 1960s by the senior professors at the Australian National University in Canberra to consider the possibility of his joining them there. He decided to remain in the UK, probably, at least in part, because funding was provided by Shell Research Ltd to establish for him and Popják the Milstead Laboratory of Chemical Enzymology at Sittingbourne. Lord (Victor) Rothschild FRS was influential in the decision to establish this laboratory; he was strongly supported by Robert Robinson, who had professional connections with Shell. Kappa and George Popják moved to Milstead in 1962 (figure 4) to become co-directors of the laboratory, and over the years Victor Rothschild and Kappa developed a warm friendship.

The main thrust of the research of Kappa and George Popják at Milstead was the study of the stereochemistry of enzymatic reactions. Rita carried out many of the syntheses of the isotopically labelled materials that the work required. This line of research continued after Popják left Milstead in 1968 to go to the University of California, Los Angeles.

Kappa's work at Milstead led directly to his being awarded the 1975 Nobel Prize in Chemistry (figures 5 and 6) jointly with Vladimir Prelog of the Eidgenössische Technische Hochschule, Zürich. It appealed greatly to Kappa's sense of humour that on the Nobel citation, rather than showing two mirror-image molecules, the artist had drawn two identical ones! The award ceremony on this occasion was held in a large sports stadium because the town hall was being refurbished. Since Kappa was unable to hear a word of what was being said, he amused himself by looking around the audience, which was largely in darkness, whereas the main stage was brightly lit. Through the gloom he could see lots of flashes of light appearing all over the stadium and he finally realized they were coming from the jewels that the women were wearing. He said later that this was the thing he remembered most clearly from the award

Figure 6. The Cornforth family at Stockholm. (Copyright © Boo Jonsson, Reportagetiänst.)

ceremony. His short but penetrating speech should be recorded here. He spoke on behalf of both recipients:

> That our work has been considered worthy of such distinction is a great satisfaction to both but I think we derive equal satisfaction from the sense of being two in the great company of those who approach the truth. In a world where it is so easy to neglect, deny, corrupt and suppress the truth, the scientist may find his discipline severe. For him, truth is so seldom the sudden light that shows new order and beauty; more often truth is the uncharted rock that sinks his ship in the dark. He respects all the more those who can accept that condition; and in returning thanks tonight we are saluting all those who make our load lighter by sharing it.

Kappa left Milstead in 1975 to take up a Royal Society Research Professorship at the University of Sussex, and he received news of the Nobel Prize shortly thereafter; later (1977) he received his knighthood (figure 7). It was in 1975 that Rita decided it was the right time to retire. They bought a lovely house in Lewes that stood high on a hillside giving a magnificent view over Sussex and, as Kappa loved to point out, of the brewery down below.

He travelled each day to the university to work experimentally at the bench (figure 8). One of his projects was to synthesize a molecule that would act as an enzyme does to catalyse a reaction; this work was unfinished. It is a sad reflection on the way in which science is supported that he had great difficulty in obtaining funds for his experiments. So he synthesized compounds that were needed by others and exchanged them for funds for his main work. He gave lectures to undergraduates until he was well into his eighties and he was always willing to discuss chemistry with them. He was particularly effective in guiding the ones who were in difficulty back onto the right track.

Figure 7. The Cornforth family at Buckingham Palace.

Kappa retained throughout his connection with Australia; he remained an Australian citizen and held both British and Australian passports. On one of his return visits to Sydney he gave an address on 'Scientists as citizens', one of a small number of papers not describing research results.

Rita's support

This memoir has referred at several points to the support that Rita gave to Kappa (figure 9); it was immense and was the solid foundation on which he stood. She organized essentially everything for him and the family. She carried the major task of running the house, arranging maintenance and repair, the shopping and cooking, all alongside her scientific work and coping with three lively children. He made the tax returns but otherwise it was Rita who did what was needed. She was the car driver, and when they travelled abroad, Rita fixed all the flights and hotels. These trips abroad started in the 1950s and included substantial periods in Canberra and the USA; Rita's presence was essential to him on these visits. How many women could have done what she did? He could not possibly have made his remarkable scientific achievements without her, and part of the Nobel award is rightly hers.

Wider interests

Kappa had many other interests, one being chess (figure 10*a*). He was a formidable chess player, having started at the age of 14 years; he had been given a Staunton Chess Set by his parents. In 1933 he won the New South Wales under-16 Championship and in 1937 he scored well in the Australian Championships in Perth. While there, he set an Australian record for simultaneous blind chess by taking on twelve Perth Club players, beating eight and drawing

Figure 8. Kappa at Sussex. (Copyright © Edward Reeves Photography.)

Figure 9. Kappa and Rita at Milstead.

Figure 10. Kappa at play. (*a*) Chess; (*b*) tennis.

with two. This record stood until the 1970s. In England he played for Hampstead, Middlesex, Sittingbourne, Brighton and Sussex. Robert Robinson also enjoyed chess, so he and Kappa played 'postal chess' against each other; the pleasure this gave to both is clear from their correspondence.

He also greatly enjoyed tennis (figure 10*b*) and he had a searing serve; he played well into his eighties.

He had a deep love of poetry, which gave him both solace and huge pleasure. Poetry for Kappa was the equivalent of music for a hearing person. His knowledge of poetry was quite remarkable, matched only by his memory of it. He could accurately recite long poems, often those he had read years before. Probably his greatest love was for the poetry of W. B. Yeats, a special favourite being 'The lake isle of Innisfree'. On one of his regular visits to see Kappa, one of us (A.R.B.) recited this poem with him; the first verse is:

> I will arise and go now, and go to Innisfree
> And a small cabin build there, of clay and wattles made:
> Nine bean-rows will I have there, a hive for the honey-bee,
> And live alone in the bee-loud glade.

Coming to the second verse, which is very moving, his eyes became moist as he recited; he was filled with emotion. Poetry was another bedrock for him.

In addition, he read prodigiously, constantly and widely and he was fond of detective fiction for relaxation. He always read the newspaper at the table, morning and evening, and this was accepted by the family because of his deafness. Initially, it was *News Chronicle*, but

Figure 11. Kappa in his latter years. (Copyright © Philippa Cornforth.) (Online version in colour.)

when publication ceased, it was *The Guardian*. His choice of newspapers shows where he always stood in his political views; in addition, *New Statesman* and *New Scientist* were read regularly.

Not only an avid reader (figure 11), he also enjoyed writing and his scientific papers are models of clarity and style. So, too, were his many letters and his translations into English of, for example, German poems.

It may have been his feeling for the rhythm, balance and structure of poetry that led to his remarkable, and very amusing, ability to compose limericks after a few moments' thought. He could do so for almost any location and on all sorts of topics. There are many, often about chemistry, but also others; the three recorded here are fine examples.

> Spittoons that are made out of platinum
> Resist all your efforts to flatten 'em
> You can also use rhodium
> But never use sodium
> For then they'd explode when you spat in 'em.

The second is very much for chemists:

> A mosquito was heard to complain
> That a chemist had poisoned her brain
> The cause of her sorrow
> Was para-dichloro-
> Diphenyltrichloroethane.

Finally, Kappa gave a definition of life and wrote a matching limerick: 'A system is alive, or has life, if it resists inevitable decay by exact replication and can evolve by occasional inexact replication';

Figure 12. Bushwalking in the Blue Mountains. (Copyright © Philippa Cornforth.)

You rot all the time you're alive
And copy yourself to survive
A copy untrue
May work better than you
If it does, you can die; it will thrive.

His interest in walking that started when he was a boy was shared by Rita, and the photo of Rita up a tree (figure 12) shows her spirit; they had fun together! He never lost the taste for walking, and he continued almost to the end of his life to walk each day. This he could do by going up a steep track behind his house in Lewes onto rolling Sussex countryside, often returning with his collection of mushrooms. He loved the natural world and especially trees and wild flowers.

Both Rita and Kappa loved gardening, a joy that started at their house in Shakespeare Road, Mill Hill. This had a splendid garden containing a vegetable area and lots of fruit trees. Kappa taught himself how to graft tasty varieties of apple onto less tasty apple trees. Later, he took delight in showing his friends around their steeply sloping garden in Lewes. They planted a quince tree there, and he and Rita made quince jelly from the fruit; also each year when Seville oranges arrived they made their own marmalade. The recipe was their own and it appears in the Royal Society collection *But the crackling is superb* (Kurti & Kurti 1988).

The family

The family life of the Cornforths was inevitably affected by Kappa's deafness, but it seems that everyone adjusted although it was not always easy. He never complained but he did have dark days, yet after working hard inside himself he came out of them to return to his usual equilibrium. There were frustrations; hard work on lip reading was needed and things happened that could be funny when viewed in retrospect. In all of this, Rita was his solid and patient support and she devoted herself to relaying the content of conversations to him, especially important when groups of people were talking. She maintained constant eye contact with Kappa that gave him the reassurance he needed to overcome the inevitable feeling that he had of being isolated and somewhat lonely.

He had a warm relationship with the children and would swing them over his head when they were small. They enjoyed the stories that he made up himself to tell, and he taught them how to play Scrabble and tennis although he always won at both! He introduced the children to the stars so that they could pick out the major constellations. More energetic 'lessons' were on swimming and the fun to be had at the seaside in rock pools. So Kappa was a 'hands-on Dad' who had close empathy with the children; he always gave good counsel when they had any sort of trouble or problem.

He enjoyed singing and had a lovely voice. He knew the songs from Gilbert and Sullivan and he liked those from the music hall; his favourite was 'Two lovely black eyes'. Remarkably, these were songs he had not heard since childhood; he would sing them to the children and grandchildren. Train journeys had their interest too. At the station, Kappa thought he knew the right platform and charged rapidly off in that direction, but the rest of the family knew he was wrong. The only way to get him back was for one of the children, feeling a bit self-conscious, to run what was by now the rather long distance after him. Such events raised a family smile as they were recalled.

Obviously, talking is possible for a deaf person but listening is not, so Kappa would recite poems and tell stories and jokes at the dinner table. After a joke he would shake with huge laughter and this was totally infectious. He was very good company, knowledgeable over a wide range of topics, and both entertaining and informative. He always got to the heart of the matter under discussion at home and also at university seminars. Even without Rita present he could follow the presentation in the seminar reasonably well from the slides. It was amazing how he could then add to the discussion a penetrating question or pertinent comment even on a topic that was quite distant from his own. He loved a vigorous argument, all with good humour, although it was very difficult for anyone to win against such a brilliant mind.

The last years

Kappa continued working at the university until Rita became infirm; at that point, in 2005, he ceased his chemical work at Sussex. He cared for Rita with great devotion, and to do so he learned the skills he had previously lacked including cooking using recipes written out by Rita. She would say, 'Chemists make good cooks'; indeed, not only was he a good cook but he also quite enjoyed it. Rita continued even at this stage to relay the conversation to Kappa when their friends visited. If ever there were a marriage of massive strength, cohesion and love, this was it. Rita's death in November 2012 was a huge blow to Kappa, and the loneliness he had felt throughout his life because of deafness was now far worse. He was, however, fortunate to have the loving support of his family to help him cope. Inevitably, there were bleak moments, but when his close friends visited he rallied and was always good company. Often the talk on such visits was of gardening, wine or hiking, and frequently poetry was recited. Chemistry came in as well, with Robert Robinson a favourite topic but also how the nature of research on chemistry differs so much in the twenty-first century from the earlier days. He doubted whether many chemistry students now would have the manipulative skills needed to crystallize and recrystallize a 20 mg sample of a radioactive compound until it reached constant specific radioactivity. It would have been a regular task for him.

Eventually his physical condition required the support of carers, and in his last year he accepted live-in care. All his carers enjoyed his company; they warmed to his jokes and laughter and he regularly played Scrabble with the closest of his devoted helpers. He and his helpers were together in this way during the morning of the day that he had the massive stroke from which he died on 8 December 2013.

John (Kappa) Cornforth was a wonderful human being and one of the greatest organic/bio-organic chemists in the world. His name will always live on in the history of science.

SCIENTIFIC WORK (D.W.Y.)

Early work

Cornforth began his academic studies at the University of Sydney and published three research papers on heterocyclic chemistry during his BSc years. One of these (1)* was the first of many with Rita, his future wife. His MSc led to a further five publications on natural product chemistry, two as sole author. Given his lifelong contributions to the field of terpenes and steroids, it was somewhat prophetic that his final publication from Sydney with J. C. Earl (2) suggested a possible triterpene structure for sarcostin, the sapogenin from the Australian plant *Sarcostemma australe* R.Br. Considering this as 'unfinished business', Cornforth returned to the subject nearly 20 years later in a solo publication (24) that helped finally to prove the correct (steroidal) structure (Mitsuhashi & Shimizu 1963).

Oxford and penicillin

In 1942, having completed his doctorate at Oxford with Robert Robinson, Cornforth joined the ongoing programme of research on the isolation and structure determination of the antibiotic penicillin. E. P. Abraham had isolated the amino acid penicillamine from the acid hydrolysis of penicillin. Belatedly it was shown that it (and therefore penicillin) contained sulfur and that it formed a thiazolidine with acetone. Several structures for penicillamine were put forward in a report (Abraham *et al.* 1943), an addendum to which stated that Dr. J. W. Cornforth had suggested the structure **4**. This had been dismissed on the basis of a low value in a Kuhn–Roth determination for C-methyl groups, but Cornforth observed that this low value might be due the presence of a *gem*-dimethyl group. Within six weeks of his suggestion, Cornforth confirmed the structure by total synthesis (4) and suggested (correctly) that it belonged to the 'unnatural' D-series of amino acids.

In addition to penicillamine **4**, acid hydrolysis of penicillin yielded the aldehyde **3**, which was also produced together with carbon dioxide and the mercaptide of penicillamine when alkali-inactivated penicillin was treated with mercuric chloride. It seemed clear that alkali

* Numbers in this form refer to the bibliography at the end of the text.

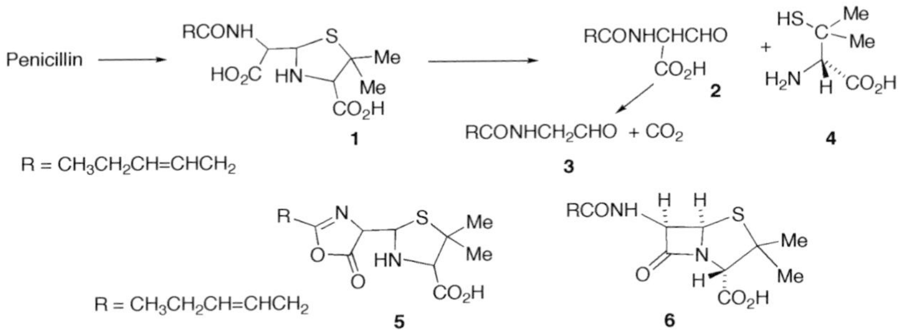

R = CH₃CH₂CH=CHCH₂

R = CH₃CH₂CH=CHCH₂

inactivation had given a thiazolidine which was then converted by mercuric chloride into **3**, **4** and CO_2. Robinson deduced that the aldehyde **3** was formed by decarboxylation of the β-carboxyaldehyde **2**, and so alkali treatment of penicillin had given the thiazolidine carboxylic acid **1**. It followed that penicillin was a dehydration product of the acid **1**, and Robinson proposed the thiazolidine-oxazolone structure **5** for the antibiotic. Abraham and Chain preferred the alternative β-lactam structure **6** as being more in keeping with the experimental results (Abraham *et al.* 1949), and this was finally confirmed by X-ray crystallographic analysis (Crowfoot *et al.* 1949).

Oxazoles, oxazolones and related heterocyclic compounds: the Cornforth rearrangement

The oxazolone structure **5** was an early target for penicillin synthesis, and Cornforth played a leading role in this work. Various heteromethylene-oxazolones such as the enol **7** were prepared and reacted with penicillamine in the hope of obtaining a compound of type **5**, and in some cases antibacterial activity was observed.

In the course of this work it was found (5) that reaction of the acid **8** with phosphorus pentachloride gave, not the expected acid chloride, but the ester **9**. In addition, Rosenmund reduction of the acid chloride **10** gave the aldehyde **11**. These and other reactions were evidently examples of a hitherto unknown rearrangement of 4-carbonyl-substituted oxazoles (**12**→**14**), which has since become known as the Cornforth rearrangement. The suggested mechanism involves the intermediacy of a nitrile-ylide **13**, and the likelihood of a given rearrangement occurring is dependent on the position of the equilibrium between reactant and product (Dewar & Turchi 1975).

After the lifting of the wartime publication embargo, all UK and US penicillin research appeared in 1949 as a book in which Cornforth (10) reviewed all of the oxazole chemistry.

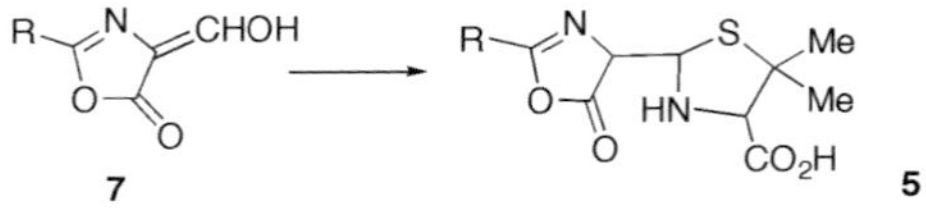

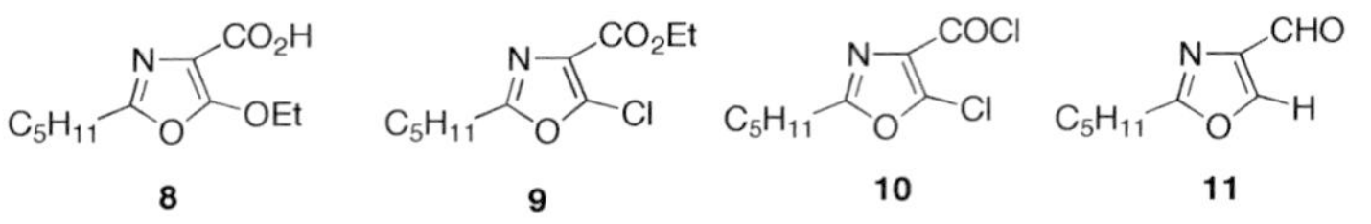

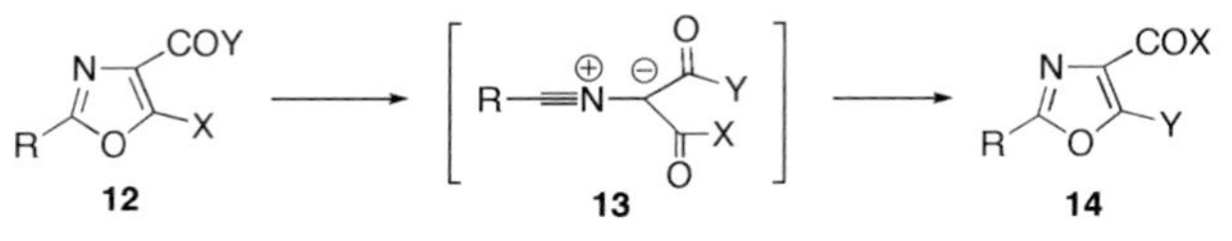

He continued to work on these and related heterocyclic compounds on moving to the National Institute for Medical Research in 1946. He developed a new, general and convenient synthesis of oxazoles and iminazoles using imidoethers of type **15** (7). Reaction of acetimidoethyl ether with ethyl glycinate gave the product **15** (R = Me, R' = Et), but with 2 mol of diethyl aminomalonate in moist air it gave the oxoiminazole **16** (R = Me). Formylation of **15** gave the salts **17**, which reacted with HCl to give the oxazoles **18**. Hydrolysis and decarboxylation then provided a synthesis of monosubstituted oxazoles **19** including the parent oxazole **19** (R = H), which had never before been prepared.

The synthesis was extended to iminazoles **20** by reacting the acid derived from ester **18** with ammonia or an amine. In an alternative method, the potassium salt **17** (R = Me, R' = Et) reacted with ethyl glycinate hydrochloride to give the iminazole **20** (R = Me, R^2 = CO$_2$Et, R^3 = CH$_2$CO$_2$Et). Extension of the synthesis (9) gave a 4-cyano-oxazole, and an alternative synthesis of an oxazole from a thioether analogue of **17** was discovered during an attempted synthesis of penicillin (8).

The first total synthesis of 'non-aromatic steroids'

Robinson began his synthesis of steroids shortly after the discovery of their structures in 1932 (reviewed in Fieser & Fieser 1959, pp. 53–89). His first targets were the 'aromatic steroids' equilenin **21** and oestrone **22**, which posed less of a stereochemical challenge than did the 'non-aromatic steroid' cholesterol **23**, which, having eight asymmetric centres, required the synthesis of one unique stereoisomer from 256 possibilities. The methods developed in this early work laid firm foundations for many future steroid syntheses. The synthesis of cholesterol **23** was begun before the discovery of its relative stereochemistry by Carlisle & Crowfoot (1945) and its absolute configuration by Cornforth in 1954 (20).

In his doctoral studies Cornforth (3) discovered a simple method of using sodium and alcohol to reduce β-methoxynaphthalenes to β-tetralones via the hydrolysis of an intermediate enol ether. The reaction was especially favourable for 1,6-dimethoxynaphthalene **24**, which yielded the tetralone **26** via the enol ether **25**. This finding was fundamental to the successful route to the 'non-aromatic steroids', which was resumed after the war both at Oxford and in Cornforth's laboratory at the National Institute for Medical Research.

Methylation of the β-tetralone **26** and use of the Robinson annulation reaction (du Feu *et al.* 1937) gave the tricyclic enone **27** (6). A second asymmetric centre was now introduced by demethylation and hydrogenation. The resultant diol **28** was stereochemically homogeneous, the A/B ring junction being assumed to be *cis* by analogy (6, 11). Partial acetylation, and hydrogenation gave a mixture of acetoxy-alcohols, which was subjected to chromic oxidation followed by alkaline hydrolysis. The resultant ketone **29** was a separable mixture of diastereoisomers. Because these were α-decalones that had been subjected to enolization, the B/C ring junction was correctly considered to be *trans* (6, 11). It subsequently turned out that the desired *cis-anti-trans* diastereoisomer was the minor one. Later work by Cornforth (16) indicated that hydrogenation/oxidation of methyl ethers related to the *cis* isomer **28** and its *trans* counterpart gave *cis-syn-trans* and *trans-anti-trans* reduction products, respectively, so that, had the A/B junction been *trans*, the predominant isomer might have had the three centres retained in the synthesis in the required relative stereochemistry.

The two diastereoisomers **29** were resolved separately and each of the four stereoisomers was converted into its corresponding α-methyl ketone, which was oxidized to the corresponding diketone. One of these four diketones proved to be identical to the 'Reich diketone' **30**, a degradation product of deoxycholic acid (Reich 1945), which could also be obtained from the cholesterol degradation product **31** known as the 'Köster–Logemann ketone' (Köster & Logemann 1940). Thus the absolute stereochemistry of the synthetic product was confirmed and intermediates were available in quantity to act as synthetic relays.

Conversion of the ketone **30** into the unsaturated ketone **32** (Billeter & Miescher 1950) was followed (12, 13) by conversion into the diol **33**. Preferential protection of the ring A hydroxyl, oxidation and deprotection then gave the 'Köster–Logemann ketone' **31**.

A fifth asymmetric centre was now introduced stereospecifically by carboxylation of the benzoate of **31** and esterification. Reformatsky reaction of the resultant ester **34** with methyl bromoacetate and hydrolysis gave two diastereoisomeric products **35**. One of these was hydrogenated, esterified, acetylated and dehydrated to give the product **36** with *trans* stereochemistry at the A/B ring junction. This was hydrogenated and the acetyl group was replaced by benzoate giving **37**, identical to a specimen prepared from cholesterol, thus confirming the stereochemistry at all seven asymmetric centres. All of the asymmetric centres of the ring system of natural steroids were now in place, and the synthesis of epiandrosterone **38** was completed by homologation and ring closure.

Previous work on the correlation of natural steroids by partial synthesis meant that this synthesis was sufficiently flexible to prepare all of the 'non-aromatic' sex hormones and many adrenal hormones. A different synthesis of 'non-aromatic' steroids was published (Woodward

Me ...CO₂Me Me ...CO₂Me Me CO₂Me Me O

35 ⟹ 36 ⟹ 37 ⟹ 38

et al. 1951, 1952) at the same time as the preliminary report (12) of this work, and both groups completed syntheses of cholesterol **23**.

Collaborative interdisciplinary work at the National Institute for Medical Research

When Cornforth moved to the National Institute for Medical Research in late 1946, conditions there were ideal for interdisciplinary collaboration and, in addition to carrying out steroid synthesis and heterocyclic studies, he became involved in several collaborative projects. In one of these, the discovery that the non-ionic surfactant Triton A-20 suppressed experimental tuberculosis in mice, led to a series of publications from 1951 to 1973 on the preparation and examination of analogous structures as antitubercular agents (48). He was also involved in a Medical Research Council research scheme into sources of the drug cortisone using the steroid sapogenin hecogenin, which was available in quantity as a byproduct in the manufacture of sisal fibre (19). His most fruitful collaboration was with George Popják, a medical biochemist. This lasted through Popják's move to direct the Medical Research Council laboratories at Hammersmith and the move of both men to the Milstead Laboratories at Sittingbourne, until in 1968 Popják moved to the University of California, Los Angeles.

Biosynthesis of cholesterol and squalene from acetate

The hydrocarbon squalene was indicated as an intermediate in cholesterol biosynthesis by early biological experiments (Channon 1926) and, when the structures of both squalene **39** (Heilbron *et al.* 1926) and cholesterol **23** became known, Robinson (1934) proposed that squalene might cyclize to cholesterol **23** as shown in conformation **39a**, with loss of the three methyl groups highlighted in red. Discovery of the structure of the triterpene lanosterol **40** (Voser *et al.* 1952) led Woodward & Bloch (1953) to suggest that squalene might first cyclize as shown in conformation **39b** with either (i) both methyl groups shown in green undergoing 1,2-shifts or (ii) one of them undergoing a 1,3-shift to give lanosterol **40**. Loss of the three methyl groups in **40** shown in red would then give cholesterol **23**.

39a — 23 — 40 — 39b

In studying the biosynthesis of glycerol in foetal rats, Popják & Beeckmans (1950) noted that [1-¹⁴C]acetate was also incorporated into cholesterol, confirming Bloch's early experiments (reviewed in (59)) showing incorporation of [²H], [¹⁴C] and [¹³C]acetates into both squalene and cholesterol, and incorporation of labelled squalene into cholesterol. Bloch (reviewed in (17, 59)) identified the site of each label incorporated from [1-¹⁴C] and [2-¹⁴C]acetate into the side chain of cholesterol by using degradative methods previously developed in the determination of its structure.

Cornforth's entry to the field gave a new dimension to unravelling the biosynthetic origin of cholesterol **23**. He began (14, 15) by examining the labelling in ring A of samples of cholesterol **23** derived from both [1-^{14}C] and [2-^{14}C]acetates by converting them into cholest-5-ene **41**. Ozonolysis to a keto-aldehyde and aldol condensation then gave the enone **42**. This was ozonolysed to yield a diketoacid, which, on heating, gave the aldehyde **43** and C6 of cholesterol as carbon dioxide. The aldehyde **43** underwent a retro-Michael reaction thus isolating ring A as the cyclohexanone **44**, which could be further degraded to allow the radioactivity of each individual carbon atom to be measured. Thus the origins of C6 in ring B, all of the ring A carbons and the C19 methyl were defined.

Bloch and Dauben (reviewed in (17)) separately identified the origin of C7 in ring B of cholesterol, and Woodward & Bloch (1953) discovered the origin of the two carbons of the C-methyl moieties C18–C13 and C19–C10, showing that C13 was derived from the methyl carbon of acetate.

Cornforth and Popják (21) now turned their attention to rings C and D. The labelled samples of cholesterol were converted into samples of the olefin **45**. Ozonolysis to the keto-aldehyde **46** and retro-Michael reaction gave **47** and **48**. Further degradation of the ketone **47** revealed the origin of C12, C13 and C18 and degradation of the aldehyde **48** the origin of C15, C16 and C17.

In a further degradation (21), the samples of cholesterol were converted into the diene **49**, which was ozonolysed to the lactone-acid **50** and a diacid, isolated as its ammonium salt **51**. Further degradation allowed the label in atoms C9, C8 and C11 to be measured as CO_2. The conclusions from the two degradations were that C8, C11, C12, C14 and C16 originate from the carboxyl group of acetate and that C9, C13, C15, C17 and C18 originate from the methyl group. Discovery of the origin of all 27 carbon atoms of cholesterol from the two atoms of acetate had now been completed.

Cornforth and Popják (18) now addressed the origin of labelling in the individual atoms of squalene **39** derived by incubating [2-^{14}C]acetate with rat liver slices. Oxidative ozonolysis of the resultant [^{14}C]squalene gave two molecules of acetone, four molecules of laevulinic acid and one molecule of succinic acid. These were separated and further degraded to identify the positions of all of the labels.

The pattern of labelling of cholesterol and squalene biosynthesized from [1-¹⁴C] and [2-¹⁴C] acetate **52** is summarized in **23b** and **39c** below. This is the result expected for the Woodward–Bloch model of squalene cyclization. The labelling pattern expected from Robinson's model is shown in **23a** and differs from that found by experiment at C7, C8, C12 and C13.

Cornforth's general stereoselective olefin synthesis: the Cornforth model for asymmetric induction; synthesis of squalene

Interest in the synthesis of natural all-*trans* squalene, and the lack of a general method for the synthesis of trisubstituted olefins of predetermined geometry, led Cornforth to develop a general stereoselective synthesis of olefins.

Although the stereochemistry of nucleophilic addition to the carbonyl group of acyclic aliphatic ketones had been rationalized on the basis of Cram's rule (Cram & Abd Elhafez 1952), it had yet to be applied to α-chlorocarbonyl compounds. Cornforth (25) realized that the dipolar repulsive interaction between a carbonyl group and an α-halogen might cause them to be *anti* as in **54**, so that attack at the carbonyl group by a nucleophile from the side of the smaller α-substituent would give a product **55** of defined relative stereochemistry.

To test this hypothesis, now referred to as 'Cornforth's rule', 3-chlorooctan-4-ol **56** was prepared by reaction of 2-chlorobutanal with either butyl magnesium bromide or butyl lithium. Reaction with alkali with inversion at the halogen-bearing carbon gave 70% *trans*-3,4-epoxyoctane **57** and 30% *cis* isomer, whether the Grignard reagent or the lithium alkyl had been used. Reaction with ketones proved more stereoselective than with aldehydes and (i) 3-chlorobutan-2-one with ethyl magnesium bromide and (ii) 4-chloropentan-3-one with methyl magnesium bromide gave the diastereoisomeric tetrasubstituted products **58** and **59**, respectively, each with 85% stereoselectivity.

Having established a new approach to epoxides from α-chlorocarbonyl compounds, a general synthesis of olefins in good yield and high stereoselectivity was completed as shown for (*E*)-3-methylpent-2-ene **65**. Synthesis of the epoxide **63** from the ketone **61** via alcohol

62 followed by conversion to the iodide **64** and *anti*-selective reductive elimination gave the olefin **65**.

61   62   63   64   65

This has proved to be a general stereoselective synthesis of tetrasubstituted and trisubstituted olefins. Extension to disubstituted olefins followed when Cornforth reduced 3-chloro-octan-4-one **66** with sodium borohydride in aqueous ethanol and completed the synthesis of the *cis* olefin **68** with 85% stereoselectivity via the epoxide **67**.

66   67   68

The method was now used to synthesize squalene **39** (26) by using 3,5-dichloropentan-2-one **60** to supply 25 of the 30 carbon atoms of the all-*trans* triterpene.

Biosynthesis of cholesterol and squalene: mevalonic acid and the methyl and hydrogen rearrangements

Bonner & Arreguin (1949) proposed that a five-membered intermediate might be involved in the biosynthesis of terpenes from acetate, and Bloch *et al.* (1954) showed that 3-methylcrotonate or biosynthetically related substances were better sources of carbon than acetate for the biosynthesis of cholesterol. When the Merck group (Wolf *et al.* 1956) isolated the natural product mevalonic acid **69** and incubated synthetic [2-^{14}C]mevalonolactone **70** with a preparation of liver enzymes, they obtained radioactive cholesterol **23** (Tavormina & Gibbs 1956; Tavormina *et al.* 1956). Unlabelled cholesterol and radioactive carbon dioxide were obtained when [1-^{14}C]mevalonolactone was used. This suggested that six units of an 'isopentane' structure arising from decarboxylation were incorporated into squalene and thence into cholesterol. Cornforth (22, 23) now showed that racemic [2-^{14}C]mevalonolactone was incorporated into the six positions shown in squalene (**39d**) and, by implication, into the five positions shown in cholesterol (**23c**).

69   70   39d   23c   69a   71

The absolute configuration of naturally occurring mevalonic acid was proved to be (*R*) (**69a**) by Eberle & Arigoni (1960), and this prompted Cornforth to 'complete' its synthesis from (−)-linalool, which had been assigned the sterochemistry **71** (Prelog & Watanabe 1957). This proved to be one of Prelog's few misapplications of 'Prelog's rule', because the synthesis yielded unnatural (*S*)-mevalonic acid. This work is the subject of the sole joint publication (28) by Cornforth and his co-recipient of the 1975 Nobel Prize in Chemistry. Synthesis of both (*R*)- and (*S*)-mevalonic acids was later accomplished with (+)- and (−)-linalools (33).

Leopold Ružička (Eschenmoser *et al*. 1955) put forward a detailed mechanism for the cyclization of squalene **39** to lanosterol **40**, amended here because the sequence is now known to involve the 2,3-epoxide **72** (van Tamelen *et al*. 1966; Corey *et al*. 1966). Cyclization of the epoxide to the cationic intermediate **73** may be followed by a concerted sequence involving (i) migration of the C17 hydrogen to C20, (ii) migration of the C13 hydrogen to C17, (iii) two 1,2-methyl migrations from C8 and C9 and finally (iv) loss of the proton from C9 to give the $\Delta^{8,9}$-olefin in lanosterol **40**.

In an approach that is now regarded as a classic, Cornforth (27) answered the question of whether the conversion of squalene **39** into lanosterol **40** involved one 1,3-shift of the methyl A in **39e** or two 1,2-shifts of the methyls A and B. [3′,4-^{13}C$_2$]Mevalonolactone **70a** was synthesized, mixed with unlabelled material and enzymatically converted into cholesterol **23d**. Oxidation allowed isolation of the CH$_3$C– groups as acetic acid. Had there been 100% ^{13}C at the C3′ and C4 of mevalonolactone, then the labelling pattern in cholesterol would have been entirely as shown in **23d** whether methyl A or B had ended up as C18. However, six different molecules of mixed labelled and unlabelled mevalonoactone are incorporated into squalene, as shown by the red lines in **39e**. Methyl A thus arises from a different molecule of mevalonolactone from that of the target atom C13, whereas methyl B and C13 arise from the same molecule of mevalonolactone. Careful calculation of the ratios ^{13}C:^{12}C in the starting mevalonolactone and that expected of cholesterol from the two possible mechanisms showed that the double 1,2-shift mechanism would give rise to twice as much doubly labelled acetate from the oxidative degradation as would the single 1,3-shift mechanism. Mass spectrometric analysis of the recovered acetate was in accord with the former mechanism.

The question of the hydrogen shifts could now be addressed (36) by obtaining cholesterol **23e** from (4*R*)-[2-^{14}C, 4-^{3}H$_1$]mevalonic acid **69b** because Cornforth showed (37) that the 4-*pro-R* hydrogens are retained in the biosynthesis of squalene **39**. By the Ružička mechanism below, on conversion to cholesterol **23e**, one tritium (at C24) will have retained its original position, two will have migrated and three will be eliminated. The 5:3 ^{14}C:^{3}H ratio found (36) in **23e** was in accord with this, and treatment with a corpus luteum preparation cleaved the bond between C20 and C21 to give progesterone **74** and isocaproic acid (4-methylpentanoic acid) with the expected 3:1 and 2:1 ^{14}C:^{3}H ratios and a loss of tritium from C20. Proof that the remaining tritium label was at C17 was obtained by Baeyer–Villiger reaction to a tetraol retaining all tritium followed by oxidation to a ketone with loss of the remaining tritium.

Cornforth and Popják had therefore provided experimental proof for the rearrangement of hydrogen atoms and methyl groups in the biosynthesis of cholesterol.

Biosynthesis of squalene from farnesyl pyrophosphate: 1

Farnesyl pyrophosphate **75** is the immediate precursor of the symmetrical molecule squalene **39** (Lynen *et al.* 1958). Cornforth and Popják (29, 30) used a squalene synthetase system to convert [2-^{14}C, 5,5-^{2}H$_2$]mevalonolactone **70b** into squalene **39f**, which contained 11 deuterium atoms rather than the expected 12. They showed that the missing deuterium was replaced by hydrogen from the coenzyme NADPH rather than from the aqueous medium. Further experiments with labelled samples of farnesyl pyrophosphate and mevalonolactone and degradation of the squalene produced (31) showed that loss of the hydrogen atom occurred at one of the two central atoms of squalene. The stereospecificity of the hydrogen transfer (32) was shown to involve the hydrogen from the β-face of NADPH and NADH.

Absolute stereochemistry of the many redox reactions involving nicotinamide adenine dinucleotide coenzymes

The pyridine nucleotide coenzymes NAD$^+$ and NADP$^+$ **76** had long been known to effect a large number of enzyme-catalysed redox reactions by stereospecific hydrogen transfer to or from one or other face of the pyridinium ring at C4 (Levy *et al.* 1962). The reactions were classified as involving the α- or β-faces of the coenzyme, but absolute stereochemistry had not been assigned to these faces. This anomaly was removed by Cornforth and colleagues (34), who used known enzyme-catalysed reactions to prepare samples of NAD^{2}H **77** labelled separately at each of the C4 hydrogens. These were degraded to the [^{2}H$_1$]succinic acids **78** (H$_A$ = ^{2}H) and **78** (H$_B$ = ^{2}H). A sample of (2R)-[^{2}H$_1$]succinic acid **78a** was prepared from (2S, 3R)-[^{2}H$_1$]malic acid **79** of well-defined stereochemistry, and optical rotatory dispersion (ORD) comparison of the three samples of [^{2}H$_1$]succinic acid showed that the absolute stereochemistry of NADH in **77** had H$_A$ (α-face) as the *pro-R* hydrogen and H$_B$ (β-face) as the *pro-S* hydrogen. Correlation of the stereospecificities of reactions involving NADH and NADPH had already been made (Nakamoto & Vennesland 1960), and so the assignment of absolute stereochemistry was applicable to all enzyme-catalysed reactions involving these coenzymes.

76   **77**   **78**   **78a**   **79**   **78b**   **39g**

Biosynthesis of squalene from farnesyl pyrophosphate: 2

The ORD method for identifying (2R)- and (2S)-succinic acids allowed Cornforth and Popják (35) to determine the stereochemistry of the condensation of the two molecules of farnesyl pyrophosphate **75** that gives the central carbon atoms of squalene **39**. Using [2-^{14}C, 5, 5-^{2}H$_2$] mevalonic acid **69c** (H$_E$ = H$_F$ = ^{2}H) and ozonolysis of the squalene produced gave [^{2}H$_3$] succinic acid, the ORD of which was comparable to that of (2S)-[2-^{2}H$_1$]succinic acid **78** (H$_B$ = ^{2}H). Its absolute configuration was therefore assigned as (S) as in **78b** and so it derived from the [^{2}H$_3$]squalene **39g**. Hence the *pro-S* hydrogen of NADH (β-face) is incorporated at either 11α or 12β of cholesterol depending on whether the squalene is cyclized from one or the other end of the symmetrical molecule.

Stereochemistry of the biosynthesis of cholesterol from (R)-mevalonic acid

(R)-Mevalonic acid **69a** is used uniquely for terpene biosynthesis. The first two steps in the biosynthesis of terpenes and steroids involve the synthesis of (i) a monophosphate and (ii) a diphosphate (pyrophosphate) **69d**. Step (ii) uses only the (R)-isomer (40) and so racemic samples of stereospecifically labelled mevalonic acid may be used to study the stereochemistry of biosynthesis. The stereochemistry of the labelled atom relative to the stereocentre C3 is the only requirement.

The first step in the biosynthesis of farnesyl pyrophosphate **75** from mevalonic acid **69c** involves decarboxylation–dehydration of the pyrophosphate **69d** to isopentenyl pyrophosphate **80**. This is then isomerized to dimethylallyl pyrophosphate **81** with the loss of one of the hydrogen atoms originally at C4 of mevalonic acid, and protonation of the olefin. A second molecule of isopentenyl pyrophosphate **80** then loses a hydrogen atom from the same carbon in substitution at C1 of dimethylallyl pyrophosphate **81** (originally C5 of mevalonic acid). This yields geranyl pyrophosphate **82**. Reaction of geranyl pyrophosphate **82** with isopentenyl pyrophosphate **80** then yields farnesyl pyrophosphate **75b**.

69c (R = H);   **80**   **81**   **82**
69d (R = P$_2$O$_6$$^{2-}$)

75b

There are many stereochemical questions to be answered here, and syntheses of samples of mevalonic acid **69c** labelled stereospecifically with deuterium and/or tritium at C2, C4 and C5 were completed in their solution.

The first objective was to determine the stereochemistry of the hydrogen (H_A or H_B) lost in the isomerization of **80** to **81** and in the two carbon–carbon bond-forming reactions in the sequence. All of these involve C2 of isopentenyl pyrophosphate **80**, which originates from C4 of mevalonic acid. (4R)- and (4S)-[4-$^2H_1$]Mevalonic acids **69c** ($H_A = {}^2H$) and **69c** ($H_B = {}^2H$) and the corresponding tritiated compounds were prepared by stereospecific synthesis (37) and incubated with a rat liver preparation to yield farnesyl pyrophosphate **75b**. Mass spectra showed that three deuterium atoms were retained when (4R)-labelled mevalonic acid had been used and no deuterium was present in the experiment using (4S)-labelled mevalonic acid. This was confirmed by using the tritiated samples and so the mevalonic acid 4-*pro-S* hydrogen H_B was lost in all three reactions leading to farnesyl pyrophosphate **75b**. Interestingly, although it is the 4-*pro-S* hydrogen that is lost in the synthesis of all-*trans*-farnesyl pyrophosphate **75** and squalene, Cornforth and colleagues (38) showed that the biosynthesis of rubber in *Hevea brasiliensis* latex involves loss of the 4-*pro-R* hydrogen, suggesting that the *cis* configuration of rubber is formed without the involvement of any *trans* intermediates.

To answer the question of the stereochemistry of carbon–carbon bond formation at C1 of isopentenyl pyrophosphate, a sample of (5R)-[$^2H_1$]mevalonic acid **69c** ($H_E = {}^2H$) was prepared (Donninger & Popják 1966) and incubated with a rat liver preparation (37) to give squalene **39** containing six deuterium atoms. Ozonolysis gave laevulinic acid, which was degraded to (R)-[$^2H_1$]succinic acid, as confirmed by ORD comparison. Thus bond formation in the synthesis of farnesyl pyrophosphate **75b** proceeded with inversion of stereochemistry at both centres C1 of **81** and **82** (C5 of **69c**).

[2, 3-$^2H_2$]Succinic acid obtained directly from the ozonolysis represents the central atoms of squalene **39**. It was known (35) that one of these atoms has the (S) configuration and, because the isolated succinic acid had zero rotation (37), it must be the *RS* (*meso*) species. This indicated that the reaction between the two molecules of farnesyl pyrophosphate **75** involves inversion of stereochemistry at that farnesyl residue, which does not exchange hydrogen.

Cornforth and Popják (39) now examined the stereochemistry of the decarboxylative dehydration of mevalonyl pyrophosphate **69d** and of the two carbon–carbon bond-forming reactions with respect to the face of the olefinic nucleophile **80** involved by synthesizing (2R)- and (2S)-[$^2H_1$]mevalonic acid **69c** ($H_D = {}^2H$) and **69c** ($H_C = {}^2H$) from the two samples of [4-$^2H_1$]mevalonic acid prepared in the previous study. Both substrates were enzymatically converted into isopentenyl pyrophosphate **80**, and the (2R)-[$^2H_1$] isomer was also converted into farnesyl pyrophosphate **75b**. A chemical method was devised to determine the steric positions of the deuterium and hydrogen atoms in isopentenol and this was applied to the products of the enzyme-catalysed decarboxylation–dehydration reaction to show that *trans*-elimination had occurred.

The sample of farnesyl pyrophosphate **75b** derived from (2R)-[2-$^2H_1$]mevalonic acid was converted into farnesol and ozonolysed to give laevulinic acid. Further oxidation gave (2R)-[$^2H_1$]succinic acid by ORD comparison. The coupling reactions, which had been shown to involve inversion of stereochemistry at one carbon (C1 of **81** and **82**, C5 of **69c**), were now also defined by the face of the double bond at the atom (C4 of **80**) involved.

Cornforth and Popják had now defined the stereochemistry of all of the steps in the conversion of mevalonic acid to squalene except for the stereochemistry of protonation in the conversion of isopentenyl pyrophosphate **80** to dimethylallyl pyrophosphate **81**. The solution to this final question would await Cornforth's development of methods for assessing chirality in methyl groups.

Although the stereochemistry of the condensation of farnesyl pyrophosphate **75** to squalene **39** was now known, there remained the question of whether it would be possible for squalene, although symmetrical, to be transferred in a spatially oriented manner from the enzyme that produces it to the enzyme that epoxidizes it. Cornforth (54) showed that this was not the case by injecting (5S)-[5-^{3}H$_1$]mevalonic acid **69c** (H$_F$ = ^{3}H) into living rats. They were killed after 45 minutes and cholesterol was isolated from their livers. Degradation showed equal labelling at the 11α and 12β positions so that squalene, when biosynthesized *in vivo*, is not transferred in a spatially oriented manner.

The chiral methyl group in enzymic reactions

There are many enzyme-catalysed reactions in which a methyl group is converted into methylene or vice versa or in which a methyl group is transferred intact from one compound to another. These reactions may be stereospecific, and Cornforth's next challenge was to develop methods to study them. His solution to the problem required the synthesis of samples of acetic acid containing the three isotopes of hydrogen disposed in a stereochemically defined manner and the development of assays for compounds containing such 'chiral methyl' groups. Because it is not possible to obtain tritium undiluted with normal hydrogen, Cornforth reasoned that if compounds were made in which every molecule containing tritium also contained deuterium, and if the method of assay involved solely the measurement of tritium, then isotopic discrimination would simply be between hydrogen and deuterium.

The reaction of acetyl-CoA **84** and glyoxylate **83** catalysed by malate synthase was chosen for study (41) because there is sufficient discrimination between the isotopes, the intramolecular tritium and deuterium isotope effects being 2.7 and 1.4, respectively. If (S)-malate **79a** were synthesized stereospecifically from acetyl-CoA **84** and if the isotope effect required that the C–H bond be broken in preference to the C–^{2}H bond, then stereospecifically labelled [^{2}H$_1$, ^{3}H$_1$]acetate will give unequal amounts of (2S, 3R)- and (2S, 3S)-[3-^{2}H$_1$, 3-^{3}H$_1$]malate **79a** (H$_B$ = ^{2}H) and **79a** (H$_A$ = ^{2}H), respectively. Because fumarase catalyses the reversible dehydration of (S)-malate **79a** to fumarate **85** by *trans*-elimination with loss of the 3-*pro-R* hydrogen, an assay of the stereochemistry of the product from the malate synthase catalysed reaction is available.

Cornforth (41) now synthesized samples of (R)- and (S)-[^{2}H$_1$, ^{3}H$_1$]acetate. [^{2}H] Phenylacetylene **86** was reduced by diimide to (Z)-[2-^{2}H$_1$]1-phenylethylene **87**. Epoxidation to the epoxides **88** followed by reduction by lithium borotritide with inversion of stereochemistry gave a racemic mixture of (1R, 2R)- and (1S, 2S)-[2-^{3}H$_1$, 2-^{2}H$_1$]1-phenylethanol **89a** and **89b**. This was mixed with unlabelled material and resolved into the (1R)- and (1S)-enantiomers of known absolute configurations. These were separately oxidized with chromic oxide and peroxytrifluoroacetic acid without loss of label and hydrolysed to (R)- and (S)-[^{2}H$_1$, ^{3}H$_1$]acetic acids **90a** and **90b**, respectively.

Each specimen of acetate was incubated with ATP, acetate kinase, phosphotransferase, coenzyme A, glyoxalate and malate synthase to give (S)-malate **79a**. The samples of malate were purified and diluted with unlabelled (S)-malate with and without added [^{14}C]malate. Tritium retention in fumarate **85** from the fumarase reaction was measured, showing 67.2% retention using (R)-[^{2}H$_1$, ^{3}H$_1$]acetate, 30.7% using (S)-[^{2}H$_1$, ^{3}H$_1$] acetate, and 48.1% using a sample of randomly labelled [^{3}H]acetate. The disparity from ideal was taken to reflect an intramolecular deuterium isotope effect of about 2.2 in malate synthase. The malate synthase reaction therefore occurs with inversion of configuration at the methyl group, and a simple method was available for determining the chirality of doubly labelled methyl groups and for studying the enzyme-catalysed reactions in which they are involved.

The preliminary report of this research (41) was published simultaneously with a report by Arigoni's group (Luthy *et al.* 1969) in which the same malate synthase/fumarase assay had been developed but a different synthesis was devised for the (R)- and (S)-[^{2}H$_1$, ^{3}H$_1$]acetates.

Chiral methyl and citric acid metabolism

Cornforth now studied the stereochemistry of the reactions catalysed by four enzymes that synthesize or cleave citric acid (42–44): *si*-citrate synthase of the tricarboxylic acid cycle, *re*-citrate synthase from *Clostridium acidi-urici*, *si*-citrate lyase, and ATP citrate lyase. An improved modified synthesis of the (R)- and (S)-acetates above was used.

si-Citrate synthase catalyses the condensation of acetyl-CoA **84** at the *si*-face of the carbonyl group of oxaloacetic acid **91**, incorporating acetyl-CoA as the *pro-S* CH$_2$CO$_2$H chain of citric acid as in **92a**, whereas the *re*-synthase incorporates it as the *pro-R* CH$_2$CO$_2$H chain as in **92b**. Both citrate lyase and ATP citrate lyase cleave citrate, with the *pro-S* CH$_2$CO$_2$H group becoming acetate **84a** and the rest of the molecule becoming oxaloacetate **91**.

The group in citrate **92b** that is cleaved to acetate **84a** using either of the citrate lyases originates from oxaloacetate in the *re*-synthase reaction, and so (3R)- and (3S)-[3-^{3}H$_1$] oxaloacetate **91** (H$_B$ = ^{3}H) and **91** (H$_A$ = ^{3}H), respectively, were separately used as substrates for *re*-citrate synthase to yield samples of labelled citrate **92b** of well-defined stereochemistry.

These were cleaved to [³H₁, ²H₁]acetate in ²H₂O using *si*-citrate lyase. The samples of acetate were analysed using the malate synthase/fumarase assay to show that cleavage of citrate by citrate lyase proceeds with inversion of configuration at the methylene group at which replacement of the four-carbon residue by hydrogen occurs.

Knowledge of the stereochemical outcome of the reaction catalysed by *si*-citrate lyase now allowed the stereochemistry of *si*-citrate synthase to be determined. This enzyme was used to convert samples of (*R*)- and (*S*)-acetate **84** separately into citrate **92a**. This was cleaved by *si*-citrate lyase to give samples of labelled acetate, which were analysed by the malate synthase/fumarase assay. (*R*)-Acetate afforded (*R*)-acetate as product over the two steps, indicating that both the synthase and lyase reactions had proceeded with inversion of stereochemistry. The same results were obtained when ATP citrate lyase replaced *si*-citrate lyase in the sequence, and so this enzyme also catalyses cleavage with inversion of stereochemistry.

When samples of (*R*)- and (*S*)-acetyl-CoA **84** were incubated with *re*-citrate synthase, the citric acid **92b** obtained had the labels from the starting acetates in the *pro-R* CH_2CO_2H group. Two methods were used to analyse the stereochemistry. In the first method, the citrates **92b** were treated with aconitase, which is known to dehydrate citrate **92** with loss of the *pro-R* hydrogen from the *pro-R* CH_2CO_2H side chain, thus defining the stereochemistry of labelling in the samples of citrate. In the second method the citrates were converted to fumarate by using *si*-citrate lyase and malate dehydrogenase. This allowed the *anti*-elimination of water by fumarase to define the stereochemistry. The results from both methods indicated that the reaction catalysed by *re*-citrate synthase proceeded with inversion of stereochemistry.

Answering the final stereochemical question in the biosynthesis of cholesterol from mevalonic acid

Isopentenyl pyrophosphate isomerase mediates the reversible transformation of isopentenyl pyrophosphate **80** into dimethylallyl pyrophosphate **81**. Cornforth and Popják (37) had shown that isomerization occurs with loss of the 2-*pro-R* hydrogen (4-*pro-S* of mevalonic acid) but the stereochemistry of protonation of the double bond had still to be elucidated. Methods for analysing chiral acetate now made this possible (46). (2*R*)- and (2*S*)-[2-³H₁] Mevalonic acids **69c** were incubated with soluble enzymes from pig liver in ²H₂O, and the farnesyl pyrophosphate **75c** isolated was converted into farnesol. Degradation and assay of the acetate produced showed that (*R*)-[³H₁, ²H₁]acetate was obtained from the sample by using (2*R*)-[2-³H₁]mevalonic acid, and (*S*)-[³H₁, ²H₁]acetate was obtained from the sample by using (2*S*)-[2-³H₁]mevalonic acid. Because (*Z*)-[³H₁]isopentenyl pyrophosphate **80** (H_D = ³H) is formed from (2*R*)-[2-³H₁]mevalonic acid **69c** (H_D = ³H), and (*E*)-[³H₁] isopentenyl pyrophosphate **80** (H_C = ³H) from (2*S*)-[2-³H₁]mevalonic acid **69c** (H_C = ³H) (37), the deuteron must have added from the 3*re*, 4*re* face of the double bond.

In his Prix Roussel lecture (47), Cornforth recognized these experiments as marking

the end of a long trail for Milstead. A molecule of squalene has 50 hydrogen atoms. In their biosynthetic origin, one was a *pro-4S* hydrogen in a molecule of reduced nicotinamide-adenine-dinucleotide phosphate; two came from water; mevalonic acid supplied five *pro-5S* hydrogens, six each of *pro-5R*, *pro-4R*, *pro-2R* and *pro-2S*; and eighteen methyl hydrogens. So far as we can ascertain, the whole process of biosynthesis is completely stereospecific.

Biosynthesis of mevalonic acid and leucine catabolism

3-Hydroxy-3-methylglutaryl-coenzyme-A synthase catalyses condensation of acetyl-CoA **84** at the *si*-face of the 3-keto group of acetoacetyl-CoA **93** to afford (3S)-3-hydroxy-3-methylglutaryl-CoA **94**, which is then reduced to (3R)-mevalonic acid **69e**. Incubation with (R)- and (S)-[$^3H_1$, $^2H_1$]acetyl-CoA **84** ($H_A = {}^3H$, $H_B = {}^2H$) and **84** ($H_A = {}^2H$, $H_B = {}^3H$), respectively, and chemical reduction of the product **94** to the lactone of mevalonic acid **69e** was followed by conversion into cholesterol and thence into androsta-1,4-diene-3,17-dione **95**. The retention of tritium in androsta-1,4-diene-3,17-dione **95** was indicative of the stereochemistry at C2 of the mevalonic acids **69e** derived from (R)- and (S)-acetate and so, given a normal hydrogen isotope effect, the synthase-catalysed condensation proceeds with inversion of configuration (49).

3-Hydroxy-3-methylglutaryl-CoA lyase and 3-methylglutaconyl-CoA hydratase are involved in the catabolism of leucine. Cornforth (50) used chemical methods to convert [(3R, 4R)- + (3S, 4S)]-[4-$^3H_1$] and [(3R, 4S)- + (3S, 4R)]-[4-$^3H_1$]mevalonic acids into samples of enzymically active (2S, 3S, 4R)- and (2R, 3S, 4S)-[2,4-$^3H_2$, 3-^{14}C]3-hydroxy-3-methylglutaryl-CoA **94** ($H_B = H_C = {}^3H$) and **94** ($H_A = H_D = {}^3H$), respectively. On incubation with the lyase in ^2H_2O and assay of the samples of (R)- and (S)-acetyl-CoA **84** obtained, it was evident that the lyase reaction had proceeded with inversion of configuration.

Treatment of the samples of labelled 3-hydroxy-3-methylglutaryl-CoA **94** with the hydratase gave (E)-3-methylglutaconyl-CoA **96**, tritium loss showing that *syn*-dehydration of **94** had occurred. In this respect it differed from all other dehydratases with the exception of 5-dehydroquinate dehydratase.

Chiral methyl: a postscript

Cornforth studied the stereochemistry of other enzyme-catalysed reactions in which methyl groups are created or reacted upon. In the oxidative decarboxylation of S-malate **79a** to pyruvate by malic enzyme it was found (45) that hydrogen replaced the carboxyl group with retention of configuration.

Biosynthesis of fatty acids involves carboxylation of acetyl-CoA **84** by acetyl-CoA carboxylase to give malonyl-CoA. Cornforth (51, 52) used (R)- and (S)-[2-^{14}C, 2-$^3H_1$, 2-$^2H_1$] acetates to show that the carboxylation occurred with retention of configuration.

Cornforth's groundbreaking work has stimulated others to study the stereochemistry of enzyme-catalysed reactions involving chiral methyl groups (Floss *et al.* 1984) and his contribution has resulted in a step change in our understanding of the mechanism of metabolic reactions.

Imitation of enzyme catalysis

Cornforth now turned from studying reactions catalysed by enzymes to the design of a compound that might mimic the catalytic properties of an enzyme. As his reaction he chose olefin hydration, which is catalysed by many hydratases and dehydratases, and envisaged ways in which it might be accelerated in the manner of an enzyme. His catalyst would have a well-defined structure containing a shaped hydrophobic cavity with a precisely placed catalytic acidic group and would operate in aqueous medium. A phosphinic acid group was chosen because it would be anchored within the cavity by two bonds. Work was begun at Sittingbourne and continued at Sussex. New synthetic methods were developed and eventually two *meso*-atropisomers **97** and **98** and the resolved racemic atropisomers **99** were prepared (55). Stereomutation of the isomers was followed by nuclear magnetic resonance spectroscopy and the activation energy was calculated.

In the final publication on imitation of enzyme catalysis (57), the phosphinic-tetraphosphonic acid **100** and phosphinic-triphosphonic acid **101** were prepared. In water at pH 2–4 these formed stable monodisperse solutions that catalysed the hydration of 2-methylpropene to *tert*-butyl alcohol more efficiently than did a *p*-toluenesulfonic acid solution of equivalent acidity. However, complexation of propene to these compounds was not comparable to that expected of an enzyme. Cornforth concluded that, to reach useful levels of catalysis, design of the cleft flanking the phosphinic acid function would need to be refined.

Other work

Cornforth's work covered many areas. In his stereochemical studies, he used a mixture of degradative, labelling and X-ray crystallographic methods to determine the absolute stereochemistry at the sulfonium centre of *S*-adenosylmethionine, the ubiquitous and versatile metabolic intermediate that is the principal metabolic donor of methyl groups (53). Over the years he published corrections to many errors in the published work of others. After his retirement he revised structures suggested erroneously in 18 different publications for a product of the Erlenmeyer–Plöchl synthesis (56) and corrected a misunderstanding on a structure thought to be 2-chloro-3*H*-indol-3-one that had been extant for more than 115 years and 40 publications (58). In a longstanding interest in the plant dormancy hormone abscisic acid he elucidated its stereochemistry and completed two different total syntheses. His research in several areas of chemistry and biochemistry has not only solved many very important questions but has greatly influenced the work of others and will continue to do so in the future.

HONOURS AND AWARDS

1939   1851 Exhibition Overseas Scholar
1953   Fellow of the Royal Society of London
        Corday–Morgan Medal and Prize (Chemical Society)
1965   Ciba Medal (Biochemical Society)
1966   Flintoff Medal (Chemical Society)
1967   Hon. Member, American Society of Biological Chemists
        Stouffer Prize
1968   Davy Medal (Royal Society of London)
        Pedler Lecturer (Chemical Society),
1969   Ernest Guenther Award (American Chemical Society)
1970   Andrews Lecturer (University of New South Wales)
        Max Tishler Lecturer (Harvard University)
1971   Robert Robinson Lecturer (Chemical Society)
1972   Commander of the Order of the British Empire (CBE)
        Prix Roussel
1973   Foreign Hon. Member, American Academy of Arts and Sciences
        Pacific Coast Lecturer
1975   Nobel Prize in Chemistry
        Australian Man of the Year
        Royal Society Research Professor, University of Sussex
        Hon. DSc, Eidgenössische Technische Hochschule Zurich
1976   Royal Medal (Royal Society of London)
        Hon. Fellow, St Catherine's College Oxford
        Hon. Fellow, Royal Australian Chemical Institute
        Hon. DSc, University of Oxford
        Hon. DSc, University of Liverpool
        Hon. DSc, University of Warwick
        Hon. ScD, Trinity College Dublin
1977   Knight Bachelor
1978   Chemical Society Award, Chemistry of Natural Products
        Corresponding Member, Australian Academy of Science
        Hon. Member, Royal Society of New South Wales
        Sandin Lecturer (University of Alberta)
        Hon. DSc, University of Aberdeen
        Hon. DSc, University of Hull
        Hon. DSc, University of Sussex
        Hon. DSc, University of Sydney

ACKNOWLEDGEMENTS

We are grateful to the Cornforth family, Philippa, Brenda and John, for providing details of Sir John's family life and to Professor J. R. Hanson, Dr C. T. Bedford and Philippa Cornforth for reading the manuscript and making helpful suggestions. We thank the Biochemical Society for their archived interview of Sir John with Professor Trevor Goodwin.

The frontispiece photograph was taken by Godfrey Argent. This and other copyright photographs are reproduced with permission.

REFERENCES TO OTHER AUTHORS

Abraham, E. P., Baker, W., Chain, E. & Robinson, R. 1943 A discussion of the structure of penicillinic acid and its derivatives. *Report to the M.R.C. Committee for Penicillin Synthesis (C.P.S.)* no. 91.

Abraham, E. P., Baker, W., Boon, W. R., Calam, C. T., Carrington, H. C., Chain, E., Florey, H. W., Freeman, G. G., Robinson, R. & Sanders, A. G. 1949 The earlier investigations relating to 2-pentenylpenicillin. In *The chemistry of penicillin* (ed. H. T. Clarke, J. R. Johnson & R. Robinson), pp. 10–37. Princeton University Press.

Billeter, J. R. & Miescher, K. 1950 Über einige Abkömmlinge des tricyclischen Oxyketons aus Cholesterin. *Helv. Chim. Acta* **33**, 388–397.

Bonner, J. & Arreguin, B. 1949 Biochemistry of rubber formation in the guayule. I. Rubber formation in seedlings. *Arch. Biochem. Biophys.* **21**, 109–124.

Bloch, K., Clark, L. C. & Harary, I. 1954 Utilisation of branched chain acids in cholesterol synthesis. *J. Biol. Chem.* **211**, 687–699.

Carlisle, C. H. & Crowfoot, D. 1945 The crystal structure of cholesteryl iodide. *Proc. R. Soc. Lond.* A **184**, 64–83.

Channon, H. J. 1926 The biological significance of the unsaponifiable matter of oils. I. Experiments with the unsaturated hydrocarbon squalene (spinacene). *Biochem. J.* **20**, 400–408.

Corey, E. J., Russey, W. E. & Ortiz de Montellano, P. R. 1966 2,3-Oxidosqualene, an intermediate in the biological synthesis of sterols from squalene. *J. Am. Chem. Soc.* **88**, 4750–4751.

Cram, D. & Abd Elhafez, F. A. 1952 Studies in stereochemistry. X. The rule of 'steric control of asymmetric induction' in the synthesis of acyclic systems. *J. Am. Chem. Soc.* **74**, 5828–5835.

Crowfoot, D., Bunn, C. W., Rodgers-Low, B. W. & Turner-Jones, A. 1949 The X-ray crystallographic investigation of the structure of penicillin. In *The chemistry of penicillin* (ed. H. T. Clarke, J. R. Johnson & R. Robinson), pp. 310–367. Princeton University Press.

Dewar, M. J. S. & Turchi, I. J. 1975 An investigation of the scope and limitations of the Cornforth rearrangement. *J. Org. Chem.* **40**, 1521–1523.

Donninger, C. & Popják, G. 1966 Studies on the biosynthesis of cholesterol. XVIII. The stereospecificity of mevaldate reductase and the biosynthesis of asymmetrically labeled farnesyl pyrophosphate. *Proc. R. Soc. Lond.* B **163**, 465–491.

du Feu, E. C., McQuillin, F. J. & Robinson, R. 1937 Experiments on the synthesis of substances related to the sterols. Part XIV. A simple synthesis of certain octalones and ketotetrahydrohydrindenes which may be of angle-methyl-substituted type. A theory of the biogenesis of the sterols. *J. Chem. Soc.*, 53–60.

Eberle, M. & Arigoni, D. 1960 Absolute Konfiguration des Mevalolactons. *Helv. Chim. Acta* **43**, 1508–1513.

Eschenmoser, A., Ruzicka, L., Jeger, O. & Arigoni, D. 1955 Zur Kenntnis der Triterpene. 190. Mitteilung. Eine stereochemische Interpretation der biogenetischen Isoprenregel bei den Triterpenen. *Helv. Chim. Acta* **38**, 1890–1904.

Fieser, L. F. & Fieser, M. 1959 *Steroids*. New York: Reinhold.

Floss, H. G., Tsai, M.-D. & Woodard, R. W. 1984 Stereochemistry of biological reactions at proprochiral centers. *Topics Stereochem.* **15**, 253–321.

Heilbron, I. M., Kamm, E. D. & Owens, W. M. 1926 The unsaponifiable matter from the oils of elasmobranch fish. Part 1. A contribution to the study of the constitution of squalene (spinacene). *J. Chem. Soc.*, 1630–1644.

Köster, H. & Logemann, W. 1940 Zur Kenntnis der Cholesterinoxydation. Isolierung von 1-Oxo-2,13-dimethyl-$\Delta^{9,14}$-dodekahydrophenanthrol-(7), einem neuen Abbauprodukt des Cholesterins, und Darstellung einiger Derivate. *Ber. Dt. Chem. Ges.* **73**, 298–304.

Kurti, N. & Kurti, G. 1988 *But the crackling is superb: an anthology on food and drink by Fellows and Foreign Members of the Royal Society*. Bristol: Adam Hilger.

Levy, H. R. Talalay P. & Venesland, B. 1962 Steric course of enzymatic reactions at meso carbon atoms—application of hydrogen isotopes. In *Progress in stereochemistry* (ed. P. B. D. de la Mare & W. Klyne), vol. 3, pp. 299–349. London: Butterworths.

Luthy, J., Retey, J. & Arigoni, D. 1969 Preparation and detection of chiral methyl groups. *Nature* **221**, 1213–1215.

Lynen, F., Eggerer, H., Henning, U. & Kessel, I. 1958 Farnesyl-pyrophosphat und 3-Methyl-Δ^3-butenyl-1-pyrophosphat, die biologischen Vorstufen des Squalens. *Angew. Chem.* **70**, 738–742.

Mitsuhashi, H. & Shimizu, Y. 1963 Structure of cyanchogenin and sarcostin. *Steroids* **2**, 373–378.

Nakamoto, T. & Vennesland, B. 1960 The enzymatic transfer of hydrogen. VIII. The reactions catalysed by glutamic and isocitric dehydrogenases. *J. Biol. Chem.* **235**, 202–204.

Popják, G. & Beeckmanns, M.-L. 1950 Synthesis of cholesterol and fatty acids in foetuses and in mammary glands of pregnant rabbits. *Biochem. J.* **46**, 547–558.

Prelog, V. & Watanabe, E. 1957 Über die Absolute Konfiguration von Linalool und über den Sterischen Verlauf der Umwandlung von Linalool in α-Terpineol. *Liebigs Annln Chem.* **603**, 1–8.

Reich, H. 1945 Über Bestandteile der Nebennierenrinde und verwandte Stoffe. 72. Mitteilung. Oxydation von Desoxycholsäure-methylester-diacetat mit Chromsäure. III. Untersuchung der 'ketonfreien' Anteile. *Helv. Chim. Acta* **28**, 892–897.

Robinson, R. 1934 Structure of cholesterol. *Chem. Ind.* **53**, 1062–1063.

Tavormina, P. A. & Gibbs, M. H. 1956 The metabolism of β,γ-dihydroxy-β-methylvaleric acid by liver homogenates. *J. Am. Chem. Soc.* **78**, 6210.

Tavormina, P. A., Gibbs, M. H. & Huff, J. W. 1956 The utilisation of β-hydroxy-β-methyl-δ-valerolactone in cholesterol biosynthesis. *J. Am. Chem. Soc.* **78**, 4498–4499.

Van Tamelen, E. E., Willett, J. D., Clayton, R. B. & Lord, K. E. 1966 Enzymatic conversion of squalene 2,3-oxide to lanosterol and cholesterol. *J. Am. Chem. Soc.* **88**, 4752–4754.

Voser, W., Mijovic, M. V., Heusser, H., Jeger, O. & Ruzicka, L. 1952 Über Steroide und Sexualhormone. 186 Mitteilung. Über die Konstitution des Lanostadienols (Lanosterins) und seine Zugehörigkeit zu den Steroiden. *Helv. Chim. Acta* **35**, 2414–2430.

Wolf, D. E., Hoffman, C. H., Aldrich, P. E., Skeggs, H. R., Wright, L. D. & Folkers, K. 1956 β-Hydroxy-β-methyl-δ-valerolactone (divalonic acid), a new biological factor. *J. Am. Chem. Soc.* **78**, 4499.

Woodward, R. B. & Bloch, K. 1953 The cyclisation of squalene in cholesterol synthesis. *J. Am. Chem. Soc.* **75**, 2023–2024.

Woodward, R. B., Sondheimer, F., Taub, D., Heusler, K. & McLamore, W. M. 1951 The total synthesis of a steroid. *J. Am. Chem. Soc.* **73**, 2403–2404.

Woodward, R. B., Sondheimer, F., Taub, D., Heusler, K. & McLamore, W. M. 1952 The total synthesis of steroids. *J. Am. Chem. Soc.* **74**, 4223–4251.

BIBLIOGRAPHY

The following publications are those referred to directly in the text. A full bibliography is available as electronic supplementary material at http://dx.doi.org/10.1098/rsbm.2015.0016 or via http://rsbm.royalsocietypublishing.org.

(1)   1938   (With G. K. Hughes, F. Lions & R. H. Harradence) Researches on indoles. Part V. Coumarono (3,2-B) indole and derivatives. *J. R. Soc. N.S.W.* **71**, 486–493.

(2)   1940   (With J. C. Earl) Sarcostin. Part I. A preliminary study of its behaviour with reagents. *J. Chem. Soc.*, 1443–1447.

(3)   1942   (With R. H. Cornforth & R. Robinson) The preparation of β-tetralone from β-naphthol and some analogous transformations. *J. Chem. Soc.*, 689–691.

(4)   1943   (With E. P. Abraham, E. Chain, W. Baker, R. H. Cornforth & R. Robinson) Further studies on the degradation of penicillin. VI. Synthesis of penicillamine. *Report to the M.R.C. Committee for Penicillin Synthesis (C.P.S.)* no. 100.

(5)   1945   (With R. H. Cornforth, E. P. Abraham, W. Baker, E. Chain & R. Robinson) Preparation of 2-n-amyl-5-chloro-oxazole-4-aldehyde and its condensation with penicillamine. *Report to the M.R.C. Committee for Penicillin Synthesis (C.P.S.)* no. 492.

(6)   1946   (With R. Robinson) Experiments on the synthesis of substances related to the sterols. Part XLV. *J. Chem. Soc.*, 676–679.

(7)   1947   (With R. H. Cornforth) A new synthesis of oxazoles and iminazoles including its application to the preparation of oxazole. *J. Chem. Soc.*, 96–102.

(8)   1948   (With H. T. Huang) Experiments on a synthesis of penicillin. *J. Chem. Soc.*, 1964–1969.

(9)   (With H. T. Huang) Synthesis of a 4-cyano-oxazole. *J. Chem. Soc.*, 1969–1971.

(10)   1949   Oxazoles and oxazolones. In *The chemistry of penicillin* (ed. H. T. Clarke, J. R. Johnson & R. Robinson), pp. 688–848. Princeton University Press.

(11)   (With R. Robinson) Experiments on the synthesis of substances related to the sterols. Part XLVIII. Synthesis of a tricyclic degradation product of cholesterol. *J. Chem. Soc.*, 1855–1865.

(12)   1951   (With H. M. E. Cardwell, S. R. Duff, H. Holtermann & R. Robinson) Total synthesis of androgenic hormones. *Chem. Ind.*, 389–390.

(13)   1953   (With H. M. E. Cardwell, S. R. Duff, H. Holtermann & R. Robinson) Experiments on the synthesis of substances related to the sterols. Part LI. Completion of the synthesis of androgenic hormones and of the cholesterol group of sterols. *J. Chem. Soc.*, 361–384.

(14)   (With G. D. Hunter & G. Popják) Studies of cholesterol biosynthesis. 1. A new chemical degradation of cholesterol. *Biochem. J.* **54**, 590–597.

(15)   (With G. D. Hunter & G. Popják) Studies of cholesterol biosynthesis. 2. Distribution of acetate carbon in the ring structure. *Biochem. J.* **54**, 597–601.

(16)   (With W. B. Renfrow) Structures of some 2-methoxy-8-keto-4a-methylperhydrophenanthrenes and related compounds. *J. Am. Chem. Soc.* **75**, 1347–1350.

(17)   1954   The biosynthesis of cholesterol. *Rev. Pure Appl. Chem.* **4**, 275–302.

(18)   (With G. Popják) Studies on the biosynthesis of cholesterol. 3. Distribution of ^{14}C in squalene biosynthesized from [Me-^{14}C]-acetate. *Biochem. J.* **58**, 403–407.

(19)   (With J. M. Osbond & G. H. Phillipps) The conversion of hecogenin acetate into 11-oxotigogenin acetate. *J. Chem. Soc.*, 907–912.

(20)   (With I. Youhotsky & G. Popják) Absolute configuration of cholesterol. *Nature* **173**, 536.

(21)   1957   (With I. Youhotsky-Gore & G. Popják) Studies on the biosynthesis of cholesterol. 4. Degradation of rings C and D. *Biochem. J.* **65**, 94–109.

(22)   (With R. H. Cornforth, G. Popják & I. Youhotsky-Gore) Biosynthesis of squalene and cholesterol from DL-β-hydroxy-β-methyl-δ-[2-^{14}C]valerolactone. *Biochem. J.* **66**, 10P.

(23)   1958   (With R. H. Cornforth, G. Popják & I. Youhotsky-Gore) Studies on the biosynthesis of cholesterol. 5. Biosynthesis of squalene from DL-3-hydroxy-3-methyl-[2-^{14}C]pentano-5-lactone. *Biochem. J.* **69**, 146–155.

(24)   1959   On the structure of sarcostin. *Chem. Ind.*, 602–603.

(25)   (With R. H. Cornforth & K. K. Mathew) A general stereoselective synthesis of olefins. *J. Chem. Soc.*, 112–127.

(26)   (With R. H. Cornforth & K. K. Mathew) A stereoselective synthesis of squalene. *J. Chem. Soc.*, 2539–2547.

(27)   (With R. H. Cornforth, A. Pelter, M. G. Horning & G. Popják) Studies on the biosynthesis of cholesterol. 7. Rearrangement of methyl groups during enzymic cyclisation of squalene. *Tetrahedron* **5**, 311–339.

(28)   1960   (With R. H. Cornforth & V. Prelog) Über die Absolute Konfiguration von Linalool, eine Berichtigung. *Liebigs Annln Chem.* **634**, 197–198.

(29)   1961   (With G. Popják, DeW. S. Goodman, R. H. Cornforth & R. Ryhage) Mechanism of squalene biosynthesis from mevalonate and farnesyl pyrophosphate. *Biochem. Biophys. Res. Commun.* **4**, 138–142.

(30)   (With G. Popják, R. H. Cornforth & DeW. S. Goodman) Synthesis of $1\text{-}T_2\text{-}2\text{-}C^{14}$ - and of $1\text{-}D_2\text{-}2\text{-}C^{14}\text{-}$ *trans-trans*-farnesyl pyrophosphate and their utilization in squalene synthesis. *Biochem. Biophys. Res. Commun.* **4**, 204–207.

(31)   (With G. Popják, DeW. S. Goodman, R. H. Cornforth & R. Ryhage) Studies on the biosynthesis of cholesterol. XV. Mechanism of squalene biosynthesis from farnesyl pyrophosphate and from mevalonate. *J. Biol. Chem.* **236**, 1934–1947.

(32)   1962   (With G. Popják & G. Schroepfer) Stereospecificity of hydrogen transfer from reduced nicotinamide-adenine dinucleotides to squalene. *Biochem. J.* **84**, 34P.

(33)   (With R. H. Cornforth & G. Popják) Preparation of *R*- and *S*-mevalonolactones. *Tetrahedron* **18**, 1351–1354.

(34)   (With G. Ryback, G. Popják, C. Donninger & G. Schroepfer Jr) Stereochemistry of enzymic hydrogen transfer to pyridine nucleotides. *Biochem. Biophys. Res. Commun.* **9**, 371–375.

(35)   1963   (With R. H. Cornforth, C. Donninger, G. Popják, G. Ryback & G. J. Schroepfer Jr) Stereospecific insertion of hydrogen atom into squalene from reduced nicotinamide adenine dinucleotides. *Biochem. Biophys. Res. Commun.* **11**, 129–134.

(36)   1965   (With R. H. Cornforth, C. Donninger, G. Popják, Y. Shimizu, S. Ichii, E. Forchielli & E. Caspi) The migration and elimination of hydrogen during biosynthesis of cholesterol from squalene. *J. Am. Chem. Soc.* **87**, 3224–3228.

(37)   1966   (With R. H. Cornforth, C. Donninger & G. Popják) Studies on the biosynthesis of cholesterol. XIX. Steric course of hydrogen eliminations and of C–C bond formations in squalene biosynthesis. *Proc. R. Soc. Lond.* B **163**, 492–514.

(38)   (With B. L. Archer, D. Barnard, E. G. Cockbain, R. H. Cornforth & G. Popják) The stereochemistry of rubber biosynthesis. *Proc. R. Soc. Lond.* B **163**, 519–523.

(39)   (With R. H. Cornforth, G. Popják & L. Yengoyan) Studies on the biosynthesis of cholesterol. XX. Steric course of decarboxylation of 5-pyrophosphomevalonate and of the carbon to carbon bond formation in the biosynthesis of farnesyl pyrophosphate. *J. Biol. Chem.* **241**, 3970–3987.

(40)   1968   Terpenoid biosynthesis. *Chem. Br.* **4**, 102–106.

(41)   1969   (With J. W. Redmond, H. Eggerer, W. Buckel & C. Gutschow) Asymmetric methyl groups and the mechanism of malate synthase. *Nature* **221**, 1212–1213.

(42)   1970   (With H. Eggerer, W. Buckel, H. Lenz, P. Wunderwald, G. Gottschalk, C. Donninger, R. Mallaby & J. W. Redmond) Stereochemistry of enzymic citrate synthesis and cleavage. *Nature* **226**, 517–519.

(43)   1971   (With H. Lenz, W. Buckel, P. Wunderwald, G. Biedermann, V. Buschmeier, H. Eggerer, J. W. Redmond & R. Mallaby) Stereochemistry of *si*-citrate synthase and ATP citrate lyase reactions. *Eur. J. Biochem.* **24**, 207–215.

(44)   (With P. Wunderwald, W. Buckel, H. Lenz, V. Buschmeier, H. Eggerer, G. Gottschalk, J. W. Redmond & R. Mallaby) Stereochemistry of the *re*-citrate synthase reaction. *Eur. J. Biochem.* **24**, 216–221.

(45)   1972   (With K. H. Clifford, C. Donninger & R. Mallaby) Stereochemical course of decarboxylation of *S*-malate on malic enzyme. *Eur. J. Biochem.* **26**, 401–406.

(46)   (With K. Clifford, R. Mallaby & G. T. Phillips) Stereochemistry of isopentenyl pyrophosphate isomerase. *Proc. R. Soc. Lond.* B **182**, 277–295.

(47)   Prix Roussel 1972. Enzymes of cholesterol biosynthesis. *Labo-Pharma, problèmes et techniques* no. 215, pp. 51–57.

(48)   1973   (With E. D. Morgan, K. T. Potts & R. J. W. Rees) Preparation of antituberculous polyoxyethylene ethers of homogeneous structure. *Tetrahedron* **29**, 1659–1667.

(49)   1974   (With G. T. Phillips, B. Messner & H. Eggerer) Substrate stereochemistry of 3-hydroxy-3-methylglutaryl-coenzyme A synthase. *Eur. J. Biochem.* **42**, 591–604.

(50)   1975   (With B. Messner, H. Eggerer & R. Mallaby) Substrate stereochemistry of the hydroxymethylglutaryl-CoA lyase and methylglutaconyl-CoA hydratase reactions *Eur. J. Biochem.* **53**, 255–264.

(51)   1977   (With B. Sedgwick) The biosynthesis of long-chain fatty acids. Stereochemical differentiation in the enzymic incorporation of chiral acetates. *Eur. J. Biochem.* **75**, 465–479.

(52)   (With B. Sedgwick, S. J. French, R. T. Gray, E. Kelstrup & P. Willadsen) The biosynthesis of long-chain fatty acids. Incorporation of radioactivity from stereospecifically tritiated malonyl thiol esters, and the stereochemistry of the acetyl-CoA carboxylase reaction. *Eur. J. Biochem.* **75**, 481–495.

(53)   (With S. A. Reichard, P. Talalay, H. L. Carrell & J. P. Glusker) Determination of the absolute configuration at the sulfonium center of *S*-adenosylmethionine. Correlation with the absolute configuration of the diastereomeric *S*-carboxymethyl-(*S*)methionine salts. *J. Am. Chem. Soc.* **99**, 7292–7300.

(54)   (With F. P. Ross) Symmetry of squalene epoxidation *in vivo*. *Proc. R. Soc. Lond.* B **199**, 213–230.

(55)   1987   (With L. M. Huguenin & J. R. H. Wilson) Synthesis of substituted dibenzophospholes. Part 8. Synthesis and resolution of atropisomers of a 4,6-diaryldibenzophosphole. *J. Chem. Soc. Perkin Trans. 1*, 871–875.

(56)   1991   (With M.-H. Du) 4-(2′-Hydroxyphenylmethylene)-2-phenyloxazol-5(4*H*)-one: a comedy of errors. *J. Chem. Soc. Perkin Trans. 1*, 2183–2187.

(57)   1996   Synthesis of substituted dibenzophospholes. Part 9. Preparation of two water-soluble phosphinic-polyphosphonic acids. *J. Chem. Soc. Perkin Trans. 1*, 2889–2893.

(58)   (With P. B. Hitchcock & P. Rozos) Isatin chloride: a phantom. Reactions of 2-(2,2-dichloro-2,3-dihydro-3-oxoindol-l-yl)-3*H*-indol-3-one. *J. Chem. Soc. Perkin Trans. 1*, 2787–2792.

(59)   2002   Sterol synthesis: the early days. *Biochem. Biophys. Res. Commun.* **292**, 1129–1138.

RICHARD HENRY DALITZ

28 February 1925 — 13 January 2006

Richard H. Dalitz

RICHARD HENRY DALITZ

28 February 1925 — 13 January 2006

Elected FRS 1960

By Ian J. R. Aitchison* and Sir Chris Llewellyn Smith‡ FRS

Rudolf Peierls Centre for Theoretical Physics, 1 Keble Road, Oxford OX1 3NP, UK

Richard (Dick) Henry Dalitz was a theoretical physicist whose principal contributions were intimately connected to some of the major breakthroughs of the twentieth century in particle and nuclear physics. His formulation of the 'τ–θ' puzzle led to the discovery that parity is not a symmetry of nature—the first of the assumed space-time symmetries to fail. He pioneered the theoretical study of hypernuclei, of strange baryon resonances, and of baryon spectroscopy in the quark model (at a time when many considered it 'naive'), to all of which he made lasting contributions. The 'Dalitz plot' and 'Dalitz pairs' are part of the vocabulary of particle physics. Throughout his career he remained in close touch with many experimentalists, and he had an encyclopaedic knowledge of the data. Many of his papers were stimulated by experimental results and were concerned with their analysis and interpretation, work that often required the forging of new phenomenological tools; many also indicated what new experiments needed to be done. As a consequence, he was a theorist exceptionally valued by experimentalists. He created and ran a strong particle theory group at Oxford, which attracted many talented students and researchers, and which has continued to thrive.

FAMILY BACKGROUND AND EARLY YEARS

Dick was born in Dimboola, a small town in western Victoria, Australia. His grandfather Heinrich had a smallholding near the town, but his main income was as a stonemason. He and his wife, Anna, had a large family of ten boys and three girls; the boys had little schooling and had to go out to work as soon as possible. Dick's father, Friedrich Wilhelm, was the eldest boy; he took work as a blacksmith in Dimboola. There he married Dick's mother, Hazel Drummond, who was a schoolteacher in the town, and was of Scottish descent.

* ijraitchison1@gmail.com
‡ chris.llewellyn-smith@physics.ox.ac.uk

© 2016 The Author(s)

http://dx.doi.org/10.1098/rsbm.2016.0019   61   Published by the Royal Society

Heinrich had been born in 1861, soon after his parents arrived in Australia. As the family had emigrated from Germany, it was generally assumed that they were originally Germans, but the name was an unusual one, and Dick was sceptical. However, it was not until after he settled in Oxford in 1963 that he found proof that they were descended from pre-German inhabitants of what later became Brandenburg, who were known as Wends, or Sorbs. With characteristic thoroughness, and with the help and encouragement of Gerald Stone, then of Nottingham University, Dick eventually identified the exact village and found his forbears listed in the parish records. He was able to trace, and then to meet in Australia, many other Sorbian families who had settled in Dimboola and elsewhere in the Wimmera district.

With Hazel's support, Dick's father passed examinations and became a government clerk in Melbourne, where Dick was educated. Dick won the first of many scholarships to attend Scotch College for the last four years of his secondary schooling. There major influences on him were Mr A. D. Ross, Senior Mathematics Master, and Mr Kaye, the Senior Physics Master. Dick graduated from Scotch College in 1941, with many prizes and scholarships, including the Ormond Exhibition in Mathematics at Ormond College, Melbourne University. He became a physics and mathematics student at the university, living at home. He profited from the teaching of Sir Thomas Cherry (FRS 1954), in mathematical analysis and the theory of functions; his interest in theoretical physics was first aroused by Dr H. C. Corben, then lecturer in mathematics and physics at Melbourne. During the summers of 1944–45 and 1945–46 Dick conducted research on the flow of compressible fluids under the guidance of Professor Cherry, as described in (1)*.

EARLY CONTRIBUTIONS AND DALITZ PAIRS

In 1946 Dick left Melbourne for Trinity College, Cambridge, supported by a travelling scholarship from the University of Melbourne, and accompanied by his wife, Valda (*née* Suiter); they had been married at Scotch College Chapel on 9 August 1946. During 1946–48 Dick worked towards his Cambridge DPhil under the supervision of Nicholas Kemmer (FRS 1956), on problems of nuclear physics and electrodynamics. By the end of the two years the money had run out and the couple had a young child, so in 1948 Dick took up a one-year post as a research assistant in the H. H. Wills Physical Laboratory at the University of Bristol, where he enjoyed close contact with the cosmic ray group of Cecil Powell (FRS 1949). Then in 1949 Dick joined the Department of Mathematical Physics at the University of Birmingham under Rudolf (later Sir Rudolf) Peierls FRS, where he would spend the next four, very formative, years.

He submitted his Cambridge thesis entitled 'Zero-zero transitions in nuclei' on 13 December 1950. It concerned primarily the transition from the first excited 0^+ state of ^{16}O at 6.05 MeV to the 0^+ ground state. Conservation of angular momentum prevents the transition from proceeding by the emission of a single photon, but it is allowed for a longitudinally polarized virtual photon that converts to an electron–positron pair. Motivated by experiments of Samuel Devons (FRS 1955) and others (Devons & Lindsey 1949; Devons *et al.* 1949), the thesis described the calculation of radiative corrections to angular correlations in such an internal pair-creation process. The techniques for higher-order calculations in quantum electrodynamics had only recently been developed in the independent work of Sin-Itiro Tomonaga, Julian Schwinger and Richard Feynman (ForMemRS 1965). Their different

* Numbers in this form refer to the bibliography at the end of the text.

formalisms had been remarkably synthesized by Freeman Dyson (FRS 1952) in 1949, who spent the years 1949–51 as a Teaching Fellow in Peierls's department. At the end of the paper (2) describing the main results of his Cambridge thesis, Dick wrote that he 'would like to acknowledge here his debt to the lectures [on quantum field theory and electrodynamics] of Mr. F. J. Dyson and to thank Professor R. E. Peierls for his continual interest in this work'. Both Dyson and Peierls, especially the latter, would exert a strong influence on Dick.

This work on internal pair creation bore fruit in the first of Dick's seminal contributions to particle physics—the realization that e^+e^- pairs ('Dalitz pairs') can be produced in the decays of neutral π-mesons (3). At the 1987 Bristol Meeting to celebrate 40 years of particle physics (50) Dick recalled how, on a weekend visit to Bristol in early 1951 to visit 'old friends on the fourth floor' (i.e. Powell's group), they showed him some of the emulsion events they were working on, after which

> they said 'Here are two peculiar pairs'. In each of these cases, the outgoing pair of tracks were clearly identified as electronic. What was peculiar about them was that the origin of each pair could not be seen as separate from the centre of the cosmic ray star from which it emerged. What could give rise to these two pairs? On my way back to Birmingham, I suddenly realized that the π^0 itself could give rise to them by a direct decay to γe^+e^-, through the process of internal pair conversion of one of its product photons,
>
> $$\pi^0 \rightarrow \gamma + \text{'}\gamma\text{'} \rightarrow \gamma + e^+e^-.$$

His thesis work was now relevant, because his calculations had shown (2) that the internal pair creation rate in that $0 \rightarrow 0$ transition in ^{16}O depended very little on the nuclear charge, and was certainly non-zero for $Z = 0$. 'So', he recalled (50), 'I calculated the rate for the internal conversion of one of the γ-rays in $\pi^0 \rightarrow \gamma\gamma$ decay for a free π^0'.

Dick obtained (3) a branching ratio of 1.185% for this π^0 decay mode, later increased to 1.195% by radiative corrections (Joseph 1960); today's value is (1.198 ± 0.032)%. At that time the Bristol group was reluctant to claim discovery of the mode from their two events; it was established a year or so later (Daniel *et al.* 1952).

Dalitz pairs became a useful tool in particle physics. For example, the decay $\Sigma^0 \rightarrow \Lambda^0 + e^+e^-$, in which the photon in the decay $\Sigma^0 \rightarrow \Lambda^0 + \gamma$ converts to a pair, was used to establish that the Σ^0 and Λ^0 have the same parity. In another example, Dick's work on the single conversion in π^0 decays was extended by N. N. Kroll and W. Wada to the double-Dalitz process $\pi^0 \rightarrow e^+e^-e^+e^-$ (Kroll & Wada 1955). Their analysis was used by Plano *et al.* (1959) to establish that the parity of the π^0 was odd, the same as that of the charged pions.

THE τ–θ PUZZLE AND THE DALITZ PLOT

Dick's analysis of τ^+-meson* decays led to a revolution in particle physics, and secured his place in the first rank of particle theorists.

His interest in strange particles had begun during the year 1948–49 at Bristol. He became well informed about the discoveries being made by Powell's group, and he continued to follow their work after moving to Birmingham. Data on the 'new' (i.e. strange) particles accumulated slowly, and in 1953 Powell organized a Royal Society Discussion Meeting, held on 29 January 1953, to review the available evidence. By then 11 events of the type

---

* Subsequently identified as the charged strange meson K⁺.

$$\tau^+ \rightarrow \pi^+\pi^+\pi^-$$

were known, and as Dick later recalled (46), 'the time was ripe to give some serious consideration to their characteristics'. The result of this consideration was first reported at the International Cosmic Ray Conference held on 6–12 July at Bagnères-de-Bigorre in the Basque country on the northern slopes of the Pyrenees.

This conference, organized by Patrick (later Lord) Blackett FRS (PRS 1965–70) and Louis Leprince-Ringuet, was a watershed in particle physics. Dick himself felt (46) that it 'was a major event in the lives of all the physicists who took part in it'. The historical account of it by James Cronin (ForMemRS 2007) is entitled 'The 1953 Cosmic Ray Conference at Bagnères-de-Bigorre: the birth of sub-atomic physics' (Cronin 2011), and he places it in the same category as the 1927 Solvay Conference and the 1947 Shelter Island Conference. It marks the moment when, in particle physics research, cosmic ray studies gave way to experiments at accelerators.*

Two contributions to the conference were particularly noteworthy. The first was given by Robert Thompson of Indiana University. He presented measurements of the decay of the 'heavy meson' $\theta^0 \rightarrow \pi^+\pi^-$ observed in a precision cloud chamber (Thompson *et al.* 1953). The mass of the θ^0 was 971 ± 10 electron masses (m_e). Because the pions were known to be spinless, the parity of the θ^0 was necessarily $(-)^J$, where J is the spin of the θ^0, which is carried away as angular momentum by the two pions.

The second was Dick's contribution, which was concerned with the analysis of the τ^+ decay process in terms of its spin-parity, and on which he had started to work in Birmingham after the Royal Society Discussion Meeting. The τ^+ was by then well established, with a mass of $970 \pm 5 \, m_e$. His talk was a brief summary of the main results obtained in the paper that he had sent to the journal (received 1 July 1953) before leaving for the conference (4). As he later recalled (46):

> It was my opinion that the amplitude for the [τ^+] decay mode should be largely calculable in form (although not in magnitude) in terms of angular momentum barrier considerations, apart from a few parameters necessary when the total angular momentum and parity could be apportioned to the internal orbital motions within the three-particle system in more than one comparable way. If so, it would then be possible to deduce the values of these internal angular momenta from the distribution of events and from them to reach some conclusions about the total spin-parity [of the τ-meson], at least to exclude some possibilities. First, a representation was needed to display the distribution of events pictorially.

That representation was, of course, the first Dalitz plot. To appreciate its construction, some kinematics have to be introduced.

The decay may first be considered in the centre-of-mass system of the two like pions (labelled 1 and 2 in figure 1), where the unlike pion (labelled 3) has momentum p and the like pions have momenta $\pm q$. The magnitudes p and q of p and q are related by the conditions of energy and momentum conservation; ℓ is the angular momentum of the like pions and L is that of the unlike pion.

It is also convenient to treat the decay in the rest frame of the τ^+-meson. The three outgoing pions then have zero total momentum and total kinetic energy $E = m_\tau - 3m_\pi$. Apart from the spatial orientation, the specification of the decay configuration requires two

---

* The proceedings of the conference were not formally published, and existed only in mimeographed form available to the participants. However, the contributions may now be found online; Dick's is at http://inspirehep.net/record/1344834/files/Rayonnement-236-238.pdf.

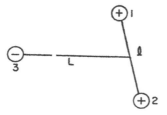

Figure 1. τ-Meson decay in the rest frame of the like pions, labelled 1 and 2. (Figure reprinted with permission from (5). Copyright © 1954 the American Physical Society.)

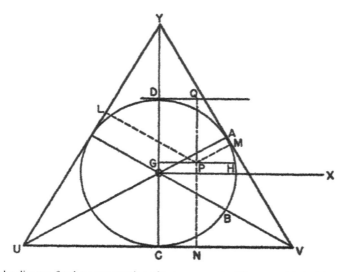

Figure 2. Triangular diagram for the representation of τ-meson events. (Figure reprinted with permission from (5). Copyright © 1954 the American Physical Society.)

parameters, for example the kinetic energies of two of the pions, say ϵ_1 and ϵ_2. At that time (July 1953) the data were not able to distinguish the charges of the outgoing mesons, and so Dick adopted a parametrization that was symmetrical between the three pions: namely, he retained all three kinetic energies ϵ_i, subject to the constraint $\epsilon_1 + \epsilon_2 + \epsilon_3 = E$. Then, referring to figure 2, an event corresponding to the kinetic energies ϵ_i may be specified by a point P in the interior of an equilateral triangle YUV of height E, such that the perpendiculars (PL, PM, PN) from P onto the three sides of the triangle are of length ϵ_i (the sum of these three perpendiculars being equal to the height of the triangle). Interchange of any two energies ϵ_i corresponds to reflection of P in a corresponding altitude of the triangle so that, because no charge information was available, the event is represented in each of the six sub-triangles of YUV. The distribution in any sub-triangle is obtainable from that in AOV by successive reflections in the altitudes, and so only that ordering of the energies for which P lies in AOV need be considered.

However, the full interior of the triangle is not kinematically available. To find the allowed region, Dick at this point moved to a non-relativistic description, for which the error is at most a few percent. Then one finds (4) that the boundary of the physical region may be written as

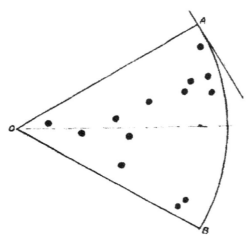

Figure 3. The data from 13 τ-decay events (from (4)).

$x^2 + y^2 = \frac{1}{9}E^2$, where* $x = (\epsilon_1 - \epsilon_2)/\sqrt{3}$, $y = \epsilon_3 - \frac{1}{3}E$. This is the circle inscribed in the triangle of figure 2, having radius $\frac{1}{3}E$. All the events must fall inside this circle. Plotting the events on this diagram results in the 'Dalitz plot'.

The crucial property of such a plot is that the distribution of events on the plot is proportional to the square of the matrix element for the decay. This follows from the fundamental fact that the density of states, up to numerical factors, is (5)

$$\delta(\epsilon_1 + \epsilon_2 + \epsilon_3 - E)\, d\epsilon_1 d\epsilon_2 d\epsilon_3 = \tfrac{1}{2}\sqrt{3}\; dx dy,$$

so that variation in the density of events on the plot is a direct consequence of non-trivial structure in the decay matrix element†. It was a brilliant construction, allowing the events themselves to reveal the physics of the decay. It perfectly united Dick's fondness for geometry and the primacy he always accorded to the data.

The key question was whether the θ^0-particle and the τ-particle could be closely related, in view of the near equality of their masses. In particular, could the τ^+ have parity $(-)^J$, as was necessarily the case for the θ^0? The matrix element for the τ decay could be expanded in a series of products $Y_{Lm_L}(\theta_p, \phi_p) Y_{\ell m_\ell}(\theta_q, \phi_q)$ (see figure 1). Bose statistics for the like pions requires ℓ to be even, so that the τ parity is $(-)^{L+1}$. Dick now argued that, given the small energy release, angular momentum barrier considerations would limit L and ℓ to low values. If the parity of τ were even, then $L = 1$ would be the most likely value. This would produce a factor p^2 in the squared matrix element, which is proportional to ϵ_3, and vanishes at the point C on figure 2, or at A in the folded plot of figure 3. More generally, when the π^- is stationary (at C) J is carried by the two π^+-mesons, and must be even by Bose statistics. Hence the density of events must vanish near C (or A) unless J^P is $0^-, 2^-, 4^-, \ldots$. A uniform distribution of events would signal $J = 0$ and odd parity.

The data he showed at Bagnères-de-Bigorre (figure 3) were too sparse to draw a firm conclusion, but Dick allowed himself the statement that 'The data available at present … offers no significant evidence for any lack of isotropy in the decay process' (4).

---

* Dick actually rescaled the variables to produce a circle of unit radius.
† Dick himself referred to his plot as 'the usual phase-space diagram'.

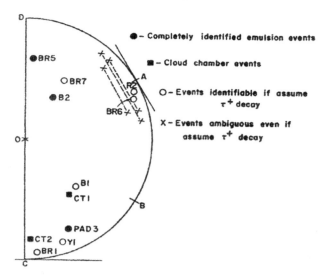

Figure 4. The data on τ-meson decay events in which the signs of τ-meson charges were established (Figure reprinted with permission from (5). Copyright © 1954 by the American Physical Society.)

The analysis of (4) had, however, provided the predicted energy distributions for the unlike pion for spin-parity combinations 0^-, $1^\pm$, 2^+ and 3^-, which were generally more sharply distinguishable than the corresponding predictions for the charge-averaged case. For example, the amplitudes for natural parities $(-)^J$ must all contain an axial vector factor $\boldsymbol{p} \times \boldsymbol{q}$, whose square vanishes on the boundary of the plot. By January 1954, 13 τ^- events with mostly identified charges could be placed on the full plot, as shown in figure 4, taken from Dick's 1954 paper in *Physical Review* (5) (the plot is symmetrical about the axis DC as a result of the symmetry of the two π^+-mesons). By this time, Dick was at Cornell, where he moved in September 1953 on a two-year leave of absence from Birmingham, having been invited by Hans Bethe (ForMemRS 1957).

There was certainly no dearth of events near the point C (slow π^-), but Dick's conclusion was still cautious: 'the number of τ-decay events giving a slow unlike π-meson rather suggests that the least L is $L = 0$, which would imply that the τ meson belongs to the class of even $[J]$ and odd $[P]$, a class for which [if P is conserved] the 2π decay is forbidden'. Two weeks after Dick's paper was received (on 9 February 1954), Fabri (1954) submitted a paper that gave a formal derivation of the decay amplitudes for the spin-parity combinations 0^-, $1^\pm$, 2^+ and 3^-, and extended the kinematics to the relativistic case.

Thus by early 1954 there was already emerging a 'τ–θ puzzle': the near equality of the masses suggested that they were simply different decay modes of a common particle (in different charge states), but that could not be the case, it seemed, because the parities were different. The puzzle came into sharper focus at the Pisa Conference the following year, when Edoardo Amaldi presented a report on τ decays based on 106 events, reaching the quite firm conclusion that the spin-parity of the 3π state from τ decay was most probably 0^-.

One resolution of the puzzle, raised at the time by Dick himself and others, was to suppose that the θ^0 and τ^+ were indeed different charge states of the same particle (i.e. a charge doublet (K^0, K^+)), but that parity was not conserved in their decays. This would imply a failure of invariance with respect to space reflections. However, as he recalled at the 1982 Paris Colloquium (46):

> How was it possible that reflection invariance should not hold, people asked—was not left–right invariance inherent in our most fundamental conceptions about space-time? The only answer available was that the occurrence of both K → 2π and K → 3π decays actually did demonstrate this, but this answer did not have compelling force because it could not point to any *explicit* empirical demonstration of parity failure. ... It required much less faith to suppose that ... there existed two distinct K-meson charge doublets, labelled τ and θ, close in mass but with different spin-parities. ... The mental obstacle [to accepting the parity violation explanation] arose from the fact that the τ–θ puzzle did not provide an explicit demonstration of parity nonconservation.

By this twice-repeated lack of 'explicit demonstration' of the failure of reflection invariance Dick meant some observable effect, the existence of which would unequivocally show that this symmetry did indeed fail. In fact, he himself came very close to predicting just such an effect. As he recalled in (59), the K → 2π and K → 3π amplitudes can interfere if they both contribute virtually to a process leading to a common final state—and such interfering amplitudes will have opposite parities. One such example is the pair of amplitudes for the processes $\Lambda \to n + \overline{K}^0 \to n + \pi^- + \pi^+ \to \pi^- + p$ and $\Lambda \to p + K^- \to p + \pi^- + \pi^+ + \pi^- \to \pi^- + p$. Dick thought of making a calculation of these processes in 1955 (59): it would have shown that a parity violation effect would be expected in the decay of *polarized* Λ-particles. But there were major theoretical uncertainties, and the effect was (mistakenly) thought likely to be small. So he did not complete the calculation.

It was, as Dick acknowledged (46, 59), the genius of Tsung Dao Lee and Chen Ning Yang (Lee & Yang 1956) to relate the question of possible parity violation in K-meson decays with the whole class of weak interactions, so that the first empirical demonstrations of parity non-conservation were not carried out with strange particles but in nuclear β decay and in π–μ–e decay. Nevertheless, it was Dick's analysis of τ decay that had led to this momentous discovery.

The discovery of parity (P) violation was soon followed by that of charge-conjugation (C) violation, and later of CP violation. Dick always maintained a strong interest in these discrete symmetries. Frank von Hippel and Dick discussed the implications of electromagnetic Λ–Σ^0 mixing for charge symmetry in Λ physics (22); and in 1986 Neil Tanner and Dick (49) drew attention to the possibilities afforded by the antiproton beam of LEAR for new measurements concerning T-, CP- and CPT-violation parameters in the K^0–$\overline{K}^0$ system.

In his first paper on the plot (4) Dick had shown how it could not only reveal the spin-parity of the decaying state but also provide information about strong pairwise interactions in the final state. Both properties made the plot a powerful tool in the exploration of the hadronic resonance spectrum in the 1960s and 1970s. The energies ϵ_i remained suitable relativistic variables, the only new feature being that the shape of the plot was no longer circular, even in the equal-mass case. An important early application was to the ω-meson, which decays to three pions; the density of events on the plot clearly vanished at the boundary, hence establishing $J^P = 1^-$ for the ω (Maglić *et al.* 1961; Stevenson *et al.* 1962).

Resonance states involving pairs of final-state particles could be immediately identified as concentrations of events (bands) near lines of constant ϵ_i. This was particularly relevant in cases where the mass of the resonance was such that it could not be directly formed in a 'beam plus target' channel. An early example was the strangeness −1 baryon Y*(1385) (now called Σ(1385)), whose mass, 1385 MeV, is below that of the K⁻p system. This was discovered in a hydrogen bubble chamber at the Berkeley Bevatron by a Dalitz plot analysis of the reaction $K^-p \rightarrow \Lambda^0 + \pi^+ + \pi^-$ (Alston *et al.* 1960). The strangeness -2 baryon $\Xi^*(1530)$ (which also can only be seen in final states) followed soon after, via the reaction $K^-p \rightarrow \Xi^- + K^+ + \pi^0$ (Pjerrou *et al.* 1962; Schlein *et al.* 1963).

As the data improved, Dalitz plots found an important new application. By exploiting the interference between different resonance bands, it proved possible to extract information about the phases of production amplitudes. Originally pioneered in the context of (inelastic) nucleon resonances (Herndon *et al.* 1975*a*, *b*), the technique has more recently been successfully applied to measure CP-violating phases (del Amo Sanchez *et al.* 2010*a*; Poluektov *et al.* 2010) and $\bar{D}^0$–D^0 mixing parameters (Zhang *et al.* 2007; del Amo Sanchez *et al.* 2010*b*). Dalitz plots produced from the B-factories now contain upwards of 10^5 events—some distance from the original 13! Dick's beautiful 'pictorial representation' is certain to remain an indispensable tool in particle physics.

Y–N, Y–Y INTERACTIONS AND HYPERNUCLEAR PHYSICS

Dick returned to Birmingham as Reader in Mathematical Physics in 1955, and then moved to the University of Chicago in 1956, where he was based for the next seven years. Enrico Fermi had died in 1954, and as Dick recalled in an interview he gave in 2003 (O'Byrne 2004), several leading theoretical physicists had left Chicago, providing a 'tremendous opportunity— to build up groups again and get things going'. It was in Chicago that his

> interest in hypernuclear events developed particularly well … because a young emulsion experimenter, Riccardo Levi-Setti, whose work I had known from his hypernuclear studies in Milan, came to the [Enrico Fermi] Institute for Nuclear Studies at this time. We benefited from each other, I think, and we got quite a lot done.

Dick worked on the physics of strange particles throughout his career. Of some 220 main publications listed in the bibliography (see the electronic supplementary material), almost one-half broadly involve strange particles; nearly one-third relate more specifically to hypernuclei, a field he pioneered and in which he was a recognized leader for 50 years.

The observation of the first hyperfragment event, in a balloon-flown photographic emulsion, was announced in Warsaw by Marian Danysz and Jerzy Pniewski (Danysz & Pniewski 1953). Subsequently, the light s-shell hypernuclei $^3_\Lambda H$, $^4_\Lambda H$, $^4_\Lambda He$ and $^5_\Lambda He$ were analysed by Dick and collaborators. In Dick's first published work on Λ hypernuclei, he focused on the near equality of the ($^4_\Lambda H$, $^4_\Lambda He$) binding energy and its origin in the charge symmetry of the Λ–N interaction; he also noted the very small binding energy of the $I = 0$ $^3_\Lambda H$, the only bound $A = 3$ hypernucleus (6). By 1958–59 Dalitz and B. W. Downs reported that the existence of a bound Λ–N system was strongly excluded and that analysis of the $I = 1$ triplet $^3_\Lambda He$, $^3_\Lambda H$, $^3_\Lambda n$ indicated that these systems were not expected to form bound states, a conclusion unaffected by the existence of moderately strong three-body forces arising from pion exchange processes (8, 9, 11).

Soon after the discovery of parity violation, Dick initiated the theory of mesonic weak decay of hypernuclei. He realized that the two-body decays $^4_\Lambda H \rightarrow {}^4He + \pi^-$ and $^3_\Lambda H \rightarrow {}^3He + \pi^-$, then being studied in photographic emulsions, could be used to extract the parent hypernuclear ground-state spins and parities, and hence provide information about the spin dependence of the Λ–N force (10). An improved calculation by Dalitz and Liu (12) provided a plot of the branching ratio ($^4_\Lambda H \rightarrow {}^4He + \pi^-$)/(all π^- decays of $^4_\Lambda H$) for the possible ground-state spins $J = 0$ and $J = 1$, as a function of the relative amounts of s-wave (parity-violating) and p-wave (parity-conserving) amplitude in the elementary decay $\Lambda \rightarrow p\pi^-$. The data at that time were not able to establish the value of J, but within a few years this type of analysis yielded the J^P assignments for $^3_\Lambda$H, $^4_\Lambda$H, $^4_\Lambda$He, $^8_\Lambda$Li, $^{11}_\Lambda$B and $^{12}_\Lambda$B (21, 33, 41) (Block *et al.* 1964; Bertrand *et al.* 1970; Ziemińska 1975). In particular, the ground-state spins 0^+ for $^4_\Lambda$H and $\frac{1}{2}^+$ for $^3_\Lambda$H showed that the s-wave Λ–N interaction was more attractive in the singlet state than in the triplet state.

The complete spin dependence of the Λ–N interaction can be obtained from the energy spacings of the $J = J_c \pm \frac{1}{2}$ spin doublets in Λ-hypernuclei, where the hyperon in the s shell couples to a ground-state nuclear core with non-zero spin J_c. Together with Avraham Gal and John Soper, Dick introduced shell-model techniques to predict the anticipated γ-ray transitions (29, 30, 39, 40). The effective Λ–N interaction contains spin–spin, spin–orbit and tensor terms, in addition to a spin-independent term. This work was further developed with Gal, John Millener and Carl Dover (48) and served as the basis for the interpretation of γ-ray spectroscopy experiments, which began in 1998 at the High Energy Accelerator Research Organization (KEK) in Japan and at Brookhaven National Laboratory in New York, and continued with systematic programmes at both laboratories (Hashimoto & Tamura 2006). The spin dependence of the effective Λ–N interaction is now rather well understood.

In addition to the mesonic modes, hypernuclear ground states also decay by non-mesonic weak decay (NMWD) modes of the type $\Lambda n \rightarrow nn$ or $\Lambda p \rightarrow np$. This is a four-fermion, $\Delta S = 1$, baryon–baryon weak interaction, and is the only practical way to obtain information on the weak process $\Lambda N \rightarrow nN$. In particular, NMWD processes offer new systems for exploring the still incompletely understood $\Delta I = \frac{1}{2}$ rule. Once again, it was Dick who led the way in the analysis of these decays. With G. Rajasekharan he proposed a simple but very effective phenomenological model (17), in which the non-mesonic rates $\Gamma_{NM}(^A_\Lambda Z)$ were expressed as linear combinations of rates R_{NJ} for the elementary $\Lambda N \rightarrow nN$ interactions, where $N = n, p$ and $J = 0, 1$. The four s-shell hypernuclei $^3_\Lambda$H, $^4_\Lambda$H, $^4_\Lambda$He and $^5_\Lambda$He were considered. Thus, for example,

$$\Gamma_{NM}(^3_\Lambda H) = \tfrac{1}{8}(3R_{n0} + R_{n1} + 3R_{p0} + R_{p1})\rho_3,$$

where ρ_3 is the average $A = 3$ nucleon density at the position of the Λ baryon. This model was then used by Dick and Martin Block (19) to determine the rates R_{NJ} from data recently obtained by Block *et al.* (1964). One interesting relation, which can be tested experimentally in principle, follows from assuming the validity of the $\Delta I = \frac{1}{2}$ rule: $R_{n0}/R_{p0} = 2$. The early data were such that no definite conclusion could be drawn about the $\Delta I = \frac{1}{2}$ rule. Indeed, even according to a much more recent analysis (Alberico & Garbarino 2000), using the phenomenological Dalitz–Rajasekharan–Block model, a pure $\Delta I = \frac{1}{2}$ rule could be excluded only at the 40% confidence level.

A final example of Dick's early and continuing pivotal role in this field concerns $\Lambda\Lambda$ double hypernuclei. The first such double hypernucleus, an example of $^{10}_{\Lambda\Lambda}$Be, was announced by the Warsaw group in 1962 (Danysz *et al.* 1963a, b), and Dick was among the first to extract information about the Λ–Λ interaction from it (20). A second event, an example of $^6_{\Lambda\Lambda}$He, was reported by D. J. Prowse in 1966 (Prowse 1966). Then, in 1977, Bob Jaffe predicted (Jaffe 1977) the existence of the H-particle, a deeply bound (by perhaps 80 MeV) six-quark system with the quark content of two Λ hyperons. The existence of such an H-particle would bring into question the existence of double hypernuclei stable against all except weak interactions, because a strong decay of the type $^6_{\Lambda\Lambda}$He $\rightarrow$ ^{4}He + H would be possible, given the much weaker binding of the two Λs in the hypernucleus. At Dick's prompting, the evidence for the two double hypernuclei was re-examined (53). An independent analysis of unpublished photomicrographs taken of the event by Peter Fowler (FRS 1964) in Bristol some 25 years earlier confirmed the interpretation of the $^{10}_{\Lambda\Lambda}$Be event, but the $^6_{\Lambda\Lambda}$He event seemed less secure; furthermore, the binding energies in the two cases were in some considerable disagreement. In 2001 the issue was resolved by the discovery of a tightly constrained $^6_{\Lambda\Lambda}$He event with a net binding energy of about 1 MeV (Takahashi *et al.* 2001); this implied that the Λ–Λ interaction is weakly attractive.

Personal accounts of Dick's career-long involvement with hypernuclear physics have been given by Don Davis (Davis 2008) and Avraham Gal (Gal 2008).

$\overline{\text{K}}$–N INTERACTIONS AND THE K-MATRIX

Nothwithstanding his attachment to hypernuclear physics, Dick was primarily a particle physicist, and a constant aim of his research was the traditional one of establishing the properties of the various states, and the nature of the forces between them. In the mid 1950s, theoretical attention was mostly focused on the interactions of pions and nucleons. Never one to follow fashion, Dick turned to the study of the strong interactions of strange particles, in the course of which he developed new and lasting phenomenological tools.

An early and very influential series of papers was concerned with low-energy $\overline{\text{K}}$N interactions. In 1959 Dick and San Fu Tuan (13) analysed the available data, using as parameters two complex $\overline{\text{K}}$N scattering lengths in the isospin 0 and 1 channels, as was then conventional. They found one solution set ('b_-') in which the real part of the $I = 0$ scattering length could indicate binding. They pointed out, for the first time, that in this case the $I = 0$ K$^-$p scattering amplitude would have a pole just below threshold, in the (unphysical) lower half-plane of the complex energy variable, reached by analytic continuation from the upper half-plane across the cut lying between the $\pi\Sigma$ and $\overline{\text{K}}$N thresholds. This focus on analytic continuation across cuts to look for poles was something quite unfamiliar in hadron phenomenology at the time. The authors noted that the imaginary part of the amplitude would exhibit a pronounced peak below the $\overline{\text{K}}$N threshold. They concluded that 'under certain circumstances, the appearance of this maximum would correspond to the existence of a resonance … in pion–hyperon scattering [i.e. in $\pi\Sigma$] for a closely related energy value'. A note added in proof stated that the situation had 'now been analysed in greater detail' in a further publication.

In this second paper (14) (confined for simplicity to the $I = 0$ channel) the authors took what would prove to be a very significant step: they introduced a new parametrization based on a two-channel K-matrix, describing the coupled $\overline{\text{K}}$N and $\pi\Sigma$ channels (all in the s-wave and $I = 0$). This parametrization was fully relativistic; further, Hermiticity of the Hamiltonian, together with time-reversal invariance, implied that K had to be a real symmetric matrix, and any such matrix would guarantee a unitary T-matrix. The authors argued that at low energies it would suffice to take the elements of K to be constant, in analogy with the scattering length approximation. Thus three parameters were required, two of which could be related to the (complex) $I = 0$ scattering length of the previous fit. The authors noted that the data pointed towards the solution b_- and the resulting pole structure found in (13), which they now interpreted as corresponding to 'the existence of a bound state in the $\overline{K}N$ channel'. The situation made it quite possible that there 'should exist a resonant state for pion–hyperon scattering at an energy of about 30 MeV below the K^-p (c.m.) threshold energy'. This state became known as the $Y_0^*(1405)$.

There soon followed a fuller description of the approach (15). Although its title still referred specifically to $\overline{K}N$ reactions, it is in fact a classic in the field of general hadron phenomenology. It set out the general K-matrix formalism in a relativistic (rather than potential theory) context, as appropriate to the analysis of particle physics experiments. The authors emphasized, in addition to the guarantee of unitarity, the utility of the formalism in dealing with strong inter-channel coupling effects—in particular (in this case) the reaction of the K^-p channel on the $\pi\Sigma$ channel. The formalism provided an economical parametrization, generalizing non-relativistic effective range theory. Detailed consideration was given to both the $I = 0$ and $I = 1$ $\overline{K}N$ channels: assuming charge independence, six real parameters were required, two more than in the previous fits. Attention was paid to the structure of the cuts in the complex energy plane associated with the branch points at the $\pi\Lambda$, $\pi\Sigma$, K^-p, $\overline{K}^0n$ thresholds. Although the implications of the b_- solution were reiterated, when the paper was submitted it no longer appeared to be favoured by the data.

By the time of the 1961 Aix-en-Provence conference, the situation had changed again, as discussed by Dick in his contribution (18). In Dick's words, 'some tentative experimental evidence was presented by Alston *et al.* (Alston *et al.* 1961)', in the reaction $K^- + p \rightarrow \Sigma^\pm + \pi^\mp + \pi^+ + \pi^-$ for K^- momentum 1.15 GeV/c. A plot of the invariant mass distribution of the $(\Sigma\pi)^0$ system showed a concentration of events near a mass of about 1405 MeV, but the sample contained only 32 events. Soon afterwards, Alexander *et al.* (1962) analysed 189 events of the type $\pi^-p \rightarrow \Sigma^\pm\pi^\mp K^0$ at 2.1 GeV/c; examination of the Dalitz plot and its projections showed a prominent enhancement in $M_{\Sigma\pi}$ at 1410 MeV. Later analyses (Thomas *et al.* 1973; Hemingway 1985) provided even stronger evidence for the state, which is now known as the $\Lambda(1405)$.

It is, perhaps, a measure of Dick's intuition in selecting this system for study 56 years ago that, although the existence of the $\Lambda(1405)$ is now accepted, its interpretation is still not settled. From the beginning he appreciated the need for a dynamical theory that went beyond the strictly phenomenological K-matrix approach. At the time, such a theory of strong interactions was provided by partial wave dispersion relations—specifically the N/D method (Chew & Mandelstam 1960). Here the N function contains the contributions from forces (particle exchanges), and D accounts for unitarity effects. In a more pedagogical follow-up (16) to his paper with Tuan (15), Dick showed how the K-matrix could be simply related to N and D (namely $K = N/\text{Re}D$ in the single-channel case). Then, with Wong and Rajasekaran (26), he showed that a $\Lambda(1405)$ state could be dynamically generated by an exchange of vector mesons between the meson and baryon fields, lending support to the idea that it was a composite system, somewhat analogous to the deuteron (a bound n–p system).

By then, of course, Dick had become intensely interested in the quark model for hadrons, as we shall discuss shortly. Here the picture of the $\Lambda(1405)$ is apparently very different. Having $J^P = \frac{1}{2}^-$, it would be an $L = 1$ SU(3)-singlet state of u, d and s quarks, coupled to the s-wave meson baryon systems. In the hadronic channels, it would be an 'elementary', not composite, particle, not generated by hadronic dynamics. But the quark model had difficulty in accounting for the large difference in mass between this state and its spin–orbit partner, the $J^P = \frac{3}{2}^-\Lambda(1520)$ (Isgur & Karl 1978). On the other hand, a purely hadronic interpretation of the

$\Lambda(1405)$ would—according to the quark model—require the existence of a new partner of the $\Lambda(1520)$ in a region already well explored.

This was a new 'puzzle', this time in hadronic physics. Which interpretation was correct? Was the state elementary or composite? Or did the truth lie somewhere between? As it happened, a formal way to insert an elementary particle into the N/D framework had been discovered by Dick, Leonardo Castillejo and Freeman Dyson in the famous 'CDD' paper (7). There is an ambiguity in the N/D procedure, which allows one or more poles to be added to the D function without spoiling the solution. Such a pole will give rise to a zero of the amplitude, but depending on the residue it may also lead to a nearby zero of ReD, which will appear as a resonance in the amplitude. Such a resonance will persist, however weak the forces represented in N, and will hence be interpreted as 'elementary'.

Dick revisited this puzzle many times (42, 43, 45, 55, 60). From today's perspective, the answer is most likely to be found from lattice quantum chromodynamics (QCD). Indeed, a recent calculation indicates that the $\Lambda(1405)$ is a $\overline{K}N$ molecule (Hall *et al.* 2015).

OXFORD AND QUARKS

When he was in Birmingham, Dick was strongly influenced by Rudolf (Rudi) Peierls, who (in Dick's words in the biographical notes he provided for the Royal Society when he became a Fellow in 1960) 'showed a stimulating enthusiasm for the questions of interest to me and discussions with him showed me a viewpoint towards physics which I found refreshing and novel'. After Peierls accepted the Wykeham Chair in Oxford, which he took up in 1963, he persuaded Dick to join him, as a Royal Society Research Professor and Fellow of All Souls College.

Dick moved to Oxford in 1963 on a trial basis, with the option of returning to Chicago. He brought with him an enormous American convertible, in which he negotiated the narrow English roads. But he eventually exchanged it for a Mini, and he was based in Oxford for the rest of his life, remaining very active after he retired in 1990.

At All Souls he pushed for the creation of a Visiting Fellows scheme, against rival proposals that had already been partly accepted. Since 1966 the scheme has brought some 700 Visiting Fellows to Oxford for between one and three terms, to the great benefit of academic life in the university. Dick and Dennis Sciama (FRS 1982) were active in persuading a series of very distinguished scientists (including, for example, Subrahmanyan Chandrasekhar FRS, John Ellis (FRS 1985) and Claude Shannon (ForMemRS 1991)) to come to Oxford on this scheme. Dick also took an active part in college elections, as a member of the college's governing body and its Academic Purposes Committee. His quiet presence was appreciated by the other Fellows who were mainly drawn from the arts and humanities, and when he chose to speak in Governing Body meetings his words carried all the more weight for being brief, to the point and authoritative.

When he arrived in Oxford, Dick also took on the role of advisor on theoretical matters at the nearby Rutherford High-Energy Laboratory, as it was then called. Experiments at the laboratory's Nimrod accelerator and elsewhere were revealing the existence of new resonances in pion–nucleon scattering. Dick's intense interest in these experiments was greatly valued by the experimentalists, and he was driven to seek an understanding of the emerging hadronic spectra in terms of the quark model. This would be a major focus of his research in Oxford, and of work by others in his group.

The idea of quarks as constituents of hadrons arose from the work of Y. Ne'eman and M. Gell-Mann (ForMemRS 1978), who proposed classifying the known baryons and mesons in the octet **8** representation of the group SU(3) (Ne'eman 1961; Gell-Mann 1961). This scheme made several successful predictions, and was generally accepted after the discovery in 1964 of the spin $\frac{3}{2}$ Ω^- baryon, with the mass predicted by Gell-Mann, who argued for its existence as the missing member of a decuplet **10** representation of SU(3).

No physical particles were then assigned to the fundamental (triplet) representation of SU(3). In August 1961 Gell-Mann lectured on the eightfold way, as he called his classification, in the first Tata Institute for Fundamental Research Summer School in Theoretical Particle Physics. Rajasekaran (2006) has reported that during one of his talks, Dick—who was also speaking in the school—repeatedly asked him why he was ignoring the SU(3) triplets, but Gell-Mann evaded the question, which was not picked up by any of the participants.

Stimulated by Serber, Gell-Mann (1964) later found it 'tempting to try to use unitary triplets as fundamental objects'. These proposed spin $\frac{1}{2}$ objects, which he dubbed quarks, would have non-integral electric charges, and he found it 'fun to speculate about the way quarks would behave if they were physical particles of finite mass (instead of purely mathematical entities as they would be in the limit of infinite mass)'. He concluded that a search for stable quarks 'would help to reassure us of the non-existence of real quarks'. Very shortly thereafter, Zweig (1964) independently proposed the existence of quarks (which he called aces) and (in contrast to Gell-Mann) used a model with quarks as constituents (the *quark model*) to explain many features of the data*.

Those who, like Dick, took the quark model seriously, assumed that, as no quarks had been observed, the lightest quark (which, as pointed out by Gell-Mann, would be stable) had a mass of at least 5 GeV. Hence, although the π-meson and K-meson have very different masses (140 and 500 MeV respectively), the binding energies of the quark–antiquark pairs—of which they are composed—would differ by 10% or less. It was therefore reasonable to believe that they have similar wave functions and properties, as implied by SU(3) symmetry. As pointed out by Morpurgo (1965), it was also reasonable to believe—as assumed by quark modellers—that, although very tightly bound, quarks would move non-relativistically inside light mesons and baryons.

Dick first took up the quark model in his 1965 Les Houches summer school lectures (23). After tracing its origin back to the Fermi–Yang model (in which the π-meson was regarded as a nucleon–antinucleon bound state) he observed:

> these bound state models have never been considered fully respectable … it is not really possible to meet all the objections that can be made to such models from a field-theoretic point of view. Yet the models are instructive and suggestive, and have at present rather more contact with the experimental data than do the more formal considerations based on group theory.

His lectures provided the first comprehensive, critical overview of the quark model, and became a bible for the relatively few who then took it seriously.

Dick focused particularly on the baryons, which are composed of three spin $\frac{1}{2}$ quarks according to the model. He faced head-on the fact that if quarks obey Fermi statistics (as required by the spin-statistics theorem), then the lowest lying baryons (in the **8** and **10** representations of SU(3)) would necessarily have spatially antisymmetric wave functions. He described this as

---

* In fact, Petermann (1965) was the first to explore the possibility of assigning particles to the triplet representation of SU(3), in a short paper written in French (received on 30 December 1963 but not published until 1965) that passed unnoticed for 50 years.

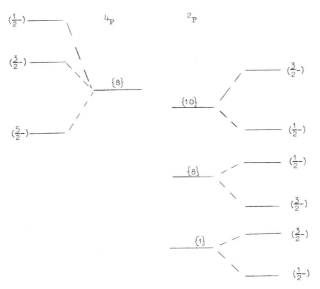

Figure 5. $L = 1$ three-quark supermultiplet (Figure 6 of (23)). Here and in figure 6, {8}, etc., denote the SU(3) assignment, and $\frac{1}{2}$, $\frac{3}{2}$, etc., denote the total angular momentum. (Figure 2 of (24); reproduced by permission of the Science and Technology Facilities Council, Rutherford Appleton Laboratory.)

'strange' and 'surprising', as the wave function would have three nodes and would therefore be expected to have high kinetic energy, but 'perfectly possible … despite many remarks to the contrary in the literature'. He then discussed briefly what inter-quark potentials could produce such a wave function, conceding that we 'know of no particularly natural mechanism' that would lead to the necessary features. Next he outlined the possibility, proposed by Greenberg (1964), that quarks obey para-statistics of order 3 and the three-quark wave is anti-symmetric in the extra three-valued variable, which would allow the space wave function to be symmetric—but he did not pursue it 'in view of the deep additional assumptions which are involved'.

The major new feature of Dick's Les Houches lectures was his description of the expected spectrum of baryon states in which one of the quarks carries one ($L = 1$) or two ($L = 2$) units of angular momentum. As in the case of the ground state, spin-dependent forces were expected to split these states, whereas spin–orbit coupling would further split the 70 negative parity $L = 1$ states into the supermultiplets shown in figure 5. These levels would in turn be split into 30 isospin multiplets as a consequence of the strange quark's being heavier than the non-strange quarks. Dick showed that the ten negative-parity baryons then known could all be assigned to one of these states. He also showed that the four positive-parity resonances that were then known fitted the $L = 2$ quark scheme (figure 6). Remarkably, resonances corresponding to all the states in the $L = 1$ and $L = 2$ level schemes first* spelled out by Dick are known today.

The specific assignments that Dick proposed at Les Houches, and subsequently as more resonances were discovered, involved making choices; for example, he assigned the lower-mass pion–nucleon resonance in the $J^P = \frac{3}{2}^-$ channel to the ^2P state and the higher to the ^4P

---

* Greenberg (1964) had previously tabulated a large number of states allowed in a three para-quark shell model (some of them, as he pointed out, spurious), including states with the quantum numbers in figures 5 and 6, but 'postpone[d] assigning the known baryons to multiplets'.

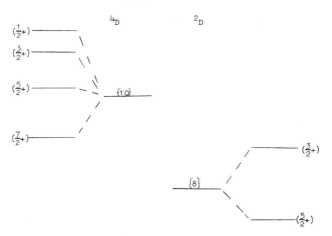

Figure 6. $L = 2$ three-quark supermultiplets (Figure 7 of (24); reproduced by permission of the Science and Technology Facilities Council, Rutherford Appleton Laboratory.).

state (anticipating the effect of the colour hyperfine interaction abstracted from quantum chromodynamics a decade later). All his assignments have stood the test of time, except those for the $Y = I = 0$ states, which are subject to large SU(3) mixing (Dick anticipated 'appreciable distortion' of the mass values expected for isolated SU(3) multiplets).

Shortly after the Les Houches School, Dick gave an invited talk (24) on resonant states and strong interactions at the 1965 Oxford International Conference on Elementary Particles, which he based on the quark model. Apart from a section on di-baryonic states, his talk mirrored his earlier lectures, albeit with a more detailed discussion of the data. In his conclusions Dick noted that 'it is remarkable that all of the baryonic resonances known to have negative parity can be accommodated [in the] $L = 1$ configuration', although he cautioned that 'it is entirely possible that whatever parallelism is found between the data and the simple quark model might simply reflect the existence of general relationships which would also hold in a more sophisticated and complicated theory of elementary particle stuff'.

This possibility had become much less likely by the time Dick spoke, a year later, as rapporteur on Symmetries and the Strong Interactions (25) at the XIII International Conference on High-Energy Physics in Berkeley, California, when he began his talk by describing three theorems that essentially ruled out any relativistic generalization of the SU(6) symmetry group. The rest of his talk was based on the quark model. He began by reviewing limits on the existence of real quarks set by several searches. After his talk, Dick was asked whether the successes of the model require the existence of real quarks. He replied, 'my opinion is that, if there do not exist real quarks, this model has no interest'.

Dick again insisted that Fermi statistics require an antisymmetric space wave function for the lowest-lying baryons, while conceding that, although logically possible, this would require dynamics that are 'not easy to understand'. He also reported the additional problem that (as first found in a model calculation by Mitra & Majumdar (1966)) 'there is a serious possibility' that antisymmetry for the baryon space wave function 'may require a zero in the baryon structure form-factor at quite low momentum transfer', in contradiction with the data (in fact a zero is almost certainly required although it can be shifted to arbitrarily high momentum transfer by constructing a sufficiently complicated wave function (32)).

Dick's Berkeley Conference talk, and his work in the following years, was well received by experimentalists, but theorists' reactions were generally not so warm, although the quark model continued to explain a growing volume of data. First, many found it hard to believe that very strongly bound—and hence presumably strongly interacting—quarks could behave as almost free, independently moving, particles as 'naively' assumed. Dick's response to such objections was that it was better to 'take [these simple] models seriously as a semi-phenomenological approach, calculating their predictions in detail and pushing forward their comparison with experiment as far as possible, rather than dwell on their shortcomings from the standpoint of theoretical physics today' (27). In support of this position, which was justified by subsequent developments, he cited initial objections to the nuclear shell model that were later understood to be invalid.

Second, an antisymmetric ground-state space wave function, on which Dick initially insisted, was generally considered highly implausible or impossible. Some thought this ruled out the quark model. Others believed that the difficulty was removed in ways already proposed (e.g. by assuming anti-symmetry in a new three-valued variable), or hoped that it would be resolved by a new idea. In fact already in 1967 Dick (28) assumed 'without comment' that three-quark wave functions for baryons should be totally symmetric in the labels of the three quarks, before noting the conflict with the spin statistics theorem, and describing para-statistics and the three triplet model of Han & Nambu (1965) as possible ways out of the dilemma. He pointed out, however, that in both cases it could not be assumed (as tacitly done in the literature) that all low-lying states would have the same permutation symmetry as the ground state, so additional states could exist.

Between 1965 and his first peer-reviewed paper on quarks in 1973, Dick reported mounting evidence for the quark model in 14 more summer school lectures and conference talks. This period witnessed a growing interest in quarks in the 'Dalitz group' in Oxford. At first he did not ask his students to work on quarks but some did so anyway. In 1967 one of us (C.Ll.S.) developed a relativistic quark model for mesons after asking Dick why the so-called Weisskopf–Van-Royen paradox had not led him to abandon quarks, and receiving the answer that he would do so if someone could derive the paradox in a relativistic framework; C.Ll.S.'s later pioneering applications of the quark–parton model to deep inelastic neutrino scattering played a role in convincing sceptics of the 'reality' of quarks and gluons.

In 1969 three visitors to Oxford (L. Copley, G. Karl and E. Obryk) successfully applied the quark model to photo-excitation of the $L = 0$, spin $\frac{3}{2}$ (Δ), and $L = 1$ and $L = 2$ states of the nucleon (Copley *et al.* 1969*a*, *b*). Many years later Karl, with Isgur (a frequent visitor to Oxford), provided a very successful description of the spectrum of *p*-wave baryons by using the inter-quark spin–spin and spin–tensor potential given by the QCD Fermi–Breit Hamiltonian (Isgur & Karl 1978). In his thesis on the separation of the centre of mass and internal motions in composite systems, F. Close (a Dalitz student from 1968 to 1970) applied his results to quarks, without any prompting from Dick. In 1972, while at Stanford Linear Accelerator Center (SLAC), Close and Gilman extended the work of Copley *et al.* to electro-production and successfully explained variations with momentum transfer that could hardly be attributed to some abstract symmetry (Close & Gilman 1972). In 1981, in one of his last papers (43) on light quarks (to which, without any prompting, he added Close's name), Dick combined results in Close's thesis with ideas derived from QCD to cast light on attempts to understand the quark–quark spin–orbit coupling in *p*-wave baryons.

In the early 1970s working on the quark model became increasingly 'politically acceptable' for various reasons: its continuing to describe all new data; Feynman's authorship with Kislinger and Ravndal (Feynman *et al.* 1971) of a paper on quarks, partly inspired by the work of Copley *et al.*; having revealed in 1968 that nucleons contain charged point-like constituents, deep inelastic electron scattering data from SLAC showed in 1969 that they have spin $\frac{1}{2}$, and increasingly suggested that they are quarks, as complementary neutrino data from CERN made clear in 1973; recognition that—as described below—the colour quantum number resolved the statistics problem, while QCD and the discovery that it is asymptotically free provided a framework in which it can be convincingly argued (if not rigorously proved) that only colour singlets should exist as free particles, whereas quarks should be forever confined.

Dick's first paper on quarks in a refereed journal (31), written with his student R. Horgan (whose name he put first), set out a formalism for constructing three quark states in a shell model, extending and generalizing earlier work by Greenberg and others. This is the first of Dick's papers that employed explicit wave functions, which were assumed to be symmetric under interchange of the quark labels. A lecture later that year on this work (32), and on Horgan's use of it to fit all the then known data (Horgan 1974), began by addressing the statistics problem. After describing para-statistics and the Han–Nambu model, Dick discussed the three-valued colour variable proposed by Gell-Mann (1972), in which the wave function can also be anti-symmetrized. He then expressed concern that, without additional dynamical assumptions, all three of these possibilities imply the existence of additional unobserved states, a problem finessed by Gell-Mann who proposed that—for a yet to be identified reason—only colour singlet states are allowed (in which case, with a corresponding assumption, order 3 para-statistics and colour make identical spectroscopic predictions).

Dick then reported that Lipkin (1973) had recently proposed that the inter-quark potential is generated by the exchange of an octet of coloured gluons; Fritzsch & Gell-Mann (1973) had noted this possibility earlier, attributing it to J. Wess. Lipkin observed that such a potential could promote all coloured states to high masses. A year later, Dick (35) pronounced himself fully satisfied with this solution, while still referring to Lipkin—although by then a relativistic field theory (QCD) that embodied his idea had been proposed (Fritzsch *et al.* 1973) and meanwhile non-Abelian gauge theories such as QCD had been shown to be asymptotically free (Gross & Wilczek 1973; Politzer 1973).

In a 1977 paper (36) with M. Jones (a visitor, who was listed as first author), Dalitz and Horgan used their earlier results to analyse the latest data. This paper and Horgan (1974) are today still the standard references for the classification of baryons expected in experiment and their masses. Dalitz and Horgan, with a postdoctoral visitor Reinders (37), went on to apply the model to $L = 3$ states.

Through the 1970s and into the 1980s Dick continued to present reviews of the successes of the quark model accompanied by meticulous comparisons of its predictions with the data, taking account of the latest experimental and theoretical developments. He discussed the spectroscopy of charmed particles (34), before they had been discovered, and of the J/ψ family (38), and in (44) and (47) the implications of QCD for hadronic spectroscopy (Isgur–Karl, etc.), the MIT bag model, and the possible existence of sub-quarks. In the 1980s Dick became interested in Monte Carlo simulations of QCD formulated on a discrete space-time lattice. With Ford (his student, who was the first author) and Hoek (51), he performed state-of-the-art calculations of the potential between two static colour charges in a pure lattice gauge theory (without dynamical quarks) on the largest lattice yet constructed (34^4).

A very productive collaboration between Dalitz and Goldstein led to a series of influential papers related to heavy quarks, published in the period 1988–99. The first (52), with R. Marshall (FRS 1995), was on correlations between the decays of heavy particle (charm, bottom or top) antiparticle pairs in back-to-back jets resulting from electron–positron annihilation into a heavy quark–antiquark pair. The standard model predicts correlations between the helicities of the initial quark–antiquark pair, which depend on how close the energy is to the Z pole. At high energy compared with the quark mass, the helicities are conserved when the quarks fragment, according to QCD. This leads in the case of charm (for example) to correlations between the spins of the charmed vector mesons (D*/anti-D*) that contain the initial charm/anti-charm quarks, which are manifested in the angular distributions of their decay products. The results of (52) were used by the ARGUS Group at the DORIS II DESY e⁺e⁻ storage ring (Albrecht *et al.* 1996) and produced the expected result.

The second paper (54), also with Marshall, proposed a way to determine the helicity of charm quarks (produced in any hard process, not necessarily in pairs) via the subsequent jet hadronization into a D plus two π-mesons. Disappointingly, the predicted effect, which depended on the interference between D* and non-resonant D plus pion, was small, as confirmed at SLAC (Abe *et al.* 1995), but the paper led to further theoretical developments related to a transverse spin-dependent fragmentation function (Collins 1993), which in turn stimulated experiments that continue to this day

In a subsequent paper (56), Dalitz and Goldstein studied the top/anti-top case in more detail and showed that the parity-violating effects in the decay chain t → bW⁺, W → l⁺v are large and will test closely the detailed spin structure of electroweak interactions involving the top quark. This is now a standard reference for experiments that study top through the so-called lepton decay channel. In (57) they showed that in collider production of a top–anti-top pair, both of which decay to leptons, the momenta of the decay products are correlated. A given configuration of momenta depends on the top mass and determines a probability distribution for possible top masses.

In (56) and (57) Dalitz and Goldstein developed a means of analysing the decays of top–anti-top pairs produced in hadronic interactions. This involved what they described as an 'illuminating' geometrical construction, reproduced here as figure 7. They applied it to a single candidate for top–anti-top pair production found by the Collider Detector at Fermilab (CDF) as an illustration of the procedure they proposed (this candidate implied a top quark mass of around 125 GeV; today the mass is known to be around 173 GeV). Although they were careful to describe this as 'pure speculation', it was not well received by CDF (and the controversy was picked up by the scientific press), but the other Fermilab collider experiment (D0) used their work, which was recently also used by the CMS collaboration in analysing data from the Large Hadron Collider (LHC).

In their next paper on top quarks (58), written with Sliwa, Dalitz and Goldstein presented a technique for separating top-quark production from standard model background events that is applicable to the channel in which one top quark decays semi-leptonically while its antiquark decays hadronically into three jets, or vice versa. They showed that the method, which was subsequently used by both the CDF and D0 collaborations, discriminates dramatically between Monte Carlo-generated events with and without simulated top quarks of mass around 120 GeV.

In 1994 the top quark was discovered by CDF and D0. In his final paper (61) on quarks, Dick—again with Goldstein—reported Monte Carlo calculations that tested the likelihood

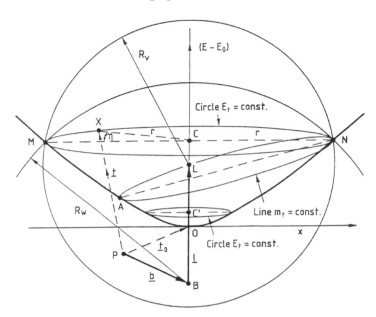

Figure 7. This construction, and the other figures in (56) and (57), are wonderful examples of Dick's love of geometry and ability to think geometrically, which was manifested in many of his papers. In an interview in 2003 (O'Byrne 2004) he said that he 'came at [the Dalitz plot] from a geometrical perspective because I visualise geometry better than numbers'.

methods they had proposed for determining the top mass for masses of order 170 GeV. Various versions of the 'matrix element/dynamic likelihood method', which is based on that paper, have been used by D0 and CDF at the Tevatron and by ATLAS and CMS at the LHC.

SCIENTIFIC STYLE AND PERSONAL CHARACTERISTICS

Dick described his pragmatic, data-driven approach to physics in an interview in October 2003 (O'Byrne 2004), which we have quoted, when the photograph in figure 8 was taken. He once said to one of us, 'My job's not to make theories—it's to understand the data.' In the same vein, when Gabriel Karl told him about a paper that considered the possible effects of a hypothetical interaction, he replied, 'But there is no such thing.' 'Yes,' said Gabriel, 'but you can *imagine* that there is'; to which Dick replied, 'In that case you must stop yourself.'

Dick immersed himself in the experimental data, of which he had an encyclopaedic knowledge until their volume became too great. Once, when wondering whether he had quoted an experimental result correctly (he had), he said to one of us, 'I used to know all the data; at one time I knew every event'. He saw his role as being to seek ways to represent data so that they directly reveal nature's secrets, as the Dalitz plot had done.

After Dick's analysis of K decays hinted that parity is violated, he might conceivably have been the first to analyse this possibility had it not been for his reluctance to speculate. Yet, ironically, his pioneering work on the quark model was regarded as outrageously speculative

Figure 8. Dick Dalitz during the 8th International Conference on Hypernuclear and Strange Particle Physics, October 2003. (Copyright: US Department of Energy's Thomas Jefferson National Accelerator Facility; reproduced with permission.) (Online version in colour.)

by many. For Dick, however, the theoretical objections were outweighed by the fact that the model provides a simple way to describe a huge quantity of data. When almost overnight in the 1970s the 'naive' quark model became accepted, Dick's seminal work was soon largely forgotten. This, and the scepticism it attracted at first, must have been hard to take, but he never publicly expressed bitterness about it.

Dick's work was characterized by great professionalism. He tackled every problem with exemplary thoroughness, and his review articles and lecture notes were wonderfully useful sources of comprehensive information, concisely presented. He worked long hours. After a burglary in the Oxford Theoretical Physics Department one Christmas, it was thought that the large electromechanical calculator that he kept next to his desk (and used with great skill well into the 1970s) was among the stolen items. But it turned out that Dick had taken it home for work over the Christmas break.

Dick's style soon became clear to his students who, within a month or two of their arrival, were set to carry out calculations of immediate relevance to experiments. They were both impressed and rather intimidated by his intellect, knowledge and reputation, and by the way in which he would reflect on a question in silence for what often seemed like minutes before supplying a highly concise answer. They also greatly appreciated the pains he took in writing long letters providing advice on career options after they had left Oxford.

Dick served on several advisory bodies including the UK's Nuclear Physics Board (1972–85), the Council of the Royal Society (1979–81) and the CERN Scientific Policy Committee (1974–78). He took detailed notes but spoke little, although the contributions that he did make were valued, and his colleagues greatly appreciated the opportunity to talk to him outside the formal sessions. As a research professor he had no formal administrative duties, but he ran the Oxford particle theory group with quiet efficiency, to the relief of others on whom the lot might have fallen. It is fitting that the flourishing group that he founded is today housed in premises known as the Dalitz Institute.

Dick was very happily married, and is survived by his wife, Valda, a son, three daughters and eleven grandchildren. He was a private person whose shy and modest exterior hid a deeply caring and kind man. He has left fond memories with his many colleagues, students and friends, as well as a great scientific legacy.

HONOURS AND AWARDS

1966   Maxwell Medal and Prize, Institute of Physics and Physical Society
1969   Bakerian Lecture, Royal Society
       Jaffe Prize, Royal Society
1975   Hughes Medal, Royal Society
1978   Corresponding Member, Australian Academy of Sciences
1980   Foreign Member, Polish Academy of Science
       J. Robert Oppenheimer Memorial Prize, University of Miami
1982   Royal Medal, Royal Society
1990   Foreign Member, National Indian Academy
       Harrie Massey Prize, Institute of Physics and Australian Institute of Physics
1991   Foreign Associate, US National Academy of Sciences
2005   Gian Carlo Wick Commemorative Gold Medal

ACKNOWLEDGEMENTS

We are grateful to Avraham Gal for comments on the section on hypernuclei, to Mike Teper for information about Dick's activities at All Souls, to Frank Close, Gary Goldstein, Ron Horgan and Gabriel Karl for advice and comments on the section on quarks, to Shyue-Rong Sha of the SLAC Library for valuable assistance, and to Valda Dalitz and Heather Kay (*née* Dalitz) for helpful comments on the manuscript.

The frontispiece photograph was taken by Walter Bird and is reproduced with permission.

REFERENCES TO OTHER AUTHORS

Abe, K. and 209 others (SLD collaboration) 1995 Search for jet handedness in hadronic Z^0 decays. *Phys. Rev. Lett.* **74**, 1512–1516 (http://dx.doi.org/10.1103/PhysRevLett.74.1512).

Alberico, W. M. & Garbarino, G. 2000 The $\Delta I = \frac{1}{2}$ rule in non-mesonic weak decay of Λ-hypernuclei. *Phys. Lett.* B **486**, 362–368 (http://dx.doi.org/10.1016/S0370-2693(00)00766-8).

Albrecht, H. and 205 others (ARGUS collaboration) 1996 Physics with ARGUS. *Phys. Rep.* **276**, 223–405 (http://dx.doi.org/10.1016/S0370-1573(96)00008-7).

Alexander, G., Kalbfleisch, G. R., Miller, D. H. & Smith, G. A. 1962 Production of strange-particle resonant states by 2.1-BeV/c π^- mesons. *Phys. Rev. Lett.* **8**, 447–450 (http://dx.doi.org/10.1103/PhysRevLett.8.447).

Alston, M., Alvarez, L. W., Eberhard, P., Good, M. L., Graziano, W., Ticho, H. K. & Wojcicki, S. G. 1960 Resonance in the $\Lambda\pi$ system. *Phys. Rev. Lett.* **5**, 520–524 (http://dx.doi.org/10.1103/PhysRevLett.5.520).

Alston, M. H., Alvarez, L. W., Eberhard, P., Good, M. L., Graziano, W., Ticho, H. K. & Wojcicki, S. G. 1961 Study of resonances of the Σ–π system. *Phys. Rev. Lett.* **6**, 698–702 (http://dx.doi.org/10.1103/PhysRevLett.6.698).

Bertrand, D., Coremans, G., Mayeur, C., Sacton, J., Vilain, P., Wilquet, G., Wickens, J. H., O'Sullivan, D., Davis, D. H. & Allen, J. E. 1970 Branching ratios for the π^- mesonic decays of the hypernuclei $_\Lambda^3$H and $_\Lambda^4$H. *Nucl. Phys.* B **16**, 77–84 (http://dx.doi.org/10.1016/0550-3213(70)90339-1).

Block, M. M., Gessaroli, R., Kopelman, J., Ratti, S., Schneeberger, M., Grimellini, L., Kikuchi, T., Lendinara, L., Monari, L., Becker, W. & Harth, E. 1964 Hyperfragment studies in the helium bubble chamber. In *Proc. Int. Conf. on Hyperfragments, St. Cergue* (ed. W. O. Lock), pp. 63–74. Geneva: CERN (http://dx.doi.org/10.5170/CERN-1964-001).

Chew, G. F. & Mandelstam, S. 1960 Theory of low-energy pion–pion interactions. *Phys. Rev.* **119**, 467–477 (http://dx.doi.org/10.1103/PhysRev.119.467)

Close, F. E. & Gilman, F. J. 1972 Helicity structure of nucleon resonance electroproduction and the symmetric quark model. *Phys. Lett.* B **38**, 541–554 (http://dx.doi.org/10.1016/0370-2693(72)90538-2).

Collins, J. 1993 Fragmentation of transversely polarized quarks probed in transverse momentum distributions. *Nucl. Phys.* B **396**, 161–182 (http://dx.doi.org/10.1016/0550-3213(93)90262-N).

Copley, L. A., Karl, G. & Obryk, E. 1969*a* Backward single pion photoproduction and the symmetric quark model. *Phys. Lett.* B **29**, 117–120 (http://dx.doi.org/10.1016/0370-2693(69)90261-5).

Copley, L. A., Karl, G. & Obryk, E. 1969*b* Single pion photoproduction in the quark model. *Nucl. Phys.* B **13**, 303–319 (http://dx.doi.org/10.1016/0550-3213(69)90237-5).

Cronin, J. W. 2011 The 1953 Cosmic Ray Conference at Bagnères-de-Bigorre: the birth of sub-atomic physics. *Eur. Phys. J.* **H36**, 183–201 (http://dx.doi.org/10.1140/epjh/e2011-20014-4).

Daniel, R. R., Davies, J. H., Mulvey, J. H. & Perkins, D. H. 1952 Nuclear interactions of great energy. Part 1. Evidence for the creation of heavy mesons. *Phil. Mag.* (7) **43**, 753–774 (http://dx.doi.org/10.1080/14786440708520992).

Danysz, M. & Pniewski, J. 1953 Delayed disintegration of a heavy nuclear fragment. 1. *Phil. Mag.* (7) **44**, 348–350 (http://dx.doi.org/10.1080/14786440308520318).

Danysz, M. and 22 others 1963*a* Observation of a double hyperfragment. *Phys. Rev. Lett.* **11**, 29–32 (http://dx.doi.org/10.1103/PhysRevLett.11.29).

Danysz, M. and 22 others 1963*b* The identification of a double hyperfragment. *Nucl. Phys.* **49**, 121–132 (http://dx.doi.org/10.1016/0029-5582(63)90080-4).

Davis, D. H. 2008 Exchange reactions with Dick Dalitz. *Nucl. Phys.* A **804**, 5–12 (http://dx.doi.org/10.1016/j.nuclphysa.2007.12.015).

del Amo Sanchez, P. and 446 others (BABAR collaboration) 2010*a* Evidence for direct *CP* violation in the measurement of the Cabibbo–Kobayashi–Maskawa angle γ with $B^\mp \to D^{(*)}K^{(*)\mp}$. *Phys. Rev. Lett.* **105**, 121801 (http://dx.doi.org/10.1103/PhysRevLett.105.121801).

del Amo Sanchez, P. and 448 others (BABAR collaboration) 2010*b* Measurement of $\overline{D}^0$–D^0 mixing parameters using $D^0 \to K_S^0\pi^+\pi^-$ and $D^0 \to K_S^0K^+K^-$ decays. *Phys. Rev. Lett.* **105**, 081803 (http://dx.doi.org/10.1103/PhysRevLett.105.081803).

Devons, S. & Lindsey, G. R. 1949 Electron pair creation by a spherically symmetrical field. *Nature* **164**, 539–540 (http://dx.doi.org/10.1038/164539a0).

Devons, S., Hereward, H. G. & Lindsey, G. R. 1949 Life-time for pair emission by spherically symmetrical excited states of the O^{16} nucleus. *Nature* **164**, 586–587 (http://dx.doi.org/10.1038/164586b0).

Fabri, E. 1954 A study of τ-meson decay. *Nuovo Cim.* **11**, 479–491 (http://dx.doi.org/10.1007/BF02781042).

Feynman, R. P., Kislinger, M. & Ravndal, F. 1971 Current matrix elements from a relativistic quark model. *Phys. Rev.* D **3**, 2706–2732 (http://dx.doi.org/10.1103/PhysRevD.3.2706).

Fritzsch, H. & Gell-Mann, M. 1972 Current algebra: quarks and what else? In *Proc. XVI Int. Conf. on High Energy Physics, 6–13 September, Batavia, IL* (ed. J. D. Jackson & A. Roberts), vol. 2, pp. 135–165. Batavia: National Accelerator Laboratory.

Fritzsch, H., Gell-Mann, M. & Leutwyler, H. 1973 Advantages of the color octet gluon picture. *Phys. Lett.* B **47**, 365–368 (http://dx.doi.org/10.1016/0370-2693(73)90625-4).

Gal, A. 2008 Hypernuclear physics legacy and heritage of Dick Dalitz. *Nucl. Phys.* A **804**, 13–24 (http://dx.doi.org/10.1016/j.nuclphysa.2008.02.297).

Gell-Mann, M. 1961 The eightfold way: a theory of strong interaction symmetry. California Institute of Technology Laboratory Report CTSL-20 (unpublished). (Reprinted in M. Gell-Mann & Y. Ne'eman, *The eightfold way*, pp. 11–57 (W. A. Benjamin, New York, 1964).)

Gell-Mann, M. 1964 A schematic model of baryons and mesons. *Phys. Lett.* **8**, 214–215 (http://dx.doi.org/10.1016/S0031-9163(64)92001-3).

Gell-Mann, M. 1972 Quarks. *Acta Phys. Austriaca Suppl.* **9**, 733–761 (http://dx.doi.org/10.1007/978-3-7091-4034-5_20).

Greenberg, O. W. 1964 Spin and unitary-spin independence in a paraquark model of baryons and mesons. *Phys. Rev. Lett.* **13**, 598–602 (http://dx.doi.org/10.1103/PhysRevLett.13.598).

Gross, D. J. & Wilczek, F. 1973 Ultraviolet behavior of non-Abelian gauge theories. *Phys. Rev. Lett.* **30**, 1343–1346 (http://dx.doi.org/10.1103/PhysRevLett.30.1343).

Hall, J. M. M. *et al.* 2015 Lattice QCD evidence that the $\Lambda(1405)$ resonance is an antikaon-nucleon molecule. *Phys. Rev. Lett.* **114**, 132002-1–132002-5 (http://dx.doi.org/10.1103/PhysRevLett.114.132002).

Han, M. Y. & Nambu, Y. 1965 Three-triplet model with double SU(3) symmetry. *Phys. Rev.* **139**, B1006–B1010 (http://dx.doi.org/10.1103/PhysRev.139.B1006).

Hashimoto, O. & Tamura, H. 2006 Spectroscopy of Λ hypernuclei. *Prog. Part. Nucl. Phys.* **57**, 564–653 (http://dx.doi.org/10.1016/j.ppnp.2005.07.001).

Hemingway, R. J. 1985 Production of $\Lambda(1405)$ in K⁻p reactions at 4.2 GeV/*c*. *Nucl. Phys.* B **253**, 742–745 (http://dx.doi.org/10.1016/0550-3213(85)90556-5).

Herndon, D. J., Söding, P. & Cashmore, R. J. 1975*a* Generalized isobar model formalism. *Phys. Rev.* D **11**, 3165–3182 (http://dx.doi.org/10.1103/PhysRevD.11.3165).

Herndon, D. J., Longacre, R., Miller, L. R., Rosenfeld, A. H., Smadja, G., Söding, P., Cashmore, R. J. & Leith, D. W. G. S. 1975*b* Partial-wave analysis of the reaction $\pi N \rightarrow \pi\pi N$ in the c.m energy range 1300–2000 MeV. *Phys. Rev.* D **11**, 3183–3213 (http://dx.doi.org/10.1103/PhysRevD.11.3183).

Horgan, R. 1974 Baryon spectroscopy and the quark shell model (II). Numerical fitting to the data and the baryonic predictions. *Nucl. Phys.* B **71**, 514–545 (http://dx.doi.org/10.1016/0550-3213(74)90199-0).

Isgur, N. & Karl, G. 1978 P-wave baryons in the quark model. *Phys. Rev.* D **18**, 4187–4205 (http://dx.doi.org/10.1103/PhysRevD.18.4187).

Jaffe, R. L. 1977 Perhaps a stable dihyperon. *Phys. Rev. Lett.* **38**, 195–195 (http://dx.doi.org/10.1103/PhysRevLett.38.195). Erratum, *Phys. Rev. Lett.* **38**, 617 (1977) (http://dx.doi.org/10.1103/PhysRevLett.38.617).

Joseph, D. 1960 Electron pair creation in $\pi + p$ capture from rest. *Nuovo Cim.* **16**, 997–1013 (http://dx.doi.org/10.1007/BF02860383).

Kroll, N. N. & Wada, W. 1955 Internal pair production associated with the emission of high-energy gamma rays. *Phys. Rev.* **98**, 1355–1359 (http://dx.doi.org/10.1103/PhysRev.98.1355).

Lee, T. D. & Yang, C. N. 1956 Question of parity conservation in weak interactions. *Phys. Rev.* **104**, 254–258 (http://dx.doi.org/10.1103/PhysRev.104.254). Erratum, *Phys. Rev.* **106**, 1371 (1957) (http://dx.doi.org/10.1103/PhysRev.106.1371).

Lipkin, H. J. 1973 Triality, exotics and the dynamical basis of the quark model. *Phys. Lett.* B **45**, 267–271 (http://dx.doi.org/10.1016/0370-2693(73)90200-1).

Maglić, B. C., Alvarez, L. W., Rosenfeld, A. H. & Stevenson, M. L. 1961 Evidence for a $T = 0$ three-pion resonance. *Phys. Rev. Lett.* **7**, 178–182 (http://dx.doi.org/10.1103/PhysRevLett.7.178).

Mitra, A. N. & Majumdar, R. 1966 Quark statistics and baryon form factors. *Phys. Rev.* **150**, 1194–1197 (http://dx.doi.org/10.1103/PhysRev.150.1194).

Morpurgo, G. 1965 Is a non-relativistic approximation possible for the internal dynamics of elementary particles? *Physics* **2**, 95–105.

Ne'eman, Y. 1961 Derivation of strong interactions from a gauge invariance. *Nucl. Phys.* **26**, 222–229 (http://dx.doi.org/10.1016/0029-5582(61)90134-1).

O'Byrne, M. 2004 In their own words, with Richard Dalitz, Emeritus Professor of Oxford University. *On Target* (February/March), 10–13. Newport News, VA: Thomas Jefferson National Accelerator Facility (https://www.jlab.org/sites/default/files/FebMarch2004.pdf).

Petermann, A. 1965 Propriétés de l'étrangeté et une formule de masse pour les mésons vectoriels. *Nucl. Phys.* **63**, 349–352 (http://dx.doi.org/10.1016/0029-5582(65)90348-2).

Pjerrou, G. M., Prowse, D. J., Schlein, P., Slater, W. E., Stork, D. H. & Ticho, H. K. 1962 Resonance in the ($\Xi\pi$) system at 1.53 GeV. *Phys. Rev. Lett.* **9**, 114–117 (http://dx.doi.org/10.1103/PhysRevLett.9.114).

Plano, R., Prodell, A., Samios, N., Schwartz, M. & Steinberger, J. 1959 Parity of the neutral pion. *Phys. Rev. Lett.* **3**, 525–527 (http://dx.doi.org/10.1103/PhysRevLett.3.525).

Politzer, H. D. 1973 Reliable perturbative results for strong interactions? *Phys. Rev. Lett.* **30**, 1346–1349 (http://dx.doi.org/10.1103/PhysRevLett.30.1346).

Poluektov, A. and 149 others (Belle collaboration) 2010 Evidence for direct *CP* violation in the decay $B^{\mp} \to D^{(*)} K^{\mp}$, $D \to K_S^0 \pi^+ \pi^-$ and measurement of the CKM phase ϕ_3. *Phys. Rev.* D **81**, 112002 (http://dx.doi.org/10.1103/PhysRevD.81.112002).

Prowse, D. J. 1966 $_{\Lambda\Lambda}^{6}$He double hyperfragment. *Phys. Rev. Lett.* **17**, 782–785 (http://dx.doi.org/10.1103/PhysRevLett.17.782).

Rajasekaran, G. 2006 From atoms to quarks and beyond: a historical panorama (https://arxiv.org/pdf/physics/0602131.pdf).

Schlein, P. E., Carmony, D. D., Pjerrou, G. M., Slater, W. E., Stork, D. H. & Ticho, H. K. 1963 Spin-parity determination of the $\Xi\pi$ resonance (1.530 GeV). *Phys. Rev. Lett.* **11**, 167–171 (http://dx.doi.org/10.1103/PhysRevLett.11.167).

Stevenson, M. L., Alvarez, L. W., Maglić, B. C. & Rosenfeld, A. H. 1962 Spin and parity of the ω meson. *Phys. Rev.* **125**, 687–690 (http://dx.doi.org/10.1103/PhysRev.125.687). Erratum, *Phys. Rev.* **125**, 2208 (1962) (http://dx.doi.org/10.1103/PhysRev.125.2208.8).

Takahashi, H. and 66 others 2001 Observation of a $_{\Lambda\Lambda}^{6}$He double hypernucleus. *Phys. Rev. Lett.* **87**, 212502 (http://dx.doi.org/10.1103/PhysRevLett.87.212502).

Thomas, D. W., Engler, A., Fisk, H. E. & Kraemer, R. W. 1973 Strange particle production from π^-p interactions at 1.69 GeV/*c*. *Nucl. Phys.* B **56**, 15–45 (http://dx.doi.org/10.1016/0550-3213(73)90217-4).

Thompson, R. W., Buskirk, A. V., Etter, R. L., Karzmark, C. J. & Rediker, R. H. 1953 The disintegration of V^0 particles. *Phys. Rev.* **90**, 329–330 (http://dx.doi.org/10.1103/PhysRev.90.329).

Zhang, L. M. *et al.* 2007 Measurement of $D^0 - \bar{D}^0$ mixing parameters in $D^0 \to K_S \pi^+ \pi^-$ decays. *Phys. Rev. Lett.* **99**, 131803 (http://dx.doi.org/10.1103/PhysRevLett.99.131803).

Ziemińska, D. 1975 The decay process $_{\Lambda}^{11}$B $\to \pi^- + {}^{11}$C. *Nucl. Phys.* A **242**, 461–466 (http://dx.doi.org/10.1016/0375-9474(75)90108-6).

Zweig, G. 1964 An SU(3) model for strong interaction symmetry and its breaking. CERN TH 401 and TH 412 (unpublished; http://inspirehep.net/record/11881/files/CM-P00042883.pdf and http://inspirehep.net/record/4674/files/cern-th-412.pdf). (Reprinted in *Developments in the quark theory of hadrons* (ed. D. B. Lichtenberg & S. P. Rosen), vol. 1 (*1964–1978*), pp. 22–101 (Hadronic Press, Nonantum, MA, 1980).)

Bibliography

The following publications are those referred to directly in the text. A full bibliography is available as electronic supplementary material at http://dx.doi.org/10.1098/rsbm.2016.0019 or via http://rsbm.royalsocietypublishing.org.

(1)   1946   Some mathematical aspects of compressible fluid flow. *Australian Council for Aeronautics Rep. ACA-20*.

(2)   1951   On radiative corrections to the angular correlation in internal pair creation. *Proc. R. Soc. Lond.* A **206** 521–538 (http://dx.doi.org/10.1098/rspa.1951.0086).

(3)   On an alternative decay process for the neutral π-meson. *Proc. Phys. Soc.* A **64**, 667–669 (http://dx.doi.org/10.1088/0370-1298/64/7/115).

(4)   1953   On the analysis of τ-meson data and the nature of the τ-meson. *Phil. Mag.* (7) **44**, 1068–1080 (http://dx.doi.org/10.1080/14786441008520365).

(5)   1954   Decay of τ mesons of known charge. *Phys. Rev.* **94**, 1046–1051 (http://dx.doi.org/10.1103/PhysRev.94.1046).

(6)   1955   Charge independence in light hyperfragments. *Phys. Rev.* **99**, 1475–1477 (http://dx.doi.org/10.1103/PhysRev.99.1475).

(7)   1956   (With L. Castillejo & F. J. Dyson) Low's scattering equation for the charged and neutral scalar theories. *Phys. Rev.* **101**, 453–458 (http://dx.doi.org/10.1103/PhysRev.101.453).

(8)   1958   (With B. W. Downs) Remarks on the hypertriton. *Phys. Rev.* **110**, 958–965 (http://dx.doi.org/10.1103/PhysRev.110.958).

(9)   (With B. W. Downs) Hypernuclear binding energies and the Λ–nucleon interaction. *Phys. Rev.* **111**, 967–986 (http://dx.doi.org/10.1103/PhysRev.111.967).

(10)   Parity nonconservation in the decay of free and bound Λ particles. *Phys. Rev.* **112**, 605–613 (http://dx.doi.org/10.1103/PhysRev.112.605).

(11)   1959   (With B. W. Downs) Analysis of the Λ-hypernuclear three-body systems. *Phys. Rev.* **114**, 593–602 (http://dx.doi.org/10.1103/PhysRev.114.593).

(12)   (With L. Liu) Pionic decay modes of light Λ hypernuclei. *Phys. Rev.* **116**, 1312–1321 (http://dx.doi.org/10.1103/PhysRev.116.1312).

(13)   (With S. F. Tuan) The energy dependence of low energy K^--proton processes. *Ann. Phys.* **8**, 100–118 (http://dx.doi.org/10.1016/0003-4916(59)90064-8).

(14)   (With S. F. Tuan) Possible resonant state in pion-hyperon scattering. *Phys. Rev. Lett.* **2**, 425–428 (http://dx.doi.org/10.1103/PhysRevLett.2.425).

(15)   1960   (With S. F. Tuan) The phenomenological representation of $\overline{K}$-nucleon scattering and reaction amplitudes. *Ann. Phys.* **10**, 307–351 (http://dx.doi.org/10.1016/0003-4916(60)90001-4).

(16)   1961   On the strong interactions of the strange particles. *Rev. Mod. Phys.* **33**, 471–492 (http://dx.doi.org/10.1103/RevModPhys.33.471).

(17)   1962   (With G. Rajasekharan) The spins and lifetimes of the light hypernuclei. *Phys. Lett.* **1**, 58–60 (http://dx.doi.org/10.1016/0031-9163(62)90437-7).

(18)   Some topics in strange particle resonances. In *Proc. Aix-en-Provence Int. Conf. on Elementary Particles, 14–20 September 1961* (ed. E. Crémieu, P. Falk-Vairant & O. Lebey), pp. 151–176. Saclay: C.E.N.

(19)   1963   (With M. M. Block) Structure of the weak interaction $\Lambda + N \rightarrow N + N$. *Phys. Rev. Lett.* **11**, 96–100 (http://dx.doi.org/10.1103/PhysRevLett.11.96).

(20)   The $\Lambda\Lambda$ hypernucleus and the Λ-Λ interaction. *Phys. Lett.* **5**, 53–56 (http://dx.doi.org/10.1016/S0375-9601(63)80027-4).

(21)   The hypernucleus $_\Lambda\mathrm{Li}^8$ and the decay process $_\Lambda\mathrm{Li}^8 \rightarrow \pi^- + {}^4\mathrm{He} + {}^4\mathrm{He}$. *Nucl. Phys.* **41**, 78–91 (http://dx.doi.org/10.1016/0029-5582(63)90481-4).

(22)   1964   (With F. von Hippel) Electromagnetic Λ–Σ^0 mixing and charge symmetry for the Λ-hyperon. *Phys. Lett.* **10**, 153–157 (http://dx.doi.org/10.1016/0031-9163(64)90617-1).

(23)   1965   Quark models for the 'elementary particles'. In *High Energy Physics: Proc. Les Houches Summer School, 1965* (ed. C. DeWitt & M. Jacob), pp. 251–323. New York: Gordon & Breach.

(24)   1966   Resonant states and strong interactions. In *Proc. Oxford Int. Conf. on Elementary Particles, 1965* (ed. R. G. Moorhouse, A. E. Taylor & T. R. Walsh), pp. 157–181. Chilton: Rutherford High-Energy Laboratory.

(25)   Symmetries and strong interactions. In *Proc. XIII Int. Conf. on High Energy Physics, Berkeley, 1966* (ed. M. Alston-Garnjost), pp. 215–236. Berkeley: University of California Press.

(26)   1967   (With T. C. Wong & G. Rajasekaran) Model calculation for $Y_0^*(1405)$ resonance state. *Phys. Rev.* **153**, 1617–1623 (http://dx.doi.org/10.1103/PhysRev.153.1617).

(27)   1969   Quarks, the hadronic sub-units? In *Contemporary Physics: Trieste Symp. 1968* (ed. L. Fonda & Abdus Salam), vol. 2, pp. 219–247. Vienna: IAEA.

(28)   Excited baryons and the baryonic supermultiplets. In *Pion Nucleon Scattering, Proc. Irvine 1967* (ed. G. L. Shaw & D. Y. Wong), pp. 187–207. New York: Wiley. (Reprinted in *Developments in the quark theory of hadrons* (ed. D. B. Lichtenberg & S. P. Rosen), vol. 1 (*1964–1978*), pp. 316–336. (Hadronic Press, Nonantum, MA, 1978).)

(29)   1971   (With A. Gal & J. M. Soper) Shell-model analysis of Λ binding energies for p-shell hypernuclei. I. Basic formulas and matrix elements for ΛN and ΛNN forces. *Ann. Phys.* **63**, 53–126 (http://dx.doi.org/10.1016/0003-4916(71)90297-1).

(30)   1972   (With A. Gal & J. M. Soper) Shell-model analysis of Λ binding energies for p-shell hypernuclei. II. Numerical fitting, interpretation and hypernuclear predictions. *Ann. Phys.* **72**, 445–488 (http://dx.doi.org/10.1016/0003-4916(72)90222-9).

(31) 1973 (With R. Horgan) Baryon spectroscopy and quark shell model. I. The framework, basic formulae, and matrix elements. *Nucl. Phys.* B **66**, 135–172 (http://dx.doi.org/10.1016/0550-3213(73)90011-4). Erratum, *Nucl. Phys.* B **71**, 546–547 (1974).

(32) 1974 The three-quark shell model and the spectrum of baryonic states. In *Hadron Interactions at Low Energies*, *Proc. Triangle Meeting, Smolenice, Slovakia, 1973* (ed. D. Krupa & J. Pisut), pp. 145–206. Bratislava: VEDA – Slovak Academy of Sciences.

(33) 1975 (With D. Ziemińska) The hypernucleus $^{12}_{\Lambda}$B and the decay process $^{12}_{\Lambda}$B → π^+ + 3α. *Nucl. Phys.* A **242**, 461–466 (http://dx.doi.org/10.1016/0375-9474(75)90476-5).

(34)   Baryonic spectroscopy and its immediate future. In *New Directions in Hadron Spectroscopy*, *Proc ANL Summer Symposium 1975* (Report ANL-HEP-CP-75-58) (ed. S. L. Kramer & E. L. Berger), pp. 383–406. Argonne: Argonne National Laboratory.

(35) 1977 Heavy particles. In *Rudolf Peierls and Theoretical Physics*, *Proc. Oxford 1974* (ed. I. J. R. Aitchison & J. E. Paton), pp. 86–100. Oxford: Pergamon.

(36)   (With M. Jones & R. R. Horgan) Reanalysis of the baryon mass spectrum using the quark shell model. *Nucl. Phys.* B **129**, 45–65 (http://dx.doi.org/10.1016/0550-3213(77)90019-0).

(37)   (With R. R. Horgan & L. J. Reinders) The new resonance ΔD35(1925) and $(56,1_3^-)$ baryonic supermultiplet. *J. Phys.* G **3**, L195–L201 (http://dx.doi.org/10.1088/0305-4616/3/9/001).

(38)   Charm and the ψ-meson family. *Proc. R. Soc. Lond.* A **355**, 601–619 (http://dx.doi.org/10.1098/rspa.1977.0114).

(39) 1978 (With A. Gal & J. M. Soper) A shell-model analysis of Λ binding energies for the p-shell hypernuclei. III. Further analysis and predictions. *Ann. Phys.* **113**, 79–97 (http://dx.doi.org/10.1016/0003-4916(78)90250-6).

(40)   (With A. Gal) The formation of, and the γ-radiation from, the *p*-shell hypernuclei. *Ann. Phys.* **116**, 167–243 (http://dx.doi.org/10.1016/0003-4916(78)90008-8).

(41)   (With D. Kielczewska & D. Ziemińska) A determination of the spin of the hypernucleus $^{12}_{\Lambda}$B: (II). A complete analysis. *Nucl. Phys.* A **333**, 367–380 (http://dx.doi.org/10.1016/0375-9474(80)90103-7).

(42) 1981 (With J. G. McGinley) Remarks bearing on the interpretation of the Λ(1405) resonance. In *Low and Intermediate Energy Kaon-nucleon Physics* (*Proc. Workshop at Inst. of Physics, Univ. of Rome*) (ed. E. Ferrari & G. Violini), pp. 381–409. Reidel: Dordrecht.

(43)   (With F. E. Close) The antisymmetric spin orbit interaction between quarks. In *Low and intermediate energy kaon-nucleon physics* (*Proc. Workshop at Inst. of Physics, Univ. of Rome*) (ed. E. Ferrari & G. Violini), pp. 411–418. Dordrecht: Reidel.

(44)   Quarks in the context of few body physics. *Nucl. Phys.* A **353**, 215c–232c (http://dx.doi.org/10.1016/0375-9474(81)90710-7).

(45) 1982 (With J. McGinley, C. Belyea & S. Anthony) Theory of low-energy kaon-nucleon scattering. In *Proc. Int. Conf. on Hypernuclear and Kaon Physics, Heidelberg, 1982* (ed. B. Povh), pp. 201–214. Heidelberg: MPI.

(46)   Strange particle theory in the cosmic ray period. In *Int. Colloq. on the History of Particle Physics: Some Discoveries, Concepts, Institutions from the Thirties to the Fifties, 21–23 July 1982, Paris, France. J. Phys., Paris* **43**, Colloque C-8 (suppl. 12), pp. C8-195–C8-205 (http://dx.doi.org/10.1051/jphyscol:1982811).

(47)   Quarks and the light hadrons. In *Quarks and the Nucleus, Proc. Int. School of Nucl. Phys., Erice, 1981* (ed. D. H. Wilkinson), *Prog. Part. Nucl. Phys.* **8**, 7–48. Oxford: Pergamon.

(48) 1985 (With D. J. Millener, A. Gal & C. B. Dover) Spin dependence of the ΛN effective interaction. *Phys. Rev.* C **31**, 499–509 (http://dx.doi.org/10.1103/PhysRevC.31.499).

(49) 1986 (With N. W. Tanner) The determination of T- and CPT-violations for the $(K^0, \overline{K}^0)$ complex by $\overline{K}^0/K^0$ comparisons. *Ann. Phys.* **171**, 463–488 (http://dx.doi.org/10.1016/0003-4916(86)90008-4).

(50) 1988 Historical remark on $\pi^0 \to \gamma e^+ e^-$ decay. In *40 Years of Particle Physics. Proc. Int. Conf. to celebrate the discovery of the π and V particles, Bristol, 1987* (ed. B. Foster & P. H. Fowler), pp. 105–108. Bristol: Adam Hilger.

(51)   (With I. J. Ford & J. Hoek) Potentials in pure QCD on 32^4 lattices. *Phys. Lett.* B **208**, 286–290 (http://dx.doi.org/10.1016/0370-2693(88)90431-5).

(52)   (With G. R. Goldstein & R. Marshall) Heavy quark spin correlations in e^+e^- annihilations. *Phys. Lett.* B **215**, 783–787 (http://dx.doi.org/10.1016/0370-2693(88)90061-5).

(53) 1989 (With D. H. Davis, P. H. Fowler, A. Montwill, J. Pniewski & J. A. Zakrzewski) The identified ΛΛ-hypernuclei and the predicted H-particle. *Proc. R. Soc.* Lond. A **426**, 1–17 (http://dx.doi.org/10.1098/rspa.1989.0115).

(54)   (With G. R. Goldstein & R. Marshall) On the helicity of charm jets. *Z. Phys.* C **42**, 441–448 (http://dx.doi.org/10.1007/BF01548450).

(55) 1991 (With A. Deloff) The shape parameters of the Λ(1405) resonance. *J. Phys.* G **17**, 289–302 (http://dx.doi.org/10.1088/0954-3899/17/3/011).

(56) 1992 (With G. R. Goldstein) Decay and polarization properties of the top quark. *Phys. Rev.* D **45**, 1531–1543 (http://dx.doi.org/10.1103/PhysRevD.45.1531).

(57)   (With G. R. Goldstein) Analysis of top-antitop production and dilepton decay events and the top quark mass. *Phys. Lett.* B **287**, 225–230 (http://dx.doi.org/10.1016/0370-2693(92)91904-N).

(58) 1993 (With G. R. Goldstein & K. Sliwa) Observing top-quark production at the Fermilab Tevatron. *Phys. Rev.* D **47**, 967–972 (http://dx.doi.org/10.1103/PhysRevD.47.967).

(59) 1996 Kaon decays to pions. The τ–θ problem. In *History of Original Ideas and Basic Discoveries in Particle Physics, Proc. NATO Adv. Workshop, Erice, 1994* (ed. H. B. Newman & T. Ypsilantis), pp. 163–181 and 183. New York: Plenum Press.

(60) 1998 (With C. Caso *et al.*) Note on the Λ(1405) resonance. In Review of particle physics, by Particle Data Group. *Eur. Phys. J.* C **3**, 676–678 (http://dx.doi.org/10.1007/s10052-998-0104-x).

(61) 1999 (With G. R. Goldstein) Test of analysis method for top–antitop production and decay events. *Proc. R. Soc.* Lond. A **455**, 2803–2834 (http://dx.doi.org/10.1098/rspa.1999.0428).

SIR HOWARD DALTON

8 February 1944 — 12 January 2008

Howard Dalton

SIR HOWARD DALTON

8 February 1944 — 12 January 2008

Elected FRS 1993

By Christopher Anthony[1]* and J. Colin Murrell[2]

[1]*Biological Sciences, University of Southampton, Southampton SO17 1BJ, UK*
[2]*School of Environmental Sciences, University of East Anglia,*
Norwich NR4 7TJ, UK

Howard Dalton was an outstanding microbiologist who, after his remarkably productive DPhil work in the Nitrogen Fixation Laboratory at the University of Sussex, and a short period in the USA, spent his research career at the University of Warwick. He devoted himself to the elucidation of the process of methane oxidation by bacteria that use this relatively inert gas as their sole source of carbon and energy. He discovered two completely novel multicomponent monooxygenase enzymes responsible for the initial oxidation of methane to methanol. He then continued to elucidate their functions, mechanisms, regulation and structures. Their wide substrate specificity led to his interest in using these and related enzymes for biocatalysis, biological transformations and bioremediation. While remaining at Warwick University he also acted as a highly appreciated Chief Scientific Advisor to the UK Government at the Department for the Environment and Rural Affairs (Defra). Howard was a highly effective scientist, a down-to-earth, self-effacing man, outgoing and witty, an inspirational colleague who above all else made science fun.

Early life

Howard Dalton was born in New Malden, Surrey, the son of Leslie Alfred Dalton, a lorry driver, and Florence Gertrude Dalton (*née* Evans). He was highly intelligent, with an enquiring mind, and his early interest in science was evident from his many exploits with cocktails of chemicals, which often had explosive consequences. In his late teens, a laboratory experiment culminated in a blast that singed his hair and eyebrows, as shown for the next decade in the passport photograph taken shortly afterwards. Dalton also showed early entrepreneurial flair,

* c.anthony@soton.ac.uk

http://dx.doi.org/10.1098/rsbm.2016.0007

Figure 1. Howard the teenager.

buying an old-fashioned printing press at the age of 14 years and developing a lucrative sideline, producing circulars and wedding and party invitations, which were particularly popular as he slightly undercut established printing firms in the area (figure 1). His ambitious mother was the guiding influence of his childhood and she was enormously proud when he passed the 11-plus examination to gain a place at Raynes Park Grammar School. Despite his father's attempts to make him leave school at 14 years of age to take up a trade like his brother (David), who became a skilled carpenter, Howard was eager to continue his academic studies. Thanks to his mother's support, he became the first member of his family to go to university when he won a place at Queen Elizabeth College at London University. He graduated in 1965 with a BSc in Microbiology.

NITROGEN FIXATION

Howard's research career started when he undertook a DPhil with Professor John Postgate (FRS 1977) at the world-renowned ARC Unit of Nitrogen Fixation, Sussex University, where he worked on nitrogen fixation in the aerobic soil bacterium *Azotobacter*; this work led to the award of DPhil in 1968. During bacterial nitrogen fixation, atmospheric nitrogen gas is reduced to ammonia in a reaction catalysed by the nitrogenase complex, which consists of two proteins containing the metals iron and molybdenum. This enzyme is famously extremely sensitive to oxygen, raising the question that formed the basis of Howard's DPhil work: How does the oxygen-sensitive nitrogenase function in bacteria in a highly aerobic environment? His approach provides an excellent example of the use of continuous culture to sort out a puzzling problem of bacterial physiology. His extensive, imaginative study showed convincingly that this problem is solved by two mechanisms: first, respiratory protection in which respiration is used to scavenge oxygen down to safe levels, and second, conformational protection in which changes in the conformation of the enzyme protect the oxygen-sensitive sites (1, 2)*.

Figure 2. Howard embracing American culture. (Online version in colour.)

Appreciating that a better understanding of nitrogenase would be based on a physico-chemical approach, Howard moved in 1968 to the USA to work for two years as a postdoctoral fellow with Professor Len Mortensen at Purdue University, Indiana, on the biochemistry of nitrogenase in the anaerobic bacterium *Clostridium*. These studies extended his expertise in protein purification, spectrophotometric analysis and electron paramagnetic resonance (EPR) spectroscopy of metal enzymes in complex multiprotein systems, all of which supported his subsequent work on methane oxidation.

A lively, outgoing man, he embraced American culture with gusto, frequently hosting convivial gatherings such as Superbowl parties for his colleagues (figure 2). He was also active in the anti-Vietnam War protest movement, and it was through this that he met his future wife, Kira Rostislavavna De Armitt Rozdestvensky, the Russian–American daughter of Rostislav Sergevich Rozdestvensky, a college professor; she was later an employment counsellor and management consultant. She advised him that he risked being drafted into the armed services, and suggested an unusual way to avoid this—by becoming a priest, one of the categories exempt from military service. Howard discovered a little-known religious group called the Universal Life Church of California which for $25 would 'ordain' anyone. He duly sent off a cheque and within days was delighted to learn that he was now a *bona fide* Minister of Religion. It became a running joke, and his friends frequently addressed letters to the Reverend Howard Dalton; as a life-long atheist, he particularly relished the irony of his new title.

Recognizing that EPR spectroscopic techniques were going to be of great importance in the study of metalloproteins, Howard returned to the University of Sussex in 1970 to work with Dr Bob Bray in the Department of Chemistry on two molybdenum-containing enzymes, nitrate reductase from *Aspergillus nidulans* and xanthine dehydrogenase from *Veillonella alcalescens*. He used EPR to study the chemical environment of their molybdenum cofactors,

* Numbers in this form refer to the bibliography at the end of the text.

and their flavin and iron–sulfur centres, providing insights into the enzyme mechanism and the partitioning of electrons between the cofactors in the enzyme.

In October 1971 Howard and Kira were married.

WARWICK AND THE OXIDATION OF METHANE

In the early 1970s Derek Burke had just set up a Department of Biological Sciences at Warwick University and had appointed Roger Whittenbury to a chair to initiate microbiology there in 1972. Roger recalls that Warwick in those days was hardly a magnet for microbiologists, offering only an abandoned chemistry laboratory containing just two pieces of equipment, a broken piano and a dartboard! A year later, after a brief chat about his background and a promise that he would work on Roger's beloved methane-oxidizing bacteria, Howard was appointed to a lectureship in the department to strengthen its microbial biochemistry and physiology in 1973, and he and Kira settled in the village of Radford Semele near Leamington Spa. This led to a long and highly successful tenure at the University of Warwick, during which his research brought him a much-deserved international reputation, yielded many seminal publications in a career generating more than 200 scientific papers and opened up whole new research fields in the microbiology of one-carbon (C_1) compounds. Howard was awarded a personal chair at Warwick in 1983.

The oxidation of methane

Methylotrophs are microbes able to grow on reduced carbon compounds containing one or more carbon atoms but containing no carbon–carbon bonds; examples are methane, methanol, methylamine and trimethylamine (Anthony 1982; Trotsenko & Murrell 2008). The end product of all anaerobic microbial degradation of organic material is methane; some of this reaches the atmosphere, where it is a powerful greenhouse gas. The methanotrophs are a major group of methylotrophs, able to use methane and so are clearly important in the carbon cycle, diminishing the amount of methane liberated into the atmosphere. They have become of considerable importance because they can be exploited in biotransformation and bioremediation processes. The methanotrophs are divided into Type I and Type II methanotrophs (Whittenbury *et al.* 1970); this was initially based on their internal membrane systems but the types also differ in their carbon assimilation pathways, genetic systems, phylogeny and so on.

Howard built up a large and vibrant research group at Warwick and pioneered work on the extremely complex process by which methane is oxidized to methanol. This is the essential first step for subsequent energy production and for the assimilation of carbon into new cells. All of the energy used for growth of methanotrophs is obtained by oxidation of methane to carbon dioxide:

$$CH_4 \rightarrow CH_3OH \rightarrow HCHO \rightarrow HCOOH \rightarrow CO_2.$$

In 1973 the first step in this process was very poorly understood, and Dalton set out to solve it using the expertise in multicomponent metal-containing enzyme systems that he had acquired during his work on nitrogenase and related enzymes. This was achieved together with his research students and postdoctoral researchers, most importantly John Colby and David Stirling. Work from many laboratories using a variety of methanotrophs had led to the

Methane oxidation

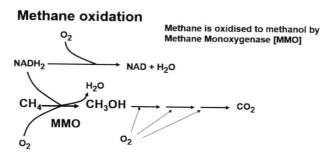

Methane is oxidised to methanol by
Methane Monoxygenase [MMO]

Figure 3. Methane oxidation by methane monooxygenase in methanotrophs. Assay of MMOs is made difficult by alternative routes for oxidation of NADH, consumption of oxygen, and metabolism of the product, methanol. (Figure taken from Anthony (2008); first published by *Science Progress* (http://www.scienceprogress.org).)

general conclusion that the first step in methane oxidation is catalysed by a mixed-function monooxygenase system. This is now called methane monooxygenase (MMO); it hydroxylates methane to methanol by using molecular oxygen and a reductant (AH_2):

$$CH_4 + AH_2 + O_2 \rightarrow CH_3OH + H_2O + A.$$

The reductant was assumed to be the usual metabolic reductant, NADH or NADPH, but there was considerable confusion and disagreement about results in the earlier studies that was often due to the use of different bacteria, different membrane preparations, different enzyme assays and so on. The obvious assay systems would involve spectrophotometric measurement of NADH disappearance, or the methane-dependent and NADH-dependent consumption of oxygen. However, most cell-free preparations used membrane fractions containing NADH oxidase, which also consumes NADH and oxygen, and the product methanol may also be further metabolized (figure 3).

An essential first step in Dalton's solution of the problem was the development of reliable, unambiguous assay systems; these systems are still in use today. They did not use the obvious substrate, methane, but were based on the use of alternative alkanes whose oxidation by MMO depended on its exceptionally wide substrate specificity (3). These methods included the oxidation of bromomethane, whose disappearance was measured by gas–liquid chromatography (GLC), and the oxidation of ethylene or propylene, the epoxy products also being measured by GLC.

Discovery of the methane monooxygenases

Application of these methods led to a definitive description of MMO, using the enzyme purified from soluble extracts of the Type I methanotroph *Methylococcus capsulatus* strain Bath, originally isolated by Roger Whittenbury from the hot springs at the Roman Baths in Bath. This soluble MMO (sMMO) was subsequently shown to be present in several, but not all, methanotrophs. It catalyses the hydroxylation of methane to methanol, with NAD(P)H as the reductant. It is made up of three components and, as with nitrogenase, sMMO contains metal ions. Resolution of this enzyme into its component proteins was a considerable achievement because only one of the components could be assayed independently of the other two. This was component C, now known as the reductase, a flavoprotein containing FAD and an iron sulfide centre as found in spinach ferredoxin and putidaredoxin. Component A is the hydroxylase and contains non-haem iron. Component B, a coupling protein, is a small colourless protein.

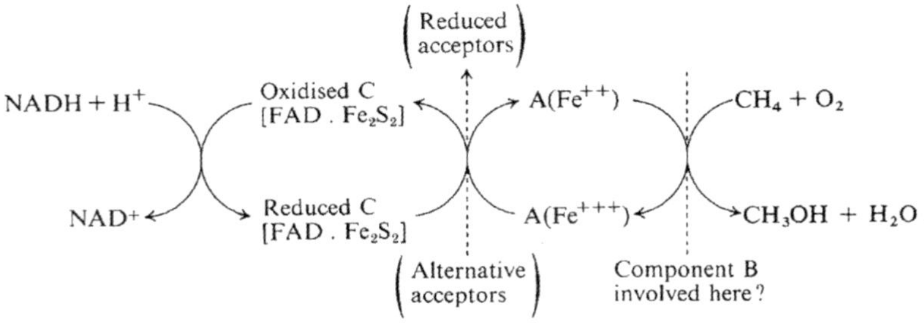

Figure 4. The pathway of electron transfer between the components of soluble MMO during the oxidation of methane to methanol by oxygen with NADH as reductant. This requires the participation of three proteins, A, B and C. (Figure taken from the published proceedings of the 3rd International Symposium on Microbial Growth on C_1 Compounds (5).)

Component C transfers electrons from the donor NADH to the hydroxylase, which catalyses the methane substrate with the use of molecular oxygen (figure 4).

At about this time a three-component MMO was partly purified by John Higgins and colleagues (Tonge *et al.* 1977) from the membranes of a Type II methanotroph, *Methylosinus trichosporium*; the electron donor was NADH in crude extracts but it was necessary to use ascorbate or cytochrome *c* in purified preparations. The enzyme was relatively unstable and some results were not always easy to reproduce. It therefore seemed that there might be two different kinds of MMO or that there might be a single membrane-bound MMO in both types of methanotroph but that it might be more readily released from its normal association with membranes to produce the sMMO.

This confusion was eventually resolved by Dalton's group in an elegant study using continuous culture, reminiscent of his work on respiratory protection of nitrogenase. It was shown that there are two completely different enzymes in *Methylococcus capsulatus*, the sMMO and also a membrane (or particulate) MMO (pMMO). Which enzyme is produced depends on the availability of copper: pMMO is produced when the copper:biomass ratio is high, whereas sMMO is produced when the copper:biomass ratio is low (6). In batch culture both MMOs may be produced, because the copper:biomass ratio cannot be as well controlled or defined (for a recent review of the role of copper in methanotrophs see Semrau *et al.* (2010)). Dalton's group subsequently developed reproducible solubilization and purification methods and showed that the membrane-bound enzyme, pMMO, also has three components and that the two types of MMO are present in other methanotrophs, regardless of the membrane type. Some methanotrophs synthesize only a single type of MMO and in that case it is most often the membrane enzyme that is produced. Remarkably, the two families of MMO share no detectable similarity in amino acid sequence or three-dimensional structure.

The substrate specificity of methane monooxygenases

A remarkable feature of the MMOs, possibly related to their normal small, unfunctionalized methane substrate, is their extraordinarily wide substrate specificity, sMMO having a wider range of substrates than pMMO. Substrates for sMMO include n-alkanes, n-alkenes, chloromethane, bromomethane, trichloromethane, nitromethane, methanol, carbon monoxide, dimethyl ether, benzene, styrene and pyridine (3). Remarkably, this enzyme is also able to oxidize ammonia, whose structure is clearly analogous to that of methane. When whole cells are used, a source of reducing equivalents must also be provided (such as methanol or formate) in addition to the potential substrate. When this is required, the oxidation of the potential substrate is referred to as co-oxidation. Dalton showed that because methanotrophs can co-oxidize a range of hydrocarbons and chlorinated pollutants they have a biotechnological interest that extends far beyond their ability to oxidize methane to methanol (7). Important examples include the industrial production of methanol from methane, the co-oxidation of propene to epoxypropane, the bioremediation of chlorinated hydrocarbons and the production of valuable recombinant proteins with the use of methane as the starting material. This interest in biotransformations stimulated his later interest in biofuels. He was a consultant for the New Jersey company Celanese and then joined the Scientific Advisory Board for the spin-out biotechnology company Celgene, which gave him considerable insight into chemical and industrial aspects of microbiology that he used to good effect in his biotransformation research.

Exploration of oxidizing enzymes for use in biotransformations

The wide substrate specificity of the methane monooxygenases made them obvious candidates as tools for the catalysis of difficult chemical reactions that might lead to useful materials.

Although Howard Dalton's earlier work at Warwick was largely based on methane monooxygenases, after 1986 his research interests increasingly involved other types of oxidoreductases. In this he was encouraged by Derek Boyd at Queen's University Belfast. They established a highly productive microbiology–chemistry collaboration that lasted about 20 years. The Warwick–Belfast link resulted in joint awards from UK Research Councils, European Union programmes and industry that funded projects on enzyme-catalysed chemistry in Warwick and Belfast resulting in 42 joint publications and 3 patents (7). At the outset of the collaboration (1986) they decided that, because demand was increasing for chiral synthons in both academic and industrial contexts, important objectives of the programme should include (i) the development of reliable methods for the assignment of structure and stereochemistry of metabolites, (ii) the discovery of new types of *cis* and *trans* dihydrodiol metabolites, (iii) the investigation of potentially competing toluene dioxygenase-catalysed reactions, and (iv) the evaluation of new applications of chiral metabolites in chemical synthesis including chiral ligands. Most of the biotransformations were conducted and analysed in Warwick before being transported to Belfast for chemical analysis on an almost weekly basis.

Derek Boyd recalls that Howard was a fearless individual who was willing to travel regularly to Belfast at times when many other academics were very reluctant to visit. Although 'the troubles in Northern Ireland' were no longer at their worst, over the years 1986–98 until the Belfast Agreement was signed, there was still an average of almost 100 terrorist-related killings annually. He recalls Howard's first lecture in Belfast 'when he tried to emphasise the wide range of substrates and reactions catalysed by a dioxygenase by stating "I would regard these dioxygenase enzymes as being really catholic in their taste"—that certainly took courage in front of a "mixed" audience!'

As a result of the Warwick–Belfast link, and of Howard's being able to demonstrate by example that it was now relatively safe to cross the Irish Sea again, several people transferred their expertise from Howard's laboratory at the University of Warwick to Queen's University Belfast; Howard's legacy, initiated in 1986 by the dioxygenase-catalysed chemistry link between Warwick and Belfast, is still continuing at the time of writing (2016).

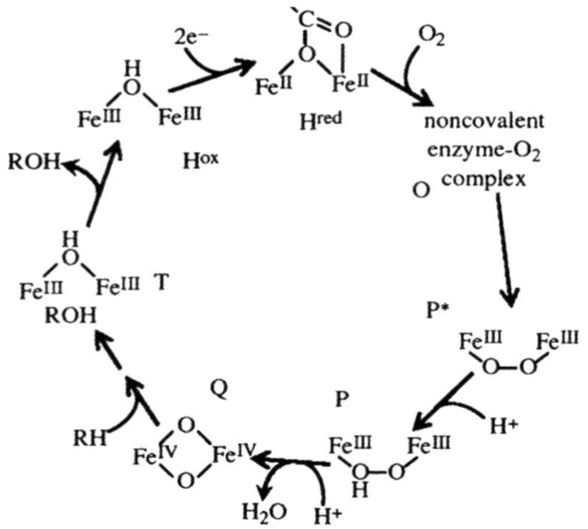

Figure 5. Principal intermediates during the sMMO catalytic cycle. This figure is based mainly on the work of the groups of Dalton, Lippard and Lipscomb; it is taken from Dalton's Leeuwenhoek Lecture 2000 (7), in which the significance of the intermediates is fully discussed.

The structure and function of methane monooxygenases

Further development of Howard's research on the methane monooxygenases was necessarily done in collaboration or was handed over to others in his group. After the purification and characterization of the two main types of methane monooxygenase, a major challenge was the molecular biology of their synthesis and regulation; this was taken up and developed in Howard's department by Colin Murrell (reviewed in Murrell *et al.* 2000).

The other major challenge was to elucidate their mechanisms and three-dimensional structures. Figure 5 shows the catalytic cycle of the soluble methane monooxygenase as determined mainly by the groups of Dalton, Lippard and Lipscomb and as described in Dalton's Leeuwenhoek Lecture in 2000 (7). The structure of the soluble enzyme was mainly determined by Lippard's group (see, for example, Rosenzweig *et al.* 1993). Howard's contribution to our understanding of the structure of the membrane enzymes was achieved by a fruitful collaboration with colleagues in Manchester and competition in the USA. Figure 6 shows the beautiful structure of one of these enzymes.

CONTRIBUTIONS TO LIFE IN AND AROUND THE UNIVERSITY OF WARWICK

Howard held many positions in the university, dealing with academic matters and other areas of university life. He was extremely generous of his time, with well over 100 PhD students and postdoctoral researchers; he was a great mentor and subsequently loyal colleague for many of his researchers who remained in the field of C_1 metabolism. He led a large and vibrant research laboratory in which training in microbial physiology and biochemistry was outstanding. While working with Howard, science was fun and there were many social gatherings at which successes such as the award of a PhD were celebrated. His 'Thanksgiving parties' at his house were also highly appreciated by all who attended, especially for some

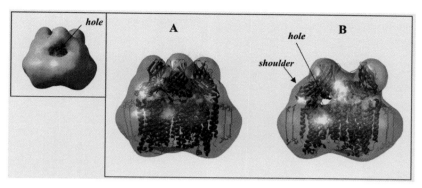

Figure 6. The structure of a membrane methane monooxygenase. Top left, the structure determined by electron microscopy and single-particle analysis at 23 Å resolution from one of Howard's last publications (8). In A and B it is shown superimposed on the crystal structure determined by Lieberman & Rosenzweig (2005). For a recent review of the structure and function of these enzymes see Sirajuddin & Rosenzweig (2015). (Taken with permission from A. Kitmitto *et al.*, *Biochemistry* **44**, 10954–10965 (2005). Copyright © 2005 American Chemical Society.) (Online version in colour.)

PhD students who were in need of a square meal. Howard was a very popular teacher at the undergraduate level, and his witty and relaxed style inspired many undergraduates to study microbiology and to pursue microbiology-related careers after graduating. In 1983 the School of Biological Sciences launched a Microbiology and Microbial Technology degree and Howard, together with his former PhD student Colin Murrell, who rejoined the department that year as a lecturer, were instrumental in developing this innovative course, one of the first of its kind in the UK. Its popularity increased over the next 10 years or so, ensuring a new generation of microbiologists who were very familiar with the use of microbes (especially methanotrophs!) in biotechnology. Throughout the 1980s and 1990s Howard led and gradually built up the Microbiology Research Group in Biological Sciences at Warwick until it was one of the biggest of its type in the UK, embracing multidisciplinary research in microbiology, often with an applied flavour. On Roger Whittenbury's retirement, Howard became Chair of the Department of Biological Sciences in 1999 and was an effective and popular leader there until he was seconded to Defra in 2002.

In 1973 a series of hugely influential International Symposia on Microbial Growth on C_1 compounds was initiated by Roger Whittenbury and Rod Quayle (FRS 1978), and these have been held every two or three years up to the present time. In 1980 the Symposium was hosted by Rod Quayle and colleagues in Sheffield, the book of proceedings being edited by Howard (4), who 12 years later was responsible, with his excellent departmental colleagues, for the 7th Symposium held in the University of Warwick (Murrell & Kelly 1993). Howard had a great influence at these symposia by his direct scientific contributions and even more perhaps by his personality. He was excellent at chairing scientific sessions in a relaxed way that encouraged participation by students and the less experienced researchers. He energetically browsed his way through most of the posters, providing entertainment and encouragement (figure 7).

Howard was a down-to-earth, self-effacing man, outgoing and witty and in the 1980s was a 'leading light' at gatherings of the staff of Biological Sciences at Warwick in weekly socials at local pubs (code-named 'Choir-Practice'!). He also enjoyed the occasional 'poker night'

Figure 7. Howard in typical happy enthusiastic conference mode. (*a*) With the authors (Chris Anthony and Colin Murrell) at the 8th International Symposium on Microbial Growth on C_1 Compounds in San Diego in 1995. (*b*) Howard at a Gordon Conference on the Molecular Basis of Microbial One-Carbon Metabolism in Oxford in 2006, chatting with his colleagues Colin Murrell (left) and Tom Smith. (Online versions in colour.)

with selected colleagues who invariably relieved him of his hard-earned cash. Howard's enthusiasm for, and extensive knowledge of, Japanese gardens was also brought into play on campus, resulting in the creation of two fine gardens at Warwick.

He was a fanatical supporter of Tottenham Hotspur Football Club (Spurs) and a highly competitive member of the Biological Sciences football team, aptly named 'Biohazard'. In the 1970s Howard performed with distinction in the 'Biohazard' team that played a friendly match with the Saudi Arabia national team, thereby adding to his illustrious international career. He also loved village cricket, turning out for a variety of local sides as a wayward but explosive fast bowler. Once, representing the nearby village of Rowington against admittedly inferior opposition, he took eight wickets for a miserly 15 runs, the highlight of his cricket career.

A great passion was real tennis and he was a member of Leamington Real Tennis Club, where his competitive spirit, guile and ability won him many tournaments. It was here, while playing in a friendly doubles tournament, that he tragically collapsed and died on 12 January 2008.

Chief Scientific Adviser to the Department for Environment, Food and Rural Affairs

Howard served as the Chief Scientific Adviser at Defra from March 2002 to September 2007. He was the first departmental Chief Scientific Adviser to be appointed by Sir David King FRS, who was then Chief Scientific Adviser to the Prime Minister. The newly created Defra had risen from the ashes of the beleaguered Ministry of Agriculture, Fisheries and Food, which was widely criticized for its handling of the bovine spongiform encephalopathy crisis and the 2001 outbreak of foot-and-mouth disease. Howard did not enter an easy atmosphere. 'It was a very inward-looking department that didn't make use of scientific resources outside', Sir David recalled. Over the next five years, Howard transformed Defra's use of science, seeking to instil scientific rigour into policy-making decisions based on sound scientific evidence. Howard led the scientific advisory team generating the UK's contingency plan for dealing with avian influenza virus and was instrumental in raising the profile of climate change as a significant threat, delivering lectures on this and other topics such as biofuels and genetically modified crops at many national and international meetings.

The following section has been kindly provided by Dame Helen Frances Ghosh, DCB, former Permanent Secretary, Defra.

SCIENCE AT THE HEART OF GOVERNMENT

By Dame Helen Ghosh DCB, former Permanent Secretary, Defra. A contribution to the Tribute to Celebrate the life of Professor Sir Howard Dalton FRS held at the University of Warwick in May 2008

As Permanent Secretary at Defra between 2005 and 2010, I had the privilege of working with Howard for almost two years. Defra is a department whose work is grounded profoundly in science, in its broadest sense: global climate to local conservation, farming and food, waste and pollution and, probably most famously, natural and sometimes man-made disasters such as flooding and animal diseases. All of these involve the most fascinating range of science, and though politicians might sometimes have found it challenging, science had to underpin all the policy that we made. Howard's work with us gave us a sure and secure—and in many areas world renowned—basis for those decisions.

No sooner had I arrived than Howard disappeared—to Antarctica. So the first image of Howard that is imprinted on my mind is a photograph of him at the bottom of a crevasse in Antarctica, reporting back to us and the public via his wonderful blog. Howard was an engaging and energizing communicator within Defra and outside, of the excitement of science and what it could do for us.

Howard was the first of Sir David King's new wave of Departmental Chief Scientific Advisors, whom he hired to be independent, authoritative and, as their title suggests, challenging.

These pioneers were asked to focus their attention on evidence-based policy making, and on ensuring that evidence was comprehensive and rigorous but above all used. Dave King also gave them the commission—when not fire-fighting on the day to day—to make space for horizon scanning.

The programme that Howard set up on his arrival focused on all these things—making sure we were doing the right science through horizon scanning, developing a science strategy, making sure we were commissioning sound and relevant evidence, and then making sure we were using it. Howard's decision to set up a Science Advisory Council to support us on all this was inspired. Initially its membership was predominantly focused on animal disease issues, which had provided the impetus for his role—and indeed the creation of Defra—in the first place. But over time its focus has expanded to the whole range of Defra science—including social science. And it has played a vital role in quality ensuring our science as a whole and also giving us immediate access—particularly in an emergency—to a range of the most distinguished scientists in their field. It was the envy of other government departments, and several followed our example.

From this concept of what his job was about, Howard pulled together a first systematic account of the science that Defra should do—the Science and Innovation Strategy—which we called 'Delivering the Evidence'. Miles Parker, our Director of Science, has reported to me that at the end of the long day of the launch of this strategy, Howard referred to it serendipitously as 'delivering the elephants'. Defra of course does have to deliver elephants, but not quite as Howard meant. That first strategy was followed a few years later by a second, ground-breaking, Evidence and Innovation Strategy.

By then it was clear that public spending constraints meant that there was no question of just carrying on with established patterns of science spend in the Defra budget, however beloved those might be with particular lobby groups, customers or—dare I say it—elements of the scientific establishment. Howard bravely argued that our spend needed to be refocused towards the issues of the day: to climate change and protecting the natural environment against the worst that humans could throw at it. That legacy lives on.

So far, so dignified and strategic, but of course what Defra gets most coverage for—however distinguished our achievements across the range of our responsibilities—is dealing with emergencies. And Howard was always there when we needed him. Howard provided a major support to the Chief Veterinary Officer (CVO) on a range of animal disease issues where his virology background and networks were used to great effect. He and CVO Debby Reynolds—particularly during the first few outbreaks of avian influenza in this country— would spend long hours closeted with Dave King and sometimes in Number 10 Downing Street, discussing the detailed science of the viruses with which we were dealing. Bovine tuberculosis was another subject for these scientific conclaves.

But Howard also had to turn his hand to the other kind of emergencies with which Defra— which we sometimes felt should be called the Department for Plague and Pestilence—had to deal. So plant disease, radioactive waste, the Buncefield fire, oil pollution and shellfish poisoning all got his attention and the benefit of his scientific experience and habits of mind. If he did not know the answer himself he generally knew a woman or man who did. When these emergencies break out, the support of the whole departmental team is vital. If my first memory of Howard will be the picture of him in Antarctica, probably my last mental image of him will be as he stood next to me at one of our early morning 'bird tables' in our National Disease Control centre in Page Street, in the early days of the outbreak of foot-and-mouth disease in 2007.

He and his wife had been in Africa when it broke out, but without a moment's apparent hesitation he came back, because of luggage delays more or less only in the clothes he stood up in. He rapidly became an expert in the Civil Service's complex rules for financing the purchase of new clothes in these circumstances, so that he could have another shirt to wear while he got his own washed! But he was still his normal optimistic, enquiring and energizing self, and made a real contribution to the emotional resilience of a team under a great deal of pressure.

Miles Parker, who probably knew him better than any of us, has commented to me, perhaps euphemistically, that 'Howard was not the most enthusiastic bureaucrat.' Despite more than 25 years as a civil servant, I think that is a real accolade.

What Howard brought was not just a new confidence and seriousness to Defra science, but also an infectious and vivid way of communicating his passions. The Antarctica blog was, I think, a first for any Whitehall scientist, and really caught the public imagination.

When Howard decided to retire from his Defra role in 2007 and return to his work at Warwick on a more full-time basis, it was a challenge for all of us. But by then and thanks to Howard, we knew what good looked like, and we were lucky—no, not just lucky, because I benefited from Howard's wise advice in the process—to be able to attract a worthy successor in Professor Bob [now Sir Robert] Watson [FRS 2011]. Howard left Bob a great legacy, which was epitomized in the excellent review of Defra science carried out by Dave King and the Office of Science and Technology shortly before the end of Howard's term with us.

Before I left Defra, I established a new award at our sports day, in the memorializing tradition of my (all-male) predecessors. Rather than call it the Helen Ghosh Cup, I decided that it should be the Howard Dalton Trophy, for the person who was the best overall performer on the day.

Howard will have lots of memorials—here in the UK and in The Gambia—but I thought that this would be one that would entertain and please him. I can just imagine him smiling— perhaps slightly embarrassed—at the idea.

In 2010 the inaugural event for the annual Howard Dalton Lecture was launched by Defra. This not only commemorates Defra's late Chief Scientific Adviser, Professor Sir Howard Dalton FRS, but also serves to acknowledge and celebrate excellence in science and policy.

But the greatest memorial to Howard's work in government is the legacy he gave us of sound science, and science at the heart of policy making. The best tribute we can pay him is to defend and protect that legacy and continue to work within the principles to which he was committed. We are very grateful to Howard for all he did for us in Defra and in government, and to the University of Warwick and to his family for lending him to us.

Howard's support for the work of Lady Kira Dalton in The Gambia

Kira says that when she decided in 2000 to give up her work as a self-employed management consultant she went to The Gambia 'looking for a project'. After meeting the headmistress of a village school at Niumi Lamin on the north bank of the Gambia river she set out to raise money in the UK for various school renovations, including fencing, toilets, roofing and furniture. During the next few years she visited for two to four weeks a year, while raising money in the UK. Howard became very interested after he visited for the first time in about 2004 and subsequently they bought a small bungalow where he set up an observatory and viewing positions for his latest hobbies, astronomy and bird-watching. At about this time James Holden had become interested in starting some charitable work in Africa and realized that he needed someone on the ground who could be trusted to deliver on whatever he decided to do. As he says, 'the very person was to cross my path in the most unlikely of places—the Leamington Tennis Court Club'. Although the club was limited to male players, Howard had persuaded them to permit Kira to put on a series of talks at the club on Leamington's history, with all proceeds going towards her school in The Gambia. This led to an invitation to James to visit, which he did in November 2004, escorted by Kira and Howard to Niumi Lamin, bringing much-needed cash that he had raised in his church in Claverdon, near Leamington, together with a large quantity of medicines. When he returned to Warwickshire he decided to start a formal charity to support the work in The Gambia. Kira had appreciated by this time that it would be sensible to start a registered charity for the sake of Gift Aid and better credibility. Thus was born the charity the African Oyster Trust (http://www.africanoystertrust.co.uk). Kira says that because the administration involved did not really appeal, it was very fortunate that James Holden had the resources and the patience to do the painstaking procedures involved in all that side of it while her interest was always with the hands-on interaction in The Gambia— especially with the young children.

Figure 8. Lady Kira Dalton at the Howard Dalton Clinic established by Kira and Howard in Jappineh, The Gambia.
(Online version in colour.)

Although Howard was very busy with Defra he loved coming out to The Gambia for a rest, staying at their bungalow. During this time he sponsored his own football team of village youngsters, whose side rejoiced in the title Brufut Hotspur, in tribute to his north London heroes Spurs. In 2007 Howard was asked to provide advice regarding Gambian water policy through a contact at Defra, Pa Ousman Jarjue, who is now Secretary of State for the Environment in The Gambia. Howard was still in the process of doing this when he died.

The other project that caught Howard's interest was the creation of a health centre up-country in Jappineh, where a nursery school had already been established. A Dutch charity had begun some building work before running out of funds. They had not got around to finishing or furnishing the place with equipment, medicines or staff. Through speaking to various contacts in the UK and America Howard was able to obtain large donations to complete that project; it is now fully established as the Howard Dalton Clinic (figure 8), supported by generous donations made in his memory after his untimely death.

FAMILY MATTERS

Howard was always supported by his happy family: Kira and their children, Amber and Jed. Kira continues to live in Warwickshire in the summer while spending much of her time working with the African Oyster Trust in The Gambia. Amber lives in Peckham with her husband and two children, Huxley Howard and Inez; she is a magazine editor and restaurant critic as well as organizing food and wine-tasting events. Jed lives in Esher with his wife and

Figure 9. Howard with his family after receiving his knighthood. (Online version in colour.)

their children, Rosie, Henry and Aja; he runs a company that provides software consultancy to energy companies. He also enjoys playing real tennis at Hampton Court in his spare time.

THE SOCIETY FOR GENERAL MICROBIOLOGY

Howard was an enthusiastic supporter of the Society for General Microbiology (SGM) (now the Microbiological Society) in the UK; he served on the Council of the Society from 1985 to 1989 and became its President, serving from 1997 to 2000. The Council of the Society decided that it would use a bequest from Howard to support attendance at an SGM meeting by a microbiology student from The Gambia, where Sir Howard and Lady Kira were involved in educational activities. Council also decided to rename the Young Microbiologist of the Year Competition, which fosters science communication in early career microbiologists, in honour of Sir Howard, the prize now being the Sir Howard Dalton Prize and Fellowship.

HONOURS

In 1993 Howard was elected a Fellow of the Royal Society and, in 2000, was awarded the Society's Leeuwenhoek Medal and Lecture, which was established to award excellence in microbiology; his lecture was entitled 'The natural and unnatural history of methane-oxidising bacteria' (7). He served as President of the Marine Biological Association from 2007 to 2008 and as President of the Society for General Microbiology from 1997 to 2000. He was named a Knight Bachelor in the 2007 New Year's Honours list for his services to science (figure 9).

ACKNOWLEDGEMENTS

We should like to thank Derek Boyd, Howard's collaborator in Belfast, for his help, Dame Helen Ghosh for her contribution about Howard's time at Defra, and Lady Kira Dalton, Amber and Jed for their enthusiastic encouragement in the production of this memoir.

The frontispiece photograph was taken in 1993 and is copyright © The Royal Society.

AUTHOR PROFILES

Professor Christopher Anthony

Christopher Anthony worked for his PhD in the Microbiology Department of the University of Reading, UK, then spent most of his professional life at the University of Southampton, UK, where he is now Emeritus Professor of Biochemistry. While there he was personal tutor to the co-author of this memoir, Colin Murrell, with whom he also played string quartets. His main interests are the biochemistry of methylotrophs during growth on C_1 and C_2 compounds. He is the author of the main textbook on these bacteria, *The biochemistry of methylotrophs*. He first discovered their unusual enzyme for oxidation of methanol (methanol dehydrogenase) and its novel prosthetic group (PQQ). He subsequently concentrated on this quinoprotein, and related quinoproteins with their associated electron transport chains, using the techniques of continuous culture, spectrophotometry, X-ray crystallography and molecular genetics.

Professor Colin Murrell

Colin Murrell studied physiology and biochemistry at the University of Southampton, where his Personal Tutor, Chris Anthony, suggested he study for a PhD with Howard Dalton. After obtaining his PhD on nitrogen metabolism in methane-oxidizing bacteria at the University of Warwick under the guidance of Howard Dalton, he spent two years as a postdoctoral researcher in Mary Lidstrom's laboratory at the University of Washington. Murrell then returned to Warwick, spending 28 years as a lecturer, senior lecturer and professor and working alongside Howard Dalton until he was seconded to Defra. In 2012 Murrell moved from Warwick to the University of East Anglia to take up the position of Director of the Earth and Life Systems Alliance. Murrell and Dalton enjoyed several fruitful collaborations and co-authored 15 papers on the biochemistry and molecular biology of methane oxidation and biotransformations using microbial enzymes. Jointly they edited a book entitled *The methane and methanol utilizers* and co-organized the Seventh International Symposium on Microbial Growth on C_1 Compounds at Warwick in 1992.

REFERENCES TO OTHER AUTHORS

Anthony, C. 1982 *The biochemistry of methylotrophs*. London: Academic Press.

Anthony, C. 2008 A tribute to Howard Dalton and methane monooxygenase. *Sci. Prog.* **91**, 401–415.

Lieberman, R. L. & Rosenzweig, A. C. 2005 Crystal structure of a membrane-bound metalloenzyme that catalyses the biological oxidation of methane. *Nature* **434**, 177–182.

Murrell, J. C. & Kelly, D. P. 1993 *Microbial growth on C_1 compounds*. Andover: Intercept Ltd.

Murrell, J. C., McDonald, I. R. & Gilbert, B. 2000 Regulation of expression of methane monooxygenases by copper ions. *Trends Microbiol.* **8**, 221–225.

Rosenzweig, A. C., Frederick, C. A., Lippard, S. J. & Nordlund, P. 1993 Crystal structure of a bacterial non-haem iron hydroxylase that catalyzes the biological oxidation of methane. *Nature* **366**, 537–543.

Semrau, J. D., DiSpirito, A. A. & Yoon, S. 2010 Methanotrophs and copper. *FEMS Microbiol. Rev.* **34**, 496–531.

Sirajuddin, S. & Rosenzweig, A. C. 2015 Enzymatic oxidation of methane. *Biochemistry* **54**, 2283–2294.

Tonge, G. M., Harrison, D. E. F. & Higgins, I. J. 1977 Purification and properties of the methane mono-oxygenase enzyme system from *Methylosinus trichosporium* OB3b. *Biochem. J.* **161**, 333–344.

Trotsenko, Y. A. & Murrell, J. C. 2008 Metabolic aspects of aerobic obligate methanotrophy. *Adv. Appl. Microbiol.* **63**, 183–229.

Whittenbury, R., Phillips, K. C. & Wilkinson, J. F. 1970 Enrichment, isolation and some properties of methane-utilizing bacteria. *J. Gen. Microbiol.* **61**, 205–218.

BIBLIOGRAPHY

The following publications are those referred to directly in the text. A full bibliography is available as electronic supplementary material at http://dx.doi.org/10.1098/rsbm.2016.0007 or via http://rsbm.royalsocietypublishing.org.

(1) 1969 (With J. R. Postgate) Effect of oxygen on growth of *Azotobacter chroococcum* in batch and continuous culture. *J. Gen. Microbiol.* **54**, 463–473.

(2)   (With J. R. Postgate) Growth and physiology of *Azotobacter chroococcum* in continuous culture. *J. Gen. Microbiol.* **56**, 307–319.

(3) 1977 (With J. Colby & D. Stirling) The soluble methane monooxygenase of *Methylococcus capsulatus* (Bath): its ability to oxygenate n-alkanes, n-alkenes, ethers, and acyclic, aromatic and heterocyclic compounds. *Biochem. J.* **165**, 395–402.

(4) 1981 (Editor) *Microbial growth on C-1 compounds*. London: Heyden & Son.

(5)   Methane mono-oxygenases from a variety of microbes. In *Microbial growth on C-1 compounds* (ed. H. Dalton), pp. 1–10. London: Heyden & Son.

(6) 1983 (With S. H. Stanley, S. D. Prior & D. J. Leak) Copper stress underlies the fundamental change in intracellular location of methane monooxygenase in methane-oxidising organisms: studies in batch and continuous cultures. *Biotechnol. Lett.* **5**, 487–492.

(7) 2005 The Leeuwenhoek Lecture 2000. The natural and unnatural history of methane-oxidizing bacteria. *Phil. Trans. R. Soc. B* **360**, 1207–1222.

(8)   (With A. Kitmitto, N. Myronova & P. Basu) Characterization and structural analysis of an active particulate methane monooxygenase trimer from *Methylococcus capsulatus* (Bath). *Biochemistry* **44**, 10954–10965.

MICHAEL ELLIOTT CBE

30 September 1924 — 17 October 2007

M. Elliott

MICHAEL ELLIOTT CBE

30 September 1924 — 17 October 2007

Elected FRS 1979

By John Pickett* FRS

Rothamsted Research, West Common, Harpenden, Herts. AL5 2JQ, UK

Michael Elliott was the leader of work at Rothamsted that invented and subsequently commercially developed the pyrethroids, a new class of insecticides. Michael made probably the greatest individual contribution to the control of insect pests that not only constrain global food production but also affect the health of ourselves and our livestock. In one of the first pioneering structure–activity relationship studies, Michael led the multidisciplinary team that invented the major pyrethroid insecticides bioresmethrin, permethrin, cypermethrin and deltamethrin. In the 1980s these represented two-thirds of the global pyrethroid market; at that time pyrethroids captured more than 25% of the total insecticide market and were used on 33 million hectares of crops (Wirtz *et al*. 2009). In 2002 deltamethrin was the world's largest-selling pyrethroid, with annual sales worth $208 million (information from Cropnosis Ltd). In terms of human health, in 2009 it was estimated that pyrethroid-treated bednets significantly decreased the number of deaths due to malaria among children under five years of age by about one-fifth as well as reducing all incidents of malaria, and in 2011 the World Health Organization recommended its vastly expanded use.

BACKGROUND

Michael Elliott was born on 30 September 1924 at Thorngrove Road, East Ham, London, to devout Anglo-Catholic parents, Thomas William and Isabel Constance Elliott (*née* Burnell). Their life centred on St Albans Church in East Ham. As an only child Michael was rather solitary, although in his childhood he played happily with two friends on Tunbridge Wells Common. He formed an early interest in scientific and technical aspects of life and was particularly impressed by its systematic order and the structure of matter. His imagination expanded not only through his formal education but also through his use of the excellent public

* john.pickett@rothamsted.ac.uk

http://dx.doi.org/10.1098/rsbm.2016.0018

library facilities in Tunbridge Wells. Passing through the Convent School at Hawkenbury, Tunbridge Wells, and then St Peter's Elementary School, he received his final schooling at Skinners Company's School, Southbridge, Kent, where he was appointed School Librarian, became a lance corporal in the army cadet corps and obtained sufficiently good grades to be awarded an Open University exhibition in 1942. Dr Harold Cordingley, the chemistry master at Skinners, having himself been a pupil of Sir Christopher Ingold FRS, encouraged Michael in this subject, introducing him to the work of both Sir Christopher and Sir Robert Robinson FRS (PRS 1945–50) on the emerging views regarding electronic theory, and this led to his university education at Southampton culminating in a BSc (external, University of London) in chemistry in 1945. His postgraduate research for his PhD was on 'Experiments on the synthesis of the pyrethrins' under Professor Stanley Harper, initially at University College Southampton from 1945 to 1946, at which time the college moved to King's College, London, until 1947. He was awarded his PhD (external, University of London) in 1952. In 1948 he joined the Department of Insecticides and Fungicides at Rothamsted Experimental Station, now renamed the Department of Biological Chemistry and Crop Protection at Rothamsted Research. His recruitment to Rothamsted by the then head of department, Charles Potter, set him on the track that took him from the lead compound pyrethrin 1, via resmethrin and its active isomer bioresmethrin, through to the photostable pyrethroids, all of which were subsequently exploited commercially. As recognition of these achievements he and his team twice earned Queen's Awards for or Technological Achievement, in 1976 and 1980.

In 1984 Michael retired from Rothamsted but continued to serve as a departmental consultant on chemistry and insecticides, his advice being eagerly sought. He also worked with his long-standing good friend and colleague, Professor John Casida (ForMemRS 1998; Member of the US National Academy of Sciences 1991), at the University of California, Berkeley, where they pioneered work on other pest toxicants that are still currently regarded industrially as potential leads for new pesticidal compounds. In 1989 Michael returned to Rothamsted as a Lawes Trust Fellow, continuing his consultancy.

INVENTION OF FIELD-STABLE PYRETHROIDS

Under Frederick Tattersfield, the first Head of the Department of Insecticides and Fungicides at Rothamsted, natural insecticides, including pyrethrum extract from the pyrethrum daisy *Tanacetum cinerariaefolium*, had been studied from the 1920s onwards. The extract from plants grown in Harpenden near Rothamsted had extremely high insecticidal activity and was supplied to Kenya to establish the pyrethrum-growing industry still extant today. In 1935 Charles Potter, who was recruited to the department in the mid 1930s, made the significant discovery that pyrethrum extract in mineral oil sprayed in darkened warehouses formed residual films that controlled pests of stored products for considerable periods and thus indicated the potential scope of pyrethrum extract and their pyrethrin components for insect control.

In 1948 Charles, having been appointed Head of Department the year before, initiated a detailed programme of research on the natural pyrethrins and allied compounds, and it was this programme that Michael joined. On the basis of his postgraduate experience studying the chemistry of the pyrethrins under Stanley Harper and in collaboration with Leslie Crombie (FRS 1973), a long-term colleague from King's College, London, but by then working at Nottingham University, he was asked to investigate relationships between the molecular structure and

Figure 1. Michael at work in Rothamsted with his colleagues Norman Janes and Bhupinder Khambay in the late 1980s. (Online version in colour.)

biological activity of pyrethrins and related analogues. Others involved or associated at various times with the programme at Rothamsted included the chemists Norman Janes, David Pulman, Bhupinder Khambay and Ian Graham-Bryce FRSE, and the insect toxicologists Paul Needham, Roman Sawicki (FRS 1987), Andrew Farnham and John Stevenson (figure 1). Michael was always keen to recognize these essential and invaluable collaborations, and also eventually many others from industry. The contribution of Norman Janes was of major significance. He joined the team in 1962 at a crucial period and brought additional expertise, specializing in nuclear magnetic resonance spectroscopy. Their recognition of the salient structural features underlying the biological activity of the pyrethroids was a major outcome of this cooperation, which enabled outstanding scientific progress.

One of the first of his studies (1)* and reviewed later (8) showed that the relative potency of isomers of allethrin, originally synthesized by Milton Schechter and colleagues in the USA (LaForge *et al.* 1956), and the natural pyrethrins varied widely between insect species. Indeed, the natural esters were much more effective against pests of agricultural importance than the corresponding allethrin isomers were. A method for isolating pure (+)-pyrethrolone† as its monohydrate made adequate quantities of pyrethrins I and II (2, 3) readily available. Direct comparison of pyrethrin I and *S*-bioallethrin indicated that the natural ester was up to 100 times more active against some insect species (figure 2).

This discovery focused attention on the importance of multiple unsaturation in the side chain of the alcoholic component and this, combined with W. F. Barthel's observation (Barthel 1961) of the potency of simple chrysanthemates such as that of 2,4-dimethylbenzyl

---

* Numbers in this form refer to the bibliography at the end of the text.
† The original nomenclature used by Michael is adopted throughout.

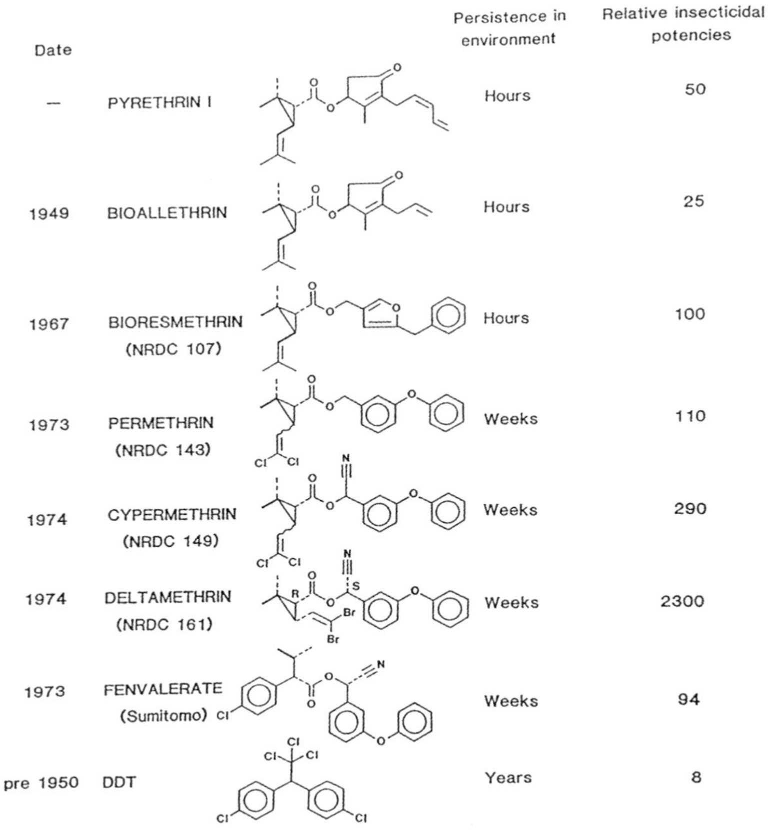

Figure 2. Development of field-stable pyrethroids. Potencies are mean values relative to 7–10 species. (Directly reproduced from original Rothamsted text.)

alcohol, stimulated an examination of alkenyl and benzyl chrysanthemates (4–7, 9–13). After synthesizing and testing many combinations of alcoholic nuclei and side chains, the particularly effective alcoholic component 5-benzyl-3-furylmethyl alcohol (12) was discovered and esterified with (+/−)-*cis–trans*-chrysanthemic acid to give resmethrin (NRDC 104), and with a new synthesis this was manufactured commercially. This in turn led to the synthesis of a resmethrin isomer, 5-benzyl-3-furylmethyl (+)-*trans*-chrysanthemate, known as bioresmethrin (NRDC 107) (figure 2), a compound that biochemical studies subsequently showed had the essential structural and stereochemical features necessary for great insecticidal activity, being relatively resistant to detoxification by insects. In addition, bioresmethrin has very low toxicity in mammals (the oral LD_{50} (the median lethal dose) for rats is more 8000 mg kg^{-1}) even compared with that of the natural pyrethrins and other pyrethroids such as allethrin (LD_{50} 500–800 mg kg^{-1}). Resmethrin and bioresmethrin were thus the first synthetic pyrethroids with greater insecticidal activity but lower mammalian toxicity than the natural compounds. Indeed, bioresmethrin has one of the greatest margins of safety (mammals : insects) of any known insecticide. The demonstration that potent insecticides could be designed by applying such principles within this group of compounds was highly significant.

Despite their valuable properties, resmethrin and bioresmethrin, like the earlier pyrethroid allethrin, are unstable in air and light and are therefore unsuitable for many applications, especially in agriculture. Nevertheless, their considerable insecticidal activity indicated the further possible potential for activity latent in their structures. John Casida's examination of the photodecomposition of bioresmethrin (Ueda *et al.* 1974) identified the isobutenyl side chain in the acid and the furan ring in the alcohol as vulnerable sites.

Michael and Norman therefore synthesized alternative acids and alcohols (18, 19, 22–24) to identify the structural features governing relative toxicity to insects and mammals and sensitivity to light and air. New compounds were designed in which the light-sensitive centres were replaced with alternative units, retaining the chemical and stereochemical characteristics of the parent molecules while maintaining their behaviour in the biochemical systems of insects and mammals (figure 2). In the most effective acid components of many synthesized, the methyl groups in the isobutenyl side chain of chrysanthemic acid were replaced by halogens, especially chlorine and bromine (15). In addition, the influence of the stereochemical form of these acid components on the insecticidal potency of esters was established (20, 22). The novel alcohol component, 3-phenoxybenzyl alcohol, was discovered independently from a consideration of the structure of 5-benzyl-3-furylmethyl alcohol almost simultaneously by Michael and his team (14) and the Sumitomo Chemical Company (Sumitomo 1971) in Japan. In this, a *meta*-substituted phenyl ring is considered to simulate the stereochemical role of the natural cyclopentenone ring or a synthetic furan ring, and a phenyl group simulates the stereochemical role of the *Z*-conjugated diene in pyrethrolone. This work led to the synthesis of permethrin (16, 17) (figure 2), the first photostable pyrethroid.

The Sumitomo scientists also showed the enhancing effect of an α-cyano group in 3-phenyoxybenzyl chrysanthemates (Matsuo *et al.* 1971; Ohno *et al.* 1974). Indeed, Michael later surprised his friend Takashi Matsuo (whose name was later changed to Noritada Matsuo) from Sumitomo by explaining that he visited London weekly to keep a close watch on such potential patent developments (figure 3). This was a key observation with far-reaching consequences made by Michael and his team, now including David Pulman, when esterification of α-cyano-3-phenoxybenzyl alcohol with the dihalovinyl acid components generated exceptionally powerful compounds (21, 22) with the combination of favourable properties not possessed by previous classes of insecticides. These showed exceptional toxicity to a wide range of insect species, persistence on foliar surfaces that was at least as great as that of established organophosphates and carbamates, and susceptibility to active metabolizing systems such as those of mammals and in the soil. Moreover, the new insecticides differed from the organochlorine compounds in three important respects: they were effectively involatile and thus not transported in the atmosphere (a major route by which DDT has been spread), they did not accumulate in fatty tissues, and they were rapidly degraded in soil, so that residues did not accumulate to contaminate the environment.

Because each α-cyano ester had three chiral centres, there were potentially eight isomers, which could all be expected to have differing biological activities. Work on the dihalovinyl esters with simpler alcohols had established that only the 1*R cis* and 1*R trans* forms (and not the 1*S cis* and 1*S trans*) were effective (20). The diastereoisomeric mixture of esters from the 1*R cis* dibromoacid (synthesized stereospecifically for the purpose) and (*RS*)-α-cyano-3-phenoxybenzyl alcohol was already recognized as a powerful insecticide, but storage in hexane yielded crystals of the α-*S*-diastereomer, which bioassays showed to be by far the more active of the two isomers. In fact, this crystalline ester, named deltamethrin, proved to be the

Figure 3. Michael and his wife, Margaret, at the Gold Shrine in Kyoto. (Photograph taken by Noritada Matsuo in the late 1990s.) (Online version in colour.)

most powerful insecticide, irrespective of class, available at the time (21). It was originally manufactured by Roussel-Uclaf in France, using an innovative commercial system to give the single crystalline isomer from eight possible isomers (Lhoste 1982) and was one of the first pure optical isomers of commercial bioactives, including pharmaceuticals.

Resmethrin and bioresmethrin and the three main photostable pyrethroids invented at Rothamsted, namely permethrin, cypermethrin and deltamethrin, have been developed commercially. These extremely potent insecticides have opened the prospect of controlling pests at lower rates of application, thus introducing much less insecticide into the environment. They are all sufficiently active to be recommended for practical application at doses from 200 g ha^{-1} down to less than 5 g ha^{-1} for deltamethrin, far below the most potent of standard insecticides of other groups particularly against a range of lepidopterous larvae. Lepidoptera and Coleoptera are highly destructive pests on many crops such as cereals, potatoes, cotton, soya, apples, pears, plums, peaches, grapes, olives, coffee and vegetables. Globally, more insecticides are used to protect cotton than any other crop, and deltamethrin is one that has been extensively used. Not only are Rothamsted pyrethroids applied to agricultural crops but they are also used in the health, garden and household markets. Permethrin is still widely used to treat clothing and mosquito nets to reduce the impact of insect-transmitted diseases, including malaria (Lengeler 2004; World Health Organization 2012).

The generally favourable toxicological and environmental properties of the photostable pyrethroids have been detailed in several authoritative reviews (for example Vijverberg & Van den Bercken 1990; Aldridge 1990). The excessive use of pyrethroids invites selection for resistance (Rothamsted Research 2004), and experiments to understand the underlying

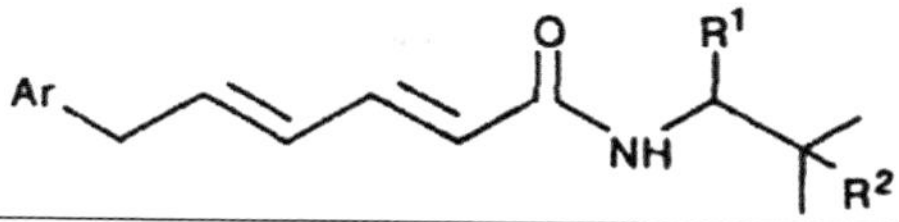

	Ar	R[1]	R[2]
a	phenyl	H	H
b	3,5-difluorophenyl	H	CH$_3$
c	dibenzofuran-3-yl	H	CH$_3$
d	dibenzofuran-3-yl	CH$_3$	H
e	5-bromonaphth-2-yl	H	CH$_3$
f	5-bromonaphth-2-yl	CH$_3$	H
g	7-fluoronaphth-2-yl	CH$_3$	H

Figure 4. Structures of synthetic isobutylamides. (Reproduced with permission from (25). Copyright © 1986 Taylor and Francis.)

mechanisms and provide strategies for limiting resistance development were pioneered by Roman Sawicki and continue at Rothamsted. Because synthetic pyrethroids have very low solubility in water and are strongly adsorbed on soil particles, they are greatly resistant to leaching through soil (Kaufman *et al.* 1981). These observations, along with the fact that very small dosages are needed for insect control, reduce the likelihood that any pyrethroid will contaminate groundwater. Despite their strong adsorptive characteristics, pyrethroids are readily biodegradable in soil, with half-lives ranging between 2–4 days and 12–16 weeks (Roberts 1981). This is in sharp contrast with the chlorinated hydrocarbon insecticides, whose soil persistences are frequently measured in years. Hydrolysis of the ester linkage is a major degradation route for all of the pyrethroids, accompanied by hydroxylation, ring cleavage and attack at the cyano group when present, leading eventually to CO_2 and water.

The value of pyrethroids, natural or synthetic, rose from about US$10 million in 1976, before the more stable compounds were available, to an estimated US$1400 million in 1990. To this total British Technology Group licensed products (invented at Rothamsted) contributed about US$800 million (59%). By 2002 the contribution remained significant at US$525 million (40%), with deltamethrin being the biggest selling pyrethroid, worth US$200 million.

Michael was keen to retain financial support, first from the Agriculture Research Council (ARC) and then the Agricultural and Food Research Council, later known as the Biotechnology and Biological Sciences Research Council, for the basic science underpinning his research. From the early 1960s the National Research Development Corporation (NRDC) funded and patented Michael's inventions, hence their NRDC numbers (figure 2), and supported the more applied aspects of the work. From 1981 this role was taken over by the British Technology Group (BTG).

FURTHER AREAS OF INTEREST

Throughout his career Michael had a vision for the discovery of novel pest control agents. In the 1980s he investigated variations in the naturally occurring isobutylamides (analogues of natural products in black pepper, *Piper nigrum*) (25, 27) (figure 4). Colleagues at Rothamsted (Andrew Farnham and Roman Sawicki) revealed the existence of negative cross-resistance to these compounds, which were up to four times more effective against houseflies resistant to pyrethroids than to susceptible strains (25).

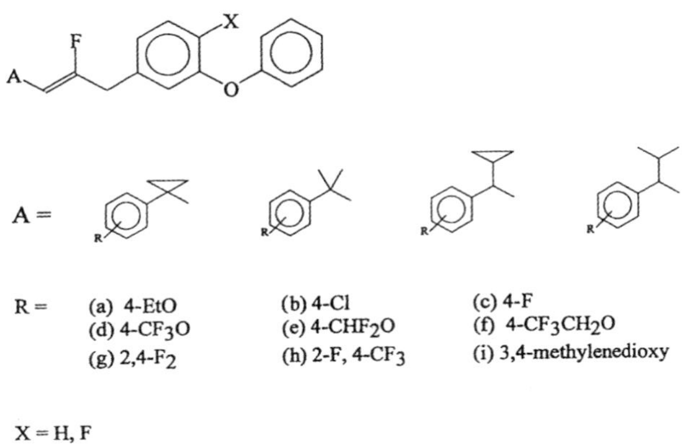

Figure 5. Active non-ester pyrethroid structures containing fluorine. (Reproduced with permission from Khambay *et al.* (1999). Copyright © 1999 John Wiley & Sons Inc.)

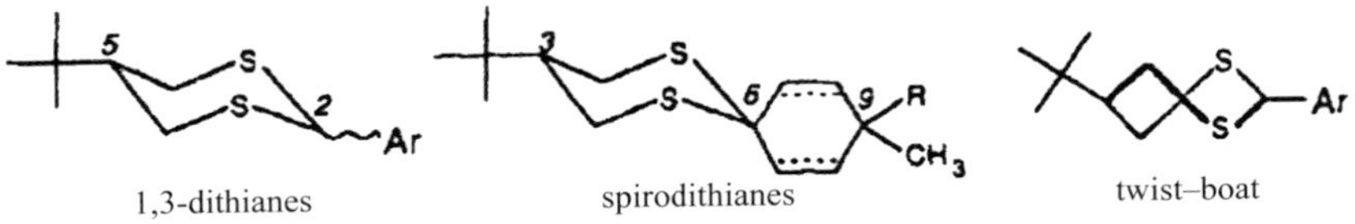

Figure 6. Dithiane structures. (Reproduced with permission from (28). Copyright © 1992 American Chemical Society.)

Just before his retirement from Rothamsted, Michael discovered a series of non-ester pyrethroids (26) in which the ester linkage, the primary site for metabolism and degradation, had been replaced by an alkyne. These compounds had low toxicity to fish and had the potential for controlling soil pests. Continuation of this work project, also funded by BTG, was progressed by Bhupinder Khambay and led to the discovery and patenting of a series of fluorinated non-ester pyrethroids (figure 5) (Khambay *et al.* 1999).

After retirement from Rothamsted, Michael visited John Casida's laboratory at Berkeley during 1986–88. There he discovered novel dithiane analogues (figure 6) (28) that interfered with the γ-aminobutyric acid-gated chloride channel with an activity comparable to that of established insecticides.

All these aspects are still very well represented in the currently active intellectual property of the global agrochemical industry.

Michael was also responsible for giving direction to my own early career studies, resulting in the first identification of aphid sex pheromones (Dawson *et al.* 1987), which arose from his long-argued recommendation for this research direction.

MICHAEL THE MAN

On 2 August 1950 Michael married Margaret Olwen James, to whom he remained devoted throughout his life; Margaret survived him by $6\frac{1}{2}$ years. Karen Mair was born in 1954 and Fiona Anne in 1955; together with their four grandchildren, Matthew, Imogen, James and

Christopher, they formed a close family, offering great support to Michael throughout his career and into his retirement until his death on 17 October 2007.

Michael was a kind, popular and modest colleague, friend and family man who, after his retirement, was known to some only as a practitioner of his favourite hobby, photography. From his early youth he had had wide interests beyond science, and his retirement enabled him to devote more time both to his family and to them. In addition to keenly following new scientific advances, he and Margaret indulged their other interests, including modern literature, art and classical music, good food and wine, hill walking and tending their immaculate house and garden; but his greatest interest was in photography. In retirement he was able to combine his scientific activities with 'spending more time with his family'. On one occasion he declined a last-minute invitation to attend a scientific meeting, saying that he had a prior engagement. He did not see the need to add that the appointment was to go bowling with his grandson.

Michael was popular with his colleagues; he showed great concern both at a personal level and in developing their career development. He always acknowledged their contributions to the work. He shared the department's interests in squash, swimming and, in the early years at Rothamsted, old cars, although this enthusiasm diminished with the advent of more reliable models.

Early in their marriage, Margaret's patience was severely tested when she found the engine of their elderly car in parts spread on the dining-room table. On his retirement he and Margaret moved to Cranleigh in Surrey to be near their daughters' families. Having installed a darkroom in the roof of the house, Michael indulged his photographic talents and became an active member of Cranleigh Photographic Club. Indeed, his grandsons Matthew and James have inherited his passion and are now accomplished wildlife photographers, concentrating on animals in their natural environment. Michael was a modest man, and his Rothamsted colleagues were not surprised to learn at his funeral that his photographic colleagues had no idea of his scientific achievements and honours.

He once said that as a young man he had seriously considered photography as a career, rather than chemistry. How fortunate it is for the world's agriculture, disease control and pest control that Michael Elliott chose chemistry.

HONOURS, DEGREES AND AWARDS

Civic honour

1982   CBE

Degrees (University of London)

1945   BSc (Lond.) (special chemistry), undergraduate at University College of Southampton
1952   PhD (external, University of London)
1971   DSc (University of London)

Fellowships

1979   Royal Society
1984   Kings' College, University of London
1984   Royal Society of Chemistry
1996   US National Academy of Sciences (Foreign Associate)

Honorary degrees

1985   DSc, University of Southampton

Other distinctions

1975   Burdick and Jackson International Award for Pesticide Research (American
              Chemical Society)
1976   Queen's Award for Technological Achievement to Rothamsted Experimental
              Station, for work on first-generation pyrethroid insecticides (NRDC 104, 107)
1977, 1980   Agricultural Research Council Awards to Inventors
1978   Second Holroyd Memorial Lecturer and Medallist, Society of Chemical
              Industry, London
1978   UNESCO Science Prize, a biennial award, to the research team at Rothamsted
              Experimental Station, for developing pyrethroid insecticides
1978/89   John Jeyes Medallist and Lecturer of the Chemical Society, London
1980   Queen's Award for Technological Achievement to Rothamsted Experimental
              Station, for work on second-generation pyrethroid insecticides (NRDC 143,
              149, 161)
1982   Royal Society Mullard Medallist
1983   Awarded la Grande Medaille de la Société Française de Phytiatrie et de
              Phytopharmacie
1984   First Royal Society of Chemistry Fine Chemicals and Medicinals Group Award
1986   British Crop Protection Council Medal for outstanding service to British crop
              protection
1988, 1992   British Technology Group (BTG) Awards to Inventors
1989   Wolf Foundation Prize in Agriculture
1989   Prix de la Fondation de la Chimie, Paris
1993   Environment Medal of the Society of Chemical Industry, London

Appointments

1948   Scientific Officer in the Department of Insecticides and Fungicides at
              Rothamsted Experimental Station
1969, 1974   Visiting lecturer at University of California, Berkeley
1979   Deputy Chief Scientific Officer, Head of Department and Deputy Director,
              Rothamsted Experimental Station
1986–88   Visiting Research Scientist at University of California, Berkeley
1989–2007   Consultant on chemistry of insecticides (UK), Lawes Trust Senior Fellow

ACKNOWLEDGEMENTS

I thank Andrew Farnham, Norman Janes, Bhupinder Khambay, David Pulman and John Stevenson for assistance in
the preparation of this memoir.

The frontispiece photograph was taken in 1984 by Godfrey Argent and is reproduced with permission.

AUTHOR PROFILE

John Pickett FRS

Having received his honours BSc chemistry degree in 1967 and his PhD in organic chemistry synthesis in 1971 from the University of Surrey, John Pickett completed his training in organic chemistry with a postdoctoral fellowship at the University of Manchester (later the University of Manchester Institute of Science and Technology) from 1970 to 1972. He joined the Brewing Industry Research Institute in 1972, studying the chemistry of malt and hops for new brewing processes. In 1976 he joined the Insecticides and Fungicides Department (later the Department of Biological Chemistry) and was appointed Head of Department in 1984 on the retirement of Michael Elliott and, concurrently in 2007, Scientific Director of the Rothamsted Centre for Sustainable Pest and Disease Management. In 2010 he relinquished these positions on being awarded the first Michael Elliott Distinguished Research Fellowship at Rothamsted. As well as fulfilling this prestigious new role, he continues to contribute to the Chemical Ecology group and is still very much involved with research activities in the UK and around the world. He has more than 520 publications and patents. John's contributions to the field of chemical ecology have been acknowledged with the 1995 Rank Prize for Nutrition and Crop Husbandry, election to the Fellowship of the Royal Society in 1996, election as a Member of the Deutsche Akademie der Naturforscher Leopoldina in 2001, award of the International Society of Chemical Ecology Medal in 2002, appointment to CBE for services to biological chemistry in 2004, and (jointly) the Wolf Foundation Prize in Agriculture in 2008, among many other international measures of esteem. He also presented, in 2008, the Royal Society's premier lecture in the biological sciences, the Croonian Prize Lecture, and in 2009 the Cornell University Lecture. In August 2012 he was awarded the International Congress of Entomology Certificate of Distinction, presented at the XXIV International Congress of Entomology in Daegu, Korea. In April 2014 he was elected a Foreign Associate of the US National Academy of Sciences. In June 2014 he became President of the Royal Entomological Society.

REFERENCES TO OTHER AUTHORS

Aldridge, W. N. 1990 An assessment of the toxicological properties of pyrethroids and their neurotoxicity. *Crit. Rev. Toxicol.* **21**, 89–104.

Barthel, W. F. 1961 Synthetic pyrethroids. In *Advances in pest control research* (ed. R. L. Metcalf), vol. 4, p. 33. New York: Interscience.

Dawson, G. W., Griffiths, D. C., Janes, N. F., Mudd, A., Pickett, J. A., Wadhams, L. J. & Woodcock, C. M. 1987 Identification of an aphid sex pheromone. *Nature* **325**, 614–616.

Kaufman, D. D., Russell, B. A., Helling, C. S. & Kayser, A. J. 1981 Movement of cypermethrin, decamethrin, permethrin, and their degradation products in soil. *J. Agric. Fd Chem.* **29**, 239–245.

Khambay, B. P. S., Farnham, A. W. & Liu, M. 1999. The pyrethrins and related compounds. Part XLII. Structure–activity relationships in fluoro-olefin non-ester pyrethroids. *Pestic. Sci.* **55**, 703–710 (http://dx.doi.org/10.1002/(SICI)1096-9063(199907)55:7<703::AID-PS17>3.0.CO;2-4).

LaForge, F. B., Green, N. & Schechter, M. S. 1956 Allethrin. Synthesis of four isomers of cis-allethrin. *J. Org. Chem.* **21**, 455–456.

Lengeler, C. 2004 *Insecticide-treated bednets and curtains for preventing malaria*. Cochrane Database of Systematic Reviews, issue 2. (Available from http://onlinelibrary.wiley.com/doi/10.1002/14651858.CD000363.pub2/pdf.)

Lhoste, J. (ed.) 1982 *Deltamethrin monograph* (ISBN 2-904125-01-9). Paris: Roussel-Uclaf.

Matsuo, T., Itaya, N., Okuno, Y., Mizutani, T. & Ohno, N. 1971 *Cyclopropancarbonsäure α-cyanbenzylester. Verfahren zu ihrer Herstellung und ihre Verwendung als Insektizide und Akarizide*. German Patent DE2231312. Sumitomo Chemical Company.

Ohno, N., Fujimoto, K., Okuno, Y., Mizutani, T., Hirano, M., Itaya, N., Honda, T. & Yoshioka, H. 1974 A new class of pyrethroidal insecticides: α-substituted phenylacetic acid esters. *Agric. Biol. Chem.* **38**, 881–883.

Roberts, T. R. 1981 The metabolism of the synthetic pyrethroids in plants and soils. *Prog. Pestic. Biochem.* **1**, 115–146.

Rothamsted Research 2004 *New resistance-busting technology developed to control the super pests*. (Available at http://www.rothamsted.ac.uk/news/resistance-busting-technology-developed-control-super-pests.)

Sumitomo 1971 *Cyclopropanecarboxylic acid esters*. UK Patent 1,243,858. Sumitomo Chemical Company.

Ueda, K., Gaughan, L. C. & Casida, J. E. 1974 Photodecomposition of resmethrin and related pyrethroids. *J. Agric. Fd Chem.* **22**, 212–220.

Vijverberg, H. P. M. & Van den Bercken, J. 1990 Neurotoxicological effects and the mode of action of pyrethroid insecticides. *Crit. Rev. Toxicol.* **21**, 106–126.

Wirtz, K., Bala, S., Amann, A. & Elbert, A. 2009 A promise extended—future roles of pyrethroids in agriculture. *Bayer CropSci. J.* **62**, 145–158.

World Health Organization 2012 *WHO recommended long-lasting insecticidal mosquito nets*. Geneva: World Health Organization. (Available at http://www.who.int/whopes/Long_lasting_insecticidal_nets_Jul_2012.pdf.)

BIBLIOGRAPHY

The following publications are those referred to directly in the text. A full bibliography is available as electronic supplementary material at http://dx.doi.org/10.1098/rsbm.2016.0018 or via http://rsbm.royalsocietypublishing.org.

(1)   1954   Allethrin. *J. Sci. Fd Agric.* **11**, 505–514.

(2)   1958   Isolation and purification of (+)-pyrethrolone from pyrethrum extract: reconstitution of pyrethrins I and II. *Chemy Ind.*, 685–686.

(3)   1964   The pyrethrins and related compounds. V. Purification of (+)-pyrethrolone as the monohydrate, and the nature of 'pyrethrolone-C'. *J. Chem. Soc.*, 5225–5228.

(4)   1965   (With N. F. Janes, K. A. Jeffs, P. H. Needham & R. M. Sawicki) New pyrethrin-like esters with high insecticidal activity. *Nature* **207**, 938–940.

(5)   1967   (With A. W. Farnham, N. F. Janes, P. H. Needham & B. C. Pearson) 5-Benzyl-3-furylmethyl chrysanthemate: a new potent insecticide. *Nature* **213**, 493–494.

(6)   (With N. F. Janes & B. C. Pearson) The pyrethrins and related compounds. IX. Alkenylbenzyl and benzylbenzyl chrysanthemates. *J. Sci. Fd Agric.* **18**, 325–321.

(7)   (With N. F. Janes) Synthesis of 4-allyl- and 4-benzyl-2,6- dimethylbromobenzene from 2,6-xylidine. *J. Chem. Soc. C*, 1780–1782.

(8)   1969   (With P. H. Needham & C. Potter) Insecticidal activity of the pyrethrins and related compounds. II. Relative toxicity of the optical and geometrical isomers of chrysanthemic, pyrethric and related acids and optical isomers of cinerolone and allethrolone. *J. Sci. Fd Agric.* **20**, 561–565.

(9)   1970   (With N. F. Janes & K. A. Jeffs) The pyrethrins and related compounds. X. The methylbenzyl chrysanthemates. *Pestic. Sci.* **1**, 49–52.

(10) 1971   (With F. Barlow, A. W. Farnham, A. D. Hadaway, N. F. Janes, P. H. Needham & J. C. Wickham) Insecticidal activity of the pyrethrins and related compounds. IV. Essential features for insecticidal toxicity in chrysanthemates and related cyclopropane esters. *Pestic. Sci.* **2**, 115–118.

(11)   (With N. F. Janes & M. C. Payne) The pyrethrins and related compounds. XI. Synthesis of insecticidal esters of 4-hydroxy-cyclopent-2-enones (nor-rethrins). *J. Chem. Soc. C*, 2548–2551.

(12)   (With N. F. Janes & B. C. Pearson) The pyrethrins and related compounds. XII. Synthesis of 5-substituted 3-furoates and 3-thenoates, intermediates for synthesis of insecticidal esters. *J. Chem. Soc. C*, 2551–2554.

(13)   (With N. F. Janes & B. C. Pearson) The pyrethrins and related compounds. XIII. Methyl-, alkenyl-, and benzyl-substituted furfuryl and furylmethyl chrysanthemates. *Pestic. Sci.* **2**, 243–248.

(14)   The relationship between the structure and the activity of pyrethroids. *Bull. Wld Hlth Org.* **44**, 315–324.

(15)   1973   (With A. W. Farnham, N. F. Janes, P. H. Needham & D. A. Pulman) Potent pyrethroid insecticides from modified cyclopropane acids. *Nature* **244**, 456–457.

(16)   (With A. W. Farnham, N. F. Janes, P. H. Needham, D. A. Pulman & J. H. Stevenson) NRDC 143, a more stable pyrethroid. In *Proc. 7th British Insecticide and Fungicide Conference*, vol. 2, p. 721. London: British Crop Protection Council.

(17)   (With A. W. Farnham, N. F. Janes, P. H. Needham, D. A. Pulman & J. H. Stevenson) Synthetic insecticide with a new order of activity. *Nature* **246**, 169.

(18)   1974   (With A. W. Farnham, N. F. Janes & P. H. Needham) Insecticidal activity of the pyrethrins and related compounds. VI. Methyl-, alkenyl-, benzyl-furfuryl and –3-furylmethyl chrysanthemates. *Pestic. Sci.* **5**, 491–496.

(19)   (With N. F. Janes & D. A. Pulman) The pyrethrins and related compounds. XVIII. Insecticidal 2,2-dimethylcyclopropanecarboxylates with new unsaturated substituents at position 3 of the cyclopropane ring. *J. Chem. Soc. Perkin Trans.* **1**, 2470–2474.

(20)   (With P. E. Burt, A. W. Farnham, N. F. Janes, P. H. Needham & D. A. Pulman) The pyrethrins and related compounds. XIX. Geometrical and optical isomers of 2,2-dimethyl-3-(dichlorovinyl) cyclopropanecarboxylic acid and insecticidal esters with 5-benzyl-3-furylmethyl and 3-phenoxybenzyl alcohols. *Pestic. Sci.* **5**, 791–799.

(21)   (With A. W. Farnham, N. F. Janes, P. H. Needham & D. A. Pulman) Synthetic insecticide with a new order of activity. *Nature* **248**, 710–711.

(22)   1975   (With A. W. Farnham, N. F. Janes, P. H. Needham & D. A. Pulman) Insecticidal activity of the pyrethrins and related compounds. VII. Insecticidal dihalovinyl analogues of *cis* and *trans* chrysanthemates. *Pestic. Sci.* **6**, 537–542.

(23)   1976   (With A. W. Farnham, N. F. Janes, P. H. Needham & D. A. Pulman) Insecticidal activity of the pyrethrins and related compounds. IX. 5-Benzyl-3-furylmethyl 2,2-dimethylcyclopropanecarboxylates with non-ethylenic substituents at position 3 on the cyclopropane ring. *Pestic. Sci.* **7**, 492–498.

(24)   (With A. W. Farnham, N. F. Janes, P. H. Needham & D. A. Pulman) Insecticidal activity of the pyrethrins and related compounds. X. 5-Benzyl-3-furylmethyl 2,2-dimethylcyclopropanecarboxylates with ethylenic substituents at position 3 on the cyclopropane ring. *Pestic. Sci.* **7**, 499–502.

(25)   1986   (With A. W. Farnham, N. F. Janes, D. M. Johnson, D. A. Pulman & R. M. Sawicki) Insecticidal amides with selective potency against a resistant (*super-kdr*) strain of houseflies (*Musca domestica* L.). *Agric. Biol. Chem.* **50**, 1347–1349 (http://dx.doi.org/10.1080/00021369.1986.10867574).

(26)   1988   (With A. E. Baydar, A. W. Farnham, N. F. Janes & B. P. S. Khambay) The pyrethrins and related compounds. Part XXXIV. Optimisation of insecticidal activity in the non-esters. *Pestic. Sci.* **23**, 247–257.

(27)   1989   (With A. W. Farnham, N. F. Janes, D. M. Johnson & D. A. Pulman) Synthesis and insecticidal activity of lipophilic amides. Part 7. Alternative aromatic groups for phenyl in 6-phenylhexa-2,4-dienamides. *Pestic. Sci.* **26**, 199–208.

(28)   1992   (With D. A. Pulman, J. P. Larkin & J. E. Casida) Insecticidal 1,3-dithianes. *J. Agric. Fd Chem.* **40**, 147–151 (http://dx.doi.org/10.1021/jf00013a029).

LLOYD THOMAS EVANS AO FAA

6 August 1927 — 23 March 2015

LLOYD THOMAS EVANS AO FAA

6 August 1927 — 23 March 2015

Elected FRS 1976

By Roderick W. King*

CSIRO, Plant Industry, Canberra ACT 2601, Australia

Lloyd Evans, a leading plant scientist, published extensively on the regulation of flowering and on crop production during a lifetime spent in research at the Commonwealth Scientific and Industrial Research Organisation (CSIRO). His significant achievements included the identification of a gibberellin plant hormone as a flowering regulator in the grass *Lolium temulentum*, the discovery of a synthetic gibberellin growth retardant that blocked endogenous gibberellin synthesis, and the discovery of a novel biological flowering clock in *Pharbitis* with a 12 h (semidian) period. In crops he established the impact on yield of photosynthate production and transport to competing sinks. Two of his books, *Crop evolution: adaptation and yield* and *Feeding the ten billion*, have had a major influence on agricultural research and policy. His ability to define research options led to many years of international advisory work. He was an Officer of the Order of Australia (AO) and was elected a Fellow of the Royal Society (FRS) and a Fellow of the Australian Academy of Science, subsequently becoming President of the latter.

In the 2003 volume of the prestigious *Annual Reviews of Plant Biology*, Lloyd Evans wrote a prefatory chapter (33)† on his life and scientific career, and together we summarized our successful search for flowering regulators of the grass *Lolium temulentum* (34). Lloyd shied away from 'grandstanding'. Here I have chosen to reveal something of the 'colour' of Lloyd's life from my recollections of events over our long friendship and, to a greater extent, gleaned from the prefatory chapter cited above and from his extensive private notes developed from his diaries‡.

---

* rwerking@gmail.com

† Numbers in this form refer to the bibliography at the end of the text.

‡ These sources are not currently publicly available, but in 2008 Lloyd and Margaret Evans requested that I use them if asked to prepare a memoir. Recently his children confirmed this permission to quote from Lloyd's diaries and his 159-page draft notes ('Memoirs of a meandering biologist') that he prepared in 2005 for his children and grandchildren.)

This memoir was commissioned by the *Historical Records of Australian Science* and will appear in volume 27 (2016). The memoir is published here with minor amendments.

http://dx.doi.org/10.1098/rsbm.2016.0008

FAMILY BACKGROUND AND EARLY LIFE

Lloyd was born on 6 August 1927 at Whanganui, New Zealand. His younger brother, Morgan Evans, was born in September 1928. Their father, Claude David Evans, was in charge of wool operations at the meatworks in Whanganui. According to Lloyd, 'Claude enjoyed an occasional beer and, late in life, even an occasional whisky, but was never seen even mildly inebriated.' Along with a strong devotion to his father, Lloyd upheld his father's moderation but with a shift from beer to sampling his substantial cellar of fine Australian wines.

Lloyd's mother, Gwendolyn Lois Maude Evans (*née* Fraser), contracted tuberculosis and died when Lloyd was 10 years old. Neither the early loss of his mother nor the hardship of food and fuel rationing during World War II seems to have affected his childhood experiences. Lloyd's main chore at that time was supplying enough firewood and, always resourceful, supplementing household supplies with fish caught in the nearby Whanganui River.

Lloyd's secondary education at Whanganui Collegiate (1941–44) was initially a shock. Studying at a level he thought was beyond him, he foundered at the first-term exam. Frank Gilligan, the headmaster, read him the riot act. By year's end, Lloyd was top of the class.

In addition to academic success, there were two especially notable 'moments' in Lloyd's high-school years. Lloyd had a very retentive memory and, during a lesson on the Romantic poets, the headmaster asked whether anyone knew Wordsworth's 'Daffodils'. Lloyd recited it verse by verse.

Years later, Lloyd's love of literature and his ability to memorize poetry came to the fore in his award in 1951 of a very prestigious New Zealand Rhodes Scholarship to Oxford. Asked what he knew of modern poetry he quoted passages from works of T. S. Eliot and W. H. Auden. In science, these skills of memory were invaluable for recalling and drawing inferences from the scientific literature. Socially, his memory of literature was also a skill that he enjoyed when interacting with his nine grandchildren and with a long-time friend and biochemist, Professor Frank Gibson (FRS 1976). These two could spend an evening, and many glasses of red wine, reciting slabs of Shakespeare to each other.

His second 'moment' involved farming. Over school vacations, Lloyd joined shearing gangs as 'rouseabout, fleeceo' and often worked as a stand-in wool classer when the regular wool classer had a bad hangover. This early exposure to farming sustained his later interest in agriculture.

UNIVERSITY EDUCATION

New Zealand

In February 1945 Lloyd began a science degree at Canterbury University College, Christchurch. His memory was of dismal botany lectures, but he then transferred to the nearby affiliate, Lincoln Agricultural College, and completed a BAgrSc. While at Lincoln he attended several brilliant public lectures on the scientific method by the world-renowned philosopher Karl Popper (FRS 1976). He also developed his practical outlook on agriculture, because the course required a full year of work on farms. Recreation involved hockey, table tennis and running. However, his greatest love was the outdoors, which he experienced through 'tramping' and mountaineering in the nearby New Zealand Alps.

His favourite subjects were soils and plant science, in the context of both farm and natural ecosystems. Most significantly for his career, Lloyd also began at Lincoln College what was to be a lifelong interaction with Otto (later Sir Otto) Frankel (FRS 1953), who at the time was Director of the nearby Wheat Research Institute. Frankel arranged seminars by renowned international scientists, including Theodosius Dobzhansky (ForMemRS 1965), Richard Goldschmidt, E. B. Ford FRS and R. A. Silow. These seminars and the chance for face-to-face discussions provided Lloyd with a career-defining richness of scientific exposure.

Awards and a scholarship in 1948, and the award of the University of New Zealand Senior Scholarship in Botany, provided the means for him to complete his BSc in botany. By 1951, with first-class honours and a masters' degree, he was employed as an assistant lecturer in agricultural botany. By then he had presented his first conference paper and published three scientific articles.

Oxford University

As a 24-year-old who had never travelled overseas, Lloyd arrived at Oxford committed to expanding his scientific horizons and to experiencing all the culture that Europe had to offer in literature, art and music. During his three years at Oxford (1951–54) he learnt to love being a part of Brasenose College. There were, however, several challenges, including the outdoor sprint across the 'quad' to have a bath at restricted hours in winter. There was also difficult after-hours access to college, but, in his words:

> the first stage involved climbing into the garden of the Rector of Lincoln. Then there was a difficult traverse of a high spiked fence (which had claimed at least one life), a traverse along the crest of the uninhabited bathroom followed by a controlled slide down its often-frost covered slate roof to a rotating row of steel spikes and, with luck, a clearing jump to the ground. On one occasion, on a frosty night, I had real problems with those rotating spikes. So I gave up working late in the lab.

Extracurricular student life was filled with sport, including hockey, and travel to Europe. The Poetry Society was particularly appealing because of the range of poets who presented their work, including Cecil Day Lewis, Arthur Waley, Kathleen Raine, Louis Macniece, Stephen Spender, Roy Campbell and, eventually after several escapes into pubs, Dylan Thomas.

Lloyd's own poetic endeavours were not without merit but were trumped in 1953 by the appearance in his life of Margaret Honor Newell (1927–2014), a fellow New Zealander*. To many people in many countries, Margaret was known as the woman who never went anywhere without her tennis racquet, and who was happy to play anywhere and with anyone. To many in Australia, England and California, Margaret was a perceptive, wise and trusted advisor and for many years she was Head Counsellor at the Australian National University (ANU) in Canberra. To yet others she was a resourceful and renowned cook and hostess, able and willing to run something up for unexpected visitors; and always a source of fun. To Lloyd, 'Margaret was the most important influence on his life, his beloved wife, counsellor, gadfly, companion, colleague and co-parent.'

Lloyd's DPhil studies were submitted in 1954 and focused on aspects of soil chemistry and pasture growth. However, it was the occasional lectures at Oxford that most inspired Lloyd, including Sir John Russell on modern agriculture, and a rambling lecture by Colin Clark on

---

* Although Margaret was born in Coimbatore, India, in 1927, the Newell family moved to New Zealand in 1930. After World War II Margaret obtained a BA at Canterbury University College in Christchurch, and in 1947 her parents moved to Geneva and then in 1949 to Sussex, UK, where they lived until 1965.

world food supply. Of more immediacy, Lloyd's imagination was fired by a lecture from Professor Fritz Went on the value for plant physiological research of the environment control facility at the Earhart Laboratory at the California Institute of Technology (Caltech), Pasadena, Los Angeles. Later, after talking with Went, Lloyd applied for and was awarded a prestigious Harkness Foundation postdoctoral fellowship.

Caltech: a postdoctoral experience

Armed with his DPhil, and now married to Margaret Newell, these two New Zealanders arrived at Caltech in mid-September 1954. Lloyd already knew of the excellence of the various scientists at Caltech including the plant biochemist and flowering physiologist James Bonner. Went, as laboratory director, was renowned for his work on environmental responses of plants.

Another physiologist at Caltech was Roy Sachs, a horticulturalist studying the flowering of *Chrysanthemum*. Roy became a lifelong friend of Lloyd and Margaret. A firm friendship was also established with W. S. (Bill) Hillman, who was a fine scientist and flowering physiologist and who in the 1970s became President of the American Society of Plant Physiologists. Not so far away, at the University of California, Los Angeles (UCLA), was Anton Lang who in 1955 became internationally famous for studies on the regulation of growth and flowering by the gibberellin class of plant hormones.

Despite all that was positive about Caltech, at that time there were strong anti-communist sentiments across the USA. Senator McCarthy and the FBI hounded many staff at Caltech, regarding it as a haven for the politically liberal and no place for the modest. Among these 'liberals' was Linus Pauling ForMemRS. Bloody but unbowed, he was protected by his recent Nobel Prize. However, it was considered a defiant act when Lloyd, Margaret and others went to hear the openly pro-Soviet Paul Robeson sing in the First Unitarian Church in Los Angeles. As a penalty, the authorities charged the church an additional $10 000 in 'taxes', with only $2000 of that sum being raised from that evening's small audience.

The 18 months that Lloyd spent at Caltech had a defining role for his subsequent career. By examining a large collection of the grass *Lolium* he isolated a unique *Lolium temulentum* genetic variant, 'Ceres', that flowered after exposure to a single long day (1). This precision in flowering of *L. temulentum* opened up many opportunities for experimentation over the next 50 years. To Lloyd, *L. temulentum* was *Lte* after his initials, but to Margaret it was '*Lolly*', regarded as Lloyd's first love because it demanded attention over Christmas and during many escapades late at night.

At Caltech, Lloyd learnt much about the design and engineering of controlled environment facilities. As a consequence and because CSIRO Plant Industry (PI) in Canberra was expanding, in 1955 Otto Frankel, its new Chief, offered Lloyd a research position and also asked him 'to take a role in the design, testing, construction and management of a new state-of-the-art plant growth facility'.

RESEARCH AT CSIRO: THE START OF A LIFETIME IN SCIENCE

In August 1956 the Evans family (now numbering three) began a four-month return to the Southern Hemisphere, but to Australia rather than New Zealand. The Harkness Fellowship required a three-month tour from western to eastern USA. Then, after revisiting England to see Margaret's parents, there was the long sea voyage to Australia. By November 1956 they had arrived in Canberra, the National Capital, then a small, sleepy, dry and dusty country town where the PI research laboratories were being developed.

Lloyd and Margaret soon established their first home for their now three children, Nicholas (born on 21 February 1956), and twins John and Catherine (born on 5 June 1958). Academically, all three children have been high achievers, and Nicholas and John are now professors at ANU. John, like his father, is a plant scientist and in 2013 was elected a Fellow of the Australian Academy of Science.

The family loved the outdoors and had ready access to bushwalking and skiing. They spent much time at the coast in the house they built in 1971 at Guerilla Bay, a two-hour drive from Canberra. Many an academic visitor experienced Lloyd and Margaret's hospitality, not just in Canberra but also at Guerilla Bay.

CERES, the Canberra Phytotron

The Canberra Phytotron was named CERES both because of the Roman goddess of agriculture and because it was an acronym for **C**ontrolled **E**nvironment **Res**earch. By world standards this was one of the larger controlled environment facilities for plant growth and it could mimic natural environments from the tropics to cold, subpolar extremes (3, 22). Its building costs were fully funded by the Australian government (a total of $1 064 000), an outcome achieved by some forcible argument by Otto Frankel. There was also substantial backing by Sir Ian Clunies-Ross, the then Chairman of CSIRO, by Sir Frederick White, his successor, by Bert Goodes, a senior public servant, and by the responsible minister, Bert Casey (later Lord Casey). In April 1958 Casey wrote: 'Cabinet tonight. I got the phytotron submission through, for the full $1,000,000. I aired myself at some length on the potentialities of this piece of equipment—and got no opposition' (White 1977).

Roger Morse, head of the CSIRO Engineering Section, understood the engineering and Lloyd the biological limitations of other phytotrons, and together they conducted extensive prototype testing (3). The building made a majestic addition to Canberra, with its large rounded feature windows and a row of 15 large controlled-environment glasshouses. Its architect, Roy Grounds, had earlier designed the Australian Academy of Science dome that had been opened in 1959; although very striking, the Academy building was frivolously referred to by locals as the Fried Egg.

CERES was opened in 1962, and the journalist and author George Johnston, writing in the *Australian* newspaper (22 August 1964), saw it as 'a compelling example of the centralizing forces at work in Canberra ... for the betterment of Australia', and of 'a new adventurous age into which we as Australians were entering'.

At the opening ceremony, the large audience was addressed first by Fred White as Chairman of CSIRO and then, brilliantly, by the Prime Minister, Bob (later Sir Robert) Menzies (FRS 1965), with a superb imitation of an Australian farmer (a 'cocky'); Otto Frankel closed the proceedings with a vote of thanks. The many distinguished scientific invitees from overseas included Fritz Went, Sterling Hendricks and Pierre Chouard. All were impressed by the speeches and by CERES, as well as by the following symposium on 'The environmental control of plant growth'.

Five years after its opening, CERES and Lloyd were featured in 'The hungry world' segment of the first live 'One world' TV link-up, watched by 500 million people. Taken for granted these days, this first world link-up on 26 June 1967 was a complex effort, especially when the USSR withdrew its satellite at a late stage. The newspapers made a meal of Lloyd's role. The Brisbane *Courier Mail* ran a headline '700 million will watch the shy scientist', a label that stuck and resurfaced several years later when Lloyd became president of the Australian and New Zealand Association for the Advancement of Science (ANZAAS). In conversation he may have appeared shy but this was not a characteristic of Lloyd. Rather, he was modest both in science and in all his dealings with people. Throughout his life he was always reluctant to use the personal pronoun 'I', an attitude reflected in 2003 in his use of a quote from Claude Bernard 'Art is I, Science is we' (33). Lloyd did not try to dominate, and was prepared to consider all options, master all the facts, draw conclusions and then reach a decision.

CERES provided Lloyd with fixed environmental conditions for his ongoing studies of the flowering of *L. temulentum*, but its huge range of available environments also allowed answers to the question of the adaptive value of particular flowering responses. For example, Lloyd wanted to know whether adaptation was seen in the flowering of Kangaroo grass, *Themeda australis*, an Australian species. So, he collected and vegetatively propagated 30 clones from latitude 6° S to 43° S. What he found was that, for flowering, the optimal daylength and temperatures determined in CERES matched conditions at their sites of origin (14). Unfortunately, the selective (that is, evolutionary) value of such adaptation has more often remained as speculation, but CERES has provided a powerful tool for unravelling flowering-time adaptation, not just for native species but for many domesticated crop and pasture species (22).

At the time of writing, CERES still operates as a valued research facility despite exceeding its originally estimated engineering life of 20 years. Other major facilities closed two or more decades ago, including those in France and Canada and the first phytotron, the Caltech facility.

The long life of CERES is testimony to the skill and planning of Lloyd Evans and Roger Morse (3), and to the efforts of its four officers-in-charge, Lloyd Evans, then Wardlaw, King and Rawson. Its output highlights Lloyd's original vision. From our 1985 review of its first two decades of operation (22), of the 520 papers published, one-quarter were by researchers outside CSIRO, a clear vindication of its conception as a national research facility. Research in CERES involved a wide range of scientific disciplines from plant pathology and microbiology to ecology, crop physiology and forestry. Fittingly, in 2013, as part of its latest upgrade, Lloyd Evans and family (figure 1) were present when he was honoured at a 50-year celebration of CERES by the placing of a plaque on its front entrance that reads, 'Celebrating five decades of controlled environment plant research, realizing the founding vision of Dr Lloyd T Evans of CSIRO'. On the opposite wall sits its original 1962 dedication: 'Cherish the Earth for man shall live by it forever', an apt creation of Lloyd's scientific mentor, Otto Frankel.

By the 1970s Lloyd had published groundbreaking papers on flowering of *Lolium* and, with his role in developing CERES, he was elected a Fellow of the Australian Academy of Science in 1971 and a Fellow of the Royal Society in 1976.

Management roles

Chief of CSIRO, Plant Industry (PI): a reluctant conscript

When the third Chief of PI, Dr John Falk, died in 1970, Lloyd resisted attempts to install him as Chief. He wrote in his diary 'I … preferred to get on with research, and I knew that

Figure 1. Family and colleagues. (*a*) John, Margaret and Lloyd Evans at the 50th anniversary of CERES.
(*b*) Ola Heide (Norway), Lloyd Evans and Rod King in the CERES entrance in 1985.

a colleague and friend Dr John Philip aspired to the position, so I did not apply.' However, apparently at the instigation of Otto Frankel, John Philip had just been appointed the first Chief of the CSIRO Environmental Mechanics group. So, after Lloyd's election as FAA in 1971, his potential as PI Chief was raised again by Frankel. There soon followed a visit from a Canberra member of the CSIRO Executive who 'invited' Lloyd to Head Office and told him to apply. Lloyd noted (in his diary entry for 15 July 1971) that he 'still wasn't keen to do so, but after talking it over with Otto and my Margaret, I sent in my application'. In his application he said:

> I would prefer to continue my full time research and that I neither enjoy administration nor am I adept at it. However, I then indicated the four broad areas where I thought the Division's research should be concentrated: (1) the productive processes of plants; (2) genetic resources and manipulation; (3) evaluation of agricultural systems; (4) the management of natural ecosystems.

His requests were accepted by the Executive, but they remained less enthusiastic about his request for a fixed-term appointment 'for something like six years, with the right to return to a research position in the Division after that.'

PI at this stage was the largest CSIRO Division. Its staff numbers were close to 400 in a government research organization of about 6000 staff spread over Australia, and with research interests ranging from agriculture to land use, radio astronomy, mining and domestic building.

As Chief, Lloyd was able to expand ecological research on fire, water use and aspects of native vegetation. He established an interdisciplinary group on storage proteins in plants and a molecular biology group under Jim Peacock, who was eventually weaned from *Drosophila* to maize, other crop plants, and the experimental plant species *Arabidopsis thaliana*. Crop research was given a further boost in 1973 by the transfer to PI of responsibility for cotton research. When Jim Peacock stepped up to the position of Chief in 1978, cotton research was further enhanced.

Up to the 1970s, the economic returns from PI's research on pastures were very impressive. By 2003, when independently analysed by the Centre for International Economics in Canberra, there were similar outstanding returns for PI's work on wheat productivity, GrazFeed and cotton breeding (benefit: cost ratios of 19, 79 and 51, respectively). All these programmes were begun or under way during Lloyd's period as Chief.

The Australian Academy of Science

In 1971, as a new FAA, Lloyd had little time to participate in the affairs of the Academy because he had just begun as PI Chief. However, by 1974 he was Chairman of the Academy's Biology Sectional Committee. In 1976, he was elected to Council and quickly saw how difficult it was to reach a consensus because its Fellows came from diverse backgrounds and were accustomed to others bowing to their unrelenting and forcible argumentation. When in 1977 he was elected Vice-President of the Academy he saw three reasons for his appointment: a shiny new FRS in 1976, he was located in Canberra, and he was one of the few plant scientists on Council. His progression to President in 1978 was not surprising.

His assessment after serving for four years as President was:

> The Academy's 25th jubilee in 1979 went well including the participation of Prince Charles, I broadened our science education activities, reached out to the Australian scientific societies, enhanced our cooperation with the other Academies, and Beauchamp House and its grounds immediately adjacent to the Academy Dome were secured for long term use.

SCIENCE

The physiology of flowering Lolium

In his first 10 years at CSIRO, Lloyd worked alone in his research on *Lolium temulentum* and elegantly established the overall picture of its floral induction. He showed that it flowered in response to longer summer daylengths, that the leaves perceived this light signal, and that a positive, transmitted floral stimulus was produced in leaves (2). These findings confirmed evidence for several other species (Lang 1965). However, he also found evidence of a transmitted inhibitor that was produced in shorter days and maintained vegetative development (2). This latter claim was severely criticized at the time by Anton Lang, who was well known

Figure 2. Lloyd Evans applying gibberellin to the young leaf of six-week-old plants of *Lolium temulentum*. This single application causes flowering.

for his extensive studies on floral induction. Interestingly, 18 years later, by using grafting techniques, Lang *et al.* (1977) provided elegant confirmation of Lloyd's claim.

This emerging picture of transmissible regulators of flowering of *Lolium* led Lloyd to application studies with two plant hormones, the gibberellins as candidates for the floral stimulus (figure 2) (5), and abscisic acid as the inhibitor (9). Then, on the basis of further application studies but with inhibitors of nucleic acid metabolism, he reported that the early events of the floral transition at the shoot apex involved the synthesis of new messenger RNA (6).

The speed with which Lloyd took his experiments to publication was quite phenomenal. His 1966 *Science* paper implicating the plant hormone abscisic acid as the *Lolium* floral inhibitor, was written in one night (9). He did this while repeating the necessary confirmatory study on the effect of applications at different times overnight.

After this early decade of research, Lloyd took great joy in the next decade in collaboration with other scientists from different backgrounds, approaches, interpretations and skills. From his diaries and private notes, his reflections of these collaborations starts with Ian Wardlaw in 1963:

Ian examined the movement of the floral stimulus from leaf to shoot apex (4) then to Bruce Knox for histochemical and autoradiographic studies of the shoot apex (10); Sterling Hendricks and Harry Borthwick (USDA Maryland USA) helped to sort out the spectral light requirements for long day induction of *Lolium* leaves (7); the enthusiastic Toon Rijven provided microchemical analyses of the shoot apices at various stages of floral induction (11). ... Much later (1980–90's), with Rod King, Dick Pharis (Calgary Canada) and Lew Mander (ANU) we renewed our studies with Lolium and established gibberellin structural requirements for flower induction as against its action on stem growth (24). Later, Rod, in collaboration with Tom Moritz at Umea, Sweden, provided ultra-sensitive measurements of the gibberellins in our *Lolium* apices (32, 35). Another very crucial collaboration was between Rod, Carl McDaniel and me; we showed that gibberellin was all that was necessary for flowering of isolated *Lolium* apices in vitro (25). With Carl, as sometimes with other collaborators, we could agree on the results while differing in our interpretations.

True collaboration never denies continued questioning and, within 10 years of Lloyd's 1966 *Science* publication (9), by using gas chromatography–mass spectrometry assays, we showed that endogenous abscisic acid was not the daylength-regulated inhibitor of floral induction in *Lolium* (17). By contrast, it took another 30 years but we did confirm that gibberellins acted as a floral stimulus in *Lolium* (34). For me, 50 years after starting our collaboration on flowering, I still feel some affinity with the sorcerer's apprentice, as Lloyd had an encyclopaedic knowledge in this field.

The final saga of work with *Lolium* involved molecular approaches with two of my PhD students: Greg Gocal and Colleen MacMillan. In confirmation of Lloyd's initial suggestion of an early unique role for nucleic acid synthesis in flowering, Greg developed beautiful *in situ* molecular information on the earliest changes in expression of specific RNAs at the shoot apex in transition to flowering. Interestingly, the very earliest increase (less than 6 h) was in expression of a potentially gibberellin-regulated gene, *LtCDKA1* (Gocal & King 2013).

Colleen provided essential gene sequence information that allowed us to show daylength upregulation of expression in leaves of a critical gibberellin 20-oxidase biosynthetic gene (MacMillan *et al.* 2005). In the leaf there was a large (more than tenfold) and rapid (less than 3 h) increase in its expression with the triggering of flowering. In association with the increase in 20-oxidase, the level of its endogenous substrate decreased while there was a matching increase in its bioactive products (35). Then, after some hours to permit transport from leaf to apex (4), there was a twofold to threefold increase in the same bioactive gibberellins at the shoot apex (32). Even more rewarding, however, was our evidence in 2008 of how turnover controlled gibberellin levels (36). In this final collaboration with Lloyd we drew a line under all the previous 22 years of our studies. Acting like a stop/go traffic light just below the shoot apex, gibberellin-degrading enzymes blocked access of some growth-active gibberellins but not of our florigenic gibberellins (36).

To reach this milestone took us 45 years of searching, 555 experiments and the growth of almost 222 000 plants of *Lolium*, with each experiment taking nine weeks to complete. After our compulsory age retirement we both continued working as Honorary Research Fellows: Lloyd starting in 1992, and me in 2008.

In 2003 we summarized our findings and predictions in a major review of gibberellins and flowering of *Lolium* (34). It was with some hesitation that we claimed to have sufficient proof that gibberellins were one of the 'florigens' of *Lolium*. Subsequently, in 2006 we had expanded this claim to allow for an additional 'florigen' after we examined the timing of expression of the gene *FT* (35). In the next year Corbesier *et al.* (2007) showed that the FT protein was a daylength-responsive, transmitted regulator of the flowering of *Arabidopsis*. It was rankling to us that many scientists were 'reluctant' to acknowledge our gibberellin studies although they were the first and still by far the more comprehensive evidence of the endogenous nature of a 'florigen' (King 2012). Although intellectual parentage drives scientific progress, a 'two-handed' approach is often wise. Fortunately, because we looked for both the positive and the contrary answer to any simple question, Lloyd and I had recognized that our 'baby' was at least twins (gibberellins and FT) and not a unique, single 'florigen'.

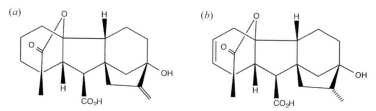

Figure 3. Close structural similarity between GA_{20} (*a*) and the synthetic contaminant 16,17-dihydroGA$_5$ (*b*), which competes with the 3-oxidase enzyme responsible for the conversion of GA_{20} to its active product.

A commercial outcome: a tale of curiosity, informed minds and tenacity

This account of work on *Lolium* has omitted our isolation and characterization of an anti-gibberellin growth retardant that decreases the height of cereals and can stop cool-season turf grass growth, a slow-grow, no-mow treatment (27, 28). A single spray on wheat led to 14–20% increases in yield for 14 sites in Europe over two years. When sprayed on turf, water use and mowing frequency were halved (29).

Lloyd was pivotal at the start because he persisted in questioning the purity of one of our chemically synthesized, natural gibberellins. To humour Lloyd, various batches of this compound were analysed by Professor Lew Mander at ANU's Research School of Chemistry and he found varying amounts of a contaminant (16,17-dihydro GA$_5$), which he then synthesized as a pure compound.

Using our work-horse, *Lolium*, we saw its powerful action as a growth retardant (27). I clearly remember that first result in June 1992 because I was listening to Beethoven's 'Ode to joy' on the radio while making the measurements of plant growth. One application of dihydro GA$_5$ blocked growth over three weeks but flowering was normal. Lloyd's meticulous data recording and tenacity led to this discovery.

Subsequently, in collaboration with Professor Olavi Junttila, a frequent Norwegian visitor, we applied molecular and chemical approaches to show that this gibberellin derivative was a competitive inhibitor of GA_{20} (figure 3), the substrate for the enzyme responsible for the last step of gibberellin biosynthesis (28). Dihydro GA$_5$ inhibited plant growth by decreasing the levels of active gibberellins.

By serendipity linked with curiosity and informed minds, we had found a plant growth retardant. Then, with patents in hand, we began a five-year collaboration with the German agrochemical company BASF. Unfortunately this tale has an unhappy ending: in 2002 the lawyers and management at BASF terminated the project because BASF was moving away from its interest in agrochemicals.

The physiology of flowering Pharbitis nil, *a short-day species*

Despite his love for *Lolium*, Lloyd saw great benefit in 'running more than one horse in a race if you wanted to succeed'. In 1966 we therefore began parallel studies on the short-day plant *Pharbitis nil*. This species kept us occupied for many years of fruitful study and highlighted similarities and differences between flowering processes of short-day and long-day plants (13).

A memorable interaction in these studies involved Professor Ola Heide from Norway, who took a sabbatical leave in Canberra in 1984 (figure 1*b*) and repeated this on two more occasions. In addition to its well-characterized 24 h circadian clock for flowering, we found that *Pharbitis* used a unique 12 h, 'semidian', biological clock (23). This remains the first report of a semidian rhythm in plants or animals, although tidal organisms can function on a 12.5 h lunar clock. Because rhythm studies go on day and night, our work became a true test of collegiality, with Lloyd arriving daily at 7 a.m. to relieve me after the night shift and Ola starting late in the day until 10 p.m.; of course we also maintained a full daytime cycle of work.

As well as enhancing our studies on *Pharbitis*, over the years much of our continuing research on flowering of wheat and *Lolium* was enhanced by often repeated sabbatical visits by no fewer than 16 international scientists.

Crop physiology

Despite great success in his studies on flowering, Lloyd recognized the value in having separate fields of research. Fifty years later in his private notes and diaries he reflected:

> Not only have these two fields, Crop Physiology and Flowering Physiology, cross-fertilized one another, but whenever I came to a road block in one, I could keep moving with the other. For example, after my initially productive burst with Lolium in the 1950s/1960s, I got stalled on the role of light (7). … It was then that I moved into crop physiology and had an exciting time through the 1970s in spite of many administrative chores. Indeed, it was crop research that kept me sane and switched on through those years, so that I could return productively to flowering physiology and then have a final fling with crops. This duality in my research along with my writing of books undoubtedly broadened my perspectives of plant biology.

As with his studies on flowering, his research programme on wheat photosynthesis and evolution involved input from colleagues, who included Bob Dunstone, Rod King, Bob Williams, Howard Rawson and Ian Wardlaw.

Cross-fertilization of ideas from flowering to crop responses arose from Ian Wardlaw's use of radioactive carbon tracers to follow the transport in *Lolium* of photosynthate (4). What was clear was that lower, more mature, leaves did not import carbon from the younger upper leaves of a plant. It was this knowledge that led to debate with a colleague, Jim Davidson, who had published a pioneering quantitative model of pasture growth (Davidson & Donald 1958). He had assumed that at high values of leaf to ground area the lower, older leaves continued to import and respire carbon as they became more and more shaded in denser crops. Thus he predicted that crop and pasture growth would reach an optimum and then decline. Lloyd disagreed and examined the relationship between leaf density and crop growth by measuring photosynthesis and dark respiration in mini crops of cotton and sunflower grown in artificially illuminated growth chambers. The results were compelling: total crop respiration levelled off at a constant value as the crop grew (8).

A pivotal step in Lloyd's developing interest in crop physiology involved our 1965 study of feedback control of the photosynthetic rate of wheat leaves. Lloyd had long wondered whether plants could produce too much photosynthetic assimilate and become 'constipated'. Inability of the rest of the plant to rapidly utilize carbon might lead to a decrease in its photosynthetic rate as a result of carbohydrate accumulation in source leaves. Many previous studies over more than six decades had suggested that there were long-term responses to a decrease in assimilate demand, but cause and effect could not be determined. In our study, the response was clear cut. The photosynthetic rate of a wheat leaf could first be depressed rapidly by 50% in 3–5 h on removing the ear of the wheat plant, its major 'sink' organ for assimilates. Then, by enhancing demand from another sink, its photosynthetic rate could be rapidly restored (12).

Figure 4. Wheat emasculation.

Our conclusion, that crop yields may be limited by the internal demand for assimilates as well as by photosynthetic supply, fashioned many of Lloyd's concepts of reproduction as a potential limit to yield, and subsequently he focused on several aspects of assimilate supply and utilization, including the following.

(i) There was potential for evolutionary differences in the rate of carbon assimilation (CER) by the leaves of ancient and modern wheats (15). Surprisingly, CER had fallen, not risen, in the course of evolution and domestication, but this conundrum was explained by evidence that, as CER had declined, individual leaf area had increased in parallel with grain yield.

(ii) Assimilate transported to the wheat grain sink comes from several sources including the leaf, the awns on the ear and from stored stem reserves (16). As in figure 4, these experiments could involve floret sterilization.

(iii) Competition for assimilates depended on sink size and its distance from the source (20). For Lloyd the message was clear: 'as in human affairs, it pays to be large, close to the source, and with direct connections to it.'

The crucial test for crop physiology is whether its insights relate to plant breeding and agronomic practice. Along with John Bingham and Roger Austin at the Plant Breeding Institute, Cambridge, UK, Lloyd confirmed that a change in assimilate partitioning did account for an increase in yield potential of 12 British wheats released by breeders since 1900 (18).

Subsequently Lloyd's appetite for looking at the past and future of agriculture led to one of his favourite and widely cited articles, 'Natural history of crop yield' (19). Then, in 1999, he concluded this adventure with crops when he and Tony Fischer published a definitive view of the meaning of the term 'yield potential' (31).

In the intervening years he was not idle. He published 15 papers with the three Marys: Lush on grain legumes, Roskams on wheat, and Cook/Bush on wheat, rice and the grasses *Echinochloa* and *Poa* (see the full bibliography in the electronic supplementary material). In addition, in 1983 he began his 'big book', *Crop evolution: adaptation and yield* (26). At 500 pages, it was 30% smaller than the first version, and its original 2500 references were cut to 1900. So far, more than 2000 copies of the book have been sold and it has received wide acclaim.

AN INTERNATIONAL AGRICULTURAL SCIENTIST

The Phytotron and IRRI: a vignette of Evans's impact on agriculture in developing countries

At the time of accepting responsibility as Chief of Division, Lloyd was nurturing an additional and rapidly growing interest in agricultural research in the Philippines. The publicity surrounding the Canberra Phytotron in the 1960s led to a visit by Robert F. Chandler, the Director of the International Rice Research Institute (IRRI) at Los Baños, the Philippines. Subsequently, with Lloyd's support, he was successful in obtaining Australian funding for the construction of a similar facility at Los Baños. Lloyd's first on-site visit was in 1970 to advise the Australian Department of Foreign Affairs on the need for and design of a phytotron at IRRI. Two years later he returned briefly and then in 1974 was an invited speaker at the symposium to mark the official opening of the phytotron; among other luminaries was the Australian Minister for Science. In the next year he returned for an extremely comprehensive review of IRRI's research as a member of the first Quinquennial Review team commissioned by TAC, the Technical Advisory Committee of CGIAR (the Consultative Group on International Agricultural Research).

Determined to mix scientific studies with his involvement in international research management, and with great admiration for IRRI's work and impact, in 1978 Lloyd spent part of a sabbatical leave there after he stepped down as Chief of PI. At that time, with agronomists and the plant physiologist S. K. DeDatta, he examined the results of rice trials that exposed for the first time the long-term decline in yields on the intensively cropped areas of the field station. R. F. Chandler had retired and it was with considerable reluctance that the new Director General, Nyle Brady, allowed the results to be published.

There followed a six-year term on the TAC committee (1978–84), and later Lloyd was also co-opted for two terms as a Trustee on the IRRI Board (1985–89). Over this period he initiated a most successful Australian Development Project in Kampuchea involving IRRI as a source of much-needed rice seed and staff back-up from IRRI agronomists.

In 1989 he left the IRRI Board with doubts about his effectiveness as a Trustee and a growing unwillingness to accept some management philosophies. However, others saw a great contribution and asked him to take on the task of the Director General of IRRI. The staff wrote, 'You have encouraged us to engage in good science to solve production problems', and the then Chairman of the IRRI Board, Wally Forman, wrote: 'There are not many bright, well-informed, level-headed, no-axe-to-grind scientists on the Boards of Centers, and you are one of them.' John Flinn, the senior economist, wrote: 'We need more interaction with distinguished scientists as yourself: people with vision, humour, and who care about people.' Regretfully, Lloyd told the IRRI Board, 'I have ties to CSIRO which I feel are not to be broken.'

Leadership in international agriculture and food production

Over time, Lloyd's contribution at IRRI as a scientist with excellent analytical skills was reproduced in his burgeoning agricultural advisory role in Australia and internationally. In 1975 he led a mission to the USSR to establish exchange visits for agricultural scientists. Two years later he was a member of an Academy delegation to China. At that time Australians knew little of agriculture there, so he published accounts of both the Russian and Chinese visits.

In the late 1970s he also began prolonged discussions on Australia's role in international agriculture with Sir John Crawford (ANU economist and Chancellor) and Jim Ingram (Director of the Australian Government Development Assistance Bureau). Then, in 1981, because the Commonwealth heads of government were to meet in Australia, the Prime Minister, Malcolm Fraser, wanted 'something dramatic to offer developing countries of the Commonwealth'. Crawford, Lloyd Evans and Ingram had the answer: the Australian Centre for International Agricultural Research (ACIAR). It fitted the bill because Fraser wanted maximum visibility overseas combined with minimum visibility in Australia. The remit for ACIAR was to support Australian agricultural scientists in truly joint research in developing countries. It was not surprising that Lloyd became a founding member of the new ACIAR advisory committee.

As an aside, Sir John Crawford (1910–84) had a major influence on Lloyd. Not only did Lloyd know Sir John as a public figure and friend, but he also succeeded him in several activities, including Overseas Fellow of Churchill College, Cambridge, President of ANZAAS, a member of TAC and a member of the ACIAR Board. Lloyd wrote in his diary:

> to have observed the arts of chairmanship by which Sir John shaped debate, elicited contributions, formulated conclusions and controlled the members with a mixture of humour, wisdom and open-mindedness, fashioned my approach to committees and decision making.

He also admired his other great scientific mentor, Sir Otto Frankel, for his perceptiveness, eloquence, courage, strategic sense, unwavering belief in the value of 'basic' research, and his loyalty to friends in the face of fire.

In 1978, at the same time as Lloyd was pushing for ACIAR to be established, he was appointed for six years to TAC, which provided oversight to CGIAR. Then, as now, CGIAR supported sustainable agriculture in developing countries and focused on crops, livestock, fisheries, forestry, land and water. Its 600 supporters in the public and private sectors in the 1980s included the World Bank, the Food and Agricultural Organization, the International Fund for Agricultural Development and the United Nations Development Programme. Over the six years of Lloyd's appointment, he attended 12 TAC meetings, generally in Rome or Washington, which were often combined with CGIAR meetings, which he attended as an observer. He also fulfilled brief review roles of the International Crops Research Institute for the Semi-Arid Tropics (ICRISAT) and the International Food Policy Research Institute (IFPRI). As he put it, 'I was not of the faith (not an economist) but I thought I would learn a lot from IFPRI's economists.' Near the end of his appointment (1984–85) Lloyd was tiring of meetings at which he heard

> the same old issues, even the same old speeches by some TAC members and the same old evasions and manipulations by chairmen. They argued a lot about who would do what, and how, and with which, and to whom!

Somewhat tongue in cheek, the French Executive Secretary, Philippe Mahler, summed up Lloyd by describing him as 'TAC's Exocet missile; he hit his targets and effected some change.'

Lloyd knew from his reputation that he had spent his time valuably and felt that CGIAR and its research centres were delivering real help to the poor and hungry. Not surprisingly, therefore, completion of his term with TAC did not end his involvement with the international research institutes. Because of his ongoing research interest in wheat, in 1990 he agreed to serve a six-year period on the Board of Trustees of CIMMYT (the International Wheat and Maize Breeding Institute) located in Mexico.

World food production

While still a high-school student in New Zealand, Lloyd had read John Boyd Orr's book *Food, health and income* (Boyd Orr 1943), and this began his interest in world food supply. Later, at Oxford, he revisited Malthusian predictions of overpopulation and insufficient food. Later still, his involvement with TAC reviews led to interaction with many able and committed agricultural scientists and economists from around the world who sharpened his thoughts on the agricultural constraints on world food production.

Such was his concern for 'the hungry world' and how many people it could hold that in the late 1990s he began his last and perhaps most significant book, *Feeding the ten billion* (30). Fittingly, this book was published in 1998, the bicentenary of Malthus's *Essay on the principle of population* (Malthus 1989 [1798]). In his diary, Lloyd recalls: 'I received the first copy of my book in October 1998, just in time to wave it around at the international symposium on World Food Security in Japan, at which I gave the opening address on "Steps towards feeding the ten billion".'

Two months later, for a study week of the Pontifical Academy of Science at the Vatican, Lloyd gave a similar talk, 'Food needs of the developing world in the early 21st century'. For Lloyd, it was a 'plus' to sleep in a cardinal's bed in St Martha's, but he regretted having no time to visit the Vatican Library or see the Sistine Chapel again. Also, he had brought with him one copy of his book (*Feeding the ten billion*), which he left on display, only to come back after lunch to find it had disappeared; he tempered his regret with the hope that the thief was too poor to buy a copy of the book. A more welcome response came from the Rockefeller demographer Joel Cohen in the first review of the book: 'Evans writes with authority, subtlety, accuracy, clarity, a marvellous richness of detail, and a very engaging human touch.'

Further praise for Lloyd's contribution to international agriculture, world food issues and his crop research came with a successful nomination to the American Society of Plant Biology for the 2004 Adolph E. Gude Jr Award for Service to Agriculture. For the Gude nomination, several leading international scientists provided me with glowing accounts of their interactions with Lloyd, and parts of three letters are detailed below.

Professor Gurdev S. Khush (Former Principal Plant Breeder at IRRI) wrote:

Lloyd has made outstanding contributions to International Agriculture and thus helped produce more food for the world's hungry.

Dr Don Duvick (Senior Vice-President Research (retired), Pioneer Hi-Bred International, Inc.) wrote:

Dr Lloyd Evans is a scientist who has made great contributions to advancement of the beneficial use of agricultural science in industrialized and (especially) in developing countries around the world. Two of his books (26, 30) have helped international policy-makers, as well as research scientists in agriculture, in food production as well as environmental protection.

Dr Tony Fischer (Honorary Research Fellow, CSIRO Plant Industry) wrote:

Lloyd was always fully informed, forthright, tolerant, solicitous and, especially, aware of and concerned about different farming cultures. … He has always been a strong advocate for continued investment in agricultural research.

LECTURES AND BOOKS

Lloyd thrived on the sudden understanding that came from research but was also delighted when he could combine insights and set them in a broader, often historical context. For example, on the centenary of Charles Darwin's death, Lloyd celebrated the event by publishing an article in *Journal of History of Biology* (21). He used Darwin's analogy between artificial and natural selection as a focus for how he and other plant biologists were approaching plant improvement.

Over his career Lloyd delivered more than 63 prestigious invited public lectures, both in Australia and overseas; about half of these were published as articles, and the other half as chapters in conference books. The invitations ranged from universities and learned societies to leading international agricultural companies including Monsanto and Du Pont and to international foundations including a very prestigious CIBA Foundation Lecture in London. There were also several addresses to the Australian Academy of Science and to meetings in the UK organized by the Royal Society.

As the titles of some of these lectures show, they were provocative; 'The two agricultures: renewable or resourceful', 'The plant physiologist as midwife' and 'The divorce of science'; others were forward-looking, for example 'Variability of cereal yields: sources of change and implications for agricultural research and policy'. Overall, with his liking for historical perspective, Lloyd first assembled the facts and then developed answers to his questions; he was a true synthesizer.

Although always heavily committed, he was an author on four prestigious articles in *Annual Reviews of Plant Physiology* and *Annual Reviews of Plant Biology* and one in *Advances in Agronomy*. He edited five books and was sole author of three books: a small university text on flowering, and his two major books, *Crop evolution: adaptation and yield* and *Feeding the ten billion* (26, 30). These last two books have had major influences on agricultural research and policy and are considered essential reading for students in this field.

Lloyd Evans's influence on Australian plant science was widely felt through his Presidency of the Australian Society of Plant Physiologists, of ANZAAS and of the Australian Academy of Science. The many honours conferred on Lloyd included Officer of the Order of Australia in 1979, one of Australia's highest civilian honours, and the Centenary Medal of Australia in 2003.

Lloyd was a legendary scientist and a true man of letters. He passed away peacefully in Canberra on 23 March 2015, a year after his wife, Margaret. He had suffered from steadily increasing dementia but was supported magnificently by all his family and friends.

ACKNOWLEDGEMENTS

It has been an honour, a privilege and a very pleasing experience to write about the life and career of Lloyd Evans, my friend and colleague of some 50 years. During the process I drew on many sources and people. For their comments and suggestions I would like to thank Lloyd's three children, Nicholas, John and Catherine, and also Robyn Diamond, Tony Fischer, Elizabeth King, John Passioura and Ian Rae. I thank especially Carl Davies and Lew Mander, who provided some of the photographs.

The frontispiece photograph was taken in 1978 by Godfrey Argent and is reproduced with permission.

REFERENCES TO OTHER AUTHORS

Boyd Orr, J. 1943 *Food and the people*. London: Pilot Press.

Corbesier, L., Vincent, C., Jang, S. H., Fornara, F., Fan, Q. Z., Searle, I., Giakountis, A., Farrona, S., Gissot, L., Turnbull, C. & Coupland, G. 2007 FT protein movement contributes to long-distance signalling in floral induction of *Arabidopsis*. *Science* **316**, 1030–1033.

Davidson, J. L. & Donald, C. M. 1958 The growth of swards of subterranean clover with particular reference to leaf area. *Aust. J. Agric. Res.* **9**, 53–72.

Gocal, G. F. W. & King, R. W. 2013 Early increased expression of a cyclin-dependant protein kinase (*LtCDKA1;1*) during inflorescence initiation of the long-day grass *Lolium temulentum* L. *Funct. Pl. Biol.* **40**, 986–995.

King, R. W. 2012 Mobile signals in daylength-regulated flowering: gibberellins, FT and sucrose. *Russ. J. Pl. Physiol.* **59**, 521–531.

Lang, A. 1965 Physiology of flower initiation. In *Encyclopaedia of plant physiology*, vol. 15, pt 1 (ed. W. Ruhland), pp. 1380–1536. Berlin: Springer

Lang, A., Chailakhyan, M. Kh. & Frolova, I. A. 1977 Promotion and inhibition of flower formation in a day-neutral plant in grafts with a short-day plant and a long-day plant. *Proc. Natl Acad. Sci. USA* **74**, 2412–2416.

MacMillan, C. P., Blundell, C. A. & King, R. W. 2005 Flowering of the grass *Lolium perenne* L. Effects of vernalization and long days on gibberellin biosynthesis and signalling. *Pl. Physiol.* **138**, 1794–1806.

Malthus, T. R. 1989 [1798] *An essay on the principle of population* (Variorum edition) (ed. P. James). Cambridge University Press.

White, F. W. G. 1977 Casey of Berwick and Westminster, Baron Richard Gardiner Casey, KG, PC, GCMG, CH, DSO, MC, KStJ, FAA, MA(Cantab.). *Rec. Aust. Acad. Sci.* **3**, 74.

BIBLIOGRAPHY

The following publications are those referred to directly in the text. A full bibliography and a curriculum vitae are available as electronic supplementary material at http://dx.doi.org/10.1098/rsbm.2016.0008 or via http://rsbm.royalsocietypublishing.org.

(1) 1958 *Lolium temulentum* L., a long-day plant requiring only one inductive photocycle. *Nature* **182**, 197–198.

(2) 1960 Inflorescence initiation in *Lolium temulentum* L. II. Evidence for inhibitory and promotive photoperiodic processes involving transmissible products. *Aust. J. Biol. Sci.* **13**, 429–440.

(3) 1962 (With R. N. Morse) Design and development of CERES—an Australian phytotron. *J. Agric. Engng Res.* **7**, 128–140.

(4) 1964 (With I. F. Wardlaw) Inflorescence initiation in *Lolium temulentum* L. IV. Translocation of the floral stimulus in relation to that of assimilates. *Aust. J. Biol. Sci.* **17**, 1–9.

(5) Inflorescence initiation in *Lolium temulentum* L. V. The role of auxins and gibberellins. *Aust. J. Biol. Sci.* **17**, 10–23.

(6) Inflorescence initiation in *Lolium temulentum* L. VI. Effects of some inhibitors of nucleic acid, protein, and steroid biosynthesis. *Aust. J. Biol. Sci.* **17**, 24–35.

(7)   1965   (With H. S. Borthwick & S. B. Hendricks) Inflorescence initiation in *Lolium temulentum* L. VII. The spectral dependence of induction. *Aust. J. Biol. Sci.* **18**, 745–762.

(8)   (With L. J. Ludwig & T. Saeki) Photosynthesis in artificial communities of cotton plants in relation to leaf area. I. Experiments with progressive defoliation of mature plants. *Aust. J. Biol. Sci.* **18**, 1103–1118.

(9)   1966   Abscisin II: inhibitory effect on flower induction in a long-day plant. *Science* **151**, 107–108.

(10)   (With R. B. Knox) Inflorescence initiation in *Lolium temulentum* L. VIII. Histochemical changes at the shoot apex during induction. *Aust. J. Biol. Sci.* **19**, 233–245.

(11) 1967   (With A. H. G. C. Rijven) Inflorescence initiation in *Lolium temulentum* L. IX. Some chemical changes in the shoot apex at induction. *Aust. J. Biol. Sci.* **20**, 1–12.

(12)   (With R. W. King & I. F. Wardlaw) Effect of assimilate utilization on photosynthetic rate in wheat. *Planta* **77**, 261–276.

(13) 1968   (With R. W. King & I. F. Wardlaw) Translocation of the floral stimulus in *Pharbitis nil* in relation to that of assimilates. *Z. PflPhysiol.* **59**, 377–388.

(14) 1969   (With R. B. Knox) Environmental control of reproduction in *Themeda australis. Aust. J. Bot.* **17**, 375–389.

(15) 1970   (With R. L. Dunstone) Some physiological aspects of evolution in wheat. *Aust. J. Biol. Sci.* **23**, 725–741.

(16) 1971   (With H. M. Rawson) Contribution of stem reserves to grain development in a range of wheat cultivars of different height. *Aust. J. Agric. Res.* **22**, 851–863.

(17) 1977   (With R. W. King & R. D. Firn) Abscisic acid and xanthoxin contents in the long-day plant *Lolium temulentum* L. in relation to daylength. *Aust. J. Pl. Physiol.* **4**, 217–223.

(18) 1980   (With R. B. Austin, J. Bingham, R. D. Blackwell, M. A. Ford, C. L. Morgan & M. Taylor) Genetic improvements in winter wheat yields since 1900 and associated physiological changes. *J. Agric. Sci.* **94**, 675–689.

(19)   Natural history of crop yield. *Am. Sci.* **68**, 388–397.

(20) 1983   (With M. G. Cook) The roles of sink size and location in the partitioning of assimilates in wheat ears. *Aust. J. Pl. Physiol.* **10**, 313–327.

(21) 1984   Darwin's use of the analogy between artificial and natural selection. *J. Hist. Biol.* **17**, 113–140.

(22) 1985   (With I. F. Wardlaw & R. W. King) Plants and environment: two decades of research at the Canberra Phytotron. *Bot. Rev.* **51**, 203–272.

(23) 1986   (With O. M. Heide & R. W. King) A semidian rhythm in the flowering response of *Pharbitis nil* to far-red light. I. Phasing in relation to the light-off signal. *Pl. Physiol.* **80**, 1020–1024.

(24) 1990   (With R. W. King, A. Chu, L. N. Mander & R. P. Pharis) Gibberellin structure and florigenic activity in *Lolium temulentum*, a long-day plant. *Planta* **182**, 97–106.

(25) 1991   (With C. N. McDaniel & R. W. King) Floral determination and *in vitro* floral differentiation in isolated shoot apices of *Lolium temulentum* L. *Planta* **185**, 9–16.

(26) 1993   *Crop evolution: adaptation and yield.* Cambridge University Press.

(27) 1994   (With R. W. King, L. N. Mander, R. P. Pharis & K. A. Duncan) The differential effects of C-16,17-dihydro gibberellins and related compounds on stem elongation and flowering in *Lolium temulentum*. *Planta* **193**, 107–114.

(28) 1997   (With O. Junttila, R. W. King, A. Poole, G. Kretchmer & R. P. Pharis) Regulation in *Lolium temulentum* of the metabolism of gibberellin A_{20} and gibberellin A_1 by 16,17-dihydro GA_5 and by the growth retardant, LAB 198999. *Aust. J. Pl. Physiol.* **24**, 359–369.

(29)   (With R. W. King, C. Blundell, L. N. Mander & J. T. Wood) Modified gibberellins retard growth of cool-season turf grasses. *Crop Sci.* **37**, 1878–1883.

(30) 1998   *Feeding the ten billion: plants and population growth.* Cambridge University Press.

(31) 1999   (With R. A. Fischer) Yield potential: its definition, measurement, and significance. *Crop Sci.* **39**, 1544–1551.

(32) 2001   (With R. W. King, T. Moritz, O. Junttila & A. J. Herlt) Long-day induction of flowering in *Lolium temulentum* involves sequential increases in specific gibberellins at the shoot apex. *Pl. Physiol.* **127**, 624–632.

(33) 2003   Conjectures, refutations and extrapolations. *Annu. Rev. Pl. Biol.* **54**, 1–21.

(34)   (With R. W. King) Gibberellins and the flowering of grasses and cereals: prizing open the lid of the 'florigen' black box. *Annu. Rev. Pl. Biol.* **54**, 307–328.

(35)   2006   (With R. W. King, T. Moritz, J. Martin, C. H. Andersen, C. Blundell, I. Kardailsky & P. M. Chandler) Gibberellin biosynthesis and the regulation of flowering in the long-day grass *Lolium temulentum* by gibberellins and the *FLOWERING LOCUS T* gene. *Pl. Physiol.* **141**, 498–507.

(36)   2008   (With R. W. King, L. N. Mander, T. Asp, C. P. MacMillan & C. A. Blundell) Selective deactivation of gibberellins below the shoot apex is critical to flowering but not to stem elongation of *Lolium*. *Mol. Pl.* **1**, 295–307.

BRIAN EYRE CBE FRENG

29 November 1933 — 28 July 2014

Biogr. Mems Fell. R. Soc. **62**, 147–166 (2016)

BRIAN EYRE CBE FREng

29 November 1933 — 28 July 2014

Elected FRS 2001

By Derek Pooley[1]* CBE, George Smith[2]‡ FRS and
Colin Windsor[3]§ FRS

[1] *11 Halls Close, Drayton OX14 4LU, UK*
[2] *Department of Materials, University of Oxford, 16 Parks Road,*
Oxford OX1 3PH, UK
[3] *Tokamak Energy, Abingdon OX14 3DB, UK*

Brian Eyre was an outstanding metallurgist who played a leading role in the development of nuclear engineering materials. His experiments on irradiated metals enabled a theoretical understanding of the mechanisms of radiation damage, and in particular the formation of voids and void swelling in structural steels. His work on the fracture of metals advanced our understanding of intergranular embrittlement and helped define the specifications of the structural components in nuclear reactors. He rose from a humble upbringing in London's East End to become Chief Executive of the UK Atomic Energy Authority (UKAEA). He was instrumental in transforming the UKAEA from a organization whose mission was to develop nuclear power generating systems into the privatized AEA Technology, which worked on a wide range of technologies on a customer–contractor basis.

The early years

Brian Eyre was born on 29 November 1933 in East London, the first child of Mabel Eyre (*née* Rumsey) and Leonard George Eyre in what he called a 'working class' family home: a small terraced house in Forest Gate.‖ His father had trained as a mechanical fitter but had periods of unemployment in the 1930's. His mother was a skilled dressmaker. Brian was six years

---

* derek_pooley@talk21.com; ‡ george.smith@materials.ox.ac.uk; § colin.windsor@tokamakenergy.co.uk
‖ Always organized, Brian left us comprehensive notes about his early life, on which we have based these first sections.

© 2016 The Author(s)
http://dx.doi.org/10.1098/rsbm.2016.0016   149   Published by the Royal Society

old when he attended his first school, Northolt Primary. At the age of 11 years he was one of very few pupils from the school to pass the 11-plus examination to be selected for Greenford Grammar School.

Brian recalled that he did not enjoy grammar school and did not relate to most of the teachers, the exceptions being a mathematics teacher in his middle years and a history teacher during his last two years. He spent much of his time on extracurricular activities. When he was 13 years old he joined the Air Training Corps, which was particularly important in broadening his experience. He was introduced to flying and obtained a glider pilot's certificate. He also spent much time with friends in aero modelling. Pocket money to finance these activities had to be earned, so he had a paper round delivering newspapers before school each day, as well as a Saturday job. The consequence was that schoolwork had a low priority and he left Greenford Grammar at 16 years of age without either matriculating or obtaining the school certificate, which were the basic qualifications at the time. Looking back he realized that getting a place in a grammar school was a privilege denied to most state-educated children, and he felt that his years there had been largely wasted.

The first employment: Fairey Aviation, 1950–55

On leaving school, his first few months were spent in dead-end jobs as an office boy and garage pump attendant. But towards the end of 1950 he obtained a place at Fairey Aviation in Hayes, Middlesex, as a technical trainee working in the materials laboratory. The pay was very low but crucially he was given one day off per week for part-time education, during which he embarked on an Ordinary National Certificate general science course at Wandsworth Technical College. He had an inspirational teacher, Mike Pay, who opened Brian's eyes to the importance of formal qualifications as a passport to a professional career.

The early 1950s were a particularly exciting time for the UK aircraft industry, and Fairey's was in the vanguard. While Brian was there the company was working on the Fairey Delta 1 and 2; the latter made a major breakthrough, increasing the world speed record to 1132 miles per hour.

Brian recalled that the atmosphere at Fairey's was rather autocratic. The Chief Metallurgist, W. E. Cooper, sat in a glass-fronted office, emerging to shout orders when he felt that his minions were not working hard enough. Brian's initial placement was working in the metallography laboratory under Arthur Greenwood, a very experienced metallurgist who was particularly knowledgeable on the microstructure and properties of alloys used in the aircraft industry. Some of the work was tedious, involving polishing sections from large alloy forgings and castings for routine examination under the microscope. Other work that he found more fascinating included learning about microstructures and the use of successive etching treatments to identify and analyse the phase distributions in alloys.

The job at Fairey's had some of the atmosphere of a school—there were about 20 trainees, all of a similar age. Formal courses for one day a week, and nine hours of evenings plus homework, as well as keeping on top of their jobs, were a major challenge. In Brian's view most of the people he studied with at night school were equal to or more able than many of the university graduates with whom he subsequently worked.

Figure 1. The Battersea Polytechnic Institute. (Illustration by James Akerman, published in
The Building News, 3 April 1891.)

THE TIN RESEARCH INSTITUTE, 1955–57

In 1955, having gained an Ordinary National Certificate, Brian moved to the Tin Research
Institute as an assistant metallurgist with responsibility for their metallography laboratory.
The institute was a much smaller organization than Fairey's. Funded by the tin producers it
provided technical support to organizations using tin-based materials.

Brian continued to receive the concession of one day off per week to continue his professional
studies: he embarked on a Higher National course at Battersea College of Technology. His manager
was the Chief Metallurgist, Dr Edwin Eldred. Under Eldred's guidance Brian published his first
two papers as sole author, on the microstructures of tin and its alloys and the phase diagram of
tin–antimony alloys (1, 2)*. This was before he had gained any professional qualifications.

BATTERSEA COLLEGE OF TECHNOLOGY, 1957–59

In September 1957, on gaining a Higher National Certificate, Brian was encouraged to continue
his education on a full-time basis and study for the newly introduced Diploma in Technology
at Battersea Polytechnic Institute (figure 1). The institute had a long and distinguished history,
having admitted its first students in 1894 and providing access to further and higher education
for the poorer inhabitants of London.

He found moving from part-time to full-time study quite a change of pace. In the early
days, working at the level of intensity to which he had become accustomed, he raced ahead on
coursework and assignments; his tutor advised him to slow down and take more time to read
around his subject. In the spring of 1959, before finals in his last year at Battersea, he suffered
a setback, which he characteristically overcame. An accident on his motorbike resulted in a
complex fracture of his left leg, requiring an extended stay in hospital. He was unable to carry
out a practical final-year project and instead conducted an extensive review of brittle fracture
in ferritic steels. This turned out to be invaluable training for his later research. Immobility

* Numbers in this form refer to the bibliography at the end of the text.

also enabled him to revise for finals more than he might otherwise have done and he gained a first-class honours Diploma in Technology (DipTech Metallurgy) at the age of 25 years.

Central Electricity Generating Board, 1959–62

On leaving Battersea in 1959 Brian was recruited by the Central Electricity Generating Board (CEGB) as a Research Officer, one of a cohort of graduate staff to form the nucleus for the planned Berkeley Nuclear Laboratories in Gloucestershire. He was to work under Bryan Edmondson on the steel surveillance-testing programme for the Magnox pressure vessel. He was seconded to the Culcheth Laboratories of the UK Atomic Energy Authority (UKAEA) near Warrington in the north of England, to work under Roy Nichols in the shielded laboratory.

Around 1959 he visited Constance Tipper, Reader in the Engineering Department at Cambridge. Tipper had worked for most of her career at Imperial College and Cambridge on the fundamental aspects of deformation and fracture in ferritic materials. She was about to retire, so she let him have a collection of iron single crystals grown by the strain anneal method; this proved to be a very fortunate event for him. Brian had the single crystals fabricated into small tensile specimens and arranged for them to be irradiated, together with some thinned, rolled and annealed sheet samples of a low-carbon iron, in the Herald reactor at the UK Atomic Weapons Establishment at Aldermaston in Berkshire. This was a small light-water-moderated research reactor, in which it was possible to achieve relatively high doses in the comparatively short time of a few months. In late 1960 he received the irradiated iron crystals and conducted tensile testing, resulting in cleavage fracture at liquid nitrogen temperatures. He used the elderly Phillips Elmiscope 100B electron microscope to study replicas taken from the fracture surfaces, exploring the effects of neutron irradiation on the topography of the fracture surfaces.

Soon after he arrived at Culcheth a potential crisis arose regarding the irradiation-induced deformation of the fuel cladding in the Magnox reactors that were shortly to come into service with the CEGB. A crash programme was mounted in late 1959 under the direction of George Hardy. The team worked on this through the Christmas holidays and developed a modification to the fuel element design that fixed the problem.

Brian moved to Berkeley Nuclear Laboratories in January 1959. Although the building work on the laboratories had been completed, the services were not fully installed. Indeed, there was no heating and the surrounding grounds were a sea of mud. He also had to find accommodation. He rented, together with Barry Jones and Arthur Smith, a house: Hornshill Farm. Barry had been president of the Sheffield University Mountaineering Club and they made frequent trips to North Wales and the Lake District for rock climbing and mountain walking. Barry and Brian remained lifelong friends, and each acted as best man at the other's wedding in the 1960s.

Brian was also encouraged by his Section Leader, Kingsley Williamson, to continue his basic research on irradiation damage in iron. Initial studies of the effects of irradiation on slip-band morphologies in iron had shown a transition from diffuse wavy slip bands in unirradiated samples to much sharper and straighter slip bands after irradiation. This transition was dependent on both irradiation dose and temperature. The observations were consistent with earlier observations on irradiated face-centred cubic metals. The sharpening of the slip bands was interpreted as being due to dislocations sweeping out irradiation damage clusters, a phenomenon called dislocation channelling (3). During this period, Brian also reported the

Figure 2. Brian Eyre (left) in 1979 with Metallurgy Division colleagues John Evans, John Williams and Merfyn Davies. (Photograph supplied by Eric Jenkins, courtesy of the NDA Photo Library.)

first-ever direct observations of neutron irradiation damage in α-iron, using the new technique of transmission electron microscopy (4). The development of dislocation configurations in irradiated material was studied, as well as the interaction of these features with point defect clusters. This was a *tour de force*, involving the development of novel methods for specimen preparation, as well as very painstaking and skilled microscopy.

HARWELL METALLURGY DIVISION, 1962–69

In the spring of 1962 Brian moved from Berkeley Nuclear Laboratories to the Metallurgy Division of the Atomic Energy Research Establishment at Harwell (figure 2). Harwell had been set up in the late 1940s under Sir John Cockcroft FRS to be the central research establishment for the UK's nuclear programme. Through the 1950s it established itself as one of the world's leading centres for research in the nuclear sciences.

On arrival Brian was given two support staff, Edgar Joyce and Arthur Bartlett. Edgar was a General Worker with responsibility for looking after the laboratory; Arthur was a Scientific Assistant with the task of assisting him in his experimental work. Brian was to build on his research on irradiation damage in iron performed at Berkeley. The facilities at Harwell, in terms of research reactors and tools for structural analysis, were excellent. In collaboration with Arthur Bartlett, a detailed study was performed on the post-irradiation annealing of neutron-irradiated iron (7). Brian was to establish an interaction with Ron Bullough (FRS 1985) in the Theoretical Physics Division that lasted the whole of his career at Harwell and beyond. Brian's systematic and rigorous approach, his emphasis on careful and thorough experimental work, his use of a range of techniques to focus on a single problem, his insistence on using the highest purity materials, and his detailed and active collaboration with leading theoreticians all made him a major international figure in the field of nuclear materials.

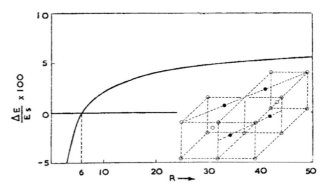

Figure 3. The percentage energy difference between equivalent square and circular interstitial loops as a function of loop size in units of the core radius (R). The inset shows the configuration of bi-interstitials in a body-centred cubic lattice, as first proposed by R. A. Johnson (Johnson 1964). (From (6).)

An early success of Brian's collaboration with Ron Bullough was a theoretical model for the development of interstitial dislocation loop geometries in body-centred cubic metals. Interstitial atoms tend to place themselves within the lattice at the point of lowest energy. The inset in figure 3 shows how two split interstitials (represented by the four black atoms) place themselves in the smallest possible loop. As the number of interstitials grows, they may form a single extra layer of interstitials—a 'stacking fault', enclosed within a dislocation loop with Burgers vector $b=(a/2)\langle 110\rangle$. Their work detailed how the stacking fault may be eliminated by lattice shears along either a $\langle 100\rangle$ or a $\langle 110\rangle$ direction to produce loops with $b = (a/2)\langle 111\rangle$ or $(a/2)\langle 100\rangle$, respectively. As the loops grow they become visible by experimental electron microscopy; many measurements of the shape, size and orientation of interstitial loops were subsequently made. These could be explained by analytical calculations of their elastic energy. Analytical calculations were made of the energy of both square and circular interstitial loops as a function of their size and orientation. The original theoretical model by Eyre and Bullough (6) correctly predicted the observations that interstitial loops are initially rectilinear but as they grow they become circular.

Early on, a young graduate, Mary Downey, joined Brian; this enabled them to broaden the irradiation damage studies to include another body-centred cubic metal, molybdenum. Thin foils of molybdenum suffer considerably less surface contamination than iron in the electron microscope, facilitating a more detailed analysis of the irradiation damage structures. They were able to analyse irradiation-induced point-defect cluster damage in molybdenum quantitatively as a function of irradiation conditions and post-irradiation annealing (5).

In the mid 1960s Dennis Maher, who had completed his PhD at Berkeley under Gareth Thomas, joined the group. Brian's group embarked on an extensive programme to study irradiation damage in molybdenum, including the nature, geometry and distribution of damage clusters as a function of a wide range of irradiation and post-irradiation annealing conditions. They developed methods for analysing the structures. This involved interacting with Ron Bullough and Roy Perrin in the Theoretical Physics Division, where computer simulation was used to analyse the geometries of small dislocation loops. This enabled them to gain insights into the development of irradiation damage structures in molybdenum and the mechanisms governing post-irradiation annealing behaviour. This work, which was reported in a series of papers in *Philosophical Magazine* (10–13), formed the most comprehensive study of irradiation damage in a body-centred cubic metal.

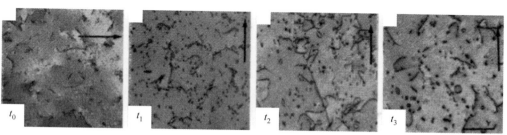

Figure 4. Electron micrographs of pure molybdenum irradiated in the Harwell DIDO reactor at 473 K and subsequently annealed at 1173 K for effective times of 0 (t_0), 12 s (t_1), 10 min (t_2) and 60 min (t_3). The scale marker (black arrow) represents 400 Å. (From (13).)

Figure 4 shows an example of the work in (13). Pure molybdenum samples irradiated to an integrated dose of 7×10^{19} neutrons cm^{-2} at 473 K in the DIDO reactor were then annealed in a furnace at 1173 K for various durations. The images show dislocation loops as multi-sided polygons. It is clear that the average size of the loops increased with the annealing time, and the paper assessed this quantitatively and fitted these measurements to analytical theories.

In the mid 1960s John Evans joined Brian's group, and they initiated experiments to determine the effects of composition on the structure and physical properties of molybdenum. A particular focus was to study the kinetics of nitrogen-rich cluster formation in quenched Mo–N alloys as a function of ageing time and temperature, using a range of techniques including transmission electron microscopy, resistivity and internal friction (8).

John Evans also conducted experiments to study damage structures in molybdenum irradiated in an accelerator at temperatures above 500 °C. He discovered the formation of a void lattice with a body-centred cubic structure; a transmission electron micrograph showing the void lattice was published on the cover of an issue of *Nature*. A seminal paper by Bullough, Eyre and Perrin on the modelling of void growth was published in 1970 (9).

On moving to Harwell in 1962, Brian initially lodged at Ridgeway House, a former Royal Air Force officers' mess used by the Atomic Energy Research Establishment as a hostel for single graduate staff. In 1963 Brian moved out to a flat in Abingdon, sharing with David Ogden from the Medical Research Council at Harwell, and Jim Hastie and Peter Ford from Culham nuclear fusion laboratory. They all had an interest in mountaineering; David and Brian joined the Oxford Mountaineering Club. A highlight during this period was to go on a British Mountaineering Association rock-climbing course in Skye in 1964, enjoying perfect weather and climbing many of the classic routes in the Black Cuillen.

Brian met Elizabeth Carol Rackham, his future wife, in 1964 on one of the weekends in Wales. She was teaching in Abingdon and was rooming with another teacher, Denise Wood, also a member of the Oxford Mountaineering Club and a strong rock climber. Carol tried rock climbing with Brian on a couple of occasions but did not take to it: there was too much waiting around. Brian and Carol were married in June 1965; she 'retired' from rock climbing and they moved to their first home in Wootton near Abingdon. They had two sons, Peter John (born in 1966) and Stephen Andrew (1967).

Biographical Memoirs

THE UNIVERSITY OF ILLINOIS, 1969–70

As a result of his vacation stays at Harwell, Howard Birnbaum invited Brian to spend a year with his group at the University of Illinois. Brian, Carol and their two sons (then two and three years old) set off on the *Queen Elizabeth 2* liner in September 1969 for Illinois via New York. Although there was research at Illinois using electron microscopy, notably by Marvin Wayman to study martensitic transformations, there was no work using diffraction contrast analysis to study defect geometries. Brian gave a course of postgraduate lectures on the principles and methods of analysis of diffraction contrast techniques. At that time he also developed a mathematical model of the annealing behaviour of irradiation-induced dislocation loops. This was related to the experimental observations he had made at Harwell working with Dennis Maher; theory and experiment were reported in a major paper (13) that completed a series of five papers on irradiation damage in molybdenum.

RETURN TO HARWELL, 1970–76

When Brian returned from Illinois, Stan Pugh had succeeded Bob Barnes as Metallurgy Division Head at Harwell, and he asked Brian to form a new group to work on the fracture of structural alloys. Walter (later Lord) Marshall (FRS 1971) had launched the so-called 'diversification programme', a new direction for Harwell aimed at winning increasing external, non-nuclear, funding for their work. This marked the beginning of the run down of the government-funded nuclear programme. Brian's group started to seek externally funded contracts as well as beginning new research programmes on fracture. New members of the group included recent graduates Tom Webster, Steve Druce, Hayden Wadley, Barry Edwards and Colin English.

In the period 1970–79 the group conducted a much broader based programme. In the irradiation damage field, Brian worked with Colin English on understanding the basic mechanisms governing the development of defect structures as radiation damage proceeds. They focused particularly on the role of displacement cascades in influencing the survival of point defects and their distributions in face-centred cubic and body-centred cubic metals (14, 16). A particularly significant outcome of this work came from Brian's continuing interaction with Ron Bullough. Together with Kanwar Krishan, a visiting scientist from India, they developed a theoretical model of how the collapse of the vacancy-rich centres of displacement cascades influenced the separation of vacancy and interstitial point defects and the effect of this on the temperature dependence of void swelling (17).

During the 1960s, void swelling in the cladding of fuel elements in fast reactors had become a major issue after observations on stainless steel cladding samples after irradiation in the Dounreay Fast Reactor. The study with Bullough and Krishan drew on the the classic work by Cottrell & Bilby (1949), on the interactions of interstitial solutes with edge dislocations in iron. They deduced that, as a result of the greater misfit strains around interstitial point defects relative to vacancies, they would interact more strongly and be lost preferentially at dislocation sinks, leaving an excess of vacancies to form voids. This work was later extended in a series of papers by Bullough and his colleagues (Brailsford & Bullough 1972) that developed a rate theory for predicting void swelling in metals and alloys under a wide range of conditions, as irradiation parameters and material structural parameters were varied. They developed a series of coupled rate equations governing all the stages and parameters of the

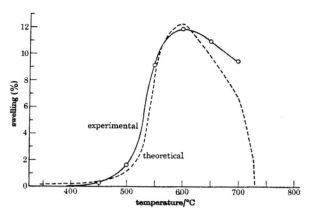

Figure 5. The swelling of type 316 stainless steel produced under irradiation by 1 MeV electrons to a total dose of 40 displacements per atom, as a function of temperature. (From (17).)

irradiation process. The irradiation dose, usually quantified as atomic displacements per atom, could be related to the simultaneous production of vacancy and interstitial atoms, or Frenkel pairs. Their aggregation into interstitial loops and their subsequent transformation into voids could all be expressed by analytical rate equations whose parameters could be deduced from experimental metallurgy. These rate equations could be solved numerically on mainframe computers to give predictions of the void swelling percentage that could be compared directly with the experimental observations, as in figure 5.

Pioneering work was also carried out on the irradiation of metals with helium ions, which results in the formation of bubble lattices (15, 19), and on irradiation with heavy ions, which provides a convenient method of producing displacement cascades that resemble the primary damage events occurring under irradiation with fast neutrons (18).

During the mid 1970s Brian worked closely with Colin English and Roy Perrin on the development of the theory of transmission electron microscope (TEM) diffraction contrast from small dislocation loops created by irradiation. In particular, they developed a programme based on two-beam dynamical theory to calculate the so-called black–white contrast of small dislocation loops lying close to the surface of a TEM foil. The fine structure of these images enabled them to determine the nature, Burgers vector and habit planes of loops in molybdenum produced by bombardment with heavy ions. They showed that $(a/2)\langle 111 \rangle$ loops often had shear components consistent with nucleation on $\{110\}$ planes, as previously predicted. They also developed a method for the determination of the nature of larger loops in particular orientations. This seminal work was reported in a series of key papers (20–23) that, decades later, still form the basis of the interpretation of TEM images of irradiation-induced defects in metals and alloys.

Brian's studies with molybdenum also continued in the field of fracture. Intergranular embrittlement had long been a problem with many metals. The problem was thought to lie in the segregation of impurity atoms on to the grain boundary surfaces within the metal. With Arvind Kumar, a visitor from India, Brian performed one of the first systematic quantitative studies of these effects. They first prepared samples of ultrapure molybdenum, containing only 6 atomic parts per million of oxygen, and then made a range of different carbon additions. Using Auger electron spectroscopy they were able to measure the concentrations of oxygen and carbon atoms on intergranular fracture surfaces, and to correlate these with the

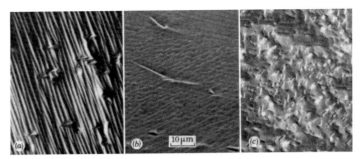

Figure 6. Scanning electron micrographs of the fracture surfaces of molybdenum containing variable amounts of carbon. The alloys contain (*a*) 1.6, (*b*) 4 and (*c*) 300 carbon atoms per 10^6 atoms and show increasing amounts of the molybdenum carbide precipitates. (From (24).)

low-temperature fracture stresses of individual grain boundaries. In a classic paper (24) they demonstrated that decreasing the grain-boundary oxygen level from 0.47 to 0.11 of saturation coverage resulted in an increase of about 60% in the work of fracture, and that this effect was partly lessened when carbon was added. Carbon was shown to partly suppress the segregation of oxygen, as well as precipitating carbides, which acted as sources of mobile dislocations and hence improved the ductility of the alloy.

Figure 6 shows scanning electron micrographs of the intergranular fracture surface of alloys containing very different amounts of carbon. Boundaries that were low in carbon but high in oxygen content showed striated or faceted structures (figure 6*a*). At intermediate oxygen and carbon levels the boundaries appeared more uniform (figure 6*b*), whereas at high carbon levels there was direct evidence of molybdenum carbide precipitation in the interfaces (figure 6*c*).

THE UNIVERSITY OF LIVERPOOL, 1979–84

In the spring of 1979 Brian was headhunted by the University of Liverpool to take the Chair of Materials Science, succeeding John Stringer. This was a difficult decision, involving a significant drop in salary as well as the challenge of teaching a range of undergraduate materials courses from scratch and setting up new research projects for the first time. At the time Liverpool did not have a strong presence in electron microscopy and Brian would have to make the case through the research councils and the university for substantial new funds.

The challenges were even more formidable than he had expected, particularly in preparations for a series of undergraduate courses for both materials and engineering students. He encountered considerable goodwill from both the university and the research councils in helping to set up his research activities in both irradiation damage and the fracture of structural alloys. Several very able research students joined his group, and considerable momentum had been established by the end of the second year.

He also became more involved in university affairs, succeeding Derek Hull (FRS 1989) as Head of Department after two years. Brian and his two sons were regular attendees at Anfield during Liverpool Football Club's great period in the late 1970s and early 1980s.

THE HIGHER MANAGEMENT YEARS, 1984–97

Brian was eventually persuaded to return to the UKAEA in the summer of 1984, replacing George Hardy, who was retiring as UKAEA Director of Fuel and Engineering. This gave him charge of the three 'Northern Research Laboratories' at Risley, Springfields and Windscale, headed respectively by Roy Nichols, John Shennan and Harry Lawton, all very able lieutenants and immensely experienced in nuclear power. Brian's job was to create, correct or strengthen the technology needed for the advanced gas-cooled reactors (AGRs) and the sodium-cooled fast reactor, and for plant decommissioning and waste management. Controlling the oxidation of the stainless steel fuel cladding and of the graphite moderator in AGRs and preventing steel cracking in the liquid sodium/water heat exchangers in the Prototype Fast Reactor at Dounreay were just two of the substantial challenges he faced.

Brian had become frustrated by the complex, anarchic management of university departments. It is therefore ironical that external events would very quickly demand major changes to the UKAEA's management arrangements that he liked so much, changes that he himself eventually had to drive through and make work. Many of his later years with the UKAEA were devoted to strategy and management, at which he proved just as effective as he had in hands-on science and technology. This was in no small measure because Brian always recognized the importance of networking; he and Carol gave a great deal of their time to making sure he knew well the people with whom he and the UKAEA had to interact, and vice versa.

Few realized it at the time, but 1984 and 1985 were the last years of a quiet, fairly stable period for nuclear power in the UK. The CEGB had largely abandoned the use of oil for high-load-factor power generation because of its cost, and the Department of Energy had forbidden the use of gas in this way because the headline North Sea reserves : production ratio was rapidly reducing as demand grew. In electricity, the Department of Energy had adopted the so-called 'CoCoNuc' (Conservation–Coal–Nuclear) strategy, with nuclear a key factor. The Thatcher government was strongly in favour of nuclear power, especially after its important role in keeping the lights on during the 1984/85 miners' strike. Walter Marshall's influence as CEGB chairman and confidant of the prime minister was considerable; he believed that the UKAEA had a useful role in nuclear technology and had much to offer other industries.

The Sizewell B Inquiry into the case for Britain's switching from AGRs to pressurized water reactors closed in March 1985. The assumption was that, once the industry had decided which reactor it should build in Britain, the government would support it and the CEGB would commission several of the chosen plants. Moreover, because nuclear power was expected to grow fairly quickly around the world it was easy enough for the UKAEA to argue that uranium prices would inevitably rise, making the fast reactor competitive. Finally, the UKAEA had been put on a 'Trading Fund' basis in 1985, giving it more flexibility to pursue commercial work through its 'AEA Technology' brand, largely out of Harwell.

The outlook changed for the worse in 1986. The disaster at Chernobyl created widespread distrust of nuclear power. The collapse in oil prices meant that new nuclear power plants no longer looked economically attractive compared with new fossil-fuel stations. The subsequent falling out between Lord Marshall and the Thatcher government over the way to privatize electricity generation, the industry's division into several companies, and Marshall's departure, eliminated his pro-nuclear influence in the electricity industry. The pressure to make use of the torrent of cheap natural gas then pouring from the North Sea was becoming irresistible, eventually leading to the 'dash for gas'. The last straw for nuclear power was the very public

Figure 7. A visit to Harwell in 1987. From the left: (standing) Ron Bullough FRS, Tony Hughes, David Livesey and Ron Sowden; (seated) Brian, David Clark and Bill Mitchell FRS. (Photograph supplied by Eric Jenkins, courtesy of the NDA Photo Library.) (Online version in colour.)

recognition that the decommissioning costs of early nuclear plants would be much larger than the value of their further generation, effectively making them impossible to privatize.

John Collier returned to the UKAEA from the CEGB in 1986, becoming its chairman in 1987, and he and Brian immediately became close partners in changing the UKAEA to cope with these difficult times and also in fighting for a continuing role for new nuclear plants for UK power generation. Collier very quickly replaced the UKAEA's geographically based management structure with a function-based one in which Brian became the board member responsible for the major nuclear 'programmes', in parallel with Graeme Low as the member for 'sites' to whom the site directors of Harwell, Dounreay, Winfrith, Culham and the Northern Laboratories reported. Brian quickly realized that the programmes that had previously been funded by the government would have to become commercial businesses if the customer base were to be broadened sufficiently to sustain the technical capabilities of the UKAEA in the future (figure 7). The global management consultants, McKinsey & Company, employed by Eyre and Collier to look at broad options for the UKAEA in these troubled times, came to the same conclusion.

There was little dissent within the UKAEA, but for a few months arguments raged about what should be its prime focus. Should it focus on the capabilities that it was trying to sustain or on the businesses that it was trying to develop? In personal terms this would determine the relative importance of site directors and business CEOs, and Brian found himself pitted in argument against Peter Iredale, who was then the director of Harwell. By this time John Collier had been asked to take over the nuclear part of Britain's power generation, which could not be privatized, to be left in the public sector for the time being. One of Brian's great strengths was persuasion, and these arguments effectively ended when he succeeded

Figure 8. The Technical Advisory Group on Structural Integrity (TAGSI) on 25 October 2005 with Ron Bullough, Sir Peter Hirsch FRS and Brian at the centre front. TAGSI was set up in 1988 with Brian as its first chairman; he held office until 1993. Originally a UKAEA committee, it was later sponsored by the nuclear industry, the Ministry of Defence and the Health and Safety Executive. It still exists today. (Photograph supplied by Eric Jenkins, courtesy of the NDA Photo Library.) (Online version in colour.)

in persuading two of the major site directors, Derek Pooley at Winfrith and Stuart Nelson at Risley, to acknowledge the supremacy of the new businesses, despite their immediate personal interest in maintaining the influence of site directors.

Brian became the overall UKAEA CEO in 1990, when Collier left to run 'Nuclear Electric' and was replaced by a non-executive chairman, John Maltby from Burmah Oil, who had been a UKAEA non-executive director for a few years. As CEO, Brian set about making the new organization work; he showed enormous enthusiasm, commitment and drive, managing to inspire his lieutenants to do the same. On the basis of McKinsey's analysis, nine businesses were set up (five nuclear and four non-nuclear), each of which set out to broaden its customer base, reduce costs and improve profit margins, mostly with considerable success.

But the UKAEA already faced a threat to its largest nuclear programme, which was fast reactor development. After 1986 it rapidly became clear that world demand for uranium would not, after all, grow very quickly. The repercussions from Chernobyl and low prices of fossil fuels effectively brought new nuclear plant orders to a complete halt. Moreover, the fuel reprocessing and plutonium-fuel fabrication that are essential for the fast reactor fuel cycle were both looking much more difficult and expensive, after various difficulties at Sellafield. The case for a continued fast reactor programme was consequently much weakened and the government decided in 1988 that the Dounreay Prototype Fast Reactor should close in 1994, leaving only a small fast reactor research programme in place. Collier and Eyre immediately and successfully campaigned to persuade the nuclear utilities to pick up some of the costs of keeping the fast reactor going. An example was the founding of the Technical Advisory Group on Structural Integrity (TAGSI) in 1998 with Brian as its first chairman (figure 8). It was later part funded by the nuclear industry and by the Health and Safety executive. They subsequently tried to pressure the government not to abandon it completely. In this they might

Figure 9. Robert Jackson MP with Brian Eyre, Stuart Nelson and Stephen White promoting AEA Technology in 1992. (Photograph supplied by Eric Jenkins, courtesy of the NDA Photo Library.) (Online version in colour.)

well have succeeded but for an ill-timed technical problem at the fast reactor that eliminated the contribution of electricity sales to its costs for some time. Oil leaking from the bearings of a pump circulating liquid sodium caused carbon build-up at some sub-assembly entry channels, restricting flow and requiring a long reactor shutdown, from which the project never fully recovered. This torpedoed the attempt to sustain its operation beyond 1994.

In addition, although Sizewell B had gone ahead in 1987 with first electrical power in 1995, there were no further orders in prospect in the UK. Both Nuclear Electric under John Collier and the UKAEA under Brian made strenuous efforts to find ways in which new plant orders could be justified in this barren period. Nuclear Electric tried to launch Sizewell C, as either a single or a twin station replicating the Sizewell B design; it was argued that the technical and project management risks would now be small. From the UKAEA, Brian had an important role in chairing a subcommittee that examined the economics of new nuclear stations in the UK. However, in the hostile environment of low fossil prices, especially the very low prices of North Sea gas (then being produced in excess of UK demand) and the tightening of restrictions on many nuclear activities after the Chernobyl disaster, the exercise was in pursuit of a forlorn hope.

Meanwhile Brian's 'day job' as UKAEA CEO in the early 1990s required him to concentrate on making sure that the new commercial businesses were successful. It had long been recognized that the formal name, United Kingdom Atomic Energy Authority, was not ideal for a commercial brand, and so 'AEA Technology' was introduced and launched commercially in 1988.

When a Monopolies and Mergers Commission review of the UKAEA was published in 1992, momentum really developed (figure 9). It endorsed Brian's approach completely, saying that AEA Technology's business activities needed to be removed from the public sector to give the organization the commercial freedom of manoeuvre that it needed. There should be a separate organization to take over the nuclear-related plant, together with the associated decommissioning and radioactive waste treatment and disposal programme.

The Commission also completely endorsed the move from the site-based organization to businesses and to corporate services. The government was persuaded. When John Maltby's term as chairman ended in June 1993, the Department of Energy appointed Sir Anthony Cleaver as chairman, to strengthen the UKAEA's top management commercial expertise for the transfer of AEA Technology to the private sector. Cleaver and Brian moved rapidly to divide the organization into three parts at the start of 1994/95: a UKAEA Government Division, with Pooley as CEO, to become the 'residual' UKAEA when privatization was complete; 'AEA Technology', with Nelson as Operations Director while a new CEO from the private sector was recruited; and a Facilities Services Division, with Andrew Hills as Managing Director, anticipating a trade sale to a sites services organization.

This was all achieved very quickly. The Facilities Services Division was sold to Procord for £12 million in March 1995. AEA Technology was vested as public limited company at the end of March 1996, and its shares were sold in September 1996 for £224 million. Brian remained as UKAEA deputy chairman and chairman of the UKAEA Government Division until formal separation was complete; he then chose to remain with AEA Technology as its deputy chairman until his retirement in 1997. For some time, AEA Technology was a darling of the stock market, its shares rising quickly more than threefold. But its character was rapidly changed by Cleaver and Watson through several trade sales and acquisitions and eventually, long after Brian had left, it failed, sinking into administration from whence it was acquired by Ricardo in 2012 for only £18 million. The UKAEA still exists, now concentrating primarily on fusion research. Its role in nuclear decommissioning and management was eventually subsumed into a new Nuclear Decommissioning Authority.

RETIREMENT, 1997–2014

No one who knew Brian was even slightly surprised to find that he worked just as hard after retirement as before. He threw himself into work with many parts of the British science and engineering community, often through his Fellowship of the Royal Academy of Engineering (1991) or of the Royal Society (2001).

Inter alia, he was a member of the Materials Commission of the Science and Engineering Research Council, a member of the Council of the Particle Physics and Astronomy Research Council and chairman of the Council of the Central Research Laboratories of the Research Councils. He was a member of Council of the Royal Academy of Engineering and of the Royal Society's Committee on the Scientific Aspects of International Security and its Plutonium Working Group. He was a visiting professor at the University of Liverpool, at University College London and at the University of Oxford, supervising postgraduate students and continuing to publish scientific papers. He was a member of the UK Ministry of Defence's 'Defence Nuclear Safety Committee' from 1994 to 2006. He had an important role in resolving the technical problems of the nuclear submarine HMS *Tireless* that caused it to be immobilized in Gibraltar, to the great annoyance of Spain, the great embarrassment of the UK and the great delight of the international media.

He was equally in demand and just as highly regarded outside the UK, becoming a foreign associate of the US National Academy of Engineering in 2009. He replaced Lord Marshall of Goring as the Senior Overseas Advisor to Kansai Electric's Institute of Nuclear Safety System Inc. (INSS) in Japan. It would probably be too much to claim that the creation of INSS and the involvement of Marshall and Eyre caused Kansai to avoid the dreadful nuclear

Figure 10. In retirement: Carol and Brian enjoying their hobby of sailing. (Photograph supplied by Carol Eyre.)
(Online version in colour.)

plant problems that later beset Tokyo Electric Power, but it certainly helped. The Japanese were anxious to establish and support the good working relations with the Oxford Materials Department that Brian helped facilitate. He was also appointed by ESKOM, the South African utility, to be an Independent Member of the Technical Advisory Committee of the Pebble Bed Modular Reactor Board. Brian had long appreciated the possible safety and efficiency of small, modular, high-temperature reactors. He was once again happy to be involved in a project that might help nuclear power make the contribution to securing future energy supplies and combating climate change that he passionately believed it should.

Despite being so busy he always tried hard to make time for his love of boats (figure 10), although as Carol's multiple sclerosis advanced, real sailing became impossible and they had to move to boats that were easier for one person to handle and easier for Carol to board and leave. Because Carol's condition became seriously debilitating, Brian was also forced to take over much of the cooking. He became an expert cook, so that being invited to dinner with the Eyres remained a high-class gastronomic experience, right to the last year or so of his life. Carol's neurological problems were a serious difficulty for them both, but Brian tackled them on all fronts, becoming chairman of the Hampshire Neurological Alliance, a charity dedicated to supporting the family and careers of people with neurological conditions in south Hampshire, where Carol and Brian had their holiday home. Only in the last few months, as the cancer finally overwhelmed him, did his remarkable energy and determination to make things happen, so characteristic of his life, finally fade.

HONOURS AND AWARDS

1992   Fellow of the Royal Academy of Engineering
1993   Commander of the British Empire
2001   Fellow of the Royal Society
2009   Foreign associate, US Academy of Engineering

ACKNOWLEDGEMENTS

The authors are grateful to the following for providing information and their recollections, on Brian's life, personality and career. First, of course, we thank his wife Carol, and sons Peter and Stephen; but then several colleagues: Mark Baker, Ron Bullough FRS, Bryan Edmondson, Colin English, Sir Peter Hirsch FRS, Sir Colin Humphreys FRS, Mike Jenkins, Barry Jones, John Knott FRS, Graeme Low and Stuart Nelson. We also thank Eric Jenkins, who was most helpful in finding suitable photographs from the UKAEA archives.

The frontispiece photograph was taken in 2001 by Prudence Cuming Associates and is reproduced with permission.

REFERENCES TO OTHER AUTHORS

Brailsford, A. D. & Bullough, R. 1972 The rate theory of swelling due to void growth in irradiated metals. *J. Nucl. Mater.* **44**, 121–135.

Cottrell, A. H. & Bilby, B. A. 1949 Dislocation theory of yielding and strain ageing of iron. *Proc. Phys. Soc.* A **62**, 49–62.

Johnson, R. A. 1964 Interstitials and vacancies in α iron. *Phys. Rev.* **134**, A1329–A1336.

BIBLIOGRAPHY

The following publications are those referred to directly in the text. A full bibliography is available as electronic supplementary material at http://dx.doi.org/10.1098/rsbm.2016.0016 or via http://rsbm.royalsocietypublishing.org.

(1)   1958   Preparation of tin and tin alloys for micro-examination. *Metallurgia* **58**, 95–106.

(2)   1959   The solid solubility of antimony in tin. *J. Inst. Metals* **88**, 223–224.

(3)   1962   Observations of slip bands in irradiated pure iron. *Phil. Mag.* **7**, 1609–1613.

(4)   Direct observations of neutron irradiation damage in α-iron. *Phil. Mag.* **7**, 2107–2113.

(5)   1965   (With M. E. Downey) Neutron irradiation damage in molybdenum. *Phil. Mag.* **11**, 53–70.

(6)   (With R. Bullough) On the formation of interstitial loops in b.c.c. metals. *Phil. Mag.* **12**, 31–39.

(7)   (With A. F. Bartlett) An electron microscope study of neutron irradiation damage in alpha-iron. *Phil. Mag.* **12**, 261–272.

(8)   1970   (With J. H. Evans) The low temperature recovery behaviour of nitrogen quenched into molybdenum. *Acta Metall.* **18**, 835–841.

(9)   (With R. Bullough & R. C. Perrin) The growth and stability of voids in irradiated metals. *Nucl. Applics Technol.* **9**, 346–356.

(10) 1971   (With D. M. Maher) Neutron irradiation damage in molybdenum. Part I._Characterisation of small perfect dislocation loops by transmission electron microscopy. *Phil. Mag.* **23**, 409–438.

(11)   (With D. M. Maher & A. F. Bartlett) Neutron irradiation damage in molybdenum. Part II. The influence of crystal perfection and irradiation temperature on the damage structure and its annealing behaviour. *Phil. Mag.* **23**, 439–465.

(12)   (With D. M. Maher & A. F. Bartlett) Neutron irradiation damage in molybdenum. Part IV. A quantitative correlation between irradiated and irradiated-annealed structures. *Phil. Mag.* **24**, 745–765.

(13)   (With D. M. Maher) Neutron irradiation damage in molybdenum. Part V. Mechanism of vacancy and interstitial loop growth during post-irradiation annealing. *Phil. Mag.* **24**, 767–797.

(14) 1973   Transmission electron microscope studies of point defect clusters in fcc and bcc metals. *J. Phys.* F **3**, 422–471.

(15)   (With S. L. Sass) Diffraction from void and bubble arrays in irradiated molybdenum. *Phil. Mag.* **27**, 1447–1453.

(16) 1975   (With C. A. English, H. Wadley & A. Y. Stathopoulos) The effect of solute atoms on collision cascades in copper and molybdenum irradiated with self-ions. In *Int. Conf. on Fundamental Aspects of*

Radiation Damage in Metals, Gatlinburg, Tennessee, USA, 6–10 October 1975 (ed. Mark T. Robinson & F. W. Young Jr), vol. 2, pp. 918–924. Oak Ridge, TN: Oak Ridge National Laboratory.

(17)   (With R. Bullough & K. Krishan) Cascade damage effects on the swelling of irradiated materials. *Proc. R. Soc. Lond.* A **346**, 81–102.

(18)   1976   (With C. A. English & M. L. Jenkins) Heavy-ion damage in α Fe. *Nature* **263**, 400–401.

(19)   1977   (With D. J. Mazey, J. H. Evans, S. K. Erents & G. M. McCracken) A transmission electron microscopy study of molybdenum irradiated with helium ions. *J. Nucl. Mater.* **64**, 145–156.

(20)   (With D. M. Maher & R. C. Perrin) Electron microscope image contrast from small dislocation loops. I. Theoretical predictions. *J. Phys.* F **7**, 1359–1369.

(21)   (With D. M. Maher & R. C. Perrin) Electron microscope image contrast from small dislocation loops. II. Application of theoretical predictions to defect analyses in irradiated metals. *J. Phys.* F **7**, 1371–1382.

(22)   1979   (With S. Holmes, C. A. English & R. C. Perrin) Electron microscope image contrast from small dislocation loops. III. Theoretical predictions for non-edge dislocation loops in a BCC crystal. *J. Phys.* F **9**, 2307–2333.

(23)   1980   (With C. A. English & S. Holmes) Electron microscope image contrast from small dislocation loops. IV. Application of theoretical predictions for non-edge loops to defect analysis in irradiated molybdenum. *J. Phys.* F **10**, 1065–1080.

(24)   (With A. Kumar) Grain boundary segregation and intergranular fracture in molybdenum. *Proc. R. Soc. Lond.* A **370**, 431–458.

PAUL FATT

13 January 1924 — 28 September 2014

Paul Fatt

PAUL FATT

13 January 1924 — 28 September 2014

Elected FRS 1969

By Jonathan F. Ashmore* FRS

*Department of Neuroscience, Physiology and Pharmacology,
University College London, London WC1E 6BT, UK*

Paul Fatt made discoveries that are fundamental to our understanding of synaptic transmission in the nervous system. He grew up in the USA and saw service in World War II, but came to London in 1948 as a research student supported by the GI Bill. His seminal work with Bernard Katz at University College London (UCL), John Eccles in Canberra, and Bernard Ginsborg at UCL was carried out during an intense period between 1950 and 1960. His work with Katz demonstrated for the first time that neurotransmitter is released in small packets, or 'quanta'. His work with Eccles (and Katz) provided an understanding of the mechanism underlying synaptic inhibition, and his work with Ginsborg identified voltage-gated calcium currents for the first time. Furthermore, in the early 1960s his electrical measurements of the muscle transverse tubule system contributed to the early models of excitation–contraction coupling in muscle. The final period of his research career was spent working on phototransduction in the visual system.

EARLY LIFE

Paul Fatt was born on 13 January 1924 in Chicago, USA, and spent his early youth there. He was the second of three sons of parents who had emigrated to the USA in the early twentieth century. His father, David (*ca.* 1880–1968), had come from Eastern Slovakia, which was then part of the Austro-Hungarian empire. It seems that his name was changed from 'Fett' (listed as such on the passenger ship *Sabraus* arriving in New York in 1899) to 'Fatt' by the filing clerk on Ellis Island. David Fatt worked in the leather business in Chicago. Paul's mother, Annie (*née* Arkin; d. 1974), was originally from Lithuania. Both were orthodox Jews and strictly kosher. Neither parent had a scientific training, but all three brothers had scientific careers.

*j.ashmore@ucl.ac.uk

http://dx.doi.org/10.1098/rsbm.2016.0005

169

Paul's elder brother, Irving (1920–96), was trained at California Institute of Technology as a chemical engineer and later, becoming known for his work on the diffusion of oxygen through contact lenses, became Dean of Optometry at the University of California (UC), Berkeley. The younger brother, Milton (1929–2011), became a mathematician, taking a PhD with Beno Eckmann at Eidgenössische Technische Hochschule in Zurich, and then taught at the California State University at Long Beach for many years. Paul had an early interest in biology and palaeontology that was fostered by regular visits to the museums of Chicago while a young boy at Grant's School in Chicago. He then spent just one term at the age of 14 years at Robert Emmet's High School, a school that he was later proud to acknowledge because it was named after an Irish nationalist and rebel leader.

In 1938 the family moved to Los Angeles and settled in the Fairfax district, made up mostly of orthodox Jews. The father ran the leather supply business until the late 1950s when a fire destroyed his stock that was kept in his garage. The move, however, allowed Irving to go to California Institute of Technology. Paul attended a junior school, Mount Vernon High School, before going to Fairfax High School and then on to Los Angeles City College. He was persuaded to specialize in civil engineering but always really wanted to study biology. He confessed that this was what had really interested him, and that his Chicago museum visits as a teenager had served to encourage this interest. Nevertheless, it was his mathematical training as an engineer that resurfaced in his wartime and subsequent scientific career.

When the USA entered World War II in 1941 after the bombing of Pearl Harbor, Paul joined as a reservist. This, at the time, permitted him to continue at City College for a short period. He was eventually called up in 1942 and underwent basic infantry training before being transferred to the eastern USA. Somehow this allowed him still to continue civil engineering in a course at the University of Kentucky in Lexington. By 1943 he was assigned to 291st Field Artillery Battalion, and with his mathematical knowledge he was put to the task of sound ranging to identify enemy guns by triangulating the sources (a method originally introduced into the British Army during World War I by William Lawrence (later Sir Lawrence) Bragg (FRS 1921)).

Paul, by then with the rank of a T4 sergeant, was sent to Europe in 1944. He arrived in France in October, landing on Omaha Beach, having travelled via Liverpool and London, where he acquired a taste for England. He moved with his battalion along with the Allied front and reached Aachen after the Battle of the Bulge on New Year's Day 1945, where he narrowly avoided being hit in a Luftwaffe attack. Towards the end of his life he recalled this traumatic episode as though it had only just happened. After seeing further action, Paul moved on with the advance, eventually crossing the Rhine and along the Lippe Canal by March 1945 and into Dortmund on the north side of the Ruhr valley. His battalion met the end of the war at the Elbe river. The summer was spent in the region until he was demobilized after Japan surrendered; he later admitted to some relief that he did not have to fight in the Pacific war.

Although already enamoured of England by 1945, Paul found himself back in the USA by the end of the year and applied to study biochemistry at the UC Berkeley, under the GI Bill. Having achieved his degree in two years, he joined the biophysics programme, also at UC Berkeley, thinking he would like to put his physics and mathematics to use rather than employ his degree to enter medical school like so many of his contemporaries. During this year he met Vernon Brooks, who was then a zoologist but later turned to neuroscience, and it was Brooks who encouraged him to write to A. V. Hill FRS at University College London, requesting to be taken on as a research student. Because he had another two years of his own GI Bill funding and because it simplified, then as now, any bureaucratic problems, Hill agreed to accept him into the Biophysics Research Unit as a research student.

Paul therefore found himself back in London in August 1948, in time to watch the London Olympics. Much to his delight, entry to the Games was free at Wembley. Hill suggested that, because there was nobody around at that time of summer, he should go down to the Marine Biological Association Laboratories at Plymouth, where Alan (later Sir Alan) Hodgkin FRS (PRS 1970–75), Andrew (later Sir Andrew) Huxley (FRS 1955; PRS 1980–85) and Bernard (later Sir Bernard) Katz (FRS 1952) were working on the action potential mechanism in the squid axon. This was Paul's introduction to using electrical methods to understand basic biological mechanisms.

THE BIOPHYSICS RESEARCH UNIT, UNIVERSITY COLLEGE LONDON

The Biophysics Research Unit, under A. V. Hill, at University College London had been newly re-established in 1946, and by 1948 Katz was working on muscle spindles in his laboratory there (Katz 1950). Back in London from Plymouth, he took on Paul as a PhD student, suggesting as a topic that he should look at the depolarization of striated muscle by acetylcholine (ACh). At the time, although some work had been done by Robert Conway at University College Dublin, who had reported that the endplate region of muscle was depolarized by ACh, there was very little understanding of the detailed mechanisms of how nerves controlled muscle, or even what the mechanism of electrical signalling entailed. It was not really even understood what factors determined the resting potential of excitable cells. Most recordings of electrical activity were carried out using extracellular recording of the potentials that surrounded active nerve cells. Indeed, Paul's first publication used an ingenious liquid electrode chamber using extracellular measurements to show that ACh depolarized the muscle endplate region (1)*. By 1948 Hodgkin and Huxley had started to use the voltage clamp, based on a technique originally devised by Kenneth ('Kacy') Cole and George Marmont at Woods Hole Laboratories, to measure currents that flowed across the membrane of the giant axon of the squid, and so initiated the modern era of membrane biophysics. The work led to the award of a Nobel Prize for Hodgkin and Huxley (together with Sir John Eccles FRS) in 1963. Instead of using extracellular electrodes, they inserted a wire into the axoplasm as a way of gaining electrical access to the inner membrane surface (Hodgkin *et al.* 1952). The idea of inserting a fine glass tube filled with a conducting saline (a 'microelectrode') into a cell had recently been introduced to the Cambridge physiology group by a visiting research fellow, William A. Nastuk, who had learnt the technique from the work of Gilbert Ling and Ralph Gerrard at the University of Chicago. Nastuk paid a visit to London and showed Paul how to make microelectrodes by using a small flame to melt a thin glass tube and pull it out to a fine tip. The electrode was then filled by boiling these electrodes under reduced pressure in a solution of 3 M potassium chloride.

Fatt and Katz started to record membrane potentials from the sartorius muscle of the frog. Eccles, Katz and Stephen Kuffler (ForMemFRS 1971) had previously looked at the endplate potential (EPP) of cat muscle when Katz was in Sydney, Australia (Eccles *et al.* 1942) and so

---

* Numbers in this form refer to the bibliography at the end of the text.

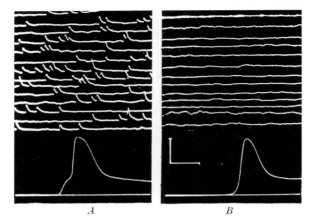

A   *B*

Figure 1. Miniature endplate potentials. The left panel shows small events about 1 mV in amplitude recorded at the
muscle endplate of a frog sartorius muscle; in the right panel the microelectrode has been moved 2 mm away.
(Reproduced from (4), with permission.)

the existence of these potentials was already known. Paul graphically described a typical day
working with Katz during his PhD:

> Leaving Katz at the entrance to the underground station I would go off for a meal at a cheap
> restaurant nearby and then return to the lab to prepare electrodes for the next day. We had the
> idea that electrodes had to be fairly fresh—no more than a day or two old, after which they would
> become brittle from soaking in the KCl filling solution and then break in use … .
>
> Katz would do the dissection and I would make the microelectrodes, then I would manipulate
> the microelectrodes while Katz ground his teeth as it wouldn't go into the muscle fibre where we
> wanted it to. And then he did the photographs. We knew about endplate potentials. And so how do
> you go from endplate potential to the whole thing? And there of course was a big problem because
> you get a contraction, you know, the thing would jump off the electrodes.

Their work showed that the EPP involved an increased ionic permeability depolarizing the
postsynaptic membrane towards zero, the first clear demonstration that synaptic receptors were
chemically gated ion channels (3). The paper, the substance of Paul's PhD thesis, characterized
for the first time the basic properties of the resultant intracellular EPP. However, the most
startling result to come out of this work was the discovery of the existence of miniature EPPs
(2, 4). These are small fluctuations of the membrane potential, of relatively uniform size, and
have come to underpin our understanding of how synapses function: they are the result of
neurotransmitter being released in packets, or 'quanta' (figure 1). This finding came out of a
chance observation in the spring of 1950: when observed at high gain, the endplate region of
the muscle was the site of spontaneous ongoing electrical activity. Although the observation
was published in *Nature* (as 'Some observations of biological noise', with a Dr P. Fatt
and Dr B. Katz as authors (2), although Paul had yet to be awarded a PhD), the origin of
'minEPPs' was unclear. They toyed with the notion that the events were non-propagated action
potentials from the fine nerve branches, induced by thermal fluctuations. When the full paper
came out in *Journal of Physiology* (with the same figure as in *Nature*), these events, dubbed
'miniature endplate potentials' (minEPPs) were unequivocally ascribed to the discharge of
multimolecular 'quanta' of ACh from the nerve terminal. In a series of elegant experiments

appearing in *Journal of Physiology* in 1952 (4), they had demonstrated that minEPPs (later more universally referred to as MEPPs), represented the 'basic coin' of chemical synaptic transmission—and that the full-sized EPP triggered by a nerve impulse represented the superposition of a large number of synchronously occurring MEPPs. They went on to characterize these quantal events in detail, paving the way for Katz's later studies with José del Castillo, Stephen Thesleff and Ricardo Miledi (FRS 1970). The EPP, and its constituent 'miniatures'—or 'minis'—became the fundamental model for explaining neurotransmission at other chemical synapses, including those in the brain.

In the original *Nature* letter they considered, but eliminated, the possibility that the events could be some sort of thermal 'noise' due to ACh colliding with receptors. Some 20 years later ACh receptor 'noise' at the neuromuscular endplate was observed by Katz and Miledi (Katz & Miledi 1970) and became the key method to analyse single-receptor channels, later growing into the full analysis of single-ionic channels by means of the patch-clamp recording methods devised by Erwin Neher (ForMemFRS 1994) and Bert Sakmann (ForMemFRS 1994) and for which they were awarded a Nobel Prize in 1991.

MARINE BIOLOGICAL ASSOCIATION, PLYMOUTH, AND CRUSTACEAN MUSCLE NEUROTRANSMISSION

In addition to their groundbreaking work on the frog endplate, Paul and Katz decamped during the summer months of 1949–51 to the Marine Biological Association Laboratories, Plymouth, to work on the readily available crustacean nerve-muscle preparation. Hodgkin and Huxley worked nearby carrying out their famous squid axon studies during the seasonal availability of the squid. It must have been an unusually fruitful environment for a graduate student. The experiments on the crustacean neuromuscular junction provided not only an elegant description of the electrical properties of invertebrate muscle but also the first real insight into synaptic inhibition, establishing that it arose from a simple shunt of membrane conductance, thereby reducing the excitatory response (5).

THE AUSTRALIAN NATIONAL UNIVERSITY AND SYNAPTIC TRANSMISSION IN THE SPINAL CORD

In the summer of 1952, after the completion of his PhD and already appointed to a position at UCL from which he resigned, Paul left UCL for the John Curtin School in Canberra to work with John ('Jack') Eccles, who had just been appointed to the chair there. He took a surface route back through the USA, visiting laboratories, and a 20-day boat voyage across the Pacific which allowed him plenty of time to read the reprints of papers that he had collected on the way.

The work he undertook with Eccles greatly extended the concepts explaining postsynaptic membrane changes that underlie excitatory and inhibitory transmission in the central nervous system. Eccles was at the time in favour of electrical transmission across nerve endings. Paul's work changed that view profoundly: 'He [Eccles] was really loud and he would shout at me abuse and then I would laugh at him and he would laugh too', Paul later recalled. This was an extremely fruitful period, although Paul remarked that Eccles's style of writing a paper—lay out all the traces on a big table and then fill in the text afterwards—was not to his taste.

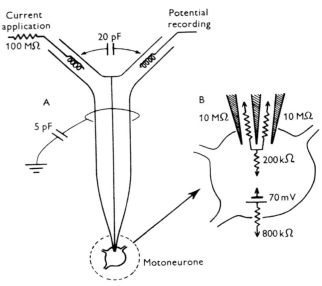

Figure 2. The recording technique developed at Canberra. (*a*) Double-barrelled microelectrode and its electrical connections. (*b*) Enlarged view of the microelectrode tip in the motoneurone. The motoneurone properties represented are the potential and resistance. For diagrammatic purposes the microelectrode tip is shown greatly magnified relative to the motoneurone. (Reproduced from (10), with permission.)

Although Eccles's laboratory had just started to use intracellular microelectrodes, Paul's work in the laboratory resulted in a significant advance in understanding synaptic transmission. The first of their series of major papers established that Ia and Ib afferents to the cat spinal cord generated distinct synaptic potentials (6), using the new developments in the engineering problem of making a micromanipulator stable enough for neuronal recording *in vivo*. The second of the papers provided the first convincing demonstration that excitatory and inhibitory synaptic potentials could be recorded intracellularly from mammalian motoneurones (7). These experiments also identified the inhibitory potentials formed by a recurrent loop onto the motoneurones from the Renshaw cells. Their work together on motoneurones identified the ionic mechanism underlying postsynaptic inhibition as arising predominantly from an increased chloride conductance. This was deduced from the observation that microelectrodes filled with the normal KCl solution led to a progressive diminution and even reversal of the inhibitory postsynaptic potential (9). During this study, Paul was involved in developing the double-barrelled microelectrode technique—two glass barrels fused and twisted together by melting, and then pulled into a fine tip with a diameter of less than 1 μm (figure 2). One barrel was used to record the synaptic potential changes, and the other injected current to alter the ionic composition or preset the membrane potential of the motoneurone. This ingenious and technically extraordinarily dextrous technique was later extended by Curtis, Eccles and colleagues in their elegant experiments on amino acid receptor pharmacology in spinal cord. Eccles was awarded a Nobel Prize in 1963 (together with Hodgkin and Huxley) for his work on excitation and inhibition in nerve cell membranes.

During his work on spinal motoneurones, Paul identified the different regions on the neuron associated with the electrical components of the spike, recognizing for the first time the ways in which the initial segment and soma dendrite determine the action potential properties of central neurons (10–12). In his investigations on the active properties of motoneurone dendrites, Paul obtained some of the first evidence, running against the conventional views of the day, for active impulse invasion of dendrites. With some difficulty he published this work after his return to London, using data he had collected in Canberra (13, 14). He has also been widely credited with the prediction (in a highly influential paper in *Physiological Reviews* (8)) that, on theoretical grounds, transmission could be mediated electrically rather than chemically but only at certain synapses, something confirmed soon afterwards in a classic study by Ed Furshpan and David Potter in the Biophysics Department at UCL (Furshpan & Potter 1959).

INHIBITION AT THE CRUSTACEAN NEUROMUSCULAR JUNCTION

Paul returned to London in 1956 to take up the position of Reader in UCL's Biophysics Department, as it now was called, to which he had been appointed in October 1955. The department was headed by Bernard Katz after A. V. Hill's retirement in 1952. Katz wanted Paul to continue working on the cat spinal cord because this was would be a natural extension of work in the department. Paul decided that the organization of a mammalian spinal cord laboratory would be too great a burden—in Canberra, Eccles had had the resources of a large laboratory to support the effort—and instead decided to take up his work again on the more accessible synapses of the crayfish neuromuscular junction.

The work with Katz before he left for Australia had examined which ions determined the crustacean muscle membrane potential and excitability. The interest in this muscle, as noted by Katz in his earlier work with Kuffler, was that the EPP could be inhibited. Paul and Katz had previously suggested that the inhibition might arise either from competition between the excitatory and inhibitory transmitters for the same postsynaptic receptor, or as a result of an induced membrane permeability increase mainly to potassium (5). The former explanation was not completely satisfactory: it was found that stimulating the inhibitory fibre alone could sometimes produce a change in the membrane potential. With Bernard Ginsborg, a research fellow with a PhD in physics but who had decided to move into physiology instead, Paul revisited the crustacean muscle (15, 16). Rather surprisingly for the time, they found that it was not only sodium that could support all-or-none action potentials, but they also demonstrated for the first time the existence of calcium-mediated action potentials and hence of one of the most important currents, the calcium current, present in biological tissues. All the techniques and the ionic substitutions used in the paper look completely contemporary to a modern reader. The range of compounds tested for substitution experiments, some of which are still used, some superseded, is really surprising. Perhaps most tantalizing of all is a small observation tucked away in a Methods section (17) of the observation by Fatt and Ginsborg that glutamate could not be used as a substitute for chloride in ion replacement experiments because it 'caused a large increase in membrane conductance, possibly through the removal of ionized calcium'. Thus Paul and Ginsborg narrowly missed identifying glutamate as a neurotransmitter for excitation at the crayfish neuromuscular junction. It is now realized to be the major neurotransmitter of the central nervous system. That honour was left to the Takeuchis, again using the crayfish, some six years later (Takeuchi & Takeuchi 1964).

Figure 3. Paul, Milton and Irving Fatt in London, *ca.* 1963.

There was one final experiment to carry out. Using his experience from Canberra and the development of new recording techniques, Paul, together with Boistel, a British Council Scholar, used two separate intracellular microelectrodes, one to pass current and the other to measure membrane potential, and found that during synaptic inhibition crayfish muscle showed an increased permeability to chloride ions (17). At least as remarkably, they provided direct evidence that the mechanism of inhibition was likely to involve γ-amino butyric acid (GABA), a newly described compound, because both GABA and activation of the inhibitory fibres increased the synaptic chloride permeability in a similar way.

MUSCLE T-TUBULE SYSTEM

Established in the Biophysics Department at UCL (figure 3), Paul turned his attention to another problem that had remained unsolved. From their earliest intracellular recordings he and Katz had noticed that the membrane capacitance of a skeletal muscle, in this case the frog sartorius muscle, was much larger than expected from the apparent surface area, given that the specific capacitance of cell membrane is about 1 $\mu F \, cm^{-2}$. Instead, the membrane capacitance was about 7–8 times greater. The problem originated with work of Cole and colleagues in the 1930s in the USA, who had measured the electrical impedance of nerve fibres at frequencies between 1 kHz and 2.5 MHz and found that any attempt to determine the impedance of the muscle fibre membrane gave a different value depending on the frequency used (Curtis & Cole 1936).

To explore this apparent paradox, Paul resorted to measurements of the sort used by Cole. The experiments were designed to use current passed extracellularly across all the fibres in a muscle. The measurement depended on a formula of Rayleigh's that had first been introduced

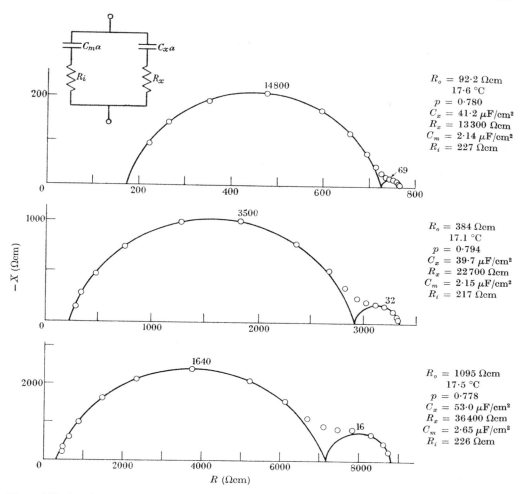

Figure 4 The impedance locus (imaginary part, X, versus real part, R) of a frog muscle as the measuring frequency is progressively increased. The large arc is due to the impedance of the sarcolemma, and the current passing through the branch C_m, R_i of the proposed equivalent circuit for Z_j shown to the right. The smaller arc is due to current through the branch C_x, R_x and was ascribed to the T-tubule system. As external sodium chloride was progressively replaced by sucrose (top to bottom), so increasing the specific resistance of the bathing medium, the relative contributions of each branch changed. (Reproduced from (18).)

for biophysical measurements in 1913. The specific impedance, Z, of a system of conducting rods, each with transverse impedance Z_j, is found to be

$$Z = R_o \frac{(1 + p)\,Z_j + (1 - p)\,R_o}{(1 - p)\,Z_j + (1 + p)\,R_o},$$

where R_o is the resistivity of the bathing medium and p is the volume fraction occupied by the rods. The 'rods' in this case are the individual muscle fibres. The advantage of the approach is that, without the bandwidth limitations imposed by using small glass microelectrodes, the impedance can be studied with great precision at frequencies well over 100 kHz, and in some cases over 1 MHz.

At these high frequencies the surface membrane capacitance can have a vanishingly small impedance and the effect of electrically resistive structures inside the cell becomes evident (figure 4). The problem, however, is that the interpretation of the data depends on a degree of mathematical sophistication that does not immediately appeal to the biologically trained. The inversion of the formula to determine Z_j depends very much on the adopted electrical model of the cell. The chosen model (figure 4) predicts that, as the measurement frequency changes, the real and imaginary components of Z change in a way that would be expected if the current could flow through two parallel arms of the circuit, one describing the surface membrane and the other any membrane system continuous with the sarcolemma (18).

It therefore is something of a surprise that Paul, having become one of the leading exponents of microelectrode recording, should resort to extracellular current measurements in his subsequent scientific work. Although teaching the techniques of recording from the neuromuscular junction to generations of students at UCL in a very popular biophysics laboratory course, he never again used microelectrode recording in his published work. That was left to his scientific collaborator, Gertrude Falk.

The careful study of the T-tubule system using extracellular impedance measurements was linked to a subsequent paper published together with Falk in the same issue of *Proceedings of the Royal Society* B. The latter used intracellular microelectrodes to explore the membrane impedance, but frequencies were limited to less than 10 kHz (19). The two papers came firmly to the conclusion that the skeletal muscle membrane needed to be represented by two conducting paths, one corresponding to the circumferential muscle membrane and the other to a system of intracellular conducting tubules, continuous with the surface, which subsequently became referred to as the T-tubule system of muscle.

The electrical measurements carried out by Paul and Falk therefore complement the direct observation by electron microscopy of the connection of the T-tubule system to the plasma membrane but are not often recognized for their painstaking effort and technical virtuosity.

A series of internal muscle membranes had been described in the electron micrographs by Porter & Palade (1957) and with hindsight can be identified in much earlier light microscopic studies (Huxley 1980). It was only with the introduction of glutaraldehyde fixation in the early 1960s that it became more widely appreciated that there was a system of transverse and highly convoluted tubules that were separate from the sarcoplasmic reticulum, the store from which calcium is released to ensure contraction. There had been earlier work by Andrew Huxley and Robert Taylor (Huxley & Taylor 1958) identifying that the activation of muscle spreads inwards from 'hotspots' on the surface muscle membrane, but evidence for the continuity of the T-tubule system with the surface membrane of muscle remained incomplete until it was shown by the electrical measurements of Paul and Falk and from the electron microscopy by Hugh Huxley FRS (Huxley 1964) and Sally Page (Page 1964), who showed that ferritin had access to the interior of the T-tubule system from the extracellular fluid. The precise molecular mechanism, of how excitation spreading along the T-tubule could couple to the calcium release mechanism in the sarcoplasmic reticulum, had to wait another 25 years for elucidation.

VISUAL TRANSDUCTION

The completion of these two projects in London after Paul's return from Australia really marks both an end of unfinished business remaining from his collaboration with Katz and a watershed in Paul's scientific career. The final 20 years of his work at UCL concerned visual transduction.

'I liked the idea of being able to excite something from a distance with the light', he said. At the time this was more of a revolutionary statement than it might now seem. From around 1963 onwards, Paul's work revolved around the mechanisms by which rhodopsin in photoreceptors could absorb light and then signal to the synapse to trigger activity in the retinal neurons. It had been known from the psychophysical experiments of Selig Hecht, Simon Schlaer and Maurice Pirenne in 1942 that rod photoreceptors could detect the absorption of a single photon. The biochemistry of rhodopsin had been extensively explored by George Wald and his colleagues at Harvard (Hubbard & Wald 1952) and eventually led to the award of a Nobel Prize to Wald in 1967. One of those colleagues was Ruth Hubbard, Wald's wife, who had also been at UCL during the period when Paul started his PhD. The emphasis in Wald's rhodopsin work had been on the early mechanisms of absorption of light and on the several photochemical steps that followed. How the absorption of a single quantum of light could be signalled to the retinal ganglion cells was completely unknown. Hypotheses abounded. The attraction to Paul of tackling one of the big problems of visual biophysics must have been irresistible. Unfortunately, he was just a little too soon: the techniques and the biochemical concepts were not yet available to solve this complex problem.

Paul's first reported experiments with Falk in vision concerned the movement of protons in suspension of rod outer segments (20). Frog rod outer segments (ROSs) are cylinders about 6 μm in diameter and 50 μm in length, and the observation that protons could be taken up in outer segments tallied with measurements of the photochemistry of extracted rhodopsin. It is likely that the ease with which such ROS could be prepared led him to believe that isolated outer segments could be used to understand visual transduction. In part this was true but it became apparent only in the next decade, through the work of W. A. ('Bill') Hagins, Mike Fuortes, Alan Hodgkin and Denis Baylor (ForMemRS 2003), that there was a circulating current from the outer to the inner segments of the photoreceptors and that the ionic gradient dissipated rapidly in the absence of an internal ATP energy source. However, in the mid 1960s Paul was using techniques similar to that which he had employed for studying muscle, except that the stimulating current covered a range of frequencies up to 1 MHz. Although there were clearly changes in the impedance of the ROS suspension on illumination with bright light, Paul and Falk with characteristic honesty were careful to point out that changes in impedance could be ascribed to the light-induced volume changes of the ROS rather than to permeability changes in the plasma membrane itself. The approach was thus less promising than expected (21).

The first convincing reports that photoreceptors signalled electrically appeared in 1965 when Tsuneo Tomita, using intracellular electrodes, reported that cones hyperpolarized when illuminated (Tomita 1965). These data were followed by results from many other groups who showed ever more convincingly that there had to be some sort of intracellular message communicating between the rhodopsin and the photoreceptor membrane conductance. From the early 1970s onwards, Paul's enthusiasm for solving the vertebrate transduction problem, although not completely extinguished, definitely waned. The nature of the visual excitation was eventually solved in 1985 by a then unheard-of group from the USSR Academy of Sciences in Moscow (Fesenko *et al.* 1985), who seemed to have stumbled on the solution almost by mistake: they found, using the new patch-clamp techniques, that the internal messenger was cyclic guanosine monophosphate (cGMP) but controlled by a cascade involving guanine nucleotide-binding proteins (G-proteins), all undiscovered in 1970. For a while, influenced by results of Penn and Hagins (Penn & Hagins 1969), Paul had nursed the idea that rhodopsin was a calcium channel, and that light gated calcium out of the ROS internal lamellae. But although there was some circumstantial evidence for this idea (in particular that a low external calcium concentration around the ROS mimicked the effect of light), by 1979 even he was beginning to have doubts about whether calcium really was the long-sought visual second messenger (23).

A short theoretical note by Paul and Falk in 1974 did, however, have a significant effect on the direction of visual physiology (22). It had been noted that the b-wave of the electroretinogram, thought to be an indicator of the second-order neuronal activity in the retina, was a much more sensitive indicator of light than the extracellular recordings of photoreceptor activity. Their note pointed out that this might arise if the so-called ON bipolar cells had a synapse with the rod photoreceptors that amplified considerably because the action of transmitter release from the rods was to close transmitter-gated channels. Knowing of other synapses for which a transmitter had a similar (unconventional) action, Paul had identified a soluble problem but one to which the conclusion was unexpected. This, as always, was an original and creative idea for the field. Gertrude Falk and I did show subsequently that there was amplification at this synapse (Ashmore & Falk 1980), but it took another 12 years for the mechanisms to be identified. The result, discovered by Falk at UCL (Shiells & Falk 1992) and by Craig Jahr in the USA (Nawy & Jahr 1991) was that, as in photo-transduction itself, ON-bipolar cell synaptic transmission amplified because it was another G-protein-modulated cGMP pathway, which this time determined the postsynaptic response.

In the early 1980s Paul had moved his laboratory and activities to the Biochemistry Department of the Royal Free Hospital. The department was part of 'greater UCL' and conveniently close to his home in Hampstead. There he found a more sympathetic attitude to his search for an oligomeric structure for rhodopsin. The summary of 10 years' work on the search for rhodopsin clusters was published as a final note in 1985 (24).

Within UCL there had been considerable and growing university pressure on the Biophysics Department after Katz's retirement in 1978, because it was seen as doing insufficient teaching and its rationale as a solely research department was less in line with the spirit of the times. Ricardo Miledi had taken over as head of the department but relations between him and Paul were strained. With the departure of Miledi in 1983, the writing was on the wall for Biophysics and it was reabsorbed by the Physiology Department, from which it had originally blossomed. Paul, perhaps with some sense of relief, stopped his scientific work in 1985 when the cGMP hypothesis came out, and he retired from UCL in 1989 at the age of 65 years. Apart from speaking movingly at a symposium in memory of Bernard Katz in 2003, his connections with UCL remained severed.

PERSONAL AND LATER LIFE

Paul eschewed honours. Although he was elected to the Fellowship of the Royal Society in 1969 (he had become a naturalized British citizen in 1965) he did not seek any further nominations or recognition of his achievements. Although it was clear that he had a large circle of influential scientific friends, when he retired all that became a separate episode in his life (figure 5). His entry in *Who's who* was a model of brevity. He was made a Professor of Biophysics at UCL at what many viewed as a surprisingly late stage, in May 1976. He was

Figure 5. From left to right: Murdoch Ritchie FRS, Paul Fatt, Bernard Ginsborg (with back to camera) and Douglas Wilkie FRS in conversation during a Physiological Society meeting at UCL, in 1978. (Photograph by Martin Rosenberg, The Physiological Society; reproduced with permission.)

completely unassuming, reluctant to put himself forward unless he really felt strongly about something, and when he was promoted to professor it was colleagues, particularly Gertrude, who had to tell people. He never would have done so.

Paul's office and laboratory in what is now the UCL Darwin Building (so named because it was built on the site of Charles Darwin's London house on Gower Street) were on the top floor of the two occupied by the Biophysics Department. From that sixth floor, Paul was adamant, it was acceptable to throw small amounts of waste liquid out of the window, because it would have evaporated by the time it reached the street. The small amount of space that he and Gertrude shared was next to the laboratory of E. J. Harris, whom Paul had known ever since joining the department. 'EJ', a stout walker who was reputed to soak his feet in formaldehyde to toughen them up, and Paul often went walking together. John Nicholls FRS recounts that he saw Paul once take a pair of scissors and cut the legs of the trousers he was wearing because Harris had said he must have shorts if they were to go camping together in Scotland (Nicholls 2015).

Paul always retained a sort of boyish and impulsive enthusiasm, the hard-working scientist, and apart from looking like a slightly hunched and dishevelled owl, he always seemed to stay more like one of a younger generation of research fellows at the laboratory bench than one of a group of older scientists with management responsibilities. His lectures on biophysics set the careers of many future neuroscientists. The undergraduate course consisted of mornings of lectures, during which Paul's spidery handwriting would gradually fill the board in a derivation of cable theory, often backtracking and rubbing out the chalk when he decided he had made a mistake. He usually ended the lecture covered in white dust, and most of the students (this was meant to be an undergraduate course) were left slightly mystified by his explanations. The rest of the day was spent in the class laboratory, during which everyone gradually did the Fatt and Katz experiments until they got the equipment to work and data to show for it. For well-primed students it was the best possible introduction to biophysics.

Paul Fatt was married three times. While in Australia he married Ione Copplestone (1926–2015) and had a son Michael (b. 1954), an epidemiologist and presently a full-time specialist GP, and two daughters, Laura (b. 1955) and Harriet (b. 1957). The Australian family changed the surname back the original name Fett after Ione and Paul divorced. When at University College London he married Gertrude Falk (1925–2008), a physiologist trained at Rochester University with an expertise in microelectrode recording who had come in 1961 on a Guggenheim Fellowship to work with Paul. They had met at a conference in Seattle at which Paul was reporting on his new work on the effects of GABA. Paul and Gertrude had a daughter Ilsa (b. 1963), now a jewellery designer. After separating from Gertrude, he married Carla Wartenberg, a freelance translator, in 1985. Paul had met her through the Labour Party. For the last 30 years of his life they lived in Hampstead in a flat overlooking Parliament Hill Fields, allowing Paul to accompany Carla across to the Ladies' Swimming Pool each morning, waiting for her with hot tea after her swim. Hampstead was where he first decided he wanted to live when he came to London in 1948.

Carla Wartenberg has written of her time with Paul. She describes him best as a passionate secular humanist who sometimes could not accept the realities of the world around him. His heroes were mostly rebels and so-called heretics, fighters against what they saw as injustice or obscurantism and who often failed or seemed to have failed. His list included Akhnaton, the Egyptian pharaoh who wished to replace a pantheon of ancient gods by one supreme impersonal deity, the Sun; Giordano Bruno, burned at the stake for refusing to hide his belief in an infinite universe; and Shelley in his aspect as a revolutionary poet. Paul even ordered a small bust of the poet, which he kept on his desk.

Paul was always independent and could be fiercely outspoken at times. He joined the Labour Party and for many years remained an active member (his idea of a good after-lunch exercise for his guests was to go out canvassing for the party) but he resigned in 2003 after the Iraq invasion, in the belief that Labour was abandoning the socialist–humanist ideals that had attracted him to it 50 years earlier. Paul joined Pugwash, the Campaign for Nuclear Disarmament and the World Disarmament campaign, went on marches and demonstrations and gave fiery talks about the horrors of nuclear war to audiences in church halls and civic centres. Paul was outraged when Margaret Thatcher was elected under Statute 12 of the Society and organized a memorandum, which several Fellows signed. Although Paul was not successful (it was pointed out that a repeal of the Statute so soon after her re-election in 1983 might be embarrassing to the Society and to Fellows who had signed) it is conceivable that ultimately he did succeed, because no other sitting prime minister has since been put up for election.

Paul and Carla travelled extensively both abroad and in Britain. Paul was a determined walker and at different times and in different stages they walked almost the whole of the South West Coast Path around from Dorset to Somerset, walked the Pennine Way and spent months staying in Scotland, mainly in the Hebrides. They were energetic travellers around most of the Mediterranean, visiting many countries independently, including Turkey, Syria and, shortly after the massacre at Luxor in 1997, Egypt, finding themselves not surrounded by all the usual tourist crowds. The attraction of being able to explore all the sites that they wanted on just a

Figure 6. Paul in Eire on holiday, *ca.* 2000. (Online version in colour.)

short trip was too much of a lure. Six weeks later they went back again. For the last years of his life, the travels were not quite so far afield but they found a particular liking for a hostel high above Zurich on the Rigiblick. They also liked, and stayed for periods in, a simple stone cottage on the Atlantic coast in southwest county Mayo, Eire (figure 6).

After we had finished a long and memorable oral history interview for the Physiological Society, Paul's parting words to me were, with typical gusto, 'I am going to live to be 100!' Unfortunately he did not achieve that aim, but died a year later, peacefully in his sleep at home on 28 September 2014 at the age of 90 years.

Paul had many opportunities to become a major figure in the organization of modern neuroscience. He chose to be a laboratory scientist first and foremost. His influence on modern neuroscience and biophysics stands in the series of decisive and original discoveries that he made.

ACKNOWLEDGEMENTS

This memoir could not have been written without the help of Paul Fatt's family, in particular Carla Wartenberg, Ilsa Fatt, Michael Fett, Laura Fett and Lois White. Much of the early biographical material comes from a revealing oral history recorded in 2013 by Paul Fatt himself for the Physiological Society Archives (http://www.physoc.org/sites/default/files/page/Paul%20Fatt.pdf) and from the transcript of the Bernard Katz Memorial Symposium at UCL in 2003. The quotations are from these sources. I am also indebted to Francisco J. Alvarez-Leefmans, Stuart Cull-Candy

FRS, Bernard Ginsborg and Sally Page, all former members of the UCL Biophysics Department, for much helpful information, additions to and corrections of my many errors. Aspects of Paul's later life are adapted from a memoir written by Carla Wartenberg.

The frontispiece is a photograph of Paul Fatt in his laboratory in 1979 taken by Francisco J. Alvarez-Leefmans, and is reproduced with permission.

AUTHOR PROFILE

Jonathan Ashmore

Jonathan Ashmore is Bernard Katz Professor of Biophysics at University College London. He completed a PhD in theoretical physics under Tom Kibble FRS and a short postdoctoral fellowship with Abdus Salam FRS at the International Centre for Theoretical Physics in Trieste, Italy, before retraining as a physiologist at UCL. He worked with Paul Fatt and Gertrude Falk between 1974 and 1977 in the Biophysics Department, UCL, on a project identifying high-gain synaptic transmission in the retina. His work since 1980 has been on hearing mechanisms, carried out first at the University of Sussex and then at the University of Bristol before returning to UCL in 1996. He was elected a Fellow of the Royal Society in the same year and was President of the Physiological Society from 2012 to 2014.

REFERENCES TO OTHER AUTHORS

Ashmore, J. F. & Falk, G. 1980 Responses of rod bipolar cells in the dark-adapted retina of the dogfish, *Scyliorhinus canicula*. *J. Physiol.* **300**, 115–150.

Curtis, H. J. & Cole, K. S. 1938 Transverse electric impedance of the squid axon. *J. Gen. Physiol.* **21**, 757–765.

Eccles, J. C., Katz, B. & Kuffler, S. W. 1942 Effect of eserine on neuromuscular transmission. *J. Neurophysiol.* **5**, 211–230.

Fesenko, E. E., Kolesnikov, S. S. & Lyubarsky, A. L. 1985 Induction by cyclic GMP of cationic conductance in plasma membrane of retinal rod outer segment. *Nature* **313**, 310–313.

Furshpan, E. J. & Potter, D. D. 1959 Transmission at the giant motor synapses of the crayfish. *J. Physiol.* **145**, 289–325.

Hodgkin, A. L., Huxley, A. F. & Katz, B. 1952 Measurement of current–voltage relations in the membrane of the giant axon of *Loligo*. *J. Physiol.* **116**, 424–448.

Hubbard, R. & Wald, G. 1952 *Cis–trans* isomers of vitamin A and retinene in the rhodopsin system. *J. Gen. Physiol.* **36**, 269–315.

Huxley, A. F. 1980 *Reflections on muscle* (The Sherrington Lectures, vol. 14). Liverpool University Press.

Huxley, A. F. & Taylor, R. E. 1958 Local activation of striated muscle fibres. *J. Physiol.* **144**, 426–441.

Huxley, H. E. 1964 Evidence for continuity between the central elements of the triads and extracellular space in frog sartorius muscle. *Nature* **202**, 1067–1071.

Katz, B. 1950 Depolarization of sensory terminals and the initiation of impulses in the muscle spindle. *J. Physiol.* **111**, 261–282.

Katz, B. & Miledi, R. 1970 Membrane noise produced by acetylcholine. *Nature* **226**, 962–963.

Nawy, S. & Jahr, C. E. 1991 cGMP-gated conductance in retinal bipolar cells is suppressed by the photoreceptor transmitter. *Neuron* **7**, 677–683.

Nicholls, J. 2015 *Pioneers of neurobiology: my brilliant eccentric heroes*. Sunderland, MA: Sinauer Associates, Inc.

Page, S. G. 1964 The organisation of the sarcoplasmic reticulum in frog muscle. *J. Physiol.* **175**, 10P–11P.

Penn, R. D. & Hagins, W. A. 1969 Signal transmission along retinal rods and the origin of the electroretinographic a-wave. *Nature* **223**, 201–204.

Porter, K. R. & Palade, G. E. 1957 Studies on the endoplasmic reticulum. III. Its form and distribution in striated muscle cells. *J. Biophys. Biochem. Cytol.* **3**, 269–300.

Shiells, R. A. & Falk, G. 1992 The glutamate-receptor linked cGMP cascade of retinal on-bipolar cells is pertussis and cholera toxin-sensitive. *Proc. Biol. Sci.* **247**, 17–20.

Takeuchi, A. & Takeuchi, N. 1964 The effect on crayfish muscle of iontophoretically applied glutamate. *J. Physiol.* **170**, 296–317.

Tomita, T. 1965 Electrophysiological study of the mechanisms subserving color coding in the fish retina. *Cold Spring Harb. Symp. Quant. Biol.* **30**, 559–566.

Bibliography

The following publications are those referred to directly in the text. A full bibliography is available as electronic supplementary material at http://dx.doi.org/10.1098/rsbm.2016.0005 or via http://rsbm.royalsocietypublishing.org.

(1)   1949   The depolarizing action of acetylcholine on muscle. *J. Physiol.* **109**, 10P.

(2)   1950   (With B. Katz) Some observations on biological noise. *Nature* **166**, 597–598.

(3)   1951   (With B. Katz) An analysis of the end-plate potential recorded with an intracellular electrode. *J. Physiol.* **115**, 320–370.

(4)   1952   (With B. Katz) Spontaneous subthreshold activity at motor nerve endings. *J. Physiol.* **117**, 109–128.

(5)   1953   (With B. Katz) The effect of inhibitory nerve impulses on a crustacean muscle fibre. *J. Physiol.* **121**, 374–389.

(6)   1954   (With J. C. Eccles, S. Landgren & G. J. Winsbury) Spinal cord potentials generated by volleys in the large muscle afferents. *J. Physiol.* **125**, 590–606.

(7)   (With J. C. Eccles & K. Koketsu) Cholinergic and inhibitory synapses in a pathway from motor-axon collaterals to motoneurones. *J. Physiol.* **126**, 524–562.

(8)   Biophysics of junctional transmission. *Physiol. Rev.* **34**, 674–710.

(9)   1955   (With J. S. Coombs & J. C. Eccles) The electrical properties of the motoneurone membrane. *J. Physiol.* **130**, 291–325.

(10)   (With J. S. Coombs & J. C. Eccles) The specific ionic conductances and the ionic movements across the motoneuronal membrane that produce the inhibitory post-synaptic potential. *J. Physiol.* **130**, 326–374.

(11)   (With J. S. Coombs & J. C. Eccles) The inhibitory suppression of reflex discharges from motoneurones. *J. Physiol.* **130**, 396–413.

(12)   (With J. S. Coombs & J. C. Eccles) Excitatory synaptic action in motoneurones. *J. Physiol.* **130**, 374–395.

(13)   1957   Electric potentials occurring around a neurone during its antidromic activation. *J. Neurophysiol.* **20**, 27–60.

(14)   Sequence of events in synaptic activation of a motoneurone. *J. Neurophysiol.* **20**, 61–80.

(15)   1958   (With B. L. Ginsborg) The ionic requirements for the production of action potentials in crustacean muscle fibres. *J. Physiol.* **142**, 516–543.

(16)   (With B. L. Ginsborg) The production of regenerative responses in crayfish muscle fibres by the action of calcium, strontium and barium. *J. Physiol.* **140**, 59P–60P.

(17)   (With J. Boistel) Membrane permeability change during inhibitory transmitter action in crustacean muscle. *J. Physiol.* **144**, 176–191.

(18)   1964   An analysis of the transverse electrical impedance of striated muscle. *Proc. R. Soc. Lond.* B **159**, 606–651.

(19)   (With G. Falk) Linear electrical properties of striated muscle fibres observed with intracellular electrodes. *Proc. R. Soc. Lond.* B **160**, 69–123.

(20) 1966 (With G. Falk) Rapid hydrogen ion uptake of rod outer segments and rhodopsin solutions on illumination. *J. Physiol.* **183**, 211–224.

(21) 1968 (With G. Falk) Conductance changes produced by light in rod outer segments. *J. Physiol.* **198**, 647–699.

(22) 1974 (With G. Falk) The dynamic voltage-transfer function for rod–bipolar cell transmission. *Vision Res.* **14**, 739–741.

(23) 1979 Decline of the calcium hypothesis of visual transduction. *Nature* **280**, 355–356.

(24) 1985 Relation of the different forms of frog rhodopsin observed by isoelectric focusing and electrophoresis to a functional model of rhodopsin clusters in the disc membrane. *Vision Res.* **25**, 1865–1867.

GEORGE WILLIAM GRAY CBE MRIA FRSE

4 September 1926 — 12 May 2013

Biogr. Mems Fell. R. Soc. **62**, 187–211 (2016)

GEORGE WILLIAM GRAY CBE MRIA FRSE

4 September 1926 — 12 May 2013

Elected FRS 1983

By John W. Goodby* FRS and Peter Raynes FRS

Department of Chemistry, The University of York, York YO10 5DD, UK

George Gray was a renowned British materials chemist, internationally distinguished for his research into liquid crystals and their applications in flat-panel displays. His seminal invention of the liquid-crystalline cyanobiphenyls underpinned the creation of the modern electronic displays industry, which began with digital watches and has continued through to smart and three-dimensional televisions. There are now more liquid crystal displays in the world than people, and these devices have engendered societal changes through social networking on the Internet. His ability to design, synthesize and utilize self-organizing materials across the various disciplines of science showed that he was a supreme molecular engineer. For his contributions to soft-matter and related advanced technologies he was made a Commander of the British Empire, Kyoto Prize laureate, Fellow of the Royal Society, Fellow of the Royal Society of Edinburgh and Honorary Member of the Royal Irish Academy.

EARLY YEARS AND FAMILY

George Gray was born to John and Jessie Gray in Denny, Scotland, on 4 September 1926. He was an ordinary, happy and mischievous boy brought up in a stable and loving family. He was the only son, but he did have a sister, Catherine, six years his senior. As a child his main interests were making models of ships, reading, and growing plants and gardening. The small town of Denny, where he grew up, was not particularly attractive because it was centred on coal mining, paper manufacture and iron production. However, as it had easy access to the surrounding and beautiful countryside, his memories were of hills and rivers, not industrial grime.

George's mother was much closer to his sister than she was to George; maybe she found him too lively, untidy and mischievous—for example, he once tied his nanny to a chair. In

* john.goodby@york.ac.uk

http://dx.doi.org/10.1098/rsbm.2016.0001

later life they came to understand one another much better. His father, on the other hand, was a great friend to him. He was the pharmacist in Denny, and a trained chemist and botanist, to whom George owed his early interest in science. George's father ran his own business, and it was through being allowed to help in weighing materials and making pills, powders and solutions that George developed a special interest in chemistry. His father used to take George on walks on Sundays, and would talk to him about plants, their medical components, and the chemistry of living processes. Thus, by the time he was 10 years old, George was conversant with atoms and molecules that constituted living and materials systems, and from that point he never wanted to be anything other than a chemist.

His father influenced him strongly along the way as George's interests in science developed. He possessed a collection of books on the history of science, from which George learned about the achievements of scientists such as Faraday, Black, Priestley, Gay-Lussac and Lavoisier. This made him keen to achieve in science, an attitude that was strengthened when he went to the University of Glasgow and was actually taught by leading research chemists such as J. W. (later Sir James) Cook FRS, the eminent steroid chemist, and J. Monteath Robertson (FRS 1945), at that time the youngest UK university professor and a famous X-ray crystallographer. In addition to studying chemistry during the war years, George also took subsidiary subjects in mathematics and physics, graduating in 1946.

Two issues then were implicated in George's move south of the border to the remote and war-torn city of Kingston upon Hull. First, George's father became seriously ill and could not afford to support him through a research degree. Second, George met Professor Monteath Robertson in a corridor in the department at Glasgow. Monteath informed George that there was a temporary post as a laboratory demonstrator at the University College of London (Hull), and that his friend Brynmor Jones was moving there from Sheffield University to become Professor of Chemistry. At that time there was only one post of professor in Hull, but as the college progressed towards receiving its Charter, Brynmor moved upwards to become its Vice Chancellor and was later knighted by the Queen. At the time George had also been offered employment with the Anglo-Iranian Company in Persia, but he turned this down for the opportunity to work in the Department of Chemistry at Hull, where he stayed for the next 40 years. George must have been successful in his first year at Hull because he was quickly appointed as an assistant lecturer. Professor Brynmor Jones pointed out that as a full member of staff he could now study for a higher degree, and suggested two topics, one in reaction kinetics and the other in liquid crystals, which Brynmor had made initial studies on (Jones 1935). George chose the riskier topic of liquid crystals and subsequently submitted his thesis in 1953 entitled 'A study of the synthesis and mesomorphism of certain aromatic carboxylic acids' for the degree of Doctor of Philosophy in the Faculty of Science of the University of London. After a number of years patiently investigating liquid crystals and cell membranes and teaching organic chemistry, George's commitment to the university was recognized by his promotion to the position of Senior Lecturer in 1960. His successes and growing reputation saw him promoted to Reader in Chemistry in 1964, and at the age of 52 years to Professor of Chemistry in 1978. Later he went on to become the Grant Professor of Chemistry and Head of Department. Reflecting on his time at Hull, Gray commented (24)*:

> It was a challenging environment in which to work, perhaps more so than in some better heeled institutions—everyone was keen to succeed, to help one another, and to recover after the lost war-

---

* Numbers in this form refer to the bibliography at the end of the text.

time years. Indeed I owe a great debt to the University of Hull, giving me as it did freedom to do research, develop my own ideas, gain promotion and work in a steadily improving environment supported by many excellent colleagues. Because of this, I remained at Hull for over 40 years before leaving in 1990, after serving as Head of Chemistry and senior Professor.

When George moved to Hull he also met Marjorie Canavan, who worked in pharmacy and nursing. They married in 1953, and subsequently had three daughters. The eldest, Veronica, has three children of her own; Elizabeth was their second daughter, who passed away a few years before George and Marjorie; and the youngest, Caroline, has a son. Possibly following in her father's footsteps, Caroline became an organic research chemist with the pharmaceutical company SmithKline Beecham, working on the synthesis of new pharmaceutical products. Marjorie and George were a loving and endearing couple, and there was always a warm and fun-loving glow around them. Talking about Marjorie, George said 'a scientist (like me) who gives a lot to science sacrifices a lot of his life and time to that process, and he needs behind him a very good woman. I was lucky to have that in my wife' (24). Thus, it was touching that they passed away within two weeks of one another.

THE UNIVERSITY OF HULL, 1946–70

To place George Gray's life of research in organic materials into context, it is worthwhile considering the nature and practical uses of liquid crystals. At the time that George began his research in Hull, liquid crystals were being investigated by only a few scientists across the world; maybe 100 at most. However, by the turn of the millennium liquid crystals used in flat displays had become ubiquitous, with more liquid crystal devices in the world than people. Moreover, their uses in communication devices have resulted in massive societal changes. Apart from displays, liquid crystals have found applications in high-yield-strength polymers (for example Kevlar), low-viscosity fluids (to lubricate computer disc drives), thermochromics (strip thermometers) and gels (for example Cif), to name but a few. They have become the quintessential organic materials of the modern era, and are thought of by many as a fourth state of matter, bridging solids and liquids. Their unique properties are based on the anisotropic shapes of their molecules, which are either rod-like (prolate) or disc-like (oblate), and on their abilities to self-organize into fluid-like phases. The fluidity of their structures permits ease of molecular reorientation by applied external stimuli, such as mechanical, magnetic and/or electrical fields (for an introduction to liquid crystals see Collings (1990) and Collings & Hird (1997)).

With the encouragement of Brynmor Jones, who had already been working on liquid crystals, Gray's methodical research into the synthesis and characterization of mesomorphic materials started in 1946. Thus Gray's early work involved the synthesis and determination of the mesomorphic properties of alkoxybenzoic and alkoxynaphthoic acids, and was probably based on the 1942 thesis by Y. M. May entitled 'Preparation and properties of 4-hydroxy-2-napthoic acids'; May was a research student of Jones's at the University of Sheffield. In his studies Gray determined the melting-point and clearing-point transition temperatures of homologous series of substituted acids as a function of terminal alkoxy chain length, and in some cases determined the presence of smectic (lamellar) phases. He was later aided in this work by his research student F. Marson, who graduated with a Master's degree in 1955 with a thesis called 'Synthesis and mesomorphism of certain substituted n-alkoxy aromatic

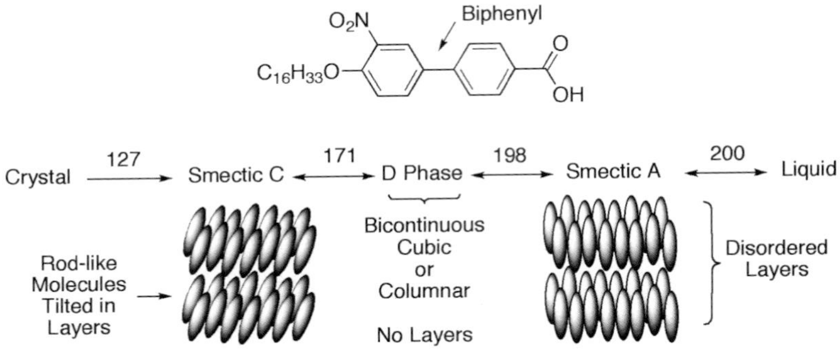

Figure 1. The formation of smectic and bicontinuous liquid crystal phases for 3'-nitro-4'-n-hexadecyloxybiphenyl carboxylic acid (temperatures in degrees Celsius).

carboxylic acids'. Two observations can be made: first, with the synthesis of substituted biphenyl carboxylic acids it was clear that Gray was already investigating the liquid crystal properties of biphenyls 20 years before he employed the same motif in the structures of the groundbreaking nematogens used in displays, and second, the enigmatic rod-like 3'-nitro-4'-n-hexadecyloxybiphenyl and 3'-nitro-4'-n-octadecyloxybiphenyl carboxylic acids were also prepared (for example see figure 1). These two remarkable materials were described by Marson as exhibiting either two or three smectic phases respectively, but today, as a result of the collaborative work with J. W. Goodby (19), A. J. Leadbetter (20) and J. E. Lydon (Lydon 1984, pp. 75–76), they are known to exhibit bicontinuous cubic (gyroid) phases sandwiched between the smectic A or liquid and C phases as a function of temperature. The fundamental underlying importance of this work was that it showed that curvature of the packing of rod-like molecules could affect the induction of mesophase formation in soft matter systems. Similar effects are now found for 'blue phases' (3), surfactants, amphiphiles, micelles, DNA complexes and di-block copolymers, among others (Bruce *et al.* 2006).

The confidence in the transition temperatures of Gray's early work can be attributed to his design and construction by the technicians in the Department of Chemistry of an electrically controlled hot stage for attachment to his optical microscope, which allowed samples to be viewed while the temperature was being raised (1). A side elevation and plan of the block are shown in figure 2*a*. The hot stage consisted of two cylindrical pieces of copper about 4.5 inches in diameter and 0.625 inches thick. Both had a centrally drilled hole 0.5 inch in diameter. A slide slot and aperture for insertion of a thermometer were cut out. Below the lower block a coil of nichrome wire 22 feet long was wound on a mica disc, which was insulated with other mica discs from the copper block and brass plate below, as shown in figure 2*b*. The heating rate was controlled by using a rheostat; the whole apparatus was insulated with asbestos and covered with a brass outer casing. Glass plates, top and bottom, were used to prevent air currents, and melting points between 40 and 300 °C were determined regularly, via standards, with a high degree of accuracy. This instrumentation was ultimately critical to the liquid crystal research of the era because no methods, other than microscopy, were available for quantitative studies. No doubt Gray's understanding of dislocations and disclinations in defect textures, and his having access to thermal polarized light microscopic analysis, gave him an internationally leading edge in the field.

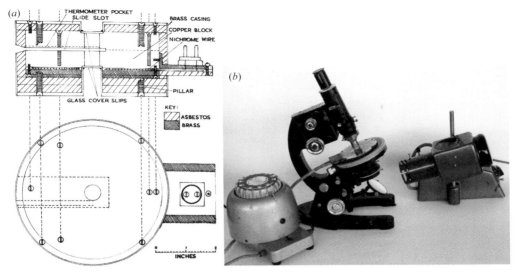

Figure 2. The microscope hot stage developed for the study of thermotropic liquid crystals. (*a*) Schematic representation of the construction of the hot stage. (*b*) The microscope, light source and rheostat of the early microscopy equipment designed and used by Gray.

In about 1952–53 Gray's research into liquid crystals expanded beyond the study of the effect of aliphatic chain length and lateral substitution on the mesomorphic properties of materials. Instead he switched his work to the investigation of the design and structure of the central aromatic core unit and the linking groups, usually Schiff bases that were attached to it. With MSc students J. B. Hartley (1954) and P. Culling (1956), and doctoral student A. Ibbotson (1957) the steric effects on the mesomorphism of polycyclic compounds were studied. In particular an attempt was made to establish whether the non-sterically affected biphenyl ring system that Gray had previously been investigating was planar, twisted at a fixed angle about the 1:1′ bond, or freely rotating about this bond in the mesomorphic states of its derivatives. This was investigated by preparing the comparative 7-n-alkoxyfluorene-2-carboxylic acids and their alkyl esters, the 2-n-alkoxybenzylideneaminofluorenes, the 2:7-di-(*p*-n-alkoxybenzylideneamino)fluorenes and the analogous fluorenone derivatives. By comparing the mesomorphic properties of these compounds, in which the tricyclic fluorene ring system was planar, with those of the biphenyl analogues, carrying substituents in the 4 or 4:4′ positions, indefinite conclusions were reached. However, they suggested that the biphenyl ring system might be planar in the smectic and nematic mesophases.

Further studies on the 4-*p*-n-alkoxybenzylideneamino-3′-2′-2- and 3-chlorobiphenyls were also made. The nematic thermal stabilities of the 2′-chloro and 2-chloro isomers were found to be much lower than those of 3′ and 3 isomers. This was explained by interannular twisting of the biphenyl rings from co-planarity by the chlorine atoms in the *ortho* positions. The isomeric mono-anils bearing bromine and methyl substituents were found to give similar results. By comparing the mesomorphic properties of mono-anils with different substituents in the 2 position they concluded that the nematic thermal stabilities decreased with increasing substituent size, i.e. with increasing interannular angle, and therefore that free rotation could not occur about the 1:1′ bond in the nematic state. The outcome was that for the biphenyl the

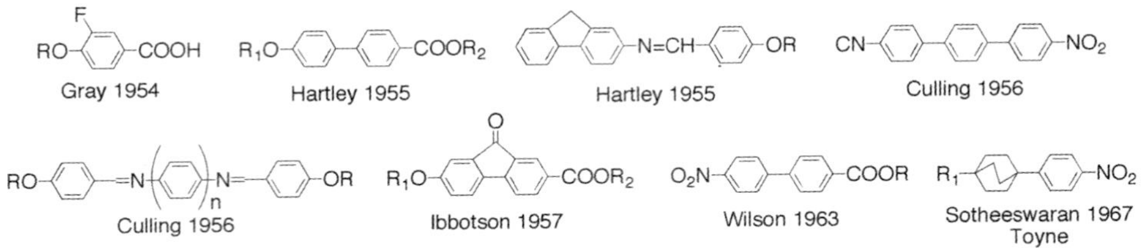

Figure 3. Early liquid crystal materials prepared in Hull.

interannular angle was suggested to be certainly much less than the 45° in solution, and might be as little as 0°, i.e. the angle for biphenyl in the crystal state.

Although these conclusions were speculative, and have not been upheld by later neutron scattering studies on molecular dynamics in liquid crystals, it is clear that Gray was starting to build property–structure correlations about mesophase formation and stability. His cumulative studies formed the basis for his 1962 book *Molecular structure and the properties of liquid crystals* (2). At the time this was the most important chemistry text ever brought out on the subject of liquid crystals, and it gave Gray international repute. However, he also viewed writing the book as particularly important because he could see a possible end to his liquid crystal research as funding became increasingly scarce.

As his early work on liquid crystals began to bear fruit, the direction of the field began to waver as a result of the subject's becoming labelled as a scientific curiosity. Looking for ways forward, Gray became influenced by the department's interest in the kinetics of organic chemical reactions, most notably in the area of the nitration of materials possessing aromatic rings, as seen in Marson's thesis. The research of Culling saw Gray extend his interests, by default, into rod-like systems based on the terphenyl motif. Although nitration and polynitration of unsubstituted *p*-terphenyl were the main topics of the work, Culling also included research into 4-cyano-*p*-terphenyl. This initial work was followed by more extensive research by D. Lewis, as reported in his doctoral thesis 'A study of the nitration of *p*-terphenyl'. Figure 3 shows the structures of some of the more relevant materials prepared in Hull on the path towards suitable materials for displays, with the nitro-substituted biphenylyl ester prepared by R. C. Wilson (whose 1963 PhD thesis was entitled 'Transmission of electronic effects in certain biphenyl systems') coming very close to the successful design used for the groundbreaking 4-n-alkyl 4'-cyanobiphenyls.

With these studies, which were published as a 13-part series of papers on mesomorphism and chemical constitution in *Journal of the Chemical Society*, Gray developed the following property–structure correlations for the molecular design of liquid crystals, which he later applied extensively in his future research on display materials:

- regular trends in liquid crystal transition temperatures within homologous series;
- the dependence of nematic thermal stability on molecular breadth and lateral substitutent size;
- the strong influence of steric twisting by a lateral group in depressing mesophase thermal stability;
- the role of aromatic core size and type on phase type and phase stability;
- core shielding effects in diminishing the depressing effects of lateral groups;
- the important nematic terminal group efficiency order;

- the more subtle dependence of smectic thermal stability on a combination of lateral group size and dipole moment.

Gray possessed the relevant knowhow and skills that underpinned the seminal invention of the liquid crystals that formed the basis of the modern flat-panel displays industry. Ten years later, opportunity arrived and the liquid-crystalline terphenyls were united with their biphenyl analogues, and thereby nematic formulations were produced that had wide operating temperatures for displays that could be used by the electronics industry for applications in the desert and the tundra alike.

However, the inventions of new display concepts were not even on the horizon in 1960, and consequently funding for research into liquid crystals was becoming scarce, particularly for universities such as Hull, and so Gray turned to industry, and in particular to Reckitt & Sons Ltd of Hull for help. Over the following decade the company funded research into bacterial and germicidal action against various organisms, and the investigation of the structures and properties of their lipopolysaccharides. Seven PhD theses resulted from these studies, and as a consequence more than 50% of Gray's research became involved in the investigation of the cell walls of bacterial membranes, which after all are another form of liquid crystals. One of Gray's students, S. G. Wilkinson (now deceased), later became Professor of Biological Chemistry at the University of Hull, and so began Gray's dynasty in the Chemistry Department. Wilkinson once remarked that during his PhD research, Gray carried on studying thermotropic liquid crystals by working at the bench, but that he (Wilkinson) never knew what he was doing. This observation was frequently made in the years to come: Gray was careful about what he divulged, even to his own researchers.

A PROGRAMME ON FLAT-PANEL DISPLAYS, 1970–72

As the 1960s progressed it became clear that funding for liquid crystals would not be forthcoming. Gray had applied to the Science Research Council for support, but was told that he should find a synthesis chemist to work with! This was a point of contention he often raised with the councils. So he seemed destined to work on biological membranes for the foreseeable future. Then in the late 1960s the Radio Company of American (RCA) started to take an interest in alternative displays to the cathode ray tube, and in particular displays based on liquid crystals. This work was not unknown to researchers at the Royal Radar Establishment (RRE) at Malvern; Tom Elliott (FRS 1988) had attended a conference at the National Bureau of Standards in Boulder, Colorado, and heard about and saw a demonstration of a liquid crystal display made by RCA (C. T. Elliott, personal communication). He wrote an internal RRE report on what he had seen, which sparked a lot of interest. The story of how RRE and Hull University began to collaborate in the research of liquid crystals is fascinating, and on such small coincidences do such big discoveries, inventions and societal changes turn. The story was delightfully recalled in his own words by Cyril Hilsum FRS, who was at the time a leading physicist at RRE (Hilsum 1984).

> It was on this scene that an exotic figure emerged. He was by no means as well known then as he has come to be, and I use 'exotic' in the sense that he was foreign to the context of science and a research laboratory, not with the alternative meaning 'bizarre'. The story really begins with him, and it is strange to think that the UK liquid crystal fraternity will always be indebted to him. He was the Minister of State for Technology, Mr John Stonehouse. In March 1967,

Mr Stonehouse paid his first visit to RRE, and the conversation with the Director, Dr—now Sir—George MacFarlane FRS ranged over many topics. They touched on the financial return from inventions—the world does not change a lot—and MacFarlane pointed out that UK royalties to RCA on the shadow-mask colour TV tube cost more than the development costs of Concorde. This impressive fact, the truth of which I have never been able to establish, remained in the mind of the Minister during his journey back to London, and festered overnight. Early next morning he rang the Director, and said he was convinced that the UK should mount a programme to invent a solid state alternative to the shadow-mask tube! George MacFarlane was certainly taken aback, but he is a resilient character who does not give in easily. He summoned to his office David Parkinson, then Head of the Physics Group, and me. He explained the situation in which he found himself, and asked what the chances were of RRE making a solid state flat panel colour TV. David turned white, and I said, 'None whatever'. Neither response offered the basis of a constructive reply to the Minister, so we agreed on the conventional Civil Service reaction—we would set up a Working Party to study the topic.

David Parkinson chaired the Working Party, and by October we were able to recommend work on semiconductor lamps, for very simple displays (Parkinson 1967). This was almost a diversion. The real task of the group was very difficult and time-consuming, because we had to assess effects and materials quite unknown to us. Among the topics brought to our notice early in 1968 were liquid crystals. Here I must digress for a moment and explain the Ministry of Defence system for procurement of electronic components for the Armed Services. Since 1938 this has been the responsibility of an organization with the initials CVD. Until 1950 the initials stood for 'Committee for Valve Development', but later it became more appropriate to change to 'Components, Valves and Devices'. CVD operates through a simple structure of committees, manned by Scientific Civil Servants, each committee dealing with one group of components. It is normal for each committee to organize two or three meetings a year with industrial and academic scientists on particular topics of interest. Now we can return to our theme.

By 1968 CVD had passed the responsibility for Displays to me, and I asked Leslie Large, a scientist in CVD, to organize a meeting on Liquid Crystals. It took place on 1 October. There is no written record of this meeting, but it remains fresh in the minds of several of the participants. The high spot was a review by the person then regarded as the UK authority, and at the end of his talk I called for questions. There being none, I attempted to fill an embarrassing gap, and having noticed that the light from the slide projector, reflected from his liquid crystal sample, cast a curiously shaped and patterned curve on the screen, asked him how this happened. He attempted an explanation, realized this was wrong, remembered a reference to the phenomenon in a book he carried, rapidly turned the pages of this book, decided that the reference was in his loose notes, upended these, dropped both the notes and the book, and then knelt on the floor picking up the pieces. The meeting was rapidly escaping from my control when a quiet voice from the back of the room said 'I wonder if I can help'. I lifted my eyes from the grovelling body of my key speaker and replied 'I'd be most obliged if you would', and my rescuer proceeded to give a succinct explanation. That was the first time I met George Gray. The rest of the meeting was distinguished for the lack of useful knowledge demonstrated by most of our community, and at the end, when Les Large asked if we had reached any conclusions. I replied, 'Yes, we must put the man from Hull on a contract'. This was easily said, but at that time we had no justification for any liquid crystal programme at all. In fact, in August, in response to a query from MOD Patents Branch, I had written (Hilsum 1984), 'I may say we are not optimistic about liquid crystals. I would be surprised if our Working Party recommends that work should be started'. I was influenced in this by two inputs to the Working Party a month earlier, one writing 'Ferroelectrics probably offer the best hope of finding large enough electrooptic effects at room temperature', and another, 'Liquid crystals may have a minor role for displays in high ambient lighting, but they will make no impact on Black and White or Colour TV'.

To counter this pessimism, there was in late October a positive report of a liquid crystal electrooptic effect, which might have display applications [Heilmeier *et al.* 1968*a, b*]. This came from Heilmeier, Zanoni & Barton of RCA, who demonstrated dynamic scattering, albeit at temperatures between 77 °C and 90 °C. They claimed to have a proprietary mixture operating at room temperature, but gave no details. The record, and all memories, go curiously flaccid at this point, and for a year nothing worthy of mention happened in the UK on liquid crystals. The Working Party ground away, by now under my chairmanship, for David Parkinson had been translated to more responsible tasks. In October 1969, one year after the CVD meeting, the first draft of the Working Party Report appeared, proposing to work on eight topics, but excluding liquid crystals.

The final version was issued in December (Hilsum 1969), and it differed from the draft in one crucial and fascinating respect. The relevant extract read, 'One system is worth immediate attention. This is the display based on liquid crystals'. Such a volte-face is difficult to explain, particularly since no earth-shattering discoveries were revealed to me in the interim.

The draft had recommended a large programme on ferroelectric ceramics, and a small exploratory contract on liquid crystals. However, Hilsum was unhappy with this and replaced everywhere the words 'ceramic ferroelectrics' with 'liquid crystals' in the final version, and in April 1970 CVD offered Gray a two-year contract to work on 'Substances exhibiting liquid crystal states at room temperature' at a maximum expenditure of £2177 per annum.

A SCIENTIFIC REVOLUTION

The work on materials started in Hull in October 1970 with two researchers, John Nash, who was a postdoctoral fellow, and Ken Harrison (see figure 4), who was appointed to the RRE contract even though he was involved in the writing of his thesis, which was entitled 'The effects of structural changes on the liquid crystalline properties of certain esters', for which he was awarded a PhD in 1972.

The initial research at Hull was not particularly well focused. Target structures for new liquid crystals were based on materials reported by RCA and IBM. The preferred devices at that time used the dynamic scattering mode, which required materials with negative dielectric anisotropy ($-\Delta\varepsilon$), and so low-melting materials with rod-like structures and lateral dipoles relative to the molecular long axes were sought. However, purities and problems for many families of materials were soon raised; they were often found to exhibit electrolytical instability, ease of oxidation, or degradation on exposure to ultraviolet radiation. Thus, the Hull group worked on a variety of Schiff bases, azobenzenes, stilbenes, carbonates, carboxylic esters and ultra-pure Schiff bases, among others, but to little effect. However, in 1970 a paper (Leslie 1970) at the 3rd International Liquid Crystal Conference in Berlin on the reorientation of nematic liquid crystals in a twisted configuration by magnetic fields by Frank Leslie (FRS 1995), who was Gray's lifelong friend, coupled with device experiments on rotating the plane of polarized light in a twisted nematic configuration by J. F. Dreyer at the same conference (Dreyer 1970) led to the invention of the twisted nematic liquid crystal display (TNLCD) by Schadt and Helfrich of Hoffmann-La Roche (Schadt & Helfrich 1971) This device required materials of positive dielectric anisotropy ($+\Delta\varepsilon$) and, as with all new materials, nematic phases at room temperature. Thus, the search was on for stable, $+\Delta\varepsilon$, low-melting nematogens that could operate over wide temperature ranges. This was a relatively tall order considering what little was known at the time about the design and synthesis of such liquid crystals for displays.

Figure 4. George Gray and Ken Harrison (early 1970s).

As with the studies on materials for dynamic scattering devices, Gray would have realized that the preparation of liquid-crystalline Schiff bases and esters was relatively straightforward, and therefore there could be a rapid turnaround in material design and construction. However, the introduction of a longitudinal dipolar unit was limited to a few functional groups. He was used to employing nitro groups in his previous studies, but he knew that such materials were often weakly yellow and had a high melting point, and thus the best option would have been a terminal nitrile moiety. Again he would have realized that most of the instabilities for such materials were associated with the incorporation of a central linking group, which actually was being employed for ease of synthesis. His bold step was to omit the linkage and, from pre-RRE research, to incorporate a terminal cyano group into the structure of biphenyl to give stable materials with a high $+\Delta\varepsilon$. This design could only lead to the synthesis of the now famous cyanobiphenyls (4). The most important of these was 4-n-pentyl-4'-cyanobiphenyl, which was first synthesized by Harrison while Gray and Nash were at the 1972 International Liquid Crystal Conference at Kent State University in the USA. They returned to find that Harrison had a flask with a beautiful nematic liquid crystal flowing around it in its mesophase at room temperature (see figure 5).

4-n-Pentyl-4'-cyanobiphenyl is commonly known as 5CB to researchers across the world, but for proprietary reasons it was called K15 (K after Ken Harrison) and ultimately a homologue of the K3n series of compounds, where n is aliphatic chain length. Thus it was the first example of a colourless, photochemically, oxidatively and electrolytically

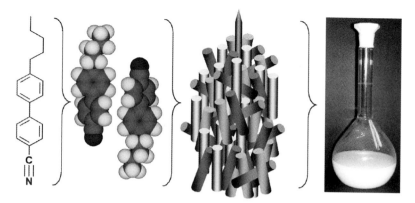

Figure 5. 4-n-Pentyl-4′-cyanobiphenyl, showing its structure, molecular architecture,
bulk mesophase structure and physical appearance.

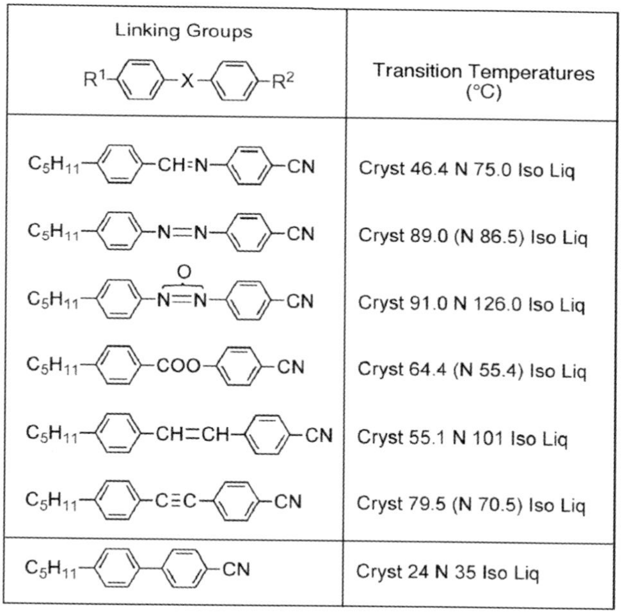

Linking Groups R¹–◯–X–◯–R²	Transition Temperatures (°C)
C_5H_{11}–◯–CH=N–◯–CN	Cryst 46.4 N 75.0 Iso Liq
C_5H_{11}–◯–N=N–◯–CN	Cryst 89.0 (N 86.5) Iso Liq
C_5H_{11}–◯–N=N(O)–◯–CN	Cryst 91.0 N 126.0 Iso Liq
C_5H_{11}–◯–COO–◯–CN	Cryst 64.4 (N 55.4) Iso Liq
C_5H_{11}–◯–CH=CH–◯–CN	Cryst 55.1 N 101 Iso Liq
C_5H_{11}–◯–C≡C–◯–CN	Cryst 79.5 (N 70.5) Iso Liq
C_5H_{11}–◯–◯–CN	Cryst 24 N 35 Iso Liq

Figure 6. The effect of linking group on transition temperatures (degrees Celsius) in comparison with the values
obtained when the linkage was omitted as for 4′-pentyl-4-cyanobiphenyl (bottom).

stable nematogen with a melting point near to room temperature, and physical properties suited for use in TNLCDs. Figure 6 shows how the mesophase behaviour of this material with the missing link compares with those of analogues having various linking groups. The figure shows that apart from the Schiff base the other materials have quite high melting points, and several exhibit monotropic nematic phases that occur below the melting point on supercooling. Without forming mixtures none of the materials could be considered suitable materials for displays. The low melting point of 5CB therefore paved the way to the creation of low-melting materials with wide mesophase temperature ranges for displays. Consequently Gray would often use the discovery of cyanobiphenyls as an example of the importance of basic research; to quote him (23):

> I knew what I was doing by using the cyano group to compensate for loss of molecular length, while at the same time providing the strongly polar molecular structure needed for the electric field to switch on the display. This I stress was not luck ... the fundamental science was secure ... we knew what we were doing.

One example of a cyanobiphenyl was obviously not enough, and realizing that mixtures consisting of homologues would need to be prepared, Harrison and Nash (and Martin Pellatt from BDH Ltd) set out to synthesize a well-chosen selection of the 4-n-alkyl-4′-cyanobiphenyls (K3n series) and 4-n-alkoxy-4′-cyanobiphenyls (M3n series; M after Martin Pellatt). From his earlier studies Gray knew that the homologous series would exhibit an odd–even effect with respect to the transition temperature from the nematic phase to the isotropic liquid, and that the members with an odd number of carbon atoms in the alkyl chain would have higher values than the even-numbered homologues for the K3n series. Thus 3CB, 5CB and 7CB would have seemed obvious choices to prepare. The melting points were shown to fall precipitously on passing from the butyl to the pentyl homologue in both series, and then to recover slowly as the chain length was increased. A length of five carbon atoms, i.e. for K15 and M15, is essentially enough to create a nanosegregated system between the non-polar aliphatic chain and the aromatic biphenylyl moiety. As the alkyl chain was increased, smectic phases were introduced in both series, thereby showing that the aliphatic parts of the materials were starting to dominate the intermolecular interactions. In essence there is a balance point between the non-polarizable and polarizable segments for the two sets of materials, which occurs between the pentyl and heptyl homologues. Such balance points are similar in nature to the hydrophobic–hydrophilic balances found for surfactants and lipids, for example.

From a practical point of view there was a need to raise the temperatures of the transitions from nematic to liquid in mixtures. This was achieved by extending the aromatic core units of the K series by one phenyl ring to give the terphenyl analogues, and the pentyl-substituted material, called 5CT (T15), was the obvious candidate. Thus the way forward for creating practical materials was in place. With patents filed on 9 November 1972, it was time to expand the research activities, to include more users and to commercialize the inventions. Eventually two consortia were created, one for devices and the other for materials, to exploit the newly developing technologies in flat-panel displays. The Materials consortium included RRE, Hull University and BDH (which became part of E. Merck in 1973). Originally ICI and Fisons had expressed interest in commercializing the materials, but previous productive R&D with BDH meant that the company was considered a more favourable collaborator. After discussions with Dr Ben Sturgeon, Director of Research, BDH accepted a contract towards the end of December 1972, and within three months had provided samples of 5CB. Thus, with the process development provided by Sturgeon and his team at BDH Chemicals (see figure 7), high-purity cyanobiphenyl and terphenyl liquid crystals found their way into the many different mixture formulations and into various forms of display, thereby becoming templates for the development of materials for TNLCDs.

With the 'three wise men', Hilsum, Gray and Sturgeon (see figure 8), in place driving forward the collaboration, the next important development towards commercialization of cyanobiphenyls was the design of mixture formulations that possessed suitable phases and transition temperatures. Peter Raynes (FRS 1987), a recent recruit to RRE from Cambridge

Figure 7. Scaling up at BDH for the chemical synthesis of cyanobiphenyls.

Figure 8. George Gray, Cyril Hilsum and Ben Sturgeon at the University of Hull for the Queen's Award for Technological Achievement, 1979.

University, introduced a step change in this process by realizing that there was a possible short-cut to determining the eutectic point for a multi-component mixture via an extension of thermodynamic theory for mixed systems. He developed a more accurate semi-empirical method to give melting points of eutectic mixtures to within 5 °C, and clearing points to within 2 °C of experimental results (Hulme *et al.* 1974; Raynes 1980). In 1974 Raynes made

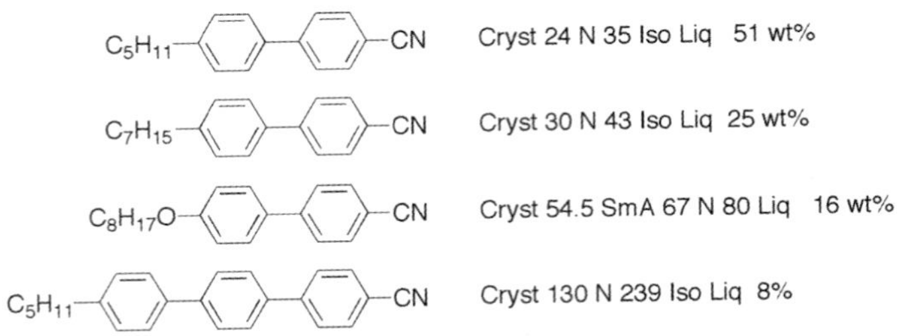

Figure 9. The composition of the technologically important nematic liquid crystal formulation E7.

Figure 10. George Gray in his synthesis laboratory and the products of his research.

a four-component eutectic mixture, called E7, that possessed a nematic phase that existed over a temperature range of −9 to +59 °C. Its composition is shown in figure 9, and at the time it met all of the specifications required by the manufacturers of watch displays, and it became a universally used nematic mixture (see figure 10).

As a consequence of the work formulating mixtures with suitable temperature ranges of operation for practical applications, it became possible to build on the more popular mixtures and to introduce additives that would be capable of 'tweaking' physical properties of the mixtures to give improved material performance for the device manufacturers. Modern mixtures are now tailor-made for device manufacturers in such a way that they are designed to respond appropriately to applied electrical fields, to possess suitable birefringence for required cell spacings in devices, to have extraordinarily low conductivities, to reduce image sticking, and so on; consequently formulation has now become a 'technical art'.

From the mid 1970s, with his research focused on the applications of his work on display materials, and with funding from CVD and RRE secure, Gray was able to use the two interconnected research drivers as springboards for new ventures into liquid crystals in the search for new materials that might upstage cyanobiphenyls. Thus, his ensuing work formed the basis of much of the fundamental materials research in the now rapidly growing subject of liquid crystals, thereby becoming a superb example of multidisciplinary nano-engineering of novel states of matter at its very best. The result was that his materials became the subjects of several thousand articles by other scientists, and numerous awards of medals and fellowships.

However, success came with a downside, as Gray noted (20):

> These results are often said to be my claim to fame but there are those (mainly non-performers) who like to stress the negative aspect that no European Display Production of any consequence developed from our materials chemistry success. I think this is supposed to upset me, and indeed the English do love to knock success and the successful. Frankly, I cared very little that UK Ltd did not benefit device-wise from the work and that this area was exploited to the full in Japan and the Far East. I was happy to see that society in its widest international sense was benefiting by my science, and was not too troubled that the coffers of Electronic Companies did not profit thereby. It did however please me that the UK chemical industry benefited financially from my work—a conveniently forgotten fact. Also, I would like to emphasize some other much wider, and to me equally important advantages and consequences, that stemmed from our simple discovery of the cyanobiphenyls.

Thus, in the following we depart from the discovery and commercialization of cyanobiphenyls and recount Gray's contributions to other aspects of fundamental and applied research in liquid crystals.

BEYOND CYANOBIPHENYLS, 1974–90

Soon after cyanobiphenyls were reaching the commercialization stage, Nash and Harrison left Hull and were replaced by postdoctoral researchers Dave Coates and Alan Mosley, and research students Damien McDonnell and John Goodby (FRS 2011). Coates and McDonnell were funded by RSRE (previously RRE) and continued research into materials for display devices, whereas Mosley and Goodby were both funded by the Science Research Council and thereby were engaged in expanding the fundamental science base of the enlarged research group. Two years later Stephen Kelly joined the group as a member of the RSRE team, and shortly afterwards Colin Waters. Waters later went on to work at RSRE, where he and Raynes invented the super-twisted nematic liquid crystal device, which became used in commercial displays with high information content (Raynes & Waters 1987). As Gray commented (24), 'The success (of biphenyls) also attracted very good people to work in the Hull Liquid Crystal Group, and probably the most able and exciting group of young researchers that I was ever privileged to work with was created.'

Mosley was funded by a joint research grant that was held between Gray and Leadbetter. At the time he met Gray, Leadbetter was at the University of Bristol studying the structures of molecular crystals and glasses by X-ray diffraction and neutron scattering. Part of his research was funded by RSRE and it was through the supervisor of the Liquid Crystal Programme, John

Kirton, that Leadbetter was encouraged to talk to Gray about obtaining some interesting liquid crystals to study. Kirton, however, warned Leadbetter that Gray did not suffer fools gladly and that he should be careful if he wanted help. Gray visited Bristol, and on the way back to the station they drafted their first research proposal. Thus continued a research collaboration that lasted 15 years, and a friendship that lasted a lifetime. Through the various forms of funding the collaboration, they extensively investigated the structure and molecular dynamics in nematic and smectic liquid crystals.

While developments of the biphenyls and their mixtures were ongoing, the increased funding enabled research to be undertaken by the Hull group on a wider front, leading to the following fundamental successes that Gray highlighted:

(i) a fuller understanding of smectics and their polymorphism consequent upon the synthesis and study of new materials exhibiting SmB, SmF and SmI phases, with Goodby in collaboration with Leadbetter (13–15);

(ii) rationalization of smectic nomenclature that was achieved at a meeting in Halle involving Goodby, Sackmannn and Demus, resolving the serious problem of the same phases being assigned different code letters by different groups (16);

(iii) development of new alicyclic mesogens (bicyclooctanes and cubanes), originated with Toyne, and in collaboration with Kelly (17, 18);

(iv) molecular factors determining SmC formation, with Goodby (6, 10);

(v) development of phase identification by optical microscopy, with Goodby (19);

(vi) synthesis of deutero-mesogens for neutron studies, with Mosley in collaboration with Leadbetter (8, 11);

(vii) development of novel chiral mesogens; work with McDonnell in which the position of a chiral centre of given optical configuration in a chiral alkyl group was shown to determine the helical twist sense in an alternating way dependent on parity (Gray–McDonnell rules) (5, 9);

(viii) high-order parameter dyes, with Coates and McDonnell (7, 12);

(ix) discovery of the 'blue phases' of chiral nematic liquid crystals, with Coates (3).

By 1980 the members of the 1970s Hull research group had mostly dispersed, Coates to Standard Telephone Laboratories, McDonnell to RSRE, Kelly to Brown Boveri et Cie in Switzerland, Mosley to GEC Hirst Research Laboratories, and Goodby to AT&T Bell Laboratories in New Jersey, USA. In the following years increasing importance was being placed on universities to report on research outputs through the Research Assessment Exercise. In Hull, Gray, who was a member of the University Grants Committee, had a strategy to expand the stronger research groups by taking in other academic staff from weaker groups, and thereby to reduce the breadth of research undertaken in the department. Thus, Dr J. Biggs, Dr R. M. Scrowston and Dr K. J. Toyne from the current staff joined Gray's Liquid Crystal Group, and Dr D. Lacey was promoted from within the group to the position of Lecturer, increasing the staff to five. For half of them the artificial make-up of the group was not one that would last, but Lacey and Toyne remained with the team until retirement, and made some significant and considerable contributions to the research effort: Lacey with side-chain liquid crystal polymers, and Toyne with ferroelectric liquid crystals. Toyne in particular brought to the group up-to-date synthetic capabilities that propelled the Hull Liquid Crystal Group back into the forefront of novel display materials.

Early in the 1980s Ken Toyne was examining ways to make monofluorinated terphenyls (21), and it had occurred to him that if one lateral fluorine substituent in terphenyl could induce beneficial mesomorphic and physical properties for ferroelectric liquid crystals, then maybe two substituents might improve those properties further. Using the Nobel prizewinning Suzuki–Miyaura boronic acid coupling technique, difluoroterphenyls were prepared by Toyne's student, Hird, as host materials for ferroelectric liquid crystals (22) (Hird *et al.* 2003). At a similar time it was realized, for nematic homologues, that it would be possible to use the materials for electrically controlled birefringence devices in which the molecules in the 'off-state or dark-state' are aligned vertically with respect to the glass substrates. Then the application of an electric field would induce the molecules to deviate from normal and so the 'on-state' would become light. For this configuration (Schiekel & Fahrenschon 1971), the first generation of devices achieved suitable switching times, and the displays provided high brightness and good viewing-angle properties, with excellent contrast. The fast response times and the possibility of creating multidomains that gave symmetrical and wide-angle viewing meant that the vertically aligned (VA) mode could be adapted to TV applications. The collaboration between Hull, RSRE and E. Merck, using the boronic acid coupling reactions to build laterally fluorinated materials, as shown with ferroelectric host materials, set the mode for research for the next generation of liquid crystal displays.

Although George Gray's priority in research was liquid crystals, he loved chemistry, which he also liked to enthuse his students with. Therefore, from his point of view he was sad to see the subject coming under attack from the media in the early 1990s. An example of this is to be found in an article in *Chemistry in Britain* in June 1991, entitled 'Chemophobia' (Kauffman 1991). Gray was obviously affected by this because he had slides made of the cover of the magazine, and he underlined certain parts of the text concerned with the carcinogenic nature of man-made materials as follows: 'the human dietary intake of "nature's pesticides" is likely to be several grams per day—probably at least 10,000 times higher than the dietary intake of man-made pesticides'. Gray felt that chemistry had given so much to society, from health care to advanced materials, and that media reporting on the subject was poorly researched and inaccurate. Gray probably reacted as he did towards the changing media landscape of research, and the willingness of many scientists to advertise their work without having the necessary scientific depth. In this context he summed up his feelings in the following words taken from his Kyoto Prize address (23):

> Is there a message in all this for the young who aspire to achieving similar things? Obviously training and education are matters to be taken very seriously, and hard work and a single minded dedication are prerequisites. Luck and good fortune may be unpredictable elements in life, but at least their likely influence can be optimised by seizing every opportunity for the advancement of your aims and ambitions. In other words, never step back from an opportunity. Mistakes are inevitable in any career, but with a sense of humor, these can be laughed off, but while smiling, always firmly resolving that the same error will not be made again. Most important of all, be 100% professional in all that you do, paying scrupulous attention to detail and accuracy, and if you can, direct what you do to be of the most benefit to humankind.

As the 1990s approached, George Gray was nearing retirement and was realizing that to maintain the impetus of the Hull group he would need to import a suitable person to take over the reins. With the help of Thorn EMI and STC he arranged for Goodby to return from AT&T Bell Laboratories to become a Reader in Industrial Chemistry. This Goodby agreed to by taking a year-long 'leave of absence' from Bell Laboratories. Unsettled in the UK, Goodby was negotiating a return to the USA, and maybe knowing this Gray decided to retire and to become a Research Coordinator at Merck in Poole, leaving Goodby to look after the group in Hull. During his time at Merck, Gray looked after the Engineering and Physical Sciences Research Council CASE student portfolio, and instigated and arranged the very successful Merck CASE Student conferences, which continue today. After a couple of years with Merck and becoming a Visiting Professor at the University of Southampton, Gray retired to become a consultant working from his home, Juniper House in Wimborne, Dorset.

Overall, George had humour, patience and irreverence. His rejection of authority and excessive administration appealed to his friends, colleagues, students and researchers alike, bringing out the best in those who knew him well, as summed up in 2015 by Hull City's Poet-in-Residence, David Osgerby:

Professor George Gray CBE

George Gray was an alchemist of his day.
Scientist, pioneer, and inventor.
He gave us the liquid crystal display.
He was a teacher; he was a mentor.
There are few who have changed the world so much.
As he, yet stayed unknown to most.
A family man who kept the common touch;
George Gray was not a man who liked to boast.
His legacy is there for all to see;
His name even carried on a train.
Imagine life without the LCD.
George's genius was everyone's gain.
He brought the world a new dimension;
A master. A father of invention.

Honours and distinctions

Gray's contributions to liquid crystals over 40 years of research were recognized in several awards:

1980	Rank Prize for Optoelectronics
1983	Elected Fellow of the Royal Society
1985	Clifford Patterson Lecturer of the Royal Society
1987	Leverhulme Gold Medal of the Royal Society
1989	Elected Fellow of the Royal Society of Edinburgh
1991	Fine Chemicals and Medicinal Group Award of the Royal Society of Chemistry
	Doctorate of Science (DSc), *honoris causa*, University of Hull
	Commander of the Most Excellent Order of the British Empire (CBE)
1993/94	Gold Medallist and Lecturer of the Society for Chemical Industry
1994	Doctorate of Science (DSc), Trent University at Nottingham
1995	Kyoto Prize and Laureate
1996	Foreign Member of the Japanese Academy of Engineering
	Doctorate of Science (DSc), *honoris causa*, University of Southampton
	Karl Ferdinand Braun Gold Medal of the Society for Information Display (SID)
1997	Freedericksz Medal of the Russian Liquid Crystal Society
	Doctorate of Science (DSc), *honoris causa*, University of East Anglia

1998	Honored Member of the International Liquid Crystal Society
1999	Visiting Senior Fellowship of the Defence Evaluation Agency (DERA)
2001	Doctorate of Science (DSc), *honoris causa*, University of Aberdeen
	Elected Honorary Member of the Royal Irish Academy
2002	Doctorate of Science (DSc), *honoris causa*, University of Exeter

Gray published more than 250 research papers and 100 patents and wrote several textbooks. His first book on liquid crystals probably remained his favourite. However, he took great delight in being the senior editor of the four-volume set of *Handbook of liquid crystals* that was published by VCH in 1998, editing the Taylor & Francis series of textbooks on liquid crystals, and being the editor of *Journal of Liquid Crystals*, published by Taylor & Francis.

His research at Hull brought recognition to the university in The Queen's Award for Technological Achievement in 1979, the first award of its type to a university in the UK, and in November 2005 a Historical Chemical Landmark was awarded to the University of Hull by the Royal Society of Chemistry.

Of these awards the one identified as the most important is the Kyoto Prize. As with the world's most important awards, Gray's research was acclaimed by the President of the USA, Bill Clinton, and the Prime Minister of the United Kingdom, John Major. The contents of their messages of congratulation are given below (23).

Congratulatory message

Bill Clinton, President of the United States of America

Read by proxy: David A. Pabst, Consul-General of American Consulate-General in Osaka-Kobe

Greetings to everyone gathered for the presentation of the 1995 Kyoto Prizes. I am pleased to congratulate this year's distinguished recipients for their contributions to the betterment of humanity.

This year the Inamori Foundation marks the beginning of its second decade of honoring lifetime achievements in the fields of Advanced Technology, Basic Sciences, and Creative Arts and Moral Sciences. The 1995 honorees have enriched our fundamental understanding of the universe, increased our ability to apply scientific knowledge to achieve technological progress, and advanced the conception and impact of art in our society.

Dr George William Gray's seminal contributions to liquid crystal research and development have provided the basis for the liquid crystal display technology essential to virtually all contemporary computer and electronic products. Dr Chushiro Hayashi's theories on the birth and evolution of the stars and on the formation of the solar system have made him one of the giants of twentieth century astrophysics. Mr Roy Lichtenstein has formed the symbols and artifacts of contemporary society into potent artworks that redefine both the nature and purposes of art.

Each of these extraordinary individuals exemplifies the deepest resources of the human spirit. For what they have given us—and continue to give—we are immensely grateful. Best wishes to all for a memorable event.

Congratulatory message

John Major, Prime Minister of the United Kingdom

Read by proxy: Anthony R. Cox, Counsellor, Science and Technology, Her Britannic Majesty's Embassy in Japan

I am delighted to have this opportunity to send my warmest congratulations to the 1995 Kyoto Prize Laureates: Dr George William Gray for his contribution to research and development of liquid crystal materials; Dr Chushiro Hayashi for his contribution to the maturation of modern astrophysics; and Mr Roy Lichtenstein for his influence on contemporary fine art.

I am particularly pleased and proud that a British scientist is among those honoured.

Figure 11. In recognition of George Gray's contributions to science and technology, and to the City of Hull, a Lord Mayor's Centenary Blue Plaque was located on the wall at the entrance to the Department of Chemistry in the University of Hull.

I warmly commend the excellent work of the Inamori Foundation to support and encourage research and for its contribution through the highly prestigious Kyoto Prizes to the recognition of outstanding achievements in Advanced Technology, Basic Sciences and Creative Arts and Moral Sciences.

On the award Gray commented, 'I would like to think too that the Award (Kyoto) also recognises my work in nurturing the careers of very many young people who began their professional careers as my PhD students, and the work I have done and enjoyed doing as Chairman of the International Liquid Crystal Society.'

However, there were three other recognitions that George had a greater fondness for. The first was his election to the Fellowship of the Royal Society. It was probably the recognition of his scientific achievements by his peers that he most appreciated, along with his name being written into history. The second was being made Commander of the Most Excellent Order of the British Empire. Recognition by Queen and Country was very special to George, although, being a proud Scot, he seemed to revel at being at the centre of the British establishment. But George also had a sense of humour bordering on irreverence, and so he also got a real thrill out of having sounded the horn of the Hull Trains 'Pioneer-class train' that was named after him. Lastly, George had a deep fondness for Hull University and the City of Hull, and he would have been proud that both recognized his contributions to science and the city with the positioning of a plaque on the wall outside the Department of Chemistry (figure 11).

ACKNOWLEDGEMENTS

We are indebted to George Gray's daughters Veronica and Caroline for reading and amending the memoir. We are also grateful to Cyril Hilsum FRS for allowing us to use his recollections of his meeting with George Gray, and to Tom Elliott FRS for his recollections on the development of LCDs at RCA.

All photographs were provided from the personal files of George Gray, John Goodby and Peter Raynes. (The online version of the frontispiece is in colour.)

Author profiles

Professor John W. Goodby FRS

Professor John Goodby studied for his first degree at the University of Hull in 1971, before becoming George Gray's Science Research Council-funded research student and postdoctoral research fellow. He left Hull to become a Member of the Technical Staff at AT&T Bell Laboratories, USA, in 1979. After becoming a supervisor leading the Liquid Crystal Materials research group, Gray arranged for him to return to Hull as the Thorn EMI, STC Reader in Industrial Chemistry. Within two years Gray retired, handing over the reins of leading the Hull Liquid Crystal Research Group to Goodby. In 2005 Goodby moved, with members of his team, to York University, where he is now Chair of Materials Chemistry. Together Goodby and Gray authored 29 papers, five patents and one textbook entitled *Smectic liquid crystals: textures and structures*. Jointly they edited the four-volume *Handbook of liquid crystals*, and the Taylor & Francis series of textbooks on liquid crystals.

Professor Peter Raynes FRS

Physicist Peter Raynes was recruited by Cyril Hilsum in 1971 to work at the Royal Radar Establishment, Malvern (later the Royal Signals and Radar Establishment; RSRE) on liquid crystal materials and devices. He immediately started working closely with George Gray and his group at Hull University, developing their liquid crystal materials, including the cyanobiphenyls, into systems suitable for use in display devices. Together with others, Gray, Hilsum and Raynes were awarded the 1980 Rank Prize for Optoelectronics. Raynes was joint author with Gray and his Hull group of six papers and eight patents, and his colleagues at Malvern included three former PhD students of Gray's. Raynes left RSRE in 1992, moving first to the Sharp Laboratories of Europe at Oxford and then, in 1998, to the Chair of Optoelectronic Engineering at Oxford University. He is currently an Honorary Visiting Professor in the Department of Chemistry at York University.

References to other authors

Bruce, D. W., Coles, H. J., Goodby, J. W. & Sambles, J. R. 2006 Discussion Meeting on new directions in liquid crystals. *Phil. Trans. R. Soc.* A **364**, 2565–2843.

Collings, P. J. 1990 *Liquid crystals, nature's delicate phase of matter.* Princeton University Press.

Collings, P. J. & Hird, M. 1997 *Introduction to liquid crystals: chemistry and physics.* London: Taylor & Francis.

Dreyer, J. F. 1970 A liquid crystal device for rotating the plane of polarized light. (Abstract.) In *Proceedings of the 3rd International Liquid Crystal Conference, Berlin, 24–28 August,* p. 25.

Heilmeier, G. H., Zanoni, L. H. & Barton, L. H. 1968a Dynamic scattering: a new electrooptic effect in certain classes of nematic liquid crystals. *Proc IEEE* **56**, 1162–1171. (http://dx.doi.org/10.1109/PROC.1968.6513)

Heilmeier, G. H., Zanoni, L. H. & Barton, L. H. 1968b Dynamic scattering in nematic liquid crystals. *Appl. Phys. Lett.* **13**, 46. (http://dx.doi.org/10.1063/1.95846)

Hilsum, C. 1969 *Final Report of RRE Working Party on Solid State Displays and Lamps.*

Hilsum, C. 1984 The anatomy of a discovery. In *Technology of chemicals and materials for technology* (ed. E. R. Howells), pp. 43–109. Chichester: Ellis Horwood.

Hird, M., Goodby, J. W., Lewis, R. A. & Toyne, K. J. 2003 The fascinating influence of fluoro substituents on the synthesis and properties of liquid crystals. *Mol. Cryst. Liq. Cryst.* **401**, 1–18. (http://dx.doi.org/10.1080/744814910)

Hulme, D. S., Raynes, E. P. & Harrison, K. J. 1974 Eutectic mixtures of nematic 4'-substituted 4-cyanobiphenyls. *Chem. Commun.*, 98–99. (http://dx.doi.org/10.1039/C39740000098)

Jones, B. 1935 Apparent cases of liquid-crystal formation in *p*-alkoxybenzoic acids. *J. Chem. Soc.*, 1874. (http://dx.doi.org/10.1039/JR9350001873)

Kauffman, G. B. 1991 Chemophobia. *Chemy Br.* **27**, 512–516.

Leslie, F. M. 1970 Distortion of twisted orientation patterns in liquid crystals by magnetic fields. *Mol. Cryst. Liq. Cryst.* **12**, 57–72. (http://dx.doi.org/10.1080/15421407008082760)

Lydon, J. E. 1984 *Smectic liquid crystals—textures and structures.* Glasgow: Leonard Hill.

Parkinson, D. H. 1967 *First Report of RRE Working Party on Solid State Displays and Lamps.*

Raynes, E. P. 1980 RSRE Memo, 3266; see also P. Raynes, in *Handbook of liquid crystals*, vol. 1 (*Fundamentals of liquid crystals*) (ed. J. W. Goodby, P. J. Collings, T. Kato, C. Tschierske, H. F. Gleeson & P. Raynes), pp. 351–363 (Wiley-VCH, Weinheim, 2014).

Raynes, E. P. & Waters, C. M. 1987 Super-twisted nematic displays. *Displays* **8**, 59–63. (http://dx.doi.org/10.1016/0141-9382(87)90038-2)

Schadt, M. & Helfrich, W. 1971 Voltage-dependent optical activity of a twisted nematic liquid crystal. *Appl. Phys. Lett.* **18**, 127–128. (http://dx.doi.org/10.1063/1.1653593)

Schiekel, M. F. & Fahrenschon, K. 1971 Deformation of nematic liquid crystals with vertical orientation in electric fields. *Appl. Phys. Lett.* **19**, 391–393. (http://dx.doi.org/10.1063/1.1653743)

BIBLIOGRAPHY

The following publications are those referred to directly in the text. A full bibliography is available as electronic supplementary material at http://dx.doi.org/10.1098/rsbm.2016.0001 or via http://rsbm.royalsocietypublishing.org.

(1)   1953   A heating instrument for the accurate determination of mesomorphic and polymorphic transition temperatures. *Nature* **172**, 1137–1140.

(2)   1962   *Molecular structure and the properties of liquid crystals.* London: Academic Press.

(3)   1973   (With D. Coates) Optical studies of the amorphous liquid–cholesteric liquid crystal transition: the 'blue phase'. *Phys. Lett.* **2**, 115–116.

(4)   (With K. J. Harrison & J. A. Nash) New family of liquid crystals for displays. *Electron. Lett.* **9**, 130–131.

(5)   1976   (With D. G. McDonnell) Synthesis and liquid crystal properties of chiral alkyl-cyano-biphenyls (and -*p*-terphenyls) and of some related chiral compounds derived from biphenyl. *Mol. Cryst. Liq. Cryst.* **37**, 189–211.

(6)   (With J. W. Goodby) Molecular structure and the polymorphism of smectic liquid crystals. *J. Phys. (Paris)* C3 **37**, 17–26.

(7)   (With D. Coates, D. G. McDonnell, J. Constant, J. Kirton, E. P. Raynes & I. A. Shanks) Pleochroic dyes with high-order parameters for liquid crystal displays. *Electron. Lett.* **12**, 514–515.

(8)   1977   (With A. Mosley) The transition temperatures of some deuteriated liquid crystals. *Mol. Cryst. Liq. Cryst Lett.* **41**, 75–79.

(9)   (With D. G. McDonnell) The relationship between helical twist sense, absolute configuration and molecular structure for non-sterol cholesteric liquid crystals. *Mol. Cryst. Liq. Cryst. Lett.* **34**, 211–217.

(10)   1978   (With J. W. Goodby) A natural progression from smectic C to tilted smectic B properties in the n-alkyl 4'-n-alkoxybiphenyl-4-carboxylates. *Mol. Cryst. Liq. Cryst* **48**, 127–149.

(11)   (With A. Mosley) The synthesis of deuteriated 4-n-alkyl-4'-cyano-biphenyls. *Mol. Cryst. Liq. Cryst.* **48**, 233–242.

(12)   (With J. Constant, E. P. Raynes, I. A. Shanks, D. Coates & D. G. McDonnell) Pleochroic dyes with high order parameters. *J. Phys.* D **11**, 479–490.

(13) 1979 (With J. W. Goodby) Smectic F trends in the 4-(2'-methylbutyl)phenyl esters of 4'-n-alkoxybiphenyl-4-carboxylic acids and 4'-n-alkylbiphenyl-4-carboxylic acids. *J. Phys. (Paris)* C3 **40**, 27–36.

(14)   (With A. J. Leadbetter, J. P. Gaughan, B. A. Kelly & J. W. Goodby) Characterization and structure of some new smectic F phases. *J. Phys. (Paris)* C3 **40**, 178–184.

(15) 1980 (With J. W. Goodby, A. J. Leadbetter & M. A. Mazid) The smectic phases of the *N*-(4-n-alkoxybenzylidene)-4'-n-alkylanilines (n0.m's)—some problems of phase identification and structure. In *Liquid crystals of one- and two-dimensional order* (ed. W. Helfrich & G. Heppke), pp. 3–18. New York: Springer.

(16)   (With D. Demus, J. W. Goodby & H. Sackmann) Recommendations for the use of the code letters G and H for smectic phases. *Mol. Cryst. Liq. Cryst. Lett.* **56**, 311–314.

(17) 1981 (With S. M. Kelly) The synthesis of 1,4-disubstituted bicyclo(2.2.2)octanes exhibiting wide-range, enantiotropic nematic phases. *J. Chem. Soc. Perkin Trans. 2*, 26–31.

(18)   (With S. M. Kelly) Phenyl- and biphenylylbicyclo(2.2.2)octane derivatives—two novel classes of nematic liquid crystals. *Angew. Chem. Int. Ed. Engl.* **20**, 393–394.

(19) 1984 (With J. W. Goodby) *Smectic liquid crystals: textures and structures.* Glasgow: Leonard Hill.

(20) 1986 (With G. Etherington, A. J. Leadbetter, X. J. Wang & A. Tajbakhsh) Structure of the smectic D phase. *Liq. Cryst.* **1**, 290–214.

(21) 1988 (With L. K. M. Chan, D. Lacey & K. J. Toyne) Synthesis and liquid crystal behaviour of further 4,4''-disubstituted 2'-fluoro-1,1':4',1''-terphenyls. *Mol. Cryst. Liq. Cryst.* **158**, 209–240.

(22) 1989 (With M. Hird, D. Lacey & K. J. Toyne) The synthesis and transition temperatures of some 4,4''-dialkyl- and 4,4''-alkoxyalkyl-1,1':4',1''-terphenyls with 2,3- or 2',3'-difluoro substituents and of their biphenyl analogues. *J. Chem. Soc. Perkin Trans. 2*, 2041–2053.

(23) 1995 Kyoto Prizes and Inamori Grants, The Inamori Foundation, Kyoto, Japan, pp. 97–119 (see http://www.kyotoprize.org/en/laureates/george_william_gray/).

(24) 1998 Reminiscences from a life with liquid crystals. *Liq. Cryst.* **24**, 5–13.

SIR JOHN HAROLD HORLOCK FREng

19 April 1928 — 22 May 2015

Biogr. Mems Fell. R. Soc. **62**, 213–232 (2016)

J. H. Horlock

SIR JOHN HAROLD HORLOCK FREng

19 April 1928 — 22 May 2015

Elected FRS 1976

BY J. D. DENTON[1]* FRS FREng AND J. P. GOSTELOW[2]‡

[1]*Department of Engineering, University of Cambridge, Whittle Laboratory,
J. J. Thompson Avenue, Cambridge CB3 0DY, UK*
[2]*Department of Engineering, University of Leicester, Leicester LE1 7RH, UK*

John Harold Horlock was one of the outstanding engineers of his generation. His expertise was in the thermodynamics and fluid mechanics of turbines and compressors, as used for jet engines and for power generation. He made major contributions to this field over 60 years. After graduating from Cambridge he worked for Rolls-Royce for two years before returning to Cambridge to study for his PhD, and was subsequently appointed a lecturer in engineering and a Fellow of St John's College. At the age of 30 he was elected to the Harrison Chair of Mechanical Engineering at Liverpool, where he remained for nine years, producing an impressive amount of individual research as well as transforming the department into one of the best in the country. Returning to a chair at Cambridge he reorganized the Mechanical Sciences Tripos and founded the Whittle Laboratory, which became one of the world's leading centres for turbomachinery research. He then became Vice-Chancellor of Salford University, remaining there for seven years before moving on to become Vice-Chancellor of the Open University. After retirement at the age of 62 he continued to be very active: as a consultant, as Treasurer and Vice President of the Royal Society, as a frequent visitor to the Whittle Laboratory and as the author of many papers and several books. Knighted in 1996, Sir John Horlock will be remembered not only for his intellectual abilities but also for his personal skills, which enabled him to interact freely with all levels of society, from cabinet ministers to graduate students.

FAMILY BACKGROUND AND SCHOOLING, 1928–46

John Harold Horlock was born in April 1928 in Edmonton, north London, the son of Harold and Olive, who already had a daughter, Beryl, seven years older than John. Harold and his

* Author for correspondence (jdd1@cam.ac.uk).
‡ jpg7@leicester.ac.uk.

http://dx.doi.org/10.1098/rsbm.2016.0009

brother Horace ran a family undertaking business in Edmonton and Enfield, the business having been in the Horlock family for several generations. His grandfather on his mother's side was a master baker who had moved to England from Germany in the 1880s and married Catherine, who was English but of German extraction. There was no family history of scientific or engineering interests.

John was beset by early medical problems, having a major operation for osteomyelitis before the age of two. This left him with a slightly shortened right leg, which caused some problems in later life. He also had an operation for appendicitis a year later. When John was born the family lived above the shop on Edmonton Green, but in the 1930s they moved to the more salubrious suburb of Winchmore Hill and in 1933 John entered Highfield Road Primary School. After a few years he moved on to another Edmonton primary school, Raglan. Here John first developed a love of football and cricket that was to remain with him throughout his life. He played for the school against other local schools and had a trial for Edmonton junior boys, but unfortunately did not make the team.

In 1938 John took the 11-plus examination, a year early at the age of 10, on the basis of which he was accepted for the Latymer School in Edmonton but had to stay on at Raglan for another year until he was 11 years old. He thus started secondary schooling just before the start of World War II and was initially evacuated to Diss in Norfolk, but he did not settle well there and because there had not yet been any air raids he returned to Edmonton after a few weeks. He subsequently spent many nights with his family in an air raid shelter in their garden.

John had fond memories of Latymer School. Although many of the pupils had been evacuated and there were frequent air raid warnings he was taught a full curriculum, including the sciences. Although the air raids eased in 1942–43, the V1 flying bombs and later the V2 rockets continued to cause disturbances at the time when he was taking the School Certificate examinations in 1944. He took part in a great variety of school sports, representing the school at football, cricket, athletics and swimming. Outside school he played cricket for Edmonton cricket club and Middlesex schoolboys, and football for a local youth club, even playing one game for Tottenham Hotspur Juniors. One suspects that it is fortunate for his future career that he was not selected for a more formal trial. He also took part in a remarkable variety of other school activities being a member of the literary and debating, science and music societies and he also acted in school plays. In the vacations John took part in school forestry and farming camps and went on long cycling tours, staying at Youth Hostel Association hostels.

After obtaining eight distinctions in the School Certificate at age 16, John went in to the sixth form to study pure mathematics, applied mathematics, physics and geography for the Higher School Certificate. He always regretted not studying chemistry at that stage. After just one year in the sixth form he took the Cambridge Scholarship examination for St Catherine's College. Because he was in competition with pupils from public schools who were in their third year of sixth-form studies it is unsurprising that he was not successful. However, at the same time he took the qualifying examination for the Cambridge Mechanical Sciences Tripos and passed it comfortably, although at that stage he showed no great interest in engineering topics. After two years in the sixth form he obtained three distinctions in his Higher School Certificate examinations, only missing out on a distinction in geography. On the strength of these results he was awarded a state scholarship and a Middlesex county scholarship. However, his father was concerned about whether he should go to university or take an apprenticeship and at one stage it was planned that he should start an apprenticeship with the aircraft firm Short Bros in Rochester. Perhaps fortunately this idea was dropped and he was entered for St John's College, Cambridge, where he was accepted as a commoner. John left Latymer School in 1946, having been Captain of School in his final year. He was full of praise for the broad education he received at the school and it is clear that he was an outstanding pupil. One important legacy of his schooldays is that he met his future wife, Sheila Stutely, at the school and they became close friends, sharing an interest in music. Although they went separate ways on leaving school they were to get together again five years later.

CAMBRIDGE, 1946–49

After John left school it was expected that he would have to do National Service before going up to Cambridge. However, despite all his sporting achievements, he was declared medically unfit because of his damaged leg, and was able to gain late entry to St John's, starting in the second week of the Michaelmas term. He started to study mathematics but soon changed to mechanical sciences under the guidance of Harry Rhoden, the Director of Studies for Engineering. This choice was surprising because John had shown no previous interest in, or aptitude for, engineering. Harry Rhoden was a specialist in the relatively new field of turbine and compressor aerodynamics and it is likely that it is from him that John got his interest in this field, which has come to be called 'turbomachinery'. At that time it was possible to take Part I of the Mechanical Sciences Tripos in two years instead of the usual three and John was enrolled on this 'fast course'. At first he found it very hard going, having missed the first few weeks of term and with many of his contemporaries having returned from the services with some engineering experience. The workload left little time for relaxation and the only other activities he took part in were football and cricket, both of which he played intermittently for the college first team. In one football match he twisted his knee badly and the injury remained with him for the rest of his life.

At the end of the first year John obtained a First in the 'preliminary examination', which covered all branches of engineering. In the long vacation it was necessary to gain workshop experience and he did this in the departmental workshops and at the de Havilland aircraft factory in Hatfield. De Havilland were one of the pioneers of jet propulsion and this experience must have contributed to his future interest in aerodynamics and jet engines. In his second year John worked hard, and in the Mechanical Sciences Tripos Part I examinations at the end of the year he won the Rex Moir prize for obtaining the top marks among the 300 or so undergraduates. In the third year he studied for Part II of the Tripos. In this it was possible to specialize in one of the main engineering disciplines and John chose the 'mechanical engineering' option, although at this stage he did not have any strong leaning to this as opposed to one of the other branches. The course covered all aspects of mechanics and thermodynamics, and John was partnered with Neville Kirby, who had worked on gas turbines with the Newcastle-based company C. A. Parsons during the war; as a result John became interested in these then-new power plants. At the end of his third year John obtained another First, but this time not the top First, which clearly disappointed him.

On the basis of his second-year performance John had received a scholarship to visit Massachusetts Institute of Technology (MIT) and he did this in the summer of 1949 after graduating from Cambridge. He travelled around the east coast of America by hitch-hiking and recounts how he was given a lift by a Princeton professor who took him into the university common room where Albert Einstein was present. John was clearly impressed by the teaching and research at MIT, where he met some distinguished engineers, and he was tempted to stay there for further study. However, he had already accepted a graduate apprenticeship with Rolls-Royce and in the late summer of 1949 returned to the UK to start on this.

Rolls-Royce, Cambridge and MIT, 1949–57

The graduate apprenticeship involved a year's practical work in several different departments of the company and ended with a spell working at the drawing board in the compressor design office. John enjoyed this experience of compressor design and at the end of his apprenticeship was allowed to stay on in the compressor office, working under Geoffrey Wilde, who subsequently was largely responsible for Rolls-Royce's development of the very successful RB211 family of three-shaft high-bypass engines. He was initially given the task of redesigning the compressor of the Avon engine, which had been in trouble because of surge. Surge is a violent instability that can occur when the compressor is being started or otherwise operated off-design and it can rapidly destroy the engine. It seems remarkable that such an important task was entrusted to a new graduate but John found that his education at Cambridge soon enabled him to pick up the methods involved. In fact the compressor was redesigned, built and tested in six weeks, a staggeringly short time. It is estimated that a similar task nowadays would require a team of engineers who would take at least a year to complete it. So much for the influence of computers! The new compressor worked first time and cured the surge problem, thus gaining John quite a reputation within the company.

After that success John worked on a variety of projects within the company, including the experimental testing of a low-speed research compressor. Outside work he played cricket for a local village team and enjoyed walks in the Derbyshire countryside. He met and worked with several experienced turbomachinery specialists and realized that there was still much that was not understood about the flow in compressors and turbines. Because of this he enquired of his old Director of Studies, Harry Rhoden, about the possibility of returning to Cambridge to study for a PhD, and in 1952 he obtained a DSIR studentship to work with Professor William (later Sir William) Hawthorne (FRS 1955), whom he had previously met at MIT.

Hawthorne was a brilliant theoretician who had worked with Frank (later Sir Frank) Whittle (FRS 1947) on combustion problems during the war but had subsequently become more interested in the aerodynamics of internal flows, including turbomachinery. He had developed a method of modelling the complex three-dimensional flow through blade rows of turbines and compressors, using a technique called 'actuator disc theory'. This replaced the blade row by a discontinuity, the actuator disc, across which the axial and radial velocities were conserved but the circumferential velocity and pressure underwent step changes. This enabled the effects of the blade row to be felt far upstream and downstream, in contrast to the radial equilibrium theory, developed in the USA and independently by Whittle, in which all changes in flow were confined to the blade rows. However, the theory was complex and was restricted to a single blade row and so was of limited use to designers. John's PhD task was to simplify the theory, apply it to multiple blade rows and try to validate it by experimental testing. The latter task was facilitated by Rolls-Royce's donating to the Engineering Department a copy of the two-stage compressor that John had tested in Derby (figure 1). His PhD thus involved a great deal of both theoretical and experimental work. Hawthorne's supervision was very 'light touch' and John was left very much to plan his own research. In fact he must have completed his

PLANE No	ANNULUS AREA	INSTRUMENTATION.
P. 1	369·45 □"	5 STATICS FRONT WALL, 5 STATICS REAR WALL. PROVISION FOR TRAVERSING.
P. 2	129·31 □"	3 ADJUSTABLE IMMERSION KIEL PROBES.
P. 3	"	3 STATICS OUTER WALL. PROVISION FOR TRAVERSING.
P 4	"	" " " " " "
P 5	"	" " " " " "
P 6	"	" " " " " "
P 7	"	" " " " " "
P 8	"	" " " " " "
P 9	"	5 OUTER WALL STATICS. 5 INNER WALL STATICS. 3 ADJUSTABLE IMMERSION KIEL PROBE
P 10	———	3 STAGNATION THERMOMETER POCKETS.

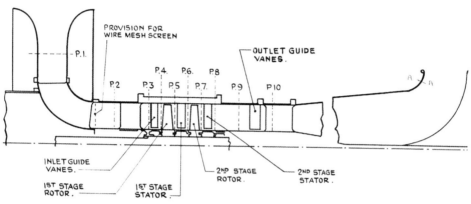

Figure 1. The two-stage compressor first used by John during his PhD research. The compressor was subsequently used by many other research students, including the first author.

original tasks early, because his PhD thesis includes the investigation of an almost unrelated problem of the secondary flow in a sinusoidal pipe, which is relevant to the meandering of rivers. Again this involved both experimental and theoretical work; in particular the theory led to a differential equation, which he solved numerically on the EDSAC computer. Hence John must have been one of the first engineers to make use of a digital computer. It is therefore surprising that his future work remained largely analytical while the field of turbomachinery aerodynamics soon became dominated by computerized numerical methods. This work was published in *Proceedings of the Royal Society* (4)* with John as the sole author, quite an achievement for a research student.

In 1953, while still working for his PhD, John was offered and accepted the position of demonstrator in the Engineering Department. Despite the title this involved him giving lectures to the undergraduates, including the large first-year class. At first he was not happy with his lecturing performance; however, he learned rapidly and after a few years, when he was giving thermodynamics lectures to the first-year students in parallel with two famous professors, Hawthorne and A. H. Shapiro (who was on leave from MIT), he attracted the larger audience.

John and Sheila had got together again after five years, and the security of John's university salary enabled them to get married in 1953. They lived in a university flat close to the department until the birth of their first daughter, Alison, in 1955, when they moved to a new house in Girton.

* Numbers in this form refer to the bibliography at the end of the text.

While still a research student John published several papers based on his PhD research and his work at Rolls-Royce (1–3) and in 1954 he was elected to a Research Fellowship at St John's. He continued to play cricket, captaining the departmental team, which at one time included three future vice-chancellors and which won the University Laboratories cup. In 1956, at the age of 28, he was appointed to a full lectureship in the Engineering Department. In the same year he accepted a year's exchange with a lecturer from MIT and the family enjoyed living in Boston for that period. At MIT John gave some lecture courses but also spent time writing his first book, *Axial flow compressors* (5), which was finished soon after his return from MIT in 1957. The book covered the whole field of compressor aerodynamics from the basics up to the latest research developments: it has had a major impact on turbomachinery designers and researchers and continues to be in widespread use.

LIVERPOOL UNIVERSITY, 1958–67

Soon after his return from MIT John was approached by Liverpool University and encouraged to apply for the Harrison Chair of Mechanical Engineering, recently vacated by Professor W. J. Kearton. He was surprised to be offered the post at the young age of 30 but accepted it without hesitation. Soon after moving to Liverpool he returned to a feast at St John's College. One of the senior fellows was heard to remark to another, 'There's that young fellow Horlock—been appointed to a chair at Liverpool.' The other replied, 'That's not a chair; it's only a stool.' Such an attitude did not go down well at Liverpool.

On arriving at Liverpool John found that the department he inherited was strong on teaching but less so on research and he set about remedying this. A principal constraint was the existence of separate and competing Civil and Electrical Engineering Departments, with engineering mathematics being taught by the Mathematics Department. Within the Mechanical Engineering Department Professor Harry Preston had built up a strong fluid mechanics group, which overlapped with John's interests. These conflicting interests naturally resulted in some in-fighting but overall the spirit of the department was friendly. The department was initially understaffed but, taking advantage of the stimulus of the 1960s energy and technology boom, and the consequent university expansion, John was able to recruit several new lecturers and quickly built up a strong turbomachinery group. This attracted outside funding that was used to set up good experimental facilities and to recruit some excellent research students, many from overseas. The Liverpool Mechanical Engineering Department was built up to become one of the strongest in the country.

This was a time before the development of computational fluid dynamics (CFD) as the dominant research and design tool that we now know. However, John supported the acquisition of the university's DEUCE computer. The computer worked well but getting a sensible run involved the student in an all-night session. Around 5 a.m. the disc would clog up with dust and the unfortunate student had to wipe it clean with a handkerchief before continuing. Woe betide any unfortunate student who became so frustrated that he 'pulled the plug'. Warm-up time was three days, and for the student the penalty was a lifetime ban. John saw the computer as an important element of the work and encouraged his colleagues and students to use it. They produced accurate potential flow solutions for two-dimensional cascades and initiated some viscous and three-dimensional approaches. However, John himself was more interested in an approach based on a balance between experimental, analytical and computational work. This approach characterized his work throughout his lifetime and is still important for turbomachinery research and design today.

The family was very happy at Liverpool, living on the Wirral peninsula, by the sea. Their son, Tim, was born soon after their return from MIT in 1958, and their second daughter, Jane, was born in 1961. The 1960s were a lively time in Liverpool. An unknown group called The Beatles played for dances in the student's union for £20 per night and the new Catholic Cathedral, fronting on to Hope Street with its legendary Philharmonic Pub, was built within sight of the engineering department offices. For the engineering students it seemed that there was never a dull moment.

John's personal research output during his time at Liverpool was prolific; he published more than 50 papers in the nine years he was there. His paper on actuator disc theory, written jointly with Hawthorne (6), was awarded the James Clayton Prize of the Institution of Mechanical Engineers in 1962. He continued his interests in turbomachinery with work on cascade aerodynamics, secondary flows, annulus boundary layers, tip leakage effects, compressor stall and unsteady flow. He also tried to diversify his interests outside turbomachinery with work on cycle analysis, magnetohydrodynamics, steam properties, marine propulsion and noise generation. His interest in cricket led to wind-tunnel experiments and a paper attempting to explain the swing of a cricket ball (9); however, he was unable to explain (nor can anyone else yet) why this is affected by the atmospheric humidity. His work on turbocharging led to good collaboration with researchers on internal combustion engines, with similar groups at the University of Manchester Institute of Science and Technology and Queen Mary College and, in industry, with Napiers and Hawker Siddeley Brush Turbines. On top of this he found time to write another book. *Axial flow turbines* (7), published in 1966, was a companion to his first book, *Axial flow compressors*, and was equally successful.

In his nine years at Liverpool University John turned around and built up the Mechanical Engineering Department into one of the foremost in the country. In this he was helped by the fact that this was the time of the 'white heat' of Harold Wilson's technological revolution. Mechanical Engineering at Liverpool was bursting at the seams and research grants and students flowed in. The department needed a new building but the main line into Lime Street station carved right through the university; the only space available was over the railway cutting. Such considerations never daunted John Horlock and he built a tower over that cutting (figure 2). This is an aspect of John's character that should be emphasized: he was a dreamer of big, but achievable, dreams.

Inevitably the job also involved a good deal of administrative work. In addition to running the Engineering Department John chaired the Departmental Grants Committee. Outside the university he was a member of the Aeronautical Research Council and the chairman of its Propulsion Committee; he was also the editor of a series of books for Pergamon Press. In the latter context he came to know the late Robert Maxwell. In 1966 he spent some time at Pennsylvania State University, where he collaborated with George Wislicenus, a pioneer of turbomachinery aerodynamics.

CAMBRIDGE AGAIN, 1967–74, AND THE WHITTLE LABORATORY

In 1967 John was offered and accepted one of three newly created chairs in engineering at Cambridge. The family moved back to Cambridge and built a house in Newnham, quite close to the Engineering Department.

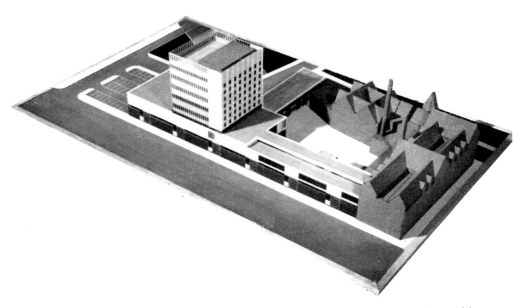

Figure 2. The new Mechanical Engineering building constructed at Liverpool under John's supervision. The building is placed on top of a railway cutting.

At first John found it difficult to be only one of several professors and no longer the head of the whole department. In particular his old supervisor, Will Hawthorne, who had recently been elected to the Royal Society, worked in the same field of research and John worked closely with Will on the fundamental flow physics of turbomachinery. He was elected into a Professorial Fellowship at St John's, where he renewed his friendship with his former Director of Studies, Harry Rhoden. In his new job John had responsibility for the allocation of teaching duties to the approximately 100 teaching staff of the department. Sir John (later Lord) Baker FRS remained as Head of the Department and he gave John the daunting task of revising the Mechanical Sciences Tripos, which was renamed the Engineering Tripos. With the help of Sir David Harrison, John steered the changes through the university's formidable bureaucracy; in the process he inevitably upset some individuals. The new course was more modern and broader than the old one and better addressed industrial requirements. Within the department professorial relations were very good, the administrative set-up was sound and the department ran well.

On the research side John was disappointed to find that the facilities at Cambridge were not as good as those he had built up at Liverpool. There was no space in the overcrowded Engineering Laboratory for major new turbomachinery facilities, which might anyhow have been too noisy. On the basis of John's experience as a member of the Mechanical Engineering Committee of the Science Research Council (SRC), John and Hawthorne applied to the SRC for funding to construct a new dedicated turbomachinery laboratory in west Cambridge. Although this was a joint application there is no doubt that the initiative came from John. The application was successful and an unprecedented grant of £272 000 was awarded. In 2015 money this is equivalent to about £10 million. This was the first time that the SRC had funded a building outside the special-purpose facilities of nuclear physics. The plan was to

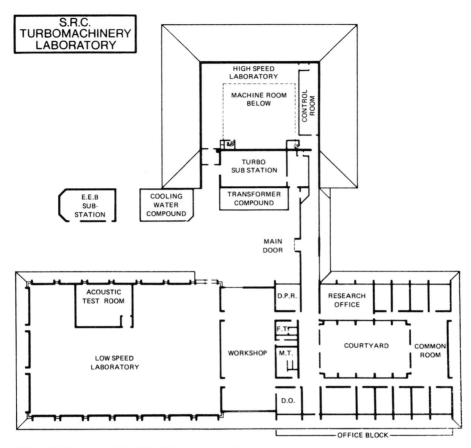

Figure 3. The layout of the Whittle Laboratory at its completion in 1971. At the time it was called the S.R.C. Turbomachinery Laboratory.

build the new laboratory on the west Cambridge site, near to the proposed new Cavendish Physics Laboratory. There was some opposition to the plans from the occupants of the nearby astronomy buildings because of possible noise and light interference. Because of this the plans were revised to place the potentially noisy compressors in an underground basement, to have no windows in the high-speed laboratory and to surround it with an earth embankment. Despite these measures the proposal attracted a 'non placet' in the Senate. John argued vigorously for the proposal and when it came to the vote it was only passed by nine votes.

Construction started in December 1969 and the laboratory was completed in May 1971. In retrospect it is surprising that such a complex laboratory could have been constructed so quickly and at such a modest cost. The building (figure 3) contained two large laboratories, a workshop, ten staff offices, a student office and a common room. The 'high-speed' laboratory included an underground basement containing two large compressors, with a combined power of almost 1 MW, driving two transonic wind tunnels at ground level; it also contained a new large (5 ft diameter) low-speed turbine. The facilities in the 'low-speed' laboratory had mainly been moved from the main department and included a large (5 ft diameter) low-speed

Figure 4. John Horlock with Sir Frank Whittle FRS at the formal opening of the Whittle Laboratory in 1973.

compressor, two large cascade wind tunnels and the two-stage compressor first used in John's thesis. The laboratory was officially opened by Sir Frank Whittle in May 1973 (figures 4 and 5) and was then called the SRC Turbomachinery Laboratory. It was renamed the Whittle Laboratory in November 1975. A new wing, named the Horlock Wing, was opened in 1997 and further extensions were added in 2013.

John became the first director of the laboratory and recruited several of his past PhD students from Liverpool to help staff it. In addition several existing teaching staff from the Engineering Department based their research in the new laboratory. The group worked closely with Rolls-Royce to improve the understanding of flows through turbines and compressors, for which small improvements in efficiency have a major impact on a jet engine's fuel consumption. After Baker's retirement in 1968 Hawthorne had become Head of the Engineering Department. He was very much a 'hands off' leader, frequently away travelling on government or university business, and one suspects that John had to do much of the running of the department, which at that time was probably the largest university department in the country. In 1973 Hawthorne's five-year spell as head came to an end and he was free to concentrate on his duties as Master of Churchill College (1968–83). John naturally hoped to be considered for the headship of the department but he was only one of several eligible professors and the headship went to Austyn Mair, the Professor of Aeronautics. John had already been approached about the Vice-Chancellorship of Salford and he decided to accept it. However, he asked for the Salford appointment to be deferred until 1974 to allow him to help get the new turbomachinery laboratory established.

Because of his increasing administrative responsibilities John was able to do less individual research. However, he continued to publish profusely during this time at Cambridge with more than 30 papers, some of which were based on his previous work at Liverpool or were

Figure 5. John Horlock, Sir Stanley Hooker FRS, Sir Frank Whittle FRS, Sir William Hawthorne FRS and Dr Bob Feilden FRS at the opening of the Whittle Laboratory in 1973.

written with co-authors. His work continued to concentrate on the physics of turbomachinery flows rather than on the development of numerical methods, which were now coming into widespread use. However, he encouraged his students and colleagues to make use of the best available numerical methods, including some unusual approaches, such as obtaining solutions in the hodograph plane.

SALFORD, 1974–80

John moved to Salford in April 1974 and initially stayed in a flat on campus while the rest of the family remained in Cambridge to enable the children to finish their school year. The family then moved into the Vice-Chancellor's house in Hale, where they settled in quickly and where Sheila became involved in a good deal of entertaining of university officials. Later Sheila became a JP on the Manchester bench.

The job of Vice-Chancellor at Salford was very different from that of an Oxbridge professor. Salford was a recently established university, having previously been a college of advanced technology. It had a large engineering department that was well staffed; but the quality of the student intake, many of whom were overseas students, was lower than average, and there was little research funding. John worked hard to try to remedy these issues. Many of the problems he encountered revolved around staffing issues, one particularly difficult problem involving a dispute between groups of students. John also spent a good deal of time outside the university trying to put it on the map nationally and he took on several tasks of national importance. He was a member of the Aeronautical Research Council, becoming its chairman in 1979, and also a member of the Finniston committee of inquiry into the engineering profession, of the Science Research Council and of the Marshall committee looking into combined heat and power. As Vice-Chancellor he became a member of the Committee of Vice-Chancellors and Principals (CVCP) and later of the Universities Committee for Non-Academic Staff. The university Chancellor was the Duke of Edinburgh. John got on well with him and found him genuinely interested in Salford and its students. The relationship led to John and Sheila's being invited to a dinner in Windsor Castle in the presence of The Queen and the then Prime Minister, Harold Wilson.

Despite these heavy duties John attempted to continue some academic research. He wrote another book, *Actuator disk theory* (10), published in 1978, which applied the ideas generated in his thesis to many related problems of internal flow. This book represented a major intellectual exercise as it contained a great deal of complex analytical theory. However, by then the topics it covered had been largely taken over by numerical methods and so the book was of limited use to designers. During his time at Salford he also published several papers and gave many invited lectures. He was elected a Fellow of the Royal Society in 1976, and a Fellow of the Royal Academy of Engineering in 1977.

Towards the end of his time at Salford John was approached about several senior positions at other universities and Oxbridge colleges, but was not tempted until he was approached by the Open University (OU). As a result of his work on the Finniston committee John was very much in favour of continuing postgraduate education for engineers. He saw the OU as an ideal vehicle for furthering this objective and so decided to accept the position of Vice-Chancellor. John and Sheila had enjoyed their time at Salford and were sad to leave; in recognition of his contribution the university awarded John an honorary degree and named a residential building after him.

THE OPEN UNIVERSITY, 1981–90

The Open University represented a major change from the traditional university that John was used to. It was based at Milton Keynes, but the large number of teaching staff were spread around the country, as were its more than 100 000 students. The move was more difficult because the registrar had retired at the same time as the previous Vice-Chancellor and John took some time to settle in. In this he was ably assisted by the new registrar, Joe Clinch, and his secretariat. The family moved into the Vice-Chancellor's house in Aspley Guise, which, by coincidence, was only a mile or so from where Sheila's grandmother had lived. Sheila was able to continue as a JP on the Bedfordshire bench and she also accompanied John to the many OU degree ceremonies around the UK.

A major difference between the OU and the more traditional universities was that the funding came directly from the government via the Department of Education and Science rather than through the University Grants Committee. This meant that John had to deal directly with government ministers and senior civil servants and it is clear that he resented this intrusion into academic freedom. A major confrontation occurred when a staff member complained directly to the Secretary of State for Education and Science, Sir Keith Joseph, alleging political bias in the material taught in a social sciences course. John's political views were not aligned with the then conservative government and one gets the impression that he and Sir Keith did not 'hit it off'. The course in question had already been comprehensively reviewed by external assessors but the government appointed three more to review it further. They expressed some reservations but John refused to withdraw the course and managed to continue it with minor modifications.

The OU was also hit by funding cuts, as the conventional universities had been rather earlier. These threatened the very existence of the OU. John led a major 'Save the OU' campaign involving the press and politicians, which involved his appearing on the radio and television. The support of the large number of students was an important part of this campaign, which probably prevented any further cuts.

The OU was very strong on teaching but most departments were not strong on research. John tried to encourage more staff research, but with limited success. He was also active in trying to encourage more women to take up engineering: this was an interest that continued throughout his whole career. His ambition to initiate postgraduate courses was handicapped when the government made it clear that any such courses would have to be self-financing. However, over time he initiated postgraduate courses in management studies, computer science and manufacturing. These increased the size of the OU student body by some 50%. John did little teaching himself but did become proficient at television presentations and interviews. The job brought him into contact with a very large number of senior politicians and other well-known personalities. The skills he required were very different from those of his early career and it is a tribute to his abilities and personality that he was able to carry such a heavy load so successfully.

Although able to do little personal research during this period he did publish 10 papers, several of them related to his work on the Marshall committee on combined heat and power plants. He also edited two books, jointly with D. E. Winterbone, *The thermodynamics and gas dynamics of internal combustion engines*, volumes 1 and 2 (11), and wrote another himself entitled *Cogeneration: combined heat and power* (12). The latter again related to his work on the Marshall committee. He was also involved in many outside activities, most notably as a member of the Engineering Council, as a director of the National Grid Company and as chairman of the Advisory Committee on Safety of Nuclear Installations. Towards the end of his 10-year term the enormous workload started to take its toll, leading to the need to take a few months' leave, and to his decision to retire from the position a few months before the end of the 10-year appointment. As at Salford, he was awarded an honorary degree by the OU, and a new building for management studies was named after him.

RETIREMENT, 1990–2015

After John's retirement from the OU, John and Sheila moved the short distance from Milton Keynes to Ampthill, near Bedford, so that Sheila could continue as a JP on the Bedfordshire bench, of which she later became chairman. She also became chair of the Bedfordshire Probation Committee. Given his vast range of outside activities and interests it was clear that John was not going to retire in the usual sense. In addition to his existing commitments he returned to his turbomachinery interests by becoming chairman of a high-level advisory committee for Rolls-Royce. This consisted of senior academics and staff from the National Gas Turbine Establishment at Farnborough and from Rolls-Royce (figure 6), who met regularly to advise the company on major technical issues. John was an ideal chairman for this group: he caught on to new developments remarkably quickly and was always eager to

Figure 6. The opening meeting of the Rolls-Royce Aerothermal panel, *ca.* 1989. John chaired the panel for more than 10 years. (Online version in colour.)

contribute ideas of his own. As chairman John had to pass the committee's recommendations on to the Rolls-Royce Engineering Director, and once every year to the main board. Hopefully, these recommendations contributed somewhat to the success of the company over the 15 years during which he was chairman.

John also renewed his turbomachinery interests by becoming a regular visitor at the Whittle Laboratory, which he had founded 20 years earlier. The laboratory had expanded greatly over that period and had earned a worldwide reputation for its research. It is appropriate that when a new wing of the laboratory was opened in 1997 it was named the Horlock Wing. John used to visit the laboratory every week, sharing an office with one of his past students, Ivor Day, now a leading expert on experimental methods and compressor stall. He interacted extremely well with the staff and research students in the laboratory, encouraging them in their research and publishing several papers jointly with students. He even learned to use numerical methods, which now dominate the subject, at both a research and a design level, to study some interesting features of flow in compressors. However, his main interests were now on the thermodynamics of gas and steam turbine cycles for power generation, especially on the effects of cooling flows on gas turbine efficiency. He published several papers on this topic in collaboration with Professor J. B. Young from Cambridge (15, 18, 19) and with L. Torbidoni from Genoa University (17, 21).

Another of John's activities after retirement was to chair the Board of Trustees of the EMF Biological Research Trust. This was an offshoot from his directorship of the National Grid Company and looked into a possible relationship between strong electromagnetic fields and cancer. It also looked at the design of electricity pylons with a view to improving their visual impact.

In the 15 years after retirement John wrote some 30 papers. He was a regular attendee and contributor at the annual American Society of Mechanical Engineers gas turbine conferences

Figure 7. Some guests at John's 70th birthday party held at St John's College, Cambridge, in 1998. From left to right: Dr Roy Smith (General Electric Company), J.H.H., Dr Bill Heiser (US Air Force), Dr Phil Ruffles FRS (Rolls-Royce). (Online version in colour.)

and received two of their major awards: the Calvin Rice lectureship in 1994 and the R. Tom Sawyer Award in 1997. In 1998 a 70th birthday party for John was held at the Whittle Laboratory and at St John's College. This included a series of seminars and was attended by many prominent colleagues from the UK and overseas (figure 7). After retirement he wrote four books related to the thermodynamics of power generation. These were *Combined power plants* in 1992 (13), *Energy for the future* (jointly with Sir Denis Rooke FRS and I. Fells) in 1995 (14), *Advanced gas turbine cycles* in 2003 (16) and *Energy: resources, utilisation, and policies* in 2009 (21). He also published an autobiography, *An open book*, in 2006 (20), which greatly helped in the preparation of this memoir.

In 1992 John became Treasurer and Vice President of the Royal Society, the first engineer to hold that office since 1843 (figure 8). This involved him in spending two or three days per week in London. In this capacity he saw the need for further independent funding of the Royal Society and initiated a fund-raising scheme named Project Science, chaired by Prince Philip, which eventually raised about £20 million for the Society. He was also responsible for the Society's policy on education, in which capacity he interacted with Lord Dearing's Committee on Higher Education and was instrumental in formulating a new career structure for school technicians. His five-year term as Treasurer and Vice President ended in 1997 and at the age of 69 John felt that he had done enough and was glad that the tenure of the position had recently been reduced from ten years to five.

For the last few years of his life John was physically handicapped but he continued to be technically active almost up to the time of his death, co-authoring his last paper in December 2014 (23). This came 46 years after an earlier paper in the same antipodean series (8) and demonstrates how consistently John retained his interest in solving the remaining physical

Figure 8. Officers of the Royal Society, 1994. Back row: Peter (now Sir Peter) Lachmann (Biological Secretary), Sir Francis Graham-Smith (Physical Secretary). Front row: J.H.H., Sir Michael Atiyah (President), Dame Anne McLaren (Foreign Secretary).

problems of flows through turbomachinery blading and how there remain many interesting issues for succeeding generations to resolve.

In 1996 John was knighted for services to science, engineering and education. The three topics correctly reflect the areas on which he has had influence but do not do justice to the magnitude of his contribution. His contribution to science was partly through his work for the Royal Society but much of his research, for example actuator disc theory and secondary flow theory, falls midway between science and engineering and he made major contributions to these fields. His contribution to education comes largely through his Vice-Chancellorship of two universities. His time at the OU was especially important and it is quite possible that the OU might have been closed down had it not been for his determined resistance. He also contributed to education through his reorganization of the Engineering Tripos at Cambridge and through his teaching and supervision of many research students. His contribution to engineering is enormous. His many research papers have aided researchers and designers over many decades, but probably the major influence has been through his books. These have been the main source of information for thousands of engineers in the field of turbomachinery aerodynamics and the thermodynamics of power generation; they are certain to continue in widespread use for decades to come. A major achievement, which alone would earn him international recognition, was his founding of the Whittle Laboratory. Judged on the number of best-paper and other awards this has grown to be the world's most successful turbomachinery research centre. John would be proud of its continued success.

However, a list of his achievements does not do justice to John as a person. In fact his achievements would not have been possible without his personality. He had a rare combination of outstanding technical and administrative abilities, coupled with the facility to communicate effectively and to relate to colleagues at all levels of society. These talents are illustrated by the fact that he rose to become chairman of almost every committee that he was invited onto. He was equally comfortable arguing over government policies with cabinet ministers or discussing detailed technical issues with research students. He had a long and happy family life and is fondly remembered by his wife Sheila, daughters Alison and Jane, son Tim and eight grandchildren and by very many past and present colleagues.

Acknowledgement

The frontispiece photograph was taken by Godfrey Argent and is reproduced with permission.

Honours

1976   Fellow of the Royal Society (Vice-President and Treasurer, 1992–97)
1977   Fellow of the Royal Academy of Engineering
1980   Hon. DSc, Heriot-Watt University
1981   Hon. DSc, University of Salford
1987   Hon. DSc, University of East Asia
       Hon. DSc, University of Liverpool
1991   Hon. Fellow, St John's College, Cambridge
       Hon. DUniv, Open University
       Hon. DSc, Council for National Academic Awards
       Hon. Fellow, University of Manchester Institute of Science and Technology
1995   Hon. DSc, De Montfort University
1996   Knighted for services to science, engineering and education
1997   Hon. DSc, Cranfield University

       Fellow of the Institution of Mechanical Engineers
       Fellow of the American Society of Mechanical Engineers
       Foreign Associate of the National Academy of Engineering, USA
       Honorary Fellow of the Royal Aeronautical Society

Awards

1962   James Clayton Prize, Institution of Mechanical Engineers
1969   Thomas Hawksley Gold Medal, Institution of Mechanical Engineers
1994   Calvin Rice lecturer, American Society of Mechanical Engineers
1997   R. Tom Sawyer Award, American Society of Mechanical Engineers
       Arthur Charles Main Prize, Institution of Mechanical Engineers
2001   Sir James Ewing Medal, Institution of Civil Engineers
2003   ISOABE Achievement Award, International Society of Air Breathing Engines

BIBLIOGRAPHY

The following publications are those referred to directly in the text. A full bibliography is available as electronic supplementary material at http://dx.doi.org/10.1098/rsbm.2016.0009 or via http://rsbm.royalsocietypublishing.org.

(1)   1952   *Some actuator-disc theories for the flow of air through an axial turbo-machine*. Aeronautical Research Council R&M 3030.

(2)   1955   *Experimental and theoretical investigation of the flow of air through two single-stage compressors*. Aeronautical Research Council R&M 3031.

(3)   Erosion in meanders. *Nature* **176**, 1034.

(4)   1956   Some experiments on the secondary flow in pipe bends. *Proc. R. Soc. Lond.* A **234**, 335–346.

(5)   1958   *Axial flow compressors—fluid mechanics and thermodynamics*. London: Butterworth.

(6)   1962   (With W. R. Hawthorne) Actuator disc theory of the incompressible flow in axial compressors. *Proc. Instn Mech. Engrs* **176**, 789–814.

(7)   1966   *Axial flow turbines—fluid mechanics and thermodynamics*. London: Butterworth.

(8)   1970   Unsteady flow in turbomachines. In *Proc. Third Australasian Conference on Hydraulics and Fluid Mechanics, Sydney, 25–29 November 1968*, pp. 221–227. Sydney: Institution of Engineers, Australia.

(9)   1973   The swing of a cricket ball. In *Proc. ASME Symp. on the Mechanics of Sport* (ed. J. L. Bleustein), vol. 4. New York: American Society of Mechanical Engineers.

(10) 1978   *Actuator disk theory*. New York: McGraw-Hill.

(11) 1982   (Editor, with D. E. Winterbone) *The thermodynamics and gas dynamics of internal combustion engines* (2 volumes). Oxford University Press.

(12) 1987   *Cogeneration—combined heat and power (CHP): thermodynamics and economics*. Oxford: Pergamon.

(13) 1992   *Combined power plants, including combined cycle gas turbine (CCGT) plants*. Oxford: Pergamon.

(14) 1995   (Editor, with D. Rooke & I. Fells) *Technology in the third millennium: energy for the future*. London: Chapman & Hall.

(15) 2002   (With R. C. Wilcock & J. B. Young) *Gas properties as a limit to gas turbine performance* (ASME paper GT-2002-30517). New York: American Society of Mechanical Engineers.

(16) 2003   *Advanced gas turbine cycles*. Oxford: Elsevier Science.

(17) 2005   (With L. Torbidoni) A new method to calculate the coolant requirements of a high-temperature gas turbine blade. *Am. Soc. Mech. Engrs J. Turbomachinery* **127**, 191–199.

(18)   (With R. C. Wilcock & J. B. Young) The effect of turbine blade cooling on the cycle efficiency of gas turbine power cycles. *Am. Soc. Mech. Engrs J. Engng Gas Turbines Power* **127**, 109–120.

(19) 2006   (With J. B. Young) Defining the efficiency of a cooled turbine. *Am. Soc. Mech. Engrs J. Turbomachinery* **128**, 658–667.

(20)   *An open book*. Durham: Memoir Club.

(21)   (With L. Torbidoni) Turbine blade cooling: the blade temperature distribution. *Proc. Inst. Mech. Engrs* A **220**, 343–353.

(22) 2009   *Energy: resources, utilisation, and policies*. Malabar, FL: Krieger Publishing Co.

(23) 2014   (With J. P. Gostelow & G. J. Walker) Some unresolved physical problems in turbomachinery flows. In *Proc. 19th Australasian Fluid Mechanics Conference, Melbourne, 8–11 December 2014* (ed. H. Chowdhury & F. Alam). Victoria: Australasian Fluid Mechanics Society (http://people.eng.unimelb.edu.au/imarusic/proceedings/19/331.pdf).

DAVID HUNTER HUBEL

27 February 1926 — 22 September 2013

DAVID HUNTER HUBEL

27 February 1926 — 22 September 2013

Elected ForMemRS 1982

BY ROBERT H. WURTZ*

National Institutes of Health, Bethesda, MD 20892, USA

David Hunter Hubel was one of the great neuroscientists of the twentieth century. His experiments revolutionized our understanding of the brain mechanisms underlying vision. His 25-year collaboration with Torsten N. Wiesel revealed the beautifully ordered activity of single neurons in the visual cortex, how innate and learned factors shape its development, and how these neurons might be assembled to ultimately produce vision. Their work ushered in the current era of analyses of neurons at multiple levels of the cerebral cortex that seek to parse out the functional brain circuits underlying behaviour. For these achievements, Hubel and Wiesel, along with Roger W. Sperry, shared the Nobel Prize for Physiology or Medicine in 1981.

EARLY LIFE: GROWING UP IN CANADA

David Hubel was born on 27 February 1926 in Windsor, Ontario. Both of his parents were American citizens, born and raised in Detroit, but because he was born in Canada he also held Canadian citizenship. His father was a chemical engineer, and his parents moved to Windsor because his father had a job with the Windsor Salt company. His mother, Elsie Hubel (*née* Izzard), was independent minded, with an interest in electricity and a regret that she had not attended college to study it. His paternal grandfather had emigrated from Germany to Detroit, where he had invented the first process for the mass production of gelatin pill capsules.

When David was three years old, his family moved to Montreal. David was fascinated by science very early, with chemistry being a central interest. That interest was probably inspired by his father's work and was further stimulated by the gift of a chemistry set that developed into a small basement laboratory. In his experiments he 'perfected' an explosive mixture of

* bob@lsr.nei.nih.gov

This memoir originally appeared in *Biographical Memoirs of the US National Academy of Sciences* and is reprinted, with slight modifications, with permission.

potassium chlorate, sugar, and potassium ferricyanide. One test produced an explosion that rocked the neighbouring houses, was heard over the Montreal suburb of Outremont, and elicited a visit from the police. A second, less explosive interest was electronics, which led to the successful construction of a one-tube radio and a lifelong interest in amateur radio. Another enduring interest in his life was the piano; David started taking lessons before he could read and continued into college.

David went to an English-speaking school in Montreal. Learning French was required in schools in the bilingual province of Quebec, but teaching was mainly for written rather than spoken French. As a result he could not speak French as readily as he could read it. In high school ten subjects were compulsory but one additional could be selected: he chose Latin. As he recalled, 'Mathematics was considered appropriate for future engineers, Latin for future doctors, and biology for dumb students.'

He had an influential teacher who required an essay every week based on ideas, not just facts, which perhaps contributed to the clarity of his writing, a skill for which he was well known later in life. After graduation from high school David planned to go to college in the USA and had interviews at MIT, but the onset of World War II disrupted that plan. He stayed in Montreal and went to McGill University. He did honours in mathematics and physics 'because these subjects fascinated me and there was almost nothing to memorize.' He graduated in 1947.

Accepted for graduate work in physics at McGill, on a whim he also applied to medical school, although he had never taken a biology course. When he decided to go to medical school his future physics adviser opined, 'Well, I admire your courage. I wish I could say the same for your judgment!'

David found medical school to be hard work, and the only course he enjoyed was biochemistry. By the second year he developed a strong interest in the brain. This was a fortunate interest, because the Montreal Neurological Institute, part of McGill, was world famous for its work on epilepsy by the neurosurgeon Wilder Penfield and the neurologist Herbert Jasper. David screwed up his courage and arranged to meet the famous Dr Penfield. It must have been a successful meeting because Penfield promptly arranged a meeting with Dr Jasper, who in turn offered David a summer job doing electronics in his physiology laboratory. This critical afternoon was stressful for David. When he got back to his car he found the engine running, with the keys locked inside. He had to take the streetcar home to get a spare key.

By the time David received his MD degree in 1951, he found that he enjoyed clinical medicine. He continued his training at McGill, doing an internship, a year of neurology residency and a fellowship year in clinical electroencephalography (EEG) with Jasper. He had worked two summers in Jasper's laboratory, and during his year-long stay he had become Jasper's assistant for interpreting EEG records. He came to regard Jasper as a major mentor.

David finally had the opportunity to move to the USA to do a second year of neurology residency at Johns Hopkins University, beginning in 1954. The move also subjected him to the doctor's draft in the USA because of his citizenship. He volunteered for the army, and successfully sought to be assigned to a laboratory, the Walter Reed Army Institute of Research in Washington DC. In 1955, close to 30 years of age, David had his first opportunity to do research on his own.

WALTER REED: FORAY INTO RESEARCH

David's mentor at Walter Reed was Michelangelo 'Mike' Fuortes, a spinal cord neurophysiologist who collaborated with Karl Frank at the National Institutes of Health (NIH) in Bethesda.

David had no experience in animal research or in electrophysiology, and he regarded himself as fortunate to have a mentor as supportive as Mike. David did an initial experiment with Mike that compared the flexor and extensor reflexes in decerebrate cats, which gave him a thorough grounding in electrophysiology. David was then casting about for his own research project when Mike suggested placing wires in the cortex of cats and recording from them while they were awake. The attempt was a failure, but the idea captured David's imagination.

He began developing techniques for recording from animals while they were awake. He first developed a tough tungsten microelectrode, and then developed an electrode advancer that moved the electrode to record from isolated neurons. Both inventions required multiple versions. The advancer required so many versions that he decided to make new ones himself, so he learned to operate a lathe. David recorded from freely moving cats during sleep and wakefulness and noted that neuronal activity was strongly affected by the level of arousal. He also recorded from primary visual cortex, and was able to confirm the main results that Richard Jung's laboratory in Germany had obtained using full-field visual stimulation in anaesthetized cats. Many neurons were not activated by full-field stimulation (as reported by Jung's group) or by David's flashlight. Some of these unresponsive neurons, however, did respond when he moved his hand in front of the cat. Some responded to hand movement in one direction but not the other, a preview of what was to be seen later in the analysis of the visual activity of the anaesthetized cat.

David was not quite the first person to record from awake, behaving animals. His mentor, Herbert Jasper, had visited David's laboratory to learn how to make tungsten electrodes. Jasper used them in experiments on classical conditioning in monkeys, which he published in 1958, a year before David published his findings from cats during wakefulness and sleep in 1959. After David joined in collaboration with Torsten Wiesel (ForMemRS 1982) he was fully occupied with anaesthetized animals with eyes paralysed, permitting the precise mapping of receptive fields. Ed Evarts at the NIH perfected a complete system for use in awake monkeys that became the standard in the field.

David never lost interest in this early work; his visits to Ed's NIH laboratory years later quickly moved to an animated comparison of recording devices between the fathers of the field. David had successfully demonstrated restrictive receptive fields in the lateral geniculate nucleus, which he said he found difficult to study 'since a waking cat seldom kept its eyes fixed for more than a few minutes.' Because a monkey moves its eyes several times per second, before the visual system could be studied in an awake monkey, the monkey had to hold its eyes steady long enough for the receptive fields to be mapped. This problem was solved by developing a behavioural procedure that rewarded the monkey for not moving its eyes. These techniques of restraining the monkeys, recording single neurons and requiring the monkeys to maintain visual fixation have become standards in the field of vision research. Although David left recording from awake animals in 1959, he left a legacy of innovations that are incorporated into methods that are taken for granted today.

LANDMARK STUDIES OF THE VISUAL CORTEX

While the insights into the nervous system that the collaboration between David Hubel and Torsten Wiesel produced are landmarks in the evolution of neuroscience, the collaboration itself was fortuitous. David and Torsten first met when Torsten visited Walter Reed to learn how to make David's tungsten electrodes. At the time Torsten was in the laboratory of Stephen

Figure 1. David Hubel and Steve Kuffler in the Neurobiology Department Library. (Courtesy of Edward Kravitz and the Photo Archive of the Department of Neurobiology, Harvard Medical School.)

Kuffler (ForMemRS 1971) in the Wilmer Institute at Johns Hopkins. Kuffler had made major discoveries about the retinas of cats but had not himself worked on vision for several years. David was planning to join the physiology department at Johns Hopkins at the invitation of Vernon Mountcastle (ForMemRS 1996). The snag was that the physiology laboratories at Hopkins were being renovated and would not be available for a year.

In view of this delay, Kuffler suggested that David spend time in his laboratory collaborating with Torsten, an ingenious solution to the space problem. In 1958 David moved to the Wilmer Institute. After discussions between Kuffler, Torsten and David, they agreed that the best research direction would be to extend the investigations that Kuffler had done on the cat retina to the visual cortex (figure 1).

It was a particularly far-sighted decision and the start of a collaboration that lasted 25 years. Throughout the long series of experiments that followed, Kuffler was their major mentor, tough critic and lifelong friend. When Kuffler moved from the Wilmer Institute at Johns Hopkins to Harvard Medical School in 1959, David and Torsten moved with him and were among the inaugural members of what eventually became the Department of Neurobiology at Harvard. They were thus not only at the forefront of studying the visual system, but they also did so in one of first departments devoted to studying the nervous system in the emerging field of neuroscience.

When they began their experiments at Johns Hopkins, David and Torsten set up in the laboratory that Kuffler had used to study the cat's retina. They incorporated instruments that were classics as well as ones that were newly developed. They initially used the projection ophthalmoscope that Kuffler had used to stimulate the retina, and for holding the anaesthetized cat's head steady they used the same stereotaxic frame used nearly 20 years earlier by Samuel Talbot and Wade Marshall to map the topography of the cat's primary visual cortex. The tungsten electrode and the electrode advancer that David had developed at Walter Reed were new additions.

Figure 2. Hubel and Wiesel mapping a receptive field in cat visual cortex using a 'crude projector and screen'. (Photo source: Harvard Medical Library in the Francis A. Countway Library of Medicine.)

The goal of David and Torsten's experiments was to see what changes occurred in visual processing beyond the retina. Individual retinal receptors break the image falling on the retina into hundreds of thousands of individual messages. Each message conveys information about one tiny part of the visual field, the visual receptive field of the individual neuron. These messages are transmitted by the optic nerve to a nucleus of the thalamus, the lateral geniculate nucleus, and from there to the primary visual area of the cerebral cortex. The task of the cerebral cortex is to reconstruct these messages so that the brain can 'see' the image. At the time of their experiments, there was little idea, much less experimental evidence, about how this reconstruction came about.

What was known about the neuronal mechanisms of the cat retina was largely based on the investigations of Steve Kuffler on the output neurons of the retina, the ganglion cells. Kuffler had shown that these retinal neurons primarily responded not to full-field illumination but to light or dark spots in the receptive field of the retinal neuron. At the start of David and Torsten's experiments, the issue was whether there would be a change in what stimuli neurons at higher levels of the visual pathway required. The answer to that came relatively quickly; they had great difficulty activating cortical visual neurons with spots of light.

But persistence enabled a serendipitous finding that changed the course of their experiments. For one neuron they were able to find only faint responses to spots of light in one part of the visual field, but when they changed the slide in the ophthalmoscope they produced a burst of activity. It was the line produced by the edge of the slide that excited the neuron, as they subsequently verified by using lines instead of spots. This preference for oriented line stimuli revealed a major feature of primary visual cortex: neurons responded to oriented lines better than to the spots of light that were effective in the retina. Subsequent experiments showed that different neurons preferred different orientations, and across a sample of neurons all orientations were represented (figure 2).

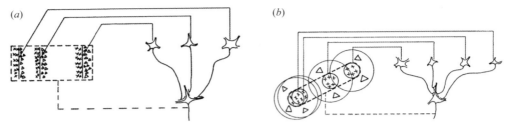

Figure 3. Drawings of the sequence of visual processing in striate cortex proposed by Hubel and Wiesel in 1962. (*a*) The transformation from circular receptive fields of the retina to the elongated fields of a simple cell in primary visual cortex. (*b*) Construction of complex cell receptive fields from inputs from simple cells. (From Hubel & Wiesel (1962).)

David and Torsten's first publication was in 1959 and reported the orientation selectivity of primary visual cortex. In 1962 they published their first *magnum opus* in which they differentiated between classes of visual neurons, described the columnar organization of these neurons (an organization previously found by Vernon Mountcastle in the somatosensory cortex) and showed that neurons within a column preferred similar orientations. They also showed that cortical neurons had ocular dominance; they received input from each eye but most had a greater response from one eye than the other.

One of the salient points of the 1962 paper was not the results but the interpretations. David and Torsten suggested that neurons in visual cortex could be categorized by the stimuli that optimally activated them. The first two classes were termed 'simple' and 'complex' cells. They went on to suggest that there was a sequential organization of the cells. Cortical simple cells responded to line stimuli as a result of the alignment of the circular receptive fields of their input neurons (figure 3*a*). Complex cells that required less precise localization of a line stimulus were driven by inputs from multiple simple cells (figure 3*b*). This was a major step suggesting how activity in one neuron class might result from the input of a previous neuron class in the sequence. This of course raised the possibility that, if the sequence were followed high enough in the visual system, the neuronal activity underlying visual perception might be understood.

Subsequent work in the cat showed a continued modification of receptive field organization in the visual areas just beyond the primary visual cortex, and in at least one visual area beyond those. David and Torsten then largely switched to studying the monkey, first going back to the lateral geniculate nucleus and showing that the receptive field centre and surrounds had a colour opponent organization (stimuli in the centre responded best to one colour; stimuli in the surround responded to a different colour). This was followed by a series of investigations on the monkey visual cortex including the organization of ocular dominance columns and orientation columns and their changes across the topographic map in primary visual cortex. A hypothesis that arose from these observations was the 'ice cube' model of cortical modules in which the ocular dominance and orientation columns ran in orthogonal directions. The series of experiments opened entirely new directions of research on visual mechanisms in the brain that are still being pursued by laboratories throughout the world.

Within three years after beginning the study of the visual cortex in adult cats, David and Torsten also began studying its development. They knew that children with congenital cataracts had substantial visual deficits even when those cataracts were removed. It seemed possible that, from their new understanding of the visual processing in cerebral cortex, the nature of the deficit, its location in the visual pathway and the extent of plasticity in the developing visual system might be determined. This turned out to be the second major direction in their research collaboration.

They first recorded from kittens at successive ages during development. They found that shortly after the kitten's eyes opened, many neurons in the primary visual cortex showed orientation selectivity similar to that in adults. They concluded that at least some neurons must have made the proper connections before the eye opened. They then tested to see whether the visual responses changed when the kitten was deprived of vision, as would be the case with a child with cataracts. In the laboratory they produced this deprivation by sewing the lids of one eye closed in newborn kittens under anaesthesia, to produce monocular deprivation. When they looked in the lateral geniculate nucleus and primary visual cortex after a few months of closure, they found reduced responses and anatomical changes in neurons receiving input from the deprived eye, whereas the neurons receiving input from the open eye appeared normal. Cortical neurons that usually received input from both eyes now usually responded only to input from the normal eye. The monocular deprivation was most severe when started before eye opening, less severe if the eyes were open for a few months and then sutured closed, and normal if the suturing was done in the adult cat.

These experiments established two fundamental points about visual development: the neuronal connections are probably largely present before the eyes open and the visual system is used, and the organization of these connections deteriorates if deprived of visual input during a critical period after birth. Subsequent experiments established that the critical period was between four and eight weeks after eye opening. For treatment of humans with cataracts or disorders of the alignment of the two eyes, it is essential to make the corrections before the end of a comparable human critical period. The findings had provided support for both sides of the old controversy between nature and nurture: there were neuronal connections at birth, which supported the nature view, but the continued use of the system was required to maintain its function, the nurture point of view.

A series of experiments followed that explored the effects of deprivation in baby monkeys, a better animal model of human visual function. Here they found that the critical period starts at birth, with high sensitivity to lid closure during the first four to six weeks, lower sensitivity for another few months, and no effect after a year. The greater precision in the organization of the monkey cortex and the use of more advanced anatomical techniques produced clear visual evidence for ocular dominance columns and their change with monocular deprivation. These experiments on the plasticity within the visual system also spawned a new field of research, including a search for the synaptic and molecular mechanisms of that plasticity.

The work on the functional structure of the visual system and its developmental plasticity were both cited by the Nobel committee when it awarded David and Torsten the Nobel Prize for Physiology or Medicine in 1981, which they shared with Roger Sperry (figure 4).

Summing up the collaboration

The collaboration between David Hubel and Torsten Wiesel flourished for 25 years, and is summarized in their 2005 book, *Brain and visual perception*. The collaboration is certainly one of the most successful in biological science and one of the longest. The two had common views about how to go about doing science, what was important and what was not. They asked

Figure 4. Torsten Wiesel, Roger Sperry and David Hubel in Stockholm, 1981. (Photo source: Harvard Medical Library in the Francis A. Countway Library of Medicine.)

the right question: how did the system work? Their respect for each other was immense, as was their realization that they each brought special abilities to the collaboration, different but complementary.

Over the years of long shared hours Torsten remarked that there was also a bonding between them, and a familiarity with each other's attitudes and habits. David recalled that when an experiment extended late into the night 'I knew we should quit when Torsten began to talk in Swedish.'

At the memorial service for David, Torsten described the collaboration as the best years of his life. David, during his lifetime, also referred to his time at Harvard collaborating with Torsten as an idyllic period. The collaboration strengthened as their discoveries multiplied; they realized that they had arrived at the visual cortex at just the right time with the right techniques, and been given a golden opportunity. Their success was due to their own insight and diligence, to luck, and to the initial research direction that was the gift of Steve Kuffler. The two repeatedly and gratefully acknowledged the critical advice and guidance provided by Kuffler. They would have been pleased to share the Nobel Prize with him, but he died in 1980, the year before they were awarded the prize.

Within a few years of their initial publications, their results attracted widespread attention. Within 10 years of the initial publications, they were so well known that they were referred to universally as H & W as if they had become a name brand, which they had.

With the perspective of a half century after the initial reports, it is interesting to review why their research was so riveting. First, they recorded single neurons from among the millions in the visual cortex, in contrast with the EEG and with evoked potential methods that averaged across pools of possibly unrelated neurons. Second, single-neuron recording allowed them to compare the change in neuronal response with changes in the visual stimulus, a comparison that many doubted would be useful in a brain with billions of neurons. Third, they proposed a specific sequential organization of individual neurons that over a series of steps offered a mechanistic explanation of why different neurons responded best to different stimuli.

Figure 5. David Hubel at the microscope.

Finally, the proposed transformations across a series of neurons offered the first glimpse of how the sequential connection between neurons might transform the signals responding to spots in the retina into the oriented lines in cortex. This in turn raised the possibility that understanding such a progression might lead to insights into the brain mechanisms underlying visual perception.

In addition, their later experiments on monkeys contributed to shifting the field of visual research to the primate brain. The addition of behavioural techniques to control fixation of the eyes, momentarily stabilizing the visual fields, to David's microelectrodes and advancer, made higher levels of the visual system the prime target for investigating higher brain functions. Thus a substantial fraction of what we know about the cerebral cortex, particularly higher behavioural functions, results from the exploration of the visual system, and the genesis of that work is the observations of Hubel and Wiesel.

David remained at Harvard for the rest of his life as the John Franklin Enders University Professor of Neurobiology. He continued to work on the visual system with several collaborators and students, including a 10-year collaboration with Marge Livingstone that included identifying the functional correlates of the submodalities of vision (such as form, contrast and colour). Torsten moved to Rockefeller University, where he concentrated on the connections within striate cortex with Charles Gilbert.

BEYOND THE LABORATORY

In addition to winning the Nobel Prize in 1981, David's contributions were recognized by election to the leading learned societies of the world, including the National Academy of Sciences in 1971, the American Academy of Arts and Sciences in 1965, the American Philosophical Society in 1982, and the Royal Society, as a Foreign Member, in 1982. He was honoured by multiple honorary lectures and awards, and received 13 honorary degrees (figure 5).

In 1954 David married Ruth Izzard shortly after she graduated from the Department of Psychology at McGill. She went to work as a laboratory technician to supplement David's minimal stipend. Ruth was warm and friendly to anyone who encountered her, and she gave David over their nearly 60-year marriage the support he needed for his life's work.

Ruth and David had three sons, Carl, Eric and Paul, born in Washington DC, Baltimore and Boston respectively. Their sons speak with fond memories of David and their home life growing up. They comment on his devotion to Ruth, and the happy dinners of the family on the nights that David was home (he and Torsten worked late into the night a couple of times per week). They comment on his endless curiosity that stimulated their own curiosity. The challenge in science is always the competing demands between life in the laboratory and life at home. Judging from the comments of his sons, David seems to have achieved an enviable balance.

David had many interests out of the laboratory, and shared several of them with his sons. Already noted was skill with a lathe that he referred to as 'occupational therapy'. According to his son Carl, David's interests outside of the laboratory included piano, flute and recorder; woodworking and metalsmithing (he made most of the household furniture, lamps and picture frames); rug and scarf weaving; ham radio and Morse code; languages (French, German and Japanese); astronomy and photography (he had a darkroom in the basement); bicycling, sailing, skiing and tennis.

During the years when he was engaged in experiments, David did little teaching, but on becoming emeritus he began teaching Harvard freshmen, which both teacher and students enjoyed. Although David and Torsten concentrated on their collaboration and had few students in the laboratory for many years, David was passionate about engaging students. I experienced his enthusiasm directly after hearing his talk at Woods Hole in 1961 when I was a graduate student. Detecting my more than casual interest, he invited me to visit their laboratory, put me up overnight and let me watch the day's experiments (long microelectrode penetrations through a cortex). It changed my life, as interactions with David changed the lives of so many others. The case was similar for many of the medical and graduate students who were fortunate enough to spend time in David and Torsten's laboratory.

David had strong opinions on many subjects, which he expressed with conviction. His opposition to animal rights activists became particularly evident when, as President of the Society for Neuroscience, he used his position and prestige to point out the tremendous benefits of animal-based research to understanding and treating human diseases. As a Nobel laureate his views were exceptionally influential.

Perhaps David expressed his strongest views on what he regarded as the best way to do science. He extolled the virtues of small groups of hands-on scientists, and the benefits that come from principal investigators spending time at the bench. He cited his time at Harvard, and particularly his collaboration with Torsten, as a period when their time was largely spent doing their own research that was designed to test their own ideas. Graduate students and postdoctoral fellows in their laboratory had similar liberty. They were part of a Neurobiology Department organized by Steve Kuffler, whose style was a model for the ideal laboratory that David envisioned. It was an era of what we might call 'mom and pop science', not a pejorative description but one of nostalgia and envy. It was a different era, in which David and others like him flourished. In David's view, why would we want to stray from such a successful system?

AUTHOR PROFILE

Dr Robert H. Wurtz

Robert Wurtz is an NIH Distinguished Investigator in the Laboratory of Sensorimotor Research of the National Eye Institute at NIH. He received his AB from Oberlin College in chemistry and his PhD in physiological psychology from the University of Michigan, where he worked under James Olds on intracranial self-stimulation. He did postdoctoral research at Washington University in St Louis, at the NIH and at the Physiological Laboratory at Cambridge University. He joined the Laboratory of Neurobiology at the National Institute of Mental Health, in 1966, where he began studies on the visual system of awake, behaving monkeys, and became the founding Chief of the Laboratory of Sensorimotor Research in 1978.

Dr Wurtz's research explores the organization of the brain underlying visual perception and the control of eye movement. He developed methods now widely used to study the visual system in awake, behaving monkeys, the best animal model available for the human visual system. This method made possible the analysis of the brain's integration of visual input from the eye with information about movement of the eye that is essential for the active vision of all primates. This approach underlies his subsequent experiments and those of others on the neuronal basis of attention and of visual cognition in general. The recent work of Dr Wurtz and his colleagues has revealed circuits within the brain that convey information used to produce stable visual perception in spite of our frequent eye movements.

Dr Wurtz has served as President of the Society for Neuroscience and has been elected to the National Academy of Sciences, the Institute of Medicine and the American Academy of Arts and Sciences. Among his awards and honours are the Karl Spencer Lashley Award of the American Philosophical Society, the Distinguished Scientific Contribution Award of the American Psychological Association, the Ralph W. Gerard Prize of the Society for Neuroscience, the Dan David Prize for Brain Sciences, and the Gruber Prize in Neuroscience.

ACKNOWLEDGEMENTS

I am indebted to Torsten Wiesel for reading a draft of this biography. I appreciate the help provided me by Carl Hubel, and I have also incorporated some comments made by Carl, Eric and Paul, particularly those made at the memorial service for David at Harvard on 16 November 2013. Recollections from David's early life are adapted from his 1996 autobiographical chapter published in the collection *The history of neuroscience in autobiography.*

The frontispiece photograph is reproduced courtesy of the US National Academy of Sciences.

SELECTED BIBLIOGRAPHY

A full bibliography and CV are available as electronic supplementary material at http://dx.doi. org/10.1098/rsbm.2016.0022 or via http://rsbm.royalsocietypublishing.org.

1957   Tungsten microelectrode for recording from single units. *Science* **125**, 549–550.
1958   Cortical unit responses to visual stimuli in non-anesthetized cats. *Am. J. Ophthalmol.* **46**, 110–122.
1959   Single unit activity in striate cortex of unrestrained cats. *J. Physiol.* **147**, 226–238.
        (With T. N. Wiesel) Receptive fields of single neurones in the cat's striate cortex. *J. Physiol.* **148**, 574–591.
1960   Single unit activity in lateral geniculate body and optic tract of unrestrained cats. *J. Physiol.* **150**, 91–104.

1962   (With T. N. Wiesel) Receptive fields, binocular interaction and functional architecture in the cat's visual cortex. *J. Physiol.* **160**, 106–154.

1963   (With T. N. Wiesel) Receptive fields of cells in striate cortex of very young, visually inexperienced kittens. *J. Neurophysiol.* **26**, 994–1002.

     (With T. N. Wiesel) Single-cell responses in striate cortex of kittens deprived of vision in one eye. *J. Neurophysiol.* **26**, 1003–1017.

1965   (With T. N. Wiesel) Receptive fields and functional architecture in two non-striate visual areas (18 and 19) of the cat. *J. Neurophysiol.* **28**, 229–289.

     (With T. N. Wiesel) Comparison of the effects of unilateral and bilateral eye closure on cortical unit responses in kittens. *J. Neurophysiol.* **28**, 1029–1040.

     (With T. N. Wiesel) Binocular interaction in striate cortex of kittens reared with artificial squint. *J. Neurophysiol.* **28**, 1041–1059.

     (With T. N. Wiesel) Extent of recovery from the effects of visual deprivation in kittens. *J. Neurophysiol.* **28**, 1060–1072.

1966   (With T. N. Wiesel) Spatial and chromatic interactions in the lateral geniculate body of the rhesus monkey. *J. Neurophysiol.* **29**, 1115–1156.

1968   (With T. N. Wiesel) Receptive fields and functional architecture of monkey striate cortex. *J. Physiol.* **195**, 215–243.

1969   (With T. N. Wiesel) Anatomical demonstration of columns in the monkey striate cortex. *Nature* **221**, 747–750.

     (With T. N. Wiesel) Visual area of the lateral suprasylvian gyrus (Clare–Bishop area) of the cat. *J. Physiol.* **202**, 251–260.

1970   (With T. N. Wiesel) The period of susceptibility to the physiological effects of unilateral eye closure in kittens. *J. Physiol.* **206**, 419–436.

1971   (With T. N. Wiesel) Aberrant visual projections in the Siamese cat. *J. Physiol.* **218**, 33–62.

1972   (With T. N. Wiesel) Laminar and columnar distribution of geniculo-cortical fibers in the macaque monkey. *J. Comp. Neurol.* **146**, 421–450.

1974   (With T. N. Wiesel) Sequence regularity and geometry of orientation columns in the monkey striate cortex. *J. Comp. Neurol.* **158**, 267–294.

     (With T. N. Wiesel) Uniformity of monkey striate cortex: a parallel relationship between field size, scatter, and magnification factor. *J. Comp. Neurol.* **158**, 295–306.

     (With T. N. Wiesel) Ordered arrangement of orientation columns in monkeys lacking visual experience. *J. Comp. Neurol.* **158**, 307–318.

1975   (With T. N. Wiesel & S. LeVay) The pattern of ocular dominance columns in macaque visual cortex revealed by a reduced silver stain. *J. Comp. Neurol.* **159**, 559–576.

1977   (With T. N. Wiesel & S. LeVay) Plasticity of ocular dominance columns in monkey striate cortex. *Phil. Trans. R. Soc. Lond.* B **278**, 377–409.

     (With T. N. Wiesel) Functional architecture of macaque monkey visual cortex [Ferrier Lecture]. *Proc. R. Soc. Lond.* B **198**, 1–59.

1980   (With T. N. Wiesel & S. LeVay) The development of ocular dominance columns in normal and visually deprived monkeys. *J. Comp. Neurol.* **191**, 1–51.

1981   (With J. C. Horton) A regular patchy distribution of cytochrome oxidase staining in primary visual cortex of the macaque monkey. *Nature* **292**, 762–764.

1982   Exploration of the primary visual cortex [Nobel Lecture]. *Nature* **299**, 515–524.

1984   (With M. S. Livingstone) Anatomy and physiology of a color system in the primate visual cortex. *J. Neurosci.* **4**, 309–356.

1987   (With M. S. Livingstone) Segregation of form, color and stereopsis in primate area 18. *J. Neurosci.* **7**, 3378–3415.

1991   Are we willing to fight for our research? *Annu. Rev. Neurosci.* **14**, 1–8.

1996   David H. Hubel. In *The history of neuroscience in autobiography*, vol. 1 (ed. L. Squire), pp. 296–317. Washington DC: Society for Neuroscience.

2002   (With S. Martinez-Conde & S. L. Macknik) The function of bursts and spikes during visual fixation in the awake lateral geniculate nucleus and primary visual cortex. *Proc. Natl Acad. Sci. USA* **99**, 13920–13925.

2005   (With T. N. Wiesel) *Brain and visual perception: the story of a 25-year collaboration.* New York: Oxford University Press.

2009   The way biomedical research is organized has dramatically changed over the past half-century: are the changes for the better? *Neuron* **64**, 161–163.

KENNETH LANGSTRETH JOHNSON

19 March 1925 — 21 September 2015

KENNETH LANGSTRETH JOHNSON

19 March 1925 — 21 September 2015

Elected FRS 1982

By Roderick A. Smith* FREng

Department of Mechanical Engineering, Imperial College London, Exhibition Road, London SW7 2BX, UK

Kenneth Johnson, born in Barrow in 1925, studied mechanical engineering at Manchester during World War II. After some years in industry and an early appointment back in Manchester, he spent most of his academic career teaching and researching at the Engineering Department of Cambridge University. He was also a long-serving Fellow of Jesus College. He was renowned for the insightful analysis of meticulous experiments in contact mechanics. He was widely acknowledged as the doyen of this area, particularly after the publication of his seminal work of the same name. His major publications included topics in friction and wear, rheology and lubrication, rolling contact and adhesion. Important applications of his insights included the prediction of corrugations and cracks in railway lines. He was gratified when, after many years of dormancy, his ideas in adhesion were used by others to explain the climbing behaviours of insects and other small animals with soft feet. He was a devoted family man, characterized by warm personal qualities that won him many friends around the world.

Background and family life

The paternal grandfather of Kenneth Langstreth Johnson (hereafter KLJ or Ken), Richard Cuthbert Johnson, formerly of Leeds and later of Lancaster, had seven children, one of whom, Frank Herbert Johnson, was bright enough to attend Lancaster Royal Grammar School and to win an Exhibition to study history at Sidney Sussex College, Cambridge. He was appointed to a teaching post at Barrow Grammar School in 1922, rose to become Senior History Master, ran the school orchestra and remained there for the rest of his teaching career until 1956. KLJ's mother, Ellen Johnson (*née* Langstreth), was a school teacher; she was born in Todmorden in 1888 and married Frank in March 1923. KLJ was born on 19 March 1925.

* roderick.smith@imperial.ac.uk

The young KLJ attended Victoria Infants' School in Barrow from 1930 to 1933. He recalled his main memory of this time as having to sit by a girl to help with his knitting, and commented that this perhaps accounted for his subsequent shyness with girls. The other memorable event at the time was the birth of his sister, Margaret Elizabeth, in August 1932. At seven years of age, he transferred to St Paul's Primary School, Abbey Road, Barrow, for a happy three-year period. He remembered the headmistress, Miss Fallows, as being 'brilliant', teaching scripture like a novel, and introducing her young charges to the novels of Charles Dickens.

This period culminated with the once dreaded (though possibly now much lamented) 11-plus examination in March, for entry to the grammar school. It comprised papers in arithmetic and English, and an intelligence test. Barrow, with a population of about 50 000, had only one grammar school, so competition was stiff, but KLJ was placed third overall in town.

Thereafter KLJ, after what he described as a conventional happy childhood, set out on an academic trajectory aimed, after his father, for Cambridge; however, he also led an active outdoor life of rugby, athletics, swimming, Boy Scouting and, later, fell walking and climbing on the nearby Western Fells in Cumbria. He recalled, 'The Grammar School for Girls stood alongside, separated by a high spiked fence. This must have been just for show, since there was easy access round the back.' Clearly the shyness was wearing off.

In the sixth form, studying mathematics, applied mathematics and physics, he received high-quality teaching from teachers who held degrees in engineering and had been recruited during the Depression. He was appointed Head Prefect and was on the school teams for rugby, swimming and athletics. His second sixth-form year, 1941, coincided with the wartime bombing of Barrow, a strategic military target. In normal circumstances he would have stayed at school for a Cambridge Scholarship year. However, the wartime need for technically qualified staff was pressing, so on taking his Higher School Certificate he became what was known as a 'Snowflake': he was interviewed by C. P. Snow (later Lord Snow), then Director of Technical Personnel at the Ministry of Labour, and offered a State Bursary on an accelerated course to read mechanical engineering at Manchester College of Technology, attached to the Ministry of Aircraft Production. It is worth noting the origins of this scheme: soon after the outbreak of the World War I in 1915, most university students (including KLJ's father) volunteered for military service in France. Of the 40 or so freshmen in Frank's year of 1913, only two returned to complete their degree. During the German rearmament in the 1930s it was recognized that further war, when it came, would be long and very dependent on science and engineering. To avoid the mistakes of 1915, Snow, a chemistry lecturer at Cambridge, was recruited to Whitehall to increase the output of science and engineering graduates.

Forgoing his Cambridge ambitions, Ken therefore went to Manchester, where he was a resident of Dalton Hall, a Quaker foundation, which provided a rewarding student experience. After just two years and three months, including one day a week spent on military training, parades being rotated though the week to give minimum disruption of the lecture timetable, he graduated in December 1944 with the top first-class degree of his year and winning the accolade of the Isobel Stoney Prize.

EARLY CAREER

After his graduation, an interview at the Ministry of Aircraft Production sent KLJ to a firm in Gloucester called Rotol, which was set up to design and manufacture aircraft propellers for use with Rolls-Royce and Bristol aero engines. The plant was located halfway between Gloucester and Cheltenham, and Ken was found accommodation in a National Service hostel that took a wide variety of 'war workers'. The single-storey huts contained about 12 identical rooms on either side of a central corridor. Each room was about 8 feet square, containing a bed, cupboard, table, wash basin and toilet.

KLJ was put to work in the Research Department, whose main concern was measuring with strain gauges the vibratory stresses in the propeller blades. For bending stresses the gauges were glued top and bottom parallel to the axis of the blade; for torsional stress the gauges were attached at 45°. The forward thrust developed by each blade of a propeller depends on its rotational speed and the length of the blade, but this is limited to keep the tip speed below the speed of sound. To convert the increasing power developed by the engine over the years it became necessary to increase the number of blades. The Spitfire fighter had started the war with three blades but had reached five when KLJ joined the firm in January 1945. The engine drove the propeller through a gear of non-simple ratio. Thus by measuring the frequency of any troublesome vibration it was possible to tell whether it originated in the engine or in the propeller. He later recalled that the introduction of a five-bladed propeller for the later versions of the Spitfire helped him to divide the pie equitably when his immediate family numbered five.

In addition to the bending vibrations, the blades were observed to vibrate torsionally if their aerofoil sections became stalled. This unstable vibration was known as 'stalled flutter'. To check whether a new design of propeller was subject to flutter it was driven on a spinning tower by a large electric motor located at Farnborough. Given the flutter problem to study, KLJ set about calculating the natural torsional frequencies of a blade, using the relaxation method of Southwell (1940).

During this period in industry he worked as a Manchester external candidate for an MSc, awarded in December 1948, on 'Stalled flutter of propeller blades'; from January 1949 he took up the post of Assistant Lecturer in Mechanical Engineering back in his old department at Manchester College of Technology and as Resident Tutor back in Dalton Hall. His experience of mechanical vibrations had led him to the conclusion that serious ignorance existed on issues related to damping, which was at that time rather vaguely attributed to hysteresis losses in the material. So in the somewhat limited time allowed by his teaching duties, he initiated a research programme into slip damping at interfaces in contact, thus beginning a lifetime study of many aspects of the contact problem. Experiments were conducted with a hard steel sphere pressed into contact with a flat steel surface and subjected to an oscillating shear force. In 1953 David Tabor, from Cambridge, who had recently published a major book with Philip Bowden, *The friction and lubrication of solids* (Bowden & Tabor 1950), visited Manchester and was impressed by Ken, particularly his careful experimental work; this proved to be the beginning of a long academic association and close friendship (Field 2008).

Teaching was always a great priority for Ken, and he took his responsibilities extremely seriously. In this period he became founding editor of the journal *Bulletin of Mechanical Engineering Education* (now *International Journal of Mechanical Engineering Education*); an early paper on laboratory teaching in the journal prompted an invitation to KLJ to speak at a conference in Cambridge, his first academic association with what became his natural home.

It is of interest that a much earlier (1908) researcher of the propeller at Manchester was the philosopher Ludwig Wittgenstein (Lemco 2007). His patent for an airscrew driven by blade-tip jets was inappropriate for use in aeroplanes but eventually found application in the Fairey

Rotodyne helicopter of the 1950s. Both KJL and Wittgenstein became Cambridge professors, but KLJ of course stayed with engineering.

Earlier, while at Rotol, Ken had met and courted Dorothy Watkins during healthy and wholesome pursuits such as walking, cycling, swimming, music and Youth Hostelling, activities that continued throughout the Manchester period. He passed auditions to become a member of the Hallé Choir and toured the country under the baton of John Barbirolli during the Festival of Britain in 1951, a tour that included Edinburgh, the new Festival Hall in London and the refurbished (from bombing) Free Trade Hall in Manchester.

In 1954 KLJ was appointed Demonstrator in Engineering at Cambridge. A short time before he began his appointment on 1 October 1954 he handed in his PhD thesis to Manchester. He and Dorothy were married on 11 September and had a brief honeymoon at Llangrannog on the Cardigan Bay coast (remembered by the smell of dead and dying rabbits struck down by myxomatosis). A final tidying-up of the Manchester work saw KLJ and Tabor, as External Examiner, travelling from Cambridge by train to Manchester, Tabor reading the thesis and Ken *The Guardian*, interrupted by questions from his interlocutor. In December 1954 KLJ was awarded a PhD for his thesis 'An experimental investigation of the effects of an oscillating tangential force at the interface between elastic bodies in contact'.

KLJ at Cambridge, 1954–2015: research

KLJ's academic career in the Cambridge University Engineering Department can be summarized thus: promoted to Lecturer in 1956 and Reader in 1970, elected *ad hominem* Professor in 1977, and served as Deputy Head of Department from 1983 to 1992, the year in which he formally retired on 30 September. He was elected to a Fellowship of Jesus College in 1957, where he served as Tutor for Graduate Students from 1963 to 1969. More will be said about the personal distinction he brought to these appointments later, but first we will consider his research activity.

A useful collection of KLJ's papers has been published (Kauzlarich & Williams 2005), and very recently a summary of his life and work has appeared (Hills *et al.* 2016). These have made the present task much easier: I have leaned rather heavily on these two publications. First, Hills *et al.* stated perceptively:

> The term 'contact mechanics' is not precisely defined, but we may sensibly think of it as the study of all the phenomena associated with the interaction between solid bodies pressed or held in contact: it includes a knowledge of the contact stress field, a characterisation of the material response both elastically and plastically, deduction of the effects of surface roughness, of lubrication, of friction, and an understanding of the physics of the interaction forces between the surfaces. Ken Johnson has contributed to all of these aspects of the problem, and in the last of these fields his efforts have been seminal.

Exactly so.

Kauzlarich & Williams classified KLJ's research into five themes and invited experts in each area to nominate what they thought to be the six most influential of Ken's publications in each of these areas. A few of the nominations appeared in more than one topic. This has made my task of selecting key publications from a distinguished list considerably easier and I, too, follow these themes. The sections below are closely based, with acknowledgements, on the descriptions and nominations of the experts.

Friction and wear (T. H. C. Childs)

When KLJ came on the scene, Bowden & Tabor (1950) had established the junction growth theory of adhesive friction and Archard (1953) had just formulated his wear law. There was clear understanding that wear could be by the direct failure of metallic junctions or could proceed via oxidation and failure of the oxide. All these theories drew attention to the fact that real surfaces are rough, that frequently the areas of real contact between loaded surfaces, at the high spots or asperities, are much less than the apparent areas, and that it is the behaviour of these real areas that govern friction and wear.

Paradoxically, KLJ's earliest contributions (about 1955–65) to studies of friction and wear were not directly in the behaviours of these real contact areas in isolation, for example their deformation and failure under combined normal and tangential loading. Rather he studied the elastic subsurface deformations and relative motions of hard steel surfaces (for example a ball and a flat) loaded together in both static and rolling contact conditions, acted on by tangential forces and spin torques insufficient to cause sliding. In such conditions the apparent contact area consists of both locked and slipping regions. Johnson's studies (for example (1, 2)*) brought together the micro (real contact area) and macro (subsurface) views of surface interactions. The insights into and interests in contact mechanics that he developed underpinned a second period of friction and wear activity (about 1965–70 and 1985–95), one that was explicitly concerned with asperity deformation and failure (for example (7, 24)). From about 1995 (for example (25, 29)) he attacked a fundamental question relating to dry friction: how does slip occur at the real contact area between two elastic bodies—rather than assuming a sliding friction coefficient value as an input to a mechanical analysis, can it, or the limiting friction stress at sliding, be derived from the material properties of the sliding surfaces themselves?

The previous paragraph sets the scene, in terms of the technical areas to which KLJ has contributed. But his influence on others working in the fields of friction and wear has been, and still is, much greater than just through these particular achievements. His approach to problem solving combined rigorous analysis (with approximations, where necessary, guided by physical insight) with conceptually and sometimes physically simple experimentation. Clear and well-thought-out diagrams supported written descriptions of difficult concepts. His presentation of large collections of data, spanning ranges of physically diverse conditions, were routinely made digestible through the use of appropriate non-dimensional groups that enabled divergences between experiments and theory to be readily identified. And, as often as not, the divergences were as interesting for the insights they produced as the areas of agreement were for the satisfaction they gave. Of course these are points that apply generally beyond the areas of friction and wear, but they constitute a significant contribution that merits attention.

Rheology and lubrication (H. P. Evans)

KLJ's first reported effort of measuring traction in disk machines was in a paper co-authored with R. Cameron (6). (Disk testing is the experimental modelling of the contact conditions in many types of machine elements simulated by the study of two disks, driver and driven, of the same or different radii and materials pressed into contact, either under lubricated or dry conditions.) In these tests the contact pressures used increased to 1.8 GPa and the form of the traction curves was described: linear behaviour at low sliding, progress to a maximum value, and then a gentle reduction as the sliding speed became large—'viscoelastic behaviour is suggested

---

* Numbers in this form refer to the bibliography at the end of the text.

by the observed decrease in apparent viscosity as the time of transit of the oil through the contact zone was reduced by increasing the rolling speed'. In interpreting the measurements, attention was concentrated on evaluating hypotheses as to the cause of decreasing traction at high sliding rates. The paper came down on the side of the theory that the film shears like a plastic solid when a critical shear stress is reached, and found that the explanation of a Newtonian fluid whose viscosity is reduced by frictional heating was not supported by the high-pressure data.

A paper co-authored with Jim Greenwood, a long-time colleague in the Engineering Department at Cambridge, and S. Y. Poon (10) is one of two theoretical papers included in this section. This paper examined mixed lubrication in which the load was supported partly by an elastohydrodynamic film and partly by direct asperity contact. It introduced an ingenious treatment to conclude that 'the surface separation, upon which the asperity contact conditions depend, can be calculated directly from the elastohydrodynamic conditions, independently of surface finish'. Electrical contact resistance measurements were also presented and compared well with predictions emerging from the model.

A paper co-authored with J. L. Tevaarwerk (11) was an experimental *tour de force*. It provided a thorough demonstration of the nonlinear Maxwell model proposed by the authors. The experimental technique used disk tests operated in two different modes: rolling with spin, and rolling with sideslip. The two modes resulted in distinctly different strain rate histories. Essentially one mode was used to establish parameters for the nonlinear Maxwell model proposed. In a 'more discriminating test' the model was then shown to correspond to the experimental results of the other mode without any adjustment of the parameters. This has become probably the most referenced paper in the field, and justifiably so.

A pair of papers were co-authored with C. R. Evans and published in 1986 (16, 17). The first ('The rheological properties of elastohydrodynamic lubricants') chronicled the way in which the important parameters identified in describing the traction response of lubricating oils vary in terms of pressure and temperature. It explained the four regimes found to occur in the extensive disk machine testing that was performed. The key parameters of viscosity, Eyring stress and limiting shear stress were determined from disk testing for three lubricating oils of different types. The paper recognized that the fourth parameter, the lubricant's elastic shear modulus, cannot be established from disk testing because it is masked by the shear deflection of the disks themselves. This much-referenced paper presented a wealth of information, not least for analysts seeking to build detailed theoretical models of the shearing lubricant.

The other twin paper ('Regimes of traction in elastohydrodynamic lubrication') (17) presented the four traction regimes established by earlier experimental work in terms of two non-dimensional groups. These were based on the contact pressure, established as being the dominant influence on traction behaviour, and on a parameter influential in determining film thickness. The paper presented maps that partitioned this parameter space into regions where each of the traction regimes (Newtonian, Eyring, viscoelastic and elastic–plastic) were expected to occur. A map was proposed for each of three lubricants subject to extensive measurement in the experimental programmes that fed into this interpretative paper. The purpose of the maps was to 'assist in a prediction of traction forces in any particular application', and the process by which this prediction could be effected was detailed. Also included was a comparison of the maximum predicted traction coefficient with those determined from experimental traction curves over a range of temperatures and contact pressures.

The final paper of this selection of contributions to lubrication ('The behaviour of transverse roughness in sliding elastohydrodynamically lubricated contacts') (20) was also co-authored with Greenwood. It sought to examine theoretically the influence of sinusoidal roughness in a sliding elastohydrodynamic contact. The paper typifies the approach seen in so many of the papers included in this collection: a simple theoretical treatment that is ingeniously developed to give a fundamental understanding of the essence of a tribological situation. This paper is particularly noteworthy for having identified the fundamental difference between elastohydrodynamic films that behave in a Newtonian way and those subject to significant non-Newtonian effects when surface roughness is included.

Contact stress analysis (D. A. Hills)

Chronologically, Johnson's first major contributions in contact mechanics began in Manchester, when he studied, both experimentally and theoretically, the problem of a fixed spherical contact subject to oscillatory shear. The results of that work, published in *Proceedings of the Royal Society* series A in 1955 (1), set the standard and pattern for the next half century: the careful devising of innovative experiments that pull out the essential physical features of the problem under consideration, the development of appropriate theory, drawing wherever possible on closed-form solutions whose interpretation and application to the experiment are clear, and, above all, the use of physical insight to explain phenomena previously obscure. The 1955 paper marked the start of Johnson's contribution to fretting (loaded contacts subjected to small oscillatory movements). The experiments he performed, developed by John O'Connor, Johnson's first research student at Cambridge and who himself went on to make major contributions to this field and later to develop the celebrated Oxford replacement knee, are still very widely quoted as demonstrations of physical evidence of partial slip in stationary contacts. An extension of the theory from spherical bodies to more general second order contacts was undertaken with P. J. Vermeulen (5). This included a deduction of the surface state of stress and this then led to the general question of the study of contacts between second-order bodies, each of which could be represented by a half-space—the Hertzian contact.

Hertz (1882) solved what we would now describe as the boundary value problem; he deduced the contact pressure between convex bodies in terms of the load and local curvature. One hundred years later, Johnson gave a seminal review lecture describing Hertz's original study, the intervening refinements and the practical application of the theory to engineering problems. Although a review, that paper (12), given at the Institution of Mechanical Engineers, provided the audience with a perfect picture of the classical study of the problem, its limitations and its extensions.

We turn now from elastic analysis to the problem of contacts involving plasticity. Finite-element (FE) methods have now given us a sledgehammer technique to investigate nonlinearities. I recall being told early in my career that engineering is the art of being exactly right rather than exactly wrong. Easy availability of FE methods that are now taken for granted came after KLJ's early work, so he turned to thinking, the application of physical insight, and dimensional argument; these processes provided real progress, in a way that contrasts with the unthinking use of commercial FE code giving additional obscurity. His insight was nowhere more acute than in his studies of the indentation test (8), and anyone wishing to learn about plasticity in general could do no better than to read KLJ's papers on indentation experiments. The paper in question, (8), makes quite clear to anyone the different possible responses that any elastic–plastic component makes to the application of load, and does so in a way that the reader can then generalize to a wide range of other problems. Of course, all elastic–plastic problems have to be solved by applying the Prandtl–Reuss equations, and KLJ's elegant solution of them 'on-axis' beneath a hardness test is a model for how careful thought can say a great deal about a potentially intractable problem. In the paper Johnson argued how, from simple kinematic considerations, the strain state on-axis beneath a sphere can be specified, and from this how the stress state must follow. He proved unambiguously that, when an indenter is removed, there must be reversed plastic flow upon unloading. The use of simple kinematic simplifications to problems involving plasticity was then applied to contact problems involving more widespread plasticity, and it also formed the basis of his studies of shakedown under rolling contact, discussed below.

The work on rolling contact was aimed at explaining several things—rail corrugation, for example—but also at determining the steady-state residual stresses that, together with the passing contact loading, give the conditions for ensuing failure. In the mid 1970s Johnson was turning his mind to the various kinds of failure that can occur. Specifically, at that time the 'delamination' theory of wear had just been introduced, and there was a suggestion that both wear and rolling contact fatigue therefore involved the propagation of some kind of 'crack'. As ever, the nature of the contact stress field makes this rather difficult, and it was left to Johnson to make significant inroads into the problem and also to recognize that the amount of plasticity present was always very significant and could not simply be ignored. He successfully found the unifying theme between wear and rolling-contact fatigue, and published key papers on this with A. D. Hearle, Alan Bower and, later, A. Kapoor (14, 19, 21).

Rolling contact (A. Kapoor)

Steel wheels rolling on steel rails provide the low-friction rolling contact that gives railways an energy-efficient way of moving passengers and freight. Wheels roll or slide (or roll *and* slide) on rails, subjecting them to repeated loading. Before replacement, a typical rail may carry some 500 million tonnes, equivalent to 50 million repeated passes of a loaded wheel. The so-called permanent way is anything but permanent: each passage of each wheel is an irreversible event. What load can be supported safely on each tiny contact patch about the size of a small coin? Naturally, answers coming out of a single application of the load will not be correct. KLJ considered the effect of this relentless loading. The material can flow plastically, leading to the development of residual stresses and strain hardening. Wear can change the contact geometry to become more conformal, thus decreasing the stress. Simple concepts from the shakedown of civil structures were applied in the late 1950s and early 1960s to produce the very first shakedown limits in rolling contact. This is, in a sense, a safe contact pressure limit for the material to remain elastic in repeated rolling contact (4, 22). The intervening 40 years saw many research groups developing these ideas further; KLJ and his co-workers continued to produce various key publications investigating the shakedown of surfaces subjected to rolling contact, sliding contact, rough surfaces and oscillating loads, the key ones of which we will now consider.

After his first shakedown paper, KLJ started to model plastic flow and residual stresses. Work on measuring and predicting plastic flow continued throughout this period. In the 1980s the Cambridge group was working on modelling plastic flow in rolling contact, using a dislocation method and traditional plasticity theories modified to model the accumulation of plastic strain with time, a process termed ratchetting (18, 19, 23). Alan Bower used considerable computational resources to solve the plasticity equations to determine the extent of ratchetting in rolling contact (19). Alas, his experiments to mimic this behaviour in twist and tension–compression tests were met by the failure of the specimen by what we now know as ratchetting failure. Ratchetting failure and ratchetting wear were next on the research agenda. All this research has found decent homes. Joe Kalousek in Canada applied 'pummelling' to design rail and wheel profiles, and ratchetting is currently being used to predict rolling contact fatigue in rails and wheels.

Rolling contact causes cracking and was dramatically brought to public attention in the UK by the catastrophic rail failure at Hatfield in October 2000. In the 1970s and 1980s KLJ had collaborated extensively with British Rail to work on squats and other fatigue cracks caused by rolling contact. Dislocations were used to model a crack parallel to the surface of a passing wheel; subsequently a research student, Bower, developed a model of rolling contact fatigue crack that is driven by Mode I (opening), Mode II (shear) and fluid pressure. These models are now being used increasingly by the railway industry to understand and control rail degradation.

The 1970s saw KLJ, with Cambridge colleagues Stuart Grassie and R. Wielie Gregory, developing dynamic analyses of wheel–rail interaction to address the formation of corrugations (longitudinal sinusoidal waviness on the rail surface, also manifested by longer wavelengths on dirt roads) leading to 'roaring rails' (13). Models incorporating vehicle, bogie, suspension, wheel, contact patch, rail, pad, sleeper, ballast and sub-base are extremely complex, and KLJ's simple semi-analytical approaches demonstrated the importance of pad resilience on dynamic loads at frequencies associated with this phenomenon, work that has led to the use of more resilient pads worldwide. Other models helped demonstrate the role of pinned–pinned response of rails between the two sleepers in developing corrugations. Much of this work has been applied subsequently to real problems by Grassie, who also collected considerable data on rail geometry and dynamic response in days when modern sophisticated equipment was not available.

Adhesion (J. A. Greenwood)

The Bowden–Tabor theory of friction suggests that friction is the force required to shear the junctions that form whenever two solids make contact. An obvious objection to the theory is that these junctions seem not to require a normal force to break them, so why do they require a tangential force? Do solids adhere, or do they not? One of KLJ's earliest publications (3) explained that elastically a circular contact must have infinite tensile stresses round its periphery if the contact area is any greater than the Hertz area for the current load, so any attempt to decrease the load without decreasing the contact radius will induce such stresses— so adhesion is not observed. Alan Roberts found (Roberts 1968) that rubber–glass contacts *were* larger than Hertz theory predicted and that significant normal forces were required to separate the two; his colleague Kevin Kendall suggested that this was perhaps due to the surface energy. An expert on elastic contact theory was brought in, and the Johnson–Kendall–Roberts (JKR) theory was born—and satisfyingly verified (9).

According to the theory, the pull-off force for a circular contact, as occurs between a sphere and a plane, will be

$$P_c = \tfrac{2}{3}\pi R\Delta\gamma,$$

where R is the radius of the sphere and $\Delta\gamma$ the surface energy, so that a direct mechanical measurement of the physical–chemical quantity $\Delta\gamma$ becomes possible. Unfortunately, the physical chemists already used a different formula, the Derjaguin equation:

$$P_c = 2\pi R\Delta\gamma.$$

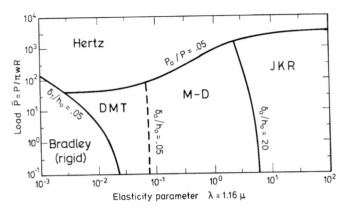

Figure 1. Adhesion map. (From (26).)

Both equations are apparently applicable to all elastic contacts even though neither contains an elastic constant. The difference lies in the contact geometry. In the JKR theory the infinite tensile stresses round the periphery mean that the contact has a neck: indeed, Maugis *et al.* (1976) reproduced the JKR equations by recognizing that this neck is the parabolic crack tip of fracture mechanics and, by applying the fracture mechanics equation, that the stress intensity factor, a measure of the stress singularity, will be

$$K = \tfrac{1}{2}(E^*\Delta\gamma/2)^{\frac{1}{2}}.$$

Tabor recognized that the height of the neck is critical because, of course, surface energy is merely an integral measure of the effect of surface forces, and these have a finite (rather small) range. The ratio of the neck height to the range of action of the surface forces gives the 'Tabor parameter',

$$\alpha = R^{\frac{1}{3}}\Delta\gamma^{\frac{2}{3}}/E^{*\frac{2}{3}},$$

and both equations are correct. The 'adhesion map' (figure 1) (26) details the behaviour of different contacts.

Origins and developments of the JKR theory (K. Kendall, A. D. Roberts and W. Federle)

KLJ's relationship with David Tabor has been mentioned above. The JKR theory was one of the most interesting fruits of their collaboration, specifically with Kendall and Roberts, two of Tabor's research students. Roberts was working to understand how windscreen wipers function. Kendall joined British Rail Research in 1969, trying to understand how rusting iron particles in the brake block stuck to carriage windows, giving them the familiar dirty brown colour. These nanoparticles stuck so hard to the glass windows that it was impossible to scrape them off. They both concluded that some kind of adhesion was taking place, giving 'greater than Hertz' contact patches. Ken was brought into the discussion and agreed to attempt the necessary modification of the Hertz theory; this he achieved the next day as his family were watching the Football Association Cup Final.

Adhesive contacts have a key role in many technological processes such as manufacturing, in which control over contaminant particles is essential, for example in wafer cleaning for semiconductors. Micromechanical devices demand better control over friction and lubrication. Particle immobilization or release, controlled positioning in reproduction devices, and settling of bio-organisms on surfaces or biotechnologies all need to be better understood for continuing progress. The rising impact of the JKR equation, starting in the 1990s, reveals the steeply growing relevance of small-scale adhesive contact theories in physics and biology.

Ken showed that that the JKR theory is particularly accurate for the analysis of contacts at the micrometre and nanometre scale (28). The interest in adhesion and friction between contacts at this length scale had markedly increased with the introduction of new measurement techniques such as the atomic force microscope and the surface force apparatus (27), as well as with progress in silicon-based microfabrication technology.

A further area of application for Ken's contributions to contact mechanics emerged recently with the field of bio-adhesion. The adhesive structures on the feet of many climbing animals, such as geckos, tree frogs, spiders and insects, are small and soft, and therefore fall within the 'JKR regime' (26). These natural adhesives work well on rough substrates, allow rapid switching between firm attachment and detachment, and possess self-cleaning properties, so that many groups worldwide have started to mimic their properties and build synthetic bio-inspired adhesives.

One of Ken's friends and neighbours in New Square was Walter Federle, also a Fellow of Jesus College, a zoologist studying the function of adhesive organs in insects. Walter often took Ken to lunch in college during his later years, and they discussed bio-adhesion research. Despite his failing health, Ken enjoyed talking about science and he was always particularly interested to hear about his former students and colleagues.

Many important developments in the bio-adhesion field build on Ken's work, such as the understanding of how animals control adhesion via shear forces and how adhesive pads compensate for surface roughness. The JKR theory also forms the basis of the 'contact splitting' principle, which suggests that splitting of a single contact into multiple smaller contacts can lead to enhanced adhesion, providing an explanation for the independent evolution of dense arrays of microscopic adhesive hairs in geckos, spiders and insects (Arzt *et al.* 2003).

Contact mechanics: the book

KLJ's *magnum opus*, his monograph, *Contact mechanics* (15), was a fitting culmination of his studies on the modelling of contact mechanics. Universally regarded as the bible of the subject, it is a source to which one returns over and over again. It is very unlikely to be surpassed or outdated. It has been translated into many languages and has pride of place on many academics' bookshelves worldwide. It will be a long-lasting memorial to KLJ's deep understanding of the topics that formed his life's research.

KLJ AT CAMBRIDGE, 1954–2015: LIFE AND FAMILY

Ken and Dorothy had three children, Marian (born in 1957), Hilary (1958) and Andrew (1962), the last of these when KLJ was enjoying a sabbatical at Brown University. At that time one crossed the Atlantic by ship; Andrew has now been an air traffic controller in the USA for many years, avoiding the sea sickness that affected the family en route to Providence, Rhode Island, on the old *Queen Mary*.

In Cambridge KLJ continued choral singing, initially with the Cambridge University Musical Society under David Willcocks, and later with Collegium Laureatum. He was

Figure 2. KLJ, an inspiring and dedicated teacher. (Online version in colour.)

President of Cambridge University Swimming Club and encouraged his family to swim, and to swim well. He was much valued as a consummate college man, and is fondly remembered by his many pupils for his well-informed supervisions and by students in the Engineering Department for inspiring and insightful lectures (figure 2). His behind-the-scenes advice was much respected, in for example introducing Sir Alan Cottrell FRS to the Jesus College election, which led to his highly successful Mastership. KLJ was unstinting in his wise advice to younger colleagues, of whom I was one. A close bond developed: I always regarded Ken as a father figure on whom I could rely. We enjoyed many family walking and climbing holidays in the Lake District (figure 3). It was my pleasure to lead Ken up C Buttress on Coniston Dow Crag, a climb he had achieved years previously in his Barrow days. Somewhat less of a pleasure was enabling him to climb Broadstand on Scafell by having him stand on my head to reach some high holds—not, I am now informed by Dorothy, because of an unsteadiness for heights on his part but because of a stiff shoulder, originally injured by a fall at Scout Camp years previously and much later replaced by some mechanical parts.

Ken and Dorothy hosted legions of students, researchers and visitors in their home at Park Terrace and latterly at New Square. Their generous entertainment almost always began with a sherry and included a delicious meal served with large helpings of convivial conversation. Most of the people I have contacted in the preparation of this memoir have extremely happy memories of their kind hospitality. All have commented on how much they valued Ken's innate good sense and stability. The people involved with his research have repeated their admiration of Ken's clever and careful experimental work and the brilliance of his analysis of the results, leading to deep insights into the physical nature of the phenomena he studied. The citation for the Royal Medal in 2003 stated: 'In recognition of his outstanding work in the field of contact mechanics. His work is characterized by elegant experiments, skilful analyses and insightful explanations of observed phenomena.'

Figure 3. KLJ and the author, together with their respective wives, Dorothy and Yayoi, walking in the Lake District in 1990. (Online version in colour.)

If a poor idea or theory was offered, his reply was 'I would be surprised if that were true.' An outrageously silly idea might provoke the reponse 'I would be extremely surprised if that were true.' Mrs Thatcher managed to render him speechless, when she introduced a conversation with him by saying 'We scientists …'.

After retirement in 1992 his life continued rather unchanged: research, college, family and friends. Many holidays were spent in Ravenglass in a cottage from which KLJ enjoyed the Western Lakes. We shared his 70th birthday on top of Bowfell, drinking champagne in the snow. Ken remained as sharp as ever and produced several publications. In the decade after his 80th birthday, mobility started to become a problem with increasing severity. Dorothy was ever supportive. In the last couple of years, life was beginning to be an effort. He welcomed visits to his book-lined home in New Square, but eventually even the short walk down to the Cam was too much (figure 4). On what proved to be his last visit to Wasdale Head in the summer of 2013, as we loaded KLJ back into the car, he said, with a small tear, 'This is the last time I shall see these hills.' Sadly, this proved to be true.

KLJ was extremely modest, a trait that has made collecting this information unusually difficult. So I shall let his modesty and dry, gentle humour speak for themselves by quoting from his acceptance speech for the 2006 Timoshenko Medal, given at the Applied Mechanics Dinner of the 2006 Winter Annual Meeting of the American Society of Mechanical Engineers (ASME), held at the Hilton Chicago Hotel on 9 November 2006 (see http://imechanica.org/node/462).

I must belong to a shrinking number of Timoshenko medallists who actually met the great man himself, that is if 'met' is the right word. It was at the 1956 IUTAM Congress in Brussels. He was always surrounded by KGB men in long black coats. It was impossible to get near enough to see the white of his beard.

However, I can claim to be a good friend of his side-kick: Norman Goodier, Timoshenko medallist in 1963 and co-author of his famous book on *The Theory of Elasticity*. Goodier graduated

Figure 4. Watercolour painted by KLJ shortly before his death.

in Engineering from Cambridge (England, that is!) and came to the United States on a scholarship to the University of Michigan, where he met Timoshenko. Interestingly for me, Goodier's Cambridge PhD Dissertation contained a report of an investigation into corrugation of railway rails. It showed rather more progress on that problem than I managed to make 50 years later.

When Timoshenko emigrated from Russia to the US, he found it an undeveloped country as far as mechanics was concerned, which led to the foundation in 1927 of the Applied Mechanics Division of ASME, with Timoshenko as first chairman. No doubt he was pleased to find an acolyte with a sound Cambridge training in mechanics. Goodier capitalized on the situation in the time honoured way, by 'marrying the boss'[s] daughter'.

[…]

In common with vibration analysts then and since, I worried about assessing the damping. I became convinced that in most practical cases of structural vibration the damping arose principally by slip at clamped joints. On returning to the university I made this the subject of my PhD. This topic brought me into close contact with R. D. Mindlin and his group at Columbia University, who were studying Hertz contact under the action of tangential friction forces. That was the start.

During my time as a Graduate Student I was profoundly influenced by three books: Timoshenko and Goodier's *Theory of Elasticity;* Den Hartog's *Mechanical Vibrations* and Bowden and Tabor's *Friction and Lubrication of Solids*. I tried to copy the simple and direct style of all three when I came to write my own book on *Contact Mechanics*. I have been fortunate that contact mechanics has become an expanding field. In the early days I had a visit from Don Conway of Cornell, who expressed surprise that anyone could fill their time with contact problems!

[…]

I must also take this opportunity to acknowledge my debt to David Tabor, who died last year aged 92. He not only invented the word 'tribology'*, but along with F. P. Bowden in the Cavendish Laboratory in Cambridge, he established the subject as a respected scientific discipline. Many members of ASME look back with pleasure and satisfaction to time spent in that laboratory.

[...]

About the time I formally retired from teaching in '92, microprobe instruments such as the Atomic Force Microscope and the Surface Force Apparatus were being developed mainly in physics departments, and used to study friction on the atomic scale. Irwin Singer of the Naval Research lab, in Washington, observed that this activity was going on in complete isolation from the traditional world of engineering tribology. He organized a NATO ISA [Advanced Study Institute] in Braunlager [Braunlage] to bring the two communities together. It was an eye opener for both sides. My activities changed quite dramatically from wheel/rail contacts, whose diameters are about 10 mm, to contacts of a few micrometres or less. At this scale molecular adhesion between the surfaces becomes a major effect. This meant that I had to make friends with physicists, for whom friction has suddenly become a fashionable subject. Maybe they will be able to explain the question that so exercised Bowden and Tabor 60 years ago: the relation between adhesion and friction. They picked up [a] paper of mine on adhesion in Hertz contacts, written in 1971 with two graduate students: Kevin Kendall and Alan Roberts which suddenly became famous as the 'JKR theory'. To bask in this celebrity, my co-author Alan Roberts recently entered JKR into Google and was rewarded by pages and pages of citations ... to J. K. Rowling, the author of Harry Potter.

HONOURS

1982 Fellow of the Royal Society
1983 Honorary Fellow, American Society of Tribologists
1987 Fellow of the Royal Academy of Engineering
1995 Honorary Fellow, University of Manchester Institute of Science and Technology

AWARDS

1961 James Clayton Prize, Institution of Mechanical Engineers (also in 1969)
1983 National Award, American Society of Lubrication Engineers
1985 Tribology Trust Gold Medal, Institution of Mechanical Engineers
1998 George Stevenson Medal, Institution of Mechanical Engineers
1999 William Prager Medal, Society of Engineering Science
2003 Queen's Medal, Royal Society
2006 Timoshenko Medal, Applied Mechanics Division of the American Society of Mechanical Engineers

* Tabor actually used the term 'tribotechnology'; Peter Jost, who died in June 2016, is usually credited with the term 'tribology' in his eponymous report written 50 years ago (Jost 1968).

ACKNOWLEDGEMENTS

KLJ's modesty meant that he did not leave lengthy detailed records of his life. I have, however, benefited greatly from the scripts of recorded interviews conducted by Professor Jim Woodhouse, Professor D. A. Hills and Professor D. Nowell together for some brief notes deposited in the Royal Society's Library by KLJ. Particular thanks go to Professor T. H. C. Childs, Professor H. P. Evans, Professor D. A. Hills, Professor A. Kapoor and Dr J. A. Greenwood for their generosity in allowing me to plunder their published work on KLJ's research contributions. I have enjoyed and benefited from discussions with Professor J. A. Williams, Professor I. Hutchinson, Dr A. D. Roberts, Professor K. Kendall and Dr W. Federle. Ken's wife, Dorothy, and his daughter Hilary have contributed their own knowledge and helped to improve my draft manuscript. The final acknowledgement must be to KLJ himself, who acted as a much-valued mentor, colleague and close friend since I first met him when he was a senior member of staff and I was a new research student arriving in Cambridge in 1971.

The frontispiece photograph was taken in 2003 and is reproduced with permission.

REFERENCES TO OTHER AUTHORS

Archard, J. F. 1953 Contact and rubbing of flat surfaces. *J. Appl. Phys.* **24**, 981–988.

Arzt, E., Gorb, S. & Spolenak, R. 2003 From micro to nano contacts in biological attachment devices. *Proc. Natl Acad. Sci. USA* **100**, 10603–10606.

Bowden, F. P. & Tabor, D. 1950 *The friction and lubrication of solids.* Oxford: Clarendon Press.

Field, J. 2008 David Tabor. *Biogr. Mems Fell. R. Soc.* **54**, 425–459.

Hertz, H. 1882 Über die Berührung fester elastischer Körper. [On the contact of elastic solids.] *J. Reine Angew. Math.* **92**, 156–171.

Hills, D. A., Nowell, D. & Barber, J. R. 2016 K. L. Johnson and contact mechanics. *Proc. Instn Mech. Engrs C J. Mech. Engng Sci.* (published online before print 17 February 2016; http://dx.doi.org/10.1177/0954406216634121).

Jost, H. P. 1968 *Committee on Tribology Report, Ministry of Technology.* London: HMSO.

Kauzlarich, J. J. & Williams, J. A. 2005 *Selected papers, Kenneth Langstreth Johnson.* Published privately.

Lemco, I. 2007 Wittgenstein's aeronautical investigation. *Notes Rec. R. Soc.* **61**, 39–51.

Maugis, D., Barquins, M. & Courtel, R. 1976 Griffith cracks and adhesion of elastic solids. *Métaux Corrosion Industrie* **26**, 1–10.

Roberts, A. D. & Tabor, D. 1968 Surface forces: direct measurement of repulsive forces due to electrical double layers on solids. *Nature* **219**, 1122–1124.

Southwell, R. V. 1940 *Relaxation methods in engineering science.* Oxford University Press.

BIBLIOGRAPHY

The following publications are those referred to directly in the text. A full bibliography is available as electronic supplementary material at http://dx.doi.org/10.1098/rsbm.2016.0012 or via http://rsbm.royalsocietypublishing.org.

(1)   1955   Surface interaction between elastically loaded bodies under tangential forces. *Proc. R. Soc. Lond.* A **230**, 531–548.

(2)   1958   Effect of a tangential contact force upon the rolling motion of an elastic sphere on a plane. *J. App. Mech. Trans. Am. Soc. Mech. Engrs* **80**, 339–346.

(3)   A note on the adhesion of elastic solids. *Br. J. Appl. Phys.* **9**, 199–200.

(4)   1962   A shakedown limit in rolling contact. In *Proc. 4th US National Congress of Appl. Mech., Berkeley, Calif., 1962* (ed. R. M. Rosenberg), pp. 971–975. New York: American Society of Mechanical Engineers.

(5)   1964   (With P. J. Vermeulen) Contact of nonspherical elastic bodies transmitting tangential forces. *J. App. Mech. Trans. Am. Soc. Mech. Engrs* **31**, 338–340.

(6)   1967   (With R. Cameron) Shear behaviour of elasto-hydrodynamic oil films at high rolling contact pressures. *Proc. Instn Mech. Engrs* **182**, 307–319.

(7)   1968   Deformation of a plastic wedge by a rigid flat die under the action of tangential force. *J. Mech. Phys. Solids* **16**, 395–402.

(8)   1970   The correlation of indentation experiments. *J. Mech. Phys. Solids* **18**, 115–126.

(9)   1971   (With K. Kendall & A. D. Roberts) Surface energy and the contact of elastic solids. *Proc. R. Soc. Lond.* A **324**, 301–313.

(10) 1972   (With J. A. Greenwood & S. Y. Poon) A simple theory of asperity contact in elastohydrodynamic lubrication. *Wear* **19**, 91–108.

(11) 1977   (With J. L. Tevaarwerk) Shear behaviour of elastohydrodynamic oil films. *Proc. R. Soc. Lond.* A **356**, 215–236.

(12) 1982   One hundred years of Hertz contact. *Proc. Instn Mech. Engrs* **196**, 363–378.

(13)   (With S. L. Grassie, R. W. Gregory & D. Harrison) The dynamic response of railway track to high frequency vertical/lateral excitation. *J. Mech. Engng Sci.* **24**, 77–99.

(14) 1985   (With A. D. Hearle) Mode II stress intensity factors for a crack parallel to the surface of an elastic half-space subjected to a moving point load. *J. Mech. Phys. Solids* **33**, 61–81.

(15)   *Contact mechanics.* Cambridge University Press.

(16) 1986   (With C. R. Evans) The rheological properties of elastohydrodynamic lubricants. *Proc. Instn Mech. Engrs C J. Mech. Engng Sci.* **200**, 303–312.

(17)   (With C. R. Evans) Regimes of traction in elastohydrodynamic lubrication. *Proc. Instn Mech. Engrs C J. Mech. Engng Sci.* **200**, 313–324.

(18) 1987   (With A. D. Hearle) Cumulative plastic flow in rolling sliding contact. *J. Appl. Mech. Trans. Am. Soc. Mech. Engrs* E **54**, 1–7.

(19) 1989   (With A. F. Bower) The influence of strain hardening on cumulative plastic deformation in rolling and sliding line contact. *J. Mech. Phys. Solids* **37**, 471–493.

(20) 1992   (With J. A. Greenwood) The behaviour of transverse roughness in sliding elastohydrodynamically lubricated contacts. *Wear* **153**, 107–117.

(21)   (With A. Kapoor) Effect of changes in contact geometry on shakedown of surfaces in rolling/sliding contact. *Int. J. Mech. Sci.* **34**, 223–240.

(22) 1994   (With A. Kapoor & J. A. Williams) The steady state sliding of rough surfaces. *Wear* **175**, 81–92.

(23)   (With A. Kapoor) Plastic ratchetting as a mechanism of metallic wear. *Proc. R. Soc. Lond.* A **445**, 367–381.

(24) 1996   (With A. Kapoor & J. A. Williams) A model for the mild ratchetting wear of metals. *Wear* **200**, 38–44.

(25) 1997   Adhesion and friction between a smooth elastic spherical asperity and a plane surface. *Proc. R. Soc. Lond.* A **453**, 163–179.

(26)   (With J. A. Greenwood) An adhesion map for the contact of elastic spheres. *J. Colloid Interf. Sci.* **192**, 326–333.

(27)   (With I. Sridhar & N. A. Fleck) Adhesion mechanics of the surface force apparatus. *J. Phys.* D **30**, 1710–1719.

(28) 1998   Mechanics of adhesion. *Tribol. Int.* **31**, 413–418.

(29) 2000   The contribution of micro/nano tribology to the interpretation of dry friction. *Proc. Instn Mech. Engrs C J. Mech. Engng Sci.* **214**, 11–22.

EPHRAIM KATCHALSKI-KATZIR

16 May 1916 — 30 May 2009

Ephraim Katchalski-Katzir

EPHRAIM KATCHALSKI-KATZIR

16 May 1916 — 30 May 2009

Elected ForMemRS 1977

By Ruth Arnon[1]*, Michael Sela[1] and Colin Shindler[2]‡

[1]*Department of Immunology, Weizmann Institute of Science, PO Box 26, Rehovot, Israel 76100*
[2]*SOAS, University of London, Thornhaugh Street, Russell Square, London WC1H 0XG, UK*

Ephraim Katchalski-Katzir was a leading researcher in the development of polyamino acids, which allowed new insights into the reactions and behaviour of proteins. His work developed pathways into the exploration and investigation of antigenicity. He was a founder of the Israel Society for Biochemistry and a founding member of the European Molecular Biology Organization. He was also president of Israel between 1973 and 1978—an unusual distinction because this post was usually held by former politicians. As head of the Israeli Association of Science, he was prominent in promoting the cause of science both as president and outside his term of office. Ephraim Katchalski-Katzir passed away in May 2009.

PART I: SCIENTIFIC CAREER

By Ruth Arnon and Michael Sela

Ephraim Katchalski-Katzir dedicated his life to science and to the State of Israel, all within the frame of his belief in the progress of humanity through science. He was one of the most prominent Israeli biological chemists of his time.

He was born in Kiev, Ukraine, in 1916 and as a six-year-old immigrated with his family to Palestine. The family first settled in Tel Aviv, then a tiny coastal city, and then moved a year later to Jerusalem.

This memoir was written in two parts by separate authors.
* ruth.arnon@weizmann.ac.il
‡ colinshindler@googlemail.com

© 2016 The Author(s)
http://dx.doi.org/10.1098/rsbm.2016.0015   269   Published by the Royal Society

He enrolled at the Hebrew University of Jerusalem, where he studied botany, zoology and bacteriology before finally concentrating on biochemistry and organic chemistry. In 1941 he completed his PhD thesis on simple synthetic polymers of amino acids. After 1945 he continued his education at the Polytechnic Institute of Brooklyn, Columbia University and Harvard University.

Soon after receiving his PhD, while still at the university, Katzir prepared the first water-soluble polypeptide, poly-L-lysine, and showed that it is digested by trypsin. It was the first demonstration of a synthetic polymer serving as a substrate for an enzyme and emphasized the potential use of polyamino acids as protein models. This was an idea first developed by Ephraim Katzir and was widely seized upon by the biochemical community. This pioneering work of Katzir opened the way to a new approach to the study of proteins, and won him international recognition almost immediately.

Katzir remained associated with the Hebrew University until 1948, when Chaim Weizmann, Israel's first president, a renowned chemist in his own right, invited Katzir and his eldest brother, Aharon, to join the fledgling Weizmann Institute. At this institution, Ephraim founded the Department of Biophysics, while Aharon, who was also a distinguished scientist, chaired the Department of Polymer Research. He held this position until his tragic death in the hands of a Japanese terrorist at the Ben-Gurion airport in 1972.

In the Department of Biophysics, Ephraim Katzir, together with his young associates, continued the research on polyamino acids (1)*. The discovery of polylysine, the first polymer of bifunctional amino acids, led to the synthesis of other polymers: polyarginine, polyproline, polyaspartic acid and many others. The investigation of their chemical, physical and biological properties led to most interesting results (2). For example, it was discovered that peptides of lysine helped penetration into cells. Poly-L-proline was discovered to exist in two completely different shapes, depending on whether the peptide bond is in *trans* or *cis* conformation, resulting in obligatory helices that are respectively right-handed or left-handed.

In addition, these synthetic polymers provided early evidence for the presence of helical structures and β-conformations in proteins. They were also useful in evaluating the role of various molecular forces, such as hydrogen bonding and hydrophobic interactions, in stabilizing the conformation of proteins. In addition they permitted a better understanding of protein denaturation. Katzir's work on polyamino acids opened the way for the preparation for the first time, by Michael Sela and Ruth Arnon in the Department of Biophysics, of synthetic antigens and their extensive application in fundamental studies of the chemical basis of antigenicity (Sela *et al.* 1962). This led to the development of the drug Copaxone, a synthetic amino acid copolymer used worldwide for the treatment of multiple sclerosis. Thanks to these fundamental contributions, Katzir occupies a unique and distinguished position in the field of protein science.

Knowledge of the physical and chemical properties of synthetic polyamino acids played a role in the work that led, in 1961, to the deciphering of the genetic code. In their first publication on the subject, Marshall Nirenberg and Heinrich Mathaei identified the poly-L-phenylalanine produced enzymically in a cell-free system in the presence of polyuridylic acid as messenger, by comparing it with poly-L-leucine, first synthesized by Katzir.

Another major success of Ephraim Katzir was the work on immobilized enzymes. Katzir developed a method for binding enzymes, which speed up numerous chemical processes,

---

* Numbers in this form refer to the bibliography at the end of the text.

to a variety of surfaces and molecules. He was among the first to prepare, in 1960, a well-characterized derivative of trypsin coupled to a synthetic polyamino acid copolymer, with full catalytic activity and enhanced stability. This was followed by the preparation of other insoluble enzymes such as chymotrypsin, papain, urease and alkaline phosphatase, several of them also as synthetic membrane–enzyme conjugates (3). This method laid the foundations for what is now called enzyme engineering, which plays an important role in the food and pharmaceutical industries. For example, it is used to produce fructose-enriched corn syrup and semi-synthetic penicillins.

In the late 1950s Katzir was among the founders of the Israel Society for Biochemistry. It was through his activities that several Israeli scientists were invited to serve as founding members of the European Molecular Biology Organization (EMBO). He was also pivotal in the efforts to create international scientific links and collaborations that led to the acceptance of Israel as a full member of the Federation of European Biochemical Societies (FEBS).

In 1973 Katzir was elected as the fourth president of the State of Israel, a position he held until 1978. (It was upon becoming president that he changed his surname from Katchalski to Katzir.) Upon completion of his term as president he returned to research at the Weizmann Institute and was named Institute Professor, a prestigious title awarded by the Weizmann faculty and administration to outstanding scientists who had made significant and meaningful contributions to science or to the State of Israel. He also devoted himself to the promotion of biotechnological research in Israel and founded the Department of Biotechnology at Tel Aviv University. The creation of this department was a continuation of his previous efforts to establish science-based industries in Israel: he had helped create several companies based on the fruits of scientific research.

In the later years of his scientific career, Professor Katzir turned to new research areas. In one project he headed a team of Weizmann scientists who won an international contest on computer modelling of proteins. In another study he was part of an interdisciplinary Institute team that revealed an important aspect of the effects of snake venom on the body.

Katzir authored hundreds of scientific papers and served on the editorial and advisory boards of numerous scientific journals. International scientific symposia were held in Rehovot and Jerusalem to celebrate his 60th, 70th, 80th and 90th birthdays.

Professor Katzir was a member of the Israeli Academy of Sciences and Humanities and of numerous other learned bodies in Israel and abroad, including the Royal Institution of Great Britain, the Royal Society of London, the National Academy of Sciences of the USA, the Académie des Sciences in France, the Scientific Academy of Argentina and the World Academy of Arts and Sciences. He was a visiting professor at Harvard University, Rockefeller University, the University of California at Los Angeles, and Battelle Seattle Research Center.

Katzir won many prizes and awards, including the Rothschild Prize, the Israel Prize in Natural Sciences (which he shared with Michael Sela), the Weizmann Prize, the Linderstrom Lang Gold Medal, the Hans Krebs Medal, the Tchernikhovski Prize for scientific translations, the Alpha Omega Achievement Medal and the Engineering Foundation's International Award in Enzyme Engineering. He was the first recipient of the Japan Prize and was appointed to France's National Order of the Legion of Honour in the rank of Commander. He received honorary doctorates from more than a dozen institutions of higher learning in Israel and abroad, including Harvard University, Northwestern University, McGill University, the University of Oxford and the Technion-Israel Institute of Technology, as well as his own Weizmann Institute of Science.

Ephraim Katzir was an incredible teacher: friendly, inspiring, patient, thorough, and always stimulating! He had dozens of PhD students and at least as many postdoctoral fellows and visiting professors on sabbaticals. Many of his doctoral students eventually became professors, and their students did so as well, resulting in seven such scientific generations, in institutions of higher learning and in the Israeli biotech industry, besides the many who returned to their own countries and excelled there.

Ephraim Katzir was a legend in his lifetime. He passed away on 30 May 2009 in his home on the grounds of the Weizmann Institute. He will be greatly missed by his many colleagues and friends and will be remembered not only as a brilliant scientist and statesman, but also for his human warmth, integrity and high moral standards.

PART II: POLITICAL CAREER

By Colin Shindler

Ephraim Katzir was born in Kiev on 16 May 1916. His father, Yehuda Katchalski, was an accountant and an adherent of Zionism. Katchalski and his wife, Tsila, originally lived in Łódź, then in the Tsarist empire, now in Poland. Łódź was a centre of socialist politics and radical endeavour. During the 1905 revolution an uprising took place in Łódź in which many workers were killed. The city's social awareness extended to the Jewish community of Łódź, which constituted approximately one-third of the population. The intense fighting between the Russians and the Germans on the Eastern Front during World War I persuaded the Katchalskis to move further eastwards to Kiev in the Ukraine.

After the end of the Great War, the Katchalskis moved to Białystok in an independent Poland. The economic crisis of the mid 1920s provided the impetus for the Polish Jewish middle class to leave Białystok for the Yishuv (Jewish settlement in Palestine) in 1925 as part of the fourth aliyah (emigration to Palestine). The family settled in Jerusalem.

Katchalski (later Katzir) attended the Rehavia Gymnasia in Jerusalem before enrolling in the newly established Hebrew University of Jerusalem.

Katzir was a member of Hanoar Haoved (the working youth), a youth group, established in 1925, which was an intrinsic part of the pioneering labour Zionist movement. Berl Katznelson, a central labour figure, was involved with the group from the outset and spoke at their gatherings.[*] He commented that Hanoar Haoved 'turned to the most neglected and impoverished circles of young people, on whom all the educators and organisers had given up … it listened and understood the lives of young people who worked every day and opened up new vistas from the everyday life to a world of culture'.[‡]

Katzir's devotion to the construction of a state of the Jews led to a cross-fertilization between his scientific interests and his national activism. In 1939 he graduated from the first non-commissioned officers' course of the Haganah, the Yishuv's self-defence force, and subsequently became commander of its student unit in the field. In view of growing military clashes between Palestinian Arabs and Zionist Jews—and the inevitability of a conflict with nationalists in the Arab world generally—Katzir contributed his scientific expertise to the defence of the Yishuv. Katzir felt that in the aftermath of the Shoah (Holocaust) the Jews

[*] *Davar*, 1 and 13 October 1926.
[‡] http://noal.org.il.

would face terrible consequences if they lost the conflict. In May 1948, at the height of Israel's war of independence, Katzir was appointed head of the Heyl Mada (HEMED)—the scientific research and development corps of the Israel Defence Forces. This in turn laid the basis for RAFAEL Advanced Defence Systems, which today is Israel's second largest defence manufacturer, employing 7000 people and responsible for the development of the Iron Dome, an anti-missile system that has protected Israeli cities from short-range rockets in recent years. In the early 1960s Katzir headed a governmental committee for the formulation of a National Scientific Policy.

In a broader sense, Katzir believed that the pursuit of science would make a contribution to the region. He was certainly inspired by his mentor, Chaim Weizmann, a former chemistry lecturer at the University of Manchester and Israel's first president. Sixty years later, Katzir reflected (4):

> I would do what I could to help establish the State of Israel and contribute to its security and its social and economic development. In addition, I would attempt to do some original research while at the same time playing my part in raising a new generation of Israeli scientists and helping to create the physical and intellectual conditions in which science and technology could flourish in this region. Like Chaim Weizmann, whose life and work served as an inspiration to many young scientists, I believed with all my heart 'that science will bring peace to this country, renew its youthful vigour and create the sources for new life, both spiritually and materially.'

His close association with Weizmann—they shared scientific interests as well as liberal values—led to a life in which he was honoured for his scientific research in Israel but also for his commitment to creating a modern state. He thus headed the Israeli Association for the Promotion of Science, but also served as Chief Scientist of the Ministry of Defence in the mid 1960s. He trained a generation of younger scientists and translated important material into Hebrew.

Katzir was heavily involved in the popularization of science from the outset. Even as a student, he organized a series of lectures on different aspects of scientific endeavour and investigation for the general public at the Hebrew University of Jerusalem and kibbutzim around the country. He often met with children to stoke their interest in science from an early age. He subsequently became the co-editor, with Shlomo Hestrin, of one of the very first Israeli popular science journals, *Mada*.

Katzir was elected the fourth president of Israel in 1973. The office of president was deemed to be above politics. Einstein was offered the presidency in succession to Weizmann in 1952, but preferred to remain at Princeton. Yet all his predecessors had previously been political figures—and like Katzir had all been members of the dominant Labour party. Since his term of office in the 1970s all successors have similarly been political figures. Katzir—while certainly a committed Labour man—was therefore unusual in that he never formally entered the bear-pit that is Israeli politics.

Katzir came into office at a crossroads in Israeli politics. The pioneering labour Left that had characterized and influenced his upbringing was in a state of disintegration, while Menahem Begin's nationalist Likud was in its ascendency. Begin won office in 1977 at his ninth attempt. Katzir decided to leave office one year later, having served only one term.

Katzir's time in office was marked by both war and peace, by violence and calm. A year before his election, his brother and fellow scientist had been killed in the attack on passengers at Israel's Lod airport by the far-Left Japanese Red Army—which was guided by the Popular

Front for the Liberation of Palestine (PFLP) with arms supplied by North Korea. In 1974— one year into Katzir's presidency—the killings of high-school children took place in Kiriat Shemonah and Ma'alot in northern Israel.

However, the central events of Katzir's presidency were the bookended occurrence of the Yom Kippur war in 1973 with Egypt and the visit of its president, Anwar Sadat, to Israel in 1977.

On taking office, the former president, Zalman Shazar, an admirer of the Lubavicher Rebbe, greeted him with the biblical invocation

> Arise, arise chosen of the nation and blessed by God in a good and auspicious time. You should merit seeing with your very eyes ... peace and righteousness reign in the land of our forefathers.*

Yet six months after his inauguration, Israel fought a bloody war with Egypt and Syria. Although the Yom Kippur war ended with the Israeli army near Cairo, the unexpected Egyptian assault and the crossing of the Suez Canal of its armed forces severely dented Israel's self-image and its confidence in being able to defend itself. Israel suffered more than 2500 killed and 7000 injured.

Katzir visited the troops on the front line, talked to bereaved parents and spouses in their homes and went to hospitals to comfort the injured. Within four years the enemy had turned into a negotiating partner—and Katzir was the first to greet president Anwar Sadat on his totally unexpected visit to Israel at the end of 1977. He later recalled Sadat with mixed emotions (4):

> [There was] the close personal relationship that I developed with President Sadat during his brief but momentous visit to Israel and until his untimely death. This was a valued friendship and one that I had hoped would help establish closer ties between our two countries. It was a bitter disappointment to find that zealots from both sides seemed to have ruined every chance for lasting peace. Sadat was murdered in Egypt by Muslim extremists, and [prime minister Yitzhak] Rabin, whom I greatly respected and admired, was assassinated by a Jewish extremist in Israel.

During his time in office, Katzir promoted a closing of the gap between the haves and the have-nots in Israel. He endorsed volunteerism and instituted the Presidential Award for Volunteerism, a prize granted annually in recognition of 12 individuals who had devoted themselves to volunteer work. Katzir also promoted the importance of science at all levels of the Israeli educational system. In the wider world, he strongly supported the expansion of Jewish studies in institutes of higher education.

Katzir carried out his duties, but he maintained his interest in scientific advances even while president. In one sense, it mollified an inevitable tedium of office. Katzir was clearly a political dove in his later years and remained an old-school Zionist pioneer. He strongly believed in a resolution of the Israel–Palestine problem through a fair settlement. In 2005 he wrote about his vision for the future (4):

> I have always thought of Israel as a pilot plant state in which dedicated people can explore all kinds of imaginative and creative possibilities aimed at improving society and the state. I feel certain that in the years to come we will continue to operate as a testing ground, drawing on the fruits of science and technology to determine the best and most satisfying ways of living in a country geared to the future. The highest standards of health care, educational practice, and cultural and recreational facilities will flow from research and development in the natural

* http://www.chabad.org.

sciences, as well as in automation, computer science, information technology, communication, transportation, and biotechnology. I believe it is possible to create such a pilot plant state by encouraging the development of science-based high technology industry and agriculture. Once it gains momentum, this core of activity will contribute significantly to the economic growth and prosperity of the country. In this pilot plant state, I would like to see a free, pluralistic society, a democracy whose citizens live by the rule of law, and a welfare state in which public services are efficiently handled. Great emphasis will be laid on excellence in science and research, literature, and the arts, thus enriching the intellectual and cultural life of every citizen.

We Jews are eternal optimists. We have always believed, even in the depths of our despair, that the Messiah will come, even if he tarries a little. I am sure that ultimately we will create our model society geared for life in the twenty-first century and founded on the great moral and ethical tenets that we have held sacred since ancient times.

The fashion in the early years of the state of Israel was to hebraize one's name. Gruen became Ben-Gurion and Persky became Peres. Katchalsky chose the surname Katzir. This means 'harvest' in Hebrew. It testified to his lifelong belief that hard work and intellectual commitment would bring its reward for the benefit of all.

ACKNOWLEDGEMENTS

Emeritus Professor Nathan Sharon, Weizmann Institute, initiated this account of Ephraim Katzir's scientific career. He passed away in 2011.

This memoir is adapted in part from Sela (2011). We recommend Katzir's autobiography *A life's tale* (Carmel Publishing House, 2009) for more information.

The frontispiece was taken by Shlomo Ben-Zvi and is used courtesy of the Weizmann Institute of Science Archives. All rights reserved to the Weizmann Institute of Science.

REFERENCES TO OTHER AUTHORS

Sela, M. 2011 Ephraim Katzir-Katchalski. *Am. Phil. Soc.* **155**, 211–215.
Sela, M., Fuchs, S. & Arnon, R. 1962 Studies on the chemical basis of the antigenicity of proteins. 5. Synthesis, characterization and immunogenicity of some multichain and linear polypeptides containing tyrosine. *Biochem J.* **85**, 223–235.

BIBLIOGRAPHY

The following publications are those referred to directly in the text.

(1)   1958   (With M. Sela) Synthesis and chemical properties of poly-alpha-amino acids. *Adv. Protein Chem.* **13**, 243–492.
(2)   1964   (With M. Sela, H. I. Silman & A. Berger) Polyamino acids as protein models. In *The proteins*, 2nd edn (ed. H. Neurath), vol. 2, pp. 405–602. New York: Academic Press.
(3)   1966   (With I. Silman) Water-insoluble derivatives of enzymes, antigens, and antibodies. *Annu. Rev. Biochem.* **35**, 873–908.
(4)   2005   My contributions to science and society. *J. Biol. Chem.* **280**, 16529–16541.

MICHAEL FRANZ LAPPERT

31 December 1928 — 28 March 2014

Michael F. Loppolt

MICHAEL FRANZ LAPPERT

31 December 1928 — 28 March 2014

Elected FRS 1979

By G. Jeffery Leigh* OBE and John F. Nixon‡ FRS

Department of Chemistry and Biochemistry, School of Life Sciences, University of Sussex, Falmer, Brighton BN1 9RQ, UK

Michael Lappert was one of the giants of twentieth-century organometallic chemistry. His research, carried out over six decades and leading to about 800 publications, had a profound and influential effect on the field, and his contributions covered almost every block of the Periodic Table. His early reputation was established by his extensive studies in boron chemistry exemplified by the reports of BCl_4^-, BN cyclobutadiene analogues, triborylamines, BCl_3-catalysed *ortho*-Claisen rearrangements and evidence for restricted rotation about the B–N bond in aminoboranes. He had a lifelong interest in amides, including those of carbon, and especially electron-rich olefins, which remarkably were the ready source of numerous transition-metal carbene complexes. The last could also be obtained directly from the Vilsmeier reagent. He was the first to show that a carbene complex may act as an initiator of olefin metathesis. Later interests concerned the syntheses of new types of compound from all blocks of the Periodic Table driven by his imaginative use of new types of ligand (either sterically crowded or having no β-hydrogen atoms, often including $SiMe_3$ or Bu^t substituents to confer lipophilicity). The use of $CH_nSiMe_{(3-n)}$ ($n = 0$, 1 or 2) to stabilize transition-metal alkyl compounds was a major advance, because at the time stable homoleptic (a term he introduced) transition-metal alkyl compounds were unknown. He showed that the $-CH(SiMe_3)_2$ ligand could stabilize both low-coordinate transition metal and lanthanide compounds. Similarly, carbene analogues of the Main Group 14 elements germanium, tin and lead were obtained. Surprisingly in the solid state, these species were weakly dimerized (for example $R_2Sn=SnR_2$), and unexpectedly exhibited a pyramidalized geometry at the heavy element. The latter had very significant bonding implications, because it differed fundamentally from the well-known planar structure of the corresponding alkenes. The first persistent or stable paramagnetic heavier Main Group element species MR_2 (M = P or As) and MR_3 (M = Ge or Sn) were also

* jeffery.leigh@sky.com

‡ Author for correspondence (j.nixon@sussex.ac.uk).

http://dx.doi.org/10.1098/rsbm.2016.0014

obtained while parallel work using $-N(SiMe_3)_2$ resulted in the corresponding Main Group amido derivatives. Other lipophilic ligands, such as β-diketiminates, were also widely used, as were bulky aryloxo and thiolato ligands, to obtain stable low-coordinate Main Group species. The first examples of d- and f-block species containing bridging alkyl groups were described. Those who worked with him cited his vast knowledge and supportive low-key advisory style, which ensured a contented and productive laboratory atmosphere. In addition to his scientific work, he was deeply interested in opera, literature and the theatre, about which he could talk knowledgeably.

EARLY LIFE AND EDUCATION

Michael Lappert (universally known as 'Mike') was born in Brno, in what was then Czechoslovakia, on 31 December 1928, the second son of Julius and Kornelie ('Nelly') Lappert (*née* Beran). Other members of the family lived in Vienna. He and his brother, Martin Josef, enjoyed an extremely happy early life, the family living in a wooden house (now preserved as being of unique architectural interest) in an estate dominated by his maternal grandparents' large mansion. The Lappert home provided a cultured and musical environment for the children: their mother, a pianist of concert standard, often accompanied their father Julius's fine baritone singing; both parents were university graduates. The daily routine was extremely full, involving piano and violin lessons, gymnastics, swimming and Hebrew lessons. Czech was spoken, but curiously in later life Mike completely lost his native language. With the Nazis' assumption of power in Czechoslovakia in 1938, he and his brother were sent by their parents to London on one of the last *Kindertransport*. Their parents died in Auschwitz, and the brothers never saw them again. The two boys arrived in London at the end of June 1939 and were placed as boarders in Cannock House School, Eltham. Already in England at that time were Dr R. Herrmann (Nelly's cousin from Brno) and Louise Gross, the daughter of Julius's cousin, who had both arrived in 1938 but without their spouses. Mike never forgot his debt to Britain for receiving him and was always fiercely and proudly British. Cannock House School was evacuated in 1939 to Sheerness, and the boys were billeted with local families, finding a happy home for about three months. Most school activity consisted of football or cricket in the mornings and lessons in the afternoons. However, this period came to an abrupt end when the town and dockyards experienced the first enemy air-raid of the war and in early 1940 the school hastily returned to Eltham, the brothers remaining as the sole boarders, teaching being carried out by just two masters. Matters came to a head after a visit by a representative of the Czech Refugee Trust Fund, the boys' guardians. It was concluded that their schooling was inadequate and the boys joined Wilson's Grammar School near Horsham, later moving to Camberwell, where in 1946 Mike obtained his Higher School Certificate in chemistry, zoology and pure and applied mathematics.

Mike's aunt Louise Gross (Auntie) had come to Britain via Palestine. Like Mike and Martin she was a refugee who had lost all her belongings to the Nazis. Although she had always directed her own house staff at home, in Britain she lived at first as a servant in the house of a wealthy shipping magnate, because such employment was then often a condition of refugees being granted British residence. She eventually found a flat of her own in north London, and that is where Mike and his brother went to live when they left boarding school. She was an excellent cook and did her utmost to act as a mother to the two boys. Mike was extremely lucky in that he was allowed maximum freedom and minimum domestic responsibilities so that he could concentrate on his studies. Later Mike's home became widely known for the generosity of its hospitality; after Auntie's death, excellent cooking and great hospitality continued to be a feature of the house that Lorna Lappert (*née* McKenzie) ran after her marriage to Mike in 1980. Lorna was born in Workington, Cumbria, where she taught after graduating in English at Manchester University in 1961. She later took a post at Marple Hall Grammar School in Cheshire, living in West Didsbury, Manchester, in a house opposite that which Michael and Auntie then occupied. This proximity led to a friendship that culminated in their long and happy marriage, in which they shared a deep interest in travel and culture.

Mike's interest in theatre, film, music and especially opera developed when he moved to London, and he began to keep a detailed written account of all his experiences of culture and science, although not a daily diary. He continued with this for the rest of his life. Wherever he travelled he recorded his experiences, especially of what he saw in a given gallery and of what he heard in specific theatres and concert halls. He noted the principal actors and musicians he heard perform, and what he thought of the productions. He developed an encyclopaedic knowledge of literature and music. When he began to lecture and to attend scientific conferences his accounts broadened. He recorded when and where he spoke, the names of notable people who heard him, the details of place and time of the many conferences all over the world that he attended, and lists of the names of eminent scientists who were also present. This record proved useful for the writing of this account, but it is not obvious why and for whom it was prepared other than for himself. It is unlikely that he intended to publish it.

EARLY ACADEMIC CAREER: NORTHERN POLYTECHNIC, 1953–59

Mike began to build himself a career for the future. Because university access in the early postwar years was dominated by returning ex-service personnel, Mike (despite feeling that he had performed well during interviews at Imperial College in both 1946 and 1947) was not offered a place and for about a year he joined a small food-analytical enterprise while also attending evening classes at the Regent Street Polytechnic, where he passed the Intermediate Physics examination. Desperate to begin his higher education, he accepted a place at the Northern Polytechnic, now part of the London Metropolitan University, on a two-year BSc course with chemistry as the major and mathematics as the minor component, subsequently fulfilling university requirements by staying for an extra year and graduating in 1949 with first-class honours.

The newly appointed head of chemistry at the Northern Polytechnic was William Gerrard, under whom Mike began his research, completing his PhD thesis entitled 'Reactions of boron trichloride with alcohols and ethers' in 1951. Mike worked on organoboron chemistry, which was then a burgeoning area of preparative chemistry. This excited considerable interest among chemists of the time because it was a new and original extension of organic chemistry to one of carbon's nearest Periodic Table neighbours. Mike quickly exhibited his drive and originality and his research gave him a profound knowledge of reaction mechanisms. When he later changed his area of study to inorganic chemistry, this gave him a unique approach to his subject because other inorganic chemists of the period were generally concerned primarily with structure.

He subsequently accepted the offer of the post of Assistant Lecturer at the Northern Polytechnic, and he enjoyed directing the research of several new entrants while acting as 'lieutenant' to Gerrard, who was greatly preoccupied with administrative tasks. In addition to his supervisory duties Mike spent his non-teaching time as an active experimentalist; significant discoveries reported were the first tetrachloro- and tetrabromo-borates (2)*, metaboric esters (5), the interaction of BCl_3 with alcohols (7), boron–nitrogen analogues of cyclobutadienes (13), and borazine polymers (8). The first published review (1) on organic compounds of boron proved influential, while another (with Gerrard) (3) covered the reactions of BCl_3 with organic compounds. Mike's co-supervision with Gerrard (3) of 11 doctoral students resulted in 47 papers. Among his co-workers was Edward W. Abel (later Professor of Chemistry at Exeter and President of the Royal Society of Chemistry).

The first detailed infrared spectroscopic characterization of organoboron compounds was reported in collaboration with L. J. Bellamy (4) and L. A. Duncanson (6). A corollary of the infrared studies was the use of trends in the carbonyl stretching frequency $v(C=O)$ of coordination complexes of ethyl acetate with various Lewis acids, initially BX_3 (X = F, Cl or Br) and subsequently several other Main Group element halides, to afford a qualitative measure of their relative Lewis acidity (9).

On becoming a Recognised Teacher of the University of London, Mike's former role ended and he was able to pursue independent research. In 1953 he was promoted to Lecturer and in 1955 to Senior Lecturer, but despite his success and impressive research productivity he became frustrated with his opportunities for further advancement at the Northern Polytechnic and in 1959 he moved to the chemistry department of the Manchester College of Science and Technology (later the University of Manchester Institute of Science and Technology, UMIST), three graduate students accompanying him to complete their PhD theses.

MANCHESTER COLLEGE OF SCIENCE AND TECHNOLOGY, 1959–64

Mike's initial appointment was to a lectureship in inorganic chemistry but he was quickly promoted to Senior Lecturer. The colloid scientist B. A. Pethica, the organic mechanistic expert G. Baddeley and the teacher and author R. B. Heslop were influential colleagues. The Chemistry Department at UMIST was experiencing a transformation under its new head of department, Professor Robert Haszeldine (FRS 1968). Before his arrival it had been a department teaching mainly applied and part-time classes in the Faculty of Technology of the University of Manchester, but Haszeldine was determined to raise it at least to parity with the more highly recognized department in the Faculty of Science in that part of the University of Manchester often referred to as 'Owens'. To this end he modernized the Chemistry Department so that up-to-date spectroscopic facilities were available, even including one of the few commercial nuclear magnetic resonance (NMR) spectrometers manufactured by AEI in Manchester. The drawback was that Haszeldine did not delegate authority and in the early 1960s he was formally the research director of about 100 graduate students via several lieutenants, all being authorities in their own right. Mike was not inclined to take part in such an arrangement and formed his own research group, obtaining independent funding from various sources, while taking advantage of the facilities that the department had to offer. He shared a large laboratory in which

---

* Numbers in this form refer to the bibliography at the end of the text.

his students worked with other researchers, not his students, who later made their own careers in chemistry; these included A. P. Lever, J. A. Connor and G. J. Leigh. Mike's work began to expand and blossom in an atmosphere that certainly encouraged him to do so, but he also took advantage of life in Manchester, cultivating his lifelong interests in music, the theatre and active sport including skiing, and in walking, often in the nearby Peak District. One consequence of his exploring the Lake District was his later purchase of the cottage at Eaglesfield (near Cockermouth in Cumbria), in which John Dalton, the proponent of the atomic theory, had been born (see below). However, still frustrated by the lack of opportunities for further promotion at UMIST, he moved to the new University of Sussex in 1964.

RESEARCH ACHIEVEMENTS AT UMIST

Mike's research at UMIST was carried out by a total of 12 postgraduates, among whom were Harry Cragg (later to occupy a senior role at the University of Kent and sometime Lord Mayor of Canterbury), T. A. George (later Professor at the University of Nebraska), K. Jones (later Reader at UMIST) and B. Prokai (later vice-president of American Cyanamid). Three postdoctoral researchers included P. N. K. Riley (later of John Dalton College), J. C. Kotz (later co-author with K. F. Purcell of a very influential inorganic chemistry textbook) and K. Brockelhurst (later Professor of Biochemistry at Queen Mary College). The first monograph on inorganic polymers (11) and in which Mike wrote one chapter (10), which appeared in 1962, was co-edited with G. Jeffery (Jeff) Leigh (later OBE, Deputy Head of the AFRC Unit of Nitrogen Fixation and Professor of Environmental Science at Sussex University), who became a lifelong friend.

The idea of π-bonding in boron compounds was explored by both proton NMR studies on the hindered rotation about the B–N bond in $BCl(NMe_2)Ph$ (24) and measurement of ionization potentials in the series $BCl_n(NMe_2)_{3-n}$ (with J. B. Pedley—the first of several joint projects) (20). A continuing theme involved the addition of $BX(L)(L')$ moieties across the multiple bond of an organic compound, for example in the chloroboration of alkynes to afford alkenylboranes (14). Other notable achievements during this period were the isolation of the first triborylamine (15), tri(primary-amino)boranes (12), the amino- and alkoxy-boration of isocyanates and isothiocyanates (16) and syntheses of a series of boron–sulfur compounds (21). Mike's initial departure from boron chemistry, exemplified by the discovery of a series of organotin amides and their use as reagents (17, 18), represented a major development in his work.

UNIVERSITY OF SUSSEX, 1964–2014

In early 1964 Mike accepted an invitation from Professor Colin Eaborn (FRS 1970), the first Dean of the School of Molecular Sciences at the recently founded (1961) University of Sussex, to join as Reader in Inorganic Chemistry, and in October that year he began to teach the final undergraduate year of the first chemistry intake. The new environment proved to be much more conducive to his research, which flourished enormously. He was promoted to full Professor in 1969 (Research Professor 1997; Emeritus Professor 2011) and showed, with other Sussex colleagues, that a chemistry department in a new university could nevertheless attain international stature as a centre of excellence.

Among Mike's fellow inorganic chemistry specialists on his arrival at Sussex were the lecturers Alan Pidcock, Michael Ford-Smith and David Smith, who had been appointed at the inception of the university, and were soon augmented in 1966 by the appointment of John Nixon (FRS 1994), also as a lecturer, who moved from his post at St Andrews University. Senior organic and physical/theoretical chemistry colleagues included A. I. Scott (FRS 1978), J. N. Murrell (FRS 1991), A. D. Jenkins and E. A. R. Peeling (who had played a major role in designing the chemistry laboratories in collaboration with the architect Sir Basil Spence). Harry Kroto (FRS 1990) (later Sir Harry, President of the Royal Society of Chemistry and Nobel laureate) had also recently joined Sussex as a Tutorial Fellow in Physical Chemistry.

The multidisciplinary Agricultural and Food Research Council (AFRC) Unit of Nitrogen Fixation led by Professor Joseph Chatt FRS had also recently moved from Queen Mary College to occupy an adjacent custom-built building on the Sussex campus. Its Deputy Director with responsibility for its biological group was John Postgate (FRS 1977). Among the AFRC personnel who actively contributed over the years both to the weekly inorganic chemistry seminar programme and to undergraduate and post-graduate teaching were Jeff Leigh, Ray Richards, Jon Dilworth, Chris Pickett and Richard Henderson. Seminars, sponsored independently by both AFRC unit and university members, were attended by both groups, and regular visits by international visitors were commonplace. It was akin to having two inorganic chemistry departments on the same campus!

Mike's research activity during his initial years at Sussex still mainly concerned boron chemistry, with little indication of the enormous range of topics that he would subsequently explore. He attracted graduate students and postdoctoral workers from all over the world, and during his career he published some 800 scientific papers, covering many different areas of the Periodic Table, a productivity that few other researchers have matched. Indeed, it was rumoured among generations of students that his ambition was to publish papers on every element in the Periodic Table, an aspiration that he came very close to fulfilling! Over his career he supervised 116 doctoral and 8 MSc students and worked with 101 postdoctoral fellows and 16 sabbatical visitors. His friendliness and helpfulness were widely appreciated and he extended personal hospitality to all his students and many visitors. His generosity was widely known and legendary.

Professor Philip Power (FRS 2005), a former student and subsequently a major international inorganic chemistry figure in his own right, has given a first-hand account of the *modus operandi* of the Lappert research team (see Power 2015), pointing out that 'virtually all the synthetic work involving air and moisture-sensitive compounds was carried out using Schlenk techniques and the group did not have a dry box, a fact which renders the synthetic accomplishments all the more impressive.' The research unit was described by Power as

an informal but well-knit team, short on ceremony and long on esprit, imagination and practical skills. Laboratory hours were flexible and Mike's direction was low-key, combining his nice sense of humour with a mastery of understatement in offering suggestions. The team was highly industrious, with no sense of pressure, since Mike strongly believed that his students should be self-motivating and persistence would eventually yield results. Group meetings stressed the importance of keeping accurate records and awareness of developments in the literature. There were frequent group discussions of important new papers, during which students quickly became aware of the huge breadth of Mike's research interests. He was perceived as an essentially private person, the group being largely unaware of other personal aspects of his life such as his fluency in German and the tragic nature of his early life. Their overall impression of him was one of warmth. On the social side the twice-yearly receptions at his home were eagerly anticipated, hosted in the early days by his 'Auntie' Louise Gross, and later by his wife Lorna.

Although Mike's contributions to chemistry at Sussex University were inevitably dominated by his research activity, he was also active on the teaching and social fronts, participating enthusiastically in initiatives such as the organometallic crash course, the chemistry-by-thesis BSc degree, and career weekends at the University White House in the Ashdown Forest. The organometallic crash course involved teaching the subject intensively over a short period of one week rather than the conventional method of spreading the material over a term or semester. Three inorganic faculty members were involved, each offering a different topic but interacting as a trio at daily problem-solving and quiz sessions. The course, which ran for several years, proved popular with faculty and students alike.

Mike also regularly participated in year-round lunchtime games of tennis on the nearby university hard courts (other participants included Sir John 'Kappa' Cornforth FRS, John Murrell, John Nixon, Tony McCaffery, Ray Richards, Malcolm Topping, Gerry Lawless and Hazel Cox), Mike being the acknowledged master of the high defensive lob! This activity certainly contributed to the excellent collegiate atmosphere and strong community spirit that prevailed at Sussex during this period. Other important features were the weekly inorganic discussion group meetings and the annual Isle of Thorns career weekends for final-year undergraduates, where the atmosphere was deliberately informal: students stayed overnight and on the Saturday evening faculty offered light-hearted 'entertainment'. The multifaceted lifestyle of chemistry faculty at Sussex during this period has been particularly well documented in *MOLSBOOK* (see Murrell 2009), with a front cover designed by Sir Harry Kroto.

In 1993, in the introduction to a special issue of *Journal of Organometallic Chemistry* dedicated to Mike, his former student, Professor David Cardin of Reading University, wrote (see Cardin 1993):

> To those of us who are fortunate enough to know Michael Lappert personally, either as students, collaborators in joint projects, or colleagues (enjoying from time to time his famous hospitality!), it seems incredible that this issue is to celebrate his 65th birthday. It seems even more incredible in view of his continuing visits around the world, frequently coupled (as at home) with visits to concerts, operas and art galleries to think of him retiring. In this connection it might be worth reflecting that Giuseppe Verdi, a composer over whose works he has been known to enthuse, did what is generally considered his best work in his eighties.

The following year a symposium and dinner was held at Sussex University in Mike's honour entitled '40 years of research'. Many of his former students attended, and the invited speakers, spanning the four decades, were his long-standing friend Professor Heinz Nöth from Munich, Professor Edward Abel, Professor Colin Raston, Professor Phil Power FRS, Professor Dave Cardin and Dr Gerry Lawless. At Mike's specific request the word 'retirement' was not mentioned during the meeting and he went on to publish a further 250 papers over the next 20 years!

The celebration in 2005 of 40 years of successful publication by the Royal Society of Chemistry journal *Chemical Communications* provided a clear indication of the continuing influence of Lappert's research work. The editors of the journal drew attention to the top 40 most-cited authors and congratulated Mike on coming top of the list with no fewer than 5913 citations (about 800 more than his nearest challenger). Another Sussex colleague, also high in the publication list, was Peter Hitchcock, who carried out most of the hundreds of X-ray crystal structure determinations on the Lappert group compounds during his Sussex period.

A significant innovation, established around that period by Mike and Heinz Nöth, was the series of Anglo-German Inorganic Chemistry Meetings (AGICHEM), inaugurated in 1991 as

Figure 1. Mike in 2007 exhibiting the plaque outside the cottage where John Dalton was born and to which it was later affixed. (Reproduced with permission.) (Online version in colour.)

a joint venture of the Gesellschaft Deutscher Chemiker and the Royal Society of Chemistry. The first meeting, held at Brighton and chaired by Mike and Heinz, was so successful that subsequent biannual conferences were held at Stuttgart (1993), Brighton (1995) and Marburg (1997) before the UK venue for the meeting became more diversified; the most recent meeting was held in Edinburgh in 2014.

A further career milestone was Mike's period as President of the Dalton Division of the Royal Society of Chemistry from 1989 to 1991. An interesting feature of his role in this office was, as previously mentioned, that he also owned the cottage at Eaglesfield in the Lake District in which John Dalton was born, which he and his wife Lorna visited on many occasions (see figure 1). Furthermore in 2003, to mark the bicentenary of Dalton's famous paper setting out his 'Table of the relative weights of the ultimate particles of gaseous and other bodies', Mike, together with his Sussex colleague John Murrell, published an article entitled 'John Dalton, the man and his legacy: the bicentenary of his Atomic Theory' (101).

Remarkably, over the 20-year period following his formal retirement in 1994, Mike continued to write, publish and review huge numbers of research papers and he regularly attended weekly chemistry seminar programmes until he had a fall while playing tennis on the Sussex university campus courts at lunchtime on 28 March 2014, sustaining injuries from which he died. A celebration of his life was held at the Meeting House on the Sussex University campus on 2 July 2014; and roughly a year after his death, former colleagues and students from all over the world packed a Royal Society of Chemistry Dalton Division one-day meeting in his honour held on 1 April 2015 in Burlington House, London. In what was widely regarded as a meeting of exceptionally high quality, lectures were delivered by distinguished speakers from the UK, the USA, Australia, New Zealand and Germany, including a contribution from Nobel laureate Professor Richard Schrock FRS. Repeated references were made to Mike's many seminal ideas in a wide variety of fields. Sussex colleagues David Smith and John Nixon described his early life and reminisced about his Sussex career. His extraordinary generosity

Figure 2. The front cover of the special Mike Lappert Memorial Issue of *Organometallics* (2015).
(Reproduced with permission of the American Chemical Society.) (Online version in colour.)

and kindness shown to students and colleagues alike was also acknowledged. At the end of the
meeting, Mike's widow, Lorna, was presented with a bound volume of his 30 most influential
papers entitled 'The influence of Michael Lappert on the chemistry landscape' (see Arnold *et
al.* 2014). Further tributes included a special issue of *Organometallics* **34**, 2035–2706 (2015),
the front cover of which is reproduced in figure 2.

Friends and colleagues at Sussex University decided that a fitting tribute to Mike would be
the placing of wooden bench at the tennis courtside at Sussex University, just a short distance
from his office. It has the following citation:

IN MEMORY OF MICHAEL LAPPERT, FRS, MUCH-LOVED COLLEAGUE, INSPIRATIONAL SCIENTIST AND
INDOMITABLE TENNIS PLAYER.

50 PRODUCTIVE YEARS AT SUSSEX

RESEARCH ACHIEVEMENTS AT SUSSEX UNIVERSITY

Period 1964–74

Boron halides were used to synthesize divalent platinum halogeno-complexes (22), and the
structure of the transient BF_2Cl was established by microwave spectroscopy, in collaboration
with H. W. Kroto (40). Calorimetric studies were introduced in 1965 on complexes of ethyl
acetate with Group 13 halides (19) and iridium(I) complexes obtained by dehydrochlorination
of iridium(III) hydrochlorides (30). Organometallic diazoalkanes (23) afforded heterocycles
via addition to 1,2-dipoles (26); a Sussex collaboration with Professor A. D. Jenkins (27),
involved kinetic studies on titanium amides as initiators for acrylonitrile polymerization.

A very important development during this period was the introduction of ligands containing
$-CH_n(SiMe_3)_{3-n}$ groups, which subsequently became very widely used by others (25, 31).

Notable syntheses based on this paradigm included [Cu{CH$_2$(SiMe$_3$)}$_4$] (32), [Y(CH$_2$(SiMe$_3$)$_3$) (thf)$_2$] (33), where thf represents tetrahydrofuran, and [Cr{CH(SiMe$_3$)$_2$}$_3$] (38).

Furthermore, the concept that kinetic rather than thermodynamic effects were crucial for the stabilization of metal or metalloid Main Group element compounds under ambient conditions led to the isolation of the first two-coordinate tin and lead alkyls, [M{CH(SiMe$_3$)$_2$}$_2$] (M = Sn or Pb) (34), which are analogous to carbenes. It was subsequently shown that although these species afford weak dimers analogous to the alkenes in the solid state, unlike their carbon counterparts they did not have planar structures but instead exhibited pyramidalization at the heteroatom. This differing behaviour of the heavier Main Group p-block elements opened up a series of major developments in this area. Electron spin resonance studies in solution revealed the existence of the persistent stannyl radical Sn{CH(SiMe$_3$)$_2$}$_3$ (35). The work, involving sabbatical visitor Professor Harold Goldwhite, stimulated studies on phosphorus and arsenic compounds and also afforded similar stable radicals (44).

A significant achievement was the direct synthesis from the electron-rich olefin (CH$_2$PhN)$_2$C=C(NPhCH$_2$)$_2$ of a platinum(II) complex of the carbene :C(NPhCH$_2$)$_2$ (28). A structurally similar NHC carbene, first reported by Arduengo and co-workers (see Arduengo *et al.* 1991) and now extremely well known, has found wide synthetic and catalytic applications. The Lappert group subsequently exploited a variety of electron-rich olefins as precursors for a wide range of carbene–transition-metal complexes (48), which featured in a comprehensive review (36) also including the extensive work of the group of E. O. Fischer in Munich. Dismutation of electron-rich olefins having different substituents at the nitrogen atoms was shown to be catalysed by rhodium(I) complexes (29). A further method of generating a carbene–transition-metal complex involved a three-fragment oxidative addition reaction (39). Similarly, oxidative addition of an alkyl halide to zerovalent platinum was shown to proceed by a radical process (37). Collaboration with Professor A. W. Johnson FRS, who had recently moved to Sussex from Nottingham, on vitamin B$_{12}$ chemistry as a model to the above carbene–metal chemistry led, *inter alia*, to a kinetic and mechanistic study of the coenzyme B$_{12}$-dependent enzyme ethanolamine ammonia-lyase (41).

Period 1975–86

The remarkable versatility of the Lappert research group is exemplified by the following selections from his published work during this period. A major review with P. Lednor of free radicals in organometallic chemistry (45) was very influential, as was the report of the synthesis of stable P(II) and As(II) alkyls and amides (46) and a method for generating either [M(η^5-C$_5$H$_4$R^1)$_2$R^2]$^-$ (M = Ti, Zr or Hf; R^1 = H or SiMe$_3$, R^2 = X(SiMe$_3$)) from the M(IV) precursor and sodium naphthalide (52).

Collaboration with Sussex colleague J. B. Pedley in the calorimetric determination of the heats of alcoholysis of Ti, Zr and Hf chlorides, alkyls, amides and alkoxides led to the observation that the M–X bond energy terms (X = C, N or O) *decreased* in the order Hf > Zr ≫ Ti and to the important conclusion that bond strengths decrease with atomic number in a Main Group element but the *reverse* is the case in the transition metals (42). A joint venture with the Haaland–Fjelderg electron diffraction team (59) led *inter alia* to the determination of the gas-phase structure of the lithium amide [Li{N(SiMe$_3$)$_2$}$_2$]$_2$.

Dark blue [Th{η^5-C$_5$H$_3$(SiMe$_3$)$_2$}$_3$], the first crystalline thorium(III) compound, was obtained by Na/K reduction of [Thη^5-(C$_5$H$_3$)(SiMe$_3$)$_2$Cl$_2$], metallic thorium being the co-product. Collaboration with Edelstein's group (using the SiMe$_2$Bu^t analogue), involving variable-temperature electron paramagnetic resonance, magnetic measurements and optical spectra, established that the green reduction product had a $6d^1$ rather than a $5f^1$ electronic ground state (66, 84). The very widely used bis-trimethylsilylcyclopentadienyl ligand, η^5-$C_5H_3(SiMe_3)_2$ (abbreviated to Cp″), was introduced in 1981 in the context of early (f^0–f^3) lanthanocene and related Sc and Y chlorides, including the synthesis and X-ray structural characterization of $[(Pr\{\eta^5-[C_5H_3(SiMe_3)_2]\}_2(\mu\text{-}Cl))_2]$ (55). This led to a detailed survey of such data for the complete 4f-metal series and of hetero-bimetallic analogues such as $[LnCp″_2(\mu\text{-}Cl)_2ML_2]$ (M = Li or Na, L = a neutral donor) or $[AsPh_4][NdCp″_2Cl_2]$ (57).

   The first examples of bridging (μ-Me)$_2$-4f-metal species $[\{MCp_2(\mu\text{-}Me)_2\}_2]$ and $[MCp_2(\mu\text{-}Me)_2AlMe_2]$ (where Cp represents cyclopentadienyl, C_5H_5) were prepared (43) and early transition metal *meso*-metallacycles $[M\{CH(SiMe_3)C_6H_4CHSiMe_3\text{-}o\}(Cp)_2]$ (M = Ti, Zr, Hf or Nb) displayed reversible one-electron reduction (60). Among extensive contributions to carbene–metal chemistry was the synthesis and structures of *cis*- and *trans*-$[Mo(CO)_4(A)_2]$ (A = carbene), complexes and a kinetic study of their interconversion (56). Surprisingly, treatment of $[Nb(\eta^5\text{-}C_5H_4Me)_2(CH_2SiMe_3)Cl]$ with Na/Hg in thf under an atmosphere of CO_2 yielded the crystalline Nb^{III}-η^2-CO_2 complex, the carbon dioxide having unexpectedly displaced the chloride ion (54).

   Attention to Main Group element chemistry was not neglected, and a series of crystalline, monomeric, thermochromic (yellow-to-red), divalent Ge, Sn or Pb amides, $M(NR^1R^2)_2$ (R^1 = $SiMe_3$, R^2 = $SiMe_3$ or Bu^t; M = Ge, Sn or Pb; or R^1 = R^2 = $GeMe_3$, $SiEt_3$ or $GePh_3$), was prepared from the appropriate lithium amide and metal(II) chloride (49). Bulky silylmethyl and related trialkyls of Group 13 metals included the X-ray-authenticated InR_3 (53). Similarly, reaction of ECl_3 (E = P or As) with $3LiNHAr$ (E = P or As; Ar = $C_6H_2Bu^t_3$-2,4,6) gave the novel, crystalline, orange (P) or red (As), two-coordinate imides $E(=NAr)(NHAr)$ (61).

   Gas chromatographic studies of homogeneous catalytic reactions included hydrosilylation (via co-condensation of metal atoms at $-196\,°C$), of isoprene with triethoxysilane below $0\,°C$, affording quantitative and regio- and stereo-selective yields of (Z)-1-triethoxysilyl-2-methyl-2-butene (50). This period ended with two major reviews. The first, 'Metal σ-hydrocarbyls, MR_n: stoichiometry, structures, stabilities, and thermal decomposition pathways', introduced the terms 'homoleptic and heteroleptic' into coordination and organometallic chemistry (47). The second, entitled 'Bridged hydrocarbyl or hydrocarbon binuclear transition-metal complexes: classification, structures, and chemistry', afforded a comprehensive survey of a topic that came into prominence after 1970 (58).

Period 1987–96

The role of heavier Group 14 element carbene analogues, MX_2 (M = Ge, Sn or Pb; X = CHR_2, NR_2, OAr or SAr; R = $SiMe_3$, Ar = $C_6H_2Bu^t_3$-2,4,6), in transition-metal chemistry was comprehensively reviewed (70). Following Denk and West's discovery of the first room-temperature-stable gaseous silylene, and its structure determination by electron diffraction, the Lappert group prepared the crystalline silylene, $Si\{N(CH_2Bu^t)\}_2C_6H_4$-1,2, and showed that it underwent oxidative-addition reactions (78).

   Other important milestones in widely differing areas of chemistry included:

   (i) identification of the chelating ligand $[\eta^2\text{-}CH_2=CHSi(Me)_2]_2O$ as a key component of the industrially important Speiers hydrosilylation catalyst (63, 73);

   (ii) a low-temperature single-crystal X-ray and neutron diffraction study of Me_2Mg, which revealed the first example of an intermolecular weak (agostic) γ-methyl-metal interaction (71);

(iii) lipophilic calcium and strontium alkyls, amides and phenoxides obtained directly from the corresponding metal, in collaboration with Sussex colleague Geoff Cloke (FRS 2007) (74);

(iv) establishment of the linear structure of MnR_2 in the gas phase (67);

(v) first examples of neutral homoleptic 4f-metal(III) alkyls, $[LnR_3]$ (Ln = La or Sm); the former being pyramidal with unusually short La$\cdots$HCH$_2$ contacts (68);

(vi) metal-vapour syntheses affording bis-(η-1,3,5-tri-t-butylbenzene) sandwich complexes of zerovalent titanium, zirconium and hafnium (65); and

(vii) metal complexes containing the novel benzene 1,4-dianion (79).

Studies, in collaboration with the groups of R. A. Andersen, J. C. Green and A. Haaland, on 3d^6, 3d^7 and 3d^8-metal amides $M(NR'_2)_2$, which are monomeric in the gas phase, were shown by electron diffraction to have an N–M–N core and by photoelectron spectroscopy and molecular orbital calculations to have $^6A_1$, $^2B_1$ and $^3A_2$ ground states, respectively (69). Novel two-coordinate germanium arylamides and related crystalline tin(II) amide $[Sn\{N(H)Ar\}_2]$ compounds were also described (72).

Particularly exciting achievements were long-sought-after examples of transition-metal complexes containing a metal–phosphorus double bond, $[MCp_2(=PAr)]$ (M = Mo or W; Ar = $C_6H_2Bu^t_3$-2,4,6), which were obtained in crystalline form, the structure of the Mo compound revealing a short Mo–P distance and a Mo–P–C angle of about 116°, consistent with the existence of a stereochemically active lone pair at phosphorus (64).

Interestingly, the first examples of neutral mononuclear 4f-metal thiolates, for example $[Sm(SAr)_3]$ and $[Yb(SAr)_2(dme)]$, could be obtained directly from the corresponding metal-alkyl precursors (75), and a further important observation was the transformation of the ubiquitous –CH(SiMe$_3$)$_2$ ligand into the corresponding β-diketiminate -N(SiMe$_3$)C(Ph)C(H)C(Ph)N(SiMe$_3$)$^-$, on treatment with PhCN (76). Such β-diketiminate ligand systems were subsequently developed extensively by the Lappert group.

Final period, 1997–2014

Mike Lappert reached the normal age of retirement of 65 years at the end of 1993, but he was granted an employment extension until 1997 to allow him to continue to supervise postgraduate research students until 2003 and to be part of the Chemistry Departmental Research submission to the University Grants Committee. Thereafter he continued as a Research Professor with postdoctoral workers until his death. From 1997 until his death he supervised 7 postgraduates and 25 postdoctoral scientists. The work during this time continued along the lines of the earlier periods described above. He continued to explore the chemistry of bulky ligands that could stabilize otherwise unusual metal complex stereochemistries and oxidation states, and expanded the chemistry of less-common metals, especially rare earths, and of low oxidation states of these and many other elements.

His work, even in single publications, often involved a wide range of topics, so that summarizing his research under specific headings is quite challenging. The references quoted should generally be regarded as typical of the subject discussed rather than a comprehensive record. Two closely related earlier communications published in 1994 (76, 77) attracted 114 citations each, showing their scientific significance. Each describes the straightforward preparation of two highly lipophilic monoanionic ligands, azaallyl and β-diketaminate, and the introduction of these ligands into early transition and Main Group metal chemistry. He was one of the first to realize that the β-diketaminato (or NacNac) ligands that he employed were suitable for supporting a wide range of coordination chemistry, providing the advantage of steric protection of a metal centre, and similar to the widely used acetylacetonate ligand. Diketiminates are formally condensation products of a ketone and an amine, and variation of the two starting materials gives rise to a wide variety of similar but different materials with a range of reaction and steric properties. Such β-diketiminate ligands became particularly popular ancillary groups in various fields of organometallic and coordination chemistry, with significant contributions using the Lappert bis(trimethylsilyl) substituted β-diketiminate. Mike himself continued to be active in this area and, along with Bourget-Merle and Severn (99), published a definitive review on the subject of NacNac ligands. These were designed to support low-oxidation-state lanthanum compounds but Mike continued to exploit their use in a wide range of transition-metal coordination compounds, in both spectator and non-spectator roles (73, 95, 100, 102, 105, 108, 112, 115, 118, 120, 125).

As mentioned earlier, an abiding interest of Mike's was the chemistry of carbenes and of analogous metal(II) derivatives from Periodic Group 14, and the olefins from which they may be derived. He published a review of his work in this area in 2005 (109). Reactions between the heavier members of this Group were investigated (80–82, 85, 86, 91, 96, 107, 110, 116) and Mike also collaborated with other independent researchers whose specialities included various spectroscopic techniques and thermochemistry, the information from which would complement that obtained from his own specific researches (83, 87, 97, 103, 111).

Of special importance are the reactions of the various divalent heavier Group 14 element carbene-analogues with carbonyl groups (80) and their ready insertion into metal–nitrogen bonds (81) and specific P–P bonds of organophosphorus cage compounds (116). Particularly interesting was the report (in collaboration with the groups of Cowley, Rankin and Power) of the spontaneous generation of stable pnictinyl radicals from 'Jack-in-the-box' dipnictines and a detailed examination of solid-state and gas-phase structures and a theoretical investigation of the origins of steric stabilization (97).

A range of sterically crowded Lappert-type ligands was used to investigate new chemistry of a wide range of metallic elements, many of which, such as the rare-earth derivatives, have become readily available only relatively recently. In addition to the examples cited above, especially noteworthy is a report of complexes of aluminium(I) (88). Later publications describe the use of the NacNac ligand with magnesium (92), cobalt, iron and zirconium (118, 104), thallium (93), a considerable number of different lanthanides (89, 106, 119, 123, 126), alkali metals (94), titanium, zirconium and iron (113), tin (114), zinc (117, 127), a wide range of further transition elements (90, 121) and even some non-metal clusters (124). Remarkably, even with this enormous output, Lappert also published a review (98) and contributed to several books (51, 62, 122).

AWARDS AND HONOURS

Mike Lappert was the recipient of the first Royal Society of Chemistry Medal for Main Group chemistry (1970). He was also an *Organometallics* Medallist (1978) and a Tilden (1972), Nyholm (1994) and Sir Edward Frankland (1998) Lecturer. He received the F. S. Kipping Award for Silicon Chemistry from the American Chemical Society in 1976 and the Alfred Stock Memorial Prize in 2008. This latter is the premier award of the Gesellschaft Deutscher Chemiker for inorganic chemistry, which is presented every two years and only rarely to a non-German scientist. Probably because of his family history, of all the honours he received during his career he was proudest of this. Since 1950 the only other UK recipient was Professor H. J. Emeléus FRS. Mike was elected a Fellow of the Royal Society in 1979 and was President of the Dalton Division of the Royal Society of Chemistry from 1989 to 1991. He was a Science and Engineering Research Council Senior Fellow (1980–85) and held honorary doctorates of the Universities of Munich (1989) and Murcia (2013). From 2000 he was an Honorary Professor of Shanxi University in China. He lectured worldwide during his academic career and also held positions as Visiting Professor at the Universities of Alabama, Alberta, Auckland, British Columbia, Chinese University of Hong Kong (where he was Royal Society Tang Professor), University of California at Davis, Rennes, Waterloo, Western Australia and Wisconsin (where he was the first McElwain Awardee for Inorganic Chemistry).

Career summary

Born 31 December 1928 in Brno, Czechoslovakia. Arrived in England in June 1939 (*Kindertransport*). Educated at Cannock House School and from 1942 to 1946 at Wilson's Grammar School. Undergraduate student at the Northern Polytechnic, London. BSc, first-class honours (1949); PhD (1951), supervisor W. Gerrard. Assistant Lecturer (1951–52), Lecturer (1952–53), Senior Lecturer (1953–59) in organic chemistry at the Northern Polytechnic. Recognised Teacher of the University of London (1956), Fellow of the Royal Institute of Chemistry (1956), DSc (1960). At UMIST: Lecturer in inorganic chemistry (1959–61), Senior Lecturer (1961–64). At Sussex University: Reader (1964–69), Professor (1969–97), Research Professor (1997–2008), Emeritus Professor (2011–14).

Acknowledgement

The frontispiece photograph was taken in about 1995 by Lorna Lappert and is reproduced with permission. (Online version in colour.)

References to other authors

Arduengo, A. J., Harlow, R. L. & Kline, M. 1991 A stable crystalline carbene. *J. Am. Chem. Soc.* **113**, 361–363.
Arnold, J., Brothers, P. J., Mountford, P., Piers, W. E., Thomas, C. M. & Tilley, T. D. 2014 The influence of Michael Lappert on the chemistry landscape. *Dalton Trans.*, 16553–16556.
Cardin, D. J. 1993 Introduction to special issue. *J. Organometall. Chem.* **462**, ix–x.
Murrell, J. 2009 *MOLSBOOK*. Private publication; copies may be obtained by writing to the Chemistry Subject Office at the University of Sussex.
Power, P. P. 2015 Editorial for the Mike Lappert Commemorative Issue. *Organometallics* **34**, 2035–2936.

Bibliography

The following publications are those referred to directly in the text.

(1)   1956   Organic compounds of boron. *Chem. Rev.* **56**, 959–1064.
(2)   1957   Pyridinium tetrachloro- and tetrabromo-borates. *Proc. Chem. Soc.*, 121.
(3)   1958   (With W. Gerrard) Reactions of boron trichloride with organic compounds. *Chem. Rev.* **58**, 1081–1111.

(4)   (With L. J. Bellamy, W. Gerrard & R. L. Williams) Infrared spectra of boron compounds. *J. Chem. Soc.*, 2412–2415.

(5)   Chemical properties of *n*-butyl metaborate. *J. Chem. Soc.*, 3256–3259.

(6)   (With L. A. Duncanson, W. Gerrard, H. Pyszora & R. Shafferman) Infrared spectra and structures of some acyloxy-derivatives of boron. *J. Chem. Soc.*, 3652–3656.

(7)   1959 (With W. Gerrard & B. A. Mountfield) Interaction of boron trichloride with catechol, quinol, resorcinol and pyrogallol. *J. Chem. Soc.*, 1529–1535.

(8)   Cyclic organoboron compounds. Part III. Cyclic B-aminoborazoles and their polycondensates. *Proc. Chem. Soc.*, 59.

(9)   1962 Coordination compounds having carboxylic esters as ligands; relative acceptor strengths of some Group III and IV halides. *J. Chem. Soc.*, 542–548.

(10)   Polymers containing boron and nitrogen. In *Developments in inorganic polymer chemistry* (ed. M. F. Lappert & G. J. Leigh), ch. 2. Amsterdam: Elsevier.

(11)   (Editor, with G. J. Leigh) *Developments in inorganic polymer chemistry*. Amsterdam: Elsevier.

(12)   (With D. W. Aubrey & M. K. Majumdar) Trisaminoboranes. *J. Chem. Soc.*, 4088–4094.

(13) 1963 (With M. K. Majumdar) 3-coordinate boron-nitrogen 4-membered ring systems (1-3-diaza-2-4-boretane). *Proc. Chem. Soc.*, 88.

(14) 1964 (With B. Prokai) Haloboration and phenylboration of acetylenes and the preparation of some alkenylboranes. *J. Organometall. Chem.* **1**, 384–400.

(15)   (With G. Srivastava) Triborylamines. *Proc. Chem. Soc.*, 121.

(16)   (With R. H. Cragg & B. P. Tilley) Aminoboration and alkoxyboration of isocyanates and isothiocyanates. *J. Chem. Soc.*, 2108–2115.

(17) 1965 (With K. Jones) Preparation of aminostannanes, stannylamines and stannazanes. *J. Chem. Soc.*, 1944–1951.

(18)   (With K. Jones) Metal amines as reagents for synthesis of organometallics; especially the reactions of aminostannanes with protic species. *J. Organometall. Chem.* **3**, 295–307.

(19)   (With J. K. Smith) The thermochemistry of the complexes of ethyl acetate with Group III halides. *J. Chem. Soc.*, 5826–5830.

(20) 1966 (With J. B. Pedley, P. N. K. Riley & A. Tweedale) Ionisation potentials and electronic spectra of halogeno- and amino-boranes and a study of some redistribution reactions. *J. Chem. Soc. Chem. Commun.*, 788.

(21)   (With R. H. Cragg) Organic boron-sulphur compounds. *Organometall. Chem. Rev.* **1**, 43–65.

(22) 1967 (With P. M. Druce & P. N. K. Riley) Boron halides as reagents in inorganic chemistry: synthesis of anhydrous metal bromides and binuclear halogen-bridged platinum(II) cations. *J. Chem. Soc. Chem. Commun.*, 486–487.

(23)   (With J. Lorberth). Organometallic diazoalkanes. *J. Chem. Soc. Chem. Commun.*, 836–837.

(24) 1968 (With A. Barfield & J. Lee) π-Bonding and hindered rotation in inorganic systems. *Trans. Faraday Soc.* **64**, 2571–2578.

(25) 1970 (With M. R. Collier & M. M. Truelock) μ-Methylene transition metal binuclear compounds: complexes with $Me_3SiCH_2^-$ and related ligands. *J. Organometall. Chem.* **25**, C36–C38.

(26) 1971 (With J. S. Poland) Heterocyclic syntheses with the co-ordinated ligand CN_2; reactions of trimethylsilyl-diazoalkanes. *J. Chem. Soc.*, 3910–3914.

(27)   (With A. D. Jenkins & R. C. Srivastava) The polymerization of acrylonitrile with titanium tetradimethylamide and related reactions. *Eur. Polym. J.* **7**, 289–302.

(28)   (With D. J. Cardin, B. Cetinkaya, Lj. Manojlovic-Muir & K. W. Muir) An electron-rich olefin as a source of coordinated carbene; synthesis of *trans*-[$PtCl_2$[$C(NPhCH_2)_2PEt_3$] *J. Chem. Soc. Chem. Commun.*, 400–401.

(29) 1972 (With D. J. Cardin & M. J. Doyle) Rhodium(I) catalysed dismutation of electron-rich olefins: rhodium(I) carbene complexes as intermediates. *J. Chem. Soc. Chem. Commun.*, 927–928.

(30)   (With D. J. Cardin) Dimethylaminotrimethylstannane, a powerful dehydrochlorinating reagent. *J. Chem. Soc. Chem. Commun.*, 1034.

(31) 1973 (With P. J. Davidson & R. Pearce) Silylmethyl and related complexes. Preparation, spectra and thermolysis of tetraneopentyls of Ti, Zr and Hf. *J. Organometall. Chem.* **57**, 269–277.

(32)   (With R. Pearce) Trimethylsilylmethylcopper, a stable copper(I) alkyl. *J. Chem. Soc. Chem. Commun.*, 24–25.

(33)   (With R. Pearce) Stable silylmethyl and neopentyl complexes of scandium and yttrium. *J. Chem. Soc. Chem. Commun.*, 126.

(34)   (With P. J. Davidson) Stabilisation of metals in a low co-ordination environment using the bis(trimethylsilyl)methyl ligand; coloured Sn and Pb alkyls, $M\{CH(SiMe_3)_2\}_2$. *J. Chem. Soc. Chem. Commun.*, 317.

(35)   (With P. J. Davidson, A. Hudson & P. W. Lednor) Tris-(bis(trimethylsilyl)methyl)tin(III), an unusually stable stannyl radical $R_3Sn\cdot$ from photolysis of R_2Sn. *J. Chem. Soc. Chem. Commun.*, 829–830.

(36)   (With D. J. Cardin & B. Cetinkaya). Transition metal–carbene complexes. *Chem. Rev.* **72**, 545–574.

(37)   (With P. W. Lednor) Free radicals as intermediates in the oxidative addition of alkyl halides to platinum(0). *J. Chem. Soc. Chem. Commun.*, 948–949.

(38)   1974   (With G. K. Barker) Stabilisation of transition metals in a low coordinate environment using the bis(trimethylsilyl)methyl ligand; a monomeric chromium alkyl, $[Cr\{CH(SiMe_3)_2\}_3]$ and related complexes. *J. Organometall. Chem.* **76**, C45–C46.

(39)   (With A. J. Oliver) A three-fragment oxidative addition reaction as a route to transition metal carbene complexes: imidoyl halides and rhodium(I) compounds as precursors for rhodium(III) carbenes. *J. Chem. Soc. Chem. Commun.*, 274–275.

(40)   1975   (With H. W. Kroto, M. Maier, J. B. Pedley, M. Vidal & M. F. Guest) The He(I) phoelectron spectra of mixed boron trihalides and the microwave spectrum of $BClF_2$. *J. Chem. Soc. Chem. Commun.*, 810–812.

(41)   (With K. N. Joblin, A. W. Johnson, M. R. Hollaway & H. A. White) Co-enzyme-B_{12} dependent enzyme reactions: a spectrophotometric rapid kinetic study of ethanolamine ammonia-lyase. *FEBS Lett.* **53**,193.

(42)   (With D. S. Patil & J. B. Pedley) Standard heats of formation and M–C bond energy terms of some homoleptic transition metal alkyls MR_n. *J. Chem. Soc. Chem. Commun.*, 830–831.

(43)   1976   (With J. Holton, D. G. H. Ballard, R. Pearce, J. L. Atwood & W. E. Hunter) Dimeric μ-dimethyl-lanthanide complexes, a new class of electron-deficient compound, and the crystal and molecular structure of $[\{Yb(\eta^5\text{-}C_5H_5)_2Me\}_2]$. *J. Chem. Soc. Chem. Commun.*, 480–481.

(44)   (With M. J. S. Gynane, A. Hudson, P. P. Power & H. Goldwhite) Synthesis and electron spin resonance study of stable dialkyls and diamides of phosphorus and arsenic R^1_2M and $(R^2_2N)_2M$. *J. Chem. Soc. Chem. Commun.*, 623.

(45)   (With P. W. Lednor) Free radicals in organometallic chemistry. *Adv. Organometall. Chem.* **14**, 345–399.

(46)   (With M. J. S. Gynane, A. Hudson & P. P. Power) Synthesis and electron spin resonance study of stable dialkyls and diamides of phosphorus and arsenic. *J. Chem. Soc. Chem. Commun.*, 623–624.

(47)   (With P. J. Davidson & R. Pearce) Metal σ-hydrocarbyls, MR_n: stoichiometry, structures, stabilities, and thermal decomposition pathways. *Chem. Rev.* **76**, 219–242.

(48)   1977   (With P. L. Pye) Carbene and related complexes of molybdenum derived from electron rich olefins. *J. Less Common Metals* **54**, 191–207.

(49)   (With M. J. S. Gynane, D. H. Harris, P. P. Power, P. Riviere & M. Riviere-Baudet) The synthesis and physical properties of thermally stable amides of germanium(II), tin(II) and lead(II). *J. Chem. Soc. Dalton Trans.*, 2004–2009.

(50)   (With A. J. Cornish & T. A. Nile) Hydrosilylation of cyclic or linear dienes using low-valent nickel complexes and related experiments. *J. Organometall. Chem.* **132**, 133–148.

(51)   1979   (With P. P. Power, A. R. Sanger & R. C. Srivastava) *Metal and metalloid amides*. Chichester: Ellis Horwood.

(52)   1980   (With T. R. Martin, C. R. C. Milne, J. L. Atwood, W. E. Hunter & R. E. Pentilla) Syntheses and structures of the Nb(IV) metallocycle $[M(\eta^5\text{-}C_5H_4SiMe_3)_2(CH_2C_6H_4CH_2\text{-}o)]$ (M = Nb, R = $SiMe_3$) and reductive cleavage of d^0 analogues (M = Ti, Zr or Hf; R = H or $SiMe_3$) by $NaC_{10}H_8$. *J. Organometall. Chem.* **192**, C35–C36.

(53)   (With A. J. Carty, M. J. S. Gynane, S. J. Miles, A. Singh & N. J. Taylor) Bulky monomeric heavy Group 13 metal trialkyls and the crystal and molecular structure of $In[CH(SiMe_3)_2]_3$. *Inorg. Chem.* **19**, 3637–3641.

(54) 1981 (With G. S. Bristow & P. B. Hitchcock) A novel carbon dioxide complex: synthesis and crystal structure of [Nb(η^5-C_5H_4Me)$_2$(CH_2SiMe_3)(η^2-CO_2)]. *J. Chem. Soc. Chem. Commun.*, 1145–1146.

(55) (With A. Singh, J. L. Atwood & W. E. Hunter) Use of the bis(trimethylsilyl)cyclo-pentadienyl ligand for stabilising early (f^0–f^3) lanthanocene chlorides; X-ray structures of [(Pr{η-[$C_5H_3(SiMe_3)_2$]}$_2$Cl)$_2$] and of isoleptic scandium and ytterbium complexes. *J. Chem. Soc. Chem. Commun.*, 1190–1191.

(56) (With P. L. Pye, A. J. Rogers & G. M. McLaughlin) Crystal structure of *trans*-tetra-carbonyl(1,3-dimethylimidazolidinylidene)molybdenum(0), [Mo(CO)$_4${CN(Me)CH_2-CH_2NMe}$_2$], structural comparison with the *cis* isomer and a kinetic study of the *trans*→*cis* isomerisation. *J. Chem. Soc. Dalton Trans.*, 701–704.

(57) 1982 (With A. Singh) Bis(cyclopentadienyl)lanthanoid(III) chlorides. *J. Organometall. Chem.* **239**, 133–141.

(58) 1983 (With J. Holton, R. Pearce & P. I. W. Yarrow) Bridged hydrocarbyl or hydrocarbon binuclear transition metal complexes: classification, structures, and chemistry. *Chem. Rev.* **83**, 135–201.

(59) 1984 (With T. Fjeldberg, P. B. Hitchcock & A. J. Thorne) Unusual molecular structures of some sterically hindered lithium amides: electron diffraction results on gaseous [Li{N(SiMe$_3$)$_2$}]$_2$ and X-ray data on crystalline monomeric Li(NHAr)-(tmeda). *J. Chem. Soc. Chem. Commun.*, 822–824.

(60) (With C. L. Raston, B. W. Skelton & A. H. White) Stereospecific synthesis of the early transition metal *meso*-metallacycles [M{CH(SiMe$_3$)C_6H_4CH(SiMe$_3$)-o}-(η-n.C_5H_5)$_2$] their reversible one-electron reduction (M = Ti, Zr, Hf, or Nb) and oxidation (M = Nb); and the X-ray crystal structure of the zirconium complex. *J. Chem. Soc. Dalton Trans.*, 893–902.

(61) 1986 (With P. B. Hitchcock, A. K. Rai & H. D. Williams) Novel arylimides of phosphorus(III) and arsenic(III) (the arsazene being the first stable compound containing an As(III)-N double bond); X-ray structure of E(=NAr)(NHAr) (E = P or As, Ar = $C_6H_2Bu^t_3$-2,4,6). *J. Chem. Soc. Chem. Commun.*, 1633–1634.

(62) (With D. J. Cardin & C. L. Raston) *Chemistry of organo-zirconium and organo-hafnium compounds.* Chichester: Ellis Horwood.

(63) 1987 (With G. Chandra, P. B. Hitchcock & P. Y. Lo) A convenient and novel route to bis(η-alkyne) platinum(0) and other platinum(0) complexes from Speier's hydrosilylation catalyst H$_2$[PtCl$_6$].xH$_2$O; X-ray structure of [Pt{(η-CH_2=CHSiMe$_2$)$_2$O}-(P^{t}Bu$_3$)], *Organometallics* **6**, 191–192.

(64) (With P. B. Hitchcock & W.-P. Leung) The first stable transition metal (molybdenum or tungsten) complexes having a metal-phosphorus(III) double bond: the phosphorus analogues of metal aryl- and alkyl-imides; X-ray structure of [Mo(Cp)$_2$(=PAr)] (Ar = $C_6H_2Bu^t_3$-2,4,6). *J. Chem. Soc. Chem. Commun.*, 1282–1283.

(65) (With F. G. N. Cloke, G. A. Lawless & A. C. Swain) Synthesis of bis(η-1,3,5-tri-t-butylbenzene) sandwich complexes of titanium, zirconium, and hafnium, and of the hafnium(0) carbonyl complex [Hf(η-Bu$^t_3$C$_6$H$_3$)$_2$(CO)]. *J. Chem. Soc. Chem. Commun.*, 1667–1668.

(66) 1988 (With W. K. Kot, G. V. Shalimoff, N. M. Edelstein & M. A. Edelman) [Th^{III}Cp$'_3$] an actinide compound with a 6d^1 ground state. *J. Am. Chem. Soc.* **110**, 986.

(67) (With R. A. Andersen, D. J. Berg, L. Fernholt, K. Faegri Jr, J. C. Green, A. Haaland, W.-P. Leung & K. Rypdal) Monomeric,base-free Mn^{II} dialkyls; synthesis, magnetic properties and molecular structure of MnR$_2$ (R = CH(SiMe$_3$)$_3$); SCF MO calculations on Mn(CH$_3$)$_2$ and photoelectron spectra of Mn(CH$_2$CMe$_3$)$_2$. *Acta Chem. Scand.* A **42**, 554–562.

(68) (With P. B. Hitchcock, R. G. Smith, R. A. Bartlett & P. P. Power) Synthesis and structural characterisation of the first neutral homoleptic lanthanide metal(III) alkyls: LnR$_3$ (Ln = La or Sm, R = CH(SiMe$_3$)$_2$). *J. Chem. Soc. Chem. Commun.*, 1007–1009.

(69) (With R. A. Andersen, K. Faegri Jr, J. C. Green, A. Haaland, W.-P. Leung & K. Rypdal) Synthesis of bis[bis(trimethylsilyl)amido]iron(II). Structure and bonding in M(NR$_2$)$_2$ (M = Mn, Fe, Co ;R = SiMe$_3$): two-coordinate transition amides. *Inorg. Chem.* **27**, 1782–1786.

(70) 1990 (With R. S. Rowe) The role of Group 14 element carbene analogues in transition metal chemistry. *Coord. Chem. Rev.* **100**, 267–292.

(71) (With P. B. Hitchcock, J. A. K. Howard, W.-P. Leung & S. A. Mason) The first example of an intermolecular weak (agostic) γ-methyl-metal interaction: the low temperature single crystal X-ray and neutron diffraction structure of (MgR$_2$)$_\infty$[R = CH(SiMe$_3$)$_2$]. *J. Chem. Soc. Chem. Commun.*, 847–849.

(72)   (With P. B. Hitchcock & A. J. Thorne) Novel two-coordinate germanium(II) arylamides: Ge(NHAr)$_2$, [{Ge(NHAr)}$_2$(μ-NAr)] **2** and [{Ge(μ-NAr)}$_2$], and the X-ray structures of **2** and Sn(NHAr)$_2$ (Ar = C$_6$H$_2$Bu$^t_3$-2,4,6). *J. Chem. Soc. Chem. Commun.*, 1587–1589.

(73)   1991   (With P. B. Hitchcock & N. J. W. Warhurst) Synthesis and structure of a *rac*-tris(di-vinyldisiloxane) diplatinum(0) complex and its reaction with maleic anhydride. *Angew. Chem. Int. Edn* **30**, 438–440.

(74)   (With F. G. N. Cloke, P. B. Hitchcock, G. A. Lawless & B. Royo) Lipophilic strontium and calcium alkyls, amides and phenoxides; X-ray structures of the crystalline square-planar [{*trans*-Sr(NR′$_2$)$_2$(μ-1,4-dioxane)}∞] and tetrahedral [CaR$_2$(1,4-dioxane)$_2$]; (R′ = SiMe$_3$, R = CH(SiMe$_3$)$_2$). *J. Chem. Soc. Chem. Commun.*, 724–726.

(75)   1992   (With B. Cetinkaya, P. B. Hitchcock & R. G. Smith) The first neutral, mono-nuclear 4f-metal thiolates and new methods for corresponding aryl oxides and bis(trimethylsilyl)amides. *J. Chem. Soc. Chem. Commun.*, 932–934.

(76)   1994   (With P. B. Hitchcock & D. S. Liu) Transformation of the bis(trimethylsilyl)methyl into a β-diketiminato ligand; the X-ray structure of [Li(L′L′)]$_2$, [SnCl(Me)$_2$(L′L′)] and [SnCl (Me)$_2$(LL)] (L′L′ = N(R)C(Ph)C(H)C(Ph)NR, LL = N(H)C(Ph)C(H)C(Ph)NH, R = SiMe$_3$). *J. Chem. Soc. Chem. Commun.*, 1699–1700.

(77)   (With P. B. Hitchcock & D. S. Liu) Transformation of the bis(trimethyl silyl) methyl into aza-allyl and β-diketinimato ligands; the X-ray structures of [Li{N(R)C(^{t}Bu)CHR}]$_2$ and [Zr{N(R)C(^{t}Bu)CHC(Ph)NR}Cl$_3$] (R = SiMe$_3$). *J. Chem. Soc. Chem. Commun.*, 2637–2638.

(78)   1995   (With B. Gehrhus, J. Heinicke, R. Boese & D. Bläser) Synthesis, structures and reactions of new thermally stable silylenes. *J. Chem. Soc. Chem. Commun.*, 1931–1932.

(79)   1996   (With M. C. Cassani, Yu. K. Gun'ko & P. B. Hitchcock) The first metal complexes containing the 1,4-cyclohexa-2,5-dienyl ligand (benzene dianion); synthesis and structures of [K(18-crown-6)] [{Ln(Cp′)$_2$}$_2$(C$_6$H$_6$)] (Ln = La, Ce). *Chem. Commun.*, 1987–1988.

(80)   1997   (With B. Gehrhus & P. B. Hitchcock) The thermally stable silylene [Si{N(CH$_2$Bu^t)}$_2$C$_6$H$_4$-1,2]: reactivity toward CO double bonds. *Organometallics* **16**, 4861–4864.

(81)   (With B. Gehrhus & P. B. Hitchcock) New reactions of a silylene: insertion into M–N bonds of M[N(SiMe$_3$)$_2$]$_2$ (M = Ge, Sn or Pb). *Angew. Chem. Int. Edn Engl.* **36**, 2514–2516.

(82)   (With P. B. Hitchcock, J. Hu, M. Layh & J. R. Severn) Variation of bonding modes in homoleptic tin(II) 1-azaallyls. *Chem. Commun.*, 1189–1190.

(83)   (With M. C. Cassani & F. Laschi) First identification by EPR spectra of lanthanum(II) organometallic intermediates (and $E_{1/2}$ for La^{3+} → La^{2+}) in the C–O bond activation of dimethoxyethane. *Chem. Commun.*, 1563–1564.

(84)   1998   (With P. C. Blake, M. A. Edelman, P. B. Hitchcock, J. Hu, S. Tian, G. Müller, J. L. Atwood & H. Zhang) The chemistry of some tris(cyclopentadienyl)actinide complexes. *J. Organometall. Chem.* **551**, 261–270.

(85)   (With B. Çetinkaya, E. Çetinkaya, J. A. Chamizo, P. B. Hitchcock, H. A. Jasim & H. Küçükbay) Synthesis and structure of 1,3,1′,3′-tetrabenzyl-2,2′-biimidazolidinylidenes (electron-rich alkenes), their aminal intermediates and their degradation products. *J. Chem. Soc. Perkin Trans.*, 2047–2054.

(86)   (With M. A. Della Bona, M. C. Cassini, J. M. Keates, G. A. Lawless, M. Stürmann & M. Weidenbruch) Magnetic resonance studies of a tetraryl-distannene and -digermene [M$_2$R$_4$] (R = C$_6$HBu^t-2-Me$_3$-4,5,6 and M = Ge or Sn). *J. Chem. Soc. Dalton Trans.*, 1187–1190.

(87)   (With R. West, J. J. Buffy, M. Haaf, T. Müller, B. Gehrhus & Y. Apeloig) Chemical shift tensors and *NICS* calculations for stable silylenes. *J. Am. Chem. Soc.* **120**, 1639–1640.

(88)   (With P. Sitzmann, C. Dohmeier, C. Üffing & H. Schnöckel) Cyclopentadienylderivative von Aluminium(I). *J. Organometall. Chem.* **561**, 203–208.

(89)   (With M. C. Cassani & D. J. Duncalf) The first example of a crystalline subvalent organolanthanum complex: [K([18]crown-6)(η^2-C$_6$H$_6$)$_2$][(LaCp^{tt}$_2$)$_2$(μ-η^6:η^6-C$_6$H$_6$)].2C$_6$H$_6$ (Cp^{tt} = η^5-C$_5$H$_3$Bu$^t_2$-1,3). *J. Am. Chem. Soc.* **120**, 12958–12959.

(90)   (With P. B. Hitchcock & M. Layh) Synthesis and molecular structure of copper(I) azaallyls. *J. Chem. Soc. Dalton Trans.*, 1619–1624.

(91)   1999   (With W. M. Boesveld, B. Gehrhus, P. B. Hitchcock & P. v. R. Schleyer) A crystalline carbene-silylene adduct 1,2-C$_6$H$_4$[N(R)]$_2$C-Si[N(R)]$_2$C$_6$H$_4$-1,2 (R = CH$_2$Bu^t): synthesis, structure and bonding in model compounds. *Chem. Commun.*, 755–756.

(92) 2000 (With J. D. Farwell, C. Marschner, C. Strissel & T. D. Tilley) The first structurally characterised oligo-silylmagnesium compound. *J. Organometall. Chem.* **603**, 185–188.

(93) (With W. M. Boesveld, P. B. Hitchcock & H. Nöth) Synthesis and structures of 1,3,5,7-tetraazaheptatrienylsodium and -thallium(I). *Angew. Chem. Int. Edn* **39**, 222–224.

(94) (With W. M. Boesveld, P. B. Hitchcock, D.-S. Liu & S. Tian) Synthesis and structures of the crystalline heavier alkali-metal alkyls: X-ray structures of [K(μ-R){O(Me)Bu^t}]$_\infty$, [(pmdeta)K(μ-R)K(μ-R)$_2$K(μ-R) K(pmdeta)], and [Cs(μ-R)(tmeda)]$_\infty$ (R = CH(SiMe$_3$)$_2$). *Organometallics* **19**, 4030–4035.

(95) 2001 (With W. M. Boesveld & P. B. Hitchcock) Substituted triazines and pyrimidenes from 1,3,5-triazine and a lithium amidinate, alkyl- or 1-azaallyl. *J. Chem. Soc. Perkin Trans. I*, 1103–1108.

(96) (With B. Gehrhus). Chemistry of thermally stable bis(amino)silylenes. *J. Organometall. Chem.* **617/618**, 209–223.

(97) (With S. L. Hinchley, C. A. Morrison, D. W. H. Rankin, C. L. B. Macdonald, R. J. Wiacek, A. Voight, A. H. Cowley, G. Gundersen, J. A. C. Clyburne & P. P. Power) Spontaneous generation of stable pnictinyl radicals from 'Jack-in-the-box' dipnictines: a solid-state, gas-phase, and theoretical investigation of the origins of steric stabilization. *J. Am. Chem. Soc.* **123**, 9045–9053.

(98) (With C. F. Caro & P. G. Merle) Review of metal 1-azaallyl complexes. *Coord. Chem. Rev.* **219–221**, 605–663.

(99) 2002 (With L. Bourget-Merle & J. R. Severn) The chemistry of β-diketiminatometal complexes. *Chem. Rev.* **102**, 3031–3066.

(100) (With A. G. Avent, P. B. Hitchcock & A. V. Khvostov) Unusual crystalline heterobimetallic trinuclear β-diketiminates Yb{L(μ-Li(thf)}$_2$] and [Yb{L'(μ-Li(thf)}$_2$·(thf)] [L, L' = {N(SiMe$_3$)C(R)}$_2$CH, R = Ph, C$_6$H$_4$Ph-4]. *Chem. Commun.*, 1410–1411.

(101) 2003 (With J. N. Murrell) John Dalton, the man and his legacy: the bicentenary of his Atomic Theory. *Dalton Trans.*, 3811–3820.

(102) (With O. Eisenstein, P. B. Hitchcock, A. V. Khvostov, L. Maron & A. V. Protchenko) Mono-, di-, and trianionic β-diketiminato ligands: a computational study and the synthesis & structure of [(YbL)$_3$(thf)], L = [{N(SiMe$_3$)C(Ph)}$_2$CH]. *J. Am. Chem. Soc.* **125**, 10790–10791.

(103) (With L. Perrin, L. Maron & O. Eisenstein) γ-Agostic C–H or β-agostic Si–C bonds in [La{CH(SiMe$_3$)$_2$}$_3$], a DFT study of the role of the ligand. *New J. Chem.* **27**, 121–127.

(104) 2004 (With J.-P. Bezombes, P. B. Hitchcock & J. E. Nycz) Synthesis and P–P cleavage reactions of [P(X)X']$_2$: X-ray structures of [Co{P(X)X'}(CO)$_3$] and P$_4$[P(X)X']$_2$ (X = NPr$^i_2$). *Dalton Trans.*, 499–501.

(105) (With A. G. Avent, P. B. Hitchcock, A. V. Khvostov & A. V. Protchenko) Reactions of Li- and Yb-coordinated *N,N'*-bis(trimethylsilyl)-β-diketiminates: one- and two-electron reductions, deprotonation, and C–N bond cleavage. *Dalton Trans.*, 2272–2280.

(106) (With P. B. Hitchcock & G. Hulkes) Oxidation in non-classical organolanthanide chemistry: synthesis, characterization and X-ray crystal structures of cerium(III) and (IV) amides. *Inorg. Chem.* **43**, 1031–1038.

(107) 2005 (With F. Antolini, B. Gehrhus & P. B. Hitchcock) Crystalline Na–Si(NN) derivatives [Si(NN) = Si{(NCH$_2$*t*Bu)$_2$C$_6$H$_4$-1,2}]: the silylenoid [Si(NN)OMe]$^-$, the dianion [(NN)-Si–Si(NN)]$^{2-}$, and the radical anion *c*[Si(NN)]$_3^-$. *Chem. Commun.*, 5112–5114.

(108) (With P. B. Hitchcock & A. V. Protchenko) New reactions of β-diketiminatolanthanoid complexes: sterically induced self-deprotonation of β-diketiminato ligands. *Chem. Commun.*, 951–953.

(109) Contributions to the chemistry of carbenemetal chemistry. *J. Organometall. Chem.* **690**, 5467–5473.

(110) 2006 (With P. B. Hitchcock & Z.-X. Wang) Bis(silylaminodiarylphosphoranylsilylmethyl-*C,N*)-tin(II) and -lead(II) complexes and their precursors: structures of H(LL'), H(LL''), Sn(LL')$_2$ and Pb(LL'')$_2$; [LL']$^-$ = [CH(SiMe$_3$)P(Ph)$_2$=NSiMe$_3$]$^-$, [LL'']$^-$ = [CH(SiMe$_3$)P(Ph){=NSi(Me$_2$)C$_6$H$_4$-1,2}]. *J. Organo-metall. Chem.* **691**, 2748–2756.

(111) (With S. K. Ibrahim, A. V. Khvostov, L. Maron, L. Perrin, C. J. Pickett & A. V. Protchenko) An electrochemical and DFT study on selected β-diketiminatometal complexes. *Dalton Trans.*, 2591–2596.

(112) (With Y. Cheng, D. J. Doyle & P. B. Hitchcock) The β-dialdiminato ligand [{N(C$_6$H$_3$Pr$^i_2$-2,6) C(H)}$_2$CPh]$^-$: the conjugate acid and Li, Al, Ga and In derivatives. *Dalton Trans.*, 4449–4460.

(113)   (With M. J. Davies) Studies on 1,2-phenylenedioxyborylcyclopentadienes and some of their metal (Ti, Zr, Fe) complexes. *Polyhedron* **25**, 397–405.

(114)   (With M. Brynda, R. Herber, P. B. Hitchcock, I. Nowik, P. P. Power, A. V. Protchenko, A. Růžička & J. Steiner) Higher-nuclearity Group 14 metalloid clusters: $[Sn_9\{Sn(NRR')\}_6]$. *Angew. Chem. Int. Edn* **45**, 4333–4337.

(115) 2007   (With P. B. Hitchcock, G. Li & A. V. Protchenko) β-Diiminato ligand (L) transformations in reactions of KL with PI_3 and I_2: L = $[\{N(C_6H_3Pr^i_2\text{-}2,6)C(H)\}_2CPh]$. *Chem. Commun.*, 846–848.

(116) 2008   (With M. M. Al-Ktaifani, P. B. Hitchcock, J. F. Nixon & P. G. H. Uiterweerd) Specific insertion reactions of a germylene, stannylene and plumbylene into the unique P–P bond of the hexaphospha-pentaprismane cage $P_6C_4Bu^t_4ER_2$ (E = Ge or Sn, R = $N(SiMe_3)_2$; E = Pb, R = $C_6H_3(NMe_2)_2\text{-}2,6$). *Dalton Trans.*, 2825–2835.

(117)   (With J. D. Farwell, P. B. Hitchcock, G. A. Luinstra, A. V. Protchenko & X.-H. Wei) Synthesis and structures of some sterically-hindered zinc complexes containing 6-membered ZnNCCCN and ZnOCCCN rings. *J. Organometall. Chem.* **693**, 1861–1869.

(118)   (With P. B. Hitchcock & Z.-X. Wang) Synthesis and characterisation of six Fe(II or III), Co(II) or Zr(IV) complexes containing the ligand $[CH(SiMe_2R)P(Ph)_2NSiMe_3]^-$ (R = Me or NEt_2) and of $[Co\{N(SiMe_3)C(Ph)C(H)P(Ph)_2NSiMe_3\}_2]$. *J. Organometall. Chem.* **693**, 3767–3770.

(119)   (With P. B. Hitchcock, L. Maron & A. V. Protchenko). Lanthanum does form stable molecular compounds in the +2 oxidation state. *Angew. Chem. Int. Edn* **47**, 1488–1491.

(120) 2009   (With P. B. Hitchcock, A. V. Khvostov & A. V. Protchenko) Heteroleptic ytterbium(II) complexes supported by a bulky β-diketiminato ligand. *Dalton Trans.*, 2383–2391.

(121)   (With P. B. Hitchcock, M. Linnolahti, R. Sablong & J. R. Severn) Synthesis and structures of the transition-metal(II) β-diketiminates $[ML_2]$ (M = Mn, Fe, Ni, Cu, Pd), $[ML'_2]$ (M = Ni, Cu) and $[M(\eta^3\text{-}C_3H_5)L]$ (M = Ni, Pd); L or L' = $[\{N(SiMe_3 \text{ or } HC(Ph)\}_2CH]$. *J. Organometall. Chem.* **694**, 667–676.

(122)   (With P. P. Power, A. V. Protchenko & A. L. Seeber) *Metal amide chemistry*. Chichester: Wiley.

(123) 2010   (With M. P. Coles, P. B. Hitchcock, A. V. Khvostov, Z. Li & A. V. Protchenko) Crystalline amidocerium(IV) oxides and a side-bridging dioxygen complex. *Dalton Trans.*, 6780–6788.

(124)   (With P. B. Hitchcock & G. Li) Synthesis and structures of lithium salts of two cluster iodoarsenates(II) and a periodohexaantimonate(III). *Inorg. Chim. Acta* **63**, 179–183.

(125) 2011   (With M. P. Coles, P. B. Hitchcock, A. V. Khvostov & L. Maron) Synthesis and structures of the $[benzamidinato]^{3-}$ complexes $[Li_3(tmeda)(L')]_2$ and $[Li(thf)_4][Li_5(L'')(OEt_2)_2]$ [L' = $N(SiMe_3)C(Ph)N(SiMe_3)$ and L'' = $N(SiMe_3)C(C_6H_4\text{-}4)NPh]$. *Dalton Trans.*, 3047–3052.

(126) 2012   (With M. P. Coles, P. B. Hitchcock & A. V. Protchenko) Synthesis and structures of the crystalline highly crowded 1,3-bis(trimethylsilyl)cyclopentadienyls $[MCp''_3]$ (M = Y, Er, Yb), $[PbCp''_2]$, $[\{YCp''_2(\mu\text{-}OH)\}_2]$, $[(ScCp''_2)_2(\mu\text{-}\eta^2{:}\eta^2\text{-}C_2H_4)]$, $[YbCp''_2Cl(\mu\text{-}Cl)K([18\text{-crown-6})]$ or $[KCp''_2]$. *Organometallics* **31**, 2682–2690.

(127) 2013   (With J. Li, J.-C. Shi, H.-G. Han, Z.-Q. Guo, H.-B. Tong, X.-H. Wei & D.-S. Liu) Synthesis, structures, and reactivities of guanidinatozinc complexes and their catalytic behavior in the Tishchenko reaction. *Organometallics* **32**, 3721–3727.

JACK LEWIS, BARON LEWIS OF NEWNHAM HonFRSC

13 February 1928 — 17 July 2014

JACK LEWIS, BARON LEWIS OF NEWNHAM HonFRSC

13 February 1928 — 17 July 2014

Elected FRS 1973

By Robin J. H. Clark[1],* CNZM FRS and Paul R. Raithby[2]

[1]*Christopher Ingold Laboratories, University College London, 20 Gordon Street, London WC1H 0AJ, UK*
[2]*Department of Chemistry, University of Bath, Claverton Down, Bath BA2 7AY, UK*

Jack Lewis was born and educated in Lancashire. He rose rapidly to become a highly renowned chemist who helped to pioneer the development of modern inorganic chemistry. He was one of the small group of scientists who led the expansion of inorganic chemistry from its renaissance, inspired by Professor Ron Nyholm in the mid 1950s, through the syntheses and study of new transition-metal and organometallic complexes. Their characterization was accomplished through the perceptive application of the newly available physical techniques of spectroscopy (electronic, vibrational and nuclear magnetic resonance), magnetism, mass spectrometry and X-ray diffraction. Jack completed his PhD at the University of Nottingham in 1952, and then held academic appointments in close succession at the University of Sheffield, Imperial College, London, and University College London (UCL) before being appointed Professor of Chemistry at the University of Manchester in early 1962. He returned to UCL as Professor of Chemistry for the period 1967–70 before being appointed the 1970 Professor of Chemistry at the University of Cambridge, a position that he held until 1995, when he was granted emeritus status. His dedication to the study and furtherance of inorganic chemistry was profound and his research achievements were made all the more remarkable when one considers his substantial additional high-profile responsibilities. In 1975 Jack became the first Warden of the newly established Robinson College in Cambridge, where he shaped and guided a progressive academic community until his retirement in 2001. Furthermore, his skill as a highly effective debater also took him, in 1989, to the House of Lords, where as a Life Peer he represented science with great enthusiasm and distinction until a few months before his death. He was a most effective chairman of the Royal Commission on Environmental Pollution from 1985 to 1992.

* r.j.h.clark@ucl.ac.uk (author for correspondence)

http://dx.doi.org/10.1098/rsbm.2015.0022

301

Figure 1. Jack and Freddie with their two children, Penny and Ian, in 1971 or 1972. (Online version in colour.)

EARLY LIFE AND EDUCATION

Jack Lewis was born in 1928 in Blackpool, the only child of Elizabeth and Robert Lewis. His father died only about two years later and, after his mother had remarried, he moved to live with his adored grandmother in Barrow-in-Furness. This was very convenient for the Barrow County Grammar School, which he attended with success from 1939 to 1946. His abiding sport at school was rugby union. From Barrow he gained entry to the University College, Nottingham, to study for the University of London External BSc degree, graduating with first-class honours in 1949. At the end of his first year Jack was elected to the student union, where he became social secretary and organized the Union Ball and other dances. Jack's excellent quickstep attracted the attention of a certain Elfreida (Freddie) Mabel Lamb (figure 1), who entered the University of Nottingham in the same year as Jack to study mathematics and physics. Married in 1951 they had thus been married for nearly 63 years at the time of Jack's passing.

Having decided that he would make his career in chemistry, Jack entered the research school at Nottingham to work under the supervision of Professor C. C. (Cliff) Addison (FRS 1970) on non-aqueous solvents. Jack's PhD research involved the study of dinitrogen tetroxide and liquid sodium. Both are important inorganic liquids, the former being a component of rocket fuel and the latter a coolant for nuclear reactors. The dissociation of liquid N_2O_4 to NO^+ and NO_3^- had earlier been established by Addison, and the research directed by him in a joint paper with Jack describes the reaction of zinc metal with liquid dinitrogen tetroxide (N_2O_4), as well as the rates and mechanism of their reaction together (1, 2)*.

---

* Numbers in this form refer to the bibliography at the end of the text.

Figure 2. Barry Smith, David Kerridge, Cedric Furmidge, Norman Greenwood, Jack Lewis, Cliff Addison and David Litherland at University of Nottingham, *ca.* 1952.

This paper was the forerunner to many other papers by Addison and his group on the reactivity of N_2O_4 with other reagents. It is a fine example of the application of physical techniques (determination of reaction rates, electrical conductivities, etc.) to inorganic preparations, a balance between measurement and preparation that exemplifies much of Jack's subsequent work. A group photograph (figure 2) taken during this period shows Jack, partly obscured behind Norman Greenwood (FRS 1987), later Professor of Inorganic Chemistry, Newcastle upon Tyne, on the left and Cliff Addison on the right. Other work on N_2O_4 at this time was carried out by his contemporary Alan Comyns at UCL, a person with whom Jack remained in touch for many years via their connection with British Titan Products and Laporte plc.

Jack obtained his PhD in 1952 and remained at Nottingham for the next two years on a postdoctoral fellowship supported by the Atomic Energy Research Establishment (AERE), Harwell, to work on the physical and chemical properties of sodium.

EARLY ACADEMIC CAREER, 1954–70

Jack chose an academic career and was appointed to an assistant lectureship, later a lectureship, at the University of Sheffield from 1954 to 1956, to a lectureship at Imperial College, London, from 1956 to 1957, and to a fellowship (1957) and lectureship (1958) at UCL, where he was promoted to a readership in September 1961. However, nothing is static: it was well known that Fred Fairbrother would be retiring from the Chair of Chemistry at the University of Manchester in September 1962. Jack applied for this position and, after very protracted negotiations about the facilities and, in particular, the start-up grant (£13 000 plus a lectureship was a lot of money to receive in those days), he was offered this chair and accepted it as from 1 October 1962. He was only 34 years of age. After a scientifically very profitable period in Manchester, Jack returned to UCL as Professor of Chemistry from 1967 to 1970, a period that was referred to locally as his 'second coming'.

Jack's research interests expanded significantly during these periods at different universities. This was partly because of the wide range of graduate and postdoctoral researchers and visiting academics with whom he became associated or who chose to work with him. Jack's close association while at UCL with the distinguished Australian inorganic chemist Ron (later Sir Ronald) Nyholm (FRS 1958) and his group also proved influential in determining the direction of Jack's research. One may examine Jack's scientific career in terms of his accomplishments at each of these universities.

RESEARCH AT THE UNIVERSITY OF SHEFFIELD, 1954–56

At the University of Sheffield Jack began an effective and lasting collaboration with Ralph Wilkins (3). Here Jack developed an interest in magnetic studies of transition-metal complexes, using both the Faraday and the Gouy methods. To undertake these pioneering studies Jack built his own magnet, winding the coils for the electromagnets himself.

Linked to his earlier work with Addison, he also carried out a groundbreaking series of studies on complexes of the nitrosyl ligand (NO). The rates of exchange of ^{36}Cl (obtained from Amersham International) between $(Me_4N)Cl$ and $(Et_4N)Cl$ with NOCl were measured: these are quite fast and were considered to arise from self-ionization of NOCl to NO^+ and Cl^-. This was later shown to have profound implications for nitrosation reactions using NOCl (3).

This difficult and dangerous work was supported by AERE Harwell and represented a new departure for both Addison and Jack (2). Plates of zinc, copper and molybdenum were dipped into liquid sodium under argon at various contact angles to study the 'wetting' of the metals by the liquid; an ingenious torsion apparatus was devised for the work. The sodium metal was a commercial sample and had to be purified by filtration at 150 °C through sintered glass. In these circumstances it was found that zinc was wetted by liquid sodium, but that copper and molybdenum were not, results that may have led to two later papers by Jack and Geoff (later Sir Geoffrey) Wilkinson (FRS 1965; Nobel laureate 1973) on solutions of alkali metals in ethers.

Jack's study with D. B. (Brian) Sowerby expanded those on ^{36}Cl exchange with NOCl, but here the substrates were $POCl_3$, $AsCl_3$ and $SeOCl_2$. It represents a rare but useful contribution that Jack made to main-group chemistry. The paper reports exchange reactions between $(R_4N)^{36}Cl$ (R = Me, Et) in CH_3CN, nitrobenzene and $CHCl_3$ with the substrates. For the first two, the formation of $[POCl_4]^-$ and $[AsCl_4]^-$ was demonstrated, there being a direct interaction between the oxychloride and $^{36}Cl^-$, first order in Cl^- and oxychloride (4).

RESEARCH AT IMPERIAL COLLEGE, LONDON, 1956–57

Jack moved to Imperial College as a Lecturer in 1956; there he established a close research association with Geoffrey Wilkinson on the synthesis and study of organometallic complexes.

He also collaborated with other inorganic colleagues, notably Denis Evans (FRS 1981), the local expert on nuclear magnetic resonance (NMR) spectroscopy, magnetism and the eating of red-hot curries. Jack co-supervised the PhD studies of William (Bill) Griffith, who comments—as did Martin Bennett (FRS 1995) (later at UCL and then at the Australian National University, Canberra)—that Jack's lectures on inorganic chemistry were excellent. It was during this period that he also got to know F. Albert Cotton (Massachusetts Institute of Technology (MIT)), the US high-flyer in inorganic chemistry, who was collaborating with Wilkinson in writing the text of *Advanced inorganic chemistry* (Cotton & Wilkinson 1962).

Eight papers based on the research of Bill Griffith when a PhD student, on metal nitrosyl complexes, were published (5). In these papers, complexes already reported in the older German literature were examined by infrared spectroscopy and other appropriate techniques such as Gouy magnetochemical measurements applied to solids as well as aqueous solutions. Here, the brown complex $[Fe(NO)(H_2O)_5]^{2+}$ (which causes the colour in the old 'brown ring' test for nitrates) was shown to contain high-spin iron with three unpaired electrons per metal atom. Both the cation in solution and various solids containing it were studied, as were several other low-spin nitrosyls of iron, cobalt and copper, with a view to understanding the bonding of the coordinated nitrosyl (NO) ligand in such species.

RESEARCH AT UNIVERSITY COLLEGE LONDON, 1957–61

Jack's stay at Imperial College lasted only 10 months: Ron Nyholm issued a call to Jack to come to UCL and join the vigorous group that he ran there. Ron had been responsible for the so-called 'renaissance of inorganic chemistry' in the mid 1950s and was attracting a large number of PhD students, postdoctoral fellows and academics from all over the world. Jack moved to UCL in late 1957, supported initially by a fellowship until he was appointed a lecturer there in early 1958. He became a Recognised Teacher of the University of London in April 1959, an appointment that, at that time, entitled a member of staff to supervise PhD students. He thus joined an international group of staff and doctoral students with a strong representation from Australasia and America. This necessitated the clarification of certain language difficulties, such as the meanings of 'crook', 'digger', 'All Blacks', 'ANZAC', 'hogget' and 'lamb'! The in-house discussions in the research school concerning who could make the most striking discoveries and precision characterizations of new compounds were intense, as was the seemingly interminable banter on the outcome of cricket and rugby internationals. Jack may have been unaware of the somewhat dangerous version of table tennis carried out after hours in a corridor near his office in the ageing William Ramsay and Ralph Forster Laboratories.

Jack and Ralph Wilkins (University of Sheffield) had realized earlier that the effective characterization of transition-metal complexes and an understanding of their bonding and structures would require a detailed knowledge of many different physical techniques. Their co-edited book *Modern coordination chemistry: principles and methods* (11) was published in 1960 and proved ideal for this purpose, with chapters by F. J. C. Rossotti (thermodynamics), D. R. Stranks (reaction rates), R. G. Wilkins and M. J. G. Williams (isomerisation), T. M. Dunn (electronic spectroscopy), F. A. Cotton (infrared spectroscopy), and B. N. Figgis and J. Lewis (magnetism). The book became important reading for PhD students and postdoctoral fellows, not only at UCL but also in countless other universities worldwide.

Jack was not really a hands-on bench-top supervisor, but he was an excellent person with whom to discuss any difficulties with the research programme, career opportunities or, indeed, life problems of any sort. His biggest impact at UCL during this period was via his excellent communication skills at colloquia. In particular the Friday lunch-time colloquia (given by two different people each week) were usually attended by Ron Nyholm, Jack Lewis, Martin Tobe, Brian Figgis, Tom Dunn, Peter Pauling and the postdoctoral fellows and PhD students, and were both highly instructive and entertaining. Visiting academics in this period included Arthur Adamson (University of Southern California), Fred Basolo, Ralph Pearson, Jim Ibers and Lou Allred (Northwestern University), Al Cotton (MIT), Earl Muerterties (Dupont), Tom Meyer (University of North Carolina), Stanley Kirschner (Wayne State), Don Watts and Jim Parker (University of Western Australia), Stan Livingston (Sydney) and many others from 'down under', along with increasing numbers of Europeans, for example Lucio Cattalini (Padova), Victor Gutmann (Vienna), Klixbuhl Jorgensen (Geneva), and Asians, for example Shoichiro Yamada (Osaka). Woe to any person who had not sufficiently prepared their 20-minute presentation (with only 24 hours notice being given) to withstand all the relevant and penetrating questions from the floor! Jack took leave for the first six months of 1960 at MIT, where he developed his association not only with Al Cotton but also with many other leading American inorganic chemists.

One of Jack's personal objectives at UCL was to understand the theory of magnetism, notably from and with Brian Figgis, who was an expert in both the experimental and theoretical side of transition-metal magnetism. The temperature-range liquid-nitrogen Gouy system built by Figgis in 1957 was very demanding in the complexity of its operation, but it did work until the mid 1960s and provided all the key results on magnetism from UCL. On the theoretical side Figgis and Jack were interested in the nature of the chemical bond in transition-metal compounds, as were many other inorganic chemists at that time. Figgis introduced the delocalization factor k, better referred to as the fraction of time that the d electrons spent on the metal ($k = 1$ represents the ionic limit when the electron spends no time on the metal) (Figgis 1966).

Much highly original research in inorganic chemistry was completed by scientists within the Nyholm–Lewis group during these years (1957/58 to 1961/62) at UCL. Five exemplar topics are discussed below to provide a snapshot of these accomplishments (6–10, 12, 13).

In the first of these (6), Jack and colleagues carried out temperature-range magnetic susceptibility measurements on osmium, ruthenium, rhenium and iridium complexes with the d^3, d^4 and d^5 configurations and discussed the results in terms of Kotani theory. The relative importance of each assumption made in this theory was examined in the light of the magnetic results. This paper was the forerunner to a long series of studies on the magnetism of transition-metal complexes with various electronic configurations (d^1, d^2, d^3, d^8 and d^9) and geometries (octahedral, distorted octahedral and tetrahedral) as well as of antiferromagnetic systems. Many such papers discuss the magnetic properties of the complexes studied with reference to the ligand field strengths, the interelectronic repulsions and the spin–orbit coupling of the ions, and the antiferromagnetism and magnetic exchange between the ions. In particular, those with David Machin and Frank Mabbs at UCL, and subsequently developed in Manchester, led to several further publications in this area.

In the second topic (7, 9), the coordination properties of the highly versatile ligand o-phenylenebisdimethylarsine, o-$C_6H_4(AsMe_2)_2$ (diars) were explored. The ligand was shown to form eight-coordinate complexes with titanium, $TiX_4.2diars$ (X = Cl or Br). The titanium

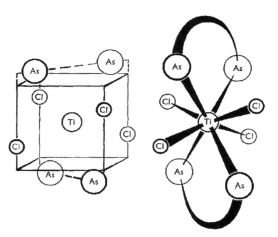

Figure 3. The structure of TiCl$_4$.2diars, showing the relationship between the coordination polyhedron and a cube.

atom is bonded to four chlorine and four arsenic atoms to form a molecule with the classical dodecahedral D_{2d} symmetry of the $[Mo(CN)_8]^{4-}$ ion. VCl$_4$.2diars was characterized similarly. This paper erased the long-held belief by inorganic chemists (including Al Cotton) that first-row transition metals such as Ti or V could not form adducts in which the metal atom had a coordination number of eight (figure 3). This research also demonstrated that ZrX$_4$ and HfX$_4$ (X = Cl or Br) formed isomorphous dodecahedral molecules (9), and later research (with David Kepert) demonstrated that NbX$_4$ similarly formed isomorphous dodecahedral complexes. These were paramagnetic owing to the d^1 electronic configuration of the niobium(IV). Moreover, it was noted (with Bill Errington) that the reaction of diarsine with ZrCl$_4$ is much faster than that with HfCl$_4$, leading to the suggestion that the very closely similar elements Zr and Hf might effectively be separated through the different rates of reaction of their halides with diarsine. Although this did prove to be the case, the procedure was not economic because diarsine remained too expensive a reagent.

In the third topic (10, 11), the chemistry of titanium(III) was studied. This oxidation state for titanium had been difficult to establish owing to the large sensitivity to air and moisture of both its starting materials and any products. The necessary vacuum-line techniques, as originally developed and described in a thesis by Herzog from Jena, Germany, enabled the syntheses and study of several titanium(III) complexes to be carried out. Their characterization established the coordination chemistry, properties, electronic spectroscopy and magnetism of titanium(III) complexes. This allowed the recognition of the features in common with those of related vanadium(III) and chromium(III) complexes. Distortion of the ligand field from octahedral was established for both the ground and excited states of each complex, and the various ligands were placed in the spectrochemical series. Much research by Robin Clark (FRS 1990) and others in the mid 1960s in this field was funded by the British Titan Products Company in Billingham, a company whose research department, managed by Alan Comyns, was keen to develop the coordination chemistry of titanium and the industrial uses of titanium compounds.

In the fourth topic (12), metal–metal bonded complexes were classified into four main types: metals, concentrated metal compounds, covalent compounds and metal–donor compounds.

Conditions favouring the formation of covalent metal–metal bonds were discussed, attention being paid to the electron configuration and the effective electronegativity of the metal atom. The electronegativity of the $d^{10}s^1$ atoms, for example in gold, was considered, and the formal similarity of these atoms to the halogens was emphasized. The compounds $Ph_3PAu[Mn(CO)_5]$, $(Ph_3PAu)_2Fe(CO)_4$ and $(Ph_3PAu)Co(CO)_4$ were synthesized and their physical properties were compared with those of $Mn(CO)_4I$ and $Fe(CO)_4I_2$. This paper led to the frequent use of the fragment Ph_3PAu as an isolobal substitute for hydride in metal carbonyl cluster chemistry. It also encouraged extensive further studies on the syntheses and properties of metal–metal bonded complexes at UCL, notably by the Lewis group during Jack's second period there, and later at Cambridge and elsewhere.

In the last of these topics, the formation was reported of chelate complexes with the general formula $[LPtX_2]$ (X = Cl, Br or I) with tertiary phosphines and arsines (L), containing the pentenyl group, having the formula $CH_2=CH(CH_2)_3ER_2$ (E = P, As). In these, both the olefinic double bond and the phosphorus or arsenic atoms were coordinated to platinum(II) metal centres. Although transition-metal complexes of Group 15 donors and of olefins had been well established by 1961, it was only then that the idea of using a 'hybrid' ligand containing both types of donor was realized (13). This was extended in the full paper (8) to the ligands 4-pentenyldiphenylphosphine, $CH_2=CH(CH_2)_3PPh_2$ and $PhE\{(CH_2)_3CH=CH_2\}_2$ (E = P or As). To extend the range of such complexes and to study the reactivity of the olefin modified by the metal, less flexible phosphorus-based or arsenic-based donors containing 2-vinylphenyl or 2-allylphenyl substituents proved to be advantageous. For example, bromination of planar $PtBr_2$ complexes of $2\text{-}CH_2=CH(CH_2)_nC_6H_4AsMe_2$ (n = 0, 1) gave octahedral Pt^{IV}-C σ-bonded species.

RESEARCH AT THE UNIVERSITY OF MANCHESTER, 1962–67

When Jack moved to Manchester as Professor of Inorganic Chemistry in October 1962 he took the magnetochemist David Machin with him from UCL to help to set up and run this area of physical inorganic chemistry. Shortly afterwards he appointed Frank Mabbs (also ex UCL) as a research fellow (1963) and then as a lecturer (1964), Mike Ware (ex Oxford) as an assistant lecturer (1964) and then as a lecturer (1966), Brian Johnson (FRS 1991) (ex Nottingham) as a research fellow funded by the Department of Scientific and Industrial Research (1964) and then as a lecturer (1965–67), and Malcolm Gerloch (ex Imperial College) as a lecturer (1966–67). Jack thus formed an effective group that remained in operation for several years and, with Brian Johnson's help, developed metal cluster chemistry during this period.

A year after Jack moved to Manchester, his close friend Ron (now Sir Ronald) Mason (FRS 1975) (an X-ray crystallographer) moved to the Chair of Chemistry at the University of Sheffield. The two young professors would occasionally meet at a hostelry in the Pennines somewhere between Manchester and Sheffield and plot out the future of inorganic chemistry in the UK, or so it was thought by the young bloods, who derived some comfort from this speculation. In Manchester Jack also became well acquainted with Geoffrey (now Sir Geoffrey) Allen (FRS 1976), and their friendship continued into the new millennium, when Allen, Mason and Lewis would lunch together at the Athenaeum Club in London several times a year to discuss science and politics.

Brian Robinson (University of Otago) has provided much information on the Manchester period. He comments that the confluence of new routine physicochemical techniques, the installation of a high-pressure facility to synthesize metal carbonyls on site and Jack's rapport with a like-minded Australian organic chemist, Arthur Birch FRS, were keys to this success. Moreover, Jack's enthusiastic approach to research and his ability to attract enthusiastic and able postgraduate students and 'lieutenants', as well as his personal vision, created a platform for his prolific research output from Manchester. Research activity during this time was concentrated in three key areas: the synthesis and spectroscopic analysis of carbonyl complexes especially metal carbonyl clusters, the reactions of coordinated ligands, and magnetochemistry. Jack's time at Manchester may therefore be seen as a period of transition, with the organometallic/carbonyl cluster research laying the groundwork for the later advances in this area at UCL and in Cambridge.

Significantly, Jack was among the first inorganic chemists to embrace modern physical techniques, including mass spectrometry and X-ray crystallography, for the characterization of the systems on which his group was working. This was especially true for his investigations of metal carbonyl complexes. These complexes lent themselves to routine mass spectrometry, a technique 'owned' at that time by the organic chemists, who were unhappy with the consequence of this inorganic intervention, namely that the probe had to be very carefully cleaned after use! This technique launched the work on metal carbonyl clusters that became a mainstay of the Lewis–Johnson collaboration over the next two decades (18).

The mass spectroscopic fragmentation patterns together with infrared spectra of carbonyl hydrides confirmed for the first time the presence of M–H–M bridges in these clusters. The mass spectra also showed the sequential loss of carbonyl groups from the metal clusters, and this, together with a careful analysis of the isotope patterns from the clusters, enabled the formulae of the clusters to be established and also provided an indication of the likely metal cluster core geometry without the need for an X-ray structure determination. The analysis of clusters by mass spectroscopy was extended successfully to include the identification of new, unusual, clusters containing interstitial non-transition elements (14, 23). The synthesis and mass spectra of many new polynuclear complexes were reported (15–17, 22) in the late 1960s.

One of Jack's other key research areas was that of understanding the reactivity of ligands coordinated to transition metals; again, the latest methods of chemical analysis were used to establish the nature of the complexes. A series of papers describing detailed studies with infrared and NMR spectroscopy, and sometimes magnetochemistry, of carbon-bonded platinum-β-acetylacetonate (19) were published. The acetylacetonate work provided a background for future studies on coordinated ligands, but it was the influence of Arthur Birch that initially produced the forward-looking research directed at the propensity of coordinated ring systems to undergo electrophilic attack. This research cemented Jack's reputation in classical organometallic chemistry and highlighted the role of transition metals, sometimes as catalysts, in many organic reactions (21). The work describes the reaction of triphenylmethyl fluoroborate on 1,3-dieneiron complexes and the subsequent reactions with nucleophiles on the resulting dienyl cation. The investigation of metal olefin complexes resulted in several papers emanating from the final years at Manchester (24).

Jack also continued his work on magnetochemistry, begun at UCL, working in collaboration with David Machin, Frank Mabbs and, later, Malcolm Gerloch, all of whom developed their independent careers. Keith Murray (Melbourne) believes that Jack's significant contribution to the development of inorganic magnetochemistry at Manchester was to introduce the subject into the curriculum via textbooks and reviews written with his collaborators and by books such as that by B. N. Figgis (1966).

The papers that had the most impact were those describing the variable temperature magnetic behaviour of the polynuclear complexes with strong linear M–O–M interactions: Cu carboxylates, Cr_3 and Fe_3 carboxylates, and, probably most importantly, $Fe^{III}OFe^{III}$ cores in [Fe(salen)]$_2$O (salen = ethylenebis(salicylimine)) (20). These d-block polynuclear complexes demonstrated strong Heisenberg exchange coupling; the complex's stereochemistry was interpreted with molecular orbital theory. The fundamental ideas on exchange coupling developed in these papers stood the test of time, predating the metalloprotein and metalloenzyme work of the 1970s onwards.

Many chemists from throughout the world will recall with great pleasure the generous hospitality of Jack and Freddie during this period.

RESEARCH AT UNIVERSITY COLLEGE LONDON, 1967–70

Jack returned to UCL as Professor of Chemistry in October 1967, accompanied by Brian Johnson and Malcolm Gerloch as lecturers. They operated during this period largely as a separate group within the Inorganic Chemistry section at UCL, although there was much joint discussion at departmental colloquia.

Ewen Smith comments that when he returned from the USA to UCL in 1967 on a fellowship to work with Ron Nyholm, he found that Ron was away at the time and that Ron's cryogenic equipment for the study of the magnetism of transition-metal complexes over a temperature range was not suitable for low-temperature single-crystal spectroscopic studies. He also needed appropriate preparative facilities. Jack immediately realized his difficulty and asked him to associate with—not join—Malcolm Gerloch's group, which had good magnetic balance facilities and also facilities with which to build the apparatus needed to grow large ion-doped single crystals. Robin Clark also made available his spectroscopic cryogenic set-up. Ewen thus made a good start and regarded Jack very highly both as a scientist and as a human being.

Memories from this period shed light on old-style chemical laboratory hazards! Jack had inherited the tiled benches in the old Ralph Forster and William Ramsay Laboratories from electrochemists via a group of biologists whose snails had, on occasion, died on the benches. Light was shed on this phenomenon when some tiles were removed to reveal pools of mercury underneath them; the human occupants of the laboratory seemed to be healthy—probably because of the thick dust film over the mercury. The large preparative laboratory was next door, and health and safety were taken seriously but in a way regarded as primitive in the present era. The open drains under the benches could lead to interesting fires if one of the many researchers poured solvent down the sink only for it to be set alight by something else further along in the drain. The most notable risk was from carbon monoxide leaking from some of the equipment. This led to shouts and evacuation of the building by everybody, including Jack, whose office was along the corridor. Ewen remembers Jack saying to him that there was a budgie kept in the laboratory at one point but it died and, after that, they relied on human detection of odours.

Figure 4. Jack (right) celebrating the award of his FRS in 1973 with Sir Alan Battersby FRS (centre) and Professor Ralph Raphael FRS. (Online version in colour.)

RESEARCH AT THE UNIVERSITY OF CAMBRIDGE, 1970–95

Jack was invited to take the Chair of Chemistry at Cambridge from 1 October 1970, and Brian Johnson and Malcolm Gerloch accompanied him from UCL. Two of the themes that emerged during the 1960s, namely the reactions of coordinated organic ligands and metal carbonyl clusters, flowered through the next decade or so (28, 30), and recognition followed rapidly for Jack (FRS in 1973, knighthood in 1982) (figure 4).

Three aspects of osmium cluster chemistry have proved to be very influential in coordination chemistry, heterogeneous catalysis and surface science. There is an appealing analogy between the reactions of ligands on a metal cluster and those occurring on a catalytic surface in heterogeneous catalytic reactions—'the cluster-surface analogy'. Jack saw clearly that by using modern spectroscopic and diffraction techniques it was easier to determine what processes were occurring on the surface of a cluster than it was in a complex heterogeneous system, and that the understanding gained from the cluster chemistry could then be applied to the real catalytic systems.

This field was transformed by the development of new methods of producing a solvation site within $[Os_3(CO)_{12}]$ by oxidizing a carbonyl group with trimethylamine oxide (30) (figure 5). The lability of the solvent molecule, CH_3CN, created a low-temperature entry point to observe the stepwise activation of ligands by the cluster. For example, C–H cleavage of the ethene in $[Os_3(CO)_{11}(H_2C=CH_2)]$ could be tracked through the vinyl complex $[Os_3H(CO)_{10}(HC=CH_2)]$ to a vinylidene, $[Os_3H_2(CO)_9(C=CH_2)]$. In each stage there is loss of a carbonyl ligand and this is offset by the coordination of the new Os–H and Os–C bonds. The C_2 ligand is initially coordinated to one osmium, moves to an edge in the vinyl complex, and spans the face of the cluster in the vinylidene. Similarly, a two-step route from $[Os_3(CO)_{12}]$ via the 'unsaturated' 46-electron cluster $[Os_3H_2(CO)_{10}]$ had been developed to yield the cyclohexa-1,3-diene complex $[Os_3(CO)_{10}(C_6H_8)]$, in which the diene was coordinated to a single osmium vertex

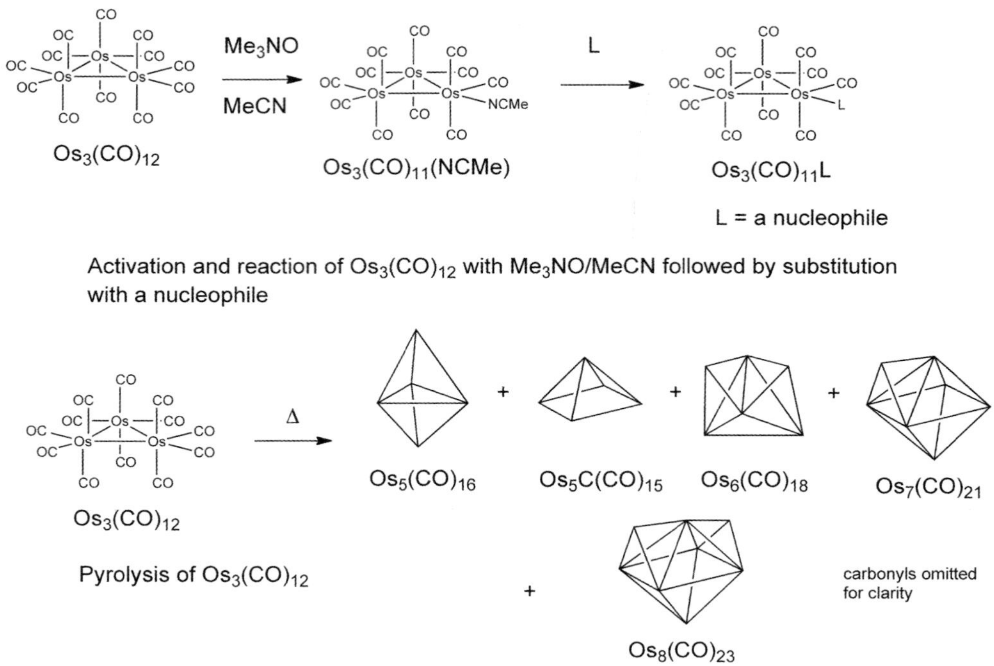

Activation and reaction of $Os_3(CO)_{12}$ with $Me_3NO/MeCN$ followed by substitution with a nucleophile

Pyrolysis of $Os_3(CO)_{12}$

Figure 5. Reactions of $Os_3(CO)_{12}$ leading to the formation of substitution complexes or high-nuclearity clusters (30).

(28, 30). The diene is also relatively labile and so the complex opened up selective ways to synthesize alkene and alkyne complexes, with different ligands being coordinated to a vertex, edge or face of the cluster.

Also related to the idea of the 'cluster-surface analogy' was the development of synthetic routes to higher nuclearity clusters in which there would effectively be a bigger metal surface with more potential coordination sites to mimic the metal surface. This field developed strongly from a detailed study of the thermolysis of $[Os_3(CO)_{12}]$, which resulted in the isolation of pentanuclear to octanuclear clusters (25). The shapes adopted by the clusters were intriguing and stimulated much development of cluster bonding theories, with these clusters showing a remarkable relationship to the electron counting methods developed by Ken Wade (Durham) (FRS 1989) in borane chemistry and then extended by Mike Mingos (Oxford) (FRS 1992). There was indeed a rationale behind the cluster in $[Os_6(CO)_{18}]$ (a capped trigonal bipyramid) not adopting an octahedral cluster framework, and $[Os_7(CO)_{21}]$ incorporating a cage with a capped octahedron geometry (29). It was also shown that reduction of $[Os_6(CO)_{18}]$ to its dianion, increasing the number of skeletal electron pairs from six to seven, did indeed result in a reorganization to an octahedral cage (26).

This work inspired the development of pathways to new high-nuclearity clusters of ruthenium and osmium at Cambridge. One of the trinuclear complexes that had been synthesized with a solvating organic ligand was $[Os_3(CO)_{11}(pyridine)]$ (30). Pyrolysis of this complex provided a route to a metallated pyridine ligand, attached to both trinuclear $[Os_3H(CO)_{10}(NC_5H_4)]$ and pentanuclear $[Os_5C(H)(CO)_{14}(NC_5H_4)]$ clusters (31), with the latter also containing a carbide ligand. After chromatography on silica, the pentanuclear hydride, $[Os_5H(CO)_{15}]^-$, was also a significant product. This may have been a precursor to the elegant $[Os_{10}C(CO)_{24}]^{2-}$ cluster, which was the predominant species after long reaction times. This complex has many features relevant to heterogeneous metal catalysts: the tetracapped octahedral cage is a fragment of the face-centred cubic metallic structure, there is an interstitial carbide, and each face is essentially a (111) surface saturated with CO. The idealized symmetry in solution is T_d and as a result the ^{13}C NMR spectrum of the cluster exhibits just two resonances for the terminal carbonyls: one from the four capping $Os(CO)_3$ and the other for the six $Os(CO)_2$ centres of the core octahedron; there is no evidence for any rapid exchange of CO between the two sites. An $Os(CO)_3$ unit contributes no electrons to the skeletal electron count, and so, with the core cluster being an octahedron, this cluster cage too could be accommodated in skeletal electron counting methods. Just as single-crystal surface science studies provide atomic-scale definition of the events on heterogeneous catalysts, with large metal particle sizes, the high-nuclearity clusters provided calibration points for nanoparticulate catalysts (Johnson 1999).

NMR spectroscopic studies showed that in many of the carbonyl complexes the carbonyls were fluxional on the NMR timescale; that is, they moved over the cluster surface. With other researchers, such as Brian Heaton (Liverpool) working with the group of Paolo Chini (Milan), characterizing the structures of these complexes in solution proved to be challenging as a result of unexpectedly simple NMR spectra at room temperature. Hopping of ligands between sites and even fluxionality of the cluster cages could be monitored by variable-temperature NMR studies. At Cambridge, an elegant and influential study was developed on $[Os_3(CO)_{10}(PEt_3)_2]$ and $[Os_3(CO)_9(PEt_3)_3]$, for which both ^{13}C and ^{31}P NMR spectroscopy were used (27). In both complexes, all the phosphines adopt the same sites: an equatorial location always with a P–Os–Os–CO axis. As a result, in the tris-phosphine complex, which has an idealized symmetry of C_{3h} local to the cluster, there are just two ^{13}CO sites: axial and equatorial (2:1 ratio). These coalesce at 20 °C, demonstrating site mobility. For the ruthenium analogue the coalescence temperature was 10–20 °C lower, and this relates well to the proposed mechanism via an intermediate with a structure like that of $Fe_3(CO)_{12}$. Generally, the relative stability of bridging sites decreases on descending a triad of transition elements. The phosphine also has a role in lowering the barrier to bridge formation. The proposed mechanism involves the pairwise formation of two bridges from one axial CO from each of two metal centres. It is a selective process along a single Os–Os edge, and for the lower-symmetry bis-phosphine complex this does not result in total CO scrambling. However, at higher temperatures the two inequivalent PEt_3 ligands exchange sites. So this second process, taken in combination with the lower-energy exchange by the bridged intermediate, does result in total CO site exchange. This kind of study probed the energy differences between ligand arrangements in the clusters, and the effects of the nature of the metal and auxiliary ligands on these energy differences. Such patterns could be relevant to the mobility of metal surfaces with or without promoters and poisons.

The early years of the 1970s were a very exciting time to be part of the Lewis/Johnson research group in Cambridge. John Evans (Southampton), who was one of Jack's first PhD students, remembers the special atmosphere of enthusiasm and optimism present, which allowed imagination to flow. Jack's leadership and provision of resources gave his students the freedom to be inventive and they took pleasure in being able to report on progress during Jack's morning rounds through the group. Jack displayed the rare capacity to keep his own pressures in the background and give each student his full attention.

Figure 6. The structure of the $[Os_{20}(CO)_{40}]^{2-}$ dianion showing the packing of the carbonyl groups on the surface of the largest osmium cluster to have been characterized crystallographically. (Online version in colour.)

Jack's passion for cluster chemistry spread internationally and he frequently welcomed leading cluster chemists from around the world, including Al Cotton, Paolo Chini and Arndt Simon (Max Planck, Munich), to interact with his group at this time. Typically, Arndt remembers not only Jack's enthusiasm for clusters but also the kindness he showed to him and others.

By the mid 1980s Jack and Brian had firmly established the Cambridge cluster group as the premier team studying cluster carbonyls of the iron triad, and had determined the archetypal structural motifs for clusters with nuclearities between three and ten metal atoms. The reactivity and manipulation of organic ligands once attached to the cluster surface continued to be of great interest. Jack's team carried out many reactions with alkenes and alkynes that were bonded to clusters, but one of the most spectacular and elegant pieces of chemistry was the formation of a trinuclear osmium cluster in which a benzene ring was coordinated parallel to the triangular osmium unit, in a new face-capping mode. The cluster $[Os_3(CO)_9(\mu_3-\eta^2:\eta^2:\eta^2-C_6H_6)]$ was obtained from the deprotonation of $[Os_3(\mu_2-H)(CO)_9(C_6H_7)]$ with $[CPh_3][BF_4]$ and 1,8-diazabicyclo[5.4.0]undec-7-ene. The cluster was characterized by ^1H NMR spectroscopy and a single-crystal X-ray diffraction study (32). A similar bonding mode for benzene was observed in the hexanuclear ruthenium cluster $[Ru_6C(CO)_{11}(\mu_3-\eta^2:\eta^2:\eta^2-C_6H_6)(\eta^6-C_6H_6)]$, obtained using a different synthetic methodology. The cluster $[Ru_6C(CO)_{14}(\eta^6-C_6H_6)]$ was initially reduced with methanolic NaOH to produce the $[Ru_6C(CO)_{12}(\eta^6-C_6H_6)]^{2-}$ dianion, which was treated with $[Ru(\eta^6-C_6H_6)(PhCN)_3]^{2+}$ to produce $[Ru_6C(CO)_{11}(\mu_3-\eta^2:\eta^2:\eta^2-C_6H_6)(\eta^6-C_6H_6)]$.

The development of new, more efficient routes to higher-nuclearity osmium clusters, containing up to 20 metal atoms, continued throughout the 1980s and 1990s (34). The synthetic routes to these materials involved the pyrolysis or thermolysis of lower-nuclearity clusters under a range of conditions. The nature and number of the products obtained were very sensitive to the conditions used and, in general, the yields of the products were low.

However, the isolation and characterization of these higher-nuclearity clusters represent the identification of some of the first nano-clusters or particles, which are now of major importance in materials chemistry and catalysis. The two largest clusters synthesized and characterized by the Lewis–Johnson group were the dianions $[Os_{17}(CO)_{36}]^{2-}$ and $[Os_{20}(CO)_{40}]^{2-}$ (figure 6). These clusters were obtained by the vacuum pyrolysis of $[Os_3(CO)_{10}(NCMe)_2]$ at temperatures above 260 °C and at initial pressures of *ca.* 10^{-3} Torr. The $[Os_{17}(CO)_{36}]^{2-}$ dianion contains a trigonal-bipyramidal core of 14 osmium atoms which is capped by three additional osmium atoms, whereas the $[Os_{20}(CO)_{40}]^{2-}$ dianion has a tetrahedral cubic close-packed metal core of 20 osmium atoms and is the only example of a totally symmetric array of metal atoms of this nuclearity. It remains the largest osmium cluster carbonyl to have been isolated and structurally characterized, and the surface of this tetrahedral cluster is analogous to a fragment of a 111 metal surface (34).

Jack was among the first to understand that if carbonyl clusters were to have practical applications in the area of catalysis the yields of these materials needed to be scaled up. It was unlikely that this goal would be achieved by thermolysis or pyrolysis methods because of the difficulties in controlling the products obtained. His group therefore started to explore cluster build-up reactions that occurred under much milder conditions, and much of this work involved addition reactions through the unsaturated cluster $[Os_3(\mu-H)_2(CO)_{10}]$ and the lightly ligated ligand cluster $[Os_3(CO)_{10}(NCMe)_2]$. However, the addition of cationic metal fragments to anionic metal clusters also proved to be a low-energy and effective way of building medium-nuclearity clusters in good yields. This approach was elegantly illustrated in one of Jack's last publications on cluster chemistry, namely the use of the $[Ru(\eta_5-C_5H_5)(NCMe)_3]^+$ cationic fragment to produce mixed-metal phosphine-stabilized clusters through anionic coupling reactions (37). Thus the room-temperature reduction of $[Os_3(CO)_{11}(PPh_3)]$ with K/Ph_2CO and subsequent coupling with $[Ru(\eta_5-C_5H_5)(NCMe)_3][PF_6]$ yielded the pentanuclear clusters $[Os_3(CO)_{11}(PPh_3)\{Ru(\eta^5-C_5H_5)\}_2]$ and $[Os_3H_2(CO)_{11}(PPh_3)\{Ru(\eta^5-C_5H_5)\}_2]$ and the tetranuclear cluster $[Os_3(CO)_{11}(PPh_3)\{Ru(\eta^5-C_5H_5)\}]$ in good yields.

Jack Lewis was considered by one of his last PhD students to work on cluster projects, Lutz Gade (Heidelberg), to be the single most influential person in shaping not only his career as a scientist but also the entire way in which he approached a scientific challenge. Jack characteristically allowed him great freedom to develop his project independently but always offered deep insight into how challenges might be overcome.

From the early 1990s, Jack opened up a new area of research involving the chemistry of monomeric, oligomeric and polymeric platinum alkyne and poly-yne materials (33). This work stemmed from the earlier transition-metal cluster studies of metal alkynes because of his realization of the interesting optical and electronic properties that these materials might have, particularly in the solid state. His research, and the complementary work in Cambridge of Richard Friend (FRS 1993) and of Andrew Holmes (FRS 2000) on related organic materials, has led to the development of a new area of materials chemistry, and groups worldwide are now developing materials related to Jack's original compounds for a range of opto-electronic applications (35). One of his first papers in the area described the synthesis of a range of new alkyne complexes of platinum and rhodium, in which new routes involving the use of *bis*-trimethylstannyl(acetylide) complexes afforded high yields of high-molar-mass organometallic rigid-rod polymers. In a later paper, in 1997, he showed elegantly that chemical manipulation of dinuclear platinum acetylide-functionalized oligothiophene complexes could be used to fine-tune the electronic properties of these systems (36).

Although Jack retired from the 1970 Chair of Chemistry at Cambridge in 1995, his interest in chemistry remained undiminished. He retained his exceptional intellect and sharpness of mind right up until his passing, and even 10 days before he died he could talk about chemistry and make insightful comments as to the way any project should be developed.

ROBINSON COLLEGE

In 1973 Robinson College was envisaged by its founder, David (later Sir David) Robinson, the entrepreneur and philanthropist, and a group of Trustees from the University of Cambridge including Professor Jack Linnett FRS, the Vice-Chancellor. From this early stage Jack was invited by the Trustees to become involved in the planning, building and development of Robinson College, and to become the first Head of House. Jack's commitment to the process was unwavering and the college was opened formally by Queen Elizabeth II in 1981 with Jack as its first Warden, a post that he held with distinction until 2001.

One of the first three Fellows appointed by Jack to join the Robinson project in early 1976 comments that there was, at that time, simply a vast building site and that besides the college Officers, there were just three other Fellows designate. Barely four decades later, the same site is the centre of a richly varied and thriving community: this is an extraordinary achievement, made possible by David Robinson's benefaction and Jack's legacy of breathing life into the college. The task with which Jack had been entrusted was immense. Whereas the older colleges had evolved over centuries, Robinson College was to be built and set up in the space of five years. Not only did a large and complex building have to be constructed, but the whole social structure also had to be put in place: Fellows, tutors, students, administrative, secretarial, domestic and gardening staff had to be appointed, chefs and porters recruited, and statutes and regulations had to be drawn up. Fellows only much later realized what sacrifices he and Freddie had been required to make: for years they were unable to be out of reach or at any great distance from Cambridge. Yet entirely positive and even joyful memories of those early years of development were cemented, especially when the first enterprising students arrived—a handful of graduates in 1977 and a pilot intake of undergraduates in 1979, then many more when the new building was taken over in 1980. Fellows retain vivid memories of a first informal concert-cum-revue in the Hall—good-humoured satire was there from the start, and testified to the positive spirit that Jack engendered around him. This nurtured a college society that is unusual in its friendliness and lack of factionalism, perhaps one of Jack's greatest achievements.

Underlying the practical decisions were important philosophical issues. Robinson was the first Cambridge college to admit both men and women undergraduates from its inception, thereby breaking with tradition. What should be the characteristics of a new college in an ancient university? Jack built a Fellowship that was totally mixed and balanced in terms of disciplines, gender and age, and was open to both new and older ideas of what a college might be. Jack understood the importance of a cohesive social structure and from the start Jack and Freddie warmly welcomed Fellows and partners to many social occasions. Jack's vision was never just domestic: he also aimed at building up an intellectually active, open-minded academic community. From the start he attracted a variety of distinguished visitors from across the world, a great privilege and enrichment for such a young college. Frequent visitors to Cambridge such as Malcolm Chisholm (FRS 1990) (Ohio State) and John Fackler (Texas

A&M) remember the warm welcome offered by Robinson College and the abiding kindness of Jack and Freddie.

When the college was finally built and staffed, Jack apparently knew everyone, whether porter, gardener, cook or housekeeper. He possessed a genuine interest in everyone he met, together with an extraordinary gift of conveying the impression that he had all the time in the world to deal with their problems. Undergraduates, too, were impressed that someone of such eminence had time to talk to them. Embedded in the chapel wall at Robinson College is a plaque recording the gratitude of the Fellows for the outstanding contribution of its founding Warden for, as the words inscribed on the staircase built in Jack's honour express it, his wisdom shaped the college and made it what it is today.

THE ROYAL COMMISSION ON ENVIRONMENTAL POLLUTION

While in Cambridge Jack became involved in politics, and his interest in the environment grew. In 1982 he was appointed to the Royal Commission on Environmental Pollution (RCEP) and succeeded Sir Richard Southwood as its chairman in 1985. During his six-year term in this role the Commission undertook five studies, leading to the 12th report on Best Practical Environmental Option (1988), the 13th report on The Release of Genetically Engineered Organisms to the Environment (1989), the 14th report on GENHAZ—a System for the Critical Appraisal of Proposals to Release Genetically Modified Organisms into the Environment, the 15th report on Emissions from Heavy Duty Diesel Vehicles, and the 16th report on Freshwater Quality.

According to Thomas Radice and Professor Susan Owen, Jack took over the reins very smoothly at the RCEP and quickly established a good rapport with the colleagues he inherited from previous enquiries. Mrs Thatcher had possibly approved of his appointment because he was considered to be a safe pair of hands, less likely to produce difficult reports as had happened under Lord Flowers FRS (Nuclear Power and the Environment) and Sir Richard Southwood FRS (Lead in the Environment).

In the event the freshwater study, initiated in 1986, took a very long time to be completed and caused some concern within Whitehall. At a time when the consequences of water privatization were requiring the establishment of a new regulatory authority and the EC Waste Water Treatment Directive was threatening to distort the investment programme of the water industry, there was some dissatisfaction that the report was not published until 1992. However, once finally published the report was acknowledged to provide an influential contribution to the determination of priorities for improving freshwater quality in the environment.

The 13th report, on the release of genetically engineered organisms, was published in July 1989, five months after Jack had taken his seat as a crossbench peer. This report heavily influenced the drafting of Part VI of the 1990 Environmental Protection Act and Jack played a major role during the course of the Bill's progress through the House of Lords in aligning the legislation yet more closely to the RCEP's recommendations. The government's response to this report was delayed until 1993, when the Secretary of State for the Environment acknowledged that, thanks to the RCEP's 13th report, the UK now had in place a comprehensive and comprehensible system for releases of genetically modified organisms, one that could be adapted to meet the needs of modern science and industry along with minimal environmental pollution.

The House of Lords and other activities

Jack's interest and work in the area of the environment led to his appointment to the House of Lords in 1989. John Selborne FRS and Thomas Radice have commented that Jack's well-received maiden speech in support of the Nature Conservancy Council on 27 July 1989 and interventions on the Environmental Protection Act established his reputation in the House of Lords as an authoritative contributor to environmental debates. He was never assertive, invariably courteous and always patient with others who might have been less familiar with some of the more intricate issues. When the Environment Bill was before the Lords in 1995 he moved amendments to promote better national management of air quality, an issue that had been highlighted in 1994 by the RCEP's 18th report on Transport and the Environment.

After retiring from the RCEP Jack took on the role of chairing the subcommittee of the House of Lords European Communities Select Committee, which had the remit to scrutinize draft European legislation that concerned environmental policies.

Among the reports produced by Jack's subcommittee was one on Packaging and Packaging Waste in 1993 and another in 1995 on Environmental Issues in Central and Eastern Europe: the PHARE Programme. After leaving the chair of the subcommittee he served on the main European Select Committee from 1997 to 2001 and was a co-opted member of the Science and Technology Committee for several inquiries that needed to call on his unrivalled expertise on environmental protection. In his later years he spoke infrequently, but when he did so he was always heard with great respect.

Jack's intellectual curiosity led to his involvement in many other fields. He was fascinated by how the world worked and how it could be made to work better. Jack always had an interest in education, and higher education in particular. In Cambridge he chaired several of the Overseas Trusts, which funded many international students in all disciplines to study at the university at every level. He also helped to create the Judge Institute (later Cambridge Judge Business School) and was chair of its first Faculty Board.

Jack maintained his passion for the environment as President of the National Society for Clean Air and Environmental Protection and through his enthusiastic support for increasing the UK's low level of woodland cover. One of Jack's greatest areas of focus was waste. He was a popular and hard-working chair of Veolia Environmental Trust, which allocates landfill taxes to good environmental causes, and was influential generally in the waste industry.

He was also interested in the medical applications of science to combat, in particular, cancer, Alzheimer's disease and arthritis, serving as President and a trustee of Arthritis Research UK from 1998 until 2012.

Over the last few years of his life Jack battled with cancer and with heart problems, but he maintained his enthusiasm for science until the very end. With great perseverance, he stoutly did his best to give his views to various environmental committees and organizations, and to provide references in support of his younger colleagues up until a few weeks before his passing.

Concluding comments

It is no exaggeration to state that Jack Lewis, Baron Lewis of Newnham, made an outstanding contribution to the scientific and academic life of the nation. Jack's development of new research areas and new groups within chemistry departments across the UK was exceptional

Figure 7. Jack Lewis at the Royal Society of Chemistry award ceremony in Birmingham in 2010 with Robin Clark (left), who nominated him for the Longstaff Medal of the Royal Society of Chemistry. (Online version in colour.)

and his work was honoured with the award of both the Royal Medal of the Royal Society (2004) and the Longstaff Medal of the Royal Society of Chemistry (2010) (figure 7). His effective chairmanship of the RCEP and of various research councils, and his wider parliamentary contribution in the House of Lords of scientific expertise and sharp intellect, were instrumental in shaping key government policies.

Jack's influence and reach were recognized internationally and he received numerous awards from all over the world. His opinion was sought widely abroad and at home, and he acted as a referee for the appointment of many scientists to academic positions at all levels, to prizes and awards of many societies, and to numerous research councils. His establishment and wardenship of Robinson College has created an ongoing legacy that nurtures new scholarship and reflects Jack's abiding interest in developing and supporting the next generation of thinkers. Indeed, Jack is remembered not only as one of the most influential scientists of his generation but also as a man whose kindness and generosity enriched the lives of those fortunate to have known him.

HONOURS

1973   Fellow of the Royal Society
1983   International Member, American Academy of Arts and Sciences
1985   Davy Medal, Royal Society
1987   Foreign Associate, US National Academy of Sciences
1994   American Philosophical Society
1993   Chevalier, Ordre des Palmes Académiques

1995   Accademia Nazionale dei Lincei
1996   Polish Academy of Arts and Sciences
       Commander, Cross of the Order of Merit (Poland)
1982   Knighted
1989   Created Baron Lewis of Newnham
2004   Royal Medal, Royal Society
2010   Longstaff Medal, Royal Society of Chemistry

Jack also received honorary doctorates from 20 universities.

ACKNOWLEDGEMENTS

We are very grateful to the Lady Freddie Lewis for providing information relating to Jack's background and early life. We are indebted to Professor Brian Johnson, Professor Bill Griffith, Professor John Evans and Professor Brian Robinson for contributions to the account of Jack's scientific achievements recently published in *Dalton Transactions* (Johnson *et al.* 2015). We thank Professor Moira Hooker and Dr Mary Stewart of Robinson College for their explanation of Jack's role in the foundation of the college. During the writing of this memoir we have also been grateful to receive several personal memories of Jack from the Earl of Selborne, Professor Dame Athene Donald DBE, Professor Martin Bennett, Professor Malcolm Chisholm, Professor John Fackler, Professor Lutz Gade, Professor Susan Owen, Professor Arndt Simon, Dr Nicky Nicholls and Mr Thomas Radice.

The frontispiece photograph was taken in February 1989 and is reproduced courtesy of the Chemistry Department, University of Cambridge.

REFERENCES TO OTHER AUTHORS

Cotton, F. A. & Wilkinson, G. 1962 *Advanced inorganic chemistry*, 1st edition. New York: Interscience.
Figgis, B. N. 1966 *Introduction to ligand fields*. London: Wiley.
Johnson, B. F. G. 1999 From clusters to nanoparticles and catalysis. *Coord. Chem. Rev.* **190–192**, 1269–1286.
Johnson, B. F. G., Griffith, W. P., Clark, R. J. H., Evans, J., Robinson, B. H. & Raithby, P. R. 2015 In memory of Lord Jack Lewis. *Dalton Trans.* **44**, 3896–3903.

BIBLIOGRAPHY

The following publications are those referred to directly in the text.

(1)   1951   (With C. C. Addison) The liquid dinitrogen tetroxide solvent system. Part X. The reaction of zinc with liquid nitrosyl chloride–dinitrogen tetroxide mixtures. *J. Chem. Soc.*, 2843–2848.

(2)   1954   (With C. C. Addison & D. H. Kerridge) Liquid metals. Part I. The surface tension of liquid sodium: the vertical-plate technique. *J. Chem. Soc.*, 2861–2866.

(3)   1955   (With R. G. Wilkins) The chemistry of nitrosyl complexes. Part I. Evidence for the self-ionisation of liquid nitrosyl chloride from tracer studies. *J. Chem. Soc.*, 56–59.

(4)   1957   (With D. B. Sowerby) Exchange of chlorine-36 between chloride ion and phosphorus oxychloride, arsenic trichloride, or selenium oxychloride. *J. Chem. Soc.*, 336–342.

(5)   1958   (With W. P. Griffith & G. Wilkinson) Some nitric oxide complexes of iron and copper. *J. Chem. Soc.*, 3993–3998.

(6)   (With B. N. Figgis, R. S. Nyholm & R. D. Peacock) Magnetic properties of some d^3, d^4 and d^5 complexes. *Discuss. Faraday Soc.* **26**, 103–109.

(7)   1961   (With R. J. H. Clark, R. S. Nyholm, P. Pauling & G. B. Robertson) Eight-coordinate diarsine complexes of quadrivalent metal halides. *Nature* **192**, 222–223.

(8)   (With H. W. Kouwenhoven & R. S. Nyholm) Complexes involving an olefinic tertiary arsine chelate group. *Proc. Chem. Soc.*, 220.

(9)   1962   (With R. J. H. Clark & R. S. Nyholm) Diarsine complexes of quadrivalent metal halides. *J. Chem. Soc.*, 2460–2465.

(10) 1963   (With R. J. H. Clark, D. J. Machin & R. S. Nyholm) Complexes of titanium trichloride. *J. Chem. Soc.*, 379–387.

(11)   (Editor, with R. G. Wilkins) *Modern coordination chemistry: principles and methods*. London: Interscience.

(12) 1964   (With C. E. Coffey & R. S. Nyholm) Metal–metal bonds. Part 1. Compounds of gold(0) with the carbonyls of manganese, iron and cobalt. *J. Chem. Soc.*, 1741–1749.

(13)   (With M. A. Bennett, H. W. Kouwenhoven & R. S. Nyholm) Metal complexes of unsaturated tertiary phosphines and arsines. *J. Chem. Soc.*, 4570–4577.

(14) 1966   (With B. F. G. Johnson, I. G. Williams & J. Wilson) Mass spectra of polynuclear carbonyls: a new polynuclear carbonyl oxide of osmium. *Chem. Commun.*, 391–392.

(15)   (With A. R. Manning, J. R. Miller & J. M. Wilson) The mass spectra of some polynuclear metal carbonyl complexes. *J. Chem. Soc.*, 1663–1670.

(16)   (With A. R. Manning & J. R. Miller) Chemistry of polynuclear compounds. Part V. The vibrational spectra of some phosphine derivatives of manganese carbonyl. *J. Chem. Soc.*, 845–854.

(17)   (With H. M. Gager & M. J. Ware) Metal–metal stretching frequencies in Raman spectra. *Chem. Commun.*, 616–617.

(18)   (With B. F. G. Johnson, R. D. Johnston & B. H. Robinson) Polynuclear metal carbonyl hydrides of manganese, ruthenium, and osmium. *Chem. Commun.*, 851–852.

(19)   (With C. Oldham) Metal-β-diketonate complexes. Part III. Metal derivatives of some platinum-carbon bonded acetylacetone complexes. *J. Chem. Soc.* A, 1456–1462.

(20) 1967   (With F. E. Mabbs & A. Richards) The preparation and magnetic properties of some oxy-bridged binuclear iron(III) Schiff-base complexes. *J. Chem. Soc.* A, 1014–1018.

(21) 1968   (With A. J. Birch, P. E. Cross, D. A. White & S. B. Wild) Iron tricarbonyl complexes of some cyclohexadienes. *J. Chem. Soc.* A, 332–340.

(22)   (With B. F. G. Johnson & P. A. Kilty) Chemistry of polynuclear compounds. Part XIII. The preparation and some reactions of dodecacarbonyltriosmium. *J. Chem. Soc.* A, 2859–2864.

(23)   (With B. F. G. Johnson & R. D. Johnston) Chemistry of polynuclear compounds. Part XIV. Hexanuclear carbidocarbonylruthenium compounds. *J. Chem. Soc.* A, 2865–2868.

(24) 1969   (With B. F. G. Johnson, T. Keating, M. S. Subramanian & D. A. White) Reactivity of cycloocta-diene and its derivatives coordinated to palladium and platinum. *J. Chem. Soc.* A, 1793–1796.

(25) 1975   (With C. R. Eady & B. F. G. Johnson) The chemistry of polynuclear compounds. Part XXVI. Products of the pyrolysis of dodecacarbonyl-*triangulo*-triruthenium and -triosmium. *J. Chem. Soc. Dalton Trans.*, 2606–2611.

(26) 1976   (With M. McPartlin, C. R. Eady & B. F. G. Johnson) X-ray structures of the hexanuclear cluster complexes $[Os_6(CO)_{18}]^{2-}$, $[HOs_6(CO)_{18}]^-$ and $[H_2Os_6(CO)_{18}]$. *J. Chem. Soc. Chem. Commun.*, 883–885.

(27)   (With B. F. G. Johnson, B. E. Reichert & K. T. Schorpp) Variable-temperature C-13 nuclear magnetic-resonance spectra of phosphine-substituted dodecarbonyl-*triangulo*-triosmium. *J. Chem. Soc. Dalton Trans.*, 1403–1404.

(28) 1977   (With E. G. Bryan & B. F. G. Johnson) 1,1,2,2,2,2,3,3,3,3-Decacarbonyl-1-(η-cyclohexa-1,3-diene)-*triangulo*-triosmium—a novel intermediate in synthetic osmium cluster chemistry. *J. Chem. Soc. Dalton Trans.*, 1328–1330.

(29)   (With C. R. Eady, B. F. G. Johnson, R. Mason, P. B. Hitchcock & K. M. Thomas) The structure of $[Os_7(CO)_{21}]$; X-ray and ^{13}C nuclear magnetic resonance analyses. *J. Chem. Soc. Chem. Commun.*, 385–386.

(30) 1981   (With B. F. G. Johnson & D. A. Pippard) The preparation, characterization, and some reactions of $[Os_3(CO)_{11}(NCMe)]$. *J. Chem. Soc. Dalton Trans.*, 407–412.

(31)   1982   (With P. F. Jackson, B. F. G. Johnson, W. J. H. Nelson & M. McPartlin) The synthesis of the cluster dianion $[Os_{10}C(CO)_{24}]_2{}^-$ by pyrolysis. X-ray structure analysis of $[N(PPh_3)_2]_2$ $[Os_{10}C(CO)_{24}]$ and $[Os_5C(CO)_{14}H(NC_5H_4)]$. *J. Chem. Soc. Dalton Trans.*, 2099–2107.

(32)   1985   (With M. P. Gomez-Sal, B. F. G. Johnson, P. R. Raithby & A. H. Wright) Benzene in a new face-capping bonding mode: molecular structures of $[Ru_6C(CO)_{11}(\mu_3-\eta^2:\eta^2:\eta^2-C_6H_6)(\eta^6-C_6H_6)]$ and $[Os_3(CO)_9(\mu_3-\eta^2:\eta^2:\eta^2-C_6H_6)]$. *J. Chem. Soc. Chem. Commun.*, 1682–1684.

(33)   1991   (With S. J. Davies, B. F. G. Johnson & M. S. Khan) Synthesis of monomeric and oligomeric bis(acetylide) complexes of platinum and rhodium. *J. Chem. Soc. Chem. Commun.*, 187–188.

(34)   1994   (With L. H. Gade, B. F. G. Johnson, M. McPartlin, H. R. Powell, P. R. Raithby & W.-T. Wong) Synthesis and structural characterisation of the osmium cluster dianions $[Os_{17}(CO)_{36}]^{2-}$ and $[Os_{20}(CO)_{40}]^{2-}$. *J. Chem. Soc. Dalton Trans.*, 521–532.

(35)   (With H. F. Wittmann, R. H. Friend & M. S. Khan) Optical spectroscopy of platinum and palladium–containing poly-ynes. *J. Chem. Phys.* **101**, 2693–2698.

(36)   1997   (With N. J. Long, P. R. Raithby, G. P. Shields, W.-Y. Wong & M. Younus) Synthesis and characterization of new acetylide-functionalised oligothiophenes and their dinuclear platinum complexes. *J. Chem. Soc. Dalton Trans.*, 4283–4288.

(37)   2000   (With R. Buntem, J. F. Gallagher, P. R. Raithby, M.-A. Rennie & G. P. Shields) Use of the fragment $[Ru(\eta^5-C_5H_5)(MeCN)_3]^+$ as an ionic coupling reagent in the synthesis of mixed-metal phosphine clusters. *J. Chem. Soc. Dalton Trans.*, 4297–4303.

SIR ALFRED CHARLES BERNARD LOVELL OBE

31 August 1913 — 6 August 2012

SIR ALFRED CHARLES BERNARD LOVELL OBE

31 August 1913 — 6 August 2012

Elected FRS 1955

By RODNEY D. DAVIES† FRS, SIR FRANCIS GRAHAM-SMITH FRS AND
ANDREW G. LYNE* FRS

*Jodrell Bank Centre for Astrophysics, Jodrell Bank Observatory,
University of Manchester, Macclesfield, Cheshire SK11 9DL*

Bernard Lovell is remembered for the iconic radio telescope at Jodrell Bank that bears his name, and for the research group at the University of Manchester that has become the Jodrell Bank Centre for Astrophysics. His enthusiasm and warm personality inspired several generations of radio astronomers, many of whom now lead their own research groups. Lovell also played a key role in the development of airborne radar during World War II.

EARLY YEARS

Alfred Charles Bernard Lovell was born on 31 August 1913 to parents Gilbert and Laura (*née* Adams), who lived in the village of Oldland Common near Kingswood on the outskirts of Bristol, Gloucestershire. At this time of settled communities, Oldland Common had been home to many generations of Lovells and Adamses. Although an only child, the young Lovell grew up surrounded by numerous cousins, uncles and aunts who engaged in the communal activities of sport, music and the Methodist chapel. The Adams family dominated musical, practical and material aspects of village life. They formed one of the earliest cricket teams; W. G. Grace was well remembered locally. Laura was captain of the Oldland Common Women's Cricket team. The chapel was the nucleus of the community with its social and musical activities. Gilbert, a tradesman, was a lay preacher with a keen knowledge of the Bible, English literature and grammar, which he instilled in his son. From the age of 10 years Bernard would play the organ for chapel services and play cricket as a substitute in the Adams cricket team. As we shall see, these influences from the two families were to play a significant part in his later life.

* andrew.g.lyne@manchester.ac.uk
† Deceased 8 November 2015, after this manuscript was completed.

http://dx.doi.org/10.1098/rsbm.2015.0026

SCHOOLING

Bernard attended the local Oldland primary school and at the age of 11 years transferred to Kingswood Secondary School, which was refounded as the Kingswood Grammar School in 1921 (it was subsequently renamed the Kingsfield School and is now the King's Oak Academy). At this time he began a passion for radio, building receivers at a stage when radio was moving from crystal set to valves. Little was he conscious of where this skill would lead in his subsequent life. His father renamed his business 'The Oldland Cycle and Radio Company' in the expectation that his son would join him when leaving school after the fifth form. By the end of the fifth form he had shown such significant progress that his headmaster successfully pleaded with his father to continue his education in the sixth form. Here his interest in science blossomed.

A pivotal event was the class visit in 1928 to the Physics Department, Bristol University, to hear Professor A. M. Tyndall (FRS 1933) give a precursor of his 1930 Royal Institution Children's Christmas Lectures on 'The electric spark'. This made a deep impression on Bernard and convinced him to continue in science. He was encouraged in this ambition by his left-wing mathematics teacher, E. R. Brown. His interest in the relation between science and religion was stimulated by discussions at home with Brown and his father and by reading the Gifford Lectures, published as *Scientific theory and religion*, by E. W. Barnes, Bishop of Birmingham. In this period Bernard became distracted from his schoolwork by cricket, in which he became the captain of the school cricket team. Nevertheless he won a Major Scholarship in the Faculty of Science in the University of Bristol to undertake a three-year honours physics course.

UNIVERSITY OF BRISTOL

Bernard Lovell entered the University of Bristol in the autumn of 1931. The H. H. Wills Physics Laboratory had been opened in 1927. Under the guidance of A. M. Tyndall it attracted an outstanding team of academics and research staff. These included the Nobel laureates C. F. Powell (FRS 1949; discoverer of the pi meson), W. Heitler (FRS 1948; quantum theory of the chemical bond) and subsequently N. F. (later Sir Nevill) Mott (FRS 1936; solid state physics). Bernard found the physics course to be so stimulating that he asked to come back in the vacations to work with the research staff on projects in crystallography and geophysics. He found the coursework so absorbing that, despite the pleas of the university cricket captain, he gave up his immediate cricket ambitions. These would find a place in his later life. In June 1934 he was awarded first-class honours in science.

During his undergraduate days Lovell enlarged his interests in music, not finding it a distraction from his science. A friendship between Bernard and a fellow physics student, Deryck Chesterman, was to develop in two significant ways. First, they were both interested in organ music, which led to his developing his skills at the organ by receiving lessons and ultimately playing on the finest organs in Bristol and Bath. The second was his meeting with Joyce, Deryck's sister, whom he was subsequently to marry.

On the basis of his first-class degree, Bernard was awarded a grant from the Department of Scientific and Industrial Research (DSIR) to undertake research for a PhD degree under the supervision of Professor Tyndall for the two-year period from September 1934 to September

1936. His research project was directed towards understanding the electrical resistance of thin films of alkali metals deposited on glass surfaces. At the time there was no consistency in the results of similar experiments conducted in leading laboratories. His immediate supervisor was E. T. S. Appleyard, who wished to investigate why the resistivity of potassium, rubidium and caesium in invisible thin surface layers was much greater than that of the bulk metal. It soon became clear that the problem was due to the cleanliness of the surface. With the assistance of the department's skilled glassblower, J. H. Burrow, an apparatus made from ultra-clean Pyrex and using ultrahigh vacua brought the values for thin layers and bulk material into agreement (1, 2). Further developments showed that the addition of even small amounts of contaminants to the surface layer greatly increased the resistivity, as found in earlier work. Lovell developed his critical and experimental skills in this project. For this work he was awarded the PhD degree in October 1936 along with a Colston Research Fellowship.

UNIVERSITY OF MANCHESTER

Professor Tyndall strongly advised Lovell to approach larger university departments, to broaden his research experience. The Physics Department of Birkbeck College, London, headed by Professor P. M. S. (later Lord) Blackett FRS (PRS 1965–70), and the Manchester Physics Department, headed by Sir Lawrence Bragg FRS, both had openings. Although Lovell preferred the cosmic ray research at Birkbeck to the X-ray work at Manchester, an Assistant Lecturer post was immediately available in Manchester. He was appointed to the three-year position on 29 September 1936. As it turned out, Lovell's wish was fulfilled a year later when Blackett succeeded Bragg, who was appointed Director of the National Physical Laboratory.

During the first year of his appointment, Lovell was able to bring his researches on the resistivity of thin metallic films to a satisfactory conclusion. This involved continuing some experiments with the Bristol group, analysing the results and publishing them (3–5).

Lovell was delighted that he had been invited to work with Blackett, a world authority on cosmic ray physics. His principal task was to take charge of the automatic counter-controlled cloud chamber required for the detection of cosmic ray showers. He made observations with the improved cloud chamber that clearly demonstrated that a more extensive programme of cosmic ray research was feasible (6). In the same period, his paper comparing his cloud chamber observations with current theoretical models of cosmic ray shower production was published (7).

RADAR

In August 1939 Lovell was preparing an expedition to the Pic du Midi Observatory, intending to observe cosmic ray showers by using a cloud chamber at high altitude. He was instead ordered by Blackett to abandon research and join the team of academic scientists rapidly assembled by J. A. Ratcliffe (FRS 1951) for the development of radar. At the declaration of war on 3 September he was at Staxton Wold, near Scarborough, observing echoes on the screen of a Chain Home (CH) radar. Among the echoes from aircraft there were transient echoes, dismissed as irrelevant by the operators, that excited his attention. Could they be echoes from ionization left by cosmic ray showers? The possibility became a driving force after the war, but it had to remain at the back of his mind through years of intense concentration on radar.

In the UK, radar had developed rapidly since the first demonstration of reflection of radio waves from aircraft in 1935. Airborne radar was already also becoming a reality, using Yagi antennas at a wavelength of 1.5 m. Lovell was soon at the embryonic Telecommunications Research Establishment (TRE), based originally in Perth, Scotland, but moved in November 1939 to an uncomfortable existence at St Athan airfield in South Wales. Here E. G. Bowen (FRS 1975), the originator of airborne radar, involved Lovell and his colleagues in the installation of AI (Airborne Interception) radar in Blenheim and Beaufighter aircraft and ASV (air to surface vessel) radar in Hudson aircraft. The group included J. W. S. Pringle (FRS 1954) and A. L. (later Sir Alan) Hodgkin (FRS 1948), who were also working on equipment using the shorter wavelength of 50 cm, with the advantages of narrower beamwidths.

In May 1940 TRE moved to Worth Matravers, near Swanage, in Dorset. Before packing for the move Lovell returned briefly (and unofficially) to cosmic ray showers by setting up one of the ASV radars on the ground, using a simple Sterba array looking upwards. No echoes were to be seen. It would be another five years before a more serious attempt could be made, but Lovell and Blackett nevertheless wrote a paper on the theoretical possibilities of echoes from cosmic ray showers, published in 1941 (9).

The successful use of the short wavelength of 10 cm depended on the resonant cavity magnetron valve developed by J. T. Boot and H. A. H. Randall in Birmingham in 1940. Valve development and production for all armed services was coordinated by the Committee for Valve Development (CVD), and contracts were placed by the Admiralty Signals Establishment (ASE). Naval radar was based at the Signal School at Eastney (Portsmouth); after a slower start than the Air Ministry, the Navy had a successful shipborne radar at 7.5 m wavelength (Type 79), and was developing 3.5 m and 1.5 m versions (see Howse 1993). The possible use of 10 cm for naval radar led to an important liaison with TRE soon after the move to Swanage.

In May 1940, P. I. Dee (FRS 1941), who had been working at the Air Defence Department of the Royal Aircraft Establishment, moved to TRE with W. E. Burcham (FRS 1957) and J. G. Wilson. Dee was then in charge of a formidable group of future FFRS who were beginning to realize the potential of 10 cm radar using the new magnetron as a transmitter. Lovell's part was the design of antenna systems. Horns were used in the initial tests, but after persuasion from H. W. B. Skinner (FRS 1942) and advice from N. F. Mott, parabolic cylinders and eventually paraboloids were adopted. Lovell explored a new technique of swinging the beam by a transverse movement of the feed dipole; this was applied at Jodrell Bank Observatory many years later.

A 10 cm radar was demonstrated to Navy visitors in October and November 1940. They were so impressed with seeing echoes from small vessels including a surfaced submarine that they immediately arranged for a copy to be built for development at the Signal School. The main problem in adapting to a shipborne installation was the narrow vertical beamwidth, which was incompatible with large angles of roll. Lovell suggested the solution: use truncated paraboloids, the now familiar 'cheese' antenna, to give a vertical fan beam. The rapid adoption by the Signal School of the TRE design led to the widely used and very successful Type 271 naval radar. This radar, which was the world's first operational 10 cm radar, went into service in April 1941.

Radar for AI developed rapidly from the 1.5 m versions through a series of 10 cm versions, first using klystrons and then adopting the magnetron. Lovell's group concentrated on the idea of lock-follow, in which a scanned radar beam could locate and lock onto an aircraft echo. Hodgkin proposed using a spiral scan, which involved rapid rotation combined with varying beam offset; in May 1941 the group successfully demonstrated automatic following on an echo from a Blenheim aircraft. Installing this in an aircraft was a formidable engineering task, which occupied the autumn of 1941. Contracts were placed in December with Metropolitan–Vickers and Ferranti for a lock-follow installation in Beaufighters. Lovell was an enthusiast for this system, but in January 1942 he was taken off the project and given charge of a new and very urgent programme for Bomber Command. This built on his hard-won experience of antenna design and aircraft installation, but it also required leadership and determination of a very high order.

In 1941 the Royal Air Force (RAF) emphasis on defence changed to attack, building up a bomber force that could strike at German towns and industry. It was, however, obvious that navigation at night or over cloud was so uncertain that many aircraft failed to find their targets. Two ground-based navigation devices GEE and OBOE, which were brought into use in February and December 1942 respectively, transformed the situation, allowing the first 1000-bomber raids on Cologne and Essen. The range of these devices was limited by the curvature of the Earth, so that the more distant targets in East Germany, and particularly Berlin, could not be reached. An autonomous onboard navigation system was urgently needed.

Dee and his group had noticed that the ground return from their 1.5 m AI radar gave a rough map of the terrain, which might be much improved by the use of a shorter wavelength such as 10 cm. There was a similar requirement for 10 cm radar from Coastal Command, in which the detection of surfaced submarines by 1.5 m airborne radar had been very successful for a few months but had been defeated by the German Metox detection system. It was possible that a centimetric radar might escape detection by submarines. The new magnetron was already in use for shipborne radar. Pressure to use the magnetron for airborne radar built up rapidly. The navigation system for the RAF became a top priority, urged on by Churchill on advice from his Scientific Advisor, Lord Cherwell FRS. It was called H2S.

The pressure to equip Bomber Command with a long-range navigation system, and the high-level decisions taken to give priority to H2S, have been set out in the biography of 'Bomber Harris' by Dudley Saward (Saward 1984*a*), who was appointed Chief Radar Officer in December 1941. Perhaps the most influential appointment was Sir Robert Renwick to the Ministry of Aircraft Production in October 1941; Lovell was to rely on his help on several important occasions when resources were particularly scarce. From this background Lovell was given extraordinary responsibility and the authority to bring H2S to operational use, preferably within a few months.* The alternative was the well-known but less powerful klystron. Lovell was pitched into the urgent requirement for a working 10 cm system, but was restricted to using the klystron. Comparative tests convinced Lovell that the higher power of the magnetron was essential, but he was officially only allowed to develop the klystron system. At this point he displayed the resourcefulness and determination that characterized the whole of his subsequent career: he led a parallel development of complete radars using both systems, installed in two different Halifax aircraft. He achieved this through a remarkable partnership

---

* There was, however, a barrier to the use of the magnetron for airborne radar. It was thought, wrongly as it turned out, that German radar engineers did not have the technique to make a magnetron, so that an aircraft crashing on enemy territory might reveal the secret of the high-powered 10 cm transmitter. As had been anticipated, a magnetron was found by German radar engineers in a crashed bomber near Rotterdam in February 1943. It was examined by a Telefunken engineer, Otto Hachenberg, who, like Lovell, after the war built a large steerable radio telescope. This coincidence, and the comparative state of centimetric radar on the two sides, was described by Lovell in 2004 (34).

with Dudley Saward, the newly appointed Chief Radar Officer of Bomber Command, and close liaisons with EMI, which developed the radar set, and with Nash & Thompson, which built the scanning antenna.

Lovell and his group were under intense pressure to produce a working H2S. Swanage, which had been a pleasant place for living and working, was increasingly under attack by air, and in May 1942 TRE moved en masse to Malvern; Lovell likened the subsequent chaos to the Marx Brothers film *Hellzapoppin'*. Much worse was the total loss on 8 June of the Halifax aircraft equipped with the only working magnetron system, with the death of key members of the EMI team including the chief EMI designer, A. D. Blumlein. The pressure only increased, culminating in a meeting with Churchill on 10 July at which he demanded 200 sets by mid October. At this stage there was no satisfactory H2S using either system; much effort had been wasted on the klystron until in July 1942 the Secretary of State ruled that the klystron work should cease. Adding to a very heavy load, Lovell was also given responsibility for providing H2S equipment for Coastal Command ASV, for which the use of the magnetron was allowed.

The dreadful shipping losses by U-boat attack in the Atlantic, which had been cut dramatically by the introduction of 1.5 m radar, rose again in January 1943 when the detection system Metox was installed on German submarines, enabling them to dive before they were detected on the surface. A new 10 cm radar was being developed for Coastal Command Wellington aircraft independently of Bomber Command, and Lovell found himself embroiled in an unpleasant controversy between competing development groups and manufacturers, which could only be resolved at the highest level. The rational solution prevailed, and Lovell's group equipped a small number of Wellingtons with modified H2S radar. The result was dramatic, and was a major factor in the Battle of the Atlantic. From March 1943 onwards the U-boats suffered losses that proved unsustainable. Later in the year American Liberator aircraft equipped with 10 cm radar took over the Atlantic patrols. Surprisingly, no 10 cm detection system was installed on the U-boats for many months; it emerged after the war that there was very little research into centimetric techniques in Germany, on the assumption that they would have no effective use during the course of the war. Another vital factor was the lack of close liaison between radar engineers and the military services, which in the UK was successfully provided by TRE.

Bomber Command first used H2S with the 10 cm magnetron in January 1943. The heavy attack on Hamburg that followed in August was guided by a Pathfinder force using H2S. It was a complete success. Reliable navigation now allowed bombers to reach Berlin, but the H2S radar map only showed the big city as a large undifferentiated mass. Effective bombing of such an extensive target required a more precise selection of targets within a detailed map, which could only be provided by the narrower beamwidth given by using a shorter wavelength.

A 3 cm version of H2S was already under development both in America and in TRE. There followed another argument about the suitability of the American equipment, and production delays in the UK. Lovell and Saward, with minimal higher authority, cut across the muddle by using local resources at TRE to produce six Pathfinder Lancasters by November equipped with 3 cm H2S. There followed raids on Berlin and Leipzig that were completely successful. Success brought a further burden: the US Bomber Command now wanted to use H2S, and TRE effort had to be diverted through the summer and autumn of 1943 to equipping Fortresses and Liberators. However, the American efforts soon took over, particularly using a 3 cm radar which they named H2X. Development of new radars, including the even shorter K-band wavelength of 1¼ cm, had become rapid and extensive. Throughout 1944 there was a

Figure 1. The dawn of astronomical research at Jodrell Bank in October 1945: a trailer of ex-military radar equipment used to study meteor trails.

confusing and stressful proliferation of proposals, including improving 3 cm H2S by using a larger (6 ft) antenna, and developing K band using American magnetron production. The early days at Swanage, when H2S was a simple aspiration, had been overwhelmed.

The story of H2S radar was told in fascinating detail by Lovell in his book *Echoes of war* (33), which was based on his personal wartime diary (now in the Royal Society archives) as well as TRE papers and material deposited in the Imperial War Museum. The close partnership between the scientists of TRE and the RAF, which was vital to the success of H2S, is best illustrated by Dudley Saward's biography of Lovell (Saward 1984*b*).

Lovell retired ill in February 1945, exhausted by superhuman effort. He seldom spoke about the vital part he had played in the devastating bombing campaign, even within his own family. He was clearly affected by the moral issues of involvement in mass bombing, but found some consolation in the vital contribution made by his anti-submarine radars in the Battle of the Atlantic.

RETURN TO MANCHESTER

In April 1945 Lovell accepted the position of Lecturer in the Physics Department of the University of Manchester. Blackett encouraged Lovell in his plan to search for radio echoes from the ionization produced by cosmic ray showers and also to follow up the sporadic echoes seen in radar systems during the war. In the autumn of 1945 Lovell brought two trailers of ex-army radar equipment back to Manchester and attempted to set up receivers in the Physics Department quadrangle. It was immediately obvious that radio interference generated by electric trams in the city centre made observations impossible. As a consequence he moved the two trailers to Jodrell Bank 20 miles south of Manchester, where the University Botany Department had a research station (figure 1).

On 14 December the first observations were made. Strong echoes were seen on the cathode ray tube. Were these the cosmic ray echoes or perhaps meteor echoes? It was soon recognized that the strongest echoes were from the ionization trail of meteors passing through the atmosphere. Lovell was seeing the Geminid meteor shower of 9–15 December. By early 1946, echoes were clearly from individual ionized meteor trails. No echoes from cosmic rays were found, as predicted by Blackett & Lovell in 1941 (9). It was subsequently found that full account had not been taken of the damping factor, which substantially reduced the strength of the echo signal. Meteor radio astronomy became the main programme at this time.

METEOR ASTRONOMY AT JODRELL BANK

The Jodrell Bank site proved to be ideal for meteor studies, with little or no radio interference and dark skies away from city lights. The first decisive radio detection of a meteor shower was of the Giacobinids of 9–10 October 1946 (12). There was a marked correlation between the naked-eye meteor rate and the radio echo rate. These echoes were seen by specular reflection from the ionized trail left by the meteor, when the direction of observation was perpendicular to the trail (12). The coincidence with optical sighting was clearly established. More quantitative data were provided by the inclusion in the team of Manning Prentice, an amateur meteor expert. He was able to provide estimates of a meteor's trajectory as well as its optical brightness (11). The electron density in the trails was deduced from the intensity of the echoes (16).

A major effort was directed towards identifying the daytime meteor streams incident on the sunlit side of the Earth. Some 13 day-time meteor streams were found during the 1947 and 1948 seasons, with well-defined radiants and with maximum rates between 10 and 60 per hour (13, 18). The streams were a recurrent phenomenon from year to year. The activity of the most intense streams was comparable with that of the well-known night-time streams such as the Geminids and the Perseids. Their radiant points are in a narrow strip of the celestial sphere following the ecliptic, as expected for objects in the Solar System.

A long-standing question in meteor astronomy had been whether or not the sporadic meteors were of interstellar origin. A critical factor in resolving this problem was a measurement of the orbital velocity of each meteor. By recording the Fresnel diffraction pattern of the echo as the meteor passed through the telescope beam, the speed could be determined with considerable accuracy. Any object moving in a closed orbit around the Sun would have a velocity relative to the Earth of between 12 and 72 km s^{-1}. Detection of velocities greater than 72 km s^{-1} would be evidence for an interstellar origin in a hyperbolic orbit. An extensive series of observations between 1948 and 1951 (19–22, 24) found no evidence for a significant hyperbolic velocity component. Some 90% of the sporadic meteors are moving in elliptical orbits with periods of about two years. Less than 1% had velocities significantly greater than 72 km s^{-1}. This result settled the debate in favour of a Solar System origin.

Bernard Lovell's book *Meteor astronomy* (23) was a masterly summary of the situation in the subject at that time.

OTHER ASTRONOMY AT JODRELL BANK BEFORE THE MK I TELESCOPE

Solar activity was detected from time to time in the meteor systems operating at 46 and 72 MHz. In the 25 July and 2 August 1946 events the radio emission was 10^4–10^5 times the normal blackbody emission of the Sun (10). This indicated that the emission was coming from coronal regions. In the period July to December 1950 a geomagnetic storm sequence resulting from a coronal M region persisted for at least seven solar rotations. There was associated metre-wavelength emission and strong auroral echoes during this period, again showing the 27-day solar rotation period.

Substantial effort by Lovell and his team was directed towards understanding the structure of the ionosphere by using the radio-echo techniques developed at Jodrell Bank (15, 17). Meteor trails were used to study the properties of the E region at heights of 60–100 km. The amplitude fluctuations of the reflected signal were caused by distortions in the ionized column left by the meteor. Fresnel diffraction theory applied to the time sequence of the echo gave the scale of the structure. Turbulent winds of the order of 20 km s^{-1} were inferred.

Radio echoes were found from a spectacular auroral activity on the night of 15–16 August 1947 (14). The most intense activity was in a faint blue cloud in the zenith, with lesser echoes from striation structures extending over distances of 400–700 km. Subsequent studies at frequencies of 46 and 72 MHz found that the true heights were 100–300 km, placing them in the E and F2 ionospheric layers. Electron densities were about 10^6 cm^{-3}, values typical of the night-time ionosphere.

Following research in World War II, J. S. Hey (FRS 1978) found radio emissions from the constellation Cygnus. Rapid fluctuations in radio brightness were interpreted as indicating the presence of a compact object, possibly Galactic. Simultaneous follow-up observations at Cambridge and Jodrell Bank at a separation of 210 km confirmed that the fluctuations were not intrinsic to the source but were most probably of local origin in the F2 layer of the ionosphere. A continuing study at Jodrell Bank showed that the fluctuations could be understood in terms of Fresnel diffraction in the ionosphere, as in the case of meteor trail echoes (Little 1951). Continuous tracking was made of the two brightest radio sources, Cygnus and Cassiopeia, which are both circumpolar at Jodrell Bank. At high elevations the fluctuations were well correlated with the ionospheric spread-F diffuse echoes at a height of about 400 km and a scale size of about 5 km on timescales of 10–40 min. At low elevations in the north, fluctuations were always present as a result of the passage of the radio waves through the continuously disturbed ionospheric and auroral regions at high magnetic latitudes.

Echoes were obtained from the Moon in 1953 (25). An array of 160 half-wave elements operating at 120 MHz was built to receive echoes from the Moon over a range of elevations at the time of meridian transit. Lunar echo signal strengths of up to 100 times the receiver noise level were recorded. A long-period (1-hour) deep fading was prominent after sunrise, which was interpreted, correctly, as being due to the Faraday rotation in the ionosphere. The experiment provided a direct measure of the electron content of the ionosphere (Murray & Hargreaves 1954).

THE 218 FT TELESCOPE

Although there were fascinating discoveries in meteor astronomy with small-area arrays in 1946 and 1947, Lovell still harboured an ambition to search for radio echoes from cosmic ray air showers. His calculations showed that a telescope with a large collecting area was required. A giant reflector paraboloid would be ideal. It would have much better angular resolution and moreover it would enable many frequencies to be used. New areas of radio astronomy including Galactic and extragalactic studies were opening up that would hugely benefit from such a

Figure 2. The construction of the 250 ft diameter Mk I telescope at Jodrell Bank in the mid 1950s.
(Online version in colour.)

telescope. This concept evolved into the fixed vertically directed 218 ft diameter paraboloid, built very simply from scaffold poles and wire, with a 126 ft mast to support radio receivers at the focus. The first observations were made in the spring of 1948. In 1949 Robert Hanbury Brown (FRS 1960), who was involved in the early development of airborne radar during World War II, joined Lovell at Jodrell Bank. He, along with research students, led a vigorous programme of observations that clearly demonstrated the potential of large-area telescopes. By tilting the mast by 15° from the zenith, Hanbury Brown showed that the Andromeda Nebula M31 and other nearby galaxies were radio sources similar to the Milky Way (Hanbury Brown & Hazard 1951). Lovell became convinced that a fully steerable radio telescope of at least the size of the fixed 218 ft paraboloid was essential for observational radio astronomy.

THE 250 FT TELESCOPE

From the start, Lovell specified the diameter as 250 ft (76.2 m), and he maintained this specification through thick and thin, overcoming difficulties and disasters of design, finance and construction. Substantial progress was made when Charles Husband was appointed as Consulting Engineer in 1949, and in 1950 a Royal Society committee gave its support to the proposed telescope, which was expected to cost between £50 000 and £100 000. The university applied to the DSIR for the costs of a preliminary study, and a formal proposal was written in 1951. The cost was estimated at £250 000. In 1952 the estimate was revised to £333 000, too much for the DSIR; fortunately the Nuffield Foundation offered to share the cost, and the project was approved in April. The 250 ft Mk I radio telescope was completed more than five years later, at more than double the cost (figure 2).

Apart from some underestimates and a serious increase in the cost of steel, there was one major design change that accounts for a large part of the increased costs. The original design was for a wire mesh reflecting surface, suitable for operation at wavelengths of 1 m and longer, but the discovery in 1951 of the hydrogen line at a wavelength of 21 cm demanded an upgrade to a solid surface. This in turn increased vulnerability to wind pressure, requiring the addition of a stabilizing wheel. This was added in 1955, and the cost reached £550 000. The DSIR held a public inquiry in January 1956, by which time the project was practically unstoppable. Responsibility for the project and its cost was shared between the university, the DSIR and Husband, but in practice it was focused on Lovell himself, whose only aim was to have a completed and working telescope. Lovell was always grateful for the support of the university. A fuller story emerged when the files were opened more than 40 years later (see, for example, the discussion on legal matters in Bromley-Davenport (2013)).

Happily the great problems with the increasing cost of the telescope were soon overtaken by immediate operational success.

On 4 October 1957 Sputnik I was launched by the USSR. The Mk I radio telescope was nearly enough complete for Lovell to install a simple radar, which by 12 October was able to track the launch vehicle. No other radar existed that could do so. Lovell's telescope suddenly made him an international hero. The cost overrun, which had reached £260 000, was met by the DSIR and the Nuffield Foundation, with the final contribution of £50 000 paid by Lord Nuffield in May 1960. The telescope could now settle down to its planned programme of research.

ASTRONOMY WITH THE 250 FT TELESCOPE

As soon as the 250 ft telescope came into operation, Bernard Lovell, with collaborators, began two observing programmes in which its large collecting area could make a significant contribution. One was the search for radio emission from stars that were known to flare optically. Was there an equivalent of the giant radio bursts from the Sun and could they be a significant contributor to the radio emission from the Galaxy? The second contribution was a measurement of the low-frequency spectrum of the strongest radio sources.

In 1950 the International Astronomical Union recognized flare stars as a new type of variable star. UV Ceti, a binary star, is the prototype. To obtain a convincing detection of radio flares, it was necessary to have an optical detection at the same time, as was the case for solar bursts. A campaign including three northern optical telescopes was run during the period September 1958 to April 1960. Fifteen significant events were detected in five flare stars at both optical and radio (100, 158 and 240 MHz) frequencies (28, 29). The radio spectrum was similar to that of solar bursts and was presumed to be via the synchrotron mechanism from relativistic electrons spiralling in enhanced magnetic fields in the stellar envelope (30). Modern interest in flare stars continues (32) and centres on high-angular-resolution radio studies in conjunction with optical spectroscopy.

The challenge to Lovell of understanding the low-frequency spectrum of the two brightest radio sources was first undertaken with the 218 ft transit telescope operating at 16.5, 19.0, 22.6 and 30 MHz (26). Observations could only be made in the summer, when Cassiopeia and Cygnus transit in darkness; at this time of day ionospheric scintillations are a minimum, as are interfering long-distance scatter signals. Both sources, which lie close to the Galactic plane, showed an abrupt fall in intensity at frequencies below 22 MHz. This was attributed

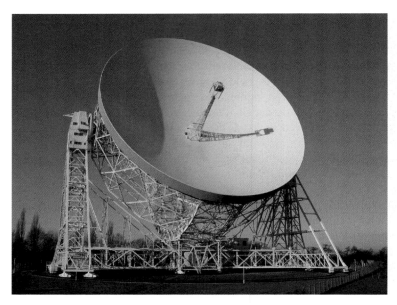

Figure 3. The 250 ft diameter telescope at Jodrell Bank in 2002, now known as the Lovell Telescope after its creator. More than 60 years since its conception, the instrument is still the third-largest fully steerable telescope in the world. (Online version in colour.)

to absorption in ionized hydrogen in the Galactic plane. Confirmation of these results was achieved when the steerable 250 ft telescope became operational (27). A 305 m baseline interferometer was constructed between the 218 ft and 250 ft telescopes working in the range 16.0–26.0 MHz. With lobe separations of 2–4°, the sources could be readily identified and their spectra determined. These results showed that their spectra were very similar, indicating that the synchrotron mechanism was at work for two quite different objects—one a Galactic supernova remnant and the other a distant extragalactic object.

The record of astronomical research up to 1970 with the Mk I telescope was well documented by Lovell (31). Since then the telescope, now affectionately known as the Lovell Telescope (figure 3), has been in almost continuous use, both as a single large aperture and as an element in interferometers such as eMERLIN and international networks.

SPACE TRACKING ACTIVITIES

The launch of Sputnik I in October 1957 was the start of the race between USSR and USA, in which Lovell and the new telescope were involved for more than a decade. Realizing that there were no operational radars capable of tracking space vehicles, he equipped the telescope with a radar that was already being developed for measuring the electron content of the ionosphere, including using echoes from future Earth orbiters such as the USA's Vanguard. This was the first radar to obtain an echo from the carrier rockets of Sputniks I and II (figure 4). This demonstrated the capability of the telescope for both tracking and communicating with spacecraft, and for detecting intercontinental ballistic missiles (ICBMs). Jodrell Bank became both a reserve radar for detecting ICBM launches while the Fylingdales radars were

Figure 4. The birth of the space race in 1957. Sir Bernard Lovell explaining to members of the press the chart of radar echo recordings from the Russian rocket that carried Sputnik I, the first man-made satellite to orbit the Earth, into space.

under construction, and at the same time a tracking station for the USA's Pioneer and Ranger series of spacecraft and the USSR's Luna and Venera series. The most notable result was the confirmation that Luna 2 had indeed hit the Moon, followed by the reception and publication of photographs of the Moon's surface by Luna 9. Throughout these activities Lovell was in the delicate position of liaison with both sides of the space race, obviously being provided by both with sensitive information on launch dates and radio frequencies and dealing with recorded data that was in demand from both sides. He maintained throughout that Jodrell Bank was dedicated to scientific research, and that all results of his observations were freely available. A detailed account of Jodrell Bank's involvement with the many space vehicle launches during this period is in the Jodrell Bank Archive (Sven Grahn, 'Jodrell's role in early space tracking activities', http://www.svengrahn.pp.se/trackind/jodrell/jodrole1.htm).

These activities took place during the height of the cold war. Lovell was invited to visit the USSR in 1958, 1963, 1975 and 1976. To his surprise, in 1963 he was invited by his hosts to visit the tracking station at Eupatoria and was shown antennas whose existence was previously unknown in the West. On his return to the UK he naturally reported these to the defence authorities with whom he was in contact, whereupon his report was classified as secret and was not made available until after his death (Bromley-Davenport 2013). His diaries from that period are held by the Royal Society.

SCIENCE AND SPACE POLICY

Lovell's wartime experience, and his plans for the Mk I telescope, inevitably drew him into consultations with government ministries. From 1953 to 1958 he served on the Air

Navigation Committee of the Aeronautical Research Council, and as a council member
from 1955. In 1957, the year in which the telescope was completed, he joined the Scientific
Advisory Council on Defence, and in 1962 the Strategic Scientific Policy Committee of the
Air Ministry. Although these appointments ended with the creation of the Ministry of Defence
in 1964, there were momentous consequences for Jodrell Bank. The unique capability of the
telescope in tracking space vehicles by radar led to the provision by the Ministry of Supply of
a powerful radar that would allow the telescope to track an ICBM launch from the USSR. This
function was eventually taken over in 1963 by the BMEWS radar at Fylingdales, but from
1960 to 1963 Jodrell Bank acted as a front-line standby. The radar was, of course, available
for scientific research on the Moon and the planets.

    With more direct relevance to science, Lovell served on an Astronomy Committee at the
formation of the DSIR in 1958, and as an original member of the Science Research Council
in 1965, chairing the Astronomy and Space Research Board in 1970.

    Lovell was an early advocate for developing a comprehensive UK space programme. By
1970 he was lamenting the demise of the Blue Streak launcher and the slow development of
spacecraft instrumentation in the UK, and he became very critical of the expense of supporting
the European Space Research Organisation. He was acutely aware of the difficult funding
situation in the 1960s, especially as he was developing new plans for radio astronomy at
Jodrell Bank.

BIGGER AND BETTER RADIO TELESCOPES

By 1960 Lovell was already looking at the possibilities for larger steerable radio telescopes.
The worst problem seemed to be the windage when looking towards the horizon; with Husband
again as consultant, Lovell proposed to expand horizontally rather than vertically, making an
elliptical reflector surface. A comparatively small version, the 38 m × 25 m Mk II, was built
in 1964 both for observational needs and as a prototype for a much larger version (figure 5).
In 1966 another of the same size was built as a much lighter structure, for use with the Mk I
as an interferometer. This, the Mk III telescope, was sited at Wardle, 24 km from Jodrell
Bank, and was intended to be demountable for erection at a more distant site. By this time the
condition of the Mk I was causing some anxiety, and in 1970 an extensive reconstruction was
undertaken. The performance was greatly improved, with a more accurate reflecting surface,
and gravitational deflections were reduced by the addition of a large new load-bearing wheel.
This conversion gave the telescope its present appearance; it was renamed the Mk IA. On its
40th birthday in 1997 it was given its present name, the Lovell Telescope. Most recently, in
2003 the surface was replaced yet again to improve its performance even further.

    The aspiration of building a bigger telescope had given way to the necessity of
reconstructing the Mk I, and to the almost simultaneous demands on the Science Research
Council by Martin (later Sir Martin) Ryle FRS to fund his One Mile Synthesis Telescope at
Lords Bridge, near Cambridge. The project did, however, continue and reached the stage of
a design for a 120 m diameter telescope, known as Mk V. When it appeared that the costs of
this would be insupportable, the emphasis switched to long-baseline interferometry, using an
array of radio telescopes distributed at distances up to 240 km. This became the Multi-Element
Radio Linked Interferometer Network, or MERLIN; after improvements in 2009 it became
the synthesis telescope eMERLIN, which is run by the Research Council as a national facility.

Figure 5. Bernard Lovell in front of the main telescopes at Jodrell Bank in 1964. The 250 ft Mk I radio telescope is in the background; the closer instrument is the smaller Mk II telescope, which was the first telescope in the world to be controlled by a digital computer.

LECTURES

Lovell was much in demand for public lectures on astronomy, cosmology, philosophy of science, and science policy. Most notably he gave the BBC Reith Lectures, published as 'The individual and the universe' (1958; http://www.bbc.co.uk/programmes/p00h9ld8/episodes/guide). Among many other named lectures, he gave the Gregynog Lectures (1962), the Halley Lecture (1964) and the Royal Institution Christmas Lecture on Exploration of the Universe (1965). In 1975 he gave the Presidential Address ('In the centre of immensities') to the British Association meeting in Guildford.

THE VISITOR CENTRE AND THE JODRELL ARBORETUM

Public interest in Jodrell Bank was encouraged by Lovell, but he was astonished by the huge crowds that came when the Mk I telescope first moved and obtained the radar echo from the carrier rocket of Sputnik I. Lectures were hastily arranged in a marquee, and soon a Visitor Centre was constructed, complete with a planetarium, which became a major educational resource for schools over a large catchment area. A rebuilt centre, known as the Discovery Centre, opened in 2011. Since its inception in 1966, the centre has welcomed an average of 100 000 visitors a year. As a uniquely accessible operational scientific instrument, the Lovell Telescope has inspired generations of schoolchildren with an interest in astronomical research and science in general.

In 1971 Lovell obtained a grant from the Granada Foundation to establish the Granada Arboretum on 35 acres adjacent to the Visitor Centre at Jodrell Bank. Some 2000 species of Northern Hemisphere trees and shrubs were planted over the next decade. These included the National Collections of *Sorbus* and *Malus* (crab apple) with a large selection of *Crataegus* (hawthorn). The planning gave interesting views of the Jodrell Bank telescopes and panoramas of the Pennines. The Heather Society's *Calluna* collection was a feature of the display at various times during the year. Lovell was pleased to see the upgrade of the Arboretum and the Discovery Centre in the new millennium. This included a redesign of the arboretum to incorporate a 'Galaxy garden' as well as seven smaller gardens by the well-known garden designer Chris Beardshaw.

The Quinta Arboretum

The Edwardian house known as The Quinta, in the Cheshire village of Swettenham, was the Lovell home from 1948. With its several acres of surrounding land, Bernard used the opportunity to establish a significant garden around a small lake. By the 1960s this had become a serious project with a wide range of trees and shrubs from around the world. The arboretum now covers 28 acres and includes more than 2000 species, some very rare. The National Collections of *Pinus* and *Fraxinus* (ash) are of particular interest, along with an extensive collection of oaks. Autumn brings a colourful display of flowering shrubs (see Lees-Milne & Verey 1982). The Quinta Arboretum is now open to the public; it is managed by the Tatton Garden Society.

Cricket

Apart from his love of the game, Bernard Lovell used cricket as a distraction from tensions of telescope acquisition and construction. As soon as the family was settled in Swettenham he joined the local Chelford Cricket Club and was soon made captain. He was mainly a bowler but was also a stylish batsman. The drying pitch on the slope of the small Chelford stream was an asset to his bowling. In the summer, Saturday afternoons were sacrosanct to the game of cricket.

A great advantage of being near Manchester was the easy access to Old Trafford, the home of Lancashire Cricket Club. His strong allegiance to Gloucestershire county (in the person of Walter Hammond) was soon switched to Lancashire (Cyril Washbrook). As Vice-president (from 1982), and subsequently President, he made his contribution to the club by proposing aids to umpires for when difficult decisions were required, particularly in areas around the stumps (for example lbw, caught-behind or run-outs). His ideas about measuring light levels under cloudy conditions were accepted by the club; light meters were installed showing both the umpires and the public the light conditions. He was an adviser to the Test and County Cricket Board in deciding the further aids to umpires that are familiar today.

Music

Throughout his life Lovell was a keen musician, playing the piano and organ and supporting local music societies. In particular, he was organist at St Peter's Church, Swettenham. He served as President of the Chopin Society and of the Guild of Church Musicians, and as Master of the Worshipful Company of Musicians.

Figure 6. The Lovell family on the occasion of Bernard's knighthood in 1961.
Clockwise from Bernard in the centre are Bryan, Judy, his wife Joyce, Philippa, Roger and Susan.

FAMILY

Bernard Lovell had a very happy family life (figure 6). His wife, Joyce, who died on 8 December 1993, was reputed to be in firm control of the enthusiastic texts of his public lectures; she was the greatest possible support for him during the many stressful periods of his career. Through their five children, the family had extended to no fewer than 14 grandchildren and 14 great-grandchildren at the time of his death.

A WIDER PERSPECTIVE

Bernard Lovell's family background and his early enthusiasm for science led him to a lifelong concern with deep questions of science and religion. This is reflected in his early essay *Science and civilization* (8), and particularly in his BBC Reith Lectures. In the last of his Reith Lectures he said:

> On the question of the validity of combining a metaphysical and physical process as a description of creation, this, as I said earlier, is the individual's problem. In my own case, I have lived my days as a scientist, but science has never claimed the whole of my existence. Some, at least, of the influence of my upbringing and environment has survived the conflict, so that I find no difficulty in accepting this conclusion. I am certainly not competent to discuss this problem of knowledge

outside that acquired by my scientific tools, and my outlook is essentially a simple one. Simple in the sense that I am no more surprised or distressed at the limitation of science when faced with this great problem of creation than I am at the limitation of the spectroscope in describing the radiance of a sunset or at the theory of counterpoint in describing the beauty of a fugue.

He is remembered with great affection by his family and by his many friends and colleagues.

ACKNOWLEDGEMENT

The frontispiece photograph is reproduced by courtesy of Jodrell Bank, University of Manchester.

AWARDS AND HONOURS

The following are a few of the numerous awards won by Lovell.

1946	Officer of the Order of the British Empire
1955	Fellow of the Royal Society
1960	Royal Medal of the Royal Society
1961	Knight Bachelor
1964	Honorary Fellow of the Society of Engineers
1967	Honorary Degree (Doctor of Science), University of Bath
1969	Lorimer Medal of the Astronomical Society of Edinburgh
1969–71	President, Royal Astronomical Society
1970	Vice-president, International Astronomical Union
1974	Member, American Philosophical Society
1975–76	President, British Association
1980	Benjamin Franklin Medal
1981	Gold Medal of the Royal Astronomical Society

REFERENCES TO OTHER AUTHORS

Bromley-Davenport, J. 2013 *Space has no frontier: the terrestrial life and times of Sir Bernard Lovell*. London: Bene Factum Publishing.

Hanbury Brown, R. & Hazard, C. 1951 Radio emission from the Andromeda nebula. *Mon. Not. R. Astron. Soc.* **111**, 357–367.

Howse, D. 1993 *Radar at sea*. London: Macmillan.

Lees-Milne, A. & Verey, R. 1982 *The Englishman's garden*. London: Allen Lane.

Little, C. G. 1951 A diffraction theory of the scintillation of stars on optical and radio wave-lengths. *Mon. Not. R. Astron. Soc.* **111**, 289–302.

Murray, W. A. S. & Hargreaves, J. K. 1954 Lunar radio echoes and the Faraday effect in the ionosphere. *Nature* **173**, 944–945.

Saward, D. 1984a *Bomber Harris: the authorized biography*. London: Cassell.

Saward, D. 1984b *Bernard Lovell: a biography*. London: Robert Hale.

Bibliography

The following publications are those referred to directly in the text. A full bibliography is available as electronic supplementary material at http://dx.doi.org/10.1098/rsbm.2015.0026 or via http://rsbm.royalsocietypublishing.org.

(1) 1936 Electrical conductivity of thin films of rubidium on glass surfaces. *Nature* **137**, 493–494.

(2) The electrical conductivity of thin metallic films. I. Rubidium on pyrex glass surfaces. *Proc. R. Soc. Lond.* A **157**, 311–330.

(3) 1937 (With E. T. S. Appleyard) The electrical conductivity of thin metallic films. II. Caesium and potassium on pyrex glass surfaces. *Proc. R. Soc. Lond.* A **158**, 718–728.

(4) The electrical conductivity of thin films of the alkali metals spontaneously deposited on glass surfaces. *Proc. Phys. Soc.* **49**, 89.

(5) 1938 The electrical conductivity of thin metallic films. III. Alkali films with the properties of the normal metal. *Proc. R. Soc. Lond.* A **166**, 270–277.

(6) 1939 (With J. G. Wilson) Investigation of cosmic ray showers of atmospheric origin, using two cloud chambers. *Nature* **144**, 863–864.

(7) Shower production by penetrating cosmic rays. *Proc. R. Soc. Lond.* A **172**, 568–582.

(8) *Science and civilization*. London: Thomas Nelson.

(9) 1941 (With P. M. S. Blackett) Radio echoes and cosmic ray showers. *Proc. R. Soc. Lond.* A **177**, 183–186.

(10) 1946 (With C. J. Banwell) Abnormal solar radiation on 72 megacycles. *Nature* **158**, 517–518.

(11) 1947 (With J. P. M. Prentice & C. J. Banwell) Radio observations of meteors. *Mon. Not. R. Astron. Soc.* **107**, 155–163.

(12) (With C. J. Banwell & J. A. Clegg) Radio echo observations of the Giacobinid meteors 1946. *Mon. Not. R. Astron. Soc.* **107**, 164–175.

(13) (With J. A. Clegg, V. A. Hughes & P. M. S. Blackett) The daylight meteor streams of 1947 May–August. *Mon. Not. R. Astron. Soc.* **107**, 369–378.

(14) (With J. A. Clegg & C. D. Elyett) Radio echoes from the Aurora Borealis. *Nature* **160**, 372.

(15) Electron density in meteor trails. *Nature* **160**, 670–671.

(16) 1948 (With J. A. Clegg) Characteristics of radio echoes from meteor trails. I. Intensity of the radio reflections and electron density in the trails. *Proc. Phys. Soc.* **60**, 491–498.

(17) Meteoric ionisation and ionospheric anomalies. *Rep. Prog. Phys.* **11**, 415–444.

(18) 1949 (With A. Aspinall & J. A. Clegg) The daytime meteor streams of 1948. I. Measurement of the activity and radiant positions. *Mon. Not. R. Astron. Soc.* **109**, 352–358.

(19) (With C. D. Ellyett) The daytime meteor streams of 1948. II. Measurement of velocities. *Mon. Not. R. Astron. Soc.* **109**, 359–364.

(20) 1950 (With M. Almond & J. G. Davies) On interstellar meteors. *Observatory* **70**, 112–113.

(21) 1951 (With M. Almond & J. G. Davies) The velocity distribution of sporadic meteors. I. *Mon. Not. R. Astron. Soc.* **111**, 585–608.

(22) 1952 (With M. Almond & J. G. Davies) The velocity distribution of sporadic meteors. II. *Mon. Not. R. Astron. Soc.* **112**, 21–39.

(23) *Meteor astronomy*. Oxford University Press.

(24) 1953 (With M. Almond & J. G. Davies) The velocity distribution of sporadic meteors. IV. Extension to magnitude +8, and final conclusions. *Mon. Not. R. Astron. Soc.* **113**, 411–427.

(25) Report on Jodrell Bank to the RAS Council 1953. *Mon. Not. R. Astron. Soc.* **114**, 318–322.

(26) 1956 (With D. J. Lamden) The low frequency spectrum of the Cygnus and Cassiopeia radio sources. *Phil. Mag.* (8) **1**, 725–737.

(27) 1960 (With H. W. Wells) The spectrum of the Cygnus and Cassiopeia radio sources below 30 mc/s. *Mon. Not. R. Astron. Soc.* **121**, 111–114.

(28) 1964 (With F. L. Whipple & L. H. Solomon) Observation of a solar type radio burst from a flare star. *Nature* **201**, 1013–1014.

(29) (With P. F. Chugainov) Simultaneous photoelectric and radio observations of flare stars. *Nature* **203**, 1213–1214.

(30)   Radio stars in the Galaxy (Halley Lecture 1964). *Observatory* **84**, 191–210.

(31)   1973   *Out of the zenith*. Oxford University Press.

(32)   1982   (With S. Kahler, L. Golub, F. R. Harnden, W. Liller, F. Seward, G. Vaiana, R. J. Davis, R. E. Spencer, D. R. Whitehouse, P. A. Feldman, M. R. Viner, B. Leslie, S. M. Kahn, K. O. Mason, M. M. Davis, C. J. Crannell, R. W. Hobbs, T. J. Schneeberger, S. P. Worden, R. A. Schommer, S. S. Vogt, B. R. Pettersen, G. D. Coleman, J. T. Karpen, M. S. Giampapa, E. K. Hege, V. Pazzani, M. Rodono, G. Romeo & P. F. Chugainov) Coordinated X-ray, optical, and radio observations of flaring activity on YZ Canis Minoris. *Astrophys. J.* **252**, 239–249.

(33)   1991   *Echoes of war*. Bristol: Adam Hilger.

(34)   2004   The cavity magnetron in World War II: was the secrecy justified? *Notes Rec. R. Soc.* **58**, 283–294.

JOHN WALTER GUERRIER LUND CBE

27 November 1912 — 21 March 2015

JOHN WALTER GUERRIER LUND CBE

27 November 1912 — 21 March 2015

Elected FRS 1963

By J. F. Talling[1] FRS and S. I. Heaney[2]*

[1] Flat 12, Woodlands, Bridge Lane, Penrith, Cumbria CA11 8GW, UK

[2] 35 Coastguard Lane, Groomsport, Bangor, Co. Down BT19 6LR, UK

John Lund's life and career were rich in the unexpected. Although his early education was deficient in science, he ultimately altered the character and practice of his adopted subject, especially in Britain. Different traditions in systematic and physiological ecology were absorbed from successive contacts with two leading authorities, and combined to good effect in his main work on the ecology of freshwater planktonic algae. Insistence on factual specifics and accuracy, and avoidance of over-generalization, were encouraged by a long wartime occupation in forensic science with consequent legal evidence. He was forthright in his opinions; he benefited and inspired a succession of younger scientists and assistants. Cooperative work with senior scientists led to some ground-breaking innovations, including that with his wife, Hilda, involving the extension of her mycological work to epidemics of chytrid parasitism in planktonic population dynamics. In retirement he devoted much time to acquiring uncommon fluency in the Russian language, which was put to good effect in private and official matters.

Early life

John Lund, born in 1912, grew up within a professional family in northwest England. Two ancestors were immigrants from Europe in the nineteenth century; one, John's great-grandfather, was a Polish Jew who came to England in 1819 and subsequently was prominent in the Oddfellows group in Britain. The other was (probably, but unconfirmed) a Scandinavian from whom the surname Lund was derived. His father, George Edward Lund, was a Manchester solicitor; his mother was Kate, *née* Hardwick. They had three children, all boys, of whom John was the youngest. His early education included a school near the Cheshire meres with which his first publication was concerned (1)†. In his teens he attended the well-known public school

* ivan@heaney35.wanadoo.co.uk (author for correspondence)
† Numbers in this form refer to the bibliography at the end of the text.

at Sedbergh in the western Yorkshire Dales, for which his memories were not affectionate. Military exercises in the Officer Training Corps earned his derision, and he was directed from a preferred science-based course to a classical one. ('Well, Lund, it's the classics that count in the after life. Latin can take you anywhere.') But the fine mountainous surroundings were enjoyed; from one hillside he witnessed a solar eclipse in about 1928.

Family fortunes were affected by the financial depression of the early 1930s. Soon after leaving school he had the prospect of an unexciting office job. A sympathetic uncle, a military man, noticed his interest in natural history—John then specialized in caterpillars, moths and butterflies—and suggested university enrolment in a biological subject. John acquired sufficient subject qualifications from a short course in a 'cram school'. He entered the University of Manchester in 1931, where he specialized in botany—after a strained relationship with the professor of zoology.

LATER EDUCATION: UNIVERSITY OF MANCHESTER

His instructors included a young Irene Manton (FRS 1961), an exceptionally incisive character, who later co-founded the introduction of electron microscopy into botany. In one course she required students to microscopically examine freshwater algae that they had personally collected from some water body. Lund later recalled that his collection included some interesting forms and generated in him a lifelong attachment to the study of algae. After receiving his first degree of BSc (with first-class honours in botany) in 1934 he went on to a short period of research on the structure of a macro-alga, a brown seaweed, for which local support from W. H. Lang FRS was available. This he completed—but never published—for the degree of MSc awarded in 1935.

UNIVERSITY OF LONDON: RESEARCH ON FRESHWATER MICRO-ALGAE

His growing interest in algae led naturally to a research studentship (1936–39) under the pre-eminent authority F. E. Fritsch FRS, at Queen Mary College of the University of London. Fritsch's influence was probably the most decisive in his scientific career. They later became close friends. He took up the taxonomic and ecological study of largely motile bottom-living micro-algae in several ponds within Richmond Park. Ecological aspects were largely linked to the behaviour of individual species. A rich assemblage of unfamiliar and partly new forms was uncovered and described in a PhD thesis and subsequent publications (2). His meticulous attention to specific detail earned the esteem of Fritsch. Fritsch had begun, for his own use, a collection of cuttings depicting individual freshwater species (figure 1). After Fritsch's death the collection was gifted to Lund, who later extended and perpetuated this as the 'Fritsch Collection' at Windermere. Fritsch had earlier transferred to his keeping the first parts of a proposed British flora of freshwater algae, which was never completed.

A second major influence came from another eminent scientist, W. H. Pearsall (FRS 1940). Pearsall combined plant physiology and ecology on an exceptionally broad front, which included pioneer work on the ecology of the English Lakes and their phytoplankton (Pearsall 1942). He was Lund's external examiner for his PhD thesis—technically an insecurely bound file, which fell to pieces in Pearsall's hands (money was short at that time). Lund later

Figure 1. An impression by F. M. Haines of his colleague F. E. Fritsch at work
assembling cut-outs as components to his collection of algal illustrations. Date about 1925.

described Pearsall as 'a legend in his own time'. His challenging science inspired Lund's later concentration at Windermere on ecological aspects of phytoplankton, as it had inspired two other early staff members (T. T. Macan and C. H. Mortimer (FRS 1958)) of the Freshwater Biological Association (FBA). This grant-aided research association ran an annual Easter course in freshwater science, which Lund attended in about 1937. Academic work continued for a short time, during which Lund was a temporary lecturer in the Department of Botany at Sheffield University.

OTHER OCCUPATIONS: FORENSIC SCIENCE IN WARTIME BRITAIN

In 1939 he was barred from war service by deficiencies of eyesight. After recommendations from others, he had entered (in 1938) a very different occupation, forensic science, at a leading forensic laboratory at Birmingham. It gave unexpected scope for his talents and expertise. He used microscopy to unearth clues—in part from soil-inhabiting diatoms—and later published extensively on soil algae (see, for example, (3)). He was an expert scientific witness in courtroom trials and learnt to distinguish between convincing and unconvincing evidence. He suffered adverse reaction from some judges with little respect for science. One summed up by advising the jury that they could neglect the scientific evidence! Later a former eminent judge, Lord Hailsham, visited the laboratory at Windermere, where Lund and he had a convivial discussion on such matters and personalities.

Figure 2. Wray Castle, near the northern shore of Windermere: the past headquarters of the
Freshwater Biological Association, 1932–49, with laboratories and staff accommodation.

WINDERMERE AND THE FRESHWATER BIOLOGICAL ASSOCIATION

Having attended the Easter field course at the FBA, Lund had some familiarity with the
laboratory and its staff. During 1944, with Fritsch's encouragement, he took up the post of
algologist with the FBA at the end of the year. The association then had headquarters and
laboratories at Wray Castle, a domestic folly by the north shore of Windermere (figure 2).
He lived in the castle for some time and took part in domestic activities. With Pearsall's
participation and support, the association had already made contributions to the study of
algae; with Lund's arrival, these were greatly enhanced. Laboratory facilities were cramped,
the staff was small, and the situation could be regarded as a 'backwater' (he later said, 'I like
backwaters'). But, with some reservations, he took up the post.

His scientific projects were soon varied and in part novel. After contemplating his
former subject of bottom-living algae—soon to be taken up by his student F. E. Round—he
decided to concentrate on phytoplankton. He continued a programme of regular sampling on
Windermere and several smaller lakes nearby, with attention to the changing phytoplankton
and environmental conditions. He made wider collections and taxonomic study of other
algae, with one broad investigation of Malham Tarn in the Pennines that showed his flair as a
naturalist (11). Pioneer work with algal cultures had already been stimulated at Windermere
(Storey 1944) by a Chinese visitor, S. P. Chu, well known to Lund personally. Lund spent
much effort in developing their application to ecological problems, in which a modification
of Chu no. 10 medium (Chu 1942) was much used. After the FBA moved from Wray Castle
to the more capacious Ferry House, he came to preside over a large laboratory in which
inverted microscopes, a multiplicity of iodized count tubes and cultures (figure 3) were richly
represented. His work included a form of biological assay, by repeated use of nutrient-replete

Figure 3. J. W. G. Lund, reading within a laboratory rich in algal cultures. Date about 1965.

cultures suspended in lake waters with growth increment controlled by physical factors (4, 12). Thus both field exposures and laboratory experimentation were involved. Growth was typically measured as 'cell divisions' (doublings) to better accommodate its exponential nature. For the same reason he generally used logarithmic scales for graphs of change in natural populations (after Pearsall), which was then unusual but was thereafter widely adopted by others in Britain.

He gave especial attention to the ecology of diatoms, and after a few years at Windermere now-classic papers were published on the contrasting seasonal cycles of *Asterionella formosa* and *Melosira italica* var. *subarctica* (later *Aulacoseira subarctica*) (4, 5, 7). Others in the FBA had appreciated the practical prominence and theoretical potential of the spring *Asterionella* maximum (Mortimer 1939; Storey 1942, 1944), and two—F. J. M. Mackereth and C. H. Mortimer (FRS 1958)—later cooperated with Lund in an exceptionally detailed investigation of its spatial distribution and associated chemical characteristics in Windermere North Basin during 1947 (14). This work, combining hydrodynamics, chemical distributions (extended by Mackereth (1953)) and population ecology, was a landmark of freshwater science in Britain.

The *Asterionella* work made use of long-term records by others in the 1930s and 1940s (see, for example, Storey 1944). As more years passed, Lund added other long-term studies, notably from his work on small centric diatoms (15), the neglected flagellate *Rhodomonas minuta* (later *Plagioselmis nanoplanktica*), very small 'μ-algae' (16) and desmids (17). Methods of study were improving, and with a colleague he published a review that incorporated local and worldwide work in limnology (8).

Soon after his arrival at Windermere he entered a new field. Hilda Canter (figure 4) took up work at the FBA, through the aegis of her professor, C. T. Ingold of Birkbeck College, London, to study the parasitism of algae by chytrid fungi. It often involved epidemics that could greatly reduce algal populations. She eventually became the leading authority on the

Figure 4. J. W. G. Lund (rear figure), with colleagues H. M. Canter (left) and C. H. Mortimer (right) on a winter ice-cover of Blelham Tarn. Date about 1947.

subject, in work that continued for more than 40 years. She collaborated with John Lund in this then novel field. She became his wife in October 1948.

After 1950 Lund became interested in the potential application of plastic enclosures to contain large delimited samples (mesocosms) of natural phytoplankton communities that were amenable to experimental modifications. There were related interests in the FBA about 1960: the use of samples in plastic bags, which Lund used at first in the lake Buttermere, or surface-open lake partitions in the small lake Blelham Tarn that could be subjected to chemical modification or vertical hydraulic mixing by 'bubble-guns' (project 'Swizzlestick'). Lund championed the use of large circular plastic (butyl rubber) enclosures that unlike small bags could maintain phytoplankton communities of natural composition. Eventually 'Lund tubes' holding about $18\,000\ m^3$ were developed, situated in Blelham Tarn, and continued in use until 1984 (figure 5). This involved much extra manpower and also local permission. Lund himself was actively engaged in the earlier stages (19), but later—approaching his retirement—the work was largely continued with a team of ecologists led by his ex-student C. S. Reynolds (Reynolds *et al.* 1982) and allowed some most profitable experimentation (22).

Throughout his career Lund was greatly helped by assistant staff, including research workers and secretaries. Secretarial assistance made feasible his wide range of activities. These included service with some chairmanships in national and international projects outside the FBA, such as those of the International Biological Programme on Loch Leven and the African Lake George, work on the productive lowland meres (Reynolds 1980) and advice to the water industry. Participation in affairs of the Royal Society—of which he was elected a Fellow in 1963—involved many overnight train journeys to London. He enjoyed exceptionally good relations with three successive helpers, Margaret Thompson, Gina Devlin and Elaine Monaghan. He gave much support to his ex-students, notably

Figure 5. 'Lund tubes', large mesocosms for phytoplankton study, in Blelham Tarn. Date about 1975.

F. E. Round, J. F. Talling (FRS 1968), Barbara Douglas, C. S. Reynolds and A. E. Bailey-Watts, who extended his work into related fields. Two—Talling and Reynolds—became colleagues at Windermere; other research colleagues there with primarily algal interests were Brenda M. Knudson, J. H. Belcher, Erica M. F. Swale, Elizabeth Y. Haworth, Kathleen Atkinson and S. I. Heaney.

ACTIVE RETIREMENT, 1977–2015

A long retirement, initially very active, began after his 65th birthday. The occasion led to the presentation of a Festschrift volume of contributions from former colleagues and friends, published by his first student, F. E. Round (Round 1988). For some years he continued to supervise the Fritsch Collection of Algal Illustrations, work that was later taken over by his colleague Elizabeth Haworth. He cooperated with others in the publication of original work, such as that with S. I. Heaney on the dinoflagellate *Ceratium* (24) and with the Czech J. Komárek on the blue-green *Spirulina platensis*. He published some thoughtful bibliographic essays such as those on Fritsch (27) and, with Elaine Monaghan, on Penelope Jenkin (28), a pioneer worker at the FBA, and provided a video tribute for the valedictory celebration for S. P. Chu in Qingdao, China. In his eighties he completed the text of a book designed to present his wife Hilda's unrivalled assembly of photomicrographs of freshwater algae (26), giving much general information on these algae. It won an American (Gerald W. Prescott) award.

He had already made efforts to improve his knowledge of the Russian language, with both scientific and social applications. For this an elderly Russian emigrée living at Ambleside, Mrs Thompson, was most helpful. He also participated in a 'Russian circle' of other learners at Windermere. During retirement he devoted much time to learning Russian and had a long correspondence with families of colleagues in Russia. Up until his 101st birthday he was still taking lessons in Russian, and he maintained his interest in the modern usage of the language. Lund's ability also helped some aspects of Russo-British cooperation, as on issues of eutrophication of enriched inland waters. He travelled widely in Russia on several occasions.

The death of Hilda after a distressing illness, and his deteriorating eyesight, marred the final decades of his life. Adaptations for limited sight, and secretarial and other help, were available, but although complete blindness eventually followed he was able to celebrate his 100th birthday with family and friends at Ambleside.

FAMILY AND HOME LIFE

John Lund's earlier years as a staff member of the FBA involved residence in Wray Castle. After marriage to Hilda he acquired an old capacious house set above the neighbouring village of Ambleside. Its agreeable surroundings included an exceptionally large garden. Both he and Hilda were enthusiastic gardeners, and the remoter regions were initially partly cleared with a machete. A traversing stream was also tended and yielded a pond, with plant life that included an algal stonewort. Hilda was especially assiduous in tending colourful plants, in consequence of which holidays elsewhere tended to be limited. John took a partly professional interest in several distinctive garden inhabitants, notably a large *Gunnera* species that harboured blue-green algae of a symbiotic association in stem-nodules. Other plants were reared indoors, including a species of the green alga *Cladophora* that formed discrete unattached 'lake balls' at the upland Malham Tarn, of which he was very proud. Hilda had a deep-seated attachment to colourful plant illustrations, which appeared as cut-outs on a screen and later as her own photographic products in a book. Each had a study for writing and occasional microscopy, for which Hilda acquired an advanced microscope by means of a grant from the Royal Society.

The family was enlarged in the 1950s by two children, Richard and Hilary. Their upbringing reduced the time that their mother could give to science, but later she returned to work at home and the FBA. John took pains to check their subsequent local schooling. Later Richard left university education and entered the Civil Service. Hilary first took up work (like John) in forensic science, but later moved to study marine chemistry and a lectureship in marine biochemistry at Bangor University. Both later married, and made frequent visits to their parents at Ambleside. There was also a grandchild, Sarah, who spent a week of her summer holidays each year visiting 'Grampy' at Ambleside.

SCIENCE: WIDTH AND PENETRATION

Lund's wider influence in his field, nationally and internationally, is incontestable. It was based on an interest in specifics rather than generalities. Algal diversity always impressed him, and averages could be misleading. Analyses at the species level were preferred. Aggregate measures such as chlorophyll *a* were at first avoided, except for dry weight summed from estimates on individual species (20). He sought to isolate the action of individual factors (16), but in an early joint work at Windermere (6) also explored factor interaction. He made possibly the widest integration of his science under the heading of eutrophication (for example (18)). He wrote several major reviews (for example (16)) and contemplated several books, including a monograph on *Asterionella*; finally a single book was produced jointly with his wife (26).

Some personal scientific features seem improbables. He was interested and skilled in taxonomy and systematics, as shown in his numerous publications under the title 'Contributions to our knowledge of British algae' and in some surveys of algal groups such as the Chrysophyceae (13). However, he tended to despise mere species lists, except in exploratory records such as for some Irish waters. Though poorly schooled in physics and chemistry, he saw their application to ecological issues as crucial, with support from plant physiology in the tradition of Pearsall. He greatly expanded the ecological application of experimental cultures of ecologically important species. Although a committed and versatile field naturalist, he avoided regional descriptions—with the exception of favourite sites, a Cheshire mere (1) and Malham Tarn (11). He made much use of chemical budgets for assessing possible nutrient limitation, but did not enter rate considerations of chemical kinetics. An early discounting of limitation of *Asterionella* by a deficiency of carbon dioxide due to the large atmospheric reservoir neglected limitations that were later investigated in detail at Windermere (Talling 1976; Maberly 1996). He did not seriously explore animal grazing on phytoplankton except at the microbial (protozoan) level, and relationships with associated zoologists were few (see, for example, (25)). One was with the eminent visitor W. T. Edmondson (Edmondson 1965). Lund defended and made use of an exceptionally long series of routine (repetitive) sampling (see, for example, (21, 23, 25)) that was unrivalled in the world.

His absence from some fields actually stimulated their exploration by several of his students and other associates. Thus partly philosophical issues involving other subjects (such as community succession and primary production) were taken up by ex-students C. S. Reynolds (see, for example, Reynolds 1997) and J. F. Talling (Talling 1993). Physical and physiological topics of algal flotation and sinking were explored in depth by A. E. Walsby (FRS 1993) (see, for example, Walsby 1988), with acknowledged guidance from an early paper by Lund (10) on these matters. Many major later advances in studies of micro-algae were made possible only by new techniques of electron microscopy and genetic analysis that remained outside his personal expertise. He did introduce some new methods into phytoplankton sampling and study, and removed much regional neglect of some older ones (9).

PERSONAL QUALITIES

He immediately impressed by his quick-wittedness and his ability to see humour in a situation. Tolerance of other viewpoints increased somewhat with age, but this did not extend to half-truths and euphemisms. As a senior scientist he made privileged use of many of the institute's facilities. In his youth he openly contested national imperialism and jingoism. He had some distaste of abstractions, preferred concrete reasoning, and respected practicalities including the financial.

He evoked loyalty and friendship in his many assistants. These extended to other colleagues with similar professional interests, although naturally there could be competition within the institute. Influential phases of shared interests existed early with several senior colleagues, with whom there was active cooperation, but later their interests tended to diverge.

In conversation he was generally entertaining. Included was a tea club in one laboratory, where he might criticize the FBA director, H. C. Gilson. Later opinion mellowed; 'we were lucky to get him'.

He had a penetrating insight into many difficult human situations. Forensic work and police courts introduced the seamier side of much human behaviour. In old age he was approached by a group seeking to gather memories of former times and personalities in Ambleside, his home village. They were impressed by the clarity and range of his recollections.

Awards and appointments

1934   BSc, University of Manchester
1935   MSc, University of Manchester
1939   PhD, University of London
1957   President, British Phycological Society
1961   DSc, University of London
1963   Fellow of the Royal Society
1967   President, International Phycological Society
       Vice-President, Freshwater Biological Association
1975   CBE

Acknowledgements

We are indebted for helpful records kindly supplied by Keith Moore of the Royal Society, by Elaine Monaghan, and by Ian Pettman, Elizabeth Haworth and Tamsin Vicary of the Freshwater Biological Association, who also supplied material used in the figures.

The frontispiece photograph was taken by Walter Bird and is copyright © Godfrey Argent Studio; reproduced with permission.

References to other authors

Chu, S. P. 1941 The influence of the mineral composition of the medium on the growth of planktonic algae. Part 1. Methods and culture media. *J. Ecol.* **30**, 284–325.

Edmondson, W. T. 1965 Reproductive rate of planktonic rotifers as related to food and temperature. *Ecol. Monogr.* **35**, 61–111.

Mackereth, F. J. M. 1953 Phosphorus utilization by *Asterionella formosa* Hass. *J. Exp. Bot.* **4**, 296–313.

Maberly, S. C. 1996 Daily, episodic and seasonal changes in pH and concentrations of inorganic carbon in a productive lake. *Freshwat. Biol.* **35**, 579–598.

Mortimer, C. H. 1939 Physical and chemical aspects of organic production in lakes. *Ann. Appl. Biol.* **26**, 167–172.

Pearsall, W. H. 1932 Phytoplankton in the English Lakes. II. The composition of the phytoplankton in relation to dissolved substances. *J. Ecol.* **20**, 241–262.

Reynolds, C. S. 1980 The limnology of the eutrophic meres of the Shropshire–Cheshire plain. *Field Stud.* **5**, 93–173.

Reynolds, C. S. 1997 *Vegetation processes in the pelagic: a model for ecosystem theory.* Oldendorf: Ecology Institute.

Reynolds, C. S., Thompson, J. M., Ferguson, A. J. D. & Wiseman, S. W. 1982 Loss processes in the population dynamics of phytoplankton maintained in closed systems. *J. Plankton Res.* **4**, 561–600.

Round, F. E. (ed.) 1988 *Algae and the aquatic environment: contributions in honour of J. W. G. Lund C.B.E., F.R.S.* Bristol: Biopress.

Storey, J. E. 1942 'The periodicity of freshwater algae with special reference to *Asterionella* in Windermere.' PhD thesis, University of Manchester.

Storey, J. M. 1944 Phytoplankton. *Annu. Rep. Freshwat. Biol. Assoc.* **12**, 17–20.

Talling, J. F. 1976 The depletion of carbon dioxide from lake water by phytoplankton. *J. Ecol.* **64**, 79–121.

Talling, J. F. 1993 Comparative seasonal changes, and inter-annual variability and stability, in a 26-year record of total phytoplankton biomass in four English lakes. *Hydrobiologia* **268**, 65–98.

Walsby, A. E. 1988 Buoyancy in relation to the ecology of the freshwater phytoplankton. In *Algae and the aquatic environment* (ed. F. E. Round), pp. 125–137. Bristol: Biopress.

Bibliography

The following publications are those referred to directly in the text. A full bibliography is available as electronic supplementary material at http://dx.doi.org/10.1098/rsbm.2015.0025 or via http://rsbm.royalsocietypublishing.org.

(1) 1935 (With M. Cohen) On the natural history of a Cheshire mere. *Naturalists Un. Year Bk*, 19–29.

(2) 1943 The marginal algae of certain ponds, with special reference to the bottom deposits. *J. Ecol.* **30**, 245–283.

(3) 1945 Observations on soil algae. I. The ecology, size and taxonomy of British soil diatoms. Part I. *New Phytol.* **44**, 196–219.

(4) 1949 Studies on *Asterionella*. I. The origin and nature of the cells producing seasonal maxima. *J. Ecol.* **37**, 389–418.

(5) 1950 Studies on *Asterionella formosa* Hass. II. Nutrient depletion and the spring maximum. Part 1. *J. Ecol.* **38**, 1–14.

(6) 1951 (With H. M. Canter) Studies on plankton parasites III. Examples of the interaction between parasites and other factors determining the growth of diatoms. *Ann. Bot.* N.S. **15**, 359–371.

(7) 1954 The seasonal cycle of the plankton diatom *Melosira italica* (Ehr.) Kütz. subsp. *subarctica* O. Müll. *J. Ecol.* **42**, 151–179.

(8) 1958 (With J. F. Talling) Botanical limnological methods, with special reference to the algae. *Bot. Rev.* **23**, 489–583.

(9) (With C. Kipling & E. D. Le Cren) The inverted microscope method of estimating algal numbers and the statistical basis of estimations by counting. *Hydrobiologia* **11**, 143–170.

(10) 1959 Buoyancy in relation to the ecology of the freshwater phytoplankton. *Br. Phycol. Bull.* no. 7, pp. 1–11.

(11) 1961 The algae of the Malham Tarn district. *Field Stud.* **1**, 85–119.

(12) (With D. Cannon & J. Siemińska) The growth of *Tabellaria flocculosa* (Roth) Kütz. var. *flocculosa* (Roth) Knudson under natural conditions of light and temperature. *J. Ecol.* **49**, 277–287.

(13) 1962 Unsolved problems in the classification of the non-motile Chrysophyceae with reference to those on parallel groups. *Preslia* **34**, 140–146.

(14) 1963 (With F. J. M. Mackereth & C. H. Mortimer) Changes in depth and time of certain chemical and physical conditions in the North Basin of Windermere in 1947. *Phil. Trans. R. Soc. Lond.* B **246**, 255–290.

(15) 1964 Primary production and periodicity of phytoplankton [Edgardo Baldi Memorial Lecture]. *Verh. Int. Verein. Theor. Angew. Limnol.* **15**, 37–56.

(16) 1965 The ecology of the freshwater phytoplankton. *Biol. Rev.* **40**, 231–293.

(17) 1971 The seasonal periodicity of three planktonic desmids in Windermere. *Mitt. Int. Verein. Theor. Angew. Limnol.* **10**, 3–25.

(18) 1972 Eutrophication. *Proc. R. Soc. Lond.* B **180**, 371–383.

(19) 1974 (With T. J. Lack) Observations and experiments on the phytoplankton of Blelham Tarn, English Lake District. *Freshwat. Biol.* **4**, 399–415.

(20) (With E. Gorham, J. E. Sanger & W. F. Dean) Some relationships between algal standing crop, water chemistry and sediment chemistry in the English Lakes. *Limnol. Oceanogr.* **19**, 601–617.

(21) 1978 Changes in the phytoplankton of an English lake, 1945–77 [in Russian]. *Gidrobiol. Zh.* **14**, 10–27.

(22)   1982   (With C. S. Reynolds) The development and operation of large limnetic enclosures in Blelham Tarn, English Lake District, and their contribution to phytoplankton ecology. *Prog. Phycol. Res.* **1**, 1–65.

(23)   1988   (With C. S. Reynolds) The phytoplankton of an enriched, soft-water lake subject to intermittent hydraulic flushing (Grasmere, English Lake District). *Freshwat. Biol.* **19**, 379–404.

(24)   (With S. I. Heaney, H. M. Canter & K. Gray) Population dynamics of *Ceratium* species in three English lakes, 1945–1985. *Hydrobiologia* **161**, 133–148.

(25)   1990   (With D. G. George, D. P. Hewitt & W. J. P. Smyly) The relative effects of enrichment and climate change on the long-term dynamics of *Daphnia* in Esthwaite Water, Cumbria. *Freshwat. Biol.* **23**, 55–70.

(26)   1995   (With H. Canter-Lund) *Freshwater algae—their microscopic world explored.* Bristol: Biopress.

(27)   1996   Felix Eugen Fritsch (1879–1954) In *Prominent phycologists of the* 20th *century* (ed. D. J. Garbury & M. J. Wynne), pp. 21–28. Moss Landing, CA: Phycological Society of America.

(28)   2000   (With E. B. Monaghan) Dr P. M. Jenkin (1902–1994) and the earliest days of the FBA's laboratory at Wray Castle. *Freshwat. Forum* **13**, 2–15.

SIR (BASIL) JOHN MASON CB

18 August 1923—6 January 2015

Godfrey Argent
'67.

B Jameson

SIR (BASIL) JOHN MASON CB

18 August 1923—6 January 2015

Elected FRS 1965

BY KEITH A. BROWNING* FRS

High Croft, Under Loughrigg, Ambleside, Cumbria LA22 9LJ, UK

Sir John Mason will be remembered for establishing cloud microphysics as a coherent discipline and for building the Meteorological Office into a leading centre of excellence on the international stage. A charismatic man, he possessed scientific vision, enthusiasm and an inspiring style of lecturing and advocacy that enabled him to recruit good scientists and raise the funds needed to achieve these ends, although his manifest self-belief and forthright manner upset some. He was highly influential within international institutions such as the World Meteorological Organization and nationally as president of many scientific bodies and Senior Vice-President and Treasurer of the Royal Society from 1976 to 1986.

EARLY LIFE

John Mason was born on 18 August 1923 in Docking, Norfolk, east of Hunstanton. His father was a farmer who died in 1936, and so his mother—a school teacher—would have been a major influence in his upbringing. When he spoke of them he tended to give the impression that his parents were simple folk who would not have understood his work or his eminence. He could already read and recite his arithmetic tables by the time he was four years old, when he started at the local village primary school. At the age of 11 years he went to the nearby Fakenham Grammar School. World War II began when he was in the sixth form, and many of his teachers were called up. As a result he had no formal teaching in mathematics or physics for his Higher School Certificate, the then equivalent of today's A-levels. A school from London was evacuated to Fakenham and its headmaster taught him mathematics in odd moments, but he more or less taught himself physics. There was, however, a very good biology teacher and so Mason concentrated on biology; in 1941 he won a scholarship to what was then University College Nottingham on the strength of his performance in biology. Once in university, however, he took up physics and mathematics. He had toyed with the idea of studying the arts but decided

* kandabrowning@googlemail.com

on physics instead because of the need for people in radar and signals during the war. He easily came to grips with physics; indeed, because many lecturers had been called up, he was given the responsibility in his second year of lecturing to first-year students. But then, in 1944, he himself was called up before he could enter the third and final year of his degree course.

He went into the Royal Air Force (RAF) and was appointed immediately as a radar officer. He had the usual six-week short-service training and was then commissioned and unusually quickly promoted to Flight Lieutenant. His first job was as Chief Instructor at the Fighter Command Radar School. He found the teaching experience very valuable. New radar-sets, mainly from the USA, were becoming available at that time and because there were virtually no manuals he had to determine how the sets worked, sometimes the previous night, before teaching people how to use and service them the next day. The work was extraordinarily demanding but he thrived on the challenge.

In early 1944 he was posted to India and Burma before being made Officer-in-charge of Signals and Telecommunications in Batavia (now Jakarta, Indonesia) in what was then the Netherlands East Indies. He was still only 21 years old but the early responsibility provided him with further remarkable experience, which stood him in good stead later. So young was he that he recalls his nonplussed Warrant Officer peevishly saying that he 'had seven children, five of whom are older than you, sir' (Royal Meteorological Society 1985). He was in the job for about 14 months before being demobilized. During that period he had had to learn quickly how to manage people.

After leaving the RAF he went back to Nottingham University. Because he returned part way through an academic year, he had only six or seven months before sitting his final examinations. During this period he had to assimilate not only the third-year material, some of which he had missed, but also revise all the things he had been taught in his first two years. Accordingly he decided that there was insufficient time for him to attend lectures or laboratory sessions and, much to his professor's annoyance, he instead read through the textbooks by himself. At this stage he was, of course, much older than most of the other students who had not been called up and he was determined not to let them beat him. He graduated in 1947 with a first-class honours degree: it was an external degree of London University because at that time Nottingham did not grant its own degrees. He was then awarded a Shirley Research Fellowship and worked on surface physics at Nottingham for a year in anticipation of going on to complete a PhD in this field. However, an attractive job opportunity arose elsewhere and he left after one year with an MSc and two research papers on surface tension to his name.

His next job was the result of a successful interview with Professor David (later Sir David) Brunt FRS, who was then head of the Department of Meteorology at Imperial College, London. Although Mason had no background in meteorology, he had been attracted by the advertisement for an assistant lecturer or lecturer in experimental physics in the department. Brunt explained that he wanted to build up the department after the war and that, apart from P. A. ('Peter') Sheppard (FRS 1964), who was then a Reader but later became Professor and Head of Department, they had nobody on the staff who did much experimental work. Mason subsequently remarked that he was very impressed by Brunt's approach, which was in stark contrast to today's tendency towards micromanagement. Indeed, Brunt's approach to management may well have influenced the style of management that Mason himself later adopted. He recalled (Royal Meteorological Society 1985) Brunt telling him at his interview:

> It doesn't matter if you don't know any meteorology. I'm told you are a very strong-minded young man who has got plenty of energy, drive and enthusiasm, and you know where you are going … so you can do anything you like. Come here and you can start from scratch; you can build up and

take any branch of atmospheric physics and just get on with it. And if I offer you an appointment and you take it, I'll tell you just one thing: I am now Physical Secretary of the Royal Society and am getting on … so I don't have much time to supervise you but if you make a good job of it and you show promise, I will back you to the hilt. If you don't, I shall kick you out!

The idea of working on his own and having a free hand captured Mason's imagination and he accepted the offer. Commenting on this later, he said:

I've often reflected whether [working on one's own] is necessarily a good thing. … That has some pros and cons: I would no doubt have learnt a great deal and would have been influenced a great deal if I had been under some great man or been in … one of the major schools of physics. On the other hand I may have grown up in their shadow and may not have developed my own independence and [gone] my own way.

The present writer, however, finds it hard to imagine Mason remaining in anyone's shadow.

IMPERIAL COLLEGE, 1947–65

Department of Meteorology

One might have thought that Mason's interest in cloud physics would have been sparked by his wartime work with radar and its ability to detect rain; however, although he was in contact with meteorologists in the RAF, he has said that this was not the case and that the main reason was Professor Brunt's personality and the opportunity he provided at Imperial College for him to do experimental work in a new field. Anyway, he started work in the Department of Meteorology in 1947 as an Assistant Lecturer at an annual salary of £400. A year later he was promoted to Lecturer and his salary increased, but only to £600. During his time in the department, it was a very lively place, with several other able and ambitious lecturers such as Richard Scorer, Eric Eady and Frank Ludlam, all eventually professors, and all prima donnas in their own way.

At the start of his new job, Mason looked around for a topic in which he could exploit his interest in experimental physics, preferably one that did not require him to have a significant background in meteorology. He found out about work under Professor G. M. B. Dobson FRS going on at Oxford University using cloud-chamber experiments, pioneered by the Nobel prize-winning physicist C. T. R. Wilson FRS, to investigate the freezing of water drops. He and Frank Ludlam also came across captured German documents describing some remarkable work on clouds carried out before and during the war by Walter Findeisen, who had a laboratory in Prague. Findeisen had not only built a big cloud chamber to try to simulate clouds but also had his own aircraft for making measurements within clouds. In addition, Mason came across the work of the American Nobel laureate, Irving Langmuir ForMemRS, who had been studying aircraft icing during the war and went on to discover, with Vincent Shaefer, that clouds can be seeded by dry ice or silver iodide to create precipitation. Against this backdrop Mason saw several threads that could be brought together in what seemed to be an area of research ripe for development.

He started by studying the nucleation of ice crystals and the supercooling of water, initially with just one or two students. His first paper was a review, published in 1950, that tried to paint a coherent picture of the nucleation of the ice phase in the atmosphere (1)*. In the same year he was invited to give one of the main lectures, on ice-crystal growth, at a meeting in

---

* Numbers in this form refer to the bibliography at the end of the text.

Oxford to mark the centenary of the Royal Meteorological Society. Here he came to the notice of international luminaries such as Carl-Gustaf Rossby, Eric Palmen and Sverre Petterssen. This was soon followed by an invitation from Brunt, then president of the Physics Section of the British Association for the Advancement of Science (BAAS), to help organize a session on cloud physics in the 1951 annual meeting of the BAAS, held in Edinburgh. What is more, still only 27 years old, he was asked to give the first talk in this session. It was on the natural and artificial production of rain. The Duke of Edinburgh was in the chair and so it was a big event nationally, which provided Mason with a very prominent platform. The success of his lecture effectively launched his public lecturing career. Another bonus from that lecture was that it inspired a young man to become Mason's first PhD student: John Monteith (FRS 1971), later Professor of Agricultural Science at Nottingham University.

While in the Department of Meteorology, Mason augmented his meagre salary by appearing frequently on radio and television programmes such as the Brains Trust, answering questions and sometimes performing experiments. He also gave public lectures around the UK and travelled abroad, often to the USA, to give lectures. However, Meteorology was a postgraduate department and so he did not have to give many formal lectures within the department. As the distinguished Swedish meteorologist Tor Bergeron had observed (and Mason himself liked to recall): 'so you're a lecturer in meteorology and you give no lectures and you know no meteorology. You'll go a long way, young man!' (Royal Meteorological Society 1985). Of course, during this time he did learn a lot of meteorology, aided especially by his friendship with fellow-lecturer Frank Ludlam, who had joined the department as a Leverhulme Research Fellow from the Meteorological (Met) Office and was one of the world's most insightful observers of the atmosphere, and of clouds in particular.

In 1951 the 28-year-old Mason was on a Rockefeller Travelling Fellowship in the USA when he was invited, together with Dr E. G. (Taffy) Bowen (FRS 1975) from Australia, to review a rain-making experiment proposed by the University of Arizona. Distinguished scientists such as Irving Langmuir were involved, but this experiment also involved commercial operators whom Mason regarded as charlatans. Although microphysics was his speciality, Mason was convinced even then that the amount and intensity of rainfall would be determined largely by the dynamics rather than the microphysics, which the would-be rain-makers were targeting. He presented his views very forcefully and argued not only for better experimental and statistical design in the experiments but, as always, also stressed the overriding need for better physical understanding. From then on, his critical attitude and emphasis on the importance of understanding the underlying physics and dynamics continued to have a moderating effect on the more exaggerated claims, and stimulated a major expansion of basic research.

In 1954 Professor Carl-Gustaf Rossby invited Mason to give a series of lectures at the University of Stockholm. As he later recalled in an interview (Taba 1995), Mason regarded Rossby as a role model who gave him a deep insight into how to manage a group of research students. By the mid-1950s Mason had built up his group to become one of the leading cloud-physics groups in the world. All the time, he and his students were producing a regular stream of research publications so that, by 1956, he was able to submit a compilation of his papers for a DSc, with Professor J. D. Bernal FRS as one of the examiners.

When Brunt retired in 1952, Peter Sheppard took over as Head of Department. John Mason had admired Brunt and owed a lot to him: not only had Brunt recruited him and given him freedom to pursue his own research agenda, but he had also engineered the platform that launched his public lecturing career. The same cannot be said of his relationship with Sheppard.

Sheppard was a very forbidding person who used to submit staff and students alike to incisive criticism when, as was the tradition, they shared their daily tea breaks with him. However, Mason stood up to him: Mason's early opportunity for leadership in the RAF had stiffened his backbone. Although Sheppard was supportive later in Mason's career, a situation of rivalry persisted for as long as Mason remained on the staff of the Meteorology Department. So it was probably a relief all round when, in 1956, he was awarded the Royal Society's Warren Research Fellowship: this independent appointment at readership level effectively gave him unfettered freedom to pursue his research with his group at Imperial College. Mason retained this Fellowship for about five years, although it was interrupted in 1959/60 when he accepted an invitation by Professor Jack Bjerknes to spend a year as a visiting professor of meteorology at the University of California in Los Angeles in the company of the renowned meteorologists Jorgen Holmboe and Zdenek Sekera. While he was there he temporarily took over both the lecturing responsibilities of Professor Morris Neiburger and the supervision of his students, one of whom was Hans Pruppacher, who later became a full professor of cloud physics.

Mason was very conscious of the general lack of knowledge regarding the basic physics of water and ice and, when he resumed his Warren Fellowship and while still located in the Meteorology Department, he set up and directed an interdepartmental research programme on the subject, funded by the Rockefeller Foundation. His idea was to break down some of the barriers that existed between departments at Imperial College: such interdisciplinary activity is common nowadays but was rather novel at the time.

Department of Physics

After discussions in 1961 with Nobel laureate and Head of the Physics Department, Lord Blackett FRS (PRS 1965–70), and with Sir Patrick Linstead FRS, Rector of Imperial College, Mason was appointed to a personal chair in the Physics Department. This was during the so-called brain drain, and Mason suspected that Blackett was concerned that Americans might have induced him to remain in the USA had he not made such an attractive offer. Thus he became the first professor in the world of the (by then) rapidly growing field of cloud physics. His entire group moved from the Meteorology Department to become an independent subdepartment of the Physics Department, where he was able to give lectures in cloud physics to undergraduates, as well as taking on other lecturing responsibilities in classical physics from Blackett. This led to an increasing number of good home-grown students joining his group, which by then was close to 20 strong. The group enjoyed smart new premises in a converted townhouse in Prince's Gardens, Kensington. Productivity was high because of the newness of the subject and the quality of students. He was a superb PhD advisor. Perhaps his greatest gift was his ability to present his students with topics to examine that were both important and tractable, a rare combination. His own enthusiasm for the research helped his students immensely through their inevitably difficult patches. Interestingly, the teatime discussions that were such a feature of life in the Meteorology Department were retained in Prince's Gardens, although generally there was less violent criticism—they were an early example of brain-storming in which half-baked ideas were put forward to be either developed further or quietly forgotten.

Personal contributions to cloud physics research

Mason's first paper on a cloud physics topic, in 1950, was on the nature of ice-forming nuclei in the atmosphere (1), but he was already showing a broad interest across the field of cloud physics and wrote a landmark review with Frank Ludlam in 1951 entitled 'The microphysics of clouds' (2), which helped him scope his ensuing research. A few years later he published a further review with Ludlam (5). Before the time of Mason's work at Imperial College, research into aspects of cloud physics had been dispersed among small groups, but Mason became the first to perform laboratory research systematically on a great number of interrelated cloud physics problems, which he later brought together in his highly acclaimed book *The physics of clouds*, published in 1957 (6) and updated in 1971. A feature of this book is the interweaving of individual facets of cloud physics into clear and authoritative descriptions of cloud properties. A version of the book more suitable for a layman audience and undergraduate students was published in 1962 (10) and helped spread interest beyond the physics and meteorology communities; a second edition was published in 1975.

Mason published about 70 papers and books on cloud physics between 1950 and 1965, and his output continued even after he left Imperial College. I shall identify just a few pioneering findings to give a flavour of their scope. Particularly well known is his equation for droplet growth, sometimes referred to as the Mason equation, which takes into account both the effects of the curvature of the droplets and of soluble or insoluble material within them. Calculations based on the Mason equation have led to the development of simplified representations of the processes in weather prediction and climate models. His equation, published in *The physics of clouds* (6), provided the basis for work on the growth of a broad spectrum of cloud and rain droplets in clouds in which ice particles are not present—so-called warm clouds. At that time, cloud condensation nuclei were believed to be primarily produced by the explosive break-up of seawater bubbles. These tiny particles, on entering the bases of warm clouds, would grow to produce cloud droplets that would increase in size and could then grow large enough to engage in coalescence and produce drizzle droplets and ultimately rain. Calculations based on the Mason equation suggested that growth by condensation alone could not lead to the formation of precipitation-sized droplets within the time and spatial scales implied by observations of real clouds. Later work by Mason and Chien (9) demonstrated the importance of entrainment of fresh nuclei to maintain a broad droplet spectrum against the narrowing effects of condensation while also needing a few large nuclei on which to grow the largest drops. There is now evidence that low concentrations of large nuclei probably do play a role in the formation of a broad spectrum of droplet sizes, leading to rapid precipitation development; however, such low concentrations were below the threshold of early observations. Mason and Chien's paper was written in the context of sea-salt nuclei, but the question of the numbers and chemistry of the most effective nuclei remains an unsolved problem for theories of droplet growth in clouds.

The above work related to the so-called warm clouds without ice, but the production of ice particles in colder clouds was also a theme of much of Mason's work. The ice particles grow by vapour deposition because the clouds are supersaturated with respect to ice; the particles then possibly collide, adhere and fall faster than their neighbours, collecting them to form snowflakes or, in related but different circumstances, producing hail or smaller graupel-pellets. In 1956/57 Mason wrote two major papers (3, 4) with his student John Hallett, who went on to become a full professor of cloud physics in the USA. These papers showed the importance of impurities in poisoning ice nuclei, explained inconsistencies in previous studies, and at the same time clarified the mechanism for direct nucleation of sublimation. They led the way for work on other methods of nucleation such as contact nucleation.

Other significant scientific contributions in cloud physics were in the field of cloud electrification. Laboratory studies in the early 1960s led by Mason, and separately by Professor Marx Brook of the New Mexico Institute of Science and Technology, established that almost all the most promising mechanisms for cloud charging and lightning initiation were too weak to promote the required electrical breakdown. Effectively Mason whittled down the number of candidate mechanisms of charging until only one survived. In 1961 a well-known paper (8) was published by Mason together with his student John Latham, who went on to found the Atmospheric Physics Research Group at the University of Manchester Institute of Technology. The mechanism, also described in Mason's Bakerian Lecture (12), entailed rebounding in-cloud collisions between ice crystals and growing graupel-pellets. In attempting to provide a quantitative explanation of this mechanism, it was suggested that regions of opposing charge were formed within the ice crystals where a temperature gradient existed. The laboratory experiments, although difficult to conduct at the time owing to instrument limitations, supported this hypothesis. Charge separation was believed to be due to dissociation and differential ionic mobility. Collisions between ice particles of different sizes falling under gravity could then lead to charge separation within the storms. Of course, the presence of a vertical electric field within the storm has a significant effect on the charge separation process, and a complete theory should really include dissipation as well as generation mechanisms. Nevertheless, the many modelling and field studies conducted over more recent years have continued to support the hypothesis that a non-inductive process (that is, one not requiring the presence of an electric field) is the most powerful one, although the precise charge transfer mechanism still remains to be established. Today there are more extensive observations of the distribution of electric charge within thunderstorms and these suggest that initial charge separation may occur through collisions between particles of ice and supercooled water. Although the Latham–Mason mechanism has not stood the test of time as being the major charge separation mechanism in clouds, there is no doubt that the thermoelectric effect, which they were the first to identify, is real.

Mason's work on thunderstorm electrification illustrates well his ability to carefully isolate one aspect of a complex physical problem and then design a laboratory experiment to test a specific theory. Two of his papers (7, 11) dealing with ice-crystal habit again demonstrate the need for careful laboratory experiments if spurious results are to be avoided. These papers nicely demonstrate how the great variety of ice crystal forms found in the atmosphere can be consistently explained simply in terms of the migration of molecules across the surface during sublimation. The capability of Mason and his group to test theories through critical laboratory studies is something that is not available in many other areas of atmospheric science. Such work is becoming almost extinct in today's financial climate. The question might be asked as to whether there was anything novel about Mason's experimental equipment: probably there was not—even his thermal-gradient diffusion chamber for growing ice crystals was not new. Rather, it was the experimental design and the careful examination of the results that delivered results. He stressed the need to look for and rule out alternative explanations: he was very critical of those who published as soon as they got a result consistent with their theory. Mason's ability to communicate ideas clearly and forcefully was usually beneficial but of course he was not always right. For example, Peter Jonas, professor of cloud physics at the University of Manchester, and Mason's former student, recalls that Mason was always dismissive of a role for turbulence in the development of raindrops in clouds. The point at issue was the relative role of cloud droplets falling and colliding versus being thrown together by small turbulent eddies (Jonas 1996).

Arguably, Mason's greatest contribution to cloud physics was in helping to build a strong international research activity in the subject, as so many of his students and research fellows moved on to form their own groups, 17 becoming full professors. Indeed, it is still true that there are few outstanding cloud physics groups that have not been influenced by involvement with scientists from his Imperial College group. Ahead of his time, Mason saw that cloud physics was crucial to the resolution of many outstanding problems in atmospheric physics. Although partly driven in the early days by interest in the possibility of weather modification, cloud microphysics remains important for the development of climate models through the microphysical properties of clouds as well as for the processing of various chemical species in the atmosphere. However, this is a difficult field of research so that, despite the huge expansion in research activity stimulated by Mason, these problems are still far from being fully resolved.

Mason's time at the Met Office is discussed in the next section but, before leaving the topic of his specific contributions to cloud physics, it is appropriate to anticipate some of his later contributions. Soon after leaving Imperial College, he initiated experiments to understand the interaction between cloud microphysics and the dynamics of cloud systems. The dynamics are responsible not only for providing the growth environment for cloud particles but also for imposing severe constraints on their subsequent development. Three observational investigations that Mason promoted in this area were Project Scillonia (Hardman *et al.* 1972), the radar studies of frontal precipitation systems by the Met Office group at the Royal Radar Establishment (RRE), Malvern (13) and, as I discuss later, the GATE project in the tropical Atlantic (WMO 1972): these all led to a better understanding of precipitation systems that was subsequently incorporated into numerical weather-prediction models. The development of these models and their use for basic atmospheric research as well as for weather prediction were areas that Mason strongly supported after he left Imperial College.

METEOROLOGICAL OFFICE, 1965–83

It became increasingly clear during the early 1960s that Mason was destined for greater things. In 1964 Sir Graham Sutton FRS, then Director-General of the Met Office, recommended him as a possible Director of the Royal Institution. The President of the RI, Lord Fleck FRS, was also keen on Mason as a candidate, describing him as 'very nearly … a "spellbinder"' in his lecturing ability (Cole 2015). In the event, George (later Lord) Porter FRS (PRS 1985–1990), was selected. However, in 1965, when Sutton was due to retire from the Met Office, Mason was invited to apply for his position. Buoyed by the fact that he had just been elected a Fellow of the Royal Society, Mason attended the selection board. He told the board that he wanted to build up the Met Office to be the best meteorological service in the world. This degree of ambition was apparently welcomed, for this was the 1960s—an era of scientific and technological optimism spurred on by Prime Minister Harold (later Lord) Wilson (FRS 1969). Mason recalls that, after his successful interview, he overheard a board member remarking, 'he'll shake 'em up a bit … but this is just what the Met Office needs' (Royal Meteorological Society 1985). Running an organization with some 3800 staff after being a research professor with fewer than 20 people would be a major step. Moreover, many of his academic colleagues regarded weather forecasting as a rather inferior occupation and the Met Office as being overly bureaucratic. But Mason had a more positive view, believing that the Office was undervalued

Figure 1. John Mason at his desk on his first day at the Met Office. (Image kindly provided by the Royal Meteorological Society and used under the Open Government Licence.)

and had made great strides since the war, with the establishment of a significant programme of research: it now had some distinguished scientists, including the turbulence expert Frank Pasquill (FRS 1977) and the dynamical meteorologist John Sawyer FRS (Director of Research 1965–76), for whom he had great respect. Figure 1 shows Mason on his first day in the Met Office, on 1 October 1965.

Widely referred to by his initials, 'BJ', by his erstwhile students, he was now referred to almost reverentially as 'DG'. At 42 years of age he was unusually young to be appointed Director-General. An apocryphal story he often told later in life concerned the parking spaces for senior Met Office staff at the Bracknell headquarters: on his first day Mason swept into the car park and parked in the appropriate slot. On entering the building he was stopped by the guard who said 'Young man, you cannot park there. It is reserved for the Director-General.' His response 'I *am* the Director-General!' would have been accompanied by his usual wide smile and laughter.

One month after becoming DG, Mason made a bold decision and, in the process, established the blueprint for his approach to creating a thrusting forward-looking organization. At that time, operational weather forecasts were being generated entirely subjectively. Mason was, however, impressed by the quality of the Office's numerical weather forecasts, which were still undergoing trials. So he overruled the caution of the staff and decreed that they should go operational without delay, together with a major publicity drive. He argued that 'if we go operational then we shall have to perform at concert pitch as opposed to a rehearsal and everyone will tighten up and the whole timescale will collapse' (Royal Meteorological Society 1985). His gamble paid off and the publicity put the Met Office in a good light: 2 November 1965 was a landmark day for Numerical Weather Prediction (NWP), and although forecasters still had to exercise judgement in the application of NWP products, this did indeed set the tone for an increasingly progressive Met Office.

Although Mason initially grew to prominence with his work on cloud physics at Imperial College and through his book *The physics of clouds*, his greatest contributions to meteorology were to come while he was in charge of the Met Office. Unlike many great scientists whose research groups are relatively narrow in their area of expertise, Mason built a research group at the Met Office that covered a huge range of expertise and in which specialists benefited from close contact with specialists in other fields—all within the same organization. Such interaction led to the development of ideas in a way that would be difficult to achieve in a much smaller, university, group. At the same time it also made for the rapid transfer of new discoveries into operational weather forecasting, which also served to identify areas where knowledge was lacking. That such a strong research activity could be built up and maintained is a testimony to Mason's abilities and foresight.

His first step towards establishing centres of excellence was to move his entire cloud physics research group into the Met Office. However, a problem that was in danger of thwarting Mason's aspiration for the Office to become a world leading institution more broadly was the ageing staff profile and lack of new blood. His response was to recruit first-rate new graduates, which he attracted by giving inspirational lectures at leading universities (24 of them in his first year as DG). He also contributed to the 'reverse brain drain' of the time by attracting leading researchers, such as Massachusetts Institute of Technology professor Raymond Hide (FRS 1971), who established a new group in the Met Office dealing with fundamental issues in geophysical fluid dynamics. Many young recruits passed through Hide's group and honed their skills to the benefit of other areas of the Office to which they were subsequently posted. He also attracted the author of this biography back from the USA to build up the Met Office group at the Royal Radar Establishment.

Against the prevailing mood of scepticism in the Met Office about the value of radar in meteorology, he promoted two new radar programmes involving the Met Office working together with the hydrological community. One of the new radar programmes, which developed over a 10-year period starting in 1966, was the Dee Weather Radar Project. This demonstrated the capability of a single radar to measure rainfall over an area as accurately as that achievable by a dense network of raingauges, and to provide the data in real time for hydrological forecasting. The evolution of this and related programmes is recounted by Collinge (1987). The other programme, which took much longer to implement in full, began in 1971 with Mason commissioning a proposal (Bulman & Browning 1971) to establish a National Weather Radar Network in which rainfall data from a distributed network of unmanned radars would be combined for use in the detailed monitoring and forecasting of the weather. The eventual outcome was the now familiar radar rainfall display covering Britain. At the same time he secured new research aircraft for the Office's Meteorological Research Flight and set up a satellite meteorology group to capitalize on the new satellite temperature soundings and cloud imagery. Other scientific areas that he was keen to support during his time in charge of the Met Office included the newly emerging atmospheric general circulation models. In particular, he foresaw their value in studying linkages between the atmosphere and oceans and in evaluating potential impacts on climate. One application was the simulation of the Milankovitch cycles leading to past ice ages. Another was the simulation of the impacts of increasing greenhouse gas concentrations in the atmosphere. Although he was cautious at first about accepting that man-made changes would dominate over naturally occurring variability, this work can be seen as a forerunner of the work of the Intergovernmental Panel on Climate Change that in due course demonstrated this beyond reasonable doubt.

A major opportunity arose when Mason, as the Permanent Representative of the UK with the World Meteorological Organization (WMO), attended the fifth session of the WMO

Figure 2. Prime Minister Edward Heath, with Director-General of the Met Office, John Mason, formally opening the new Richardson Wing at Bracknell in 1972. (Image kindly provided by the Royal Meteorological Society and used under the Open Government Licence.)

Executive Committee (EC) in 1967. The WMO at the time was planning a major programme, the World Weather Watch (WWW), to improve the world-wide observing network and to develop facilities for exploiting the new data in operational weather forecasting. Ahead of the EC meeting, Mason successfully lobbied the UK government for funding to support the Met Office at Bracknell becoming a Regional Telecommunications Hub and a Regional Meteorological Centre as part of WWW, together with a substantial training programme. The WMO EC backed the resulting proposal and a major expansion followed at Bracknell, notably a new telecommunications centre and a powerful new computer, under the charge of a new Deputy Directorate for communications and computing, all housed in a new building named after the early pioneer of Numerical Weather Prediction, L. F. Richardson FRS. Figure 2 shows Prime Minister Edward Heath with John Mason, formally opening the Richardson Wing in 1972.

Mason was proud of his ability to deliver speeches and was fond of telling the story that when the Prime Minister came to Bracknell to open the Richardson Wing, Heath told him that only once before had anyone sent him the text of his speech and then had afterwards given it word-for-word as Mason had done—without notes and seemingly spontaneously. That other person had been General de Gaulle.

At about the same time as the Met Office facilities were expanding rapidly at Bracknell, Mason persuaded the Ministry of Defence to transfer the RAF Flying Training Command Headquarters facility at nearby Shinfield Park to the Met Office for use as its new residential college. Stan Cornford, then principal of the college, recalls that Mason was justifiably proud of achieving this: not only was a residential college just what was needed in view of the dispersed nature of the many Met Office outstations but it was also close to the Department of Meteorology at Reading University, with which there was eventually an agreement to exchange students. Another of Mason's initiatives impacted the Met Office College soon after the college was established at Shinfield Park. Prime Minister Heath's government had continued to be very supportive and it was not long before Mason, bolstered by the greatly improved capabilities of the Met Office and a promise of further funding from the UK government, was able to persuade a reluctant European Community to set up the new European Centre for Medium-Range Weather Forecasts (ECMWF) in new premises adjacent to the Met Office College. The work of Mason and his staff that led to the ECMWF's being located at Shinfield Park, including Mason's discussion with Prime Minister Heath persuading him of the benefits of having the ECMWF in the UK, are mentioned in a book on the Centre's history (Woods 2006). The distinctive voice of Mason welcoming the ECMWF to the UK during the Centre's first council session in November 1975 can be heard on the website at http://www.ecmwf.int/en/about/who-we-are/history. Initially two-thirds of the scientists at ECMWF were recruited from the Met Office: along with modelling and other software from the USA, this influx of Met Office staff gave the ECMWF a flying start on its trajectory towards becoming a world leader in its own right.

Mason retired from the Met Office in 1983 at the then compulsory retirement age of 60 years. He had transformed not only the Office's facilities but also its intellectual capital. The downside of his success was that there was a touch of Fortress Bracknell and, to some extent, a downplaying of the role of outstanding meteorologists and oceanographers in the universities. However, there can be no disputing the fact that the reputation of the Office had grown enormously, to the extent that, in his last year as DG, there were about 860 applicants for 15 posts, allowing the opportunity to recruit only the brightest young mathematicians and physicists. Indeed, there was one year in which the Met Office had more applicants than the whole of the rest of the Scientific Civil Service put together. Mason justifiably claimed that his ability to attract good people was one of his greatest achievements. At the same time he also increased the reputation of the Met Office through the publicity he gained from his many awards, honorary degrees and special lectures, and through being Senior Vice-President of the Royal Society and president of many other scientific societies during (and after) his time as Director-General (listed at the end of this memoir). Mason was President of the Royal Meteorological Society at the time it moved its headquarters from Cromwell Road, near Imperial College, to Bracknell. This was financially an unfortunate move because of subsequent property inflation in London, which would have been difficult to foresee at the time; however, the move was consistent with his determination to build a meteorological powerhouse at Bracknell.

Mason's own account of his time in the Met Office has been published by the Royal Meteorological Society (17).

THE ROYAL SOCIETY

Mason was Senior Vice-President and Treasurer of the Royal Society from 1976 to 1986. Dr Peter Warren was Deputy Executive Secretary of the Royal Society during much of this time, and the following paragraphs are adapted from a eulogy that he delivered in February 2015.

Mason took up office at a challenging time for the Society: there were growing financial pressures on universities and on science, yet the Society's influence with government was at a low ebb. However, Mason, benefiting from his managerial experience as Director-General of the Met Office, and sharing a common vision with Lord Todd, the President, set about rectifying that situation. By the end of his tenure the Society was proffering advice to government and parliament, had published some 17 reports, had a fledgling Policy Studies Unit, and had re-established itself as a force to be listened to and consulted.

As a former Royal Society Research Fellow, Mason was keen for the Society to increase research appointments for outstanding young scientists. However, cuts in university budgets in the early 1980s were seriously reducing opportunities for even the best postgraduates to remain in research so as to be able to fill tenured posts as they arose. This threatened the quality of future university staff and risked a resurgence of the brain drain. Research Councils sought 'new blood' schemes, and Mason was in the forefront in seeking support for an equivalent scheme for the Society—the University Research Fellowships (URFs)—to be paid for through its Parliamentary Grant-in-Aid. With no new money forthcoming at first, he had to oversee a radical shift in the use of the existing grant from research grants to research fellowships, including the demise of the sizeable Scientific Investigations Grants scheme begun in 1849. Thirty URFs were created in 1983 and, although there were setbacks, Mason ensured that the Society could retain the then target of a steady state of 100 and, with subsequent additions to that grant, achieve that target and more. The ultimate scale of success was in no small measure the result of Mason's annual presentation of the Society's bid for its whole Grant-in-Aid, which rose from £1.7 million in 1975–76 to some £6 million in 1986 to cover International Exchanges and Research Grants, etc., as well as research appointments. Success breeds success: there are now more than 300 URFs in post and past URFs are spread far and wide across the scientific community.

The Finance Officer at the time, Nigel Parfitt, recalls that Mason also considered himself quite 'investment savvy' and at Investment Advisory Committee meetings he would come up with several proposals for changing the Society's investments: apparently the committee would always agree to one of his proposals 'to keep him happy'. Mason's energies were not restricted to higher matters: he also took a keen interest in reforming the Society's catering arrangements.

INTERNATIONAL ACTIVITIES

The World Meteorological Organization

As Permanent Representative of the UK with the WMO, Mason was voted onto its 24-member EC in 1965. According to Professor John Zillman of Australia, a fellow member of the EC from 1979 onwards, it was very clear to those involved, even from first impressions, that Mason was *the* towering intellect and dominant personality, and everyone took notice of his interventions in debates. He recalls that Mason worked closely with WMO President Alf Nyberg of Sweden, Bob White of the USA, E. K. Federov of the USSR, Bill Gibbs of Australia, Eric Sussenberger of West Germany and Jean Bessemoulin of France. He was enthusiastically supportive and involved in the planning of WMO's WWW and of the Global Atmospheric Research Programme (GARP), a 15-year international research programme, crucially bringing together WMO (representing the operational community) and the International Council of

Scientific Unions (representing the academic community). GARP played a vital role with its pioneering influence in the use of computers for modelling the global atmospheric circulation, and in the use of satellites for continuous global observation of the Earth. Mason pushed the EC hard for it to lead the way in the exploitation of satellites. Weather modification issues also came up in the WMO and, not surprisingly, he had strong views on these. He successfully coerced the WMO into a scientifically tough line in the design of the WMO Precipitation Enhancement Project (PEP).

The Met Office funded equipment for the meteorological services of developing countries, and for fellowships for staff from these services, mostly to study at its college at Shinfield Park: Mason insisted on approving each fellowship personally. He was mostly liked by EC members from the developing countries but he could be quite contemptuous of their scientific knowledge and often caused offence. Once he remarked, 'If knowledge of the First Law of Thermodynamics were the criterion for EC election, this room would be almost empty!' Also, the day before the election of EC members at the 1975 Congress, he made an intervention along the lines of 'I don't support scientific prizes like this for [some] little countries and, next week in EC, I will make sure we change the rules to get them excluded.' Members of about 100 delegations muttered under their breaths 'provided you get elected', and sure enough, the next day, the unheard-of happened and, for the first time ever, the UK Permanent Representative did not get enough votes for election onto the new EC. Mason was devastated by the vote but he was back on the EC, only slightly chastened, two years later. It is widely believed that this incident and his generally forthright style are why he, as the leading meteorologist of his age, was never given the WMO's top award: the IMO (International Meteorological Organization) Prize. Although he was close to winning it several times, his prospects were not helped by the arcane system for choosing the award winner and his antipathy towards WMO's Secretary-General, Patrick Obasi.

Mason's contribution was not restricted to his work on the EC itself; he also made a major contribution to the WMO at a more detailed level scientifically. After the sixth World Meteorological Congress in 1971, the EC agreed to mount one of the biggest ever international scientific expeditions: GATE, the GARP Atlantic Tropical Experiment (WMO 1972). Mason was the chairman of the planning board for that experiment. The purpose of GATE was to study the exchange of heat and moisture between the tropical oceans and the atmosphere, and the interaction between the meteorology of the tropics and the rest of the globe. It was the first major experiment of GARP, whose wider goal was to understand the predictability of the atmosphere and extend the time range of weather forecasts from days to more than two weeks. The experiment took place in the summer of 1974 in an area that covered the tropical Atlantic Ocean from Africa to South America. The work was truly international in scope and involved 39 research ships, 13 research aircraft and numerous buoys from 20 countries, all equipped to obtain the observations specified in the scientific plan. The long-term impact of GATE was considerable: its vast database contributed to studies that led to the first World Climate Conference in 1979 and it can be seen as one of the forerunners of the work of the Intergovernmental Panel on Climate Change.

The Surface Waters Acidification Project

In June 1983, the Royal Swedish Academy of Sciences and the Norwegian Academy of Science and Letters were asked by the Royal Society to join in a cooperative scientific project aimed at acquiring a better understanding of the causes of surface water acidification and fishery decline in southern Scandinavia. The project was the Surface Waters Acidification Programme (SWAP). It was hoped that this effort would make it possible to evaluate the role of acid deposition from anthropogenic emissions and to assess the improvement in the aquatic environment that might be gained from a decrease in such emissions, particularly those emanating from the UK. The SWAP project was an unusual policy project for the Royal Society to undertake because it involved doing new research rather than merely synthesizing existing knowledge. Having recently retired from his Met Office position, Mason was able to take on the task of SWAP Programme Director, with a secretariat based at Imperial College. Between the times of the first two meetings of the management group, Mason prepared a joint background document with SWAP's Scandinavian consultant, Professor H. M. Seip (14). The report contained proposals for research and represented a consensus of the scientists involved in the management of the project.

The SWAP project had 300 scientists from 30 institutions in the three participating countries. Its management committee was chaired by Sir Richard Southwood FRS, who until 1985 was chairman of the Royal Commission on Environmental Pollution. The committee travelled extensively as a social group; Professor Jack Talling FRS, another member of the committee, recalls that the official workings between Mason and Southwood were cordial and efficient, although they had very different characters. Mason's meteorological experience and overall scientific vision were valuable, but Southwood's tact in the face of local feelings was helpful. Their decisions were of course politically sensitive. There was some feeling that grants should be given to those working in Sweden and Norway, and not to those in Britain, but Mason held strongly to the view that all three countries were eligible to benefit. There was also sensitivity to the fact that the Central Electricity Generating Board (CEGB) burnt coal that was thought to produce much of the acidification of natural waters, so that their research opinions were liable to be questioned by those overseas. A representative of CEGB, which provided funding for SWAP, was initially a member of the management committee but eventually resigned. Despite these difficulties, the project did much to remove earlier suspicion and dissension between the nations involved, and cordiality prevailed in its meetings.

After the project was over, Mason edited the project report (15) and, although having no formal qualifications in chemistry, wrote a book on the chemical processes involved in acidification and its biological impact on freshwater life (16). The book demonstrates Mason's wide grasp of issues and contains chapters on emissions, transport and deposition of acid pollution; hydrochemical studies in catchments; catchment process studies; catchment manipulation experiments; the role of hydrology and soil chemistry; palaeolimnological studies; the toxic effects of acidification on fish and other aquatic life; and catchment modelling studies.

An important factor was that Prime Minister Margaret Thatcher FRS had great faith in Mason's scientific judgement and independence. As he was guarantor of the independence, quality and authority of its conclusions, the final report in 1990 provided a sound basis for subsequent public policy-making in all three countries. Because Mrs Thatcher trusted his judgement she agreed to fund a £700 million programme to clean up UK emissions. No less important were the overall lessons learned from the way in which Mason ran this collaborative project: above all, he ensured that only the best scientists were engaged, and that measurements were taken with standardized techniques and with an agreed protocol for their use before conclusions were drawn. The project was thus able to provide the collaborating academies, and the governments they advised, with broad-based collective and independent scientific evidence.

STYLE AND PERSONALITY

Mason had a strong, dominating personality: he rather took over any social group he was in. His duties required him to fraternize with royalty, prime ministers and many other notable people with whom, being self-assured and verbally adept, he could readily hold his own. He was always happy to recount, very fluently, stories of these encounters. In his later years he became very aware that he had become the most senior Grade 2 Civil Servant, not just in the Ministry of Defence but in the UK Civil Service as a whole. So when he visited Geneva on business he would, unabashed, requisition the Ambassador's official limousine for both himself and his personal assistant. Most regarded these practices as part of his natural exuberance, but it made him unpopular with some who felt that modesty should prevail.

Mason did not suffer fools gladly. He was a formidable presence at conferences: he always sat in the front row and, almost without exception, would ask the first question. He would rise to deliver it, facing the audience, a very tall imposing man, closer to the audience than the lecturer, who became a diminutive figure. If he disagreed with the speaker, he made that very clear. If he considered the speaker was talking nonsense or being devious, he said so very plainly. He insisted that his sole objective in doing so was to establish the truth. He got on well with Prime Minister Margaret Thatcher: they were two of a type. She, too, was an admirer of those who knew what they wanted and 'told it as it was'.

Mason worked phenomenally hard. As he rapidly moved up in the scientific world he did not change his work ethic or how he managed his staff. He expected a lot from his staff, or in the early days his students, but once they had earned his confidence he was very supportive. David Axford, one of Mason's deputies at the Met Office and later Deputy Secretary-General at the WMO, recalls that a feature of Mason's time as Director-General was to have regular lunches with staff down to Principal Scientific Officer grade. They brought their own sandwiches to his office, sat around his conference table and discussed whatever was of topical interest in an almost rank-free manner. This was a management style that Mason had developed during his time at Imperial College.

Although the 'world' was apt to see an aggressive exterior, Mason's overt self-esteem was just a personal quirk that was overlaid by other desirable qualities: not only was he exceptionally able to make decisions quickly and clearly, but on a more human level he had a great sense of humour: for example, when in charge of the Met Office he delighted in showing visiting politicians his set of African rain-making stones. More importantly, there was a kind and caring man underneath. When he was invited to the homes of staff or ex-students, he loved watching their children play and holding them on his lap. If colleagues were ill he would visit them, however distinguished or lowly. One of his former PhD students relates that, although their paths had seldom crossed over the course of 20 years, when he subsequently had complex surgery Mason had phoned him in hospital every day to ask about his progress and wish him a safe recovery. This was not an isolated occurrence: he was always concerned—genuinely so—when he heard of a student or member of staff being sick or receiving bad news. The death of Frank Ludlam, his closest colleague during his time at Imperial College, affected him immensely. Although Mason may not have said much in public, he was proud of his students' work and was pleased when they got good positions, as they so often did, after they received their PhDs. He was very supportive of his students and staff, and for the most part they were correspondingly loyal to him.

Although his work was central to his life—it was a hobby as well as a job—he had a rich and happy domestic life. His wife, Doreen (whom he predeceased), was his first love: they married in 1948 when he was a few days short of his 25th birthday and she just 20 years old. Doreen was a home-loving person who provided the stability and support that underpinned his home life. She brought up their two sons, Barry and Nigel, and seldom travelled with her husband after the children were born. However, she enjoyed the social events that went with his being Vice-President of the Royal Society and was the perfect hostess for his many visitors and friends, not least because she was an excellent cook and he was known to enjoy good food and wine.

As a family man, Mason adored his two sons and was proud of them, although he admitted he did not spend as much time with them as he would have liked while they were growing up. The elder son, Barry, became a leading economist in the Civil Service, and the younger son, Nigel, followed his father into science to become a professor of physics (currently at The Open University). Mason was very pleased to have been able to co-author a paper in his later years with Nigel. The award of the OBE to Nigel in 2007 gave him immense pleasure, and attending Buckingham Palace to see Nigel presented with this award was a lovely counterpoint to when Nigel had attended Sir John's investiture. He was a kind father-in-law to Jane, Nigel's wife, challenging her culinary skills at times: happily he lived to see them adopt their daughter Megan and enjoyed being a 'grandad'.

Outside science he did have hobbies. He greatly enjoyed classical music and often went to concerts at the Royal Albert Hall, a habit begun when he worked nearby at Imperial College. Family holidays were nearly always based in the UK and involved visits to many historical houses (he was a long-time member of National Trust). Although not religious, he particularly liked church architecture, stating he believed he had visited all the cathedrals in the UK; Durham and Salisbury were his favourites. Though he did not pursue sport after his student days, he was a passionate supporter of Arsenal and could name the 1930 Championship teams. He was a keen follower of cricket and shared this passion with two close friends, Sir Bernard Lovell FRS and Sir George Edwards FRS. In his later years he looked after Doreen wonderfully well throughout a long period of illness until he himself suffered the first of two strokes. He recovered from the first stroke well enough to write his own account of his time in the Met Office (17). His second stroke left him housebound but he remained at home with Doreen, cared for by Barry.

A proud but also humane man, he leaves behind a large cohort of scientists whose careers blossomed in different ways because of him: something of which he was most proud. His portrait resides in the National Portrait Gallery.

HONOURS, POSTS AND AWARDS

Appointments

1944–46	Commission in Radar Branch, Royal Air Force
1947–48	Shirley Research Fellow, University of Nottingham
1948–57	Lecturer in Meteorology, Imperial College, London
1957–61	Warren Research Fellow, the Royal Society
1959–60	Visiting Professor, University of California
1961–65	Professor of Cloud Physics, Imperial College, London

1965–75	Member, Executive Committee of the WMO
1965–83	Director-General, Meteorological Office
1965–83	Permanent Representative of the UK with the WMO
1968–70	President, Royal Meteorological Society
1970–75	Chairman of Council, University of Surrey
1971–76	Chairman, International Tropical Experiment Board
1976–78	President, Institute of Physics
1976–86	Treasurer and Senior Vice-President, the Royal Society
1977–83	Member, Executive Committee of the WMO
1979–85	Pro-Chancellor, University of Surrey
1982–83	President, British Association for the Advancement of Science
1983–87	Member, Advisory Board of the Research Councils
1983–90	Director, Anglo-Scandinavian Research Programme on Acidification of Surface Waters
1985–89	Chairman, International Scientific Committee, World Climate Research Programme
1986–96	President, then Chancellor, University of Manchester Institute of Science and Technology
1987–91	Chairman, Co-ordinating Committee on Marine Science and Technology
1989–91	President, National Society for Clean Air and Environmental Protection
1992–93	President, Association for Science Education
1990–2000	Senior adviser to the Global Environment Research Centre, Imperial College

Honours

1965	Fellow of the Royal Society
1973	Companion of the Order of the Bath
1979	Knight Bachelor
1988	Member, Academia Europaea
	Honorary Member, Royal Meteorological Society
1989	Honorary Member, American Meteorological Society
2004	Mason Centre for Environmental Flows opened at University of Manchester
2006	Mason Gold Medal established by Royal Meteorological Society (endowed by Mason)
2007	Honorary Fellow, Institute of Physics

Honorary degrees (DSc)

1966	Nottingham
1970	Durham
1975	Strathclyde
1980	City of London
1983	Sussex
1988	East Anglia
1990	Plymouth Polytechnic
	Heriot-Watt
	Edinburgh
1998	Reading

Honorary fellowships

1974	Imperial College
1979	University of Manchester Institute of Science and Technology (UMIST)

Awards

1959	Hugh Robert Mill Medal, Royal Meteorological Society
1965	Charles Chree Medal and Prize, Institute of Physics
1972	Bakerian Lecture and Prize, the Royal Society
	Rumford Medal, the Royal Society
	Glazebrook Medal, Institute of Physics
1975	Symons Memorial Gold Medal, Royal Meteorological Society
1979	Naylor Prize, London Mathematical Society
1988	Plymouth Marine Science Medal
1990	British Coal Science Gold Medal
	Royal Medal, the Royal Society

Special lectureships

1967	James Forest, Institute of Civil Engineers
1968	Kelvin, Institute of Electrical Engineers
	Dalton, Royal Institute of Chemistry
1975	Hugh MacMillan Memorial, Institute of Engineers & Shipbuilders in Scotland
1976	Symons, Royal Meteorological Society
1977	Halley, Oxford University
1978	Oliver Dodge, Birmingham University
1979	Larmor, Queen's University, Belfast
1985	Macaulay, Macaulay Land Use Research Institute, Aberdeen
1987	Jesse Boot, Nottingham University
	Ramanathan Memorial, India
	Bhattacharya Memorial, India
1989	Larmor, Cambridge University
	Rayleigh, Harrow School
	Bowden, UMIST
1990	Cockcroft, UMIST
	Linacre, Oxford University
	Rutherford Memorial, Royal Society, in Canada
	H. L. Welch Memorial, University of Toronto
	British Coal Science

ACKNOWLEDGEMENTS

The author is grateful to Keith Moore of the Royal Society, and to Liz Bentley and Tim Jennings of the Royal Meteorological Society, for obtaining documents from archives. Particular thanks are due to the following for sharing their knowledge and experiences: David Axford, Peter Collins, Stan Cornford, Sylvia Hobbs, Julian Hunt, Peter Jonas, John Latham, Nigel Parfitt, Jack Talling, Peter Warren, Austin Woods and John Zillman.

The frontispiece photograph was taken in 1967 by Godfrey Argent and is reproduced with permission.

REFERENCES TO OTHER AUTHORS

Bulman, P. J. & Browning, K. A. 1971 *National weather radar network*. Royal Radar Establishment Report, July. (17 pages.)

Cole, R. 2015 The importance of picking Porter. *Notes Rec.* **69**, 191–216.

Collinge, V. K. 1987 The development of weather radar in the United Kingdom. In *Weather radar and flood forecasting* (ed. V. K. Collinge & C. Kirby), pp. 3–18. Chichester: Wiley.

Hardman, M. E., James, D. G. & Goldsmith, P. 1972 The measurement of mesoscale vertical motions in the atmosphere. *Q. J. R. Meteorol. Soc.* **98**, 38–47.

Royal Meteorological Society 1985 Transcript of interview of Sir John Mason by R. J. Ogden at the premises of the Royal Society, Carlton House Terrace, London. 4 June 1985. (53 pages.)

Jonas, P. R. 1996 Turbulence and cloud microphysics. *Atmos. Res.* **40** (2), 283–306.

Taba, H. T. 1995 The *Bulletin* interviews—Sir John Mason. *WMO Bull.* **44**, 315–325.

WMO 1972 Experiment design proposal for the GARP Atlantic Tropical Experiment (excluding annexes). Geneva: World Meteorological Organization (WMO), Global Atmospheric Research Programme (GARP), GARP Atlantic Tropical Experiment (GATE). (vii + 188 pages.) QC/993.5/G6324/no.1.

Woods, A. 2006 *Medium-range weather prediction: the European approach*. New York: Springer. (288 pages.)

BIBLIOGRAPHY

The following articles and books are those referred to directly in the text and constitute a small subset of more than 250 papers by John Mason, published mainly in meteorological and physics journals.

(1) 1950 The nature of ice-forming nuclei in the atmosphere. *Q. J. R. Meteorol. Soc.* **76**, 59–74.

(2) 1951 (With F. H. Ludlam) The microphysics of clouds. *Rep. Prog. Phys.* **14**, 147–195.

(3) 1956 (With J. Hallett) Artificial ice-forming nuclei. *Nature* **177**, 681–683.

(4) 1957 (With J. Hallett) Ice-forming nuclei. *Nature* **179**, 357–359.

(5) (With F. H. Ludlam) *The physics of clouds* (*Handbuch der Physik* (ed J. Bartels), vol. 10, pp. 479–540). Berlin: Springer.

(6) *The physics of clouds*. Oxford: Clarendon Press. (481 pages.)

(7) 1958 (With J. Hallett) The influence of temperature and supersaturation on the habit of ice crystals grown from the vapour. *Proc. R. Soc. Lond.* A **247**, 440–453.

(8) 1961 (With J. Latham) Electric charge transfer associated with temperature gradients in ice. *Proc. R. Soc. Lond.* A **260**, 523–536.

(9) 1962 (With C. W. Chien) Cloud droplet growth by condensation in cumulus. *Q. J. R. Meteorol. Soc.*, **83**, 136–142.

(10) *Clouds, rain and rainmaking*. Cambridge University Press. (145 pages.)

(11) 1963 (With G. W. Bryant & A. P. Van Den Heuvel) The growth habits and surface structure of ice crystals. *Phil. Mag.* **8**, 505–526.

(12) 1972 The Bakerian Lecture, 1971. The physics of the thunderstorm. *Proc. R. Soc. Lond.* A **327**, 433–466.

(13) 1981 (With K. A. Browning) Air motion and precipitation growth in frontal systems. *PAGEOPH* (Bergeron Memorial Volume) **119**, 577–593.

(14) 1985 (With H. M. Seip) The current state of knowledge of surface waters and guidelines for further research. *Ambio* **14**, 45–51.

(15) 1990 (Editor) *Results of the Anglo-Scandinavian Acid Rain Research Programme*. Cambridge University Press.

(16) 1992 *Acid rain: its causes and its effects on inland waters*. Oxford: Clarendon Press. (136 pages.)

(17) 2010 *The Meteorological Office (1965–83): reflections by Sir John Mason CB DSc FRS on his time as Director-General of the Meteorological Office*. Royal Meteorological Society report. (28 pages.)

JOHN BRYCE McLEOD

23 December 1929 — 20 August 2014

JOHN BRYCE McLEOD

23 December 1929 — 20 August 2014

Elected FRS 1992

By Stuart Hastings*

Professor Emeritus of Mathematics, University of Pittsburgh, Pittsburgh, USA

J. B. McLeod was a brilliant solver of problems in mathematical analysis, primarily differential equations. He received his FRS in 1992, and the citation reads in part: 'Distinguished for many significant contributions to applied analysis, particularly to the theory of partial differential equations with applications to practical problems. ... By the exemplary precision and power of his publications and his lectures, he has become internationally recognized as the leading British authority on the useful applications of functional analysis.' In addition, in 2011 McLeod was awarded the Naylor Prize and Lectureship of the London Mathematical Society 'in recognition of his important and versatile achievements in the analysis of nonlinear equations arising in applications to mechanics, physics, and biology.' He collaborated widely, and was a resource for many applied mathematicians who wanted to have a more rigorous foundation for their work. He leaves a hole that will be hard to fill.

1. Overview

When Bryce McLeod was 10 years old, his home city of Aberdeen was under threat of German bombs. As a result, his schooling was partly interrupted, and so his parents sent him to his grandfather, a former Head of Mathematics at Aberdeen Grammar School, for instruction. Apparently, this gentleman had lost track of what mathematics a 10-year-old would have been exposed to, and he began the first lesson with algebra, completing linear equations in about 15 minutes and then delving into the quadratic equation. Young Bryce, having seen nothing beyond arithmetic before, had no idea what these x's and y's were about, but was too in awe of his grandfather to admit this. He went home with an assignment, and agonized for hours

* sph@math.pitt.edu

http://dx.doi.org/10.1098/rsbm.2015.0031

Published by the Royal Society

trying to determine what was going on. But when he returned the next day he was able to solve every quadratic equation his grandfather gave him*,†.

John Bryce McLeod was born on 23 December 1929, in Aberdeen. His parents were John McLeod, an engineer, and Adeline Annie Bryce. His paternal grandfather was raised on a farm but had been recognized by his teachers as bright, and he was encouraged to attend Aberdeen University.

Bryce's father and one of his uncles were engineers, and another uncle read mathematics at Cambridge, so he was following in a family tradition when at the age of 16 years he went off to study mathematics at Aberdeen University. Upon graduation he was awarded a stipend enabling him to continue his education at Oxford, where he received his second first-class honours degree, again in mathematics. After an interlude for study abroad and National Service he completed his DPhil at Oxford in 1958, under the direction of E. C. Titchmarsh FRS, the leading analyst there at the time.

He took a position at Edinburgh University, but in 1960 he accepted a Fellowship back in Oxford, at Wadham College. He became a University Lecturer, and his research in what is now called 'applied analysis' flourished.

Applied analysis is largely the rigorous study of differential equations and optimization problems arising in the sciences and engineering. McLeod's research in this area was widely recognized in the UK and abroad, but not so much in Oxford, for reasons I will discuss later. Dissatisfaction with his situation within Oxford Mathematics, and also the mandatory retirement he saw looming, led to his departure for the University of Pittsburgh in 1987. Pittsburgh had strong people in differential equations, and neighbouring Carnegie Mellon University also had a first-class group in this area.

He stayed in Pittsburgh for 20 productive years. During this period, ironically, he received an enquiry from a senior mathematician at Cambridge inviting him to apply for a chair there. He had to reply that he was beyond the mandatory retirement age.

McLeod's influence did much to resuscitate applied analysis in the UK. One indication of this was his FRS, awarded while he was in Pittsburgh. Others around Britain, including John Ball, were encouraged in their interest in differential equations by his work. His Oxford graduate students gained professorships at Exeter (later Canterbury), EPFL Lausanne, Heriot-Watt, Michigan and North Carolina State, and in Brazil.

McLeod collaborated widely in differential equations, where he was recognized as a problem solver of genius. These collaborations frequently developed when another mathematician had a problem from an applied area that he found intractable and brought it to McLeod's attention. Very often the result would be a new but simple way of looking at the problem that led to an ingenious solution.

It is symbolic of the revival of applied analysis in the UK in the past 30 years that the 2011 Naylor Prize and Lectureship of the London Mathematical Society was presented to J. B. McLeod, 'in recognition of his important and versatile achievements in the analysis of nonlinear equations arising in applications to mechanics, physics, and biology.'

---

* This story, and some other material in this memoir, came from the interview that McLeod did with Sir John Ball FRS of Oxford University in January 2014. Both participants realized the seriousness of McLeod's illness at the time of the interview, a video of which is available online at https://www.maths.ox.ac.uk/node/891.
† Much of this section was taken from Hastings (2014).

In addition to the honours mentioned above, McLeod was awarded the Whittaker Prize of the Edinburgh Mathematical Society in 1965 and the Keith Medal and Prize of the Royal Society of Edinburgh in 1987, and was elected a Fellow of the Royal Society of Edinburgh in 1974. He died on 20 August 2014 and is survived by his wife, four children and three grandchildren.

2. STUDENT YEARS

Bryce, his father, and very probably his grandfather were each the top student ('dux') in their turn at Aberdeen Grammar School, and hence had their pictures posted in a hallway. Many years later Bryce paid a return visit to the school, out of term. He was spotted by a custodian, who ordered this very casually dressed visitor to leave. Unfortunately, there had been a fire at the school in which the dux pictures were destroyed, and so Bryce was unable to point out his photo to the custodian as evidence that he should not be turned out.

It was assumed in those days that bright students from northern Scotland would go to Aberdeen University. Bryce had known from his early teens that he wanted to study mathematics, and at Aberdeen he found a more than competent mathematical faculty. The best-known mathematician there during Bryce's time was E. M. Wright, co-author with G. H. Hardy FRS of a classic book on number theory and winner of the Senior Berwick Prize of the London Mathematical Society in 1978. It was Wright who encouraged Bryce to go further in mathematics and probably Wright who found the funds that enabled him to do so at Oxford. At that time he envisaged a life as a school teacher, following in the footsteps of his grandfather.

At Oxford, Bryce fell under the influence of Theodore Chaundy, a mathematician remembered today especially for his work in hypergeometric functions. Bryce admired Chaundy greatly, and nearly 20 years later, having completed his DPhil with Titchmarsh and established himself in research, he wrote that when he came up to Christ Church as an undergraduate to read mathematics, he 'became exposed to a mathematical mind which for sheer speed and restlessness, was quite unequalled in my experience then – or, for that matter, since' (11)*.

After completing his first-class honours in mathematics at Oxford, Bryce took a somewhat unusual path. He was, under circumstances that he was unable to remember during the Ball interview, awarded a Rotary scholarship, apparently as a result of actions taken in Aberdeen. This enabled him to travel 'anywhere in the world', presumably to study mathematics. Here, it appears to this outside observer, Chaundy's advice was a bit strange, for he recommended going to the University of British Columbia, not a powerhouse in pure mathematics at that time. Bryce duly followed this suggestion, and in (31) he expressed no regrets; on the contrary he was very positive about the contacts he made there, especially a long-time friend who, as I will describe later, proved very helpful in his subsequent mathematical career.

The time at UBC apparently did cause him to shift his interest permanently from school teaching to mathematical research. When he returned, he was required to do national service, which involved low-level teaching as an Education Officer in the RAF. After this he started his research with Titchmarsh.

Bryce's first publication, joint with Chaundy, appeared in print in 1958, the year of his DPhil (1). The reviewer for *Mathematical Reviews* said: 'By an ingenious sequence of

* Numbers in this form refer to the bibliography at the end of the text.

formal manipulations the authors prove that the form of the solution depends on a quadratic characteristic equation.' His second paper (2) had the surprising title 'On the commutator subring'; surprising because I doubt that many of his friends realize that he had a publication in algebra. The reviewer wrote: 'By a simple but ingenious computation, it is shown that the subring of S generated by all commutators $rs - sr$ is a two-sided ideal in S.' Again, 'ingenious', a word not used lightly by mathematicians. But it can be said to apply to a large number of the proofs of J. B. McLeod (as he preferred to sign his papers)*.

In (31) Bryce tells this story. Titchmarsh gave regular seminars on his work, often with Bryce as the only member of the audience, during one of which he mentioned a point that was still unresolved. Bryce thought he could say something about this, and after couple of days put some notes on the problem in Titchmarsh's 'pigeonhole'. In a week he found in his own pigeonhole the complete manuscript of a paper by McLeod and Titchmarsh. Apparently there was not one word exchanged between them in the preparation of this paper. In later years, and in the Ball video, Bryce made it clear that mathematical and social interchanges with other mathematicians were among his principal rewards for tackling such a hard topic as mathematics. It seems that there was none of this with his advisor.

3. Family

Bryce had a happy childhood, and his parents, both intelligent people, accepted his inclination to disappear into his room to study mathematics. Like Bryce, his sister Morag obtained a first-class honours degree at Aberdeen University, hers being in chemistry.

Bryce met his future wife, Eunice Martin Third, while they were both at school. Eunice chose to skip university and become a nurse, continuing to work in the medical field after their marriage in 1956 and the concurrent move to Oxford. Their first two children, Kevin and Callum, were born in the UK, and the last two, twins Bridget and Patrick, came on the scene in Madison, Wisconsin, where Bryce took a year's leave in 1964–65.

Kevin was the only child who went into mathematics, obtaining his PhD at the University of Minnesota under the direction of James Serrin and making his career at the University of Wisconsin, Milwaukee. He has one joint paper with his father. Callum became a musician, working in a mixture of classical music, as conductor and performer, and theatrical music, conducting performances of *Phantom of the Opera* in London for many years. Bridget went into school teaching, becoming a head teacher in Berkshire and organizing many school musical performances. Patrick took a degree in chemical engineering and became a vice-president at Dow Corning Corporation, working at various times in Belgium, France and China. Bryce, with good reason, was proud of all his children. He was, however, much engrossed in his work, so we should give considerable credit to Eunice for their success. Beyond that, Eunice undoubtedly made Bryce's career possible with her so-called 'supporting role' at home.

In 1964–65 Bryce took leave at the Mathematics Research Center at the University of Wisconsin, Madison, accompanied by his family. He had made contact with the group there

---

* Co-authors sometimes persuaded him to be less formal, using J. Bryce McLeod or even, in few instances, Bryce McLeod.

Figure 1. Kevin, Callum, Bridget, Eunice, Patrick and Bryce, around 1965. (Online version in colour.)

with the help of Tommy Hull, the friend from Vancouver whom I mentioned above (31). This year was rewarding for Bryce mathematically and for the whole family socially. He found the MRC a revelation, particularly because he felt that applied analysis was properly appreciated there. From then until 1986 he spent most summers in Madison, with his family joining him for parts of these visits.

During those summers the family journeyed several times across the USA in the Winnebago camper van that Bryce had bought to live in while there. At Bryce's funeral Patrick spoke of these journeys:

> I look back with great fondness on those road trips around the US—Mexico, the Canyon lands, Mesa Verde, the Badlands, California and the West Coast, New England during the bicentenary year, Banff, the Canadian National Parks. There were times, of course, when the experiences weren't fully appreciated by the rest of the family, and that would annoy Dad, but his intentions were always to provide us with opportunities to learn and to develop interests that many children of our ages would never have had.

Bryce was the family photographer and documented their travels. The photograph in figure 1 is one of the very few that the family have of Bryce himself. It was taken on one of those cross-country trips.

Although Bryce and his family travelled to many parts of the world, established temporary homes during sabbaticals in Wisconsin, Minnesota and Sydney, and moved for 20 years to Pittsburgh, the house they bought in Abingdon in 1960 remained in many ways the centre of their lives together. They kept this house throughout all of their sojourns abroad.

Nevertheless, from 1987 to 2007 Eunice and Bryce made a home in Pittsburgh, enjoying particularly the local classical music scene. Their Pittsburgh home, like the house in Abingdon, held a grand piano, for Bryce to play and accompany Eunice on. It was with mixed feelings that they moved back to Abingdon after his retirement from Pitt.

Bryce was an excellent after-dinner speaker. In my experience one of his best speeches was at the conference organized in Oxford for his 70th birthday. After Bryce died, a Pittsburgh colleague, Carson Chow, wrote:

> One of the highlights of my career was being invited to a conference in his honour in Oxford in 2001. At the conference dinner, Bryce gave the most perfectly constructed speech I have ever heard. It was just like the way he did mathematics—elegantly and sublimely.

His family remembers particularly a speech he gave at his daughter Bridget's wedding, which brought her into a family with surname McGregor. His version of the history of the McGregors, perhaps not entirely favourable to that ancient clan, had both families in stitches.

It appears, however, that mathematical audiences were not always so able to take his wit in stride. On at least two occasions speeches he gave at birthday celebrations for a mathematician were interpreted by some in the audience as veiled criticisms of the celebrant, couched in humour. But his family, who of course knew Bryce best, are sure that he was much too straightforward for such a device. They maintain, for example, that when one honouree was described as being like Pooh-Bah in *The Mikado*, who held many important positions simultaneously, this was solely for its humorous effect.

4. HIS MATHEMATICS

McLeod's mathematical specialty, applied analysis, is a bridge between pure and applied mathematics. In the 1940s and 1950s, major figures in this area in the UK included Titchmarsh, M. L. (later Dame Mary) Cartwright FRS and J. E. Littlewood FRS, but then the subject fell in stature in comparison with such areas as abstract algebra and topology. After Titchmarsh's death in 1966, no specialist in differential equations held a chair at Oxford (or Cambridge) until John Ball FRS was appointed Sedleian Professor 30 years later. I have included below a section about the reasons for the lack of interest in applied analysis at Oxford in the 1970s and 1980s, but first I shall describe a selection of McLeod's most influential papers*.

4.1. Linear problems

Of McLeod's first 34 published papers, 30 were in differential equations; of these, most were on linear ordinary differential equations. This was to be expected for a student of Titchmarsh, whose mastery of the linear ordinary differential equation (ODE) domain was unsurpassed. Of his subsequent 128 papers, from 1968 to 2015, only 10 can be characterized as linear. And among his most cited papers, including two before 1968, all except one are on nonlinear problems. So my relative incompetence in linear ODEs is not the only reason that I will emphasize the nonlinear work here.

However, some of McLeod's papers on linear problems do bear particular mention. A striking indication of the importance of his early work is that many of these papers continue to be cited in the twenty-first century. Using Google Scholar I have found that about half of McLeod's 34 papers published before 1968 had citations from the year 2000 or later. Among those on linear topics were papers on Schrödinger's equation (3, 8), and the number of L^2

---

* A suggestion to readers not trained in mathematics, taken from an excellent book (Yandell 2002): if you come to material you don't understand, 'skip a bit if you want—the biographical narrative will pick up again. Pretend you are reading *Moby Dick*, and have come to another chapter on whaling.'

solutions of a class of ODEs (4, 6). Some of the early papers had citations 50 years or more after they were written.

The best known of McLeod's papers on linear equations is work he did in about 1970 with Tosio Kato of the University of California at Berkeley (13). Kato, one of the most eminent of McLeod's collaborators, visited Oxford in the early 1970s. The problem he and McLeod worked on was about 'wave motion in the overhead supply line to an electrified railway system'. They obtained several results, but the work was unfinished when Kato returned to Berkeley. Later, when McLeod sent him a solution to the problem they had been stuck on, Kato wrote back: 'How on earth did you think of that?' (31). Many of McLeod's collaborators over the years had the same question.

The functional–differential equation

$$y'(x) = ay(\lambda x) + by(x) \text{ for } x > 0, \qquad [1]$$

$$\lim_{x \to 0^+} y(x) = 1. \qquad [2]$$

This equation, derived by Ockendon & Taylor (1971), is not an ordinary differential equation unless $\lambda = 1$. In (13) a may be complex, b is real, and λ is real and non-negative, but here I will consider only the physical case of real solutions with a real.

The cases $\lambda = 0$ and $\lambda = 1$ being trivial, we assume that $0 < \lambda < 1$ or $\lambda > 1$*. The theory is more complete if $\lambda < 1$. In this case, setting $x = e^s$, $\lambda = e^c$ and $y(x) = z(s)$ gives a delay equation in standard form,

$$z'(s) = az(s + c) + bz(s),$$

where $c < 0$ since $\lambda < 1$. From this it is seen that the standard existence and uniqueness theory for linear delay differential equations applies. The interest then is in the asymptotic behaviour of solutions for large x.

In the case $b < 0$, for example, McLeod and Kato were able to show that if $\lambda < 1$, then every solution of [1] can be written in the form

$$y(x) = x^k [g(\log x) + o(1)] \text{ as } x \to \infty,$$

where

$$k = \log\left(-\frac{b}{a}\right) / \log \lambda$$

and g is a C^∞ periodic function of period $|\log \lambda|$. There is such a solution for any such g.

Perhaps the most interesting twist in this paper is a relation that is revealed between the asymptotic behaviours for $\lambda < 1$ and $\lambda > 1$. This result is too technical to give here, but I suspect that it was the cause of Kato's laudatory question mentioned above.

4.2. Nonlinearity—before and after Edinburgh

4.2.1. Coagulation

But still, most of McLeod's influence eventually is likely to be from his papers on nonlinear differential equations, all except two of which were published after a 1968 conference in Edinburgh that he helped organize and where he met James Serrin. It was in Serrin's Edinburgh

---

* Both cases are discussed in Ockendon & Taylor (1971).

lectures that McLeod first began to appreciate the interest and importance of nonlinearity in applied analysis. I start, though, with the paper from 1962 (5).

On an infinite set of nonlinear differential equations

This paper was far ahead of its time. It received almost four times as many citations in the years 2011–14 as it did up to 1980. In the video (31), McLeod tells the story of meeting the theoretical chemist William Byers Brown, later Professor at the University of Manchester, while each was fulfilling his national service requirement by teaching at the Royal Air Force Technical College in Henlow, Bedfordshire. Byers Brown, a friend for many years thereafter, introduced McLeod to coagulation theory, and this was the subject of his first paper on nonlinear differential equations.

The title above is rather general but now it might be 'On the discrete form of Smoluchowski's equation'. This equation was developed in 1916 by a pioneer in statistical physics, Marian Smoluchowski, who worked at the University of Lwów in Poland. It is usually written as a single integral equation:

$$\frac{\partial n(x, t)}{\partial t} = \frac{1}{2} \int_0^x K(x - y)n(x - y, t)n(y, t) - \int_0^\infty K(x, y)n(x, t)n(y, t)\mathrm{d}y.$$

The discrete version considered by McLeod in the first of his papers on the topic is, as his title indicates, an infinite system:

$$\frac{\mathrm{d}n_1}{\mathrm{d}t} = -n_1 \sum_{i=1}^{\infty} K_{1i}n_i,$$

$$\frac{\mathrm{d}n_i}{\mathrm{d}t} = \frac{1}{2} \sum_{j=1}^{i-1} K_{j,i-j}n_j n_{i-j} - n_i \sum_{j=1}^{\infty} K_{ij}n_j, \ i \geq 2. \tag{3}$$

The standard initial conditions are

$$n_1(0) = 1,$$
$$n_i(0) = 0 \text{ if } i \geq 1. \tag{4}$$

Smoluchowski's model has been studied extensively by mathematicians for the past 30 years, but in 1962 it was all but unknown in the mathematical community. McLeod states that the only previous pure mathematical work on the equation was for cases where the kernel K is bounded.

He first considered a distinctly unbounded case, $K(i, j) = ij$. What motivated him to do so is not made clear, but it is this part of the paper that has been most influential in the subsequent decades. His analysis of this case can be repeated in full:

For $i \geq 2$ multiply the equations by i and then sum over i, giving

$$\sum_{i=1}^{\infty} i \frac{\mathrm{d}n_i}{\mathrm{d}t} = \frac{1}{2} \sum_{i=1}^{\infty} i \sum_{j=1}^{i-1} j(i - j)n_j n_{i-j} - \sum_{i=1}^{\infty} i^2 n_i \sum_{j=1}^{\infty} ji\, n_j. \tag{5}$$

Proceed 'by noting that' if either term is multiplied out, then the total coefficient of $n_i n_j$ is $(i + j)ij$.

This and [4] imply that

$$\sum_{i=1}^{\infty} i \frac{dn_i}{dt} = 0,$$

$$\sum_{i=1}^{\infty} i \, n_i = 1,$$

and so

$$n_1' = n_1,$$
$$n_1(t) = e^t.$$

This allows one to solve successively for $n_2, n_3, \cdots$ and there results the exact solution

$$n_j(t) = \frac{t^{j-1} j^{j-2}}{j! e^{jt}}, \ 0 \leq t < 1.$$

It is remarkable that one can find an exact solution for such a complicated system. Perhaps the major step here was to hope that one could do so.

4.2.2. One of Serrin's problems

The existence of similar solutions for some laminar boundary value problems
(1968, with James Serrin)

The equations are those of K. Stewartson (FRS 1965) (Stewartson 1949) for similarity solutions of the boundary-layer equations for compressible flow over a surface. They are

$$f''' + ff'' + \mu(h - f'^2) = 0,$$
$$h'' + fh' = 0,$$

[6]

with boundary conditions

$$f(0) = f'(0) = 0, \ h(0) = a,$$
$$\lim_{x \to \infty} f'(x) = \lim_{x \to \infty} h(x) = 1.$$

[7]

The problem addressed by McLeod and Serrin in (9) was the existence of a solution to this problem.

This was the first of many uses by McLeod of the so-called 'shooting method' for proving the existence of a solution to an ODE boundary-value problem. Although the method had been used earlier, for example by Wazewski, I suspect that McLeod was not aware of this and came up with it himself, developing a more straightforward version.

In the shooting method, one assumes enough additional initial conditions to specify a unique solution and then tries to find values for these additional initial conditions such that the boundary conditions at infinity are satisfied. Thus, suppose that

$$f''(0) = \alpha, \ h'(0) = \beta.$$

[8]

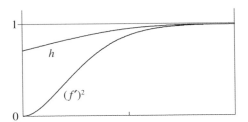

Figure 2. An expected solution to [6]–[7].

The goal is to choose α and β so that [7] is satisfied. The idea is to sort out various ways in which the solution can go wrong and fail to satisfy the boundary conditions at infinity. On the basis of numerical computations one can expect graphs of $(f')^2$ and h for a solution satisfying [7] to look like figure 2. In particular, we look for a solution with f' increasing. My presentation below is slightly simplified from that of McLeod and Serrin because they treated a more general class of systems, including one other important application. For the problem [6]–[7], one can find two specific ways in which the solution (f, h) to [6]–[8] can go wrong and not solve [7], or even the conditions $f'' \geq 0$ and $f'(\infty)^2 = h(\infty)$.

(i) $f'' > 0$ and $(f')^2$ increases above h. This happens if, for a given $\beta = h'(0)$, α is very large;

(ii) f'' becomes negative. This happens if α is zero, because $f'''(0) < 0$.

Suppose that $\mathcal{A}$ is the set of initial conditions $(\alpha, \beta) \in R^2$ such that (i) occurs, and $\mathcal{B}$ is the set of (α, β) such that (ii) occurs.

McLeod and Serrin show, essentially, that there is a rectangle R in the (α, β) plane such that the left side of R is contained in $\mathcal{A}$ and the right side of R is contained in $\mathcal{B}$ (figure 3). Also, $\mathcal{A}$ and $\mathcal{B}$ are disjoint and open. Then they use the following result from point set topology.

Lemma 4.1. *Under the given conditions on $\mathcal{A}$ and $\mathcal{B}$ there is a continuum $\Gamma \subset R$ that intersects neither A nor B and which connects the top and the bottom of R*.*

It is easy to show that if $(\alpha, \beta) \in \Gamma$ then $f'(\infty)^2$ and $h'(\infty)$ exist and are equal.

Their final step, relatively straightforward, is to show that the limits above are continuous functions of (α, β) in Γ and that R can be chosen so that at every point in the top of $R \cap \Gamma$ the two limits are above 1 and at every point in the bottom of $R \cap \Gamma$ these limits are below 1. The result follows.

4.3. Swirling flow

In the period 1969–75 McLeod wrote seven papers on the general problem of the symmetric flow above an infinite rotating disk, or between two infinite rotating disks. These problems were introduced by von Kármán and are called problems in 'swirling flow'. Here I will briefly describe the results in two of these papers.

---

* Topologists today would prove this by using some form of degree theory or algebraic topology. McLeod and Serrin give an elementary proof 'from scratch'.

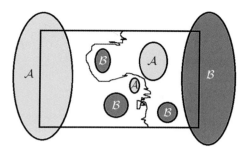

Figure 3. The plane of initial conditions α, β. One expects that the sets $\mathcal{A}$ and $\mathcal{B}$ fill the entire plane except for a set of measure zero.

4.3.1. Flow between two disks

On the flow between two counter-rotating infinite plane disks
(1969, with S. Parter)

One of the contacts whom McLeod made at the Mathematics Research Center in Madison was S. V. Parter, with whom he wrote two papers on swirling flow. One of these (14) resolved a dispute between two distinguished applied mathematicians about the boundary-layer behaviour of the flow.

In the situation where the angular velocities of the two rotating disks were of equal magnitude but opposite in signs, K. Stewartson had maintained that the main body of the flow was at rest, with boundary layers at each plate (Stewartson 1953), whereas G. K. Batchelor (FRS 1957) argued that the transition between the angular velocities of the two plates occurred in a narrow region in the middle (Batchelor 1951). By making the asymptotic analysis of Stewartson rigorous, McLeod and Parter disproved the conjecture of Batchelor.

To me this paper beautifully illustrates one role that applied analysis can play for applied mathematicians. Other papers of McLeod's in which rigorous mathematics was used to disprove 'results' that had been obtained by formal asymptotic arguments include (20) and (27). Among papers in which he confirmed the results of more applied researchers I can mention (10), (28) and, I presume, most of the papers that he co-authored with applied mathematicians, such as (29), (21) and (19).

4.3.2. Flow above a single disk—use of continuation

The existence of axially symmetric flow above a rotating disk
(1971)

Paper (12) solved perhaps the most basic problem in the area, one that had eluded some excellent mathematicians since von Kármán developed the model in 1921. I chose it to discuss for two reasons: it is an impressive piece of analysis, and it marks McLeod's first use of a technique that he was to use again in some important work in areas unrelated to fluid mechanics: the technique of continuation.

The idealized physical problem studied here is that of single infinite disk rotating with angular velocity Ω_0, and fluid occupying the half-space $x > 0$ above this disk. The fluid is assumed to have an imposed angular velocity of Ω_∞ at $x = \infty$. Von Kármán showed that the problem reduces to the study of two ODEs with boundary conditions:

$$f''' + ff'' + \tfrac{1}{2}(g^2 - f'^2) = \tfrac{1}{2}\Omega_\infty^2, \tag{9}$$

$$g'' + fg' = f'g, \tag{10}$$

$$f(0) = a, \; f'(0) = 0, \tag{11}$$

$$g(0) = \Omega_0, \; f'(\infty) = 0, \; g(\infty) = \Omega_\infty. \tag{12}$$

Here a is a parameter measuring possible suction at the plate. The problem with this term in it was brought to McLeod's attention by his colleague Hilary Ockendon.

The relation of x, f and g to physical quantities is via a similarity substitution in the original partial differential equations, and we omit those details.

McLeod had previously proved the existence of a solution to this problem when $\Omega_\infty = 0$. In this paper he proves existence if Ω_0 and Ω_∞ have the same sign, for any value of a. In assessing this proof we must remember that this was done in the years before 'bifurcation' theory became a prominent topic in applied analysis. What he does here anticipates this theory by analysing the bifurcation curve of solutions in, for example, the $(\Omega_0, f''(0))$ plane. I point out the following remark in the paper:

> There is evidently a close affinity between this pattern of proof and the general existence theorem of Leray & Schauder (1934). There the existence of a non-zero index (which is closely allied to the idea of an odd number of solutions) for one value of a parameter is used to prove the existence for other values of the parameter. It must be possible, if not probable, that the existence theorem of the present paper can be treated as an application (although a highly non-trivial one) of the Leray–Schauder result, but it does seem that the work involved in approaching the problem from this angle leads to a more complicated presentation rather than a simpler one, and it is not attempted here.

In this sentence we can see the essence of McLeod's approach to problems of this sort. He believed, and often showed, that in many cases getting to the heart of a particular problem with standard analysis yields more insights and easier proofs than application of wide-ranging theories.

In McLeod's proof Ω_∞ is considered fixed, and positive for definiteness, and Ω_0 is a parameter. There is a trivial (constant) solution when $\Omega_0 = \Omega_\infty$. He shows, importantly, that this solution is unique, and by methods akin to the implicit function theorem, but in infinite dimensions, he then shows that there is a locally unique solution for $\Omega_0 - \Omega_\infty$ small. Assuming that $\Omega_0 > \Omega_\infty$ and a solution exists for Ω_0 in some interval $(\Omega_\infty, \Omega^*)$, he concludes that a solution exists if $\Omega_0 = \Omega^*$. Further, he proves that these solutions can be chosen so that $g > 0$, meaning that the whole body of fluid is rotating in the same direction.

He wishes to show that solutions exist for $\Omega_0 > \Omega^*$ and close to Ω^*. Using series expansions and some deep but classical results from analysis, he finds that if this is not the case then there must be a second branch of solutions that goes back from Ω^* and merges with the first branch at $\Omega_0 = \Omega_\infty$. But this contradicts the local uniqueness near Ω_∞ proved earlier, and this is the basic step in proving existence for all $\Omega_0 > \Omega_\infty$. A similar proof gives existence for $0 < \Omega_0 < \Omega_\infty$.

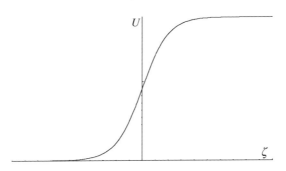

Figure 4. Front moves to the left.

5. Two important papers on partial differential equations

The term differential equation is usually taken to refer to one of two types: ordinary differential equations, in which there is only one independent variable, often time, and partial differential equations (PDEs), in which there are several independent variables, such as the three spatial coordinates. The majority of McLeod's work in differential equations involved ODEs, although often these are of a type derived from a PDE. However, of his six most cited papers, only one can be considered purely a problem in ODEs. The three with the greatest number of citations are all on PDEs, which is an indication of the greater importance attached by much of the modern applied analysis community to work in multivariable problems. I will now give some details on two of these three.

5.1. Limiting behaviour of time dependent solutions

The approach of solutions of nonlinear diffusion equations to travelling front solutions
(with Paul Fife, 1977)

Many authors refer to this article (15) as the 'classic paper of Fife and McLeod'. The general topic is nonlinear diffusion in a homogeneous medium where there can also occur chemical reactions. Fife and McLeod considered so-called 'excitable media', in which an initial stimulus at one point develops into a wave travelling out from the initial point at a steady speed. With one spatial variable the relevant PDE is of the form used by R. FitzHugh and by J. Nagumo:

$$u_t = u_{xx} + u(1 - u)(u - a), \qquad [13]$$

where $0 < a < \frac{1}{2}$ and initial conditions are assumed:

$$u(x, 0) = \phi(x), \quad -\infty < x < \infty.$$

First one looks for travelling wave solutions, by which is meant a solution of the form $u(x, t) = U(x + ct)$. A physically relevant solution must be bounded, and it is not hard to show that if $0 < a < \frac{1}{2}$ and $c > 0$ then a non-constant bounded travelling wave solution must satisfy (figure 4)

$$\lim_{\zeta \to -\infty} U(\zeta) = 0, \quad \lim_{\zeta \to \infty} U(\zeta) = 1.$$

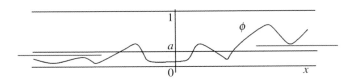

Figure 5. A typical initial condition satisfying the hypotheses of Theorem 5.2.

The following result is straightforward using the 'shooting method' mentioned above:

Theorem 5.1. *There is a unique value of c for which such a solution exists.*

We can then ask: Is this wave front stable?

Stability theorems for nonlinear PDEs are almost all local. If the initial condition is 'sufficiently close' in some sense to the exact wave form, then solutions tend to a translation of this wave as $t \to \infty$. The result of Fife and McLeod is very different.

Theorem 5.2. *Suppose that ϕ is continuous and $0 < \phi(x) < 1$ for all x. Suppose also that*

$$\lim_{x \to -\infty} \sup_{y < x} \phi(y) < a, \quad \lim_{x \to -\infty} \inf_{y > x} \phi(y) > a.$$

Then for some x_0 and positive constants K and ω,

$$|u(x, t) - U(x + ct - x_0)| < K e^{-\omega t}$$

for all x and all $t > 0$.

This is a very strong result because the initial condition has only the restriction that it be physically reasonable ($0 < \phi(x) < 1$) and lie at least some small amount below the 'threshold' a for large negative x and at least some small amount above a for large positive x. As shown in figure 5, this allows a wide variety of initial conditions. The principal tools used in the proof are a priori estimates and comparison theorems for parabolic equations.

5.2. Use of the maximum principle

Blow-up of positive solutions of semilinear heat equations
(with Avner Friedman, 1985)

McLeod wrote two papers with Friedman on this topic. Both have been widely cited. Here we will discuss one of their results for the following class of problems.

$$u_t = \Delta u + f(u) \text{ in } \Omega,$$

$$u(x, 0) = \phi(x) \text{ if } x \in \Omega,$$

$$u(x, t) = 0 \text{ if } x \in \partial\Omega, \ 0 < t < T,$$

$$\Omega \subset R^n \text{ bounded}, \ C^2 \text{ boundary}.$$

Denote the closure of Ω by $\bar{\Omega}$ and assume that

$$\lim_{t \to T^-} \max_{x \in \bar{\Omega}} u(x, t) = \infty.$$

Then the problem is to identify the blow-up set

$$\left\{ x \mid \lim_{t \to T^-} u(x, t) = \infty \right\}.$$

A special case is when the domain and initial data are radially symmetric:

$$\Omega = B_R,$$

$$\phi = \phi(r),$$

and with

$$f(u) = u^p$$

for some $p > 1$.

Theorem 5.3. *If $\phi'(r) < 0$ for $r > 0$ then blowup occurs only at $r = 0$.*

The proof uses the maximal principle four times. Friedman and McLeod introduce the function $w(r) = r^{n-1} u_r$, showing by the maximal principle that it is negative for $r > 0$ and $0 < t < T$. They then consider a function

$$J = w + c(r) F(u),$$

where c and F are to be determined. They impose several conditions on the functions c and F, including for example that

$$f'F - fF' - \frac{2c'}{r^{n-1}} F'F + \frac{2(n-1)}{r^n} cF'F + \left(c^n - \frac{n-1}{r} c' \right) \frac{F}{c} \geq 0.$$

They eventually find that if $c(r) = \varepsilon r^n$ and $F(u) = u^\gamma$ with $1 < \gamma < p$ then their conditions are satisfied. Further use of the maximal principle allows them to conclude that for any $\gamma \in (1, p)$ there is an $\varepsilon > 0$ such that if $r > 0$ then

$$\int_{u(r,t)}^{\infty} \frac{1}{s^\gamma} ds \geq \frac{1}{2} \varepsilon r^2$$

for $0 < t < T$. This beautiful inequality implies that for $r > 0$, $u(r, t)$ is bounded on $(0, T)$, proving the Theorem.

5.3. A partial success

I suspect that the problem that McLeod most wanted to solve among those where he was unsuccessful was the Stokes conjecture on the 'wave of greatest height'. This conjecture was made by Lord Stokes (Stokes 1880) and involves waves in deep water. Stokes's conjecture is the existence of a wave of greatest height and the validity of a clever formal argument he gave showing that the angle formed at the crest of this wave is $\frac{2}{3}\pi$.

An important step in proving this conjecture was taken in 1921 by A. Nekrasov (Nekrasov 1921). By what is known in fluid mechanics as a hodograph transformation, the region under one period, with wavelength λ, can be mapped onto the unit disk in the complex plane. Nekrasov showed that if $\phi(s)$ is the slope of the wave profile at the point corresponding to the point e^{is} on the unit circle, then ϕ satisfies the integral equation

$$\phi(s) = \frac{1}{3} \int_{-\pi}^{\pi} \frac{1}{\pi} \log \frac{\sin \frac{1}{2}(s+t)}{\sin \frac{1}{2}|s-t|} \frac{\sin \phi(t)}{1/\mu + \int_0^t \sin \phi(w) dw} dt. \qquad [14]$$

Here μ is defined in terms of the wave speed c and other physical parameters.

In 1961 Y. Krasovski (Krasovski 1961) showed that for each β with $0 < \beta < \frac{1}{6}\pi$ there is a μ and a corresponding solution of [14] such that $\phi \geq 0$ and

$$\sup_{0 \leq s \leq \pi} \phi(s) = \beta. \qquad [15]$$

However, this does not give the range of μ for which there are solutions to [14]. In 1978 it was shown by G. Keady and J. Norbury (Keady & Norbury 1978) that there is a solution for every $\mu > 3$. Each of the resulting waves is smooth at the crest.

The case $\mu = \infty$ corresponds to a stagnation point at the wave crest, and it is the case where, for a given c, the wave reaches the greatest height. Note that [14] makes sense without the term $1/\mu$. The Stokes conjecture is that [14] has a solution ϕ_∞ in this case, the wave slope $\phi_\infty(s)$ is discontinuous at the crest ($s = 0$), and $\lim_{|s| \to 0} \phi_\infty(s) = \pm\frac{1}{6}\pi$. Krasovski conjectured that $|\phi_\infty(s)| \leq \frac{1}{6}\pi$ for all s in $[-\pi, \pi]$, but in (16) McLeod showed that ϕ_∞ takes on values above $\frac{1}{6}\pi$ for large μ. In that paper as well he greatly improved on a proof the year before by Toland (1978) that the solution ϕ_∞ exists. The validity of Stokes's limiting argument remained a challenge, however.

The full Stokes conjecture was finally proved in a paper by C. Amick, E. Fraenkel and J. Toland (Amick *et al.* 1982), in which the authors made use of the following approximation to [14]:

$$\theta(x) = \frac{1}{3} \int_0^\infty k(x, y) \frac{\sin \theta(y)}{\int_0^y \sin \theta(t) dt} dy, \qquad 0 < x < \infty, \qquad [16]$$

where $k(x, y) = (1/\pi) \log[(x+y)/(|x-y|)]$. (McLeod had used a similar approximation in (16).)

The advantage of [16] is that it admits the exact solution $\Theta(x) = \frac{1}{6}\pi$. A key step in Amick *et al.* (1982) is their

Theorem 5.4. *If* $\phi(x) = \frac{1}{6}\pi$ *is the only solution of [16] taking values in* $(0, \frac{1}{3}\pi]$, *then any solution satisfying*

$$\liminf_{s \to 0} \theta(s) > 0, \quad \sup_{s \in (0,\infty)} \theta(s) \leq \frac{1}{3}\pi \qquad [17]$$

has the property $\theta(s) \mapsto \frac{1}{6}\pi$ *as* $s \mapsto 0$.

Of this result the authors of Amick *et al.* (1982) wrote in a prominently displayed acknowledgement:

We are heavily indebted to J. B. McLeod for an emphatic statement of Theorem 5.4 (for $\lambda < \infty$) to one of us, during a conversation in January 1980. Although we were aware already of the usefulness of the approximate kernel k, it was McLeod's remark that ultimately led us to concentrate attention on the approximate integral equation.

6. THE PAINLEVÉ EQUATIONS

McLeod wrote seven papers on a now famous set of six nonlinear ordinary differential equations due to Painlevé. I was fortunate to be involved in the first of these (17).

This is not the place to explain the background or theory of these equations, which have become an important part of mathematical physics. See, for example, the article 'Painlevé equations—nonlinear special functions' by Peter Clarkson (Clarkson 2003), a student of Bryce's who has become the leading authority on Painlevé equations since writing his DPhil thesis on one of them in 1984. Here I will describe how I came upon the problem we wrote about, and how Bryce solved it.

In 1978 I spent some time at Cornell, where I talked with G. S. S. Ludford, a leading applied mathematical authority on combustion theory. He showed me the equation

$$y'' - xy = 2y^{2\tau+1},$$

where τ is a positive constant, which he had encountered in work with C. deBoer (Ludford & deBoer 1975). The simplest version of the problem they posed 'for a mathematician' was to prove that this equation has exactly one non-constant solution that exists on $(-\infty, \infty)$. Ludford and deBoer also pointed out that when $\tau = 1$ this is the so-called 'second Painlevé transcendent'.

I had been using the 'shooting method', mentioned earlier, for about as long as Bryce, having learned a rudimentary form of the technique from an offhand remark of my PhD advisor, N. Levinson. I thought the problem could be done that way, and perhaps, though my memory is unclear, had an outline of a proof before I talked about it with Bryce when I visited him in Madison later that year. But during that Madison visit I learned of some numerical computations being done by students of Gerald Whitham FRS at Caltech that raised the problem to a different level.

These computations were for the Painlevé case $\tau = 1$:

$$y'' - xy = 2y^3 \tag{18}$$

It is not hard to show that the solution being sought, call it y_*, tends to zero at infinity, and it is reasonable to conclude that its asymptotics for large x resemble those for the well-known Airy equation

$$y'' - xy = 0. \tag{19}$$

One expects that

$$\lim_{k \to \infty} \frac{y(x)}{Ai(x)} = k,$$

Ai being the so-called Airy function from mathematical physics and k some positive constant. What the Caltech group had shown numerically was that, to many decimal places, the solution of [18] that exists on $(-\infty, \infty)$ is characterized by having $k = 1$. The obvious question is: Why?

Bryce, as a student of Titchmarsh, knew all about Airy functions. I will never forget the question he asked me when I arrived at his office one morning: 'Did you notice that by using the Airy transform you can get an exact solution of the Painlevé?'

No, I had not noticed. But this insight, plus Bryce's unparalleled technical competence in handling asymptotic analysis of this sort, led to a proof that $k = 1$, a remarkable result on what can be called the 'connection' problem of relating the behaviour of the solution as $x \to \infty$ to its continued existence as $x \to -\infty$. The importance of this result in the area of solitons only seems to grow over time.

7. Oxford

McLeod was clearly stimulated by the mathematical atmosphere at Oxford. Initially he interacted mostly with Chaundy and Titchmarsh, but after the pivotal 1968 conference in Edinburgh mentioned above, his horizons broadened tremendously. I described earlier one of the ODE boundary-value problems from fluid mechanics presented in Edinburgh by James Serrin, and McLeod's work on these marked the beginning of his almost complete shift to nonlinear differential equations.

During much of McLeod's time at Oxford he was well supported by outside funding from the SRC and its successors, enabling him to bring important visitors to the Mathematical Institute, such as Serrin, Tosio Kato, Paul Fife and Avner Friedman. He also benefited from the lively Oxford applied mathematics group spearheaded by Alan Tayler, John Ockendon (FRS 1999), Hilary Ockendon, Sam Howison and later Jon Chapman. In particular, the important collaboration between McLeod and Kato, which I discussed above, originated from a Study Group on mathematics in industry, one of a long and ongoing series pioneered by Leslie Fox and Alan Tayler. The particular model studied by McLeod and Kato was formulated by Tayler and John Ockendon in Ockendon & Tayler (1971). Several other papers, such as (23) and (21), were either in collaboration with Oxford applied mathematicians or inspired by their work, and McLeod had some joint grant support with members of this group. In addition he co-advised some applied mathematics doctoral students.

He had some outstanding DPhil students at Oxford, including Jack Carr, Peter Clarkson, Joe Conlon, Michael Shearer and Charles Stuart, some of whom brought their skills to industry and the City. According to his wife, Eunice, the thing that Bryce most enjoyed about Oxford was the teaching, both undergraduate and graduate, because the students were so good. The undergraduate teaching was through Wadham College, and he said that life in Wadham was one of the things that made it difficult to leave when they went to Pittsburgh (31).

There were two conferences organized in his honour between 2001 and 2007. The first, mentioned above, was for his 70th birthday and was held in Oxford; the second was on the occasion of his retirement from Pittsburgh. At each conference several of his Oxford students gave talks, and without exception they began by expressing their gratitude for the positive attitude that McLeod brought to their collaboration. As one said, 'Bryce encouraged [his students] ... to get on with it.'

Oxford, like other major mathematical centres, has an amazing number of visitors, and these provide constant cross-fertilization of mathematical ideas from around the world. This alone must have made it difficult to leave. So why did he leave Oxford for Pittsburgh?

As he said in (31),

> The (Oxford University) faculty board in mathematics, I think it has to be said, just wasn't interested in applied analysis. ... There was always the feeling that Oxford wasn't supporting the subject as it should.

Research mathematicians, particularly so-called 'pure' mathematicians, are sometimes categorized as either 'problem solvers' or 'theory builders'. McLeod was definitely a problem solver, and described himself as such in the introduction to (30).

An illuminating essay on this subject was written by Timothy Gowers FRS (Gowers 2000). In this essay Gowers, a Fields medallist and theory-building mathematician, argues for the importance of both theory-building and problem-solving mathematics. Gowers refers to writings of Sir Michael Atiyah FRS, also a Fields medallist and perhaps the dominant voice in pure mathematics at Oxford from 1972 to 1989, and he includes the following quote from an interview for *The Mathematical Intelligencer* in 1984:

Interviewer: How do you select a problem to study?

Atiyah: I think that presupposes an answer. I don't think that's the way I work at all. Some people may sit back and say, 'I want to solve this problem' and they sit down and say, 'How do I solve this problem?' I don't. ... I'm interested in mathematics; I talk, I learn, I discuss and then interesting questions simply emerge. I have never started off with a particular goal, except the goal of understanding mathematics.'

Gowers says:

...the subjects that appeal to theory-builders are, at the moment, much more fashionable than the ones that appeal to problem-solvers. Moreover, mathematicians in the theory-building areas often regard what they are doing as the central core (Atiyah uses this exact phrase*) of mathematics, with (problem oriented subjects) thought of as peripheral....

By contrast, the problems that McLeod worked on could often be described as quite special, and not part of a general theory. He wrote (11): '... differential equations ... are very individual things and have to be tackled most often in a very individual way.'

Another factor at Oxford was the rather sharp line that was drawn between pure and applied mathematics. McLeod was the Tutor in Pure Mathematics at Wadham college, and the senior pure mathematicians at Oxford in the 1970s and 1980s did not encourage work of his sort. For example, the quotes above show that Atiyah had a very different view of what constituted important mathematical research from McLeod.

It is not clear, however, that McLeod would have been happier if he had been officially in the Oxford applied mathematics group. He was a pure mathematician in the sense that, to him, it was crucial to give rigorous proofs of results. This is usually not the principal concern of applied mathematicians, particularly of the British school, who mostly look for what are sometimes called 'formal' arguments, based on sophisticated, sometimes ingenious, manipulations and calculations, without worrying too much about the analytical details.

Today also there is a very sharp line between pure and applied mathematics in Oxford. That line, or maybe it is a half-plane, is the one that separates the 'pure mathematics' wing of the magnificent new Mathematical Institute building from the 'applied mathematics' wing. What changed from the 1980s was that for the short time that McLeod had an office in the new building, it was in the applied wing, although his mathematics was of the same type as before. Indeed, during all his years in Pittsburgh he maintained an office for use in the summers in the quarters occupied by the Oxford Centre for Industrial and Applied Mathematics, led for much of that time by John Ockendon. In addition, the Oxford Center for Nonlinear Partial

---

* In Atiyah (1984).

Differential Equations, headed by John Ball, is housed in the applied wing of the new building. Thus for several reasons it was natural that Bryce would have a retirement office in that wing.

Fortunately, the physical separation of pure and applied mathematicians ceases in the basement, where the classrooms and cafeteria are located. From experience I know that it is possible to descend in one elevator to this level and then inadvertently take the wrong elevator back up, and find yourself in the opposite wing from where you started. Let us hope that mathematical ideas can take the same path. Indeed, McLeod's work shows that they can.

I end this section with a quote from Gilbert Strang of Massachusetts Institute of Technology, a distinguished mathematician with wide-ranging interests and much influence through his writings: 'Bryce was a true analyst—he solved problems! His papers gave answers rather than abstractions and they led the subject onward.'

8. Pittsburgh

Bryce published at a greater rate in Pittsburgh than he had in Oxford, probably because his teaching duties were fewer. The best known of the Pittsburgh papers was written with his colleague Bard Ermentrout, a leading mathematical biologist.

8.1. A problem from neurobiology

Existence of travelling waves for a neural network
(with Bard Ermentrout, 1991)

Ermentrout brought to McLeod the equation

$$u_t = -u + \int_{-\infty}^{\infty} k(x - y)S(u(y, t))\mathrm{d}y, \qquad [20]$$

an equation derived from a limiting process in which a large number of neurons are connected in a one-dimensional array, with excitatory 'all-to-all' synaptic interaction. The goal is to obtain a travelling front, as in the Fife–McLeod paper discussed earlier. But in general the equation does not reduce to a system of PDEs, and so the mathematics is even more difficult.

In (24) Ermentrout and McLeod obtained the existence of fronts for a wide range of symmetric positive kernels k with $\int_{-\infty}^{\infty} k(s)\mathrm{d}s = 1$, and firing functions S that are smooth, increasing and bounded. The basic method was continuation, which we saw above in McLeod's work on swirling flow. But here the setting is infinite-dimensional.

This paper has often been cited by subsequent users of continuation in similar settings. As Ermentrout and McLeod described it, the idea is to move continuously 'from the general problem to one where everything is known.' (Actually, they started at the known end and moved to the general problem.)

The starting point is to use the kernel

$$k(s) = \tfrac{1}{2}\mathrm{e}^{-|s|}.$$

In this case the equation does reduce to a PDE, by use of the Fourier transform in the convolution. The resulting equation,

$$u_t = u_{xx} + S(u) - u,$$

turns out to be similar to the problem of Fife and McLeod. Making the travelling wave substitution $u = u(x - ct)$ gives

$$-cu' = u'' + S(u) - u,$$

and choosing S so that $\int_0^1 (S(u) - u) = 0$, it is easily shown by a phase plane argument that there is a standing wave $(c = 0)$ connecting $u = 0$ to $u = 1$. (In dynamical system terms, this is a heteroclinic orbit in the (u, u') phase plane.)

Then they vary S and k gradually, finding a wave speed c at each point, until one reaches the given S and k of the problem. The linearized operator in the continuation is

$$L\phi = \int_{-\infty}^{\infty} k(x + cs - y) S'(u(y)) \phi(y) \mathrm{d}y,$$

considered on $C_0(-\infty, \infty)$. It is shown that this operator is Fredholm with index 0 and has 1 as a simple eigenvalue, which is what enables continuation to proceed. The paper illustrates McLeod's mastery of modern functional analysis techniques when required.

9. LATER WORK

While the paper with Ermentrout is probably the best-known of McLeod's later papers, several others have achieved significant recognition. In particular the papers 'On the uniqueness of flow of a Navier–Stokes fluid due to a stretching boundary', with K. R. Rajagopal (19), and 'Smooth static solutions of the Einstein/Yang–Mills equations' with J. Smoller, A. G. Wasserman and S. T. Yau (22), have been particularly influential in their respective areas. We mention also (20), (26) and (25).

The last of these was written with C.-K. Law, one of the most active researchers among McLeod's Pittsburgh doctoral students and a leading applied analyst in Taiwan. Another active Pitt student, C.-B. Wang, wrote an excellent dissertation on Painlevé III and continued to work with McLeod through the 2000s. His recent well-reviewed monograph (Wang 2013) was published by Springer.

McLeod collaborated with at least five other Pitt mathematics faculty members, most often W. C. Troy and me; and K. R. Rajagopal, mentioned above, was in the Pitt Engineering School. He also had many discussions with mathematicians from neighbouring Carnegie Mellon University, and in particular wrote an interesting paper with D. Kinderlehrer.

In the period after his retirement Bryce and I wrote the book *Classical methods in ordinary differential equations* (30). With a focus on existence theory for ODE boundary-value problems, it was designed as a text for students with a background that included the basic existence theorem for initial-value problems due to Picard and the analysis of phase planes. It contains some new proofs of known results and also some previously unpublished theorems. In the course of writing this book Bryce came up with a beautiful new proof of an important result due to A. C. Lazer and D. E. Leach (Lazer & Leach 1969), one of several on ODEs and PDEs that Lazer wrote with two collaborators in about 1970 and that have been widely cited in the 50 years since. I will end this memoir by giving the crux of Bryce's proof, because to me it encapsulates his ability to look at a problem from a totally new angle and thereby obtain deep new insights.

The problem, in simplest form, is about periodic solutions for equations of the form

$$y'' + n^2 y + g(y) = p(t), \tag{21}$$

where n is a non-zero integer, p is continuous and periodic, say with period 2π, g is smooth,

$$\lim_{y \to \infty} g(y) \text{ and } \lim_{y \to -\infty} g(y) \text{ exist,}$$

and for all y,

$$g(-\infty) < g(y) < g(\infty).$$

The Lazer–Leach result is a surprising blend of simple harmonic analysis and nonlinear ODE theory. It states that a necessary and sufficient condition for [21] to have a periodic solution is that

$$\sqrt{A^2 + B^2} < 2(g(\infty) - g(-\infty)),$$

where

$$A = \int_0^{2\pi} p(s) \sin ns \, ds, \quad B = \int_0^{2\pi} p(s) \cos ns \, ds.$$

The original proof was an elegant application of Schauder's fixed-point theorem, and we included it in our book*. Bryce had not known of the work until I called it to his attention, sometime around 2010 when he was in England and I in the USA. I wrote to him suggesting that we include it in the book for its elegance and importance, and attached a copy of the paper. A few weeks later Bryce wrote back that he had not read the Lazer–Leach proof, for fear of prejudicing his view of the problem, but that he had his own proof, which began with the following result:

Lemma 9.1. *Suppose that in addition to the hypotheses above g satisfies a local Lipschitz condition. For any $r > 0$ consider [21] with the following initial conditions:*

$$y(0) = r \cos \beta, \quad y'(0) = r \sin \beta.$$

If r is sufficiently large, say $r > r_0$, then for every β this solution satisfies

$$(y(2\pi) - y(0)) \cos \beta - (y'(2\pi) - y'(0)) \sin \beta > 0.$$

This lemma is not hard to prove, and the local Lipschitz condition is easily removed at the end of the proof of the theorem. Now assume that there is no periodic solution. For every r and β there are R and γ, both depending continuously on r and β, such that

$$y(2\pi) - y(0) = R \sin \gamma, \quad y'(2\pi) - y'(0) = R \cos \gamma.$$

The lemma implies that if $r > r_0$ then $\sin(\gamma - \beta) > 0$. As β goes from 0 to 2π, γ must increase by 2π because the initial conditions at $\beta = 0$ and $\beta = 2\pi$ are the same.

If there is no periodic solution then as r decreases from above r_0, γ and R continue to be well defined, for all $\beta > 0$. Also, since γ is continuous in r and β, it must continue to increase by 2π as β goes from 0 to 2π. As $r \to 0$, however, R is bounded away from 0; say $R \geq \delta > 0$, because we are assuming that at $R = 0$ the solution is not periodic. For very small

---

* One goal of our book was to show different ways of attacking the same problem.

r the solution varies only a little for initial conditions on the circle of radius r, so with $R \geq \delta$, γ cannot increase by 2π, a contradiction.

Bryce found this proof when he was over 80 years old.

ACKNOWLEDGEMENTS

I thank Hilary and John Ockendon, Edward Fraenkel, Eunice McLeod, Trevor Stuart FRS and two anonymous referees for advice and comments.

The frontispiece photograph was taken in 1992 by A. C. Cooper and is copyright The Royal Society.

AUTHOR PROFILE

Stuart Hastings

Stuart Hastings is Professor Emeritus of Mathematics at the University of Pittsburgh. A PhD student of Norman Levinson at Massachusetts Institute of Technology, he held positions at Case Western Reserve University and State University of New York, Buffalo, before coming to Pittsburgh as Chair of the Mathematics Department in 1987, the same year in which Bryce McLeod joined the Pitt department. He had first met McLeod in 1967, at a conference in Edinburgh that McLeod had helped organize. He and his British-born wife, Eileen, spent the 1973–74 academic year in Oxford, hosted by McLeod, but their first joint paper appeared in 1980, based on work started during one of McLeod's many visits to the University of Wisconsin in Madison. They subsequently wrote another 14 papers together, and also a book, *Classical methods in ordinary differential equations*, published by the American Mathematical Society in 2012.

REFERENCES TO OTHER AUTHORS

Amick, C. K., Fraenkel, L. E. & Toland, J. F. 1982 On the Stokes conjecture for the wave of extreme form. *Acta Math.* **148**, 193–214.

Atiyah, M. 1984 An interview with Michael Atiyah. *Mathematical Intelligencer* **6**, 9–19.

Batchelor, G. K. 1951 Note on a class of solutions of the Navier–Stokes equations representing steady rotationally-symmetric flow. *Q. J. Mech. Appl. Math.* **4**, 29–41.

Clarkson, P. 2003 Painlevé equations—nonlinear special functions. *J. Comp. Appl. Math.* **153**, 127–140.

Gowers, T. 2000 The two cultures in mathematics. In *Mathematics: frontiers and perspectives* (ed. V. I. Arnold, Michael Atiyah, Peter D. Lax & Barry Mazur), pp. 65–78. Providence, RI: American Mathematical Society.

Hastings, S. P. 2014 Obituary of J. Bryce McLeod. *Independent*, 22 September.

Keady, G. & Norbury, J. 1978 On the existence theory for irrotational water waves. *Math. Proc. Camb. Phil. Soc.* **83**, 135–157.

Krasovski, Yu. P. 1961 On the theory of steady state waves of large amplitude. *USSR Comp. Math. Math. Phys.* **1**, 996–1018.

Lazer, A. C. & Leach, D. E. 1969 Bounded perturbations of forced harmonic oscillators at resonance. *Ann. Mat. Pura Appl.* **82**, 49–68.

Ludford, G. S. S. & deBoer, C. 1975 Spherical electric probe in a continuum gas. *Plasma Phys.* **17**, 29–43.

Nekrasov, A. 1921 The exact theory of steady state waves on the surface of a heavy liquid. *Izv. Ivanovo-Vosnesensk. Politehn. Inst.* **3**, 52–65; English translation in Technical Summary Report No. 813, Mathematical Research Center, University of Wisconsin, 1967.

Ockendon, J. & Tayler, A. 1971 The dynamics of a current collection system for an electric locomotive. *Proc. R. Soc. Lond.* A **322**, 447–468.

Stewartson, K. 1949 Correlated compressible and incompressible boundary layers. *Proc. R. Soc. Lond.* A **200**, 84–100.

Stokes, G. G. 1880 Considerations relative to the greatest height of oscillatory irrotational waves which can be propagated without change of form. *Math. Phys. Pap.* **1**, 225–228.

Toland, J. F. 1978 On the existence of a wave of greatest height and Stokes's conjecture. *Proc. R. Soc. Lond.* A **363**, 469–485.

Wang, C.-B. 2013 *Application of integrable systems to phase transitions*. Berlin: Springer.

Yandell, B. H. 2002 *The honors class, Hilbert's problems and their solvers*. Natick, MA: A. K. Peters.

BIBLIOGRAPHY

The following publications are those referred to directly in the text. A full bibliography is available as electronic supplementary material at http://dx.doi.org/10.1098/rsbm.2015.0031 or via http://rsbm.royalsocietypublishing.org.

(1)　1958　(With T. W. Chaundy) On a functional equation. *Q. J. Math.* **9**, 202–206.

(2)　　　On the commutator subring. *Q. J. Math.* **9**, 207–209.

(3)　1961　The distribution of the eigenvalues for the hydrogen atom and similar cases. *Proc. Lond. Math. Soc.* **11**, 139–158.

(4)　　　Eigenfunction expansions associated with a complex differential operator of the second order. *Q. J. Math.* **2**, 291–303.

(5)　1962　On an infinite set of non-linear differential equations. *Q. J. Math.* **13**, 119–128.

(6)　　　Square-integrable solutions of a second-order differential equation with complex coefficients. *Q. J. Math.* **13**, 129–133.

(7)　1966　The number of integrable-square solutions of ordinary differential equations. *Q. J. Math.* **17**, 285–290.

(8)　　　(With C. Dolph & D. Thoe) The analytic continuation of the resolvent kernel and scattering operator associated with the Schrödinger operator. *J. Math. Anal. Appl.* **16**, 311–332.

(9)　1968　(With J. Serrin) The existence of similar solutions for some laminar boundary value problems. *Arch. Rat. Mech. Anal.* **31**, 288–303.

(10)　1969　Von Karman's swirling flow problem. *Arch. Rat. Mech. Anal.* **33**, 91–102.

(11)　　　Introduction to *Elementary differential equations*, by W. T. Chaundy. Oxford: Clarendon Press.

(12)　1971　The existence of axially symmetric flow above a rotating disk. *Proc. R. Soc. Lond.* A **324**, 391–414.

(13)　　　(With T. Kato) The functional–differential equation $y'(x) = ay(\lambda x + by(x))$. *Bull. Am. Math. Soc.* **77**, 891–937.

(14)　1974　(With S. V. Parter) On the flow between two counter-rotating infinite plane disks. *Arch. Rat. Mech. Anal.* **54**, 301–327.

(15)　1977　(With P. Fife) The approach of solutions of nonlinear diffusion equations to travelling wave solutions. *Arch. Rat. Mech. Anal.* **65**, 335–361.

(16)　1979　*The Stokes and Krasovskii conjectures for the wave of greatest height*. Math. Res. Ctr Rep. no. 2041, University of Wisconsin, Madison. Published in *Stud. Appl. Math.* **98**, 311–334 (1997).

(17)　1980　(With S. P. Hastings) A boundary value problem associated with the second Painlevé transcendent and the Korteweg–deVries equation. *Arch. Rat. Mech. Anal.* **73**, 31–51.

(18)　1985　(With A. Friedman) Blow-up of positive solutions of semilinear heat equations. *Indiana Math. J.* **34**, 425–477.

(19)　1987　(With K. R. Rajagopal) On the uniqueness of flow of a Navier–Stokes fluid due to a stretching boundary. *Arch. Rat. Mech. Anal.* **98**, 385–393.

(20) 1990 (With C. J. Amick) A singular perturbation problem in needle crystals. *Arch. Rat. Mech. Anal.* **109**, 139–171.

(21) 1991 (With S. J. Chapman, S. D. Howison & J. R. Ockendon) Normal/superconducting transitions in Landau–Ginzburg theory. *Proc. R. Soc. Edin.* A **119**, 117–124.

(22) (With J. A. Smoller, A. G. Wasserman & S. T. Yau) Smooth static solutions of the Einstein/Yang–Mills equations. *Commun. Math. Phys.* **143**, 115–147.

(23) (With S. P. Hastings) On the periodic solutions of a forced second-order equation. *J. Nonlin. Sci.* **1**, 225–245.

(24) 1993 (With G. B. Ermentrout) Existence of travelling waves for a neural network. *Proc. R. Soc. Edin.* A **123**, 461–478.

(25) 1994 (With A. V. Kitaev & C. K. Law) Rational solutions of the fifth Painlevé equation. *Diff. Integr. Equns* **7**, 967–1000.

(26) 1996 (With G. Friesecke) Dynamics as a mechanism preventing the formation of finer and finer microstructure. *Arch. Rat. Mech. Anal.* **133**, 199–247.

(27) 1997 (With S. V. Raghavan & W. C. Troy) A singular perturbation problem arising from the Kuramoto–Sivashinsky equation. *Diff. Integr. Equns* **10**, 1–36.

(28) 2009 (With S. P. Hastings) An elementary approach to a model problem of Lagerstrom. *SIAM J. Math. Anal.* **40**, 2421–2436.

(29) 2010 (With E. S. Benilov, S. J. Chapman, J. R. Ockendon & V. S. Zubkov) On liquid films on an inclined plate. *J. Fluid. Mech.* **663**, 53–69.

(30) 2012 (With S. P. Hastings) *Classical methods in ordinary differential equations.* Providence, RI: American Mathematical Society.

(31) 2014 Bryce McLeod, a life in mathematics; video interview conducted by Sir John Ball in January, 2014. Available at https://www.maths.ox.ac.uk/node/891.

DONALD METCALF AC

26 February 1929 — 15 December 2014

DONALD METCALF AC

26 February 1929 — 15 December 2014

Elected FRS 1983

By Nicos A. Nicola*

The Walter and Eliza Hall Institute of Medical Research, 1G Royal Parade, Parkville, Victoria 3050, Australia

and

Department of Medical Biology, University of Melbourne, Royal Parade, Victoria 3050, Australia

Donald Metcalf was one of Australia's most distinguished medical researchers and is acknowledged internationally as the father of the modern field of haemopoietic growth factors. He defined the hierarchy of haemopoietic progenitor cells, purified and cloned the major molecular regulators of their growth and maturation, determined their mechanisms of action and participated in their development for clinical use in cancer patients. He received numerous awards and distinctions during his career, but was most pleased by the fact that his life's work improved human health.

EARLY DAYS

Donald Metcalf was born on 26 February 1929 in Mittagong, New South Wales (NSW), the middle child with older and younger sisters, Rosalind and Beryl (figure 1). His father, Donald Davidson Metcalf, was the son of a Scottish migrant; his mother, Enid Victoria Metcalf (*née* Thomas), came from a wealthy farming family in Shepparton, Victoria. They were both associated with the education department and consequently moved from town to town through rural NSW every two to three years, including Womboota, Kingsvale, Goulburn, Wallerawang, Inverell, Lithgow and Tamworth. This made it difficult for young Donald to

* nicola@wehi.edu.au

This memoir was commissioned by the *Historical Records of Australian Science* and will appear in the December issue. The memoir is published here with minor amendments.

http://dx.doi.org/10.1098/rsbm.2016.0013

Figure 1. Donald Metcalf with his mother Enid and sisters Rosalind and Beryl in 1935.
(Photograph courtesy of the family of Donald Metcalf.)

form lasting friendships with his schoolmates, and he developed a relatively solitary and self-sufficient character.

Metcalf's father was ambitious and often took night-study courses, gradually moving up the ranks within the NSW education department until he eventually became headmaster of demonstration schools responsible for training new teachers in Tamworth, then Wagga then Lane Cove. Metcalf's mother was a solemn person who also taught needlework at her husband's schools and as a result Metcalf was present at these schools from a very early age and learnt to read before he was three. He was thus enrolled into first grade at age three, two years younger than his classmates. He started high school at age nine and to avoid entering university at age 14 he had to repeat his intermediate year at Lithgow and leaving year at Tamworth, being Dux of the school in both years.

The Great Depression and World War II came and went during Metcalf's childhood. He was somewhat isolated from these events by living in the country on a small farm with cows and chickens. Nevertheless he was aware of the light horsemen training in Goulburn, the mining and arms manufacture in Lithgow and the Tiger Moth flight training in Tamworth.

Metcalf studied science subjects at high school, including mathematics and chemistry, but it is unclear what led him to enrol in the medical course at Sydney University in 1945 just before his 17th birthday. Perhaps there was some parental influence for him to join a respectable profession. This was the first intake after the war, and the numbers were swollen to about 650 with returned servicemen and others wishing to make a new career. With such

Figure 2. Metcalf, Jacques Miller and Gustav Nossal all studied in the same research laboratory in Sydney, moved to the Walter and Eliza Hall Institute in Melbourne and 'retired' together at an official event in 1996. (Photograph courtesy of the Walter and Eliza Hall Institute.) (Online version in colour.)

large classes personal tuition and access to human dissection was minimal, and Metcalf found the whole time quite stressful, believing he had a poor memory for the detail required in examinations. During this time he boarded at various private houses and was house-master at Sydney Grammar School in Clovelly.

Sydney University introduced a new one-year research degree (Bachelor of Medical Science) in 1950 and Metcalf was eager to join, apparently frustrated at the lack of treatments for so many of the diseases about which he was being taught (Blythe 1998). He joined the laboratory of Patrick de Burgh in the Department of Bacteriology to work on the ectromelia ('mouse pox') virus and the liver pathology it caused. De Burgh served as an army medical officer in Northern Australia and New Guinea, where he encountered several tropical viruses that led to his interest in the pathology of infectious diseases. It is remarkable that in the space of a few years some of Australia's most eminent medical researchers and immunologists were to pass through his laboratory, including Jacques Miller (FRS 1970), Gustav (later Sir Gustav) Nossal (FRS 1982), Kay Ellem and Christopher Burrell (figure 2). Although the equipment and conditions in the laboratory were rather primitive, the eccentric professors (de Burgh and Hugh Ward, both of whom had studied at Harvard with the famous bacteriologist Hans Zissner) spent a lot of time discussing the latest research findings with their two students. For his opinion to be taken seriously was revelatory for Metcalf, who had felt invisible in a class of 650 medical students. Despite not publishing any papers from his time with de Burgh, Metcalf became hooked on academic research.

Metcalf finished his medical degree with a residency at the Royal Prince Alfred Hospital (RPAH), a major teaching hospital adjacent to Sydney University. He most enjoyed working in the emergency department with the constant roll call of colourful and sometimes shady characters. It was there that he first met Josephine (Jo) Lentaigne, a young nurse who sometimes worked with him. He was taken by her 'bright eyes and her wit and liveliness'. They began seeing each other, were soon engaged and were married in 1954.

Jo's parents were John Gerald Lentaigne (a doctor) and Eileen Garvey from Bangalow, NSW, and she had three older sisters, Mary, Margaret and Ann, and a younger sister, Genevieve. Donald and Jo Metcalf were also to have four daughters: Katherine (Kate), Mary-Ann, Penelope and Johanna. Kate and Johanna took up senior positions in the Victorian legal system, Mary-Ann became a teacher and Penelope became an accomplished visual artist.

The medical residency at RPAH convinced Metcalf that he was more suited to medical research than practice and that research was the only way to improve the appalling state of ignorance about human disease and cures. As it turned out, an executive member of the then Anti Cancer Council of Victoria, Esmond Venner (Bill) Keogh (1895–1970) was a wartime friend of Hugh Ward and approached him for suggestions regarding someone to take up the new Carden Fellowship in cancer research. A wealthy businessman and Melbourne City councillor, George Frederick Carden, as a result of family disagreements had bequeathed much of his money to the Cancer Council in 1947, the income from which was to be used to 'find the cause and cure of cancer'. The Council had failed to find a suitably experienced overseas researcher to take on this role and so offered the Fellowship to Metcalf in 1954. Metcalf, quite conscious of his lack of experience, offered to take on the position at half salary.

Keogh worked at the Commonwealth Serum Laboratories but was also a close friend and work colleague of the previous Director of the Walter and Eliza Hall Institute of Medical Research (WEHI), Charles Kellaway FRS, and had formed a close working relationship with Sir Macfarlane Burnet FRS by the time the latter was Director of WEHI. Keogh persuaded the somewhat reluctant Burnet to house the new Carden Fellow at WEHI, and so it came to be that Metcalf moved from Sydney to Melbourne to begin his research career in earnest.

Early research career at the Walter and Eliza Hall Institute of Medical Research

Metcalf's first meeting with Burnet was not what he had expected. Within the first few minutes Burnet told him that cancer was an inevitable part of the ageing process, could not be prevented, and was incurable. Anyone who worked on the disease was either a fool or a rogue! The main focus of the institute at that time was virology, and Burnet insisted that if Metcalf were to pursue research in cancer he would first have to work in virology for two years, and if that was successful then he could do cancer research. To make matters worse, Burnet offered only primitive laboratory space in the animal house, accessible by underground tunnel through the Royal Melbourne Hospital. This arrangement added to Metcalf's feelings of estrangement from the main research life of WEHI, and his discomfort was exacerbated by his strong allergy to mice and other experimental animals.

Metcalf obediently worked on vaccinia virus, using Burnet's favoured model of growth on the choriallantoic membrane of embryonated chicken eggs, but he also found time to

Figure 3. Metcalf with Jacob Furth at Harvard Medical School in Boston around 1956.
(Photograph courtesy of the family of Donald Metcalf.)

publish papers on the age incidence of various cancers from Australian statistics (1)* and on pseudoneoplastic changes in the allantois after viral inoculation (2). He found a way to marry virology with his true interest in blood cell cancers by studying virus-induced chicken leukaemias.

Metcalf had noted Jacob Furth's work on chicken leukaemias and was fascinated by Furth's demonstration that spontaneous lymphoid leukaemia formation in AKR mice could be prevented by removing the thymus, an organ of unknown function at the time. Furth had also discovered that the incidence of several types of tumours (especially endocrine tumours) could be increased by an altered balance of target hormones. Putting this together, Metcalf began searching for factors (hormones) that might stimulate lymphomatosis in mice. First he showed that plasma from patients with chronic lymphocytic leukaemia or lymphosarcoma could induce increased lymphocyte numbers in mice (that is, it contained a lymphocytosis stimulating factor, LSF) (3). He went on to show that LSF activity was also present in thymus extracts and that serum levels of LSF were dependent on an intact thymus (3). However, he did not have the resources to pursue the purification of this factor at the time, and its identity still remains a mystery.

Metcalf's interest in Furth's ideas about growth factor control of cancer and the role of the thymus in leukaemia led him to undertake a sabbatical with Furth at the Children's Cancer Research Foundation, Harvard Medical School in Boston (figure 3). In 1956 he, Josephine and young daughter Katherine moved to Boston, where in the next two years Jo gave birth to Mary-Ann and Penelope. Both births were at the Boston's Women's Lying-In Hospital, which

---

* Numbers in this form refer to the bibliography at the end of the text.

in 1981 was sold to Genetics Institute, a biotechnology company that was later to develop granulocyte/macrophage colony-stimulating factor (GM-CSF). Metcalf later reflected on the irony of the three births in the same building! Because Furth was an experimental pathologist, Metcalf learnt his trade as a mouse pathologist with him, and also learnt about leukaemia-causing viruses in the mouse, specifically the Friend virus that causes erythroleukaemia.

During this time and upon his return to WEHI, Metcalf continued his studies on LSF and the role of the thymus in its production and in controlling lymphocyte numbers (3). He showed that thymectomy in young but not old mice had profound effects on lymphocyte numbers in the periphery (spleen and lymph nodes), and that additional thymus grafts under the skin of mice acted as autonomous units regulating their own lymphocyte numbers independently of each other despite the host origin of lymphocytes in the graft—a phenomenon that Metcalf speculated arose from seeding by bone-marrow-derived stem cells. One exception was during pregnancy, when the original thymus involuted but the grafted thymus remained unchanged. After these observations, Metcalf made detailed examinations of the birth rates of lymphocytes in the thymus (using autoradiographic analysis of the incorporation of radioactive thymidine into cells), and compared these with the steady-state numbers of lymphocytes. He concluded that most of the lymphocytes born in the thymus must also die there, a concept that few were willing to accept at the time because it seemed so wasteful. Metcalf, however, was never afraid of the truth based on his sound scientific observations and spoke it regardless of the consequences. In time it became clear that this massive cell death in the thymus reflected the very important immunological processes of positive selection as well as negative selection against self-reactivity.

While Metcalf was in Boston, Burnet transformed WEHI from a virology institute to one focused on immunology and the host response to infection. Despite this and Metcalf's work on the thymus and lymphocytes, he remained banished to the animal house. It was not until 1966, when Gus Nossal succeeded Burnet as Director, that Metcalf was welcomed back into the fold, was given new laboratories in the main building, and was even appointed as Nossal's Assistant Director. Metcalf likened this event to the Beethoven opera *Fidelio*, where the prisoners come out of the underground prison, push open the grate and emerge into the sunlight (Hughes 2006)—only he was saved not by his wife but by a new Director!

DISCOVERY OF HAEMOPOIETIC COLONY ASSAYS AND THE COLONY-STIMULATING FACTORS

In the early 1950s Ray Bradley at the Physiology Department at Melbourne University (led by Douglas 'Pansy' Wright) was studying tumour growth, and to pursue these studies he spent some time in Michael Potter's group at the National Cancer Institute in Bethesda studying plasmacytomas. He also spent time at the Imperial Cancer Research Fund in London learning to grow transformed fibroblasts in agar. At that time it was believed that only virally transformed cells could grow as anchorage-independent clones in agar. Developments by the early 1960s in perfecting tissue culture media for mammalian cell growth (by Earle and Eagle; see Evans *et al.* (1956) and Eagle (1959)), the use of animal sera and the demonstration by Theodore T. Puck that single cells could grow if the medium had been 'conditioned' by other cells all converged to set Bradley on the path of trying to grow leukaemic lymphocytes in semi-solid agar by using appropriate feeder cells. To do this he used glass Petri dishes in which he applied first an underlayer of feeder cells and a top layer of leukaemic cells in agar.

Figure 4. Staff of the Cancer Research Unit, just after they had moved out of the institute's animal house in 1966–67. From left to right: Dr Malcolm Moore, Dr Noel Warner, Unit head Professor Donald Metcalf, Dr Bill Robinson and Dr Richard Stanley. (Photograph courtesy of the Walter and Eliza Hall Institute.)

Bradley asked Metcalf to supply him with thymic lymphoma cells that develop spontaneously in AKR mice, and he attempted to grow these cells using underlayers of various cell types and tissues. One of the underlayers consisted of mouse bone marrow cells, and to Metcalf and Bradley's surprise colonies did develop but in the underlayer of bone marrow cells rather than the top layer of lymphoma cells. When he came across to WEHI in 1964 to show these to Metcalf, and to seek his advice on what cells were growing in the colonies, he initiated Metcalf's lifetime fascination with the power of this simple assay to define the control mechanisms of normal blood development and their transformation to leukaemias. Metcalf was staggered by the appearance of these cultures under the indirect light of a dissecting microscope—he likened the sight to one in a spaceship flying through dark space, but approaching a myriad of sparkling galaxies of varied shapes and sizes.

Bradley and Metcalf determined that these colonies consisted of monocytes (full of phagocytosed metachromatic agar granules) and polymorphonuclear granulocytes (4). At about the same time Dov Pluznik and Leo Sachs (FRS 1997) at the Weizmann Institute in Rehovot, Israel, described a very similar assay using mouse spleen cells in agar with feeder layers of embryonic cells, but reported that the colonies contained 'mast' cells because of the metachromatic granules in the cells (Pluznik & Sachs 1965). Though these observations were independent, bitterness grew between the two groups, with Sachs accusing the Australians of having 'acquired' his ideas because of his slightly earlier publication date. Unfortunately this bitterness prevented any collaboration or exchange of materials between the two groups in the ensuing years.

Following the hypothesis that excess growth factors might be associated with the development of leukaemia, Bradley and Metcalf went on to show that AKR mice with lymphoid leukaemia had elevated levels of the colony-stimulating activity (CSA) in their sera (5). William (Bill) Robinson (figure 4), a physician from Denver doing his PhD with Metcalf, expanded these studies, as did Roger Foster when Metcalf did a sabbatical with him at the Roswell Park Memorial Institute in Buffalo, New York, from 1966 to 1967. They showed that mice with other virally induced leukaemias also had elevated levels of CSA in their sera (6, 7). They also showed that the activity was filterable. These studies were important indicators to Metcalf that CSA might represent a biological regulator or growth factor that controlled blood cell growth, but in the back of his mind was always the possibility that CSA was in fact a combination of essential metabolites, secreted by feeder cells, that were missing from the culture medium, or that it was a transforming virus. He therefore sought evidence of regulated levels of CSA in body fluids comparable to the altered levels of the only known blood cell regulator at the time, erythropoietin, in response to hypoxia or a loss of red blood cells. The elevated levels of CSA in the sera of leukaemic patients and patients with viral and other infections gave him some comfort (8).

In 1967 Malcolm Moore (figure 4), a recent PhD graduate from Oxford University, joined Metcalf's Cancer Research Unit at WEHI to study the regulation of normal and leukaemic stem cells by the colony-stimulating factors (CSFs). There he became interested in the development of the haemopoietic system from the earliest embryonic stages and, with Metcalf, showed that the yolk sac was the source of haemopoietic stem cells that would later repopulate the fetal liver and bone marrow (10).

PURIFICATION AND CLONING OF THE CSFs

Richard Stanley (figure 4) came from Perth, Western Australia, in 1967 to do a PhD with Metcalf (on sabbatical at the Roswell Park Memorial Institute at Buffalo, New York, at the time of Stanley's arrival), and following the lead of erythropoietin he set about trying to identify the CSF in human urine. He determined that it was macromolecular, proteinaceous and probably not a virus (9). This again allayed Metcalf's fears about the nature of CSFs, but the CSF in urine stimulated almost exclusively macrophage colonies and thus seemed different from CSFs from other sources. Stanley performed heroically in attempting to purify this CSF from a somewhat unpleasant source, but the separative technologies available at the time were not sufficient to achieve this task. It was not until 1977, after he had moved to the Ontario Cancer Institute, Toronto, and later Albert Einstein College of Medicine in New York, that macrophage colony-stimulating factor (M-CSF or CSF-1) from L-cell-conditioned medium was purified and shown to be highly related to human urine CSF (Stanley & Heard 1977).

In the meantime, Metcalf went on to show that there were many different cellular sources of CSFs, and that the types of colonies stimulated varied significantly with the different sources. In particular he showed with John Parker and John Sheridan that the CSF produced by activated lymphocytes or obtained from endotoxin-primed mouse lungs was antigenically different from M-CSF, was of a smaller size, and stimulated a greater proportion of granulocyte (G) or mixed granulocyte/macrophage (GM) colonies (11, 12). Attempts to purify this GM-CSF began with John Sheridan and were continued with Jim Camakaris.

Antony Burgess (figure 5) joined Metcalf's group in 1974. A protein chemist, Burgess trained in Sydney Leach's laboratory at the Biochemistry Department at Melbourne University. While working with Harold Scheraga at Cornell University in Ithaca, New York, Burgess spent time at the Weizmann Institute to access computer time and there became fascinated

Figure 5. Metcalf mentored hundreds of researchers at the Walter and Eliza Hall Institute. From left to right: Dr Nicos Nicola, Dr Justin McCarthy, Dr Antony Burgess, Dr Greg Johnson, Professor Donald Metcalf and Ms Sue Russell. Date: 1978. (Photograph courtesy of the Walter and Eliza Hall Institute.)

with blood cell formation after hearing a talk by Sachs. By an extraordinary coincidence he met Metcalf in Israel and obtained a postdoctoral position in his laboratory to purify CSFs. Burgess went on with Metcalf to purify GM-CSF to apparent homogeneity from mouse-lung-conditioned medium by 1977 (13). In 1976 Burgess invited Nicos Nicola (figure 5) (who had also trained with Syd Leach) to join him and Metcalf in the biochemical characterization of the CSFs. The three continued to fractionate CSFs from various mouse and human sources to try to define how many separate CSFs there were. Working with human-placenta-conditioned medium, they showed that two distinct GM-CSFs (termed α and β) could be separated from each other, and that they induced different kinetics of colony formation and different ratios of granulocyte to macrophage colonies (15). The former was ultimately called G-CSF (indicating its preference for stimulating granulocytic colonies), and the latter simply GM-CSF.

Around this time, Metcalf returned to his core idea that growth regulator balance might be able to control the growth of cancer cells. Using a mouse myelomonocytic leukaemic cell line (WEHI-3B) that he had generated with Noel Warner (figure 4) in 1969, he searched for sources of growth factors that could terminally differentiate these cells and extinguish their growth. He found that the sera of mice injected with bacterial endotoxin were a potent source of such a differentiation factor. In contrast, the differentiation activity of GM-CSF was rather weak. With Burgess he showed that the differentiation-inducing activity did not coincide with the majority of CSF in the serum but rather with a minor subspecies of CSF that favoured granulocyte colony formation (16). Because mouse-lung-conditioned medium from endotoxin-injected mice was an abundant source of GM-CSF, G-CSF and the WEHI-3B differentiation-inducing activity, he and Nicola embarked on a purification strategy that would separately monitor all three activities. By 1983 G-CSF had been purified to homogeneity and shown to be identical to the WEHI-3B differentiation-inducing activity and separate from GM-CSF (17).

In 1980 Burgess moved to a wing of the adjacent Royal Melbourne Hospital to become inaugural Director of the Melbourne branch of the Ludwig Institute for Cancer Research. He recruited Ashley Dunn from the Cold Spring Harbor Laboratories in Long Island, New York, and together with Nick Gough, an ex-WEHI PhD student of Jerry Adams, they embarked on a programme to clone the mouse GM-CSF gene. By collaborating with Lee Hood at California Institute of Technology, who was expert at gas-phase micro-amino acid sequencing, they obtained an N-terminal peptide sequence from material purified by Burgess with Lindsay Sparrow at the Commonwealth Scientific and Industrial Research Organization. From this sequence they generated redundant coding oligonucleotides that they used to select clones from a mouse lung complementary DNA (cDNA) library. These clones in turn were used to hybridize to mRNA from mouse lung or a T-cell line, and the selected mRNA was then translated into protein in frog oocytes. The protein thus produced was tested for GM-CSF biological activity by using microwell cultures of haemopoietic progenitor cells purified by flow cytometry. This allowed the molecular cloning of mouse GM-CSF cDNA and thus the capacity to generate large amounts of recombinant GM-CSF for testing *in vivo* (18).

Beginning during his sabbatical at the Swiss Institute for Cancer Research in Lausanne, Switzerland, in 1974–75 and continuing with Greg Johnson (figure 5) back in Melbourne, Metcalf showed that lectin-stimulated spleen cells produced colony-stimulating activity with the unique capacity to generate colonies that contained erythroid cells, megakaryocytes and eosinophils as well as granulocytes and macrophages (14). This activity, termed multi-CSF, was purified by Metcalf and Rob Cutler in 1985 (20) but by that time it had become apparent that multi-CSF was identical to a cytokine called interleukin-3 that had been purified by Jim Ihle in 1983 (Ihle *et al.* 1983) in the USA and cloned by Ian Young in 1984 (Fung *et al.* 1984) at the Australian National University. This completed the formal characterization of the four species of CSFs.

In vivo testing of CSFs and clinical trials

As the recombinant CSFs became available, Metcalf participated in determining their *in vivo* actions in mice and was immensely relieved that they proved to be genuine regulators of blood cell production as well as regulating the functional activation of granulocytes and macrophages and the migration of these cells into the tissues (22, 24).

The patent on GM-CSF was jointly owned by the Ludwig Institute for Cancer Research and the Walter and Eliza Hall Institute, and was ultimately licensed to the pharmaceutical company Schering-Plough for clinical development. Several clinical trials by competing groups and companies around the world were published from 1987 onwards, including studies by George Morstyn, Richard Fox, William Sheridan and Graham Lieschke conducted at the adjacent Melbourne Hospital (26, 30). They showed that immediately after an injection of GM-CSF there was a decrease in circulating granulocytes, macrophages and eosinophils followed by an increase 5–6 hours later, the kinetics suggesting that these effects were due to their egress from the blood into the tissues followed by their release from the bone marrow back into the blood. This was then sustained by increased haemopoiesis in the bone marrow. These activities of GM-CSF led to clinical trials for treating the neutropenia of AIDS patients, marrow failure in myelodysplastic syndromes and aplastic anaemia, neutropenias caused by radiation accidents, and neutropenias caused by chemotherapeutic treatments for cancer. It was also

Figure 6. The Spanish opera singer Señor José Carreras was an early recipient of colony-stimulating factors as part of his treatment for leukaemia, and in 1991 he visited Professor Metcalf at the Walter and Eliza Hall Institute. (Photograph courtesy of the Walter and Eliza Hall Institute.)

used to stimulate bone marrow recovery after transplantation, and one of the first patients to receive this experimental treatment was the famed opera tenor José Carreras (figure 6), whose bone marrow transplant, after his leukaemia treatment, failed to take until GM-CSF was administered. This was a particular source of pride for Metcalf, who, along with his wife, was a devoted opera fan. Carreras was grateful to Metcalf and offered him and his family and colleagues front-row seats to the Three Tenors (Carreras, Placido Domingo and Luciano Pavarotti) concert at the Melbourne Cricket Ground in 1997 as well as singing Happy Birthday to him on the occasion of his 70th birthday at the Melbourne Arts Centre in the same year.

Metcalf and Dunn's teams were beaten to the cloning of G-CSF by independent groups in Japan and the USA. The US pharmaceutical company Amgen decided to conduct some of its earliest clinical trials of recombinant G-CSF in Australia to benefit from the expertise of Metcalf and his collaborators. George Morstyn and Richard Fox again oversaw these trials at the Royal Melbourne Hospital (26, 30). As with GM-CSF, they observed a rapid decrease in blood granulocytes immediately after G-CSF injection, which was followed by an even more marked and sustained increase in blood neutrophils than seen with GM-CSF. These early studies showed that G-CSF abrogated or decreased the period of neutropenia after single-agent or combination chemotherapy for cancer, resulting in fewer days on antibiotics or days in hospital and also in some cases allowing dose escalation of the chemotherapy to attempt to eradicate the tumour.

During these studies Morstyn, Metcalf and Uli Duhrsen (a visiting scientist from Germany) were examining the blood of G-CSF-treated patients for haemopoietic colony-forming cells and noticed a marked 10–100-fold increase in all types of progenitor cells, peaking at four to six days after treatment with G-CSF (27). This critical observation led eventually to the realization that haemopoietic stem cells were also being mobilized into the peripheral blood after G-CSF administration. Further clinical trials led by Bill Sheridan (Sheridan *et al.* 1992) subsequently validated this observation and allowed the use of G-CSF-mobilized peripheral blood stem cells, collected by apheresis, to essentially replace the more invasive procedure of bone marrow transplants for haemopoietic reconstitution after myeloablative chemotherapy. This is not only an easier and safer method of obtaining stem cells from autologous or volunteer donors but it also seems more effective than bone marrow transplantation because of more rapid reconstitution of platelets and haemopoietic cells. Other clinical trials led by Memorial Sloan-Kettering Cancer Centre/Amgen researchers and David Dale (Dale *et al.* 1993) also revealed that G-CSF could ameliorate the neutropenia associated with severe chronic neutropenias, thus transforming the lives of such children.

The results of the first trials of GM-CSF and G-CSF on humans followed by subsequent trials for specific indications were a cause of great relief and satisfaction for Metcalf. For many years he had had niggling doubts that the CSFs might prove to be *in vitro* artefacts. In the ensuing 25 years he would see more than 20 million (mostly cancer) patients benefit from the use of CSFs (GM-CSF and G-CSF). He finally felt that his Fellowship from the Cancer Council had been justified.

CSF AND OTHER CYTOKINE RECEPTORS

Shortly after the purification of the CSFs, Metcalf, Burgess and Nicola used the precious few micrograms of purified CSFs available to radio-iodinate them and use them as probes to identify and characterize their cellular receptors. The CSFs were easily damaged by oxidizing conditions, so methods had to be developed that were essentially stoichiometric for incorporation of radioactive iodine. Their studies showed that several CSF receptors came in two forms—low affinity with equilibrium dissociation constants (K_d) in the nanomolar range and high affinity in the picomolar range, the latter correlating with the doses required for biological activity. Responding haemopoietic cells displayed remarkably small numbers of the high-affinity receptors at the cell surface, usually in the range 1–300 (19, 21, 23).

Metcalf used microscopic autoradiography to map the distribution of CSF receptors on different haemopoietic cells, and showed that the receptor distribution faithfully matched the cell types known to respond to each type of CSF (19, 21, 23). During these studies it became apparent that microscopic autoradiography could be a very powerful technique to detect cells that had acquired a CSF receptor, with the use of cDNA library expression screening. He, Nicola and David Gearing used this technique to screen a human placental cDNA library in COS cells and were able to clone a low-affinity form of the human GM-CSF receptor (Gearing *et al.* 1989) (31). By comparing its amino acid sequence with those of other recently cloned cytokine receptors they were able to define the unique sequence characteristics of this family of receptors. One of these defining sequences was a tryptophan–serine repeat (Trp-Ser-Xaa-Trp-Ser, where Xaa is any amino acid) in the extracellular domain that was particularly useful to define unique coding DNA sequences for cytokine receptors. Metcalf and Douglas Hilton used this method to clone additional new cytokine receptors, including the interleukin 11 (33) and interleukin 13 (34) receptors and showed that in each case the low-affinity form of the receptor was converted to high affinity by association with additional receptor subunits. They also generated neutralizing antibodies against the GM-CSF (32) and interleukin 13 (Redpath *et al.* 2013) receptors that are in clinical development for treating inflammatory and allergic diseases.

Leukaemia inhibitory factor

Although G-CSF was clearly the most potent cytokine stimulating the differentiation of WEHI-3B cells, work from Leo Sach's group in Israel using a different mouse myeloid leukaemic cell line (M1) pointed to a differentiation-inducing factor with properties different from those of G-CSF. Metcalf, Douglas Hilton and Nicola imported the M1 cell line from Japan and undertook direct comparisons with WEHI-3B cells in response to G-CSF, other cytokines and media conditioned by various cell lines. M1 cells did not respond to G-CSF or other CSFs, but instead a factor present in medium conditioned with Krebs ascites cells differentiated the M1 cells powerfully (25, 28). In fact at high concentrations of this putative factor, M1 cells failed to form colonies at all, so this novel activity was termed leukaemia inhibitory factor (LIF). Having learnt from the many years purifying CSFs, the group rapidly purified, sequenced (with Richard Simpson), cloned (with David Gearing and Nick Gough) and patented LIF (25, 28).

Shortly thereafter, Lindsay Williams (originally from the European Molecular Biology Laboratory in Heidelberg, Germany, but at that time working with Ashley Dunn at the Ludwig Institute in Melbourne), Nicholas Gough and Metcalf showed that LIF had precisely the opposite effect on embryonic stem cells—it was the long-sought-after factor that maintained them in a totipotent state and prevented differentiation into mature cell lineages (29). This surprising pleiotropy was reinforced in the next few years when various biological activities were purified and/or cloned and shown to be identical to LIF (Hilton 1992). These included adipocyte lipoprotein lipase activity, cholinergic neuronal differentiation factor, inducers of the acute phase response in liver hepatocytes, and a proliferation-inducing factor for myeloid DA1 cells. LIF was also shown to have effects on osteoblasts to stimulate bone formation and remodelling, to stimulate adrenocorticotrophic hormone release from the anterior pituitary during stress responses and to have an essential role in fertility by being required for blastocyst implantation into the endometrium and for the proper development of the placenta (Nicola & Babon 2015).

Suppressors of cytokine signalling (SOCS proteins)

The powerful differentiation and clonal suppression of M1 cells by LIF and, as subsequently shown, interleukin 6 (IL-6) made this cell line an ideal screening system for inhibitors of LIF or IL-6 action. Hilton, Robyn Starr and Metcalf used M1 colony growth in agar in the presence of IL-6 to screen cDNA libraries for expressed proteins that would prevent clonal suppression by IL-6. They found such a protein and called it suppressor of cytokine signalling 1 (SOCS1) (35). Overexpression of SOCS1 inhibited the actions of many cytokines that used the Janus tyrosine kinase/signal transducer and activator of transcription (JAK/STAT) signalling pathway. The group ultimately discovered eight members of the SOCS family (cytokine-inducible SH2-containing protein (CIS) and SOCS1–7), each of which contained a central Src homology 2 (SH2) domain (which recognizes tyrosine-phosphorylated protein sequences) and a conserved C-terminal domain called the SOCS box (36). In conjunction with Jian-Guo Zhang and Richard Simpson, the group showed that the SOCS box recruited elongins B and C and Cullin 5 to form an E3 ubiquitin ligase complex that ubiquitinated and targeted for proteasomal destruction any protein bound to the SH2 domain (37). In addition, two of the

Figure 7. Celebrating 50 years as a medical researcher in 2004 at a function at Government House organized by the Cancer Council Victoria. Here Metcalf (left) is joined by his four daughters (left to right: Penelope, Johanna, Kate and Mary-Ann) and his wife, Josephine (centre). (Photograph courtesy of the Walter and Eliza Hall Institute.) (Online version in colour.)

SOCS proteins (SOCS1 and SOCS3) contained an N-terminal sequence that could directly inhibit the catalytic activity of JAKs by binding in the substrate recognition domain of JAKs (Babon *et al*. 2012).

Despite the apparent broad specificity of SOCS proteins in inhibiting various cytokines, gene deletion studies in mice conducted by Warren Alexander and Metcalf revealed significant physiological specificity. Loss of SOCS1 caused perinatal lethality due to massive inflammation in the liver that could be abrogated by concomitant loss of interferon γ (38). Loss of SOCS3 was embryonic-lethal owing to a failure of placentation that could be prevented by breeding the SOCS3 knock-out mice to have only a single copy of the gene for LIF (42). Selective loss of SOCS3 in haemopoietic cells showed altered responsiveness only to the cytokines G-CSF and IL-6 (40, 41). Loss of SOCS2 resulted in gigantism due to enhanced growth hormone signalling (39), whereas the loss of other SOCS genes led to relatively milder phenotypes.

LATER DAYS

After turning 65 years of age, Metcalf retired from his positions as Division Head and Assistant Director at WEHI; however, there was no reduction to his contributions to science (figure 7). He continued to arrive at work at 6.30 a.m. although he left work a little earlier than in his younger days. As in most of his career he spent his days scoring haemopoietic colony assays, re-cloning colonies and acting as resident mouse pathologist to WEHI, systematically

Figure 8. Metcalf, escorted by his wife, Josephine, and Nicos Nicola, passing through a guard of honour of appreciative staff at WEHI celebrating his career shortly before his death. (Photograph courtesy of the Walter and Eliza Hall Institute.) (Online version in colour.)

scanning thousands of tissue sections for every genetically modified mouse strain or mouse leukaemia model created at the institute. This gruelling workload bent over a microscope meant he suffered from painful back problems throughout his career, but he was never more satisfied than being made to work long and hard hours, and was never happy unless there was sufficient work to keep him occupied.

In 2014, on the return flight from one of his beloved educational cruises, Metcalf felt considerable discomfort and sought a medical opinion when back in Melbourne. His symptoms were eventually determined to be due to disseminated pancreatic cancer, a disease with a very poor prognosis. Metcalf soldiered on at work while undergoing treatment until he was too unwell to work at the institute (figure 8). Even then he requested that his favourite microscope be transported to, and installed in, his home so he could continue to provide data to his various collaborators. Slides were ferried to him each day from WEHI, and the return trip consisted of precise and detailed pathological notes on the examined material.

Eventually Metcalf had to move into hospice care, where he was visited daily by his close family and devoted research colleagues from WEHI. To the end he remained alert and positive. He died on 15 December 2014 at the age of 85 years. His service was held at the Scots Presbyterian Church on 22 December, and he was buried at Melbourne General Cemetery in Parkville, just a stone's throw from the institute in which he had spent almost his entire working life.

Metcalf's work has provided a powerful legacy for medical science. Throughout his career he was recognized as the outstanding figurehead of modern haemopoietic research and the father of the field of molecular regulation of haemopoiesis. His many young students and postdoctoral fellows have carved out important careers throughout the world, testaments to his mentorship and vision. Metcalf's achievements were recognized at the highest levels, both nationally and internationally, as listed below.

Most important to Metcalf would be the fact that his research led directly to improved outcomes for millions of cancer patients worldwide. He always believed, and often 'preached', that the use of discoveries to help patients was the only purpose of medical research.

HONOURS

Civic

1976   Officer, Order of Australia (AO)
1993   Companion in the Order of Australia (AC)
2003   Centenary Medal, Australia

Scientific

1964   Syme Prize for Research, University of Melbourne
1966   Britannica Australia Award for Medicine
1968   AMA–BMA Prize for Medical Research
        Mollison Prize of AMA for Research on Pathology
1969   Fellow of the Australian Academy of Science
1974   Royal Society of Victoria Research Medal
1980   Gold Medal, Australian Cancer Society
1983   Fellow of the Royal Society of London
1986   James Cook Medal, Royal Society of NSW
        Wellcome Prize, Royal Society of London
1987   Foreign Associate, US National Academy of Sciences
        Bristol Myers Award for Distinguished Achievement in Cancer Research, USA
1988   Armand Hammer Prize for Cancer Research, USA
        Robert Koch Stiftung eV Prize, Germany
1989   Giovanni Lorenzini Prize for Basic Medical Research, USA/Italy
        Sloan Prize, General Motors Cancer Research Foundation, USA
1990   Rabbi Shai Shacknai Prize, University of Jerusalem, Israel
1991   The Clunies Ross National Science and Technology Award, Australia
1993   Albert Lasker Clinical Medical Research Award, USA
        Kantor Family Prize for Cancer Research Excellence, USA
        Louisa Gross Horwitz Prize, Columbia University, USA
        Kantor Family Prize for Cancer Research Excellence, USA
        Burnet Medal, Australian Academy of Science
1994   Jessie Stevenson Kovalenko Medal, US National Academy of Sciences
        Gairdner Foundation International Award, Canada
        Caledonian Research Foundation Prize, Scotland
        Torch of Learning Award, Friends of the Hebrew University of Jerusalem
1995   Ernst Neumann Award, International Society for Experimental Hematology
        Royal Medal, Royal Society of London

1996 Amgen Australia Prize
      Warren Alpert Foundation Prize, Harvard Medical School
1999 Chiron International Award, National Academy of Medicine, Italy
2000 The Victoria Prize, Victoria, Australia
2001 The Prime Minister's Prize for Science, Australia
2002 President's Medal, Australia and New Zealand Society for Cell and Developmental Biology
2004 Donnall Thomas Prize, American Society of Hematology
      Days of Molecular Medicine Foundation Mentorship Award
2005 Inaugural Salk Institute Medal for Research Excellence, USA
2006 Lifetime Achievement Award, Faculty of Medicine, Nursing and Health Sciences, Monash University, Australia
2007 Lifetime Achievement Award, American Association for Cancer Research
2008 Grand Hamdan International Award (UAE), Dubai
2013 Foundation Fellow of the American Association for Cancer Research (AACR) Academy

ACKNOWLEDGEMENTS

I am very grateful to Donald Metcalf's devoted wife, Jo, and his four daughters, Kate, Mary-Ann, Penelope and Johanna, for their friendship and advice during the writing of this memoir. I also thank Tony Burgess, Warren Alexander, Ashley Ng and Doug Hilton for their thoughtful comments and suggestions about the text.

The frontispiece photograph was taken in about 1980 and is reproduced by courtesy of the Walter and Eliza Hall Institute of Medical Research.

AUTHOR PROFILE

Nicos Nicola

Nicos Nicola obtained his PhD in the Biochemistry Department at Melbourne University and after a short postdoctoral period in Boston joined Donald Metcalf's Cancer Research Unit at the Walter and Eliza Hall Institute in 1977. He worked continuously with Metcalf until the latter's passing in 2014, and they co-authored 250 papers in that time. Nicola was responsible for leading purification efforts for G-CSF and LIF, the identification and cloning of cytokine receptors and the analysis of cell signalling pathways, all done in close collaboration with Metcalf. They developed a close and productive relationship, and Nicola was honoured to be asked by the family to deliver Metcalf's funeral oration in 2014.

REFERENCES TO OTHER AUTHORS

Babon, J. J., Kershaw, N. J., Murphy, J. M., Varghese, L. N., Laktyushin, A., Young, S. N., Lucet, I. S., Norton, R. S. & Nicola, N. A. 2012 Suppression of cytokine signaling by SOCS3: characterization of the mode of inhibition and the basis of its specificity. *Immunity* **36**, 239–250 (http://dx.doi.org/10.1016/j.immuni.2011.12.015).

Blythe, M. 1998 Professor Donald Metcalf (1929–2014), physiologist [online] (available at http://www.science.org. au/learning/general-audience/history/interviews-australian-scientists/professor-donald-metcalf-1929).

Dale, D. C., Bonilla, M. A., Davis, M. W., Nakanishi, A. M., Hammond, W. P., Kurtzberg, J., Wang, W., Jakubowski, A., Winton, E. & Lalezari, P. 1993 A randomized controlled phase III trial of recombinant human granulocyte colony-stimulating factor (filgrastim) for treatment of severe chronic neutropenia. *Blood* **81**, 2496–2502 (available at http://www.bloodjournal.org/content/bloodjournal/81/10/2496.full.pdf).

Eagle, H. 1959 Amino acid metabolism in mammalian cell cultures. *Science* **130**, 432–437 (http://dx.doi.org/10.1126/science.130.3373.432).

Evans, V. J., Bryant, J. C., Fioramonti, M. C., McQuilkin, W. T., Sanford, K. K. & Earle, W. R. 1956 Studies of nutrient media for tissue cells *in vitro*. I. A protein-free chemically defined medium for cultivation of strain L cells. *Cancer Res.* **16**, 77–86.

Fung, M. C., Hapel, A. J., Ymer, S., Cohen, D. R., Johnson, R. M., Campbell, H. D. & Young, I. G. 1984 Molecular cloning of cDNA for murine interleukin-3. *Nature* **307**, 233–237 (http://dx.doi.org/10.1038/307233a0).

Gearing, D. P., King, J. A., Gough, N. M. & Nicola, N. A. 1989 Expression cloning of a receptor for human granulocyte-macrophage colony-stimulating factor. *EMBO J.* **8**, 3667–3676.

Hilton, D. J. 1992 LIF: lots of interesting functions. *Trends Biochem. Sci.* **17**, 72–76 (http://dx.doi.org/10.1016/0968-0004(92)90505-4).

Hughes, R. 2006 Australian Biography. Full interview transcript: Donald Metcalf [online] (available at http://www.australianbiography.gov.au/subjects/metcalf/interview1.html).

Ihle, J. N., Keller, J., Oroszlan, S., Henderson, L. E., Copeland, T. D., Fitch, F., Prystowsky, M. B., Goldwasser, E., Schrader, J. W., Palaszynski, E., Dy, M. & Lebel, B. 1983 Biologic properties of homogeneous interleukin 3. I. Demonstration of WEHI-3 growth factor activity, mast cell growth factor activity, p cell-stimulating factor activity, colony-stimulating factor activity, and histamine-producing cell-stimulating factor activity. *J. Immunol.* **131**, 282–287.

Nicola, N. A. & Babon, J. J. 2015 Leukemia inhibitory factor (LIF). *Cytokine Growth Factor Rev.* **26**, 533–544 (http://dx.doi.org/10.1016/j.cytogfr.2015.07.001).

Pluznik, D. H. & Sachs, L. 1965 The cloning of normal 'mast' cells in tissue culture. *J. Cell. Physiol.* **66**, 319–324 (http://dx.doi.org/10.1002/jcp.1030660309).

Redpath, N. T., Xu, Y., Wilson, N. J., Fabri, L. J., Baca, M., Andrews, A. E., Braley, H., Lu, P., Ireland, C., Ernst, R. E., Woods, A., Forrest, G., An, Z., Zaller, D. M., Strohl, W. R., Luo, C. S., Czabotar, P. E., Garrett, T. P., Hilton, D. J., Nash, A. D., Zhang, J. G. & Nicola, N. A. 2013 Production of a human neutralizing monoclonal antibody and its crystal structure in complex with ectodomain 3 of the interleukin-13 receptor α1. *Biochem. J.* **451**, 165–175 (http://dx.doi.org/10.1042/BJ20121819).

Sheridan, W. P., Begley, C. G., Juttner, C. A., Szer, J., To, L. B., Maher, D., McGrath, K. M., Morstyn, G. & Fox, R. M. 1992 Effect of peripheral-blood progenitor cells mobilised by filgrastim (G-CSF) on platelet recovery after high-dose chemotherapy. *Lancet* **339**, 640–644 (http://dx.doi.org/10.1016/0140-6736(92)90795-5).

Stanley, E. R. & Heard, P. M. 1977 Factors regulating macrophage production and growth. Purification and some properties of the colony stimulating factor from medium conditioned by mouse L cells. *J. Biol. Chem.* **252**, 4305–4312.

Bibliography

The following publications are those referred to directly in the text. A full bibliography is available as electronic supplementary material at http://dx.doi.org/10.1098/rsbm.2016.0013 or via http://rsbm.royalsocietypublishing.org.

(1)   1955   The aetiological significance of differing patterns in the age incidence of cancer mortality. *Med. J. Aust.* **42**, 874–878.

(2)   Pseudoneoplastic nonspecific proliferative lesions on the chorio-allantois of the chick embryo. *Br. J. Cancer* **9**, 222–228 (http://dx.doi.org/10.1038/bjc.1955.18).

(3)   1956   A lymphocytosis stimulating factor in the plasma of chronic lymphatic leukaemic patients. *Br. J. Cancer* **10**, 169–178 (http://dx.doi.org/10.1038/bjc.1956.20).

(4)   1966   (With T. R. Bradley) The growth of mouse bone marrow cells *in vitro*. *Aust. J. Exp. Biol. Med. Sci.* **44**, 287–299.

(5)   1967   (With T. R. Bradley & W. Robinson) Stimulation by leukaemic sera of colony formation in solid agar cultures by proliferation of mouse bone marrow cells. *Nature* **213**, 926–927 (http://dx.doi.org/10.1038/213926a0).

(6)   (With R. Foster) Bone marrow colony-stimulating activity of serum from mice with viral-induced leukemia. *J. Natl Cancer Inst.* **39**, 1235–1245.

(7)   (With W. Robinson & T. R. Bradley) Stimulation by normal and leukemic mouse sera of colony formation *in vitro* by mouse bone marrow cells. *J. Cell. Physiol.* **69**, 83–92 (http://dx.doi.org/10.1002/jcp.1040690111).

(8)   1968   (With R. Foster Jr, W. A. Robinson & T. R. Bradley) Bone marrow colony stimulating activity in human sera. Results of two independent surveys in Buffalo and Melbourne. *Br. J. Haematol.* **15**, 147–159 (http://dx.doi.org/10.1111/j.1365-2141.1968.tb01524.x).

(9)   1969   (With E. R. Stanley) Partial purification and some properties of the factor in normal and leukaemic human urine stimulating mouse bone marrow colony growth *in vitro*. *Aust. J. Exp. Biol. Med. Sci.* **47**, 467–483.

(10) 1970   (With M. A. Moore) Ontogeny of the haemopoietic system: yolk sac origin of in vivo and in vitro colony forming cells in the developing mouse embryo. *Br. J. Haematol.* **18**, 279–296 (http://dx.doi.org/10.1111/j.1365-2141.1970.tb01443.x).

(11) 1973   (With J. W. Sheridan) A low molecular weight factor in lung-conditioned medium stimulating granulocyte and monocyte colony formation in vitro. *J. Cell. Physiol.* **81**, 11–24 (http://dx.doi.org/10.1002/jcp.1040810103).

(12) 1974   (With J. W. Parker) Production of colony-stimulating factor in mitogen-stimulated lymphocyte cultures. *J. Immunol.* **112**, 502–510.

(13) 1977   (With A. W. Burgess & J. Camakaris) Purification and properties of colony-stimulating factor from mouse lung-conditioned medium. *J. Biol. Chem.* **252**, 1998–2003.

(14)   (With G. R. Johnson) Pure and mixed erythroid colony formation in vitro stimulated by spleen conditioned medium with no detectable erythropoietin. *Proc. Natl Acad. Sci. USA* **74**, 3879–3882 (http://dx.doi.org/10.1073/pnas.74.9.3879).

(15) 1979   (With N. A. Nicola, G. R. Johnson & A. W. Burgess) Separation of functionally distinct human granulocyte-macrophage colony-stimulating factors. *Blood* **54**, 614–627.

(16) 1980   (With A. W. Burgess) Characterization of a serum factor stimulating the differentiation of myelomonocytic leukemic cells. *Int. J. Cancer* **26**, 647–654 (http://dx.doi.org/10.1002/ijc.2910260517).

(17) 1983   (With N. A. Nicola, M. Matsumoto & G. R. Johnson) Purification of a factor inducing differentiation in murine myelomonocytic leukemia cells. Identification as granulocyte colony-stimulating factor. *J. Biol. Chem.* **258**, 9017–9023.

(18) 1984   (With N. M. Gough, J. Gough, A. Kelso, D. Grail, N. A. Nicola, A. W. Burgess & A. R. Dunn) Molecular cloning of cDNA encoding a murine haematopoietic growth regulator, granulocyte-macrophage colony stimulating factor. *Nature* **309**, 763–767 (http://dx.doi.org/10.1038/309763a0).

(19)   (With N. A. Nicola) Binding of the differentiation-inducer, granulocyte-colony-stimulating factor, to responsive but not unresponsive leukemic cell lines. *Proc. Natl Acad. Sci. USA* **81**, 3765–3769 (http://dx.doi.org/10.1073/pnas.81.12.3765).

(20) 1985   (With R. L. Cutler, N. A. Nicola & G. R. Johnson) Purification of a multipotential colony-stimulating factor from pokeweed mitogen-stimulated mouse spleen cell conditioned medium. *J. Biol. Chem.* **260**, 6579–6587.

(21)   (With N. A. Nicola) Binding of ^{125}I-labeled granulocyte colony-stimulating factor to normal murine hemopoietic cells. *J. Cell. Physiol.* **124**, 313–321 (http://dx.doi.org/10.1002/jcp.1041240222).

(22) 1986   (With C. G. Begley, G. R. Johnson, N. A. Nicola, A. F. Lopez & D. J. Williamson) Effects of purified bacterially synthesized murine multi-CSF (IL-3) on hematopoiesis in normal adult mice. *Blood* **68**, 46–57.

(23)   (With N. A. Nicola) Binding of iodinated multipotential colony-stimulating factor (interleukin-3) to murine bone marrow cells. *J. Cell. Physiol.* **128**, 180–188 (http://dx.doi.org/10.1002/jcp.1041280207).

(24) 1987 (With C. G. Begley, D. J. Williamson, E. C. Nice, J. De Lamarter, J. J. Mermod, D. Thatcher & A. Schmidt) Hemopoietic responses in mice injected with purified recombinant murine GM-CSF. *Exp. Hematol.* **15**, 1–9.

(25)   (With D. P. Gearing, N. M. Gough, J. A. King, D. J. Hilton, N. A. Nicola, R. J. Simpson, E. C. Nice & A. Kelso) Molecular cloning and expression of cDNA encoding a murine myeloid leukaemia inhibitory factor (LIF). *EMBO J.* **6**, 3995–4002.

(26) 1988 (With G. Morstyn, L. Campbell, L. M. Souza, N. K. Alton, J. Keech, M. Green, W. Sheridan & R. Fox) Effect of granulocyte colony stimulating factor on neutropenia induced by cytotoxic chemotherapy. *Lancet* **331**, 667–672 (http://dx.doi.org/10.1016/S0140-6736(88)91475-4).

(27)   (With U. Duhrsen, J. L. Villeval, J. Boyd, G. Kannourakis & G. Morstyn) Effects of recombinant human granulocyte colony-stimulating factor on hematopoietic progenitor cells in cancer patients. *Blood* **72**, 2074–2081.

(28)   (With D. J. Hilton, N. A. Nicola & N. M. Gough) Resolution and purification of three distinct factors produced by Krebs ascites cells which have differentiation-inducing activity on murine myeloid leukemic cell lines. *J. Biol. Chem.* **263**, 9238–9243.

(29)   (With R. L. Williams, D. J. Hilton, S. Pease, T. A. Willson, C. Stewart, D. P. Gearing, E. F. Wagner, N. A. Nicola & N. M. Gough) Myeloid leukaemia inhibitory factor maintains the developmental potential of embryonic stem cells. *Nature* **336**, 684–687 (http://dx.doi.org/10.1038/336684a0).

(30) 1989 (With G. J. Lieschke, D. Maher, J. Cebon, M. O'Connor, M. Green, W. Sheridan, A. Boyd, M. Rallings, E. Bonnem, A. W. Burgess, K. McGrath, R. M. Fox & G. Morstyn) Effects of bacterially synthesized recombinant human granulocyte-macrophage colony-stimulating factor in patients with advanced malignancy. *Ann. Intern. Med.* **110**, 357–364 (http://dx.doi.org/10.7326/0003-4819-110-5-357).

(31) 1990 (With N. A. Nicola, D. P. Gearing & N. M. Gough) Low-affinity placenta-derived receptors for human granulocyte-macrophage colony-stimulating factor can deliver a proliferative signal to murine hemopoietic cells. *Proc. Natl Acad. Sci. USA* **87**, 4670–4674 (http://www.pnas.org/content/87/12/4670).

(32) 1993 (With N. A. Nicola, K. Wycherley, A. W. Boyd, J. E. Layton & D. Cary) Neutralizing and nonneutralizing monoclonal antibodies to the human granulocyte-macrophage colony-stimulating factor receptor alpha-chain. *Blood* **82**, 1724–1731.

(33) 1994 (With D. J. Hilton, A. A. Hilton, A. Raicevic, S. Rakar, M. Harrison-Smith, N. M. Gough, C. G. Begley, N. A. Nicola & T. A. Willson) Cloning of a murine IL-11 receptor α-chain; requirement for gp130 for high affinity binding and signal transduction. *EMBO J.* **13**, 4765–4775.

(34) 1996 (With D. J. Hilton, J. G. Zhang, W. S. Alexander, N. A. Nicola & T. A. Willson) Cloning and characterization of a binding subunit of the interleukin 13 receptor that is also a component of the interleukin 4 receptor. *Proc. Natl Acad. Sci. USA* **93**, 497–501 (http://dx.doi.org/10.1073/pnas.93.1.497).

(35) 1997 (With R. Starr, T. A. Willson, E. M. Viney, L. J. Murray, J. R. Rayner, B. J. Jenkins, T. J. Gonda, W. S. Alexander, N. A. Nicola & D. J. Hilton) A family of cytokine-inducible inhibitors of signalling. *Nature* **387**, 917–921 (http://dx.doi.org/10.1038/43206).

(36) 1998 (With D. J. Hilton, R. T. Richardson, W. S. Alexander, E. M. Viney, T. A. Willson, N. S. Sprigg, R. Starr, S. E. Nicholson & N. A. Nicola) Twenty proteins containing a C-terminal SOCS box form five structural classes. *Proc. Natl Acad. Sci. USA* **95**, 114–119 (http://dx.doi.org/10.1073/pnas.95.1.114).

(37) 1999 (With J.-G. Zhang, A. Farley, S. E. Nicholson, T. A. Willson, L. M. Zugaro, R. J. Simpson, R. L. Moritz, D. Cary, R. Richardson, G. Hausmann, B. T. Kile, S. B. Kent, W. S. Alexander, D. J. Hilton, N. A. Nicola & M. Baca) The conserved SOCS box motif in suppressors of cytokine signaling binds to elongins B and C and may couple bound proteins to proteasomal degradation. *Proc. Natl Acad. Sci. USA* **96**, 2071–2076 (http://dx.doi.org/10.1073/pnas.96.5.2071).

(38)   (With W. S. Alexander, R. Starr, J. E. Fenner, C. L. Scott, E. Handman, N. S. Sprigg, J. E. Corbin, A. L. Cornish, R. Darwiche, C. M. Owczarek, T. W. Kay, N. A. Nicola, P. Hertzog & D. J. Hilton) SOCS1 is a critical inhibitor of interferon γ signaling and prevents the potentially fatal neonatal actions of this cytokine. *Cell* **98**, 597–608 (http://dx.doi.org/10.1016/S0092-8674(00)80047-1).

(39) 2000 (With C. J. Greenhalgh, E. Viney, T. A. Willson, R. Starr, N. A. Nicola, D. J. Hilton & W. S. Alexander) Gigantism in mice lacking suppressor of cytokine signalling-2. *Nature* **405**, 1069–1073 (http://dx.doi. org/10.1038/35016611).

(40) 2003 (With B. A. Croker, D. L. Krebs, J. G. Zhang, S. Wormald, T. A. Willson, E. G. Stanley, L. Robb, C. J. Greenhalgh, I. Forster, B. E. Clausen, N. A. Nicola, D. J. Hilton, A. W. Roberts & W. S. Alexander) SOCS3 negatively regulates IL-6 signaling *in vivo*. *Nature Immunol.* **4**, 540–545 (http://dx.doi. org/10.1038/ni931).

(41) 2004 (With B. A. Croker, L. Robb, W. Wei, S. Mifsud, L. Dirago, L. A. Cluse, K. D. Sutherland, L. Hartley, E. Williams, J. G. Zhang, D. J. Hilton, N. A. Nicola, W. S. Alexander & A. W. Roberts) SOCS3 is a critical physiological negative regulator of G-CSF signaling and emergency granulopoiesis. *Immunity* **20**, 153–165 (http://dx.doi.org/10.1016/S1074-7613(04)00022-6).

(42) 2005 (With L. Robb, K. Boyle, S. Rakar, L. Hartley, J. Lochland, A. W. Roberts & W. S. Alexander) Genetic reduction of embryonic leukemia-inhibitory factor production rescues placentation in SOCS3-null embryos but does not prevent inflammatory disease. *Proc. Natl Acad. Sci. USA* **102**, 16333–16338 (http://dx.doi.org/10.1073/pnas.0508023102).

LESLIE SYDNEY DENNIS MORLEY FREng FRAeS

23 May 1924 — 16 June 2011

LESLIE SYDNEY DENNIS MORLEY FREng FRAeS

23 May 1924 — 16 June 2011

Elected FRS 1992

By A. J. Morris FREng FRAeS

Cranfield University, Cranfield, Bedford MK43 0AL, UK

Leslie Morley's research focused on modelling structural behaviour, with particular emphasis on plates and shells. He developed the Morley shell equation, which has been acknowledged as the simplest equation consistent with first-order shell theory. As the finite element method rose to prominence he developed elements for both plates and shells. He then worked on developing a set of new finite elements able to handle complex shell behaviour in both the linear and nonlinear regimes. He also observed that it was possible to augment the finite element solution by using singular solutions to calculate the stress intensity factor at a crack tip in a thin-walled metal structure and thereby to compute crack propagation rates. In undertaking his research Morley probed into the mathematical and physical depths of the problems he confronted, and produced some outstanding and significant results.

EARLY YEARS

Leslie Morley, or 'Les' as he liked to be known, was born on 23 May 1924 in Brighton, Sussex. He was the only child of Sydney Victor Morley and Doris May Huntley Morley.

In 1926, when the family moved to Portsmouth, Les's father was an Able Seaman in the Royal Navy and the family means were modest. By 1937 his father had reached the rank of Chief Petty Officer on the battle cruiser HMS *Hood*, flagship of the Royal Navy. He specialized in the Hood's main armament, its 15-inch gunnery, and was highly regarded as one of HMS *Hood*'s longest-serving ratings. Les recalled that his father was also a leading exponent of the prewar Royal Tournament naval gun competitions, both as a participant and later as an instructor for the Portsmouth team.

During his early childhood Les suffered a serious speech impediment that persisted throughout his life, although it became less evident in later life. This limited his ability to

* a.j.morris@cranfield.ac.uk

http://dx.doi.org/10.1098/rsbm.2015.0029

435

undertake public speaking or lecturing duties. However, he derived much encouragement in his educational pursuits from his father and mother, who had themselves received only an elementary education. He recalled that as a child he had a fascination for numbers and each evening would keenly prepare his own arithmetical exercises for completion.

His father had developed a passion for trigonometry as part of his naval training in gunnery. His direct influence on Les's developing mathematical interests was, however, limited by the necessities of his naval service. This required his father's serving commissions of two and a half years at sea followed by a similar period at home, based in Portsmouth.

Four years after his promotion to Chief Petty Officer, Les's father was lost in action in the fateful encounter between HMS *Hood* and the battleship *Bismarck* in the Denmark Strait on 24 May 1941, a day after Les's 17th birthday. For the duration of the war Les elected to remain with his mother at Portsmouth until her untimely death in 1945.

EDUCATION AND EMPLOYMENT

Les was 15 years of age at the outbreak of World War II, and Portsmouth, with its Royal Navy dockyard, was regarded by Germany as an important target. At the time he was a student at Portsmouth Northern Secondary School and was offered the opportunity to evacuate with the school to the safer haven of Peter Symonds School in Winchester. It was decided, however, that he should leave school to remain in Portsmouth with his mother, who would have otherwise been on her own while his father was away on active service.

In 1940 Les obtained employment with the Portsmouth-based Airspeed Limited aircraft company and commenced a five-year indentured apprenticeship as a tool room fitter. He started in the machine shop with deburring operations before progressing to work on the capstan lathes.

The next two years of his apprenticeship from 1941 to 1943 were spent in the tool room itself, the centre of precision engineering. Here Les learned the skills and craftsmanship that served him well throughout his life. He gained experience in jig assembly and tool making. He soon developed an interest in the design and development of multiple-action press tools to blank and bend light alloy sheet into intricate components in a single operation.

This period coincided with the commencement of German air raids on Portsmouth, during which Les served with the Home Guard, helping to man the anti-aircraft batteries of rocket guns on Southsea front adjacent to the Dockyard. He retained vivid memories of Messerschmitt fighters coming in over the Isle of Wight to shoot down the defensive balloons. These fighters were soon followed by Stuka bombers taking up formation to dive-bomb the Royal Navy dockyards and the RAF fighter base at Thorney Island. Les recalled that during these raids they would launch some 50 rockets at a time in formation. Each rocket was about 4 feet long and some 3 inches in diameter. He recalled that it was a frightening experience as the rockets left the rails and that the noise of the launch was horrendous! Les always wondered how the German pilots must have felt when these exploded simultaneously in a box-like array in the sky.

His apprenticeship continued with a move, in 1943, to the Airspeed Aircraft Drawing Office to help prepare drawings for the Horsa gliders, which played such a prominent part in the Battle of Arnhem. He then transferred to Airspeed's Stress Office, which subsequently changed location in 1944 to Christchurch (near Bournemouth) to work on the design and development of the postwar civilian Airspeed Ambassador airliner. During 1944–45 Les worked on door cut-outs in the fuselage of the Ambassador airliner.

During the course of his apprenticeship Les attended part-time classes at Portsmouth Municipal Technical School. By 1943 he had completed his studies and was awarded the Ordinary National Certificate in Mechanical Engineering, with special reference to Aeronautics. This was followed by part-time studies at Southampton University College, where in 1945 he gained a Higher National Certificate in mathematics, strength of materials and structures, and applied aerodynamics.

By 1945 Les had completed his apprenticeship and had by then, unfortunately, lost both of his parents. His Certificate of Industry from Airspeed Limited dated 23 May 1945 read:

> An outstanding Apprentice in every respect. Consistent in every regard and full of initiative. At part time studies he has worked extremely hard under difficult war conditions and obtained the Ordinary National Certificate and the Higher National Certificate during his Apprenticeship. Deserving of every encouragement.

Les continued his employment with Airspeed Limited as a 'stressman' in the Stress Office until 1946, when, by chance, he noticed a column in the *Daily Mirror* that announced the setting up of a new College of Aeronautics at Cranfield. He applied and had the good fortune to gain a place with the first batch of students as well as obtaining a Hampshire County Council grant to pay the fees and maintenance.

From 1946 to 1948 Les was a founder student on the Post Graduate Diploma Course in the Theory of Structures at Cranfield, studying aerodynamics, aircraft design and mathematics, and completed a project entitled 'Stress analysis of openings in reinforced thin walled cylinders'. He remembered Cranfield with great affection and that Professor W. S. Hemp had provided much inspiration and encouragement both at this time and also in his later research work.

From 1948 to 1949 Les gained employment with the National Luchtvaartlaboratorium (NLR) in Amsterdam as a Research Officer. His work concerned structures research investigating the behaviour of thin-walled plates and shells. He also undertook work on the flexibility of aircraft during landing impact. It was here that Les published his first three original research papers in the *Reports Transactions of the NLR*.

In 1949, Les returned to the UK and was employed as a Technical Assistant at the Bristol Aeroplane Company, Filton, Bristol. Here he was involved in stress work on the Brabazon Mk 2 fuselage with special reference to the strength of undercarriage frames subjected to concentrated impact loads. He was also involved with determining the flutter speed of highly swept-back wing designs of single-mission expendable aircraft. He joined the staff of the Royal Aircraft Establishment (RAE) at Farnborough as a Senior Scientific Officer in 1952 and remained until his retirement in 1984 as a Deputy Chief Scientific Officer (Individual Merit).

Shortly before he was due to retire from the RAE Les wrote to John Whiteman, Director of the Brunel Institute of Computational Mathematics (BICOM), at Brunel University asking if a position could be found for him; BICOM research concentrates on finite element methods and their applications, including fracture. John obtained contracts for work on shell finite elements and in 1985 was able to appoint Les as a Professorial Research Fellow in BICOM. Professor R. E. D. Bishop FRS, then Vice Chancellor of Brunel University, delighted in saying to John, 'How on earth did you persuade Morley to join BICOM!' Les remained at BICOM for 10 years, supervising research students Michael Mould and Tim Bangemann, providing wise advice and input to the research programme, and being involved in the organizing of the triennial 'The Mathematics of Finite Elements and Applications' (MAFELAP) conferences. He related very positively to and had a strong empathy with his students, frequently saying that his time at BICOM was one of the happiest periods of his working life.

This was followed from 1999 to 2002 by a collaborative research venture with Imperial College and the Ministry of Defence. In both posts he continued his research and supervised a succession of PhD students, which he found a particularly rewarding activity.

RESEARCH ACHIEVEMENTS

Morley started his research career at the NLR in Amsterdam, where he produced several internal publications on the behaviour of stiffened plates and reinforced monocoque structures. Although this did not result in any external publications, it introduced him to the world of research.

Shortly after Morley joined the RAE in 1952, the UK's first civil jet airliner, the de Havilland Comet, crashed and became the subject of investigation at the RAE under Arnold (later Sir Arnold) Hall (FRS 1953), the then Director of the Establishment. Initially, the Head of Structures Department, P. D. Walker, thought that the cause might be high stress levels induced by stress waves (or, as Les once expressed it to me, 'he had a bee in his bonnet'). Morley was asked to look at this possibility and studied the stress waves that occur in a reinforced shell structure disintegrating under internal air pressure as the result of fuselage failure. This was a potentially significant factor in establishing the root cause of the Comet disaster because there was a possibility that stress waves, generated early during the disintegration, might have caused a secondary fracture capable of misleading the accident investigators. Unfortunately, this work was not published, with the exception of one paper on stress waves in a naturally curved rod (3)*, which appeared long after the cause of the Comet crash was fully understood and identified as fatigue failure of the fuselage structure.

After this early diversion, Morley focused his research objectives on the behaviour of plates and shells. This was before the introduction of digital computers, so the limitations in calculating power meant that his early papers on plates and shells were often devoted to the application of methods that were specific to a class of problem. In many of the papers, however, Morley was clearly looking for approaches that had a more general domain of application. One outstanding example is his 1956 paper entitled 'The approximate solution of plate problems' (1). Here Morley employed a superposition of particular functions, each satisfying the governing differential equations on the interior of the plate but not on the plate boundary. The lack of compatibility was accounted for by minimizing a potential energy function. This anticipated the approach used in creating finite elements through the application of a variational principle. So it is no surprise that once the finite element method appeared he immediately recognized that this provided the key for obtaining solutions for general analysis problems that arise in the design of structures operating in complex loading environments. He returned to this topic in a subsequent paper (6) in which he derived variational principles for plate bending problems in which the boundary was part clamped or simply supported, or where boundary tractions were prescribed.

* Numbers in this form refer to the bibliography at the end of the text.

Turning his attention to thin shells, Morley showed that the equations that govern the small deflection behaviour of a cylindrical shell could be expressed by a relatively simple equation that improved on that presented by Donnell (2). This equation, known as the Morley shell equation, is acknowledged as the simplest possible equation consistent with the errors of first-approximation shell theory. He then employed the equation to solve the problem of elastic thin-walled cylindrical shells subjected to radial point loads.

Morley's continued researches in this early period culminated in the publication of his monograph *Skew plates and structures* (5), which has had wide application in aeronautical and civil engineering structures. Although published in 1963, the monograph remains a classic and is still frequently cited. Results from the monograph and those from an earlier paper on the bending of rhombic plates (4) have been extensively used by the finite element community as a source for benchmark cases.

Although his early work was significant, particularly that presented in the monograph, Morley's reputation was built on his work in developing the finite elements for the solution of thin-walled plates and shells. In the period 1962–65 several papers had appeared that introduced triangular finite elements for plate bending problems. These displacement-based elements could be either conforming (preserving displacement continuity across element junctions) or non-conforming (where such continuity is not preserved); conforming elements tended to exhibit over-stiffness, whereas non-conforming elements did not guarantee convergence. These problems were circumvented by the introduction of equilibrium elements in which the element internal variables were bending moments and inter-element continuity was enforced by Lagrange multipliers modelled by edge displacement, a technique originally introduced by Fraeijs de Veubeke (1965) and exploited by Herrman (1967) and particularly by Allman (1970). Such elements are somewhat complicated and in the case of Fraeijs de Vuebeke and Allman the use of mid-side connection quantities created difficulties in that it gave rise to a rank deficient matrix. Morley sought for simplicity. In satisfying this quest he proposed a non-conforming displacement triangular finite element that was derived from quadratically varying displacements and was therefore a constant-bending moment element (7, 10). Morley showed that this simple element gave identical results to those given by Allman's element that and this ensured convergence as successively finer meshes were employed. The element also satisfied the patch tests used to ensure the quality of the element's performance. Morley's triangular plate bending element proved to be a seminal contribution in the finite element analysis of flat plates and has been employed in numerous finite element packages. It was a key development, which he exploited in working on the creation of thin-shell finite elements. Morley's flat-facet triangular bending element, which continues to be known in the literature as the 'Morley element', has been and continues to be exploited by workers in computational mechanics and particularly in thin-shell behaviour (see, for example, Ming & Xu 2006).

Morley subsequently generalized this element to cover intrinsic geometrically nonlinear situations (20). This generalization represented a considerable achievement because, for the first time, it allowed the calculation of the strain energy employing Fréchet directional derivatives, essential for the rational analysis of the discrete finite element equations governing the stability of equilibrium at singular points in the equilibrium path where, for example, the global tangent stiffness matrix is singular.

Morley recognized that the approach he employed in solutions of plate and shell problems could be adapted to problems with inherent stress singularities. In addressing this problem

(8) he proposed a modification to the Rayleigh–Ritz method that employed a superposition of analytic solutions and piecewise continuous finite element trial functions. In doing so the finite element solution itself was partitioned into recognizable parts. The implementation resolved into four successive stages:

(i) a first part of the solution is the conventional finite element approximation of the base problem using piecewise polynomials;

(ii) each individual discontinuity or singularity is isolated and its analytical structure described in terms of an analytic solution that satisfies exactly the governing equations over the domain, but not the boundary conditions;

(iii) the boundary conditions and body forces arising from stage (ii) provide further individual problems, each contributing to the overall finite element solution;

(iv) the differences between the analytic functions and their finite element solutions generated in stages (iii) and (ii) provides the extension to the field of definition of the coordinate functions. Their amplitude is determined by minimizing the potential energy to reveal the stress concentration factor.

Morley then employed this approach to evaluate the stress concentration factor for a simply supported square flat plate under a uniformly distributed load with a square hole (9). He then moved to consider (12) how this could be developed to allow the finite element method to be used to provide estimates of the stress intensity factor (SIF) used to estimate crack growth rate. The SIF is a measure of the amplitude of the dominant singularity at the ends of a crack and can therefore be computed by Morley's method deployed with a finite element model. After the initial publication of this ground-breaking work, Morley left further development of the method to P. Bartholomew (Bartholomew 1978) while he returned to considering the solution of cylindrical shell problems but now in the context of the finite element method.

He soon realized that the finite element analysis of thin-walled shells is not as straightforward as the corresponding analysis for flat plates. It was clear to him that no work had been done to examine the nature of the mathematical solutions for loaded thin-walled cylindrical shells, which could then be compared with those delivered by finite element models. In developing the Morley shell theory, Morley had implicitly employed the fact that first-order thin-shell theory admits small differences in the physical quantities of the same order as those due to the inherently neglected transverse normal and shearing strains, a conjecture rigorously demonstrated by Koiter (1969). In a paper (11) Morley re-derived his governing partial differential equation for cylindrical shells on a consistent basis within the context of Koiter's first-approximation theory. He then derived a complete set of complementary function solutions in terms of low-degree polynomials in the shell surface coordinates. These provided a basis for evaluating finite elements that use surface coordinates. This work was developed in conjunction with A. J. Morris (14) to explore the situation in which smooth distributions of displacements give rise to inextensional deformations. These solutions were termed 'sensitive solutions' because many finite element formulations produced extraordinarily inaccurate results when attempting to recover these fundamental solutions. The root cause for this problem is an element's inability to capture stress states induced by inextensional behaviour without also introducing artificial stresses under rigid-body movement.

Morley further explored solutions for cylindrical thin shells in a major paper (13) published in 1976. In this paper he clearly indentified the set of solution types required to cover all the deformation states for finite elements purporting to solve this class of problem. The set includes membrane actions, inextensional deformations and some edge effects. He then developed a triangular finite element based on the Fraeijs de Veubeke and Allman flat-plate elements to create a hybrid shell element. This employed polynomial approximations to stress resultants on the interior of the element and a line distribution of normal displacements along the element boundaries to act as Lagrange multipliers to ensure inter-element stress continuity. This approach led to the requirement for mid-side connection quantities with its ensuing problems. Allman, working in the same group at the RAE as Morley, had proposed a procedure for avoiding the problems of mid-side nodes. Morley asserted that this was too complicated to be applied to shell elements so he conducted numerical experiments to find suitable trial functions through which he could eliminate mid-side connection quantities. This allowed him to develop a triangular shell element that could adequately represent the required solution set.

Morley continued his study of the equations of first-approximation shell theory in his paper published in 1982 (15). There he developed solutions for inextensional bending of thin shells but focused on solutions for a class of elements that could have positive, zero or negative Gaussian curvature. The paper presents closed-form exact polynomial solutions to the inextensional bending problem and represents a significant improvement on Flügge (1960), which pertained to spherical shells only. In essence, achieving exact solutions could only be obtained for slowly varying curvature, as would occur in shallow shell elements. However, such a characteristic would be typical of the elements normally employed in the finite element analysis of thin shells. In a subsequent paper (16) Morley pointed out that his inextensional bending solutions could be applied to homogeneous membrane actions from Gol'denveizer's static-geometric analogue. He then generated a set of simple solutions that could be used as criteria for assessing finite elements for shells of revolution, non-circular cylindrical cylinders and cones.

The role of bending in the finite element analysis of thin shells was addressed in depth by Morley working with M. Mould, and the results of this work were reported in a seminal paper (17) and developed subsequently (19). In undertaking their investigation a new simple flat triangular element was devised using a combined constant strain element (essentially the Turner, Clough, Martin & Topp element (Turner *et al.* 1956)) and Morley's constant-bending-moment element. This combined element was termed a 'vehicle element' and had displacement connectors at each vertex and a single rotation connector at each mid-side. A 'transitional element' was then generated by giving the element a vanishingly small flexural rigidity, which was then further degenerated to form a 'membrane element' by removing the mid-side rotation connector. This was a very versatile combination of elements allowing Morley and Mould to examine a comprehensive set of solutions covering membrane states, inextensional bending, edge effects and rigid-body movement. The work revealed two quite different roles for bending freedoms. One concerned inextensional bending moments extending over a whole shell model. The other concerned local rotational movements accompanying the curvature changes of inextensional bending and edge effects. The paper presented extensive numerical comparisons with solutions obtained from classical first-order thin-shell theory. Morley did not feel this work provided the definitive treatment of thin-shell finite elements: the paper contained the statement

In this attempt to promote a better understanding of the finite element method in its application to the linear theory of thin shells it has become clear   that   much   opportunity   remains   for further work both in the method of assessment and in the field of mathematical abstraction.

It is also worth pointing out that the 'vehicle element' devised for this study was itself extremely effective in the analysis of thin-shell problems.

Morley's researches gave stimulating insights into the fundamentals of finite element analysis in its application to thin-walled shells. This highlighted the difficulty of applying the finite element method in the solution of thin-shell analysis problems. It is unfortunate that the commercial suppliers of modern finite element software packages and their users consider that the use of three-dimensional elements relieves them of any obligation to take into account Morley's research. This introduces a degree of unreliability into finite element solutions of real-world thin-shell structures; the analysis of thin-shell structures is not a situation in which ignorance is bliss.

In working on the development of finite elements for curved shells Morley formulated the defining equations using tensor calculus and then transformed the tensor formulation into what have been termed physical components. This involves the unwieldy and often daunting task of interpreting the components of general vector and tensor equations referred to curvilinear coordinates. Morley observed that the commonly used concept of physical components, introduced by Truesdell (1953), is useful, but these are referred to tensor coordinate directions and consequently they relate directly to measurable quantities only in the coordinate directions and only where the coordinates are orthogonal. Morley recognized that this represented a deficiency and for finite element applications for curved structures it required measurable quantities that had orthogonal components oriented with respect to the tensor coordinates, whether these are orthogonal or oblique. He therefore returned to considering a method for deriving such measurable quantities based on employing anholonomic coordinates and termed these 'practical' components (18). He did not regard this paper as the final word, commenting that the method described in his paper was intended solely as an illustration.

We may conclude this review of Morley's research and publications by noting that his life's work has coherence and represents a series of steps in the development of methods for the solution of thin-plate and thin-shell problems. He had a clear mind and a way of probing into the mathematical and physical depths of the problems he addressed that produced some outstanding and significant results.

Morley had a writing style that was both elegant and precise. He adopted a policy of placing drafts of his written papers in his desk and leaving them for several weeks. After this, the papers were carefully read with a fresh eye and then redrafted to enhance clarity. He had a very disciplined approach to his writing, deleting any word not deemed 'absolutely essential'; this is a trait he passed on to those of us who had the privilege of working with him.

His contribution to his field of research was formally recognized by the award of Cranfield University's first DSc degree, by his election as a Fellow of the Royal Aerospace Society (1962), the Institute for Mathematics and its Applications (1964), the Royal Academy of Engineering (1982) and the Royal Society (1992).

PERSONAL LIFE

Les's background as an apprentice tool room fitter equipped him with many useful practical engineering skills. As a young man in the 1940s Les had developed a great interest in and owned several classic British motorcycles of the time, including a Rudge, a Chater-Lea, a

Figure 1. Les on his Vincent HRD Comet circa 1945.

Triumph Speed Twin, a BSA Star Twin and—the pride of his collection—a Vincent HRD Comet (figure 1). He was a competent mechanic and enjoyed maintaining and servicing his motorcycles.

Les met and married Norma Baker in 1951 in Bristol. When he took up his appointment at the RAE they set about looking at the possibilities of building their own home. This was realized in 1953, when Les became a leading instigator in setting up the RAE and Farnborough Self Build Association. It involved 25 employees from the RAE, all fellow scientists, engineers and technicians, building 25 houses and bungalows of traditional design in their spare time outside work hours. This was a considerable undertaking for all concerned, and Les saw the scheme through to completion, taking some six years of hard work. As none were time-served building craftsmen, each man acquired and mastered a building skill. Les specialized in plastering, together with floor and wall tiling. Over subsequent years he put his building skills to good use on his own home with a succession of projects. This included extensive landscaping of the garden and the building of a substantial extension to his garage.

During the 1950s Les's family was growing, with the arrival of Sydney (1952), Peter (1955) and Sally (1958), so his passion for motorcycles necessarily moved to the practicalities of car ownership, in particular Volvos, which never went near a commercial garage: he carried out all his own automobile servicing and repair work, including major engine overhauls. His practical mechanical engineering skills enabled him to design and build many specialized tools, which proved invaluable. These ranged from heavy-duty engine hoists to intricate handmade tools for detailed work.

Les was very much a family man, and he and Norma would take their three children on continental camping holidays. He would take most of his annual leave in one 'lump', enabling the family to enjoy a long holiday during the summer months of the 1960s and 1970s. He would drive considerable distances, and memorable family camping holidays were spent visiting most countries of Western Europe.

Throughout his working life Les was generous with his advice and time to colleagues and students alike. His enthusiasm for his research work continued throughout his retirement. In later life he sometimes reflected on his humble educational origins and would often remark to his family how lucky he had been to enjoy a long career, both at work and in retirement, in a subject he loved.

Les continued with his research into his eighties but his failing health made this task increasingly difficult. He quietly accepted that he could no longer apply the academic rigour that his work demanded. Instead, Les turned his attention to enjoying the outdoor life and looked forward to walks with members of the family and the opportunity to reminisce about his childhood and past times. Norma supported Les at home as his health continued to decline. He died on 16 June 2011 aged 87 years.

ACKNOWLEDGEMENTS

The author is grateful to the Morley family for details of his personal life and to Dr Peter Bartholomew and Professor John Whiteman for contributing to this memoir.

The frontispiece photograph was taken in 1992 and is copyright © The Royal Society.

REFERENCES TO OTHER AUTHORS

Allman, D. J. 1970 Triangular finite elements for plate bending with constant and linear moments. In *Proc. IUTAM Symp. on High-Speed Computing Elastic Structures, Liège, 23–28 August 1970* (ed. B. Fraeijs de Veubeke), pp. 105–136. Université de Liège.

Bartholomew, P. 1978 Solution of elastic crack problems by superposition of finite elements and singular fields. *Computer Methods Appl. Mech. Engng* **13**, 59–78.

Flügge, W. 1960 *Stresses in shells*. Berlin: Springer.

Fraeijs de Veubeke, B. 1965 Bending and stretching of plates—special models for upper and lower bounds. In *Proc. Conf. on Matrix Methods in Structural Mechanics* (Tech Report AFFDL-TR-66-80), pp 861–886. Dayton, OH: Air Force Institute of Technology, Wright Patterson Air Force Base.

Herrmann, L. R. 1967 Finite-element bending analysis for plates. *J. Engng Mech. Div. Am. Soc. Civ. Engrs* **93**, EM5.

Koiter, W. T. 1969 Theory of elastic shells. In *2nd IUTAM Symp on the on the Theory of Thin Shells, Copenhagen, 1967* (ed. F. I. Niordson), p. 61. Berlin: Springer.

Ming, W. & Xu, J. 2006 The Morley element for fourth order elliptic equations in any dimensions. *Numer. Math.* **103**, 155–169.

Truesdell, C. 1953 The physical components of vectors and tensors. *Z. Angew. Math Mech.* **33**, 345.

Turner, M. J., Clough, R. W., Martin, M. C. & Topp, L. J. 1956 Stiffness and deflexion analysis of complex structures. *J. Aeronaut. Sci.* **23**, 805–824.

BIBLIOGRAPHY

The following publications are those referred to directly in the text. A more complete bibliography is available as electronic supplementary material at http://dx.doi.org/10.1098/rsbm.2015.0029 or via http://rsbm.royalsocietypublishing.org.

(1)   1956   The approximate solution of plate problems. In *Proc. IXth Int. Congr. on Applied Mechanics, Brussels.*

(2)   1959   An improvement on Donnell's approximation for thin-walled circular cylinders. *Q. J. Mech. Appl. Math.* **12**, 89–99.

(3)   1961   Elastic waves in a naturally curved rod. *Q. J. Mech. Appl. Math.* **15**, 155–172.

(4)   1962   Bending of a simply supported rhombic plate under uniform pressure. *Q. J. Mech. Appl. Math.* **15**, 413–426.

(5)   1963   *Skew plates and structures* (International Series of Monographs in Aeronautics and Astronautics, no. 5). Oxford: Pergamon.

(6)   1966   Some variational principles in plate bending problems. Q. J. Mech. Appl. Math. **19**, 371–386.

(7)   1968   The triangular equilibrium element in the solution of plate bending problems. *Aeronaut. Q.* **19**, 149–169.

(8)   1969   A modification of the Rayleigh–Ritz method for stress concentration problems in elastostatics. *J. Mech. Phys. Solids* **17**, 73–82.

(9)   1970   A finite element application of the modified Rayleigh–Ritz method. *Int. J. Num. Methods Engng* **2**, 85–98.

(10)   1971   On the constant-moment plate-bending element. *J. Strain Analysis Engng Des.* **6**, 20–24.

(11)   1972   Polynomial stress states in first approximation theory of circular cylindrical shells. *Q. J. Mech. Appl. Math.* **25**, 463–488.

(12)   1973   Finite element solution of boundary-value problems with non-removable singularities. *Phil. Trans. R. Soc. Lond.* A **275**, 463–488.

(13)   1976   Analysis of developable shells with special reference to the finite element method and circular cylinders. *Phil. Trans. R. Soc. Lond.* A **281**, 133–170.

(14)   1978   (With A. J. Morris) Conflict between finite elements and shell theory. In *2nd World Congress on Finite Element Methods*, pp 531–562. Bournemouth: Robinson and Associates.

(15)   1982   Inextensional bending of a shell triangular element in quadratic parametric representation. *Int. J. Solids Struct.* **281**, 919–935.

(16)   1984   Finite element criteria for some shells. *Int. J. Num. Methods Engng* **20**, 1711–1728.

(17)   1987   (With M. P. Mould) Role of bending in the finite element analysis of thin shells. *Finite Elem. Analysis Design* **3**, 213–240.

(18)   'Practical' components of vectors and tensors. *Int. J. Engng Sci.* **25**, 37–53.

(19)   1988   (With M. P. Mould) Mechanisms and bending in the finite element analysis of thin shells. In *The mathematics of finite elements and applications VI* (ed. J. R. Whiteman), pp. 241–248. London: Academic Press.

(20)   1991   Geometrically non-linear constant moment triangle which passes the von Kármán patch test. *Int. J. Num. Methods Engng* **31**, 241–263.

RONALD CHARLES NEWMAN FInstP

10 December 1931 — 30 July 2014

R.C. Newman

RONALD CHARLES NEWMAN FInstP

10 December 1931 — 30 July 2014

Elected FRS 1998

By Bruce A. Joyce* FRS

Department of Physics, Blackett Laboratory, Imperial College London, South Kensington, London SW7 2AZ, UK

Ronald Charles (Ron) Newman was one of the most versatile semiconductor physicists of his generation and is distinguished for his work in several different areas, most notably epitaxial growth and the behaviour of impurities and dopants in a range of device-related materials, mainly silicon and gallium arsenide. His most significant contributions came from the application of local vibrational-mode spectroscopy to studies of the segregation and diffusion of oxygen and hydrogen in silicon. The results were of fundamental importance in the fabrication of integrated circuits.

EARLY YEARS

Ronald Charles Newman (Ron to family, friends and colleagues) was born on 10 December 1931 in Edmonton, north London. He was the only son of Charles and Margaret Newman but had a younger sister, Rita May. Like many of that generation, his father was unable, for financial reasons, to take up a scholarship, but nevertheless had a successful career in the Post Office and took a keen, if non-professional, interest in science and mathematics. As a result he strongly encouraged Ron during his early education

Ron's schooling started at the Bruce Grove Infant School in Edmonton, from where he moved on to the Junior School. Despite the Blitz, his family decided to stay together in London, so Ron was not evacuated and he believed this meant that his education was less impaired than those of his peer group who were evacuated. His final school move was to the Tottenham Grammar School in White Hart Lane, where in 1949 he passed the 'standard four' Higher School Certificate subjects for potential physical science degree students (pure mathematics, applied mathematics, chemistry and physics), but was disappointed not to be awarded a State Scholarship.

* b.a.joyce@imperial.ac.uk

http://dx.doi.org/10.1098/rsbm.2016.0004

He was also disappointed that his applications to several universities to study physics, based on these results, were unsuccessful and he was told he should remain at school for a further year. However, Imperial College, which had its own entrance examination, offered him a place provided that he passed their examination, which he duly did and he started his undergraduate studies in September 1949. He enjoyed his course and fulfilled his early promise when he was awarded a first-class honours BSc degree in physics in 1952.

Postgraduate research at Imperial College

After graduation, Ron was offered a research studentship to work in the group of the then Head of Department, Sir George Thomson FRS, on electron diffraction, although he had expressed a strong preference to study high-energy nuclear reactions and cosmic rays. These were, however, the days when research students did not choose their own topic but instead followed the requirements of the Head of Department or Group. So Ron worked on electron diffraction with a grant of £220 per year provided by the Department of Scientific and Industrial Research, one of the precursors of the present Engineering and Physical Sciences Research Council (EPSRC). This was the start of Ron's work on thin films, one of the two main areas he pursued during his research career. The other was local vibrational-mode (LVM) spectroscopy (see below). His thin-film work in the modern idiom would be characterized as 'nanoscience', but it took almost another 50 years for this 'new' subject to be 'invented' and to spawn a plethora of books, papers, conferences and popular articles.

Sir George, known as GP, soon moved to become Master of Corpus Christi College, Cambridge; Ron's new supervisor was Professor Morris Blackman (FRS 1962) and he also collaborated with the late Don Pashley, who was then a postdoctoral research assistant and subsequently Professor D. W. Pashley (FRS 1968). This relationship was to be resumed at Imperial College, London, many years later (see below).

The basic equipment that Ron used for his research was an electron diffraction camera that had been built in the department in the prewar years but which had a few deficiencies in its vacuum system that had to be resolved. His initial topic concerned the growth and characterization by reflection high-energy electron diffraction of electrodeposited Ni films on single-crystal Cu substrates. Earlier work by Dr W. Cochrane at Imperial College had proved to be ambiguous because it involved the concept of pseudomorphism, a very contentious issue at the time among those groups working on epitaxy. The basic idea is very simple: the growing film takes up the lattice parameter of the substrate and so becomes distorted. Blackman was very reluctant to accept this, but F. C. (later Sir Charles) Frank (FRS 1954) and J. H. (later Professor) van der Merwe published a theory of epitaxy in which the initial stage of film growth was a pseudomorphic monolayer (Frank & van der Merwe 1949a,b, 1950). As the thickness of the growing film increased, a transition occurred to give a strain-free oriented deposit. Ron therefore had to solve what at the time was the very difficult problem of measuring the thickness of very thin films, down to sub-monolayer dimensions. He used a method based on radioactive deposits and chose electrodeposited ^{60}Co on Cu, but he found that there was dissolution and then redeposition of the Cu substrate atoms, which confused the effect of the Co. As a result it was concluded that pseudomorphic growth had not occurred; however, subsequent work showed that it could happen and the use of radioactive materials could provide thickness measurement for monolayer films.

Following a suggestion by Blackman, Ron's PhD studies moved to the deposition of thin films by evaporation *in situ* in a new diffraction camera, which was built very successfully in the department's workshop. It even had a facility for automatic photographic recording of the diffraction pattern as a function of time, and the machine drawings were subsequently used by Surrey and Queen's (Belfast) universities, as well as the Atomic Weapons Research Establishment and the Atomic Energy Research Establishment, Harwell. The only problem was that vacuum pumps available at the time could not produce a low enough base pressure to avoid surface contamination. Nevertheless Ron was able to study thin epitaxial films of several different metals on single-crystal Ag substrates, that were able in large part to resist contamination. The comparatively poor vacuum did, however, result in some surface contamination, which explained the absence of pseudomorphic growth in these experiments.

Ron was awarded a PhD in September 1955 for a thesis entitled 'The deposition and orientation of thin metallic films on single crystal substrates'. Armed with this PhD he quickly secured an appointment at the Central Research Laboratories of AEI at Aldermaston Court in Berkshire, and as a result was not called up for National Service by virtue of certain government contracts having been awarded to that establishment.

ASSOCIATED ELECTRIC INDUSTRIES (AEI) CENTRAL RESEARCH LABORATORIES, ALDERMASTON COURT, BERKSHIRE, 1955–63

Having accepted this offer from the director, Professor T. E. Allibone FRS, to join the laboratory, Ron commenced work on single-crystal silicon, the 'wonder material' of the time. Support came from Ministry of Defence contracts and, as was common then, Ron was able to choose his own research topic from within the scope of the contract, which came as something of a surprise. It did, however, give him the opportunity to pursue several rather different areas. His first project was to study the surface morphology of silicon after the high-temperature treatment used in dopant diffusion experiments. For this, he developed the technique of reflection electron microscopy at a Bragg angle to reduce inelastic scattering (1)*, but although the results were encouraging the subject was not pursued further until work at the Nippon Telegraph and Telephone Laboratories in Japan in 1988, when the same technique was used to study step growth on silicon and gallium arsenide layers grown by molecular beam epitaxy.

The most important work Ron undertook at this stage of his career was in collaboration with Dr (later Professor) Ron Bullough (FRS 1985). They joined the AEI Laboratories on the same day, and became lifelong family friends. Their joint study at this time concerned investigations of impurity diffusion in metals and semiconductors and combined theory with experiment, with Ron (Newman) being largely responsible for the experimental work (2–6). This was carried out principally on silicon using infrared microscopy and absorption measurements and enabled impurity precipitation of oxygen and carbon on dislocations and grain boundaries to be directly observed in thin silicon wafers. Ron found this combination of theory and experiment to be an ideal way of working, and throughout the rest of his career he collaborated with several other theorists, including Dr Mike Sangster and Dr Roy Leigh at Reading University and Professor Bob Jones at Exeter University.

---

* Numbers in this form refer to the bibliography at the end of the text.

The identification and quantification of various spurious impurities in silicon ingots was an important outcome of this project, and included silicon carbide particles and isotopes of carbon. These analyses were carried out by measuring the integrated carbon LVMs, and this technique probably became the most important of Ron's contributions to the basic science of semiconductor materials. Certainly, the work on carbon in silicon (7) proved to be of fundamental importance in the fabrication of silicon integrated circuits, which were developed some years after these studies.

During this period of his career he also had a brief involvement with the homoepitaxial growth of silicon and germanium films, but AEI showed little or no interest in the subject and it was dropped. When AEI moved its semiconductor activities to Rugby in 1963 Ron moved there briefly, but it was not a happy experience and in the following year he moved to the Physics Department at Reading University.

PHYSICS DEPARTMENT, UNIVERSITY OF READING, 1964–88

Ron took up a lectureship at Reading, offered by William (Bill) (later Sir William) Mitchell (FRS 1986) in 1964, but his early experiences there were inauspicious. He had no laboratory space, no equipment, no research funds, no research students and very little teaching and was not helped by other members of staff 'doing their own thing'. This was a bleak state of affairs by any reckoning. His first application for funding was to the government's Defence Committee for Valve Development (DCVD) for work on silicon, but it was rejected on the grounds that 'they knew all that was necessary to make the devices they needed'. Such a response to a materials physicist from the bureaucrats is not unheard of in today's world of 'impact rating' used by the Research Councils.

However, after a visit to Professor Cyril Hilsum (FRS 1979), then at the Royal Signals and Radar Establishment (RSRE), Malvern, his next application, for the study of optical crystals containing rare-earth and hydrogen (or deuterium) impurities, was much more successful. This activity involved combined LVM and electron paramagnetic resonance measurements and led to the understanding of the structure and symmetries of rare-earth–hydrogen (deuterium) complexes in cadmium fluoride, strontium fluoride and related optical crystals. It marked the beginning of his work on hydrogen pairing with impurities in silicon and several III–V compound semiconductors, including gallium arsenide, aluminium arsenide, indium phosphide and indium gallium arsenide. It was evident from the LVM measurements on Czochralski-grown silicon that considerable improvements in crystal quality were required, a finding that vindicated his original proposal to DCVD on silicon.

Despite a very significant body of work being produced at Reading, including collaboration with several national groups, together with Ron's promotion to Reader in 1969 and to a personal chair in 1975, it became clear over time that the department was rather rapidly reducing staff numbers and that no finances were available to replace them. He was, however, able to solve a difficult scientific problem during this period, related to the limited intrinsic resolution of infrared measurements of the LVMs of impurities in semiconductors. He was using a grating spectrometer at the time in the study of thin epitaxial films, but the solution was to replace it with a Fourier transform infrared (FTIR) spectrometer that had become commercially available. This greatly improved the resolution and provided the mainstay for much of Ron's subsequent work.

It was around this time that Bill Mitchell managed to persuade the then Prime Minister, Margaret Thatcher FRS, that it would be a good idea to set up so-called Interdisciplinary Research Centres (IRCs) within universities because existing departments were too concerned with their own subjects rather than looking at the broader aspects of research topics. The decision to go ahead with these centres was almost certainly inspired by the award of the Nobel Prize in Physics to Alex Müller and Georg Bednorz in 1987 for their discovery of high-temperature superconductors. Mrs Thatcher saw the commercial potential (never fully realized) of these materials, but learned that there was no related work in the UK; the first IRC was set up in Cambridge soon afterwards for the study of this topic. It involved a number of departments of the university, including Physics, Materials Science and Electrical Engineering, working under a single director with generous Research Council backing. Bill Mitchell was a keen proponent of such centres and several more soon followed, including one for Semiconductor Materials based at Imperial College, London (then Imperial College of Science, Technology and Medicine), but University College London and Queen Mary College, London, were also directly involved.

With the gradual demise of physics at Reading, and probably encouraged by his old mentor, Bill Mitchell, who was then at Oxford, Ron was offered and accepted a post as an associate director of the Semiconductor Materials IRC, commencing work there in 1989.

Return to Imperial College and the IRC for Semiconductor Materials, 1989–99

Along with two colleagues from Reading, Dr (now Professor) Ray Murray and Mr John Tucker, Ron moved back to Imperial College on 1 January 1989 as an associate director of the IRC, but it cannot be said that he was overjoyed with the situation he found there. The promised new accommodation did not materialize, because Imperial College was rather more concerned with the establishment of a new School of Business Studies at the time, and the allocation of space was less than ideal. In the event, however, Ron was provided with a large refurbished laboratory very close to the IRC administrative offices and he relocated four infrared spectrometers, including the FTIR machine and other equipment from Reading, with the help of Ray Murray and John Tucker. He was also very pleased to meet up with an old colleague from his AEI days, Mr Jim Neave, who had moved from Philips Research Laboratories (PRL), Redhill, with the director of the IRC, Professor Bruce Joyce (FRS 2000). Ray Murray did not stay with Ron for very long, though, because he preferred to set up his own activity on photoluminescence, an area of considerable importance to the overall IRC programme. John Tucker stayed rather longer, but he eventually moved to an administrative role within the IRC. Ron did, however, recruit some excellent postdoctoral workers and research students to help support his work.

His other main disappointment in the early stages was not being invited to meetings on epitaxy for the growth of low-dimensional semiconductor structures, one of the main topics of the IRC's programme. However, this probably more reflected the differences in formality between Ron and the IRC's director, Bruce Joyce, who was keen to establish the very informal regime he had enjoyed at PRL, where meetings tended to occur over coffee. Whatever the reason, it was clear that Ron was unhappy during the early days of the IRC, but it is perhaps worth noting that an IRC represented something very different from a conventional university department. They had responsibility only for research, not undergraduate teaching, and also had a maximum lifespan of 10 years. Ron did, however, have a real champion during this time in the form of the late Professor Tony Stradling, a member of the Physics Department, who very much shared Ron's views on protocol.

IRCs were also committed to collaboration with UK industry, unfortunately just at the time when virtually all of the industrial semiconductor laboratories either had closed or were in the process of closing. Nevertheless, the IRC was told by the EPSRC that it must formally collaborate with UK industry or its funding would not continue. To this end, Professor Gareth Parry, then at University College London and an expert on semiconductor lasers, was made co-director, while £800 000 of the IRC funding was transferred annually to the EPSRC-supported III–V Centre at the University of Sheffield to pursue a more device and industry-focused programme. Apart from PRL's very generous help to Bruce Joyce, with gifts of equipment and laboratory space with associated running costs, there was no support at all from any other company within the semiconductor sector of UK industry. Fortunately, however, the Japanese Government provided £5 million for a joint project directed by Professor Dimitri Vvedensky, associate director of the IRC, and Bruce Joyce, with no strings attached to the nature of the work to be undertaken.

Despite these internal difficulties, which were mainly procedural, Ron's work on infrared flourished and included several collaborations with other universities and also with industry. As well as extending particular investigations, this was a requirement imposed by the EPSRC on the manner in which IRCs must operate: they were well funded, but the degree of control of their programmes was significant. Ron's principal area of interest during this time related to identifying and understanding the properties of crystal defects and impurity atoms in Si and a range of III–V compound semiconductors, mainly using infrared absorption, but collaboratively including the use of Raman, X-ray and neutron scattering. His infrared work was greatly facilitated by the purchase of a Bruker interferometer by the IRC, with a resolution of 0.01 cm^{-1} and a very low noise level. The studies also benefited significantly from inputs by the theorists at Exeter and Reading universities.

It seems appropriate at this point to include a little more scientific detail of Ron's major area of activity on silicon (8–18), because it is such a vital material in all our lives today. Work on all aspects of silicon technology is a huge worldwide effort to develop and produce the devices that underpin our present lifestyles, but without knowledge of its basic material behaviour, none of this would be possible. Ron was truly one of the pioneers of understanding diffusion and impurity effects in silicon crystals. The principal impurity in this context is oxygen and its importance to intrinsic gettering. Oxygen can form small clusters at temperatures below 500 °C and precipitates of SiO_2 at temperatures above 600 °C. Fast-diffusing metallic impurities, which are extremely detrimental to device action, can be trapped by these particles. The rate of oxygen diffusion is enhanced by hydrogen, and Ron's group examined in detail several aspects of this: (i) small oxygen clusters complexed with a hydrogen atom; (ii) an oxygen atom paired with a hydrogen atom; (iii) the possibility of O_2 molecules being present in boron-doped silicon; and (iv) the solubility of hydrogen as a function of the Fermi level at the annealing temperature.

By heating Czochralski silicon in either hydrogen or deuterium gas at 1300 °C and atmospheric pressure, followed by quenching and subsequent heating at 470 °C, the group showed that families of shallow donors and thermal shallow donor centres with progressively larger oxygen clusters were formed. From shifts in the infrared spectra they deduced that anharmonic coupling of the H atom to other atoms in the core of the centres occurred, and concluded that hydrogen atoms diffused to thermal donor defects and were then trapped to form single donors.

The effects occurring with hydrogen in boron-doped silicon, which related to the fabrication of high-quality microprocessor devices based on active structures in a p-type epitaxial layer grown on a p^+ substrate, were also investigated. When boron-doped silicon is heated at high temperature (*ca.* 900 °C) in hydrogen at atmospheric pressure, the molecules dissociate at the surface and the atoms diffuse very rapidly throughout the sample. If such samples are quenched, some of the diffusing atoms become trapped by the boron acceptors and form close pairs. About 30% of the in-diffused H forms such pairs and the remainder is non-active. A low-temperature (*ca.* 175 °C) anneal, however, activates these remaining H atoms, but details of this 'double activation' are not clear. Nor is the location of the H atoms before the low-temperature pairing occurs. Nevertheless, Ron did propose a possible mechanism by invoking a fast-diffusing metallic impurity species that catalysed the dissociation of H_2 molecules. In addition, Ron and his group were also the first to detect the presence of hydrogen *molecules* in Si, and to measure the solubility of hydrogen together with its low-temperature diffusivity, using infrared absorption spectroscopy.

POST-IRC: THE CENTRE FOR ELECTRONIC MATERIALS AND DEVICES AT IMPERIAL COLLEGE, LONDON

The rule established by the EPSRC for the IRCs was that they were to be funded for only 10 years, after which time they would be closed or would transform into different organizations with alternative funding. In the case of the Semiconductor Materials IRC, funding formally ceased in April 1999 and it became the Centre for Electronic Materials and Devices, directed by Professor Gareth Parry, a co-director of the IRC. The other co-director, Professor Bruce Joyce, became an Emeritus Professor and Senior Research Investigator in the Department of Physics. Ron spent 18 months in the new centre before he retired, but one of the consequences was that his co-workers at the time, Dr Ashwin, Dr Pritchard and Dr Davidson, all moved to new projects, while John Tucker formally retired and left Imperial College. Ron's main area of activity during his time with the new centre was to study further the behaviour of hydrogen in Si.

During this period, as well as being appointed an Emeritus Professor and Senior Research Investigator at Imperial College London, Ron also continued his Visiting Professorship at Reading University and was appointed to a Visiting Professorship at the then University of Manchester Institute of Science and Technology, and as an EPSRC consultant, to enable him to continue his work on hydrogen in silicon.

In the year leading up to the change, Ron learned that he had been elected a Fellow of the Royal Society and he returned early from a Gordon Research Conference in New Hampshire, USA, to attend the formal ceremony with his wife Jill, other members of his family and Professor and Mrs Bullough. His election gave him enormous pleasure.

Figure 1. Ron enjoyed deep-sea fishing in the English Channel,
where he caught numerous cod and ray. (Online version in colour.)

PROFESSIONAL AND PERSONAL INTERESTS AND ACHIEVEMENTS

Ron Newman was internationally renowned as a semiconductor physicist whose major achievements were in the field of impurity and dopant behaviour in silicon and III–V compounds. It was his application of LVM spectroscopy in particular that led to his being regarded as a leading world figure, especially for his work on carbon and oxygen impurities in silicon. Even conventional retirement did not see the end of his research contributions, and his favourite quotation in this regard, attributed to Harold Macmillan FRS, was 'The past should be a springboard, not a sofa.'

Ron was a stereotypical Englishman, perhaps best illustrated by the way in which he sought out the nearest McDonald's on visits to countries where exotic food was served, most notably Japan. Nevertheless, overseas travel was one of his favourite pastimes, and he visited many parts of the world, accompanied by his wife when work was not involved.

He met his wife, Jill Weeks, at a church youth club when he was only 16 years old, and 8 years later they were married, on 7 April 1956. They had two daughters: Susan, born in 1959, and Vivienne, born in 1962, and eventually four grandchildren. Susan worked in banking and stockbroking and married Michael Lee; they have two children, a boy and girl. Vivienne worked in local government, specializing in software problems, and married Christopher Cadman; they have two daughters.

There is little doubt that science, and of course his family, had a very dominant influence on Ron's life, but especially in his younger days he had several outside interests and hobbies that were well removed from the laboratory. These included cycling and the Youth Hostel Association, sea fishing in the English Channel (figure 1), walking in the Scottish Highlands,

Figure 2. Ron loved foreign travel and visited numerous countries. One of his favourites was Australia despite having to wear a mosquito net! (Online version in colour.)

Snowdonia and the Lake District, and music—he played the piano daily for relaxation and pleasure. His enthusiasm for foreign travel is illustrated in figure 2.

Unfortunately, Ron's later years were blighted by ill-health, but he received devoted care from Jill and his family during this time.

AWARDS AND COMMITTEE APPOINTMENTS

1971	Fellow of the Institute of Physics
1974–80	Ministry of Defence (MoD) Materials Committee, Electronics Research Council
1975–77	Editorial Board, *Journal of Physics* C
1982–85	Defence Scientific and Advisory Council: Electronic Materials and Devices, MoD
1985–88	Physics Committee, Science and Engineering Research Council (SERC)
	Semiconductor and Surfaces Subcommittee, SERC
	Neutron Beam Research Committee, SERC
	Semiconductor Group Committee, Institute of Physics
1988–91	Silicon Technology Committee, SERC/Department of Trade and Industry
1998	Fellow of the Royal Society
2000–02	Editorial Board, *Journal of Physics Condensed Matter*

Acknowledgements

I am indebted to Mrs Jill Newman, who requested me to write this memoir of her husband and for providing me with a copy of Ron's autobiographical notes. I am also very grateful to Ron's son-in-law, Mr Chris Cadman, for an electronic version of Ron's complete list of publications.

The frontispiece photograph was taken in 2000 by Prudence Cuming Associates and is copyright © The Royal Society.

References to other authors

Frank, F. C. & van der Merwe, J. H. 1949*a* One-dimensional dislocations. I. Static theory. *Proc R. Soc. Lond.* A **198**, 205–216.

Frank, F. C. & van der Merwe, J. H. 1949*b* One-dimensional dislocations. II. Misfitting monolayers and oriented overgrowth. *Proc. R. Soc. Lond.* A **198**, 216–225.

Frank, F. C. & van der Merwe, J. H. 1950 One-dimensional dislocations. III. Influence of the second harmonic term in the potential representation, on the properties of the model. *Proc. R. Soc. Lond.* A **200**, 125–134.

Bibliography

The following publications are those referred to directly in the text. A full bibliography is available as electronic supplementary material at http://dx.doi.org/10.1098/rsbm.2016.0004 or via http://rsbm.royalsocietypublishing.org.

(1)   1960   (With J. S. Halliday) Reflexion electron microscopy using diffracted electrons. *Br. J. Appl. Phys.* **11**, 158–162.

(2)   The identification of precipitate particles in single crystals of silicon by reflection electron diffraction. *Proc. Phys. Soc.* **76**, 993–996.

(3)   1961   (With R. Bullough) The kinetics of impurity precipitation on dislocations; small drift theory. *Phil. Mag.* **6**, 403–417.

(4)   1962   (With R. Bullough) The growth of impurity atmospheres round dislocations. *Proc. R. Soc. Lond.* A **266**, 198–208.

(5)   (With R. Bullough) Impurity precipitation on dislocations—a theory of strain ageing. *Proc. R. Soc. Lond.* A **266**, 209–221.

(6)   (With R. Bullough) The interaction of vacancies with dislocations. *Phil. Mag.* **7**, 529–531.

(7)   1965   (With J. B. Willis) Vibrational absorption of carbon in silicon. *J. Phys. Chem. Solids* **26**, 373–379.

(8)   1991   (With J. H. Tucker, A. R. Brown & S. A. McQuaid) Hydrogen diffusion and the catalysis of enhanced oxygen diffusion in silicon at temperatures below 500 °C. *J. Appl. Phys.* **70**, 3061–3070.

(9)   (With S. A. McQuaid, J. H. Tucker, E. C. Lightowlers, R. A. A. Kubiak & M. Goulding) The concentration of atomic hydrogen diffused into silicon in the temperature range 900 °C to 1300 °C. *Appl. Phys. Lett.* **58**, 2933–2935.

(10) 1993   (With C. A. Londos, M. J. Binns, A. R. Brown & S. A. McQuaid) Effect of oxygen concentration on thermal donor formation in silicon at temperatures between 350 °C and 500 °C. *Appl. Phys. Lett.* **62**, 1525–1526.

(11)   (With S. A. McQuaid, M. J. Binns, E. C. Lightowlers & J. B. Clegg) The solubility of hydrogen in silicon at 1300 °C. *Appl. Phys. Lett.* **62**, 1612–1614.

(12)   (With M. J. Binns, S. A. McQuaid & E. C. Lightowlers) Hydrogen solubility in silicon and hydrogen defects present after quenching. *Semicond. Sci. Technol.* **8**, 1908–1911.

(13) 1994   (With S. A. McQuaid & E. C. Lightowlers) Hydrogen related shallow donors in Czochralski silicon. *Semicond. Sci. Technol.* **9**, 1736–1739.

(14)   (With S. A. McQuaid, M. J. Binns, C. A. Londos, J. H. Tucker & A. R. Brown) Oxygen loss during thermal donor formation in Czochralski silicon—new insights into oxygen diffusion mechanisms. *J. Appl. Phys.* **77**, 1427–1442.

(15)   1997   (With R. E. Pritchard, M. J. Ashwin, J. H. Tucker, E. C. Lightowlers, M. J. Binns, S. A. McQuaid & R. Falster) The interaction of hydrogen molecules with bond-centered interstitial oxygen and another defect center in silicon. *Phys. Rev.* B **56**, 13118–13125.

(16)   1998   (With R. E. Pritchard, M. J. Ashwin & J. H. Tucker) Isolated interstitial hydrogen molecules in hydrogenated crystalline silicon. *Phys. Rev.* B **57**, R15048–R15051.

(17)   1999   (With R. E. Pritchard, J. H. Tucker & E. C. Lightowlers) Hydrogen molecules in boron-doped crystalline silicon. *Semicond. Sci. Technol.* **14**, 77–80.

(18)   (With R. E. Pritchard, J. H. Tucker & E. C. Lightowlers) Dipole moments of H_2, D_2 and HD molecules in Czochralski silicon. *Phys. Rev.* B **60**, 12775–12780.

PAUL EMANUEL POLANI

1 January 1914 — 18 February 2006

PAUL EMANUEL POLANI

1 January 1914 — 18 February 2006

Elected FRS 1973

By F. Giannelli* FRCP

47 Woodcrest Road, Purley, Surrey CR8 4JD, UK

Paul Emanuel Polani: an indefatigable man of medium height and athletic constitution, with piercing brown eyes and warm, gentle manners; a sharp, deeply cultured intellect with an unquenchable desire to learn; a mind always seeking deeper understanding through study, observation and correlation; a person of deep controlled emotions, lasting affections, strong morals, and profound respect for his fellow human beings; a life affected by the troubled Italian politics of the 1920s and 1930s, and forced by war to delay dreams of genetic research and to show instead great medical and surgical prowess. In his late thirties Paul Polani began to fulfil his research dreams. He realized that, contrary to expectations, sex determination in humans did not follow the *Drosophila*-based model, because humans with an XO sex chromosome complement are female, while those with a Y chromosome are male even when they have two X chromosomes. He also discovered that Down syndrome is sometimes caused by chromosomal translocations that, if inherited from unaffected carriers, may cause familial clustering of the disease. This was the first stimulus to the development of prenatal chromosomal tests. Then in 1960 he established a multidisciplinary unit at Guy's Hospital, London, to investigate diseases of mainly genetic aetiology, and apply research findings to clinical care, while adhering to clear ethical principles. In doing so he demonstrated originality, breadth of vision, and inspiring leadership, and is rightly considered one of the most influential founders of modern medical genetics.

Family, education and emigration

Paul was born on 1 January 1914 in Trieste, then part of the Austro-Hungarian Empire. His father, Enrico, had been born in Bohemia in 1883, attended business school in Vienna, and moved to Trieste, where he became Head of Forwarding at the Compagnia Adriatica.

* francesco.giannelli1@btinternet.com

http://dx.doi.org/10.1098/rsbm.2016.0003

His mother, Elisabetta (Elsa) Zennaro, born in Trieste in 1889, graduated from the Scuola Commerciale and became a secretary at the Compagnia Adriatica, where she met Enrico and married him in 1912. From the summer of 1914 Enrico served in the Austro-Hungarian army as an infantry officer on the Serbian front, and then as a garrison officer in Ototac (now in Croatia). At the end of World War I he returned to Trieste, which had become part of Italy, and Paul's younger brother, Renato (Ray), was born there in 1923.

Enrico and Elsa complemented each other perfectly, providing a rich education for their children. Enrico, scrupulously honest and hard-working, instilled discipline by example, and deeper values through love, logic, equanimity, consistency and dialogue. Elsa, highly intelligent and perceptive, was a patient dedicated teacher with an infectious thirst for knowledge. She taught herself French, German, mathematics and music, and enjoyed playing the piano. Paul felt that he and his family had been very fortunate in having her as wife and mother, since she was a paragon of sensibility, gentleness and caring love. Enrico was not religious, but Elsa was Catholic, and their children were raised with strong Christian values. Paul described his religious beliefs as simple and primitive, with an intuitive faith in a personal God.

Paul's parents were liberal social democrats, and Elsa strongly supported female emancipation. Both Paul and Renato were raised in this political spirit. Postwar depression, political change and diminished trading activity in Trieste combined to thwart Enrico's efforts to improve his family's standard of living by establishing his own forwarding agency.

Paul, during his secondary education at the Liceo Classico Francesco Petrarca, achieved marks high enough to exempt him from school fees. He enjoyed all subjects, but especially the arts; biology had to be supplemented by private reading, and it was then that Paul became intrigued by genetics, which had the allure of mystery and the prospect of new discoveries.

Paul's leisure was occupied by riding and sailing. His closest school friend was Gaetano (Tano) Kanizsa, with whom he shared ideas, principles and an enthusiasm for learning. Their interests were reciprocally stimulating: Tano was interested in neuropsychiatry and psychology and, later, Gestaltism, whereas Paul was interested in medicine and genetics. They spent hours discussing and trying to fathom out obscure concepts in their respective fields of interest, sometimes moonlighting to attend to their extracurricular activities undisturbed. Paul lost track of Tano during the war and was told that he had died. However, many years later, while reading Francis Crick's *The astonishing hypothesis*, Paul had the joy of seeing Tano's name mentioned in relation to Gestalt psychology: he, too, had survived the war and made his professional mark!

In 1932 Paul graduated from the Liceo Francesco Petrarca with excellent marks, and applied to the universities of Padua and Siena to study medicine. Both universities offered him scholarships, but Paul chose Siena, where the ratio of students to academics was a favourable 6:1. Most senior teachers had high academic standards, and for ambitious younger teachers Siena was a stepping-stone demanding industry and commitment to teaching and research. Medicine apart, Siena offered admirable artistic opportunities, including concerts at the famous Accademia Chigiana.

Teaching at Siena was excellent, and students were encouraged to assist with research. In his first year Paul became an intern in biology with Professor Umberto D'Ancona, and chose genetics as his special topic. D'Ancona's department was well run, with opportunities for practical work and a very good reference library including classics in Italian, German, French and English. Paul was excited by the genetics course, which included discussions of Thomas

Hunt Morgan's work on *Drosophila*, and frequent reference to the 'gold standard' text by Edward Beecher Wilson. Furthermore, D'Ancona was convinced that humans would occupy a central place in genetics, and in support of this view he often quoted British scientists.

In his second year, Paul came into closer contact with medicine, and found the courses admirable, enjoyable and exciting. He became an intern in anatomy and, in his third year, a dissection room demonstrator. With Dr Fausto Sistini, Paul also worked on the distribution of the abdominal sympathetic fibres in the frog, using microdissection of fibres selectively stained with quinacrine, under ultraviolet, and published his findings.

Paul next applied for a three-year internship in the Department of Physiology. However, in 1935 he gained a place, won in open competition, at the National Medical College of the Scuola Normale Superiore di Pisa, an institution of the highest standing and stringently selective. Fortunately, the Professor of Physiology in Siena, Igino Spadolini, also moved to Pisa, and Paul continued his physiology internship under his guidance. He graduated in medicine in 1938, with an honours MD and a thesis entitled 'The humoral transmission of the nervous impulse and the distribution of cholinesterase'. Then, after a year of rotating internship in Trieste General Hospital, he obtained the state qualification to practise medicine.

At that time membership of the Fascist Party was essential for employment, and for this reason Paul left Italy. On 1 August 1939 he arrived in Guernsey to stay with friends, and a month later he travelled to London and registered with the General Medical Council, which had a reciprocity agreement with Italy.

EFFECTS OF WORLD WAR II ON PAUL'S LIFE AND CAREER

Career

Paul intended to follow a postgraduate crash course at Hammersmith Hospital, but the start of the war put an end to this idea. A few lean and spartan months followed. Nights as a dishwasher at Kettner's in Soho provided some income, and days spent reading in the British Medical Association's library provided knowledge, warmth and comfort. As learning English was essential, watching films (two performances at a time for the price of one) was an obligation, not a luxury.

Towards the end of 1939 Paul enrolled as a Surgeon Lieutenant on SS *Adrastus*, bound for the Far East. She was a naval auxiliary on convoy duty and had the Convoy Commodore on board; the skipper, Captain Lesley, was an ex-RN Cornishman. Paul, well accepted and only gently teased by the crew, had several sick or injured sailors to attend to.

During the return journey from the Far East, Italy entered the war. Captain Lesley called Paul to his cabin and told him that from that moment he had to be considered an enemy alien; he then poured two glasses of sherry and proposed a toast to their friendship.

On arrival home Paul was met by the police and interned with other Italians, first at Lingfield Racecourse, and then in a former cotton mill in Bury St Edmunds. From there he was supposed to sail for Canada in SS *Arandora Star* but, at the last minute, a Maltese intelligence officer sent him to the Isle of Man where a doctor was needed in an internment camp. This saved Paul's life, as the *Arandora Star* was sunk by the Germans.

Paul helped to set up a hospital at Grenville Camp in Douglas, which turned out to be quite busy (see Chappell 1984). He remained there until March 1941, when he passed the scrutiny of the Camp Tribunal and was released to go to London, where doctors were needed. The Emergency Medical Service was organizing a research appointment with Professor Owen de Wesselow, to work on crush injuries and wound shock, when Paul was asked to do a stint as locum at the Evelina Hospital for Sick Children in Southwark. As the post holder did not return, Paul was appointed Resident Medical and Surgical Officer, in charge of the borough's first aid post.

Until 1946/47 Paul remained the only Resident at the Evelina, but a part-time outpatients officer was found to help with outpatients and on the wards. Two consultant paediatricians did weekly outpatient clinics and consultations on the wards. The only consultant general surgeon was the senior surgical registrar at Guy's (Sam Wass), a busy man indeed. He and the two paediatric specialists were on call, but most of the clinical and surgical work was left in the hands of junior doctors, helped by the extremely able and knowledgeable sisters.

Students from Guy's hospital came to clerk and be taught at the Evelina Hospital, because the children's wards at Guy's had been closed. Thus Paul had the stimulus and satisfaction of teaching at the bedside.

When the consultants returned from wartime service, and hospitals were resuming their normal working pattern, Paul felt it was time to go. For some years he had had day-to-day responsibility for more than 100 children requiring medical or surgical attention, and had performed some 1500 surgical operations. He had found the work incredibly satisfying and rewarding, sobering, and conducive to maturation and thought. Administrators had been supportive and friendly and he noted, in a personal communication to me, that the courageous, uncomplaining, adaptable, humorous, jolly and unimaginably kind people of Southwark had accepted him without ever asking why he was there. He was clearly an oddity but, he was there with them and they had given him a new home and indelible memories to treasure in his heart.

These feelings were obviously reciprocated. Some 15 years later I discovered some fruit-sellers near London Bridge station who remembered Paul tending to them as children. They proudly showed me the fading marks of his surgical work, and adopted me as their friend, on his account. My family doctor, who had trained at Guy's during the war, also remembered Paul, whom he defined as a human dynamo with inspirational teaching ability.

Family

In 1942 Paul met Nina Sullam, and they married in 1944. Nina was born in Poland in 1921, the only daughter of an Ottoman diplomat and Juliette Rossolato, of French origin but born in Istanbul. Nina attended junior school in Trieste, and then the Milan Conservatorio, where she obtained a concert pianist diploma. In 1938, after moving to London with her family, Nina abandoned her musical career for secretarial work in the Italian Section of the BBC European Services, which she left in 1962 to train in biology and statistics.

Nina had charm and character, and proved able to do whatever she set her mind to. Paul described her as an admirable companion and colleague: loyal, intelligent, alert, willing, active, able, tireless, highly motivated and modest. Paul and Nina shared a passion for horse-riding. They bred and broke a thoroughbred, which learned to utter three phonemes: one for Paul, one for Nina and one for horses. Skiing was Paul and Nina's holiday passion, with music and reading their other hobbies (Paul read poems in five European languages, and a few in ancient Greek and Latin). Nina and Paul had no children, but they shared every aspect of life in intense and perfect harmony.

The war interrupted Paul's contact with his family in Trieste, to his great regret. Paul's father died on 14 March 1945, but Paul could not be at his bedside. On 25 July 1944 Paul's brother Renato joined the partisan Brigata Garibaldi 'Fratelli Fontanot' to fight the Germans in the mountains of Slovenia, returning to Trieste on 17 May 1945. When Tito occupied Trieste, Renato went to Venice as an Allied court interpreter, returning to Trieste 40 days later, when Tito was evicted by the Allied forces. He then returned to his medical studies at Padua University, but wartime deprivation affected his health. He became seriously ill in 1946 and had to abandon his studies for 18 months of medical treatment, supported by his mother, Elsa, and financially by Paul. When Elsa died in 1962, Paul expressed his pain at this loss of family contact during the long war years.

RETURN TO RESEARCH AND TO GENETICS

In 1948 Sam Wass advised Paul to specialize in surgery because he was so gifted, but Paul wished to fulfil his youthful dream of research in genetics. Richard Ellis, consultant paediatrician to Guy's and the Evelina, and his successor, Philip Evans, supported Paul's wish to do research. He obtained a two-year National Birthday Trust paediatric research fellowship working on clinical kernicterus (brain damage induced by bile pigment (1)*) and subsequently became assistant to Evans, then the director of the Paediatric Department, with whom Paul and his wife Nina established a lifelong friendship. This job gave Paul time to absorb the theory of human genetics and, from 1950, to begin genetic research under the stimulating influence of the staff of the Galton Laboratory, where he was attached to Professor Lionel Penrose (FRS 1953) as a visitor.

At Guy's Paul had established good relationships with Peter Bishop, the sex endocrinologist, and Maurice Campbell, the cardiologist. Guy's Hospital was the Mecca for patients with congenital heart disease, and Paul began a series of studies on the genetics of these defects. At the same time he collected data on Turner syndrome, and females with ovarian agenesis, in collaboration with Peter Bishop's two registrars (Maurice Lessof and Joe Briggs) and an overseas visitor (Carlos De Almeida).

Guided by Penrose, Paul set about disentangling the influence of maternal and paternal age, and parity, on congenital heart disease, while trying to explore other factors: gender, consanguinity, association with other anomalies, infection and other environmental variables. Penrose followed and advised on this work, and was particularly intrigued by a small but significant effect of paternal age in coarctation of the aorta (a narrowing of the aorta in the region of insertion of the ductus arteriosus). Paul was more intrigued by the observation that coarctation of the aorta was clearly a vascular defect disproportionately affecting males, and yet was very common in females with Turner syndrome and so-called ovarian agenesis (3). He therefore wondered whether these females could have an XO sex chromosome constitution. Penrose, with a natural antipathy to hypotheses based on slim evidence, disliked Paul's idea, with its implication that sex determination in humans would differ from the *Drosophila* model (in which XO individuals are males and XXY are females). However, working with various collaborators Paul first showed (2) that cells from women with Turner syndrome/ovarian agenesis were sex chromatin negative, like

---

* Numbers in this form refer to the bibliography at the end of the text.

male cells, thus supporting the XO hypothesis. Second, he demonstrated that these females had a male frequency of colour blindness, whereas males with Klinefelter syndrome, whose cells were sex chromatin positive, had a female frequency of this X-linked defect (4, 5). Thus, genetic data indicated the presence of a single X chromosome in females with ovarian agenesis, and the presence of two X chromosomes in Klinefelter syndrome males. This strongly suggested that in humans sex determination was not based on the ratio of X chromosomes to autosomes, as in *Drosophila*.

Since 1955, Paul—who had by then become research physician for the National Spastic Society (NSS) and director of their Medical Research Section, based at Guy's Hospital—had wished to find a direct proof or refutation of his unorthodox views on the sex chromosome constitution of Turner females and Klinefelter males. An attempt with Dr Gordon Thomas did not yield adequate chromosome preparations and, after an unsuccessful approach to Peo Koller, Paul turned to Charles Ford (FRS 1965). He had come to know Ford through the work on sex chromatin and colour blindness, and they had become better acquainted after Paul suggested that Ford should be invited to the 1957 Nuclear Sexing Symposium at King's College Hospital. Ford's collaborator John Hamerton was also at the meeting and a collaboration was started to study human anomalies of sex differentiation. In the spring of 1958 Paul received Ford's preprint of a method for the study of human chromosomes in bone marrow cells, and he immediately sent Ford bone marrow from himself and patients with Turner and Klinefelter syndromes.

At the end of the summer of 1958, at the request of the World Health Organization Regional Office for Europe (WHO/Europe), Paul was seconded by the NSS to work on a large investigation of pregnancy wastage being planned in the USA. The headquarters of WHO/Europe were in Copenhagen, where Paul enjoyed free access to the university library, and the opportunity to discuss sex determination with Mogens Westergaard, who had identified the male-determining role of the Y chromosome in *Melandrium* and was sympathetic to Paul's theory of sex determination in humans.

Browsing and re-reading classic human chromosome papers, and especially Ford and Hamerton's meiotic *in vivo* confirmation (Ford & Hamerton 1956) of the human chromosome number (23 pairs), Paul recalled Ursula Mittwoch's paper on a male with Down syndrome whose meiotic chromosome count appeared to be 24 (Mittwoch 1952). He then went on to wonder whether Mittwoch had miscounted, or whether the chromosome number in Down syndrome was abnormal.

Towards the end of 1958 Paul received from Ford the exciting news that the bone marrow from a female patient with Turner syndrome had shown 45 chromosomes, and an XO sex chromosome complement. Furthermore, a male patient with Klinefelter syndrome had been shown to have 47 chromosomes, and an XXY sex chromosome complement, as well as some cells with a 46,XX karyotype; he was thus probably a sex chromosome mosaic. This good news, together with Paul's reflections on the role of the Y chromosome in sex determination, and on Mittwoch's Down syndrome paper, required discussion and planning for further action. Accordingly, in January 1959 Paul arranged to meet Ford at Heathrow, en route from Copenhagen to the National Institutes of Health (NIH) in Bethesda. It was decided to publish the findings from the Turner syndrome patient in the *Lancet*, because this journal had previously shown interest in Turner syndrome (6). The findings in this patient, and in the male with Klinefelter syndrome, clearly indicated that the Y chromosome acted as a male factor, and that sex determination in humans therefore differed from that in *Drosophila*, as Paul had earlier proposed. The patient with Klinefelter syndrome also appeared to be a mosaic, and *Nature* seemed the appropriate journal for these findings (7). Ford was also to report these matters at the forthcoming meeting of the Medical Research Society. In addition, Paul and Ford needed to investigate the chromosomes of patients with Down syndrome as a matter of urgency, because they felt that trisomy of a small chromosome was feasible. Paul, aware of Penrose's observations on the maternal age effect in Down syndrome, was particularly interested in patients born to young mothers, not only because they represented an exception to the common rule but also because some young mothers had more than one child with Down syndrome. However, as these patients were rare, their investigation was postponed to a later time. Paul then continued his journey to Bethesda.

At the NIH Paul, acting as a consultant/observer for WHO/Europe, was attached to the National Institute of Neurological Disease and Blindness, directed by Richard L. Masland, who also directed the Pregnancy Wastage Collaborative Study on which Paul was to work. This sought to identify factors responsible for abnormal development, leading to mental, neurological and physical abnormalities. The prospective study was to start by enlisting 40 000 newly pregnant women and their subsequent offspring. Each woman was to be monitored throughout pregnancy in 14 university hospitals, using detailed, standardized, clinical and biological investigations, and their offspring were to be studied in a comparable manner at delivery, and again later if they survived. Paul's task was to determine whether it seemed desirable and feasible to undertake parallel work in the UK, Eire and Scandinavia.

As soon as Paul arrived at Bethesda, Ford rang him to report that Jerome Lejeune had found that patients with Down syndrome had 47 chromosomes and were trisomic for a small acrocentric chromosome, later called no. 21.

It was likely that Lejeune *et al.* (1959) had examined patients born to old mothers, as they were the most common. Paul and Ford therefore went on to examine patients with Down syndrome born to young mothers. In this way they identified 'Down syndrome with 46 chromosomes', because the trisomy was 'hidden' by the centric fusion of chromosome 21 with a larger acrocentric, resulting in a single abnormal submetacentric chromosome (8). This abnormality was transmissible through asymptomatic translocation carriers, with a chromosome count of 45 (9). Paul reported this at the December meeting of the American Neurological Society.

It was for this work, and particularly that on Turner and Klinefelter syndrome, with their bearing on sex determination in humans, that, 14 years later, Paul was elected a Fellow of the Royal Society.

FOUNDATION OF THE PAEDIATRIC RESEARCH UNIT

Paul's work for WHO in Europe and the USA necessitated frequent transatlantic crossing, and attendance at planning and standardization meetings. This allowed him to get a clear idea of the American academic set-up, and he was able to meet American groups interested in the development of cytogenetics and other aspects of human genetics. Furthermore, when Paul presented his work on sex chromosome abnormalities and sex determination in humans to an audience of specialists meeting in Syracuse in the summer of 1959 (10), at the invitation of Lytt Gardner, he had the opportunity to meet such people as Francis Crick FRS, Barton Childs and James Neel, and also William Russell, who presented work on the mouse that paralleled Paul's work in humans. For Paul it was a rich time for discussions that helped the development of his thoughts on research.

In 1960 Paul reported to WHO/Europe on his observations in the USA and on his consultations in the UK, Eire and Scandinavia. It was agreed that the American study would be critically important to a variety of matters relating to pregnancy and its outcome. However, it was thought that a similar European study was not feasible because the intricacies of the work and the need to build the necessary facilities and to ensure standardization required an impracticable level of investment and commitment. Nevertheless, it seemed useful to duplicate specific parts of the project in those European Units where these issues were under active consideration.

In the UK, the NSS, under the influence of its progressive director and Medical Advisory Council (MAC), had begun to consider a strategy for future research into prevention in 1959. At the suggestion of the MAC, the NSS had set up a Research Advisory Council (RAC), chaired by Sir Alan Moncrieff. Its members were Professor G. Daniel (neuropathology), Dr Ronnie MacKeith (paediatric neurology), Professor Lionel Penrose (genetics), Dr P. Phillips (neurophysiology) and Sir Charles Symons (neurology), together with senior members of the NSS executive and members of the MAC.

The RAC agreed that research should focus on primary prevention. They considered two aspects: first, that research should be comprehensive and cognizant of the variety of neurodevelopmental disorders that manifest as neurological diseases, learning disability or cognitive, emotional or sensory dysfunction; and second, that research should be fundamental and basic, considering development generally (including the origin of malignancy), and more specifically developmental neurobiology. Paul suggested that an integral aim should be the immediate practical application of research findings for the benefit of patients through diagnosis, counselling and prevention.

The RAC considered that this programme could be implemented by supporting different facets of research in different centres—each concerned with a different disorder—or by establishing and supporting a single dedicated centre capable of developing the required comprehensive approach. The latter option would allow easier integration of approaches, technical facilities and methods, together with more purposeful and direct translation of research findings into clinical practice. The need for expertise in different areas would be met by multidisciplinary staffing.

At the end of his secondment to WHO/Europe, Paul reported his observations on the Pregnancy Wastage Collaborative Study and on his concurrent genetic research, to both MAC and RAC. After this, the chairman of the NSS asked him to prepare a blueprint for a comprehensive, unitary approach that would meet the objectives and research principles set out by the RAC. Paul did so, stipulating that the proposed multidisciplinary unit should have a genetic leitmotif. His plan was accepted and on 1 October 1960 the Paediatric Research Unit (PRU), an academic unit based at Guy's Hospital, was founded. Paul, appointed by the University of London as the first Prince Philip Professor of Paediatric Research at Guy's Hospital Medical School, became the director of the Unit, geneticist to Guy's Hospital and Medical School, and honorary paediatrician to the hospital (figure 1).

Figure 1. Paul Polani at his microscope in the Paediatric Research Unit in 1976.

INITIAL STRUCTURE OF THE PRU

Paul's idea of a multidisciplinary research unit with a genetic philosophy and a structure suited to the rapid translation of research findings into clinical practice was original. That the NSS accepted its format and aims was a reflection of the esteem that Paul had garnered during his association with the Society. The Unit itself bore witness to Paul's ability to guide and inspire through example, commitment and fellowship. It also adapted rapidly to changes in its field of research, thus demonstrating both the validity of Paul's research philosophy and his ability to nurture wide-ranging research interests. In essence the PRU was the embodiment of Paul's boldness and foresight, and it illustrated his belief that medical genetics was not merely that branch of medicine caring for families affected by diseases with a mainly genetic aetiology, but it must also include the multidisciplinary research necessary to understand such diseases, and the rapid and ethical translation of research findings into clinical care. Because he realized this vision, Paul has been recognized as a founder of the modern field of medical genetics, and the individual who did more than almost anyone else to influence the development of medical genetics, particularly in Europe (Harper 2007).

The NSS made a generous endowment of £2 million, spread over a period of 10 years, to cover (i) interim accommodation, (ii) the conversion of the Down warehouse into research premises (Cameron House), (iii) the progressive establishment of senior university research posts, (iv) the employment of ancillary graduates, technical and administrative staff, (v) library services, an animal station, photography, administration and secretarial assistance, (vi) the initial and provisional running of research projects, (vii) uncommitted funds for pump-priming of new research projects and strategic developments, and (viii) contributions to new laboratories and to the children's wards in Guy's Tower.

At the outset John Hamerton was appointed Senior Lecturer and head of the Cytogenetics section, and with him Paul planned the restructuring of the Down warehouse, which was completed in 1962. Until then Cytogenetics, a 'Clinical' group and an 'Epidemiology and Statistics' group (related to Paul's previous position as director of the NSS Medical Research Unit) were housed in temporary accommodation.

In 1961 the PRU established an Experimental Biology section, with Roy Spector as Senior Lecturer, and in 1962 a genetic service, dealing mostly with regional referrals. The Biochemistry section, with Philip Benson as Senior Lecturer, followed in 1963. In 1964, after his retirement, John Fraser Roberts FRS joined the Unit as consultant geneticist, and in 1965 the Developmental Immunology section, with Matteo Adinolfi as Senior Lecturer, completed the Unit's research structure.

Paul ensured that each part of the Unit worked smoothly and that the different parts worked well together. He offered encouragement, advice, ideas and help to optimize efficiency. His directing skill was based on warmth, cheerful empathy, generous modesty and the ability to enjoy people's successes more than they did themselves.

Paul's own research focused principally on Down syndrome and on the sex chromosome abnormalities associated with anomalies of sex. In 1961 the first evidence was obtained that, in Down syndrome families, the rate of transmission of translocations involving chromosome 21 and a large acrocentric chromosome (a D/G_{21} translocation, in 1960s terminology) was lower from male than from female carriers (11). After the accumulation of a large amount of data, the first estimate of the population frequency of Down syndrome due to translocations involving chromosome 21 (that is, D/G_{21} and G_{21}/G in 1960s terminology) was obtained, and Paul calculated the mutation rates for these translocations (14). This was the first estimate of the rate at which centric fusions between acrocentric chromosomes occurred in a human population. For the families of translocation Down syndrome individuals, prenatal diagnosis was essential. Paul strongly encouraged the development of appropriate methods, and the first prenatal diagnoses for chromosomal disorders were undertaken in 1969, shortly after the UK abortion laws allowed.

Paul's analysis of phenotypic variation among patients with Down syndrome indicated that somatic mosaicism, resulting in patients with a significant proportion of cells with a normal karyotype, was associated with a milder phenotype (13).This induced him to develop an experimental system to explore the possible curative effects of transplanting normal cells. In collaboration with Dr Mary Seller of the Experimental Biology section, cells from normal mice were transplanted into mice with a congenital anaemia, which cured their anaemia (16). Paul and his wife, Nina, also examined the dermatoglyphics of mosaic individuals with Down syndrome, to investigate the subtler effects of mosaicism (17).

Paul also examined a large number of women with abnormalities of sexual development. This helped, first, to assign the genes for the Xg blood group, which were known to escape X chromosome inactivation, to the short arm of the X chromosome (12) and then to show that these genes did not escape inactivation when they were on structurally abnormal X chromosomes (19).

Paul's clinical expertise was much sought after by his colleagues at Guy's Hospital, and one of these interactions led to the identification of a new syndrome of cardiomyopathy and lentiginosis (15, 20).

Paul was, and remained, in high demand as a writer of reviews, and he dealt with these rigorously and with insight. For example, while reviewing autosomal abnormalities, he noted the frequent occurrence of retinoblastoma in patients with deletions in the long arm of a D chromosome (18), thus highlighting data relevant to the position of the 'retinoblastoma' gene. In a review on pairing of the X and Y chromosomes, he brought a variety of data to bear on the location of the 'maleness' gene on the Y chromosome, and on the role played by illegitimate unequal crossing-over between the X and Y chromosome short arms in causing discrepancies of sex determination (31).

EVOLUTION OF THE PRU

By the 1970s the PRU was ready for further expansion. The discovery by Caspersson *et al.* (1968), that fluorescent staining methods allowed precise chromosome identification and detailed analysis, permitted the extension of cytogenetic diagnosis to subchromosomal levels, and hence its application to a new range of disorders. This required the recruitment of new staff both in the laboratory and in the clinic. The development of cell fusion and hybridization also opened new research fields. From this point onwards, funding for the Unit's research activities was essentially based on grants from national research-supporting bodies.

In 1971 John Hamerton left to take up the Chair of Genetics at the University of Manitoba, and Michael Daker was appointed Lecturer in charge of cytogenetic diagnoses, and Mary McGuire, whom John Hamerton had recruited as a tissue culturist, became chief technician in charge of tissue culture services. Paul also inspired and supported a systematic cytogenetic study of spontaneous abortion (overseen by Eva Alberman), to determine the contribution of different chromosomal abnormalities to the aetiology of early pregnancy loss (Creasy *et al.* 1976).

I had the task of establishing a cell biology research group; this required additional tissue culture facilities, which were funded by a private donation to Paul. I decided to investigate diseases manifesting abnormal sensitivity to DNA-damaging agents, and predisposition to cancer. Paul was interested in some of these diseases, particularly Bloom syndrome (23, 26), and he encouraged the development of prenatal testing for families with these disorders (see, for example, Ramsay *et al.* 1974; Giannelli *et al.* 1982).

In 1971 the diagnostic work of the Unit was partly funded by the National Health Service (NHS). Diagnostic activity expanded further in 1972, with the development of prenatal tests for neural tube defects, based on increased levels of α-fetoprotein in amniotic fluid (Seller *et al.* 1973). Paul also encouraged Mary Seller's participation in the exploration of the importance of environmental and nutritional factors in the aetiology of neural tube defects. This collaborative venture identified maternal vitamin status, and in particular folic acid deficiency, as the principal causative factors, and led to the effective prevention of neural tube defects (Smithells *et al.* 1980). Mouse models were also used for in-depth studies of neural tube development and its abnormalities (27).

In 1973 the Supra-Regional Laboratory for Genetic Enzyme Defects was established within the Biochemistry section, with Anthony Fensom as Principal Scientist and Lecturer, and by 1974 some of the metabolic defects investigated could be detected prenatally (22). In 1974 Caroline Berry joined the Unit. She became a consultant clinical geneticist in 1979 and remained the Unit's senior clinical geneticist until her retirement in 1997. In 1975 the PRU moved to floors 7 and 8 of Guy's Tower and various services were expanded.

In 1976 the South-East Thames Regional Genetic Centre, fully supported by the NHS, was established within the PRU. In 1979 Paul and his colleagues published a review of the genetic service that had been provided by the PRU over the previous 16 years (28). Paul also helped to establish a centralized facility for automated cell and chromosome sorting, used by Matteo Adinolfi to investigate whether fetal cells in the maternal circulation might allow non-invasive prenatal diagnostic tests (Adinolfi 1982).

In the late 1970s molecular genetics burst onto the scene, leading Paul to try to introduce this 'new genetics' to the PRU, through meetings involving interested London groups. However, he soon realized that deeper involvement was necessary. New funds were needed both to enter this field and to provide for the future of the PRU. In 1976 a fund-raiser was appointed, but proved insufficient to our needs. Accordingly, in 1978 Paul tried fund-raising through the medium of personally motivated individuals with a wide range of useful contacts. On the advice of the director of the NSS (Tim Yeo), the Generation Trust was set up. Through Yeo's contacts Paul attracted Philip (later Lord) Harris, who quickly organized a group of influential trustees. These were joined by Nils Taube, whom Paul had met by mere coincidence when they shared the same flight. Under the patronage of Prince Philip, it was hoped that the Trust would soon be in a position to contribute substantial funds. At this point, Paul asked whether I would like to take a sabbatical year in a molecular biology laboratory, and then establish a PRU Molecular Genetics section.

I was lucky enough to be able to spend this sabbatical at the laboratory of George Brownlee (FRS 1987) in the Sir William Dunn School of Pathology at Oxford University. It was 1982, and I was assigned to a fast-moving project that enabled me to learn a variety of techniques, meet several able young scientists, and learn about the work of John (now Sir John) Sulston (FRS 1986) on the genome of *Caenorhabditis elegans*.

On my return to London a molecular genetics laboratory was soon established (figure 2), initially with a small donation from the Medical School and a research grant. Then the work expanded and, when funds from the Generation Trust became available, we were able to buy essential equipment and appoint a senior scientist, Dr David Bentley, whom I had met during my sabbatical. In short order we developed rapid methods of mutation detection (Montandon *et al.* 1989; Rowley *et al.* 1995), implemented a national strategy to optimize genetic counselling for families with diseases characterized by high mutational heterogeneity, for example for patients with haemophilia B (Giannelli *et al.* 1992), and developed and applied procedures necessary for the construction of cloned maps of human chromosomes (see, for example, Bentley *et al.* 1992; Holland *et al.* 1993).

By this time Paul had officially retired, but he continued to come in daily to the PRU, to pursue his personal research with his very talented assistant John Crolla, attend the Generation Trust meetings and watch over the health and continued growth of the Unit he had created and nurtured for so many years. He continued to offer advice in the fields of genetics and paediatrics, both nationally and internationally, well into the 1990s. He was invited to deliver named lectures until 1996 and to contribute keynote addresses to genetic meetings until 2005. His successors as directors of the Unit were Professor Martin Bobrow (1983–94; FRS 2004) and Professor Ellen Solomon (1995–2008).

Figure 2. Paul Polani (left) accompanying Prince Philip, Patron of the Generation Trust, on a visit to the PRU's newly established molecular genetics laboratory (1983).

RESEARCH ON MEIOSIS AND PAUL'S LAST LIFE CHALLENGES

In 1969 Paul took a sabbatical to study meiosis, a focus of his personal research and a passion he shared with Georgiana Jagiello, a frequent visitor to the PRU, who later became Professor of Human Development and Genetics at Columbia University.

Paul compared the behaviour of chiasmata and centromeres in male and female murine meiosis (21) and used electron microscopy to examine the pairing and segregation of Robertsonian translocations in trisomic mice (32, 33). In infertile men, he demonstrated the contribution of meiotic chromosome abnormalities to their infertility (24). With Georgiana Jagiello, Paul made a first attempt (25) at testing the production line hypothesis of Henderson & Edwards (1968) in mice: this suggested that a decrease in the number of chiasmata in the oocytes, as the age at conception increased, might explain the maternal age effect in aneuploidy. The results appeared partly to support this proposition. Then Paul, with the help of Mary Seller and John Crolla, devised a second experiment in mice to test the basic idea that the first oocytes that mature in the embryo are also the first to be released from the ovary after puberty, whereas the converse is true of later-maturing ova. This test required the development of a technique involving ovary explantation, *in vitro* maintenance, and reimplantation in spayed females, so that fetal oocytes could be radioactively labelled at different times *in vitro* and then harvested at different times after puberty and maturation *in vivo* (29). The results that Paul obtained supported the production line hypothesis in mouse oogenesis (34). This *in vitro/in vivo* method of oocyte analysis was also developed to observe meiotically paired chromosomes, each with sister chromatids differentially labelled with bromodeoxyuridine, to study what happens at chiasmata (30). This was an important step in unravelling the complex story of chromosome recombination through breakage and reunion, and its relation to chiasmata and their possible terminalization.

Seeing Paul, after his retirement in 1982, coming into his laboratory every day was a joy for all his old staff. His agile, energetic step, his warm smile and his youthful, piercing eyes seemed to tell us that time was passing much more slowly than it really was. Then, late in 1989, he unexpectedly stopped coming. We were sad and wondered what might have happened, but Paul was certainly entitled to a peaceful retirement and we respected his privacy. Obviously he was well and active, because he was making intense use of the Unit library services, publishing papers and filling national and international advisory roles. I rang him from time to time. Paul liked to receive copies of our papers, and also photocopies of any interesting publications we came across. In the early 1990s, when his wife, Nina, answered the phone, she seemed reluctant to converse, and frequently failed to pass messages to Paul; I wondered whether she considered phone calls a bit of an intrusion. Then, in the spring of 1998, Paul wrote me a letter saying that in 1987 Nina had begun to show signs of a progressive neurological degenerative disease, which was now seriously advanced. His letter detailed Nina's current needs and listed useful addresses so that she could receive the best possible care if he suddenly became unable to provide it. I thought then that Paul's sudden disappearance from the Unit was explained by the need to look after Nina. Sadly her decline worsened, and she died at home on 29 December 1999.

In the new millennium Paul returned to the Unit (figure 3); he visited new members of staff to hear about their research, regularly attended the annual Unit Research Days when Unit members communicated their results, and always contributed to the discussion. He spent many days in the library of the Royal Society of Medicine, and published papers until 2004. He went to Trieste and Udine frequently, and spoke at length to his brother Renato and his only niece (Julia Polani Ause), in Oregon, on a daily basis.

In the summer of 2005 Paul was invited to chair a medical genetics meeting in Italy. He left full of enthusiasm, as he planned to revisit places he had loved in his youth. However, on his (delayed) return, I learned that an acute illness had frustrated his plans. His voice was as firm as ever, and his health had apparently recovered. I rang him before Christmas, to convey seasonal good wishes and to arrange a visit after my return from Christmas with my family. On my return I rang him repeatedly, but without an answer, and Matteo Adinolfi also failed to contact him. From a neighbour we learned that Paul was in hospital—he had not told us that his illness in the summer had been acute leukaemia. He seemed stable, and was receiving treatment when I went to visit him. I expected to see some scientific journals in his room, but there were none. When I asked him what he was reading, he told me that he had the writings of St John the Evangelist and St Paul.

In early February Paul's brother, Renato, who had flown over from Portland with his wife, Anita, rang to say that Paul's treatment had been unsuccessful, and that he wished to say goodbye. For the first time he looked frail. He asked me about the Unit, and when I told him that it was going from strength to strength he smiled. We had a warm goodbye, and a few days later, on 18 February 2006, Paul died.

Figure 3. Paul Polani in 2005, at the official opening of the newly refurbished PRU, now known as the Henry Wellcome Laboratories of Medical and Molecular Genetics, Division of Medical and Molecular Genetics. (Photograph copyright © Professor M. J. Seller.) (Online version in colour.)

HONOURS

1961 Fellow of the Royal College of Physicians, London
1973 Fellow of the Royal Society
1979 Fellow *ad eundem* of the Royal College of Obstetricians and Gynaecologists
1980 Emeritus Professor of Paediatric Research, University of London
Honorary Fellow of the Associazione di Genetica Italiana
1981 Commendatore of the Order of Merit, Republic of Italy
1982 President of the Association of Clinical Cytogeneticists of Great Britain
1984 Honorary Member of the British Paediatric Association for outstanding contribution to Paediatrics
Honorary Fellow of the Royal College of Pathologists
1985 Senior Member of the Association of British Neurology
1989 Honorary Fellow of the Royal College of Physicians of Ireland
1994 Honorary Fellow of Guy's and St Thomas' Hospitals Medical Schools
1995 Life Member of the British Medical Association
1997 Honorary Fellow of the Royal College of Paediatrics and Child Health
1998 Fellow of King's College, London
1999 Honorary Fellow of the Società Italiana di Genetica Umana

Awards

1974 Kenneth Craik Research Award, University of Cambridge
1984 Sanremo International Award and Prize for Genetic Research
1985 Baly Medal of the Royal College of Physicians for distinguished genetic research
1986 Gold Medal of the International Cerebral Palsy Society for genetic and cerebral palsy research
1994 Gold Florin of Florence
2005 Gold Medal of the Universities of Modena and Reggio Emilia, Italy, for contribution to Genetic Research

Named lectures

1961 The Harveian Society of London Lecture
1962 The Wartenberg Lecture, American Academy of Neurology, New York
1965 The Bartholomew Mosse Lecture, Rotunda Hospital, Dublin
The Scientific Basis of Medicine Annual Review Lecture, British Postgraduate Medical Federation, London
The Woodhull Lecture, Royal Institution of Great Britain, London
1969 The Fundación Jiménez Díaz Lecture, Madrid
The Mental Health Foundation Lecture, London
1974 The Kenneth Craik Lecture, University of Cambridge
1976 The Harveian Society of London Lecture
The European Society of Paediatric Research Lecture, Rotterdam
1978 The Scientific Basis of Medicine Annual Review Lecture, British Postgraduate Medical Federation, London
The George Frederic Still Lecture, British Paediatric Association, York
1979 The Holme Lecture, University College Hospital Medical School, University of London
1980 The Fison Memorial Lecture, Guy's Hospital Medical School, University of London
1981 The Blake Marsh Memorial Lecture, Royal College of Psychiatrists, London
1982 The Linnean Society Lecture, London
The Messtitz Memorial Lecture, Sussex Postgraduate Centre
1983 The Ronnie MacKeith Memorial Lecture, Association of British Paediatric Neurologists, Oxford
The Fison Memorial Lecture, Guy's Hospital Medical School, University of London
1984 The Langdon Brown Memorial Lecture, Royal College of Physicians, London
1988 The Harveian Oration, Royal College of Physicians, London
1994 Key address, International Congress of Human Genetics
1996 The Carter Lecture, British Society for Human Genetics, York
2005 Keynote Address, International Symposium on Prenatal Diagnosis, Modena

Acknowledgements

This memoir, based on 46 years of association and friendship and on notes by Paul, has been enriched by contributions from Renato Polani, Julia Polani Ause and my colleagues Dr John Crolla and Professor Mary J. Seller. I am greatly indebted to Miss Elizabeth Manners, formerly research secretary to Paul, for contributing to this memoir in many ways including the careful editing of the manuscript, the compilation of the full list of Paul's publications and the preparation of the figures.

The frontispiece photograph was taken in 1976 by Godfrey Argent and is reproduced with permission.

Author Profile

Francesco Giannelli

In 1958 I obtained an MD degree *cum maxima laude* from Rome University. During the preparation of my thesis I had become aware of Paul Polani's work on the aetiology of congenital heart disease. I first met him in 1959, when the Medical Faculty of Rome University invited him to give a lecture on his research on human chromosome abnormalities. At the end of the lecture I approached him and asked whether I could spend some time in his laboratory. Paul replied that if I succeeded in obtaining a travelling scholarship I should let him know. I made a successful application to the Consiglio Nazionale delle Ricerche (CNR) and accordingly, on 1 October 1960, I began a placement in the newly established Paediatric Research Unit (PRU), at Guy's Hospital. Four months later, when my CNR funding came to an end, I was offered a six-month scholarship funded by the PRU, and then a two-year research fellowship. This was the start of 46 happy years working in and for the PRU, comprising 10 years in Cytogenetics, 12 in Cell Biology and 24 in Molecular Genetics. Throughout this period Paul Polani was my mentor and my friend.

References to Other Authors

Adinolfi, M. 1982 The immunosuppressive role of alfaprotein and the transfer of lymphocytes across the placenta: two controversial issues in the materno-fetal relationship. In *Clinics in developmental medicine*, vol. 83 (*Paediatric research: a genetic approach*) (Festschrift for Paul Polani) (ed. M. Adinolfi, P. Benson, F. Giannelli & M. Seller), pp. 183–196. London: Spastics International Medical Publications, in association with William Heinemann Medical Books.

Bentley, D. R., Todd, C., Collins, J., Holland, J., Dunham, I., Hassock, S., Bankier, A. & Giannelli, F. 1992 The development and application of automated gridding for efficient screening of yeast and bacterial ordered libraries. *Genomics* **12**, 534–541.

Caspersson, T., Faber, S., Foley, G. E., Kudynowski, J., Modest, E. J., Simonsson, E., Wagh, U. & Zech, L. 1968 Chemical differentiation along metaphase chromosomes. *Exp. Cell Res.* **49**, 219–222.

Chappell, C. 1984 *Island of barbed wire: the remarkable story of World War Two Internment on the Isle of Man.* London: Corgi.

Creasy, M. R., Crolla, J. A. & Alberman, E. D. 1976 A cytogenetic study of human spontaneous abortions using banding techniques. *Hum. Genet.* **31**, 177–196.

Ford, C. E. & Hamerton, J. L. 1956 The chromosomes of man. *Nature* **178**, 1020–1021.

Giannelli, F., Avery, J. A., Pembrey, M. E. & Blunt, S. 1982 Prenatal exclusion of ataxia-telangiectasia. In *Ataxia-telangiectasia—a link between cancer, neuropathology and immune deficiency* (ed. B. A. Bridges & D. G. Harnden), pp. 393–400. Chichester: John Wiley & Sons.

Giannelli, F., Saad, S., Montandon, A. J., Bentley, D. R. & Green, P. M. 1992 A new strategy for the genetic counselling of diseases of marked mutational heterogeneity: haemophilia B as a model. *J. Med. Genet.* **29**, 602–607.

Harper, P. S. 2007 Paul Polani and the development of medical genetics. *Hum. Genet.* **120**, 723–731.

Henderson, S. A. & Edwards, R. G. 1968 Chiasma frequency and maternal age in mammals. *Nature* **218**, 22–28.

Holland, J., Coffey, A. J., Giannelli, F. & Bentley, D. R. 1993 Vertical integration of cosmid and YAC resources for interval mapping of the X chromosome. *Genomics* **15**, 297–304.

Lejeune, J., Gautier, M. & Turpin, R. 1959 Études des chromosomes somatiques de neuf enfants mongoliens. *C. R. Acad. Sci.* **248**, 1721–1722.

Mittwoch, U. 1952 The chromosomal complement in a mongolian imbecile. *Ann. Eugen. (Lond.)* **17**, 37.

Montandon, A. J., Green, P. M., Giannelli, F. & Bentley, D. R. 1989 Direct detection of point mutations by mismatch analysis: application to haemophilia B. *Nucleic Acids Res.* **17**, 3347–3358.

Ramsay, C. A., Coltart, T. M., Blunt, S., Pawsey, S. A. & Giannelli, F. 1974 Prenatal diagnosis of xeroderma pigmentosum. Report of the first successful case. *Lancet* **ii**, 1109–1112.

Rowley, G., Saad, S., Giannelli, F. & Green, P. M. 1995 Ultra-rapid mutation detection by multiplex, solid phase chemical cleavage. *Genomics* **30**, 574–582.

Seller, M. J., Campbell, S., Coltart, T. M. & Singer, J. D. 1973 Early termination of anencephalic pregnancy after detection of raised alpha-fetoprotein levels. *Lancet* **ii**, 73.

Smithells, R. W., Sheppard, S., Schorah, C. J., Seller, M. J., Nevin, N. C., Harris, R., Read, A. P. & Fielding, D. W. 1980 Possible prevention of neural tube defects by preconceptional vitamin supplementation. *Lancet* **i**, 339–340.

BIBLIOGRAPHY

The following publications are those referred to directly in the text. A full bibliography is available as electronic supplementary material at http://dx.doi.org/10.1098/rsbm.2016.0003 or via http://rsbm.royalsocietypublishing.org.

(1) 1950 (With P. R. Evans) The neurological sequelae of Rh sensitization. *Q. J. Med.* **19**, 129–149.

(2) 1954 (With W. F. Hunter & B. Lennox) Chromosomal sex in Turner's syndrome with coarctation of the aorta. *Lancet* **ii**, 120–121.

(3) 1955 (With M. Campbell) An aetiological study of congenital heart disease. *Ann. Hum. Genet.* **19**, 209–230.

(4) 1956 (With M. H. Lessof & P. M. F. Bishop) Colour blindness in 'ovarian agenesis' (gonadal dysplasia). *Lancet* **ii**, 118–120.

(5) 1958 (With P. M. F. Bishop, B. Lennox, M. A. Ferguson-Smith, J. S. S. Stewart & A. Prader) Colour vision studies and the chromosome constitution of patients with Klinefelter's syndrome. *Nature* **82**, 1092–1093.

(6) 1959 (With C. E. Ford, K. W. Jones, J. C. De Almeida & J. H. Briggs) A sex chromosome anomaly in a case of gonadal dysgenesis (Turner's syndrome). *Lancet* **i**, 711–713.

(7) 1959 (With C. E. Ford, J. H. Briggs & P. M. F. Bishop) A presumptive human XXY/XX mosaic. *Nature* **183**, 1030–1032.

(8) 1960 (With J. H. Briggs, C. E. Ford, C. M. Clarke & J. M. Berg) A mongol girl with 46 chromosomes. *Lancet* **i**, 721–724.

(9) 1960 (With C. O. Carter, J. L. Hamerton, A. Gunalp & S. D. V. Weller) Chromosome translocations as a cause of familial mongolism. *Lancet* **ii**, 678–680.

(10) 1961 The sex chromosomes in Klinefelter's syndrome and gonadal dysplasia. Evidence for non-disjunction, cleavage loss or other sex-chromosome aberration in man and the function of the Y chromosome. In *Molecular genetics and human disease* (ed. L. I. Gardner), pp. 153–181. Springfield, IL: Charles C. Thomas.

(11) 1961 (With J. L. Hamerton, V. A. Cowie, F. Giannelli & S. M. Briggs) Differential transmission of Down's syndrome (mongolism) through male and female translocation carriers. *Lancet* **ii**, 956–958.

(12) 1963 (With J. Lindsten, M. Fraccaro, J. L. Hamerton, R. Sanger & R. R. Race) Evidence that the Xg blood group genes are on the short arm of the X chromosome. *Nature* **197**, 648–649.

(13) 1965 (With J. L. Hamerton & F. Giannelli) Cytogenetics of Down's syndrome (mongolism). I. Data on a consecutive series of patients referred for genetic counselling and diagnosis. *Cytogenetics* **4**, 171–185.

(14) 1965 (With J. L. Hamerton, F. Giannelli & C. O. Carter) Cytogenetics of Down's syndrome (mongolism). III. Frequency of interchange trisomies and mutation rate of chromosome interchanges. *Cytogenetics* **4**, 193–206.

(15) 1968 (With E. J. Moynahan) Progressive, profuse lentiginosis, progressive cardiomyopathy, short stature with delayed puberty, mental retardation or psychic infantilism and other development anomalies: a new syndrome. In *13th Congressus Internationalis Dermatologiae*, vol. 2 (ed. W. I. Jadassohn & C. G. S. Schirren), pp. 1543–1544. Berlin: Springer.

(16) 1969 (With M. J. Seller) Transplantation of allogenic haemopoietic tissue in adult anaemic mice of the W series using antilymphocytic serum. *Lancet* **i**, 18–21.

(17) 1969 (With N. Polani) Chromosome anomalies, mosaicism and dermatoglyphic asymmetry. *Ann. Hum. Genet.* **32**, 391–402.

(18) 1969 Autosomal imbalance and its syndromes, excluding Down's. *Br. Med. Bull.* **25**, 81–93.

(19) 1970 (With R. Angell, F. Giannelli, A. de la Chapelle, R. R. Race & R. Sanger) Evidence that the Xg locus is inactivated in structurally abnormal X chromosomes. *Nature* **227**, 613–616.

(20) 1972 (With E. J. Moynahan) Progressive cardiomyopathic lentiginosis. *Q. J. Med.* **41**, 205–225.

(21) 1972 Centromere localization at meiosis and the position of chiasmata in the male and female mouse. *Chromosoma* **36**, 343–374.

(22) 1975 (With P. F. Benson, S. Blunt, A. H. Fensom & T. M. Coltart) Prenatal diagnosis of metabolic disorders. *Lancet* **ii**, 552–553.

(23) 1976 Cytogenetics of Fanconi anaemia and related chromosome disorders. In *Ciba Foundation Symposia (New Series)*, vol. 37 (*Congenital disorders of erythropoiesis*) (ed. D. W. Fitzsimons), pp. 261–306. Amsterdam: Associated Scientific Publishers.

(24) 1976 (With W. F. Hendry, R. C. B. Pugh, I. F. Sommerville & D. M. Wallace) 200 infertile males: correlation of chromosome, histological, endocrine and clinical studies. *Br. J. Urol.* **47**, 899–908.

(25) 1976 (With G. Jagiello) Chiasmata, meiotic univalents and age in relation to aneuploid imbalance in mice. *Cytogenet. Cell Genet.* **16**, 505–529.

(26) 1977 (With F. Giannelli, P. F. Benson & S. A. Powsey) Ultraviolet light sensitivity and delayed DNA chain maturation in Bloom's syndrome fibroblasts. *Nature* **265**, 466–469.

(27) 1979 (With S. Embury, M. J. Seller & M. Adinolfi) Neural tube defects in curly-tail mice. I. Incidence, expression and similarity to the human condition. *Proc. R. Soc. Lond.* B **206**, 85–94.

(28) 1979 (With E. Alberman, B. J. Alexander, P. F. Benson, A. C. Berry, S. Blunt, M. G. Daker, A. H. Fensom, D. M. Garrett, V. M. McGuire, J. A. Fraser Roberts, M. J. Seller & J. D. Singer) Sixteen years experience of counselling, diagnosis and prenatal detection in one Genetic Centre: progress, results and problems. *J. Med. Genet.* **16**, 166–175.

(29) 1979 (With J. A. Crolla, M. J. Seller & F. Moir) Meiotic crossing over exchange in the female mouse visualised by BUdR substitution. *Nature* **278**, 348–349.

(30) 1981 (With J. A. Crolla & M. J. Seller) An experimental approach to female mammalian meiosis: differential chromosome labelling and analysis of chiasmata in the female mouse. In *Bioregulators of reproduction* (ed. G. Jagiello & H. J. Vogel), pp. 59–87. New York: Academic Press.

(31) 1982 Pairing of X and Y chromosomes, non-inactivation of X-linked genes and the maleness factor. *Hum. Genet.* **60**, 207–211.

(32) 1989 (With J. A. Crolla & H. J. Roberts) Meiosis in female mice with Robertsonian translocations. I. Prophase pairing. *Cytogenet. Cell Genet.* **52**, 111–117.

(33) 1989 (With J. A. Crolla) Meiosis in trisomic female mice with Robertsonian translocations. II. Chromosome behaviour at first and second meiotic metaphases. *Cytogenet. Cell Genet.* **52**, 118–123.

(34) 1991 (With J. A. Crolla) A test of the production line hypothesis of mammalian oogenesis. *Hum. Genet.* **88**, 64–70.

JOHN RAYMOND POSTGATE FIBiol

24 June 1922 — 22 October 2014

JOHN RAYMOND POSTGATE FIBiol

24 June 1922 — 22 October 2014

Elected FRS 1977

By Rob Robson[1], Barry Smith[2] and Ray Dixon FRS[3]*

[1] *43 Priest Hill, Caversham, Reading RG4 7RY, UK*
[2] *61 Church Lane, Eaton, Norwich NR4 6NY, UK*
[3] *Department of Molecular Microbiology, John Innes Centre, Norwich Research Park, Norwich NR4 7UH, UK*

John Postgate was one of the foremost microbiologists of his generation. He is most famous for his lifelong research on sulfate-reducing bacteria and nitrogen fixation and for his seminal contributions to understanding the survival and death of bacteria. John Postgate is also known for his specialist and non-specialist books on science, most notably *Microbes and man*, first published in 1986 and now in several editions and translated into several languages. He played an important role in the development and dissemination of microbiology and in the leadership of science in the UK. John will also be remembered warmly as the supervisor and mentor of aspiring young microbiologists, several of whom have gone on to distinguished careers in microbiology. His other great love was jazz: he was an amateur cornet player of note, the leader of several jazz groups and a highly knowledgeable writer, reviewer and author of two books on the subject.

THE EARLY DAYS

John Postgate was born in London on 24 June 1922, the son of Raymond and Daisy Postgate (*née* Lansbury). His father was a historian, classics scholar, socialist writer, journalist and broadcaster and a gourmet most famously remembered for founding and editing *The good food guide*. His mother was the daughter of George Lansbury, Labour MP for Bow and Bromley, the socialist reformer and leader of the Labour Party from 1932 to 1935. John's younger brother was Oliver Postgate, who with Peter Firmin wrote, produced and performed

* ray.dixon@jic.ac.uk

http://dx.doi.org/10.1098/rsbm.2016.0006

in classic TV children's programmes such as *Noggin the Nog*, *Bagpuss* and *Clangers*. John grew up in a relaxed family background in homes in Hendon and then Finchley in North London that were visited by left-wing politicians and luminaries but few scientists. John's interest in science seemed self-engendered and founded on his menagerie of fish, rodents, lizards, felines and other pets, the building of radios, conducting alarming experiments with the household electricity and sometimes even riskier fun with his chemistry set performed in the garden shed.

John's early schooling took place in Woodstock School in Golders Green with fellow pupils from many different countries. After passing the 11-plus exam he attended the forward-looking Kingsbury County School in London, where he studied chemistry, physics, biology and zoology for his Higher School Certificate. This period of his schooling coincided with the outbreak of war in 1939, and John and his brother were evacuated to Totnes, Devon, where he studied at Hele's School in Exeter, which he credited with having good teachers who instilled the need for hard work and success in examinations. For family reasons he returned to Kingsbury County School to complete his schooling during the Blitz. Success in his 'Highers' won him a minor scholarship to Balliol College, Oxford, and with his scholarship supplemented by family, the county and a qualification in Latin, he set off for Oxford in October 1941.

It was during his early teenage years that John discovered his great love for jazz. He was not enthused by formal music lessons at school and indeed never learned to read sheet music. It was listening to the radio in his mid teens on his home-made radios that John first became excited by the big dance bands and swing music. Just before leaving for Oxford he exchanged a barely played accordion for a hard-to-play vintage cornet in a second-hand shop and this propelled him into his amateur jazz career.

It is evident that by the end of his teenage years there emerged in John lifelong attitudes and passions. These included his somewhat left-wing, mildly non-conformist and anti-establishment views, probably developed during his early family and home life. We can also see the genesis and love of science and scientific experimentation encouraged by 'garden-shed' hobbies, and his passion for listening to, studying and playing jazz.

OXFORD

Much to his surprise, John found himself studying chemistry, not zoology, at Oxford. He attended some zoology lectures but soon abandoned these because of the exacting nature of the chemistry course. John was adept in the laboratory, and in friend and fellow-student Christopher Longuet-Higgins (FRS 1958) he found a complementary study 'buddy' who was an exceptional theorist and who later became Professor of Theoretical Chemistry at Cambridge. In his third year he took biochemistry tutorials in the Department of Physiology with the physical biochemist and analytical ultracentrifugation expert, Alexander 'Sandy' G. Ogston (FRS 1955).

John undertook his fourth-year Part II research project with the influential Professor (later Sir) Cyril Hinshelwood FRS, who with Nikolai Semenov (ForMemRS 1958) won the 1956 Nobel Prize in Chemistry for their research into the mechanism of chemical reactions. In the late 1940s Hinshelwood became interested in applying chemical kinetics principles to the multiplication and variation of bacteria (Thompson 1973). John became interested in the project and this was his first experience of working with bacteria, in particular *Bacterium lactis, B. aerogenes* (now *Klebsiella aerogenes*) and *B. coli mutabile* (now *Escherichia coli*). The project set out to study how bacteria grown on glucose adapted to use other sugars. This involved tediously counting the number of bacteria in replicate cultures, using a calibrated microscope slide called a haemocytometer. In 1946 this work became John's first publication in *Transactions of the Faraday Society* (1)*. John enjoyed working in Hinshelwood's supportive and friendly research group. Finding the esteemed Professor Hinshelwood clearing up a flood in the lab taught John the lesson that performing menial tasks in the lab was not beneath anyone. Those who worked with John in his senior positions often observed him carrying out humble laboratory tasks, thus passing on the lesson to others. John was also to learn another valuable lesson from his early work: Hinshelwood's aesthetically pleasing mathematical theory for bacterial adaptation was proved wrong when its genetic basis was discovered.

John's interest in a career in academia rather than in industry or the scientific civil service was sparked by his experience in Hinshelwood's lab, but he realized that this required a research degree. John was taken on as the first PhD student of Dr Donald D. Woods (FRS 1962), who had just moved to Oxford's Biochemistry Department. As a chemist, John was allowed a year to broaden his knowledge of biology by attending lectures and tutorials in several Oxford departments, and one of his first tasks was to help Woods and other colleagues paint the ceilings and walls of their new lab. This would amuse today's academics and PhD students and horrify university campus service managers.

John started his research on the resistance of the bacterium *Acetobacter suboxydans* to sulfonamides. Woods had discovered that *p*-aminobenzoic acid (pAB) at very low levels was an antagonist of the sulfonamide drugs used in the 1930s and 1940s to fight pneumonia, puerperal fever, gonorrhoea and other diseases (Gale & Fildes 1965). The hypothesis was that sulfonamides negatively affected some process that required pAB. *A. suboxydans* was chosen as an organism to study because it was not a pathogen, could be grown on a chemically defined medium, required pAB for growth and was sensitive to sulfonamides. John set out to train the organism to withstand sulfonamides by using the technique he had learned from Hinshelwood involving serial subculture with increasing levels of the drug.

The work in the lab fell into a routine, which enabled John to enjoy the general Oxford milieu, and especially the jazz scene. Here he formed and led an amateur traditional jazz group called the Dixieland Bandits. They played at college dances and when required had to play dance music for waltzes and even the Hokey-Cokey, the dance sensation of the time. At one time or another, the group included various amateur musicians who became notable public figures including, on saxophone, clarinet and piano, Mervyn Brown, later Sir Mervyn Brown of the Foreign Office and, on clarinet, Paul Vaughan, later to become a well-known BBC broadcaster and presenter. Contemporaries and followers of jazz at Oxford during those days who would have heard the Bandits included the novelist Kingsley Amis and the poet Philip Larkin.

John drafted a short paper on his work but it was never published. This was allegedly due to Woods's perfectionism and indecision and to John's becoming engrossed in his first job. John also drafted other manuscripts but felt these were not of a standard that he would have liked, so he chose not to submit them. He learned early on the importance and necessity of

---

* Numbers in this form refer to the bibliography at the end of the text.

publishing good quality research, which he was keen to encourage in younger colleagues in whom procrastinating over publishing was not looked on kindly.

From this early time John moved among illustrious figures in British microbiology and found particularly useful participation in several microbiology summer schools focused on recent developments in chemical microbiology. They were organized by stars of the Cambridge school of microbiology including Marjory Stephenson FRS, Sidney Elsdon and Ernest Gale (FRS 1952) as well as Woods himself. This was also the era of the establishment of the Society for General Microbiology, whose founding members included Woods, Kenneth ('Butch') Butlin and B. C. J. G. ('Gabe') Knight. John attended a few of the early meetings of the Society but found he was terrified of speaking in public. This phobia took him 25 years to overcome fully and even determined his ultimate career, which lay in research establishments and not universities, with their requirement for lecturing.

By the end of three years, he started to work on his thesis. Woods found the science solid, though with some loose ends and the writing lacking in clarity and organization, which John felt 'pernickety' and chose to ignore. This would return to haunt him. Two events delayed completion of the thesis. In 1948 John married Mary Stewart, who had already graduated in English from St Hilda's. He also found a job with 'Butch' Butlin's small research group at the government's Chemical Research Laboratory, Teddington, in southwest London, where the role of bacteria in metal corrosion was being studied.

TEDDINGTON

Once established and enjoying his new job, John resumed work on his thesis, which he submitted in late 1949. After the *viva voce* in Oxford, Woods informed him that he had failed not because of the science but for the poor presentation. This came as a deep shock but a saviour was close at hand. Mary, his wife, was an English graduate and she pointed out several non-scientific problems in the writing, which was an education that John's tutors and research supervisor had neglected. In due course he resubmitted and passed without further trouble. This experience strongly influenced his lucid writing style in scientific papers and books. Many of his students and colleagues benefited from his advice about writing. He also became an editor, then Editor-in-Chief, of *Journal of General Microbiology*, where his editorial skills were bestowed on colleagues worldwide to their benefit but sometimes their chagrin.

In the late 1940s and early 1950s the cost of sulfur, mostly imported from the USA to produce the sulfuric acid needed by British industry, was very high. At Teddington, Butlin revisited an earlier idea to manufacture sulfuric acid from hydrogen sulfide (H_2S) produced by sulfate-reducing bacteria (SRBs). SRBs are obligate anaerobes and not easy to grow. They require cultures to be established in media free of O_2 in closed culture tubes and vessels. In addition, H_2S smells unpleasant and is highly noxious. Initial experiments suggested that the biological process might be uneconomic, but John's laboratory skills soon produced dense viable cultures that could be grown with H_2 as a source of reducing power in addition to sodium lactate. The consumption of H_2 was measured with Warburg manometers, which were once common in biochemistry labs but were eventually superseded by gas chromatography and polarographic techniques. He showed that fresh actively growing cultures of *Desulfovibrio vulgaris* Hildenborough could produce H_2S at rates potentially

Figure 1. Collecting samples in North Africa. (*a*) John Postgate during his visit to Libya in 1950. (*b*) Portable laboratory, specially constructed in the Chemical Research Laboratory at Teddington for the Libya visit.

70 times higher than previously recorded. This suggested a feasible industrial process. The government's Department of Scientific and Industrial Research (DSIR) was enthusiastic about the news, and the focus of Butlin's group shifted somewhat away from its original focus of understanding the role of SRBs in metal corrosion. However, scale-up proved disappointing and the idea emerged of finding more active new species of SRBs from known sulfur pools in North Africa. John travelled with Butlin via Benghazi to sample three sulfur-spring-fed lakes near El Agheila in North Africa (figure 1). They collected many samples and also described other life forms, including small fish living in the noxious environment of the pools, which were of interest to ichthyologists. The trip received worldwide attention, being heralded by the DSIR, and John gave interviews to the BBC's Radio Newsreel. Britain's sulfur shortage seemed to be over just at a time when it was most severe. The samples proved rich in SRBs, but these were not more active than local strains. However, work on the process continued for another nine years as Butlin's lab grew. A pilot plant based on sewage and calcium sulfate was built and operated by London County Council. However, the cost of sulfur imports dropped slowly and the biological process became uneconomic.

During this time John took the lead in providing a more fundamental understanding of SRBs. He showed that selenate was a competitive inhibitor of sulfate reduction (2) and contributed papers on the carbon metabolism of these organisms and the biochemistry of the sulfate-reduction process. One of the most fundamental advances in the understanding of biological sulfate reduction arose from his insight and skill in designing media in which to obtain good yields of the organisms not obscured by the black iron sulfide precipitate normally produced when H_2S reacted with iron salts in the medium (3). This produced cell pastes with a pink hue. The absorption spectra of these pink cell suspensions were examined by June Lascelles, an outstanding young Australian scientist then on a Fellowship in Woods's lab and who later became an expert in photosynthetic bacteria and a professor at the University of California, Los Angeles. June used a Hartridge reversion spectroscope that was perfected in the early 1920s to measure the level of carbon monoxide in blood and which is still used nowadays to examine gem stones. This was an ideal instrument with which to characterize the visible spectra of translucent cell suspensions. She observed two clear absorption bands in the green area of the spectrum, which were bleached on exposure to air. Such bands had previously been seen only in aerobic bacteria containing cytochromes, leading to the dogma that cytochromes were present only in aerobes and not obligate anaerobes. It was suggested that John's cultures were contaminated with aerobic organisms. However, his findings were confirmed with suspensions of repurified bacteria. It was proposed that SRBs contained a cytochrome that was spectroscopically distinct from cytochrome c from yeast or muscle.

John took extracts of his cells to the world authorities on cytochromes, David Keilin FRS and E. F. Hartree at the Molteno Institute at Cambridge, who were strong proponents of the exclusivity of cytochromes to aerobes. They confirmed both the presence of a new type of cytochrome and the presence of another novel substance characterized by an absorption band at the red end of the spectrum.

John first reported finding the new cytochrome to an International Microbiological Congress in Rome in 1953 and a year later produced two short communications naming it cytochrome c_3 and the substance responsible for the red absorption 'desulphoviridin' (4, 5). Also in 1953 Dr M. Ishimoto in Japan reported finding a cytochrome in a different species of SRB, and Martin Kamen in California found cytochromes in anaerobic photosynthetic bacteria. The 'cytochrome' dogma had been truly rebuffed. At that time, Butlin's group were growing SRBs in continuous culture, a technique learned from the Microbiology Research Department in the then Ministry of Supply's biological warfare research unit, at Porton Down near Salisbury in Wiltshire. Continuous culture provided John with a good supply of SRBs from which to extract and purify both cytochrome c_3 and desulfoviridin (6).

Our understanding of the nature of cytochrome c_3 and its role in dissimilatory sulfate reduction expanded dramatically as others applied new techniques to study sulfate reduction by SRBs. Soon it was shown that John's preparations were not fully active or pure and even contained two other cytochromes. This does not detract from the importance of his original discovery, and today the crucial roles of cytochrome c_3 and desulfoviridin in energy conservation in SRBs have been elucidated (figure 2).

The ground-breaking discovery of cytochrome c_3 and other work on SRBs led to greater exposure of the work in Butlin's group and to visits to Teddington by many distinguished microbiologists and biochemists. These meetings enhanced John's reputation and led to invitations to speak at international conferences. In 1957 he embarked on an extended scientific visit to the USA arranged around an invitation to talk on the relationship of SRBs to the secondary recovery of oil, at a small symposium at St Bonaventure University in upstate New York. The tour took in a fortnight's working visit to C. B. van Neil's lab in Hopkins Marine Station in Pacific Grove, Monterey. The aim was to examine SRBs that Van Neil had isolated from marine environments. The 'sluggardly' revival of the cultures allowed John time to explore the Californian coast and sample local wine, which he found better than its reputation at that time in Britain. He also gave an invited seminar at University of California, Berkeley, in San Francisco, home to several distinguished US microbiologists, notably Roger Stanier (FRS 1978) and H. L. Barker. At the end of the visit he met A. I. Krasna at New York's Columbia University to learn more about the enzyme hydrogenase that SRBs can use to fuel sulfate reduction.

An ulterior motive for John to go to New York was to visit the fountainhead of jazz. He took time out in Manhattan to explore record shops and listen to a lot of live jazz from some

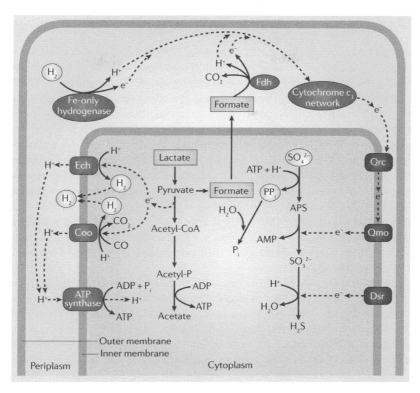

Figure 2. Current model for the role of the cytochrome c_3 network (top right) in the electron transport pathway for sulfate reduction (red components on the right) during growth of *Desulfovibrio vulgaris* Hildenborough on lactate and sulfate. Electrons are proposed to be transferred from cytochrome c_3 to the quinone reductase complex (Qrc) and then onto the quinone-interacting membrane-bound oxidoreductase complex (Qmo), which passes electrons to the adenosine phosphosulfate (APS) reductase for the reduction of sulfate to sulfite. Electrons are also transferred by an unknown mechanism to desulfoviridin, now known as dissimilatory sulfite reductase (Dsr), which catalyses the final step in sulfate reduction to reduce bisulfite to hydrogen sulfide. P_i, inorganic phosphate. (Reprinted by permission from Macmillan Publishers Ltd: J. Zhou *et al.*, *Nature Reviews Microbiology* **9**, 452–466, copyright © 2011.) (Online version in colour.)

great artists of the day, including trumpeters Sidney de Paris, Bobby Hackett and Charlie Shavers and the tenor saxophonist Coleman Hawkins. John published an article about his Manhattan experience in *Jazz Monthly* magazine in May 1958.

In the mid to late 1950s, and despite the scientific successes of Butlin's group, its economic *raison d'être* was being questioned by its masters at the DSIR. In the spring of 1959 and despite vigorous lobbying, the group was disbanded and Kenneth Butlin retired. A reason for the furore among the scientific community was that, as part of the early expansion of the group in 1951, it acquired from the Medical Research Council the custodianship of the National Collection of Type Cultures. This nationally important collection was then expanded to include microbes of economic importance and renamed the National Collection of Industrial Bacteria (NCIB). On the group's closure the NCIB was moved to the Torrey Research Station in Aberdeen and amalgamated with the National Collection of Marine Bacteria, becoming the National Collection of Industrial and Marine Bacteria, which exists to this day.

MICROBIOLOGICAL RESEARCH ESTABLISHMENT, PORTON DOWN

Just at this time, a senior vacancy opened up at the Microbiological Research Establishment (MRE) in Porton Down, then headed by Donald Henderson. John accepted the post and the family moved to Salisbury in the spring of 1959. He joined a biochemically focused section under the microbiologist Dennis Herbert, famed for being the first person to crystallize a bacterial enzyme, catalase, and an expert in continuous culture.

The fundamental goal of the MRE towards biological weapons development and defence did not align with John's political and generally pacifist views. However, the MRE was then possibly the UK's foremost microbiology research group, from which emerged fundamental advances in continuous, single-cell culture, mass cell culture, preservation of bacteria, microbial genetics, bacterial sporulation, mechanisms of animal pathogenesis, and propagation of viruses in cell tissue culture. John rapidly appreciated the value of the MRE's multidisciplinary approach and collegiality. It was to prove an important cornerstone of his belief of how science could be best advanced, a belief he was later to put into practice when eventually he had the chance to direct a scientific programme at the Unit of Nitrogen Fixation at the University of Sussex.

John could not directly continue his research on SRBs but was encouraged to look into bacterial survival and death, which was already being studied by Dick Strange at the MRE but by few others worldwide. John's work on bacterial survival and death soon proved productive once a method had been found to distinguish between dead and viable organisms. Of the several methods for doing this he settled on microscopic observations of the ability of individual bacteria to grow and divide on slide cultures. This was already in use at the MRE by Owen Powell to study the kinetics of bacterial growth and division. For this work John returned to the bacterium *Klebsiella aerogenes*, which he had studied in Hinshelwood's lab. In one strand of experiments he and his team of Janet Crumpton and John Hunter looked at the effects of starvation on the viability of cultures. To provide a consistent source of organisms, cultures were first grown in continuous culture. Samples were withdrawn and subjected to starvation; from these, further samples were taken at timed intervals. These were inoculated into a thin layer of a nutrient-rich agar in a cavity created between a microscope slide and a coverslip suspended slightly above the slide by a metal ring. Cells were observed microscopically for their ability to divide or not. There remained difficulties in determining whether a bacterium is actually dead as opposed to being incapable of growth and division. Nevertheless a number of novel observations were published by Postgate and Hunter in their very detailed 1962 paper (7). They showed that bacteria consumed their own constituents such as carbohydrate, protein and nucleic acids to preserve vital functions, but once approximately half of those had been consumed they were unable to recover and divide. In a series of papers in the early 1960s Postgate and Hunter explored the survival of frozen bacteria and described the phenomenon of 'substrate-accelerated death' of *K. aerogenes*, *E. coli* and *Serratia marcescens*, in which death was hastened by the resupply of growth substrates of which organisms had previously been starved (8). They also described the phenomenon of 'cryptic growth', particularly in dense bacterial populations, where the dead bacteria leak nutrients that can support the growth and division of viable organisms.

Early in 1962 John received an offer of a year-long Visiting Professorship at the Microbiology Department at the University of Illinois, Urbana, with Leon Campbell and Ralph Wolfe as co-hosts. The MRE was content with a shorter stay and agreed that John could resume his work with SRBs, which interested Campbell. John and Mary and their three young daughters, Selina, Lucy and Joanna, set off for the USA in the early autumn of 1962. This was his first experience of working as a university 'academic' but he had few lecturing and examination commitments, for which he was rather glad. This allowed him time to clear up some loose ends from his earlier work at Teddington and to examine some bacteria that Campbell had isolated. In only a few months he and Campbell had done sufficient work to publish six papers from their research over the period 1963–66. These included the description of novel SRBs and studies of the taxonomy of both spore-forming and non-spore-forming desulfovibrios.

Before John had left for the USA, the MRE had been looking to 'civilianize' its work by studying more of the microbiology of economic processes. John returned to the UK at the height of the Cold War and the international nuclear stalemate, and there was concern in the government that the UK needed its research on weapons and defences for biological warfare. He saw his future being constrained by this prospect and did not agree that the impressive facilities of the MRE should be devoted to defence purposes. He therefore decided to look for another job.

THE UNIT OF NITROGEN FIXATION

At the end of this sojourn John was tempted to take up a firm offer of an academic position in the USA, but he heard from Donald Woods that the Agricultural Research Council (ARC) was looking for an experienced microbiologist to join a new research group to work on nitrogen fixation. Indeed, this was one of the microbial processes that attracted the attention of the reports arguing for the civilianization of the MRE. John was told that he could meet the Director Designate *en passant* in New York.

N_2 fixation is the process, restricted to a few prokaryotic organisms (bacteria and archaea), that converts atmospheric N_2 to NH_4^+. This 'fixed' N is used by all organisms such as plants as a starting point for the biosynthesis of protein, RNA and DNA and other cell components. The provision of fixed N either through biological N_2 fixation or the industrial Haber Process is essential to agriculture. On a global scale, N_2 fixation is an essential limb of the global nitrogen cycle sustaining all life on Earth.

An earlier report, commissioned by Shell and conducted by the now retired Kenneth Butlin, surveyed the study of this process since its discovery in 1886 and the research currently being undertaken in the UK and in particular in the USA. It noted an important breakthrough made in 1960 by the Dupont de Nemours Chemical Corporation at Wilmington, Delaware. Their research team of J. E. Carnahan, L. E. Mortenson, H. F. Mower and J. E. Castle had shown that the enzyme system responsible for this process could be made to work *in vitro* (Carnahan *et al.* 1960). This made tractable the study of the biochemistry and chemistry of N_2 fixation and rapidly led to several papers on the essential characteristics and requirements of the enzyme system, called nitrogenase.

Although Shell decided not to set up a research team in this area, the ARC realized that it fell squarely in their remit and decided to set up a Unit to study the fundamentals of the biochemistry and chemistry of the process. It would leave the broader aspects to several other established university research groups around the UK. These included the diversity of nitrogen-fixing organisms and N_2-fixing symbioses especially with leguminous crops, such as peas and beans, which through their *Rhizobium*-containing root nodules are self-sufficient in fixed N.

John's meeting in New York in 1963 was with the Unit's Director Designate, Professor Joseph Chatt FRS, a distinguished inorganic chemist. The plan was to develop the Unit along interdisciplinary lines. It would be the largest ARC Unit, with 10 senior scientists, 15 support staff and research students. John was appointed as Assistant Director.

The Unit started life divided between two sites in London, the chemistry side at Queen Mary College and the biology at the Royal Veterinary College in Camden Town. The first two additional senior research staff (Dr Ray Richards and Dr Michael Kelly) were appointed and PhD students were taken on. Eventually the Unit became known as the Unit of Nitrogen Fixation (UNF) and was consolidated in 1965 at the newly established University of Sussex in Brighton. In 1968 it moved into a custom-designed building.

An important strategic decision was the initial focus of the biological research, including the selection of organisms to study. It should complement but not directly compete with work elsewhere in the world. The strategy that emerged was influenced by John's attendance at a symposium of world experts at Butternut Lake, Wisconsin, in 1964 sponsored by the C. F. Kettering Research Foundation. While in the USA he also visited several labs, especially at the University of Wisconsin, a historically important centre of academic research in N_2 fixation, where important figures in the field, including Perry Wilson, Bob Burris and Winston Brill, were located.

It was known that nitrogenase from the obligate anaerobe *Clostridum pasteurianum* studied by Carnahan and his group was destroyed by exposure to O_2. However, in the mid 1960s, W. A. Bulen, R. C. Burns and J. R. LeComte, working at the C. F. Kettering Research Laboratory in Ohio, described a much more O_2-resistant nitrogenase system from *Azotobacter vinelandii*, a bacterium capable of fixing N_2 in air (Bulen *et al.* 1964). *A. vinelandii* was then a workhorse in biochemistry, for example in seminal work on the enzymology of RNA synthesis and studies of enzyme kinetics (Lineweaver & Burk 1934).

In the mid to late 1960s John and his colleague Mike Kelly, the first senior scientific appointee on the biochemical side, studied the biochemistry of N_2 fixation in *Azotobacter chroococcum*, an O_2-tolerant N_2 fixer. They demonstrated that nitrogenase could reduce cyanide and isothiocyanate, an early example of the Unit's interdisciplinary approach (9). They also confirmed that nitrogenase could reduce acetylene to ethylene, which could be measured by gas chromatography. This remains a standard assay for nitrogenase in both whole organisms and cell extracts.

An important biological problem, addressed early in the Unit's programme, was to determine which microorganisms are capable of fixing nitrogen. Together with Susan Hill, a member of staff, John examined both continuous and batch cultures of seven microbial strains from collections, plus three local isolates, using isotopes of N_2 and acetylene and isocyanide as nitrogenase substrates. Of these only two strains were able to fix N_2, although some simulated fixation impressively in cultural tests but eventually proved simply to be very efficient scavengers of fixed nitrogen (11).

In the early 1960s Russian workers reported the isolation of nitrogen-fixing strains of *Mycobacterium* from acidic soils. It was thought that these strains might be important nitrogen fixers in soils since they are more acid-tolerant than the azotobacters. Therefore John, with a student, David Biggins, conducted a detailed physiological and biochemical examination of nitrogen fixation by *Mycobacterium flavum* 301. They concluded that the nitrogenase from this organism catalysed the same reactions as enzymes from other organisms but was more similar to that of the azotobacters in being particulate, whereas that from clostridia was soluble. However, nitrogenase in the crude extracts form *Mycobacterium* was more sensitive to O_2 than the enzyme in *A. chroococcum* extracts. This suggested that the protective mechanism was more primitive. The enzyme was purified from *M. flavum* 301, and immunological cross reactions were observed with nitrogenases isolated from some other organisms but not from the strict anaerobe *C. pasteurianum* (13). The nitrogenases from azotobacters were recognized as being particulate, suggesting that the enzyme might be protected from oxygen damage in the particles. It was later shown that the particles contained, in addition to the two component proteins in nitrogenase, a third protein (later to become known as the Shethna II protein) that was oxidized by oxygen and then formed a protected particle with nitrogenase (Haaker & Veeger 1977; Robson 1979).

In the mid to late 1960s John and research student, Howard Dalton (the late Sir Howard Dalton FRS; see Anthony & Murrell 2016), studied N_2 fixation in *A. chroococcum*, in batch and continuous cultures under a variety of conditions. They concluded that two mechanisms existed to protect the nitrogenase from damage by oxygen: first, enhanced respiration to scavenge excess oxygen, and second, a conformational state of the enzyme that prevented damage by oxygen (10). In subsequent work with another student, Jan Drozd, John confirmed these proposals and was able to demonstrate the switching on and off of nitrogenase activity and the limits of the two mechanisms (12).

John was keen to encourage other scientists to take sabbaticals working in the Unit. An example was Howard Lees from the University of Manitoba, Canada, who worked with John on oxygen- and phosphate-limited cultures of *A. chroococcum*. Their findings supported the view that respiration provided, at least in part, a protective function for nitrogenase (22). They and Britton Chance (ForMemRS 1981) also published a theoretical *Nature* note clarifying the meaning of the terms 'reversed electron flow' and 'high energy electron' in biochemistry (15).

In another collaboration, with W. S. Silver, John considered the evolution of asymbiotic nitrogen fixation, which they noted was restricted to prokaryotic organisms, particularly those considered to have 'primitive' properties. They suggested that nitrogen fixation may have evolved before significant amounts of oxygen appeared in the atmosphere. They suggested that because there would have been adequate ammonia available for the growth of these organisms, the original role of nitrogenase might have been to detoxify the environment by removing chemicals such as cyanide and/or cyanogen (20). Later, with the emergence of an oxidizing atmosphere, facultative and aerobic nitrogen-fixing organisms could only retain nitrogenase if it was protected from inactivation in some way. In the Azotobacteraceae this is achieved by 'conformational protection' and in filamentous cyanobacteria by compartmentalization.

John combined his new enthusiasm for nitrogen fixation with his interest in SRBs and confirmed the presence of nitrogenase in *D. desulfuricans* and other *Desulfovibrio* strains. One strain exists in the sheep rumen, and with an assistant, David Ware, and in collaboration with colleagues from the Rowett Research Institute in Aberdeen, John attempted to assess whether the organism might contribute to the sheep's nutrition. They concluded that although some activity was detected it was insufficient to make a significant contribution (21).

In 1969 the biochemical effort at the Unit was boosted by the addition of two new senior scientists: Bob Eady, a biochemist, and Barry Smith, a physical chemist interested in applying spectroscopic techniques to biological problems. Under John's guidance, the new Unit members and a student, Keith Cook, studied in detail nitrogenase from the facultative anaerobe, *K. pneumoniae* M5a1 (now renamed *K. oxytoca*) (16). The outcome was the most comprehensive description of a nitrogenase available in one place. This publication had the effect of putting the Unit at the forefront of world nitrogenase biochemistry. Later John appointed two more important members to the biochemical team, David Lowe and Roger Thorneley, who developed a conceptual model for the mechanism of action of nitrogenase, which they then computerized. This model was able to describe and predict the enzyme's activity in considerable detail.

Probably John's most important contribution to the scientific output of the Unit was his decision in 1969 to initiate, with research student Ray Dixon (FRS 1999), the study of the genetics of nitrogen fixation. Dixon and Postgate chose to study *K. pneumoniae* M5a1, an enteric bacterium that was likely to be genetically tractable because it was related to the extremely well-studied model bacterium *E. coli*. They established a conjugation system in *K. pneumoniae* M5a1 that enabled the transfer of genes between strains and discovered that genes required for nitrogen fixation (*nif*) were located next to the genes for histidine biosynthesis (14). The conjugation system also proved to be useful for inter-specific transfer of genetic material. Initially they tested the potential for genetic transfer of genes for histidine biosynthesis from *K. pneumoniae* M5a1 to a histidine-requiring (His$^-$) strain of *E. coli*. Remarkably, some of the His$^+$ transconjugants of *E. coli* gained the ability to fix nitrogen, demonstrating that all the genes required for nitrogen fixation were located next to the histidine operon in *K. pneumoniae* M5a1 (17). The creation of the world's first engineered diazotroph created a stir in the scientific community and sensational reporting in the media.

John became fascinated with the idea of transferring nitrogen fixation to 'alien' genetic backgrounds. Together with a visitor, Viji Krishnapillai, and his assistant Helen Kent, he studied the transfer of *nif* genes from *K. pneumoniae* M5a1 to various representatives of the γ-proteobacteria (25, 28). Although these studies were of limited practical value, because diazotrophy is already represented in related organisms that inhabit similar environmental niches, they did show the evolutionary advantages of *nif* gene clusters and their potential to mediate horizontal gene transfer.

The breakthrough in the transfer of the *nif* genes to *E. coli* and the adoption of the then new tools of recombinant DNA technology and DNA sequencing led to the steady expansion of the genetics group with the appointment of Christina Kennedy, Frank Cannon, Mike Merrick, Martin Drummond and Martin Buck (FRS 2009). The work led to significant advances in the identification and function of the large cluster of more than 20 *nif* genes in *K. pneumoniae* M5a1, in particular in the synthesis of the complex iron- and molybdenum-containing metal centres in the enzyme and the supply of reducing power. A strong focus was the complex regulation of expression of the *nif* genes in response to fixed nitrogen and O_2 and the way in which this regulatory system was subordinate to the global nitrogen and oxygen regulatory systems in the organism. Studies on the biochemistry and physiology of *Azotobacter* were expanded by the early appointment of Geoff Yates and later Rob Robson and Richard Pau. Advances were made in understanding the role of hydrogenase in recovering the energy lost by the hydrogen produced as a by-product of nitrogenase activity. Studies of the mechanisms of protection of nitrogenase from O_2 yielded novel findings, and the development of molecular genetic tools for *Azotobacter* led to the discovery of the vanadium nitrogenase system.

The year 1977 was important for John. First, he was elected to the Fellowship of the Royal Society on the basis of the many advances he had made in microbiology. Second, towards the end of the year he undertook a sabbatical for a year in Harold Evans's laboratory at Oregon State University, whom he met originally at the Butternut Lake conference. Together with Robert Maier he isolated hydrogenase-deficient mutants of the legume symbiont *Bradyrhizobium japonicum* (23). This was an important initial step in determining the role of the uptake hydrogenase in recovering the energy lost by nitrogenase as a consequence of its obligatory hydrogen-evolving activity.

When Joseph Chatt retired in 1980, the ARC appointed John as the new Director of the Unit. This was a golden age for the Unit, which was renowned as a world-leading group for nitrogen fixation research that at its peak had a staff complement of about 45.

During this time the Unit made great contributions to the understanding of nitrogen fixation, including the function and regulation of the *nif* genes, the role of hydrogen metabolism in nitrogen fixers, the properties of the complex Mo-, Fe- and S-containing metal centres in nitrogenase and its reaction mechanism and kinetics, and the discovery of a genetically distinct vanadium-requiring nitrogenase enzyme system in *A. chroococcum*, which was produced when Mo was not available (29).

John had a delightful 'hands-off' approach to staff management, both when leading the 'biologists and biochemists' and later when directing the whole Unit. This is clearly explained in John's book *Microbes, music and me*, in which he likened his leadership style to that of a big band leader:

> I like to think that my leadership echoed in some ways Duke Ellington's approach to his orchestra. He never managed his musicians: he had a collection of brilliant, disparate and individualistic soloists and he gave them their heads musically. His contribution was simply to co-ordinate them, which he did in such a masterly fashion that he created the greatest jazz orchestra of the century.

Despite the heavy administrative load associated with his interactions with the Agricultural and Food Research Council (AFRC) and his duties as Director, John still found time to do some bench work and could frequently be seen in his lab coat, streaking out strains in his small laboratory (figure 3). But other responsibilities restricted his research activities. He became President of the Institute of Biology (now the Royal Society of Biology) in 1982, and in 1984 he was made President of the Society for General Microbiology (now the Microbiology Society). He had previously served on the Society's Council and had been Editor-in-Chief of its *Journal of General Microbiology*, for which he was renowned as being extremely fastidious in the maintenance of editorial standards, perhaps as a consequence of the difficulties he himself experienced in writing his PhD thesis.

SCIENCE AND OTHER WRITING

Quite apart from John's scientific papers and reviews he was a relatively prolific author of books over 38 years. These covered three areas: specialized scientific monographs, contributions to the public understanding of science and jazz, and biographies. His scientific monographs comprise an important early review of the sulfate-reducing bacteria (24), two monographs on nitrogen fixation entitled *Nitrogen fixation*, first published in 1978 and now in its 3rd edition (33), and *The fundamentals of nitrogen fixation* (26). His biographies were of his grandfather John Postgate, an early pioneer of food safety, entitled *Lethal lozenges and tainted tea* (35), and of his father, Raymond Postgate, entitled *A stomach for dissent*, which

Figure 3. John in his laboratory at the Unit of Nitrogen Fixation in the late 1970s.

he co-authored with his wife, Mary (31). John co-authored with Bob Weir a biography and discography of the jazz trumpeter Frankie Newton (36). He also published a rather ill-fated guide aimed at increasing the public's appreciation of jazz (19). Unfortunately the publisher experienced financial difficulties and the whole edition was seized by the Official Receiver with only a few copies sold as remainders. John's last book was his 2013 memoir entitled *Music, microbes and me: a life in science*, which is self-revealing and also wryly amusing in many places (37).

In 1965, when the Unit of Nitrogen Fixation was still in its infancy, John was commissioned by Penguin publishers to write an introduction to microbiology, accessible to the general reader, that would focus on the impact of microbes on people's daily lives. *Microbes and man* finally emerged as a paperback in 1969. It soon gained popular acclaim, serving as both a teaching aid and an easy-to-read introduction to the world of microbes, illuminating both the positive and negative aspects of the huge microbial community on our planet. *Microbes and man* has undergone four revisions, been translated into nine languages and is still in print today (34). John also published *The outer reaches of life* (32), in which with typical clarity he provided an entertaining description of microbial life in a wide range of environments, some seemingly hostile to life but in which microbes have evolved to inhabit and thrive.

Figure 4. John playing his cornet at the 'King and Queen' in Brighton, May 1977.

John was also concerned about broader societal issues that could perhaps benefit from scientific intervention. Concerned by the increasing world population and consequent shortages of food and raw materials, he wrote a notorious article in 1973 for *New Scientist* entitled 'Bat's chance in hell' in which he advocated the use of a 'man child' pill in developing countries as a means to control the population (18). This created a furore, particularly in the feminist community. Far less controversial was an article published in 1984, 'Biology in the eighties—and beyond', which again alluded to world population growth and the depletion of energy resources (27). Drawing on his expertise in both sulfur and N_2 reduction, John enthusiastically promoted biotechnology as a means to supplement energy-depleting chemical production with cleaner biological processes. He also argued that this new revolution in biology would help to counter the growing wave of anti-science sentiment that blames science and technology for exacerbating humanity's problems rather than alleviating them (27).

It would be remiss to omit John's contributions to jazz (figure 4). Not only did he continue to play in and lead semi-professional jazz groups until his early eighties, he was a renowned writer and reviewer on jazz for more than 45 years for *Jazz Monthly*, *Jazz Journal* and *Gramophone*. His reviewing activity may have been encouraged by Mary, who was renowned for publishing many reviews of spoken word recordings from the 1960s.

Post-retirement activities

John's retirement in 1987 was mandatory and he became an emeritus professor at the University of Sussex. He never lost his lively interest in scientific matters and their communication to the general public. This continued past the loss of Mary, who died in 2008. They had been married for 60 years. At the time of his death in 2014 he had contributed approximately 50 reviews, letters and opinion pieces, mostly published in *New Scientist* and *The Times Literary Supplement* but several in mainstream scientific journals, including a history of the first 50 years of the Society for Microbiology.

John was concerned about the public understanding of science and the growth of anti-science attitudes. He felt that this was at least partly the fault of scientists themselves, who responded to anti-science criticisms by emphasizing the benefits deriving from the applications of science instead of defending science itself as a cultural activity. Contrary to the assertion that science does not impose moral values, John insisted that science imposes a stern, austere morality on its adherents, constantly open to challenge and modification, with no dogmas, there being no absolute truth because science only approaches the truth asymptotically and never gets there.

Most of his writings reflected his academic interests in nitrogen fixation, microbial sulfur metabolism and microbial survival and death, but some also broke new ground. For example he proposed a system (based on army practice) whereby professional scientists would be appointed for a fixed term of, say, 25 years and then (mainly) promoted one grade and retired on half pay. A few, outstanding, individuals would be retained for, say, another 10 years, after which a further assessment of their capability would occur. This system would prevent senior scientists who had effectively 'run out of steam' from blocking the promotion prospects of their younger, more productive and innovative colleagues and would also release capable, middle-aged individuals into the workforce for other roles.

A recurrent theme was to emphasize the difficulty of distinguishing between real and apparent observations. A good example is nitrogen fixation, for which several 'ghosts' have been reported, such as: How do termites and woodworm obtain enough nitrogen to grow when their diets seemingly consist only of the carbohydrate from wood? Can these organisms fix nitrogen from the atmosphere to make ammonia? The upshot of careful investigations is that only certain bacteria can fix nitrogen. Other organisms that have been reported to do so are either associated with such bacteria, for example the symbiosis between legumes and *Rhizobium* species, or are extremely effective at scavenging ammonia or other nitrogen compounds from the environment.

Another area where it is difficult to ascertain the validity of claims is that of microbial longevity. In 'The microbial way of death' (30) John explained that it was difficult to determine whether bacteria are dead or senescent. In a comment on a 1995 article in *Microbiology*, John examined the authors' claims concerning the possible age of spores of a strain of *Bacillus sphericus* isolated from the gut of bees entrapped in amber between 25 and 40 million years ago. John felt that its veracity must await determination of whether over this length of time the amber could have been permeable to nutrients in liquid or vapour, which could have sustained the organism. If the putative age of the organisms is correct, then current views on the 'tenacity of life', the stability of DNA, the resistance of spores to radiation damage and aspects of bacterial evolution will need to be radically revised. John also questioned claims of viable spores in 8000-year-old sediments and viable non-spore-forming microbes isolated from the interior of 2400-year-old Egyptian bricks. Clearly this issue remains to be settled.

Concluding remark

Quite apart from all of John's many important contributions to science and its public understanding and to the development of the careers of many younger scientists, and also his writing and performance of jazz, John was rightly proud of his own family and their background. A typically non-religious memorial service for John that took place in Brighton in 2014 highlighted some of the many caring and amusing sides of John as a husband and father, of which many of those who worked with him were unaware.

Honours and awards

1965	DSc, Oxford University
	Fellow of the Institute of Biology
1977	Fellow of the Royal Society
1978	Member, European Molecular Biology Organization (EMBO)
1981	Honorary Member, Society for Applied Bacteriology
1982–84	President, Institute of Biology
1984–87	President, Society of General Microbiology
1988	Honorary Member, Society of General Microbiology
1990	Honorary DSc, University of Bath
1992	Royal Society Leeuwenhoek Lecture: 'Bacterial evolution and the nitrogen-fixing plant'
1997	Honorary LLD, University of Dundee

Acknowledgements

We thank members of the Postgate family (Lucy, Selina and Joanna) for their helpful comments on the manuscript and for providing us with photographs of John.

The frontispiece photograph was taken in 1985 by Godfrey Argent and is reproduced with permission.

Author profiles

Rob Robson

Rob Robson was recruited by John Postgate as a Scientific Officer at the Unit of Nitrogen Fixation, which he joined in 1977. He was attracted by the Unit's scientific focus and multidisciplinarity and carried out research on the molecular biology of nitrogen fixation in *Azotobacter chroococcum*. Supported by John, his work led to insights into O_2 protection systems, the molecular genetics of N_2 fixation, including the important discovery of the vanadium nitrogenase system, and, with colleague Geoff Yates, the genetics and role of the uptake hydrogenase system. Rob left the Unit in 1987 and was a founding member of the multidisciplinary Centre for Metalloenzyme Studies at the University of Georgia at Athens in the USA. He returned to the UK in 1994 as Professor of Microbiology at the University of Reading. He retired in 2012, having been a Pro-Vice Chancellor during his last six years there. With some leftover research funds he started a project to sequence the genome of *A. chroococcum*, the organism that John had chosen for the Unit to work on in at its inception. The paper reporting the genome sequence of this organism was published in June 2015, sadly after John's death but nevertheless a fitting tribute to the opportunity and support he had given Rob earlier in his career.

Barry Smith

Barry Smith's first and second degrees and postdoctoral appointments were in chemistry. In 1969 he was appointed by Professor Chatt and Professor Postgate as a Senior Scientific Officer at the Unit of Nitrogen Fixation. His initial role was to apply spectroscopic and biochemical methods to analyse the structure and function of the enzyme nitrogenase, which is responsible for biological nitrogen fixation. This approach, which involved collaborations both within the Unit and with academic groups expert in various techniques, was timely and successful. When John Postgate retired in 1987 the Unit was combined with some other AFRC establishments, and Smith was appointed as Head of the Laboratory, which then became part of the John Innes Centre in Norwich.

Ray Dixon FRS

Ray Dixon joined the Unit of Nitrogen Fixation in 1969 as a DPhil student under John's supervision. With John's support and guidance he developed genetic techniques to identify nitrogen fixation genes in *K. pneumoniae* (now renamed *K. oxytoca*). In 1972 they successfully transferred the complete cluster of nitrogen fixation (*nif*) genes from *K. pneumoniae* to *E. coli*, thus creating the first engineered diazotroph. Ray was appointed as a Scientific Officer at the Unit in 1975 and continued to perform research on the genetics and regulation of nitrogen fixation until the Nitrogen Fixation Laboratory at Sussex was disbanded in 1995. He then moved to the John Innes Centre (JIC), where he has pioneered studies on signal transduction and transcriptional regulation of nitrogen fixation. He is currently the director of a joint research centre established by the Chinese Academy of Sciences and the JIC, known as the Centre of Excellence for Plant and Microbial Science, located across campuses in Norwich, Beijing and Shanghai.

REFERENCES TO OTHER AUTHORS

Anthony, C. & Murrell, J. C. 2016 Sir Howard Dalton, 1944–2008. *Biogr. Mems Fell. R. Soc.* **62**, 89–107 (this volume; http://dx.doi.org/10.1098/rsbm.2016.0007).

Bulen, W. A., Burns, R. C. & LeComte, J. R. 1964 Nitrogen fixation: cell-free system with extracts of *Azotobacter*. *Biochem. Biophys. Res. Commun.* **17**, 265–271.

Carnahan, J. E., Mortenson, L. E., Mower, H. F. & Castle, J. E. 1960 Nitrogen fixation in cell-free extracts of *Clostridium pasteurianum. Biochim. Biophys. Acta* **38**, 188–189.

Gale, E. F. & Fildes, P. 1965 Donald Devereux Woods, 1912–1964. *Biogr. Mems Fell. R. Soc.* **11**, 202–219.

Haaker, H. & Veeger, C. 1977 Involvement of the cytoplasmic membrane in nitrogen fixation by *Azotobacter vinelandii. Eur. J. Biochem.* **77**, 1–10.

Lineweaver, H. & Burk, D. 1934 The determination of enzyme dissociation constants. *J. Am. Chem. Soc.* **56**, 658–666.

Robson, R. L. 1979 Characterization of an oxygen-stable nitrogenase complex isolated from *Azotobacter chroococcum. Biochem. J.* **181**, 569–575.

Thompson, H. 1973 Cyril Norman Hinshelwood, 1897–1967. *Biogr. Mems Fell. R. Soc.* **19**, 374–431.

BIBLIOGRAPHY

The following publications are those referred to directly in the text. A full bibliography is available as electronic supplementary material at http://dx.doi.org/10.1098/rsbm.2016.0006 or via http://rsbm.royalsocietypublishing.org.

(1) 1946 (With C. N. Hinshelwood) The adaptation of *Bact. lactis aerogenes* and *Bact. coli mutabile* to various carbohydrates. *Trans. Faraday Soc.* **42**, 45–56.

(2) 1949 Competitive inhibition of sulphate reduction by selenate. *Nature* **164**, 670–671.

(3) 1953 (With J. P. Grossman) Cultivation of sulphate-reducing bacteria. *Nature* **171**, 600–602.

(4)   Presence of cytochrome in an obligate anaerobe. *Biochem. J.* **56**, xi–xii.

(5) 1954 Dependence of sulphate reduction and oxygen utilization on a cytochrome in *Desulphovibrio. Biochem. J.* **58**, ix.

(6) 1956 Cytochrome c_3 and desulphoviridin; pigments of the anaerobe *Desulphovibrio desulphuricans. J. Gen. Microbiol.* **14**, 545–572.

(7) 1962 (With J. R. Hunter) The survival of starved bacteria. *J. Gen. Microbiol.* **29**, 233–263.

(8) 1963 (With J. R. Hunter) Acceleration of bacterial death by growth substrates. *Nature* **198**, 273.

(9) 1967 (With M. Kelly & R. L. Richards) Reduction of cyanide and isocyanide by nitrogenase of *Azotobacter chroococcum. Biochem. J.* **102**, 1C–3C.

(10) 1969 (With H. Dalton) Effect of oxygen on growth of *Azotobacter chroococcum* in batch and continuous cultures. *J. Gen. Microbiol.* **54**, 463–473.

(11)   (With S. Hill) Failure of putative nitrogen-fixing bacteria to fix nitrogen. *J. Gen. Microbiol.* **58**, 277–285.

(12) 1970 (With J. Drozd & J. R. Postgate) Effects of oxygen on acetylene reduction, cytochrome content and respiratory activity of *Azotobacter chroococcum. J. Gen. Microbiol.* **63**, 63–73.

(13) 1971 (With D. R. Biggins & M. Kelly) Resolution of nitrogenase of *Mycobacterium flavum* 301 into two components and cross reaction with nitrogenase components from other bacteria. *Eur. J. Biochem.* **20**, 140–143.

(14)   (With R. A. Dixon) Transfer of nitrogen-fixation genes by conjugation in *Klebsiella pneumoniae. Nature* **234**, 47–48.

(15) 1972 (With B. Chance & H. Lees) The meaning of 'reversed electron flow' and 'high energy electron' in biochemistry. *Nature* **238**, 330–331.

(16)   (With R. R. Eady, B. E. Smith & K. A. Cook) Nitrogenase of *Klebsiella pneumoniae*. Purification and properties of the component proteins. *Biochem. J.* **128**, 655–675.

(17)   (With R. A. Dixon) Genetic transfer of nitrogen fixation from *Klebsiella pneumoniae* to *Escherichia coli. Nature* **237**, 102–103.

(18) 1973 Bat's chance in hell. *New Scient.* **58**, 12–16.

(19)   *A plain man's guide to jazz.* London: Hanover Books.

(20)   (With W. S. Silver) Evolution of asymbiotic nitrogen fixation. *J. Theor. Biol.* **40**, 1–10.

(21)   (With P. N. Hobson, R. Summers & D. A. Ware) Nitrogen fixation in the rumen of a living sheep. *J. Gen. Microbiol.* **77**, 225–226.

(22)   (With H. Lees) The behaviour of *Azotobacter chroococcum* in oxygen- and phosphate-limited chemostat culture. *J. Gen. Microbiol.* **75**, 161–166.

(23)   1978   (With R. J. Maier & H. J. Evans) *Rhizobium japonicum* mutants unable to use hydrogen. *Nature* **276**, 494–495.

(24)   1979   *The sulphate-reducing bacteria.* Cambridge University Press.

(25)   1980   (With V. Krishnapillai) Expression of *Klebsiella his* and *nif* genes in *Serratia marcescens*, *Erwinia herbicola* and *Proteus mirabilis*. *Arch. Microbiol.* **127**, 115–118.

(26)   1982   *The fundamentals of nitrogen fixation.* Cambridge University Press.

(27)   1984   Biology in the eighties—and beyond. *New Scient.* **103**, 47–48.

(28)   1985   (With H. M. Kent) Expression of *Klebsiella pneumoniae nif* genes in *Proteus mirabilis*. *Arch. Microbiol.* **142**, 289–294.

(29)   1986   (With R. L. Robson, R. R. Eady, T. H. Richardson, R. W. Miller & M. Hawkins) The alternative nitrogenase of *Azotobacter chroococcum* is a vanadium enzyme. *Nature* **322**, 388–390.

(30)   1989   The microbial way of death. *New Scient.* **122**, 43–47.

(31)   1994   (With M. Postgate) *A stomach for dissent: the life of Raymond Postgate, 1896–1971.* Keele University Press.

(32)   1995   *The outer reaches of life.* Cambridge University Press.

(33)   1998   *Nitrogen fixation*, 3rd edn. Cambridge University Press.

(34)   2000   *Microbes and man*, 4th edn. Cambridge University Press.

(35)   2001   *Lethal lozenges and tainted tea: a biography of John Postgate (1820–1881).* Studley: Brewin Books.

(36)   2003   (With B. Weir) *Looking for Frankie: a bio-discography of the jazz trumpeter Frankie Newton.* Cardiff: Bob Weir.

(37)   2013   *Microbes, music and me: a life in science.* Cirencester: Mereo Books.

BENTON SEYMOUR RABINOVITCH

19 February 1919 — 2 August 2014

BENTON SEYMOUR RABINOVITCH

19 February 1919 — 2 August 2014

Elected FRS 1987

By Charles T. Campbell[1]* and Ruth A. Rabinovitch

[1]*Department of Chemistry, University of Washington, Seattle, WA 98195-1700, USA*

Benton Seymour Rabinovitch was one of the pioneers of chemical dynamics. His brilliant experiments performed during his four decades as a Professor of Chemistry at the University of Washington in Seattle provided most of our early quantitative measurements of the efficiency with which energy is transferred between molecules in gas-phase molecule–molecule collisions and in collisions of molecules with solid surfaces. More importantly, his work provided quantitative estimates of the rates with which vibrational energy deposited locally within a molecule is redistributed among the many vibrational modes within that molecule, proving that the equilibration of this vibrational energy among these modes almost always occurs in approximately one picosecond. He further showed that this validates (in most cases) the assumptions of Rice–Ramsperger–Kassel–Marcus (RRKM) theory. He also developed several widely used mathematical shortcuts for using RRKM theory to make important predictions about physical chemistry. These shortcuts greatly increased both the applications and impact of RRKM theory, so that it has become one of the most important theories of physical chemistry. It continues to guide much of our fundamental understanding of chemical dynamics and reaction kinetics even today. In addition to being a great scientist, Seymour Rabinovitch was a devoted husband and father. He raised four accomplished children, and later in life became an expert in the art of silversmithing, a writer of children's books, and a philanthropist. His offspring are following beautifully in his footsteps in their kindness to fellow human beings, their excellence in scholarship, science and art, and in their energetic dedication to improving the world through teaching, research, service and philanthropy. The same can be said for his academic offspring as well.

* charliec@uw.edu (corresponding author)

http://dx.doi.org/10.1098/rsbm.2015.0021

Early years

Benton Seymour Rabinovitch was born in Montreal, Canada, on 19 February 1919, the youngest of the seven children of Rochelle (*née* Schacter) and Samuel Rabinovitch. Rochelle came to Canada as a teenager from Botosani, Romania, and in Montreal met her future husband, Samuel, who had emigrated from Bessarabia (now part of Moldova and the Ukraine). Seymour was raised by devoted parents and six elder siblings, all of whom provided moral and financial support during his education; he was the only one among them to receive an advanced degree.

At five years of age, Seymour declared that he wanted to be a lawyer, advance to Prime Minister, and be seated to the right of the King of England. During his sophomore year in high school, he was taught by his chemistry teacher, Mr Aiken, that at a temperature of zero kelvins all matter would disappear. Seymour found this concept so intriguing that he changed his career direction to chemistry.

Seymour attended the Strathcona Academy, in the Montreal suburb of Outremont. After the depression hit and the family's real estate business foundered, Seymour would watch his father leave the house each morning to try to find odd jobs to provide food for his family. His two brothers, for their part, left high school to help support the family and ensure that Seymour could continue his education. Seymour became fluent in French, because many of the courses attended by the English-speaking children in Quebec were taught in this language. He loved poetry and memorized a tremendous amount of it, entertaining himself and family with recitations. As a youth, he also enjoyed playing chess, making a name for himself as a young champion on the Montreal street park scene and continuing to play until the last months of his life.

Seymour entered McGill University in 1936 as a second-year student majoring in chemistry (figure 1). Although his studies kept him busy, he also found time for membership in clubs devoted to social problems and to the peace movement. He earned his Bachelor of Science degree in chemistry in 1939, with first-class honours (figure 2). While in college, Seymour lived at home, walking more than three miles each way; he spent the summer months selling magazines to businesses and homes in Montreal's environs, helping fund his education; he served as a crew leader during his last year. During weekends in winter he enjoyed skiing, the physical benefits of this activity being enhanced considerably by the lack of tow lifts on the ski slopes.

Montreal neighbourhoods were often separated by ethnicity, such as Jewish or Italian. There were some areas from which Jews were excluded, such as Mount Royal. Discriminatory practices that were applied in residential areas gradually disappeared after World War II, as did certain ethnicity-based university policies affecting student admissions and faculty life. When Seymour entered college, a quota system governing the admission of Jews to McGill was still in force, which meant that he needed a near 'A' average in high school to be admitted. The same quota system applied to the medical and professional schools, which troubled Seymour greatly and left a lasting impression upon him. He remained a strong advocate of minority rights throughout his life.

PhD studies and service during World War II

Shortly after Canada entered World War II (on 10 September 1939, a week after Britain), Seymour received a letter from the Dean of the Graduate School of McGill University enjoining him to stay with his original plan of commencing doctoral studies, pointing out

Figure 1. At the laboratory bench, Biology Building, McGill University, in 1939.

Figure 2. Graduation in 1939: BSc in chemistry, McGill University.

Figure 3. PhD graduation in 1942, McGill University. Seymour Rabinovitch is at the far left; his PhD advisor, Professor Carl Winkler, is in the middle.

that the department's energies would be directed towards research that contributed to the war effort. Seymour duly entered graduate school in autumn 1939 and completed his PhD with Professor Carl Winkler in February 1942 (figure 3), shortly before Rudy Marcus, a fellow student also in Winkler's laboratory. Seymour's thesis was entitled 'Studies in chemical kinetics (academic research) and the detection of vesicants (war research)'. Although chemical kinetics became his life's work, a detour during the war years into the field of vesicant detection was his contribution to the Allied war effort. Seymour initially entered the Chemical Warfare Laboratory in Ottawa as a civilian, but in December 1942 he went to a training camp for officers at Gordon Head, in Victoria, British Columbia. In 1943 Seymour was sent to England as a captain in the Canadian Army, remaining there until 1946 (figure 4). He was stationed first at Leatherhead with training at two chemical warfare establishments, one at Porton Down in Wiltshire and a second near the border with Scotland.

While in London as a Jewish officer, Seymour received hospitality from the family of Harry and Yetta Clifford, enjoying meals and family life and forming a lifelong friendship. During this period he developed a simple colorimetric method for detecting the presence of mustard gas by impregnating cloth swatches with appropriate dyestuffs or resin and placing them on battlefields or clothing. These were to be inspected early on a day of troop advancement. This method was an outgrowth of Seymour's PhD research and yielded excellent results. After the war, Seymour was sent to Washington DC to participate in a US National Chemical Panel on War Research, where he presented his work on chemical warfare. Throughout his life he savoured the memory of being asked, 'Hmmm, Rabinovitch … do you have anything to do with the guy who invented the mustard gas detector?'

On 12 June 1944, Seymour's unit was posted to Portsmouth. At the end of July, more than a month after D-day, they landed in Courseulles-sur-mer, France. He recalled digging slit

Figure 4. Captain, Mobile Lab Unit Canadian Chemical Warfare Division, Western Europe, during World War II.

trenches, three feet long, to accommodate a camp cot, conceding that most of the actual spade work was done by his batman. After St Lô was captured, Seymour's unit advanced rapidly to Ghent, followed by Antwerp, Breda, Tilburg, Leiden, Raubkammer bei Münster, and Apeldoorn. He led a team of young scientists who investigated German munitions factories and battlefields as the Germans retreated, looking for violations of the Geneva Convention on Weaponry. In Raubkammer bei Münster, his unit was the first to enter the German command centre where manufacturing and experimentation had been done. Fluorophosphate esters and nerve gases were among the substances they found.

POSTDOCTORAL STUDIES

After the war, Seymour taught physical chemistry to former soldiers at the Khaki College, the Veterans Rehabilitation College of Canada, situated in Watford, England. He was awarded Milton and Royal Society of Canada fellowships, enabling him to conduct postdoctoral studies in physical chemistry at Harvard University, under Professor George Kistiakowsky. It was at this time that he began to date his future wife, Marilyn Werby of Boston (figure 5).

FOUR DECADES AS PROFESSOR AT THE UNIVERSITY OF WASHINGTON

In 1948 Seymour joined the Department of Chemistry at the University of Washington, where he remained throughout his academic career. He and Marilyn had a long-distance engagement and married in 1949, making Seattle their home. He attained the rank of full professor there in 1957.

Figure 5. In 1947 with his fiancée, Marilyn, at a beach party in or near Boston given by his postdoctoral advisor at Harvard University, Professor George Kistiakowsky.

Seymour felt strongly that to not form lifelong friendships with one's graduate students was a lost opportunity. He formed lasting attachments to these students, who numbered 41 over the course of his career. He also mentored some 60 postdoctoral and visiting faculty associates. He and Marilyn greatly enjoyed hosting parties for the graduate students and postdoctoral researchers, occasionally also organizing large festive summer weekend reunions in Seattle. Seymour and Marilyn's marriage of 24 years was loving and full. Together they shared the joys of raising four children: Peter, Ruth, Judith and Frank, all of whom went on to have successful careers of their own. Their family enjoyed two sabbaticals: one in Ottawa in 1962, and a second at Oxford, during 1972. They also took several car trips across America and Canada in their station wagon, visiting friends and relatives. Marilyn's untimely death from cancer in 1974 was a tremendous loss and bereavement; Seymour was fortunate in having several of his children living with him or nearby during this period. In January 1980 he married Flora Reitman of Montreal, and together they enjoyed 34 years of loving marriage, pursuing many shared interests, which included travel, long walks and collecting antiques. They purchased a flat in London in the early 1980s, spending several months there every year. Seymour and Flora helped establish a graduate student space in Bagley Hall, the University of Washington Chemistry Building. Rab's Room, as it was affectionately called, was envisioned as a place for refreshments, the exchange of ideas, and the development of friendships and camaraderie among graduate students. Rab's Room owed its inspiration to similar facilities that Seymour had been impressed by during his sabbatical in England.

Seymour taught and conducted research at the University of Washington for four decades. During his career he became a virtuoso of experimental physical chemistry; his work provided the first experimental verification of important theories of molecular dynamics and energy transfer within molecules in the gas phase. A brief summary of his research contributions

Figure 6. Seymour Rabinovitch with his wife Flora attending the 1992 Nobel Award Dinner, as guest of Rudolph A. Marcus, recipient of the 1992 Nobel Prize in Chemistry. (Online version in colour.)

while at the University of Washington is provided below. Altogether, he co-authored more than 230 scientific papers as well as a widely used book on physical chemistry. He retired as Professor Emeritus in 1986, although he continued to come in regularly 'to work' for another 20 years. During those later years he had many important roles, including advising and mentoring young faculty, serving as a role model, and engendering warm personal interactions among the faculty, students and staff. One of us (C.T.C.) benefited tremendously from these interactions and will remain forever grateful to have enjoyed them, although he deeply regrets not having taken greater advantage of his opportunities to spend time with Seymour.

Seymour received numerous awards for his scientific contributions, including the American Chemical Society's 1983 Peter Debye Award and the 1984 Polanyi Medal bestowed by the Royal Society. He was elected a member of the American Academy of Arts and Sciences in 1979 and a Fellow of the Royal Society in 1987. In 1991 he received an honorary Doctorate of Science from the Technion – Israel Institute of Technology, in recognition of his extraordinary work in the field of reactions and intermolecular energy transfer dynamics. He served as an editor for *Journal of the American Chemical Society* and was Chairman of the Division of Physical Chemistry of the American Chemical Society. In 2005 the University of Washington established the B. S. Rabinovitch Endowed Chair of Chemistry in his honour. Seymour and his students made such extensive use of and contributions to RRKM theory that, when Professor Rudolph A. Marcus was awarded the Nobel Prize in Chemistry in 1992, he joked that Seymour was the missing R in RRKM. He also invited Seymour and his wife Flora to attend the week of festivities and celebration in Stockholm (figure 6).

SCIENTIFIC CONTRIBUTIONS WHILE AT THE UNIVERSITY OF WASHINGTON, 1948–90

Seymour became a Professor at the University of Washington in 1948 and continued publishing scientific papers from there until 1990. The major foci of his research during those 42 years were: (i) unimolecular reaction kinetics, (ii) intermolecular energy transfer, (iii) intramolecular energy relaxation and (iv) energy transfer when molecules collide with solid surfaces. These topics resulted from his deep interest in the rates and kinetics of chemical reactions, particularly for elementary reaction processes. This interest dated back to his research for his PhD dissertation under the direction of Carl Winkler, which involved the study of bimolecular reaction kinetics. Bimolecular reactions are reactions that result from the collision between two molecules to produce products, shown schematically as

$$A + B \rightarrow C + D. \tag{1}$$

The rate for such an elementary reaction is typically proportional to the concentrations of each reactant, [A] and [B]:

$$\text{rate} = k(T)[A][B].$$

The temperature dependence of the rate constant generally follows the classic Arrhenius Law,

$$k(T) = v \exp(-E_{act}/RT),$$

where E_{act} is the activation energy or activation barrier to reaction. As Seymour stated in his dissertation, according to 'Lewis's fundamental formulation', the rate of such a bimolecular reaction can also be expressed as

$$\text{rate} = Z_{AB} \exp(-E_{act}/RT),$$

where Z_{AB} is the number of A–B collisions per unit time (which is also proportional to [A][B]) and where $\exp(-E_{act}/RT)$ is 'the Boltzmann expression for the fraction of collisions in which the joint energy along the line of centers exceeds E_{act}'.

   At the University of Washington, Seymour turned his attention to the presumably simpler case of gas-phase unimolecular reactions, of the general class

$$A \rightarrow \text{product(s)}. \tag{2}$$

Here again the rate can be expressed as proportional to the concentrations of each reactant with a proportionality or rate constant, $k(T)$, that follows the Arrhenius Law,

$$\text{rate} = k(T)[A] = v \exp(-E_{act}/RT)[A].$$

However, this reaction becomes more complicated than bimolecular reactions when one tries to understand how the reactant gets to a high enough energy to exceed the activation barrier. It still needs a collision to activate A above the energy barrier, E_{act}. Seymour's early work asked the question: How exactly does that happen?

   Instead of being a single elementary step as implied by the reaction equation A → products, it requires three steps, hence its added complexity:

$$A + M \rightarrow A^* + M \quad \text{(excitation)}, \tag{3}$$

$$A^* + M \rightarrow A + M \quad \text{(de-excitation)}, \tag{4}$$

$$A^* \rightarrow \text{product(s)} \quad \text{(reaction)}, \qquad [5]$$

where M can be another molecule of A, any bath gas, or a solid surface, and the asterisk signifies a molecule that has been excited to an energy state higher than average. These three elementary steps highlight the areas of his most important research contributions. The first two steps refer to *intermolecular energy transfer*; that is, the transfer of energy between molecules (or between a molecule and a solid) in gas-phase collisions. The last step involves *intramolecular energy relaxation*, wherein the excess energy in molecule A denoted by the asterisk (which starts out highly localized in a part of A) redistributes itself within that molecule, so that it can break or rearrange chemical bonds to give the product(s).

His experiments were marked by brilliant research design, whereby he simplified a problem to its barest essential ingredients. As an example, consider his 1955 study of the kinetics of *cis–trans* isomerization reactions of olefins, one of the most important and commonly studied classes of reactions in organic chemistry. To simplify its study, he chose as the reactant *trans*-dideuteroethylene (1)*, which is absolutely the simplest example of this entire class of reactions:

$$
\begin{array}{ccc}
\text{D} \quad \text{H} & & \text{D} \quad \text{D} \\
\diagdown \ \diagup & & \diagdown \ \diagup \\
\text{C}=\text{C} & \rightarrow & \text{C}=\text{C} \\
\diagup \ \diagdown & & \diagup \ \diagdown \\
\text{H} \quad \text{D} & & \text{H} \quad \text{H}
\end{array}
\qquad [6]
$$

Ethylene is the smallest olefin, and the only difference between reactants and products is the swapping of the location of one of the two D atoms for one of the two H atoms from the *trans* to the *cis* location across the C=C double bond. Because D is an isotope of H, the product is nearly identical to the reactant, with negligible change in the electronic structure upon reaction, and the product has nearly the same energy as the reactant. It thus provided the easiest case to model theoretically using a combination of quantum mechanical and statistical mechanical calculations. He proved this to be a homogeneous, unimolecular reaction and determined a high-pressure limit with a true activation energy (E_{act}) of 65 kcal mol^{-1} and a frequency factor (ν) of 10^{13} s^{-1}. He showed these values to be consistent with calculations using quantum mechanics, transition state theory and statistical mechanics. This set a high standard for depth of understanding in the kinetics of organic chemical reactions.

Similarly, Seymour performed many experiments that were very cleverly designed to critically test proposed theoretical models for intermolecular energy transfer—that is, reactions [3] and [4] above—thus showing which models worked best, as well as the ranges of validity of their intrinsic assumptions (8). As an example of his approach in this area and the intensity of his efforts, let us examine how he addressed the crucial question: How does the efficiency of energy transfer in an A–M collision depend upon the choice of M, the so-called 'bath gas'? To this end, he studied the kinetics of isomerization of methyl isocyanide using 109 different inert bath gases (4). As shown in figure 7, he found that the relative activation–deactivation efficiency per collision, β_c, increased with the boiling point of M up to a saturation value of unity (corresponding to full energy equilibration upon a single collision). From this he concluded that attractive nature of the A–M interaction is important. Indeed, he found that polarizability, dipole moment and H-bonding ability of the bath molecule all increased efficiency. These experiments provided some of the earliest

* Numbers in this form refer to the bibliography at the end of the text.

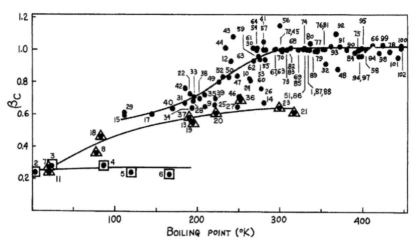

Figure 7. A plot of the relative activation–deactivation efficiency per collision, β_c, of methyl isocyanide (A) with 109 different bath gases (M) against the boiling point of the bath gas. The three solid curves correspond, from the bottom up, to (i) monatomic, (ii) diatomic and linear, and (iii) complex nonlinear molecules. These efficiencies were measured by detailed kinetic studies of the isomerization of methyl isocyanide. (Reproduced from (4), with permission.)

support for the very important realization that such collisions involve the formation of a transient A–M complex, whose lifetime increases with the strength of A–M attraction. He also concluded that efficiency increases in general with the number of transitional modes of the collision complex (which increases with the number of atoms in the A–M complex). Closer inspection of figure 7 shows that he found three subcorrelations, namely for (i) monatomic, (ii) diatomic and linear, and (iii) complex nonlinear molecules, reflecting the importance of dynamical considerations associated with the conservation of angular momentum in the energy transfer process.

Seymour next addressed the last step in this three-step unimolecular reaction mechanism (steps [3] to [5] above): A* → product(s). He asked: Once the reactant A is excited by a collision with M, what specifically happens before it delivers its products, and, if given options as to what those products might be, how do the details of this energy redistribution within the molecule A determine which products are made? This involves the very important general topic known as intramolecular energy relaxation. Through a series of very clever experiments, he proved unequivocally that highly excited reactive polyatomic molecules behave ergodically (that is, statistically) in this respect, at least on timescales longer than *ca.* 1 ps. He also found the first exceptions to this, which require extremely fast reactions that occur with a characteristic time constant near *ca.* 10^{-12} s (that is, very similar to the rate of internal energy randomization) or faster.

This question of ergodicity asks: Is newly deposited energy in molecule A distributed among all the modes of the molecule's internal motion with equal probability by the time its reaction occurs, or is this energy more localized to the part of the molecule where it originated? Ergodic behaviour is the basic assumption of RRKM theory (1951–52) and is also inherent in transition state theory (albeit in a much less general way); his elegant proof of this concept therefore had a huge impact on research in physical chemistry and chemical physics, and one that is still important today.

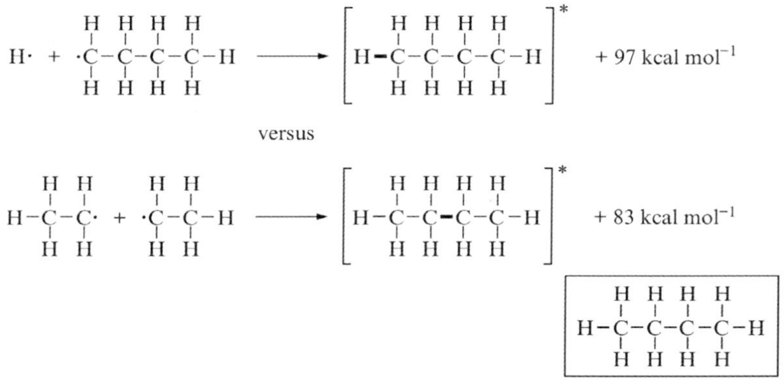

$$H\cdot \; + \; \cdot\overset{\overset{\displaystyle H}{|}}{\underset{\underset{\displaystyle H}{|}}{C}}-\overset{\overset{\displaystyle H}{|}}{\underset{\underset{\displaystyle H}{|}}{C}}-\overset{\overset{\displaystyle H}{|}}{\underset{\underset{\displaystyle H}{|}}{C}}-\overset{\overset{\displaystyle H}{|}}{\underset{\underset{\displaystyle H}{|}}{C}}-H \longrightarrow \left[H-\overset{\overset{\displaystyle H}{|}}{\underset{\underset{\displaystyle H}{|}}{C}}-\overset{\overset{\displaystyle H}{|}}{\underset{\underset{\displaystyle H}{|}}{C}}-\overset{\overset{\displaystyle H}{|}}{\underset{\underset{\displaystyle H}{|}}{C}}-\overset{\overset{\displaystyle H}{|}}{\underset{\underset{\displaystyle H}{|}}{C}}-H \right]^{*} \; +\,97\;\mathrm{kcal\;mol^{-1}}$$

versus

$$H-\overset{\overset{\displaystyle H}{|}}{\underset{\underset{\displaystyle H}{|}}{C}}-\overset{\overset{\displaystyle H}{|}}{\underset{\underset{\displaystyle H}{|}}{C}}\cdot \; + \; \cdot\overset{\overset{\displaystyle H}{|}}{\underset{\underset{\displaystyle H}{|}}{C}}-\overset{\overset{\displaystyle H}{|}}{\underset{\underset{\displaystyle H}{|}}{C}}-H \longrightarrow \left[H-\overset{\overset{\displaystyle H}{|}}{\underset{\underset{\displaystyle H}{|}}{C}}-\overset{\overset{\displaystyle H}{|}}{\underset{\underset{\displaystyle H}{|}}{C}}-\overset{\overset{\displaystyle H}{|}}{\underset{\underset{\displaystyle H}{|}}{C}}-\overset{\overset{\displaystyle H}{|}}{\underset{\underset{\displaystyle H}{|}}{C}}-H \right]^{*} \; +\,83\;\mathrm{kcal\;mol^{-1}}$$

$$\boxed{H-\overset{\overset{\displaystyle H}{|}}{\underset{\underset{\displaystyle H}{|}}{C}}-\overset{\overset{\displaystyle H}{|}}{\underset{\underset{\displaystyle H}{|}}{C}}-\overset{\overset{\displaystyle H}{|}}{\underset{\underset{\displaystyle H}{|}}{C}}-\overset{\overset{\displaystyle H}{|}}{\underset{\underset{\displaystyle H}{|}}{C}}-H}$$

Figure 8. Rabinovitch's 'chemical activation' method: an example of chemical activation, the production of an excited reactant, A*, by a previous chemical reaction that unequivocally deposits energy into some well-defined part of A, shown by the bold bonds in these two reactions that deposit nearly the same energy when producing butane. The selectivities to different products resulting from such differently excited reactants were generally found to be the same, indicating that the energy equilibrated throughout the bonds in the molecule (indicated schematically by the boxed molecule at the end) on a timescale faster than the evolution of products, thus proving the validity of RRKM theory and its ergodicity hypothesis (9).

To prove the assumption of ergodicity, he invented an approach called 'chemical activation', whereby the excited A* molecule is not produced by a collision with M, but instead by an exothermic association reaction that simultaneously forms and excites A. In this way, energy can be deposited very locally into a specific chemical bond. If the excitation level is above the critical threshold for reaction, E_{act}, then a unimolecular reaction to some other product(s) may occur:

$$A^{*} \to P. \tag{7}$$

In competition with this, the excited molecule may deactivate upon collision with a bath gas, M, thus quenching it to levels below E_{act}, resulting in the stabilization of the initial product, A. The first use of the method was reported in 1960 by Harrington, Rabinovitch and Hoare (2), with the main purpose of studying the efficiency of collisional deactivation (that is, step [4] above). Seymour later showed that by increasing the pressure of M and its collisional energy transfer efficiency (as in figure 7), he could tune the speed of such collisional deactivation, and thereby use it as a clock to time the events that happen in step [5]—the evolution of A* to another product or products.

By choosing the chemical activation reaction that produces A*, he was able to controllably place the resulting excitation energy at different bonds in the molecule (9). A schematic example is shown in figure 8.

In another important example, he studied the addition of the CD_2 diradical to the $C=C$ double bond in hexafluorovinylcyclopropane to produce a highly excited bi-cyclopropane that is totally symmetric except for its D isotopic substitutions on one side (5):

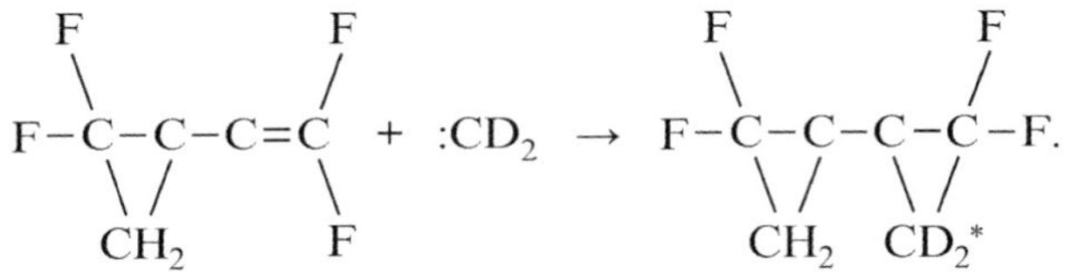

$$F-\underset{\underset{\displaystyle CH_2}{\diagdown\diagup}}{\overset{\overset{\displaystyle F}{\diagdown}}{C}}-C-C=\underset{\underset{\displaystyle F}{\diagdown}}{\overset{\overset{\displaystyle F}{\diagup}}{C}} \; + \; :CD_2 \; \to \; F-\underset{\underset{\displaystyle CH_2}{\diagdown\diagup}}{\overset{\overset{\displaystyle F}{\diagdown}}{C}}-C-\underset{\underset{\displaystyle CD_2}{\diagdown\diagup}}{\overset{\overset{\displaystyle F}{\diagup}}{C}}-C-F. \tag{8}$$

This excited molecule then decomposes quickly to liberate CF_2 either from the same end of the molecule,

$$
\begin{array}{c}
\text{F} \qquad\quad \text{F} \\
\big\backslash \qquad\ / \\
\text{F--C--C--C--C--F} \\
\ \big\backslash\ /\ \ \big\backslash\ / \\
\text{CH}_2 \quad \text{CD}_2{}^*
\end{array}
\ \rightarrow\
\begin{array}{c}
\text{F} \qquad\quad \text{D} \\
\big\backslash \qquad\ / \\
\text{F--C--C--C=C} \\
\ \big\backslash\ /\quad\ \big\backslash \\
\text{CH}_2 \qquad \text{D}
\end{array}
\ +\ :\!CF_2, \qquad [9]
$$

or from the other side,

$$
\begin{array}{c}
\text{F} \qquad\quad \text{F} \\
\big\backslash \qquad\ / \\
\text{F--C--C--C--C--F} \\
\ \big\backslash\ /\ \ \big\backslash\ / \\
\text{CH}_2 \quad \text{CD}_2{}^*
\end{array}
\ \rightarrow\
\begin{array}{c}
\text{F} \qquad\quad \text{H} \\
\big\backslash \qquad\ / \\
\text{F--C--C--C=C} \\
\ \big\backslash\ /\quad\ \big\backslash \\
\text{CD}_2 \qquad \text{H}
\end{array}
\ +\ :\!CF_2. \qquad [10]
$$

He differentiated these products by measuring the location of its D, whether on the double bond or in the cyclopropane part. If the energy deposited by the CD_2 addition remained localized to that end of the molecule, only direct reaction to the former product, reaction [9], would be expected. In contrast, nearly equal amounts of both products [9] and [10] were actually observed, indicating that the extra vibrational energy is statistically redistributed throughout the whole molecule first, before this decomposition reaction occurs. By increasing the pressure to generate more frequent collisions with bath gas, quenching the initially excited molecule and preventing its reaction, he set a clock on this reaction's time. Because he knew the rate of quenching by a bath gas from his intensive studies of intermolecular energy transfer (see above), he was able to prove that it occurs in less than 10^{-10} s.

In a later study, he increased the bath-gas pressure further and found that the fraction of product from reaction [9] increased at very high pressures until more than 25% of the total product corresponded to reactants whose internal excitation remained near its original location (6). He explained this by recognizing that the initial non-randomly excited reactant was quenched by collisions, but this molecule also had a second chance for quenching *after* internal energy randomization. This additional quenching reaction is not available on the direct route to non-random product via reaction [9], so its relative yield increases with bath gas pressure. If the rate constants for internal energy randomization and non-random product formation are known, this variation is predictable from modelling of this multi-step kinetic competition. By finding values that fitted the data, he determined the rate constants for internal energy randomization and non-random product formation to be *ca.* 1.1×10^{12} s^{-1} and *ca.* 3.5×10^{11} s^{-1}, respectively (6).

To our knowledge, this was the first study to prove that some chemical reactions indeed occur before internal energy randomization, and the first study to measure the rate constants for such a kinetic competition and thereby the quantitative extent to which it competes with internal energy randomization. This classic experiment is discussed in chemical reaction dynamics courses today as a first step towards state-selected chemistry (for example Chemistry 762 when taught by Professor F. Fleming Crim at the University of Wisconsin – Madison).

Later, in similar studies using the chemical activation technique on various fluorocarbons and hydrocarbons that extended to higher pressures (shorter times), he showed that the statistical redistribution of vibrational energy throughout the whole molecule generally occurs within *ca.* 10^{-12} s (9, 11).

In discussing these results, he introduced the idea of the 'characteristic time constant for local vibrational energy to distribute throughout the molecule', a concept that guides much of our thinking about chemical dynamics today. Thus, he deduced internal energy relaxation times with a model whereby he assumed that a vibrational subset (moiety) of the radical is initially excited, and that its excess energy decays exponentially with time in a manner crudely characterized by a single time-independent average relaxation constant τ (11, 12). He ultimately concluded that 'relaxation times (τ) of magnitude less than 10^{-12} s signify the applicability of statistical methods, such as RRKM theory, for the calculation of unimolecular rate constants of magnitude below 10^{12} s^{-1}.'

Some raised the question of whether the rate of this intramolecular energy relaxation process might be much slower if probed at much lower excitation levels where intermode coupling mechanisms may be weakened. To test this, he measured the rates of intramolecular vibrational energy relaxation in systems that reacted at much lower levels of excitation (43 kcal mol^{-1}) than previously studied (110 kcal mol^{-1}), using the technique of state selection by chemical activation, and found similarly fast times (11). Others raised the possibility that a heavy atom, through inertia, might block internal energy transfer in excited species. He investigated this by a chemical activation study of 4-(trimethyl lead)-2-butyl and 5-(trimethyl tin)-2-pentyl radicals, prepared and excited by the reaction of H atoms with the corresponding 1-olefins (13). Again, energy randomization among the vibrational modes was found to occur on a subpicosecond timescale (less than 10^{-12} s) in all the radicals studied.

Seymour's studies validated RRKM theory and showed when it might break down. This understanding is now central to all of physical chemistry and chemical physics! He even coined the name 'RRKM theory'. In his own papers, he cited as the advent of this theory two papers from Rudolph A. Marcus (Marcus & Rice 1951; Marcus 1952). The 1992 Nobel Prize in Chemistry was awarded to Marcus 'for his contributions to the theory of electron transfer reactions in chemical systems', for which RRKM theory provided an important conceptual foundation.

Seymour also developed several widely used mathematical shortcuts for applying RRKM theory to make important predictions about reaction kinetics, chemical dynamics and other aspects of physical chemistry. These shortcuts made RRKM calculations much easier to conduct, and greatly increased both the applications and the impact of RRKM theory. RRKM has become one of the most important theories of physical chemistry, guiding much of our fundamental understanding of chemical dynamics and reaction kinetics even today. Many papers have used his 'Whitten–Rabinovitch (WR) approximation' (3) when doing the vibrational energy-level sums needed for RRKM calculations. Even more have used his approximation for the evaluation of internal energy-level sums and densities that include anharmonic oscillators and hindered rotors (7). Indeed, these two theoretical works are his most highly cited papers!

Seymour also studied the transfer of energy when gas molecules collide with solid surfaces. He pioneered the 'variable encounter method' involving the study of the relaxation of an initial vibrationally cold ensemble of molecules into a vibrationally hot distribution by a known and variable number of successive collisions with a hot wall (10). He used reactions such as the ring opening isomerization of 1,1-cyclopropane-d$_2$ to propene, measuring the reaction probability per reactant-molecule collision with walls of increasing temperature for reactors of different lengths, as shown in figure 9.

From such experiments, he determined that a steady-state population of vibrational energy levels at the surface temperature is reached in a small number of collisions (10–20) even at high surface temperatures, and that this decreases towards a single collision at low

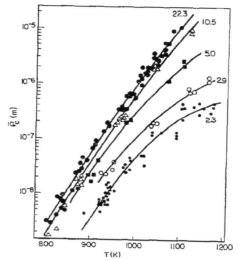

Figure 9. An example of the variable encounter method, showing a plot of the reaction probability per collision with walls for reactors of different lengths against temperature for the ring-opening isomerization of 1,1-cyclopropane-d₂ to propene. The curves from top to bottom correspond to tube lengths in which the average number of collisions with fused quartz surfaces increases from 2.3 to 22.3. (Reproduced from (10), with permission.)

temperature. This increase in the efficiency of energy transfer at lower surface temperature was early evidence that molecules at low temperature experience temporary trapping on the surface followed by desorption, and that they establish a Boltzmann population of energy levels corresponding to the surface temperature in their transient lifetime on the surface, now commonly referred to as 'trapping–desorption' encounters (with unit sticking probability). He showed, for example, that such vibrational accommodation is complete in one collision for cyclobutene at temperatures below 425 K on Pyrex and seasoned silica surfaces, and at temperatures below 550 K on seasoned gold surfaces (14).

In summary, the research of Seymour Rabinovitch and his group at the University of Washington has had a huge positive impact on the course of physical chemistry research worldwide. It led us into the modern era of chemical dynamics and provided many of its most basic concepts. Given the importance of chemical dynamics and kinetics in energy and environmental technologies, and indeed in all aspects of chemical industry, his research has been of tremendous benefit to mankind. His mentoring of graduate students, postdoctoral associates and younger faculty also made an equally important contribution to the greater scientific community. He did all this while always maintaining a wonderful gentlemanly nature. His kindly nature even came through in his papers, in which he often acknowledged a referee for helpful suggestions.

POST-RETIREMENT YEARS: SILVERSMITH, WRITER OF CHILDREN'S BOOKS, AND PHILANTHROPIST

While on sabbatical in England with Marilyn and the children in 1971, Seymour became interested in learning about silversmithing, silver patinas and the science of Sheffield silver.

His interest began during a search for a silver anniversary present for his brother: he had bought a piece of what he believed to be old Sheffield, only to discover later that it was instead electroplated. He decided to continue the search for a genuine piece and gradually became intrigued with the culture of English antiques shops and silver merchants, and with the history of English silver more generally. He started collecting antique fish and cake slices, enchanted with the varied adornments of piercing, chasing and engraving and the different shapes. What had begun as a modest collection of slices from the eighteenth and nineteenth centuries broadened after Marilyn's death, and he became an ardent collector, acquiring pieces in the USA, Britain and Europe. The slices satisfied his aesthetic sense and had the added advantage of being small, easy to store and not as costly or as difficult to transport as hollowware. At the same time, he felt that his new hobby required something more, and he decided that, besides collecting the pieces, he would also study the evolution of their patterns and forms. His earliest slice was made in 1723, and he carried his investigations through to the end of the nineteenth century, eventually conducting scholarship on silver of the twentieth century, an area with relatively little documentation. Seymour authored three books on silver servers: *Antique silver servers for the dining table* (16), *Contemporary silver* (19), co-authored with Helen Clifford, and *Contemporary silver, part II: recent commissions* (20). He wrote scholarly pieces on the chemistry of silver patinas, including 'A new method for gilding silver: use of organic gold sols', published in *Metalsmith* (17), 'The look of antique silver', in *Silver Magazine* (18), and 'The patina of antique silver: a scientific appraisal', in *Silver Society Journal* (15).

Seymour later began taking lessons in silver working, to learn at first hand how pieces were made; he went on to design and create a broad-bladed server himself. After getting to know several silversmiths, he decided to make a study of contemporary work, and in the late 1980s began commissioning the creation of contemporary servers. In so doing, he had two objectives in mind: first, to provide support, in a modest way, for independent silversmiths and the craft; and second, to make a comparative study of contemporary styles in metalsmithing relating to one particular type of object: the broad-bladed server. In 1995 an exhibition titled 'Slices of silver' held at Goldsmiths' Hall in London introduced to the public a mesmerizing collection of 42 sterling silver fish servers and cake slices created by contemporary British and American silversmiths. The collection consisted entirely of pieces commissioned by Seymour over a 20-year period and showcased the skills and artistic diversity of these contemporary silversmiths. He developed a close rapport with each artist, always encouraging freedom of creative expression. Seymour continued to sponsor new pieces, resulting in the growth of his collection to more than 100 items.

Over the years, Seymour's collection has been exhibited at the Winnipeg Art Gallery, the National Ornamental Metal Museum in Memphis, the Seattle Art Museum, the Schneider Art Museum in Ashland, Oregon, the Aberdeen Art Gallery in Scotland, the Nottingham Castle Museum and Art Gallery, and Goldsmiths' Hall. Seymour's collection and his passion for craftsmanship became the subject of magazine articles, including 'Fish get a slice of the action', published in *Country Life*, 'Slices of silver', in *Winnipeg Art Gallery Tableau*, May/June 2003, and 'On collecting', in *Silver Magazine*. He was an invited speaker at New York University's 'Sterling Modernities' conference in 2002, giving a presentation on broad-bladed slices. In 2005, through the American Friends of the Victoria and Albert Museum, Seymour donated the entire collection to this London landmark, where it resides today.

Seymour was a member of the Silver Society (London) and the American Academy of Arts and Sciences. He was honoured with the National Metalsmiths Hall of Fame award, and was

Figure 10. Seymour Rabinovitch in 2013 with all of his children celebrating the wedding of his granddaughter. From the left: son Frank B. Rabinovitch, daughter Dr Judith N. Rabinovitch (Karashima Professor of Japanese Language and Culture at the University of Montana), Seymour himself, bride Rachele Treger (daughter of Ruth), groom Ari Altman, daughter Dr Ruth Rabinovitch (infectious disease specialist) and son Dr Peter S. Rabinovitch (Professor of Pathology, University of Washington). (Online version in colour.)

named by *Silver Magazine* as a 'world personality in silver'. In 2000 he was inducted into the Worshipful Company of Goldsmiths, London, as an Honorary Liveryman—a rare honour for someone not born in the UK.

Seymour's passion for collecting led to the exploration of many small towns in Britain and America with his wife Flora, the search for new treasures becoming part of the daily adventure of travel. His passion for collecting influenced his children, all of whom appreciate art and antiques. He established a memorial endowment at the University of Washington School of Arts' Metal Design Program in Marilyn's memory, to recognize and encourage the work of young metalsmiths.

Growing up with four older sisters and two brothers, Seymour had little opportunity to cook as a boy. However, while raising his children he enjoyed dabbling in the kitchen. His recipe 'Boiled can: a delectable caramel sauce' was included in *But the crackling is superb, an anthology on food and drink by Fellows and Foreign Members of the Royal Society* (Kurti & Kurti 1997).

In recent years, Seymour authored a children's storybook entitled *Higgledy piggledy: a tale of four little pigs* (21), based on an original tale he used to tell his children when they were young. In the introduction, 'What's in a name?', and in his story, he illustrated the themes of facing challenges in life and treating others kindly, and the importance of showing resourcefulness in difficult situations.

Seymour led an extraordinarily rich and productive life, one of abiding devotion to his family and his work. He died at his home in Seattle on 2 August 2014 at the age of 95 years, surrounded by his family. His memory is a continuing inspiration to friends and family, and his generosity, warmth, philanthropy and charm are cherished. He is survived by his wife Flora, children Peter (wife Jacqueline), Ruth (husband Thomas), Judith (husband Tim), Frank (wife Karen), stepchildren Howard (wife Ramona) and Ellen Reitman, twelve grandchildren and three great-grandchildren (figure 10).

ACKNOWLEDGEMENTS

C.T.C. gratefully acknowledges Professor Fleming Crim for helping him to understand the scientific papers and contributions of B. S. Rabinovitch. The authors thank Professor Paul Hopkins and Stephanie Hemmingson for proof reading the manuscript, and a reviewer for helpful comments.

The frontispiece photograph was taken in about 2000 (photographer unknown).

REFERENCE TO OTHER AUTHORS

Kurti, N. & Kurti, G. (eds) 1997 *But the crackling is superb, an anthology on food and drink by Fellows and Foreign Members of the Royal Society*. Bristol: Adam Hilger.
Marcus, R. A. 1952 Unimolecular dissociations and free radical recombination reactions. *J. Chem. Phys.* **20**, 359–364.
Marcus, R. A. & Rice, O. K. 1951 The kinetics of the recombination of methyl radicals and iodine atoms. *J. Phys. Colloid Chem.* **55**, 894–908.

BIBLIOGRAPHY

The following publications are those referred to directly in the text. A full bibliography and curriculum vitae are available as electronic supplementary material at http://dx.doi.org/10.1098/rsbm.2015.0021 or via http://rsbm.royalsocietypublishing.org.

(1) 1955 (With J. E. Douglas & F. S. Looney) Kinetics of the thermal *cis–trans* isomerization of dideuteroethylene. *J. Chem. Phys.* **23**, 315–323.

(2) 1960 (With R. E. Harrington & M. R. Hoare) Collisional deactivation of vibrationally excited *sec*-butyl-d_1 radicals produced by chemical activation. *J. Chem. Phys.* **33**, 744–747.

(3) 1963 (With G. Z. Whitten) Accurate and facile approximation for vibrational energy-level sums. *J. Chem. Phys.* **38**, 2466–2473.

(4) 1970 (With S. C. Chan, J. T. Bryant, L. D. Spicer, T. Fujimoto, Y. N. Lin & S. P. Pavlou) Energy transfer in thermal methyl isocyanide isomerisation—a comprehensive investigation. *J. Phys. Chem.* **74**, 3160–3176.

(5)   (With J. D. Rynbrandt) Intramolecular energy relaxation. Novel and direct test of the RRK-RRKM postulate. *J. Phys. Chem.* **74**, 4175–4176.

(6) 1971 (With J. D. Rynbrandt) Intramolecular energy relaxation. Nonrandom decomposition of hexafluorobicyclopropyl. *J. Phys. Chem.* **75**, 2164–2171.

(7) 1973 (With S. E. Stein) Accurate evaluation of internal energy-level sums and densities including anharmonic oscillators and hindered rotors. *J. Chem. Phys.* **58**, 2438–2445.

(8) 1977 (With D. C. Tardy) Intermolecular vibrational energy transfer in thermal unimolecular systems. *Chem. Rev.* **77**, 369–408.

(9) 1979 (With I. Oref) Do highly excited reactive polyatomic molecules behave ergodically? *Accts Chem. Res.* **12**, 166–175.

(10) 1980 (With D. F. Kelley & L. Zalotai) Collisional relaxation of transient vibrational energy distributions in a thermal unimolecular system. The variable encounter method. *Chem. Phys.* **46**, 379–391.

(11) 1982 (With A. B. Trenwith) Rate of intramolecular relaxation of vibrational energy. Initial state selection in chemically activated 3-hexyl radicals. *J. Phys. Chem.* **86**, 3447–3453.

(12)   (With A. B. Trenwith & F. C. Wolters) Intramolecular vibrational relaxation in hexyl-3 radicals. *J. Chem. Phys.* **76**, 1586–1587.

(13) 1983 (With S. P. Wrigley) On heavy-atom blocking of intramolecular vibrational energy transfer in the 4-(trimethyl tin)butyl-2 radical. *Chem. Phys. Lett.* **98**, 386–392.

(14) 1984 (With W. Yuan) Study of vibrational energy transfer at a surface by a time-of-flight method. *J. Chem. Phys.* **80**, 1687–1690.

(15) 1990 The patina of antique silver: a scientific appraisal. *Silver Soc. J.* (winter), 13.

(16) 1991 *Antique silver servers for the dining table. Style, function, foods and social history.* Northampton, MA: Joslin Hall.

(17) 1994 A new method for gilding silver: use of organic gold sols. *Metalsmith* **14** (4), 40–43.

(18)   The look of antique silver. *Silver Mag.* (July–August).

(19) 2000 (With H. Clifford) *Contemporary silver: commissioning, designing, collecting.* London: Merrell.

(20) 2005 *Contemporary silver. Part II: recent commissions.* Seattle, WA: RAB Associates.

(21) 2013 (With R. S. Treger, M. G. Stein & R. A. Rabinovitch) *Higgledy Piggledy: a tale of four little pigs.* Medford, OR: Roxy Ann Press.

RAYMOND EDWARD SMALLMAN CBE FREng

4 August 1929 — 25 February 2015

R. Smallman

RAYMOND EDWARD SMALLMAN CBE FRENG

4 August 1929 — 25 February 2015

Elected FRS 1986

BY P. J. GOODHEW* FRENG

School of Engineering, University of Liverpool, Liverpool L69 3GH, UK

Raymond Edward Smallman was one of Britain's leading physical metallurgists. His books influenced many generations of undergraduates, and his research group spawned more than a dozen professors of metallurgy and materials science, a university vice-chancellor and at least two directors of major metal companies. Smallman's range was immense and during an active research and teaching life of more than 60 years he made important contributions, often using electron microscopy, to our understanding of crystal defects and deformation behaviour in metals, alloys, intermetallic compounds and ceramics. His professional career was based at the University of Birmingham for more than 50 years and he contributed hugely to the success of one of the country's leading schools of metallurgy and materials.

FAMILY BACKGROUND AND EARLY YEARS

Raymond Edward Smallman† was born in a public house in Wolverhampton in the West Midlands on 4 August 1929. He attended Brownhills infant school for a year before the family moved to take over a fish and chip shop in Bridgtown near Cannock—now dominated by the M6 toll motorway. Here Ray stayed until he went to university. He passed the '11-plus' examination at the precocious age of nine and went to Rugeley Grammar School, where he started on 4 September 1939, the day after war broke out. The end of the war and the return of his father enabled him to enter the sixth form and take his Higher School Certificate, which opened up the possibility of going to university.

Ray's father, David, and his mother, Edith (*née* French), were both born in Wolverhampton and for most of his schooldays they ran the shop and kept pigs and chickens. Ray was the third of their five children and during the whole of his time at school had to help with the chores associated with the family shop. These included delivering orders and peeling potatoes, both

---

* goodhew@liverpool.ac.uk

† He was actually christened Edward Raymond Smallman but never used this sequence of names.

http://dx.doi.org/10.1098/rsbm.2015.0030

of which had to take precedence over school homework. When he entered secondary school, the potatoes for the day had to be peeled before Ray caught the 8.30 a.m. train to Rugeley. Despite this load, Ray did well in his Higher School Certificate in mathematics, higher mathematics, physics and chemistry and was awarded a County Scholarship.

EDUCATION AND PhD STUDIES, 1947–53

Although he initially preferred physics, Ray was accepted into the University of Birmingham in 1947 to study for a BSc in metallurgy. In this period after the war, returning ex-servicemen were given priority for university entrance and there were fewer than 10% 'grammar-school boys' on most courses. Ray had been told that the metallurgy course led to a physics-based specialism in theoretical and structural metallurgy designed by Alan (later Sir Alan) Cottrell (FRS 1955). Fifty-five years later, Ray would be the co-author of the Royal Society's biographical memoir of Sir Alan (48)*.

The Department of Metallurgy was led by Professor Daniel Hanson and during his undergraduate course Ray was fortunate to be taught by a range of outstanding staff, many of whom were already Fellows of the Royal Society. He remembered Professors P. B. Moon and Mark (later Sir Marcus) Oliphant in Physics, George Watson (a Fellow who had then just received the Sylvester Medal) in Mathematics, Walter Haworth (Nobel laureate in 1937) in Chemistry, and Cottrell, G. V. Raynor, B. A. Bilby and F. R. N. Nabarro (all Fellows) in Metallurgy and Physics. Ray did indeed take, in his final year, the theoretical and structural metallurgy option, whereas most students took the industrial metallurgy route. His chosen option involved two research projects, supervised by Bruce Bilby (on carbon-induced damping in iron) and W. H. Hall (using X-rays to examine the defect structure of aluminium). In 1950 he graduated with first-class honours and was awarded a university research scholarship to study for a PhD.

Ray had by now developed an interest in X-ray diffraction and chose to embark on his PhD studies under the supervision of Dr Hall. However, Hall left after a few months and Ray carried on with a project entitled 'The structure of cold worked metals' under the guidance of Alan Cottrell but supervised on a day-to-day basis by Kingsley (Dr G. K.) Williamson. He thus found himself a member of two research teams, doubling the benefit that a research student gets from seminars, discussions and visitors.

Dislocations in metals were first made directly visible by transmission electron microscopy in the mid 1950s. In 1950, when Ray started his PhD work, the usual way to determine dislocation densities was with X-ray spectrometry. In his PhD work, Ray improved a Geiger-counter X-ray spectrometer to measure diffraction line shapes and intensities from deformed metals—effectively turning it into an X-ray diffractometer. He was thus able to determine the interstitial position of carbon in α-iron, the effect of cold work on dislocation locking and—retrospectively most satisfying to him—to determine dislocation densities in some cold-worked and annealed metals just before they were observed by electron microscopy in 1956.

Ray was awarded his PhD in 1953, and his first two papers (1, 2) were published in the first volume of the new journal *Acta Metallurgica*.

---

* Numbers in this form refer to the bibliography at the end of the text.

HARWELL, 1953–58

In 1953, with his PhD completed, Ray was offered a post as Scientific Officer in the Metallurgy Division at the Atomic Energy Research Establishment, Harwell. He worked for a short time under Bill Mott using X-ray diffraction to study the structure of liquid metals, specifically mercury and mercury–thallium alloys, eventually using radial distribution functions to show the strong association of atoms in the liquid state that was a precursor to compound formation in the solid.

The Head of Division, Monty (later Sir Monty) Finniston (FRS 1969), took an interest in Ray and suggested that he look at textures that had become of interest in nuclear technology in both canning materials and fuel. He built a texture goniometer and produced results on the influence of alloying on textures in face-centred cubic (fcc) metals, explaining the results in terms of stacking fault energy—which was to become a theme in his work for a couple of decades. Finniston was impressed enough to put Ray up for promotion to Senior Scientific Officer at the early age of 25 years.

Alan Cottrell left Birmingham at this time to lead the Irradiation Studies Group at Harwell, and Ray joined his group as a section leader looking into the structure of irradiation damage. It proved difficult to discover much with conventional X-ray diffraction techniques so Ray decided to apply small-angle X-ray scattering to irradiated samples. Together with Ken Westmacott (then one of Harwell's carpentry technicians!) he built a small-angle spectrometer and made the crucial decision to study quenched aluminium and copper because he expected the defect structures to be simpler, with interstitial concentrations being very low and thus only vacancies involved. They soon found evidence that small defects (later clarified as voids and dislocation loops) were present. Cottrell suggested that their estimated size of 100–1000 Å (10–100 nm) should make them visible in a transmission electron microscope (TEM). P. B. (now Sir Peter) Hirsch (FRS 1963), Bob Horne and Mike Whelan (FRS 1976) had just published the first images of dislocations in aluminium (Hirsch *et al.* 1956), so Ray used one of the early EM6 microscopes at AEI's nearby laboratories and was able to produce (rather low-quality) images of prismatic dislocation loops. Collaboration with the Cambridge group soon produced much better images of Frank loops containing stacking faults.

Despite this early success of the TEM, senior staff at Harwell were not persuaded to invest in a high-quality instrument at that time, and some momentum was lost. Ray had always been attracted to teaching and in 1958 accepted a lectureship in the Department of Physical Metallurgy at Birmingham (now the School of Metallurgy and Materials), where he was to spend the rest of his career.

UNIVERSITY OF BIRMINGHAM, 1958–93

Ray started as a lecturer in 1958, was promoted to senior lecturer in 1963, and thence to a personal chair in 1964 at the age of 34 years, becoming the youngest professor in the university. In 1969 he was appointed Feeney Professor of Metallurgy and Materials Science and Head of the Department of Physical Metallurgy and Science of Materials. In the 1980s he was successively Deputy Dean and Dean of the Faculty of Science and Engineering and then Dean of the newly created Faculty of Engineering, while remaining Head of Department until 1988. From 1987 to 1992 he was Vice-Principal of the university. After his retirement in 1993 Ray became an emeritus professor and was an active member of the school until his death.

In addition to his considerable research achievements, detailed below, Ray made a substantial impact on his school, faculty and university. He was successful in integrating the separate (and sometimes warring) departments of Industrial Metallurgy and Physical Metallurgy into a single Department of Metallurgy and Materials and stimulating his colleagues to high-quality research, which was in due course recognized by a 5* rating in the 1992 Research Assessment Exercise (RAE), the best score in Birmingham's Faculties of Science, Engineering and Medicine. In 1985 he argued successfully for the formation of a Faculty of Engineering, seeking to establish parity of esteem with Science. He became its first Dean and restructured it to reduce the number of small departments. At about this time (1986) he was elected FRS.

In the same year Michael Thompson (a former colleague at Harwell in the 1950s) was appointed Vice-Chancellor and he soon asked Ray to become his Vice-Principal. The major achievement of these years was the development of a new financial model for the university, which involved a very successful new relationship between administrative departments and academic budget centres.

Ray's increasingly successful scientific career was conducted, between 1963 and 1975, against the background of a bizarre professional harassment case. The details are not relevant to this account, but it should be recorded that for a dozen years Ray's research and teaching were conducted in an environment in which he, his colleagues and his superiors were bombarded with abusive correspondence and outrageous claims of malpractice, all of which were eventually found to be unsubstantiated. I was a student under Ray's supervision during this period and such was Ray's dignity and calm under this duress that his students were unaware of the case. Despite the time it must have consumed, the affair was not allowed to interfere with research, supervision or teaching, although it must have caused considerable distress to Ray himself.

RESEARCH AND ELECTRON MICROSCOPY

Ray Smallman's research career lasted for 65 years, during which time the technology available to pursue an understanding of the physical world changed dramatically. Transmission electron microscopy, with the added facility of obtaining diffraction information from small volumes, was developed over the same period. In 1959 Ray won a grant from the Department of Scientific and Industrial Research (DSIR) that enabled Birmingham to buy its first metallurgical TEM—an AEI EM6G—for £11 000. Computing arrived in the mid 1960s, and its usefulness developed rapidly. Ray was always keen to apply each newly developed technique but had little interest in instrument development or computing *per se*. The principal theme running through his work is the understanding of microstructures associated with deformation and damage in metals and ceramics. He worked on a very wide range of metals, alloys and ceramics, with a wide range of structures—among them fcc, body-centred cubic, hexagonal close-packed (hcp) and ordered intermetallic compounds.

A second theme is texture, which started with thorium in 1954 (3), emerged in a review paper with I. L. Dillamore in 1974 (35), flourished again in the 1980s when 1 MeV microscopy became available, and finally in the 1990s led to a major series of papers with C. S. Lee and B. J. Duggan (for example (41)).

Throughout his career Ray showed a supreme talent for enthusing and working with a series of brilliant practitioners—principally but not solely microscopists—on significant problems in physical metallurgy. He was not himself a brilliant technical microscopist but could always see the potential of a new technique and had the persuasive arts to find the money to fund the equipment, the researchers and the travel to disseminate the results. In the (long) days before the Internet his students would haunt the journals section of the library waiting for the latest issues to check that they had not been scooped by research teams in Japan or the USA, while Ray would be out visiting the rival groups. Early research students included Ken Ashbee, Trevor Lindley, John Terry and Jeff Edington; they were followed by about 100 more.

Eminent among Ray's long-term collaborators were M. H. Loretto, I. P. Jones, K. H. Westmacott and B. J. Duggan. He published more than 60 papers with Loretto and more than 50 with Jones, both of whom remained at Birmingham with Ray for more than 30 years. Other significant collaborators who joined Ray on the academic staff were P. S. Dobson, I. R. Harris and I. L. Dillamore, the last of whom left in 1969 to follow a career in industry.

The period from 1953 to 1968 was incredibly productive for Ray, with several of his papers from this time becoming citation classics. It is noteworthy that his four most cited papers were on four quite different topics: dislocation densities measured using X-rays in cold-worked and annealed metals with Kingsley Williamson in 1956 (4), stacking faults in fcc metals and alloys with Ken Westmacott in 1957 (5), dislocation loops in quenched aluminium with Westmacott and Hirsch and J. Silcox at Cambridge in 1958 (8), and the plasticity of NiAl with Tony Ball in 1966 (22). X-ray techniques took a back seat after the 1950s, but the other three classic papers initiated major lines of work that Ray pursued for the next three decades.

Early dislocation theory implied that dislocation densities in metals should increase during cold work. Ray's work with Kingsley Williamson from 1953 to 1956 demonstrated, using Debye–Scherrer X-ray analysis, that this was indeed the case (4). They measured the line broadening in several annealed and cold-worked metals and alloys and rather ingeniously deduced the dislocation density by comparing measurements of 'particle size' and 'strain' in aluminium, tungsten, molybdenum and α-brass which had been filed or annealed. Using this somewhat crude methodology they were able to determine dislocation densities across the range 10^7–10^{11} cm^{-2}. This was a great achievement at the time.

A second major strand of work arose from the seminal 1958 paper (8) with Hirsch's group on dislocation loops in quenched aluminium. Clustered vacancy defects are of course not only important in themselves but have a big role in irradiation damage in both fission and fusion reactor technology. The original work on aluminium was essentially a proof of principle and was exploited to study both point-defect aggregation and dislocation source behaviour in a series of papers with Westmacott (9, 10), Edington (14), Dobson (19), Goodhew (23) and Kritzinger (24) on aluminium, and with Eikum (16), Hales (25), Johnston (26), Fraser (31) and Hollox (20) on a range of other metals and ceramics. Later studies revealed that there can be many configurations of vacancy clusters and, as well as faulted (Frank) loops and prismatic loops, both voids and tetrahedral arrangements of stacking faults ('stacking fault tetrahedra') can form under specific vacancy supersaturation conditions.

The observation that condensed vacancy loops in many materials are initially sessile and faulted (containing a stacking fault) before 'unzipping' to become mobile prismatic loops led to some ingenious experiments to determine the stacking fault energy in materials in which its value is high and therefore measurement by determining the separation of partial dislocations is impracticable. This work formed a significant part of a third strand of Smallman's work centred on stacking faults and their role in controlling deformation. As early as 1957 Ray had published observations of stacking faults with Ken Westmacott (5), and this led to a series of papers on stacking faults in titanium dioxide with Ashbee and Williamson (12) and in a wide range of metals with Dillamore (15), I. R. (Rex) Harris (13) and Beeston (18). Ray was quick to connect the behaviour of crystal defects (in this instance stacking faults) to macroscopic phenomena (such as rolling texture) that have a significant effect on mechanical properties.

The Birmingham group was one of the first to exploit the possibility of heating metallic specimens in the TEM. Hot-stage annealing, with temperatures up to 200 °C, proved useful in studying dislocation loop behaviour in low-melting-point metals such as aluminium, and oxidation-driven behaviour in other metals such as zinc and magnesium. In combination with a simple movie camera this became quantitative microscopy, not just interesting snapshot observations. Ray's suggestion, implemented initially by Dobson and Goodhew (23), was to measure stacking fault energy by the rate of shrinkage of faulted dislocation loops.

The third strand of work, which sprang from early work on ordered NiAl with Tony Ball (21), involved the plasticity of NiAl, then a rather new material. They identified the operative slip systems as well as the nature of the vacancy defects. Ray's increasing interest in the often complex relationships between defect structure and mechanical behaviour led to work on such diverse problems as creep in dispersion-strengthened Ni–Co (with Hancock and Dillamore (32)), deviation from stoichiometry in titanium oxides (with Vere (28)), yielding in ordered alloys (with Besag (29)), cracking in irons and steels (with Webster and Dillamore (30)), further studies of the plastic deformation of NiAl (with Fraser and Loretto (33)), yielding in Cu_3Au (with Morris and Besag (34)), ordering in Ni_3Fe (with Morris, Brown and Piller (37)), martensite formation in steels (with Brooks and Loretto (38)) and the strength and hardness of Ti alloys (with Woodfield, Postans and Loretto (40)). This is not by any means a complete list but it gives a flavour of the huge range of metallurgical topics in which Ray became involved and to which he contributed key data and understanding.

One of Ray's early competitive successes was the award to Birmingham of one of the UK's half-dozen high-voltage electron microscopes (HVEMs). These operated with electron energies up to 1 MeV and enabled thicker specimens to be penetrated. Additionally (and inevitably) the displacement of atoms by these high-energy electrons became frequent enough to be a problem (by modifying the structure of the specimen before it could be recorded) or an opportunity (by allowing radiation damage to be studied directly). The Birmingham microscope was installed in 1972 and enabled Ray to return to the issue of radiation damage, among other things. He had been active in the topic in the 1950s at Harwell (with Willis (6), Churchman, Makin and Harries (7) and Westmacott (9)) but the HVEM allowed him to exploit electron damage in a series of papers with Loretto in the 1970s and 1980s, largely in hcp metals such as zinc, titanium and zirconium (39). The HVEM operated until 1989, when its building was used to house a plasma melter that formed part of the Interdisciplinary Research Centre (IRC) in Materials for High Performance Applications.

Ray's contribution across a vast range of materials was partly made possible by the strength and range of the Department of Metallurgy and Materials, which he himself had built. He always had plenty of colleagues working on interesting problems right across the field. In the 1980s and 1990s, when Ray was in his fifties and sixties, he was still publishing leading papers on intermetallic compounds, aluminium and copper alloys, cast iron, and high-temperature superconductors. To give a flavour of this range, in one 12-month period in 1997–98 Ray published papers on superdislocation dissociation in twist boundaries (with Rong and Jones (43)), on the effect of silicon content on the transformation kinetics of austempered ductile iron (ADI; with Mallia and Grech (44)) and on the orientation dependence of creep in Ni_3Al (with Zhu, Fort and Jones (45)).

To summarize Ray's research impact is almost impossible. He contributed to work on the microstructure of many metals, alloys, compounds and ceramics; he always tried to relate microstructure to its effect on properties and behaviour; he collaborated with, and inspired, hundreds of co-workers and he continued to do this long after conventional retirement.

BOOKS

For undergraduate students of metallurgy in the 1950s and early 1960s, the most influential book on physical metallurgy was Alan Cottrell's *Theoretical structural metallurgy*, first published in 1948, and revised in 1955, just after Cottrell left Birmingham for Harwell (Cottrell 1948). This was too late for Ray to benefit from it as a student but he soon followed Cottrell's example in writing an undergraduate text covering all of physical metallurgy as it was then understood. The first edition of *Modern physical metallurgy* appeared in 1962 (11), when Ray was still a lecturer of only four years' standing. It was a *tour de force* by such a young man and has been a standard text around the world for 50 years. *Modern physical metallurgy* went through four editions by 1985; subsequently—with collaborators R. J. Bishop and A. H. W. Ngan—four further editions and variants have appeared (42, 46).

Ray also found time to co-author *Modern metallography* with K. H. G. Ashbee—his first PhD student—in 1966 (17) and *Defect analysis in electron microscopy* with M. H. Loretto in 1975 (36) and in 1969 to revise and update W. Hume-Rothery and C. W. Haworth's *The structure of metals and alloys* (27).

ACADEMIC LEADERSHIP

Ray Smallman was never content to work within a system when he thought that he could change it for the better. His loyalty to the University of Birmingham was unwavering but he frequently found himself discontented with aspects of its organization. His initial reaction on taking over as Head of the Department of Physical Metallurgy in 1969 was to negotiate its merger with the Department of Industrial Metallurgy, correctly perceiving that metallurgy (and subsequently materials science) was not just a science to be pursued for academic interest but a key enabling technology for much of engineering. The same reasoning led him to argue for a distinct Faculty of Engineering at Birmingham, and almost inevitably to become its first Dean in 1985. The standards set by Ray were largely responsible for the department's excellent performance in the first—and all subsequent—national research assessment exercises. He quickly saw the need to do more than just good research: to publish and publicize it, to collaborate with industry to exploit it, to win funding for dedicated national and regional centres (first the HVEM, then—led by Mike Loretto—the IRC in Materials for High Performance Applications, then—led by Paul Bowen—the Rolls-Royce University Technology Centre), and also (dear to his heart) to devise and implement budgetary funding models within the university to ensure that funds clearly came to those whose excellent research earned them.

In 1987, under new Vice-Chancellor Michael Thompson, Ray became Vice-Principal of the university and eventually had to give up the headship of his beloved department in 1988. He continued lecturing, against his Vice-Chancellor's advice, throughout his stint as Vice-Principal and indeed afterwards in nominal retirement. His approach to fitting his teaching commitments into the busy life of a Vice-Principal was characteristically pragmatic. He asked for all his classes to be scheduled at 12 noon. He then had a perfect excuse to draw morning meetings to a close in good time, or to escape from a long meeting if he was not in the chair.

It was during his period as Vice-Principal that Ray devised and pushed through a new resource allocation model for the university and ensured that the university library was computerized, rather against the inclination of the administration. Personal charm must have played a significant part in getting these reforms accepted, particularly as (he subsequently boasted) the new models happened to benefit the Department of Metallurgy and Materials.

Beyond the university Ray played a leading role both locally (for example in the Birmingham Metallurgical Association) and nationally, in the Institute of Metals, the Metals Society and the Institute of Materials, in which he served as Vice-President. For more than 20 years he was chair of the Editorial Committee of *Metal Science Journal* and he served on the Science and Engineering Research Council (SERC).

Later years: impact on other institutions, 1993–2015

Although remaining devoted to Birmingham, Ray hugely enjoyed travel both for its own sake and for the opportunities for involvement with overseas scientists and their laboratories. At various times he held visiting professor positions at the universities of Pennsylvania and Stanford, California, Berkeley (with Gareth Thomas), Case Western Reserve, Cape Town (with Tony Ball), Hong Kong (with Brian Duggan), New South Wales and Novi Sad in (then) Yugoslavia (with Professor L. Sidjanin). He also acted as an advisor to the University of Queensland, the University of Topi in Pakistan and the University of Dhaka in Bangladesh. He was an Honorary Foreign Member of the China Ordnance Society and of the Czech Society for Metal Science.

An anecdote arising from Ray's visits to Novi Sad illustrates the serendipitous effect of travel on one's home institution. Professor Sidjanin introduced Ray to ADI and together they studied its microstructure by electron microscopy. On returning to Birmingham Ray discovered that his colleague Voya Kondic and his students had in fact been studying this system for several years but had declined to use electron microscopy to elucidate its microstructure, principally because of the friction (at the time) between the departments of Physical and Industrial Metallurgy.

Ray also played a significant part in the early success of the Federation of European Materials Societies (FEMS), becoming Vice-President in 1992 and President in 1994, just after he retired from his position as Vice-Principal and a full-time academic. After this demanding role in FEMS, rather than cutting back on his professional activities Ray undertook still more. In addition to continuing to lecture at Birmingham he went to Australia to review the Department of Mining and Metallurgical Engineering at the University of Queensland, prepared yet another revised edition of *Modern physical metallurgy*, accepted a position as academic advisor to the Vice-Chancellor of Hong Kong University, where he

Figure 1. Ray and Doreen with their children, grandchildren and partners. (Online version in colour.)

attempted to introduce an RAE-like system for research assessment, and became a Warden of the Birmingham Assay Office and a non-executive director of the University Hospital Birmingham National Health Service Trust.

Throughout his retirement Ray remained active in research, and his last technical publication was with Sidjanin on ADI in 2010 (47), 20 years after he had been introduced to the topic in Novi Sad.

FAMILY LIFE

On 6 September 1952 Ray married Doreen Faulkner in St Luke's Church, Cannock. Their marriage lasted until Ray's death and they had two children, Lesley-Ann (a pathologist) and Robert (a GP), and seven grandchildren.

The above account of Ray's professional life might give the impression of a man wholly dedicated to science in our universities. This would be to ignore an important aspect of this family man, who found the time and energy to write not one but two family memoirs. *Base metal to gold* is subtitled 'Memoirs of an academic metallurgist' and devotes about half of its 150 pages to Ray's activities with his family and friends. *Family heritage and social history*, which was completed in 2011, describes the background of the Smallman and Faulkner families, starting with Ray and Doreen's great-great-grandfathers at the beginning of the nineteenth century. Almost its only defect as a source is its lack of page numbers—an uncharacteristic detail of omission! Figure 1 shows Ray and Doreen among many of their extended family at one of their regular gatherings.

Figure 2. Ray and Doreen at Buckingham Palace in 1992 with Lesley-Ann and Robert. (Online version in colour.)

In addition to describing the development of Ray's extended family, both memoirs reveal Ray's love of travel, almost always with Doreen, and his knack of making lifelong friendships. One friend revealed at a recent event that he and Ray would have a regularly weekly phone call (between Hong Kong and the UK) 'just to keep in touch'. Ray was also proud of the recognition represented by the award of a CBE in 1992. Figure 2 shows Ray and Doreen at Buckingham Palace with their daughter Lesley-Ann and son Robert.

Honours

1986   Fellow of the Royal Society
1990   Honorary DSc, University of Wales
        Honorary DSc, University of Novi Sad, Yugoslavia
1991   Fellow of the Royal Academy of Engineering
1992   Companion of the British Empire (CBE)
        Foreign Member of the China Ordnance Society, China
1993   Foreign Member of the Czech Society for Metal Science, Czech Republic
2000   Honorary DSc, Cranfield University
2005   Foreign Associate of the US National Academy of Engineering

AWARDS

1969   Sir George Beilby Gold Medal, Institute of Metals and Society of Chemical Industry
1972   Rosenhain Medal, Institute of Metals
1978   Elegant Work Prize, Metals Society
       Van Horn Distinguished Lecture Award
1989   Platinum Medal, Institute of Materials
2004   *Acta Materialia* Gold Medal

ACKNOWLEDGEMENTS

The author gratefully acknowledges advice and support in writing this memoir from Professor Ian Jones and Professor Rex Harris FREng, longstanding colleagues of Ray Smallman at the University of Birmingham and from Ray's children, Lesley-Ann and Robert. He also wishes it to be known that it was Ray's wish that Professor John Knott FRS FREng should be a co-author but that Professor Knott's illness prevented him from being able to make a major contribution to the memoir.

The frontispiece photograph was taken in 1986 by Godfrey Argent and is reproduced with permission.

REFERENCES TO OTHER AUTHORS

Cottrell, A. H. 1948 *Theoretical structural metallurgy*. London: Edward Arnold. (2nd revised edition, 1955.)
Hirsch, P. B., Horne, R. W. & Whelan, M. J. 1956 Direct observations of the arrangement and motion of dislocations in aluminium. *Phil. Mag.* **1**, 677–684.

BIBLIOGRAPHY

The following publications are those referred to directly in the text. A full bibliography is available as electronic supplementary material at http://dx.doi.org/10.1098/rsbm.2015.0030 or via http://rsbm.royalsocietypublishing.org.

(1)   1953   (With G. K. Williamson) The growth of strain-anneal crystals of pre-determined orientation. *Acta Metall.* **1**, 487.
(2)   (With G. K. Williamson & G. Ardley) Yield points in aluminium alloy single crystals. *Acta Metall.* **1**, 126.
(3)   1954   Deformation and annealing textures in thorium. *J. Inst. Metals* **83**, 408.
(4)   1956   (With G. K. Williamson) Dislocation densities in some cold-worked and annealed metals from measurements on the Debye–Scherrer spectrum. *Phil. Mag.* **1**, 34.
(5)   1957   (With K. H. Westmacott) Stacking faults in face-centred cubic metals and alloys. *Phil. Mag.* **2**, 669.
(6)   (With B. N. T. Willis) An X-ray study of neutron-irradiated lithium fluoride. *Phil. Mag.* **2**, 1018.
(7)   1958   (With A. N. Churchman, J. Makin & D. Harries) The mechanical properties, embrittlement and metallurgical stability of irradiated metals and alloys. In *Second United Nations International Conference on Peaceful Uses of Atomic Energy*, p. 446. Geneva: United Nations.
(8)   (With P. B. Hirsch, J. Silcox & K. H. Westmacott) Dislocation loops in quenched aluminium. *Phil. Mag.* **3**, 897.
(9)   1959   (With K. H. Westmacott) Structure of quenched and irradiated metals. *J. Appl. Phys.* **30**, 603.
(10)   (With K. H. Westmacott & J. Coiley) Clustered vacancy defects in face-centred cubic metals and alloys. *J. Inst. Metals* **88**, 127.

(11)	1962	*Modern physical metallurgy*. London: Butterworth.

(12)	1963	(With K. H. G. Ashbee & G. K. Williamson) Stacking faults and dislocations in titanium dioxide with special reference to non-stoichiometry. *Proc. R. Soc. Lond.* A **276**, 542.

(13)	1964	(With I. L. Dillamore & I. R. Harris) The rolling texture and stacking fault energy of thorium, cerium and thorium–cerium alloys. *Acta Metall.* **12**, 156.

(14)		(With J. W. Edington & T. C. Lindley) Strain-ageing in vanadium. *Acta Metall.* **12**, 1025.

(15)	1965	(With I. L. Dillamore) The stacking fault energy of fcc metals. *Phil. Mag.* **12**, 115.

(16)		(With A. Eikum) A note on the transformation in non-stoichiometric rutile. *Phil. Mag.* **11**, 627.

(17)	1966	(With K. H. G. Ashbee) *Modern metallography*. Oxford: Pergamon Press.

(18)		(With I. R. Harris, I. L. Dillamore & B. E. P. Beeston) The influence of d-band structure on stacking fault energy. *Phil. Mag.* **14**, 325.

(19)		(With P. S. Dobson) The annealing of faulted loops. *Phil. Mag.* **14**, 357.

(20)		(With G. E. Hollox) Plastic behaviour of titanium carbide. *J. Appl. Phys.* **237**, 818.

(21)		(With A. Ball) Deformation properties and electron microscopy studies of the intermetallic compound NiAl. *Acta Metall.* **14**, 1349.

(22)		(With A. Ball) The operative slip system and general plasticity of NiAl. *Acta Metall.* **14**, 1517.

(23)	1967	(With P. S. Dobson & P. J. Goodhew) Climb kinetics of dislocation loops in aluminium. *Phil. Mag.* **16**, 9.

(24)		(With S. Kritzinger & P. S. Dobson) The influence of dilute magnesium addition on the growth and shrinkage of dislocation loops in aluminium. *Phil. Mag.* **16**, 217.

(25)	1968	(With R. Hales & P. S. Dobson) Formation and growth of vacancy loops in magnesium. *Proc. R. Soc. Lond.* A **307**, 71.

(26)		(With I. A. Johnston & P. S. Dobson) The effect of multiple quenching on the stability and growth of defect tetrahedra. *Phil. Mag.* **17**, 1289.

(27)	1969	(With W. Hume-Rothery & C. W. Haworth) *The structure of metals and alloys*, 5th edition. London: Metals and Metallurgy Trust of the Institute of Metals and the Institution of Metallurgists.

(28)	1970	(With A. W. Vere) The effect of temperature and deviation from stoichiometry on the mechanical properties of titanium monoxide. *Mater. Sci. Engng* **5**, 279.

(29)		(With F. M. C. Besag) Discontinuous yielding in ordered alloys. *Acta Metall.* **18**, 429.

(30)	1971	(With T. H. Webster & I. L. Dillamore) The microcracking behaviour of textured rimming steel at 77 K. *Metal Sci. J.* **5**, 68.

(31)		(With H. L. Fraser & M. H. Loretto) Direct observations of the annealing of stacking fault tetrahedra in gold and voids in NiAl. *Jerkont. Ann.* **155**, 410.

(32)	1972	(With J. Hancock & I. L. Dillamore) The creep of dispersion-strengthened Ni-Co alloys. *Metal Sci. J.* **6**, 152.

(33)	1973	(With H. L. Fraser & M. H. Loretto) The plastic deformation of NiAl single crystals between 300 K and 1050 K. *Phil. Mag.* **28**, 651.

(34)		(With D. G. Morris & F. M. C. Besag) Discontinuous yielding dislocation locking in Cu_3Au. *Acta Metall.* **22**, 801.

(35)	1974	(With I. L. Dillamore) The status of research on textures in metals. *Metal Sci. J.* **6**, 184.

(36)	1975	(With M. H. Loretto) *Defect analysis in electron microscopy*. London: Chapman & Hall.

(37)	1976	(With D. G. Morris, G. T. Brown & R. C. Piller) Ordering and domain growth in Ni_3Fe. *Acta Metall.* **24**, 21.

(38)	1979	(With J. W. Brooks & M. H. Loretto) In situ observations of the formation of martensite in stainless steel: direct observations of martensite nuclei in stainless steel. *Acta Metall.* **27**, 1829.

(39)	1983	(With M. Griffiths & M. H. Loretto) Electron damage in zirconium. I. Defect structure and loop character. *J. Nuclear Mater.* **115**, 313.

(40)	1988	(With A. P. Woodfield, P. J. Postans & M. H. Loretto) The effect of long term high temperature exposure on the structure and properties of the Ti alloy Ti5331S. *Acta Metall.* **36**, 507.

(41)	1993	(With C. S. Lee & B. J. Duggan) A theory of deformation banding in cold rolling. *Acta Metall. Mater.* **41**, 2265.

(42)	1995	(With R. J. Bishop) *Metals and materials; science, processes, applications*. Oxford: Butterworth-Heinemann.

(43) 1997 (With T. S. Rong & I. P. Jones) Superdislocation dissociation in twist boundaries. *Scr. Metall.* **36**, 861.

(44)   (With J. Mallia & M. Grech) Effect of silicon content on impact properties of austempered ductile iron. *Mater. Sci. Technol.* **13**, 408.

(45) 1998 (With W. H. Zhu, D. Fort & I. P. Jones) Orientation dependence of creep on Ni_3Al at intermediate temperatures. *Acta Mater*. **46**, 3873.

(46) 1999 (With R. J. Bishop) *Modern physical metallurgy and materials engineering*. Oxford: Butterworth-Heinemann.

(47) 2010 (With L. Sidjanin, D. Rajnovic & O. Eric) Austempering study of unalloyed and alloyed ductile irons. *Mater. Sci. Technol.* **26**, 567.

(48) 2013 (With J. F. Knott) Sir Alan Cottrell FREng. *Biogr. Mems Fell. R. Soc.* **59**, 93–124.

ROBERT JOSEPH PATON WILLIAMS MBE

25 February 1926 – 21 March 2015

CrossMark
click for updates

ROBERT JOSEPH PATON WILLIAMS MBE

25 February 1926 − 21 March 2015

Elected FRS 1972

By H. A. O. Hill[1] FRS and A. J. Thomson[2]* OBE FRS

[1]*The Queen's College, Oxford University, Oxford OX1 4AW, UK*
[2]*School of Chemistry, University of East Anglia, Norwich NR4 7TJ, UK*

Robert J. P. Williams was a pioneer in advancing our understanding of the roles of chemical elements, especially the metals, in biology and in biological evolution. During the first half of his career of more than 60 years at Oxford University he studied the thermodynamic stabilities of transition-metal complexes with organic ligands, their redox properties, magnetism and colour, to understand their biological function. In parallel he collaborated with biologists and biophysicists, for example with Bert Vallee, studying zinc in proteins. Williams was the first to describe how proton gradients could be used to drive the formation of the universal biological fuel, ATP (adenosine triphosphate), a fundamental step in biological energetics. From the late 1960s he studied many proteins that use metal ions for catalysis, for electron transfer and cellular regulation. A leading figure in the establishment of the Oxford Enzyme Group, Williams developed high-field nuclear magnetic resonance (NMR) to study the mobility and dynamics of many protein structures, leading to a deeper understanding of protein function. He held the Royal Society Napier Research Professorship from 1974 until his retirement in 1991. Subsequently he published several books setting out his understanding of the roles of metal ions in biology, and their wider significance in evolution. Bob Williams's deep insights across many disciplines made him a charismatic teacher. His lateral style of thinking never failed to inspire. His legacy lies in the successful careers of his many students and collaborators worldwide and the vigour of the new discipline of bioinorganic chemistry that he helped to establish.

Early life and education

Robert Joseph Paton Williams was born in Wallasey, Cheshire, to Ernest Ivor Williams, a customs and excise officer at Liverpool, and Alice Williams (*née* Roberts), a milliner. Both

* a.thomson@uea.ac.uk

© 2016 The Author(s)
Published by the Royal Society

sides of the family were involved in the use of steam to drive engines both at sea and on the railways. His father was a veteran of World War I, an experience that deeply changed him. Bob, as he was always known, was the second child of four, Greta being the first, Gerald the third and Kathleen the last.

From 1931 to 1937 Bob attended St George's School in Wallasey. In his early teens, and his last year at primary school, he suffered from diphtheria and was unable to go to school for six months. As a consequence he failed to win a place at the local school, Wallasey Grammar. Fortunately his parents could afford to pay the fees to allow him to attend the grammar school. There he began to show his academic potential. But he was also fond of sport—so much so that, at the age of 15 years, after taking his School Certificate, he dropped chemistry in favour of cricket! His father insisted that he take up the subject again. In addition to chemistry he studied physics and pure and applied mathematics for his Higher School Certificate. Mr Livesey, the chemistry teacher, was a man of wide general knowledge and enthusiasm. He was a Cambridge graduate who had become a schoolmaster after losing his post with a metallurgical company in the 1930s. An intellectual and interesting teacher, he was insistent that his pupils learn the subject in depth and detail. Mr Eggleshaw, the mathematics teacher, was also highly influential on the young Williams. He, too, was a Cambridge graduate, an all-round sportsman who had been in the cross-country running team at Cambridge. He had a wide interest in science, music and poetry and supplied his pupils with books to read on science subjects such as James Jeans on the Universe and even quantum theory. Some of the teaching, especially from Mr Eggleshaw, took place while pupils were fire-watching from the school rooftops during the German bombing raids over Liverpool in World War II. Those nights between 8 p.m. and midnight became an extension of Bob Williams's education and contributed to the development of an insatiable curiosity that was to last throughout his life.

In addition to fire-watching, schoolboys were encouraged to work during the school holidays in agricultural and forestry camps to help the war effort. There Bob learnt that certain chemicals were applied to growing crops, lime to control soil pH, and potassium phosphate. Indeed, agriculturalists already knew that various trace elements were required, such as boron for plants and cobalt licks for sheep. It occurred to him that such elements must be an essential part of biological systems. He had already read Darwin's *Voyage of the Beagle*, one of the few books owned by his father. This stimulated in him an ambition to understand the chemistry of life although, ironically, at school he was not permitted to study biology. Importantly, it led him to the proposition, rather precociously for a teenager, that if Darwin was correct, the best of all chemistry for life had already been discovered. It posed many questions: How many of the chemical elements did life depend on? What was their particular chemistry? What were their biological roles? The search for answers was to preoccupy Bob Williams for the rest of his scientific life.

Towards the end of his schooling, Bob was encouraged by the school to apply to Cambridge and Oxford. Having failed to win a place at Cambridge he travelled to Oxford to take the Scholarship Entrance Examination in December 1943. Thus he sat his first Oxford examination in the Hall of Wadham College, where he was later to become a fellow for more than 50 years. In January 1944 he learnt that he had been awarded a major scholarship, a Postmastership, at Merton College. Because he had no Latin qualification he had to pass a national examination in Latin to secure entry to Oxford. Although having less than six months to learn Latin from scratch, a challenging task, he nevertheless succeeded. Thus Bob Williams went up to Merton College in October 1944. Within six months he had forgotten all his Latin.

Oxford University

Undergraduate and postgraduate studies

Bob Williams's time at Oxford started somewhat inauspiciously. His sense of deprivation in his first term living in a large cold room in Merton College was increased by the prevailing food rationing and by college regulations. But these discomforts were little compared with his dismay at the tutorial system. The war had deprived Oxford of many of its younger teaching fellows. Thus his first chemistry tutor, although a kindly, well-meaning older man, seemed to know little of the revolution in scientific outlook after about 1920. Tutorial topics of the first term were dull, mere descriptions of laboratory facts not leading to any principles. There was little to discuss in tutorials.

At the end of his first term Bob seriously considered leaving Oxford and moving to Liverpool University, a place where he had friends. But he resolved to return to Oxford, determined to change things. He plucked up courage to request a change of tutor, explaining that he wanted to know the basic nature of chemical systems in modern times. The next term his new, younger tutors taught him the disciplines of thermodynamics and wave mechanics, how to think about colour and magnetism, about structure, chemical combination and reaction rates. Slowly he began to grasp chemistry.

The following extract from Bob's own writing describes vividly, after his initial negative impressions of Oxford, how he came to feel about the place in which he was to spend the rest of his life and to which he became devoted:

> I was intellectually awake and had become emotionally aware and alive as I had been when I was eighteen. I punted, often alone, on the River Cherwell; I cycled deep into the country, again often alone; I discovered Wytham Hill; I went to lectures on history, poetry and on Art. My spirits lifted. My overwhelming desire was now to show that I could succeed at Oxford. I became a very independent, dedicated spirit and I began to love the place. The idea that anything other than science, for example politics or administration, could be a way forward for me meant nothing then and means rather little now. I wanted to understand, not to manipulate. I wanted to find a satisfying relationship between living and dead objects—both were chemistry. The world in action was, and is, a somewhat shabby affair often in science as well as in everything else, but knowledge is not spoilt by that.

From 1946 onwards Oxford was changed further as demobilized servicemen who had started courses anything up to seven years earlier returned in numbers to Merton. The college became, instead of a continuation of public school life, a lively place of study. Although they studied seriously, the students rebelled against the rules. Suddenly undergraduates were allowed in pubs, and girls came into college. Many of these ex-servicemen had a more direct interest in the future, whereas those directly out of school had little thought for a career.

After sitting final examination papers at the end of three years, Bob Williams was given to understand that he could expect a first-class honours degree provided that he performed an outstanding fourth and final year, the Part II. This was a research year with a short thesis. He still wished to study chemical elements in biological systems but had little idea how to begin. His tutor for part of his third year was an analytical chemist, Dr Harry M. N. H. Irving, whose laboratory interest was organic reagents that could select metal ions from solution as coloured complexes in order to determine the concentrations of those metal ions in water. This topic attracted Bob. He saw in this work a possible parallel with the selective uptake of metal ions by organisms. To work with Irving was something of a risk, however, because the latter did

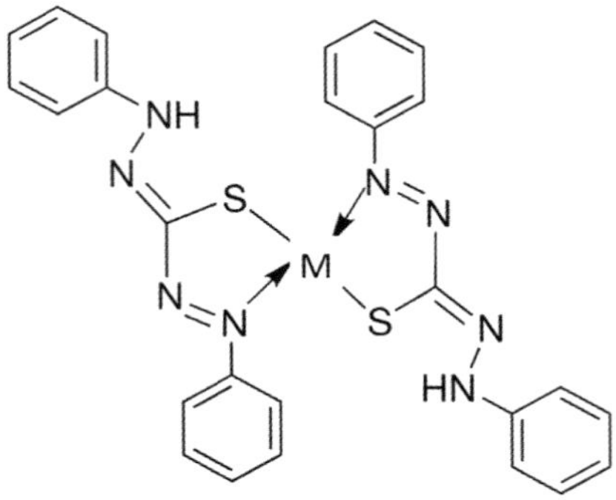

Figure 1. Metal dithizone complex, in which M can be a divalent metal ion such as the second half
of the first transition-metal series Mn(II), Fe(II), Co(II), Ni(II), Cu(II) or Zn(II).

not then have a distinguished career and had few, if any, publications. The particular work that
Irving proposed to Bob was to find a way to analyse for traces of zinc in water solutions by
using dithizone (figure 1), an organic molecule with two sulfur atoms that would bind zinc ions.

Bob found that the experiments were slow and laborious, involving shaking by hand for
1–30 minutes in a separating funnel containing a chloroform solution of the organic reagent,
green dithizone. This reagent extracted from water a zinc dithizone complex that was red.
Each experiment had to be repeated many times, because the reagent dithizone was not
very stable. So Bob devised a shaking machine to enable him to leave the laboratory to play
hockey while waiting for equilibrium to be established. Eventually, he was able to derive
expressions for the extraction process involving the metal–ligand equilibrium constant,
the acid dissociation constant of the ligand and the partition coefficient between water and
chloroform. This was a considerable achievement. He could now select the best conditions for
analysis. Further questions then arose: Was the reagent selective for zinc? What other metal
ions lying in the same region of the Periodic Table could bind to dithizone? Bob therefore
tested manganese(II), iron(II), cobalt(II), nickel(II) and copper(II). Within six months of
starting work, by Easter 1948, he had established an order of the selectivity of the binding of
the organic reagent dithizone for the metal ions thus:

$$Mg^{2+} < Mn^{2+} < Fe^{2+} < Co^{2+} < Ni^{2+} < Zn^{2+} < Cu^{2+} .$$

By chance Bob then came across elegant work carried out between 1940 and 1944 in
Copenhagen by Jannick Bjerrum on the stability constants of ammonia and ethylenediamine
complexes with metal ions in water and was immediately struck that the order of stabilities
was the same as he had found, although Bjerrum himself had not noted it (Schäffer 1994).
He convinced Irving that they should urgently submit a paper. It was published in *Nature* in
1948 (1)*. This won Bob a first-class honours degree and made something of a reputation
for himself as well as for Irving. This order of stability was to become widely known as the
Irving–Williams series and today can be found in every inorganic textbook.

Bob recounted an amusing anecdote from that initial year of research. In the front row of
his first research seminar presenting his work on the Irving–Williams series sat the world-

* Numbers in this form refer to the bibliography at the end of the text.

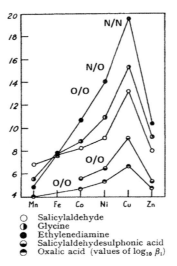

Figure 2. Irving–Williams series of thermodynamic stabilities ($\log_{10} \beta_1$) of divalent transition-metal complexes with various ligands that differ in the nature of the non-metal atoms that ligate the metal ions. (Adapted from (3), with permission of the Royal Society of Chemistry.)

famous American chemist, Dr Linus Pauling (ForMemRS 1948), a hero of Bob's, who was visiting Oxford as the Eastman Professor. Throughout his talk, Bob was frequently interrupted by Pauling until eventually he told Dr Pauling that if he persisted in interrupting his talk he would not be able to continue. Pauling then listened as Bob explained that Pauling's view of complex ion stability did not fit Bob's data. After the lecture, Pauling complained to Irving that Bob had been rude to him. On learning that Bob was still an undergraduate, Pauling immediately apologized to him. This anecdote reveals that Bob, even as a young man, had remarkable self-assurance and determination.

Supported by a Harmsworth Scholarship at Merton, for a further two years Bob continued studies with Irving on the stability of complexes of transition metals, obtaining his DPhil degree in 1950. The main aim during the doctorate was further experimentation to demonstrate the generality of the Irving–Williams series (figure 2). However, before beginning his DPhil work, during the summer of 1948 Bob visited Denmark and Sweden with the help of a Merton College travel grant. In Copenhagen he finally met Jannick Bjerrum and his father Niels, one of the great names of Danish science. He greatly enjoyed the free exchange of views about science. He learned from the Bjerrums how to use glass electrodes to measure H^+ ions released when organic acids complex with metal ions. During his subsequent doctoral work, a major experimental task was to make glass electrodes and to devise a meter to measure H^+ concentrations. This allowed him to confirm that the order he had previously found was general, but with one or two exceptions of special significance. In the case of Fe(II) ions, certain strong-field ligands changed the magnetic character of the iron and increased its stability many fold. This was an early observation of the chemical significance of changes in the electronic spin states of transition-metal ions. Later his knowledge of the function of glass electrodes in which a gradient of protons across a thin (glass) membrane is driven by an electric field was to inform his discussion with Peter Mitchell (FRS 1974) about chemiosmosis. His doctoral work was included in a lengthy paper published in 1953 (3).

Figure 3. Bob Williams in the laboratory of Professor Tiselius during his research fellowship in Sweden in 1950. (Reproduced with kind permission of the family of R. J. P. Williams.)

RESEARCH FELLOWSHIP

During the trip to Sweden between his Part II year and his doctoral studies, Bob visited the laboratory at Uppsala University of Professor Arne Tiselius (ForMemRS 1957), the well-known biochemist and Nobel laureate, and also met Professor Stig Claeson. Both were involved in the development of chromatographic techniques for protein separation. Bob was impressed with laboratory facilities compared with those at Oxford. He therefore returned to work in these laboratories in 1950, after his DPhil degree, with the support of a Rotary International Fellowship, to learn about protein purification (figure 3). Within the first three months he had devised a new method for the separation of molecules using a form of chromatography called gradient elution analysis (2). The method is widely used to this day in most biochemical and many chemical laboratories.

While in Sweden, Bob collected together his ideas for a review entitled 'Metal ions in biological systems'. *Chemical Society Reviews* refused to publish it because it did not contain new experimental material. However, it was published in the journal *Biological Reviews* in 1953 (4). Because many biologists but few chemists read it, several were to contact Bob, some eventually becoming collaborators and he their chemical mentor.

COLLEGE FELLOWSHIP AND UNIVERSITY LECTURESHIP

Towards the end of his stay in Sweden, and at the invitation of his friend Courtney Phillips, a newly elected chemistry fellow at Merton College, Oxford, Bob won a Junior Research Fellowship at Merton. He held the fellowship at Merton followed by an additional year as a lecturer at the college, and a junior demonstratorship in the Chemistry Laboratory from 1951 to 1954. Out of the blue, in 1954, Sir Cyril Hinshelwood FRS, then Oxford Professor of Chemistry, asked to see Bob. Hinshelwood was a powerful and forbidding figure, President of the Royal Society and sometime head of the Classical Society. He told Bob that three colleges—Christ Church, Pembroke and Wadham—needed a tutor in chemistry. Each one, Bob was told, will invite you to dine. Come back again in two weeks to give me your decision. Thus in 1955 Bob Williams joined Wadham College as its only chemistry tutor. He was to remain there for the rest of his life.

RESEARCH, 1951–65

The work on the stability of metal-ion complexes continued in the Irving group, which was strengthened greatly by two outstanding students, Hazel and Francis Rossotti. Together the group systematized a great deal of analytical practice in inorganic chemistry. By his own admission Bob was not a dextrous experimentalist; rather, his strength lay in bringing together apparently disparate facts and drawing out interesting correlations. In 1953 he and Irving published a paper (3) setting out a comprehensive account of the stabilities of complexes formed between organic ligands and ions of the first series of transition elements from Mn to Zn. This work confirmed that the *sequence* was independent of the chemical nature of the ligand, although it did reveal the importance of ligand denticity. The paper also discussed the electronic factors controlling the stability of metal ions underlying this sequence in terms of Pauling's theory of ionic and covalent bonds using hybridization of d, p and s orbitals. It concluded that the interaction cannot be purely electrostatic but must involve increasing covalence along the series.

At the same time a different explanation was provided by L. E. Orgel (FRS 1962), a Fellow of Magdalen College, Oxford, in a seminal paper entitled 'The effects of crystal fields on the properties of transition metal ions' (Orgel 1952). This paper introduced the chemical world to the ideas of crystal field theory first developed by two physicists (Schlapp & Penney 1932). They had shown how, in a crystal lattice, the symmetry of the local electrostatic field, provided by a set of negative ligands, split the energies of the d orbitals of a positively charged transition-metal ion. Orgel developed this idea, describing how the symmetry of the surrounding electric field from the ligands leads to a stabilization of certain d orbitals and hence can account for the increase in the heats of hydration along the series from Mn^{2+} to Zn^{2+}. In his paper Orgel did not refer to the Irving–Williams series of metal-ion complex stability published in 1948 (1). Williams later admitted that, until Orgel explained this theory, he could not understand the physics well enough to apply it. Nevertheless, a lively debate continued over the next few years between Williams and the crystal field adherents, including Orgel and J. S. Griffiths, about the relative contributions to the stabilities from symmetry effects and covalence (Jørgensen *et al.* 1958).

From 1956 until the mid 1960s, Bob Williams carried out research in the Inorganic Chemistry Laboratory with groups of Part II and DPhil students as well as research fellows. The research was focused on the chemical properties of transition-metal complex ions then known to have roles in the capture of biological energy mainly through the transfer of electrons. Electron transfer depends on a change in oxidation state of a metal ion, so key properties include the relative stability of oxidation states in a given environment, measured by the redox potentials. With students J. Tomkinson (6) and B. James (12) Bob analysed oxidation–reduction potentials of Fe(III) and Fe(II) and of Cu(II) and Cu(I), two metals of biological importance. They showed how the covalency, size and charge of metal ions affect redox potentials. Potentials could also be controlled by the use of different donor atoms of organic ligands or by changing the stereochemistry around the metal ions. Thus it was possible to generate a sequence of redox potentials of metal-ion complexes from high to low, matching the potentials from O_2/H_2O (+0.8 V) to H_2/H_2O (−0.45 V) used in biological cells. An additional important feature of the Fe(III)/Fe(II) complexes was the effect of a change in electron spin state that would become crucial to understanding the functions of haemoglobin and cytochromes (13).

Little was understood of the mechanism of electron transfer between metal centres in organic matrices including proteins, a process essential to respiration. So Williams began investigating electron conduction in solid matrices between metal ions and their complexes. Paul Braterman and Beverly Phipps, his first students in this area, studied the electrical conductivity of the pigment Prussian blue, a compound of iron cyanides containing two oxidation states, Fe(II) and Fe(III), a mixed-valence compound (15). They recognized that the intense colour arose in part from optical electron transitions from the Fe(II) to Fe(III) ions, so-called intervalence transitions. Hence a growing interest in the assignment of the optical spectra of transition-metal complexes led to a seminal review of the optical spectra of haemoproteins, revealing key connections between the haem absorption spectra and the electronic spin states of Fe ions (16). The paramagnetism of haemoglobin that depended on the state of oxygenation of the haems, first described by Pauling & Coryell (1936), could now be read out from its absorption spectrum. This was later to prove crucial to understanding haem–haem cooperativity in haemoglobin (16). Peter Day (FRS 1986), a Part II then DPhil student, followed Braterman, measuring photo-induced conductivity in metal phthalocyanines and investigated the origin of colour in mixed-valence Cu(I) and Cu(II) complexes (21). Day was later to build a distinguished career, independently of Bob, in the field of mixed-valence and magnetic materials.

It had been known since the 1930s that molybdenum was essential to healthy plant growth. Bob started to explore molybdenum chemistry with student Phillip Mitchell (14) using the thiocyanate ion, SCN^-, known as an ambidentate ligand, to probe binding to a metal ion through either the sulfur or the nitrogen atom. Mitchell used infrared spectroscopy to distinguish between the two modes of binding.

Vitamin B_{12} and cobalt

Vitamin B_{12}, the anti-pernicious-anaemia factor, became available for chemical study in the 1950s from large-scale bacterial cultures. With a team in Oxford, Dorothy Crowfoot Hodgkin FRS determined the molecular structure by crystallography in 1956 with material obtained from Dr Lester Smith of the Glaxo drug company (Dodson 2002).

This revealed one of the most complex structures of any of the vitamins, with several unusual chemical features. It contained a cobalt ion in the centre of a novel tetrapyrrole ring (known as corrin) that lacked one methine bridge, causing the ring to pucker. This cofactor was responsible for the red colour of the vitamin. But quite unexpected was the presence of a direct cobalt–carbon bond between the 5′ carbon of the sugar component of the 5′-deoxyadenosyl moiety (the sugar part) and the cobalt ion in the coenzyme form of vitamin B_{12} (figure 4). Bob Williams, working in the same building as Dorothy Hodgkin, became intrigued by the chemistry of this new cobalt complex. He was initially sceptical of Dorothy's evidence for a stable cobalt–carbon bond, given that all the metal-alkyls then known, such as Grignard reagents, were immediately hydrolysed on contact with water. He saw both the importance of studying the reactivity of the cobalt ion in B_{12} and the potential

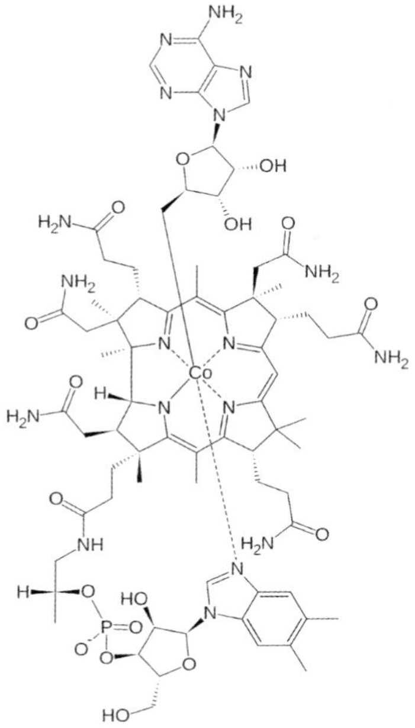

Figure 4. Structure of the coenzyme of vitamin B_{12} showing the direct bond between the central cobalt ion (Co) and the alkyl group ($-CH_2-$) of the sugar moiety. (Taken from https://commons.wikimedia.org/w/index. php?curid=2034238.)

for using optical and other spectroscopic methods. Over the years between 1961 and 1973 Bob published some 26 papers, mostly in *Journal of the Chemical Society*, on the chemistry of B_{12}; he had a strong team of co-workers led by J. M. Pratt, who obtained his DPhil in 1963, and H. A. O. Hill (FRS 1990), a research fellow from Queen's University Belfast, trained in organic chemistry.

The group analysed a wide range of the chemical properties of the vitamin, described in a comprehensive monograph by Pratt (1972). Studies included ligand substitution reactions at the cobalt site, and characterization of the cobalt ion redox states Co(I), Co(II) and Co(III). The latter were prepared by Hill, using coulometry (22). The complexes were also characterized by NMR and electron paramagnetic resonance (EPR) spectroscopies, introducing these powerful analytical techniques into the Inorganic Chemistry Laboratory (24). The group showed that vitamin B_{12} will bind and transfer the methyl group ($-CH_3$) to other metals including mercury and platinum (25). Methyl mercury ion, $[CH_3-Hg^+]$, produced in bacteria by transfer of the methyl group from B_{12} to polluting Hg, caused poisoning in the Japanese fishing community of Minimata as it was passed up the food chain to people via fish. Studies of a dioldehydrase, a B_{12}-containing enzyme, in collaboration with M. A. Foster in an early application of EPR spectroscopy, detected radical intermediates produced during turnover implying the *homolytic* fission of the Co–C bond (27). Hill's introduction of electrochemical techniques to prepare defined oxidation states of B_{12} led to the development of methods for obtaining the direct interaction between redox proteins and a graphite electrode. From this work came a handheld electrochemical sensor of glucose concentrations in a finger-prick of blood, allowing diabetics easily to monitor blood-sugar levels quantitatively.

Early biological work

Zinc and Bert Vallee

Alongside his research at the Inorganic Chemistry Laboratory on the chemistry of transition-metal ions, Bob Williams began to study their roles in biology through correspondence, and collaboration, with biologists. He had neither the experimental expertise himself nor access to laboratories appropriately equipped for work on proteins. This work proceeded largely unknown to his research group working in the Inorganic Chemistry Laboratory. After publication of his seminal 1953 review (4) he was contacted by Bert Vallee, a medical doctor at Harvard, who was analysing the zinc content of various biological cells with the use of the colorimetric reagent dithizone, which Bob himself had studied with Irving. Vallee had observed that red cells from blood contained a relatively high concentration of iron, owing to the presence of haemoglobin, but a very low concentration of zinc, whereas white cells had little iron but surprisingly large quantities of zinc. He wondered whether the observation had wider significance, because zinc was not then known to be of importance in biology. Vallee visited Bob in Oxford in 1955 just after he had analysed the enzyme carboxypeptidase, a major hydrolytic enzyme in pancreatic digestive juices. Hans Neurath, who had first isolated the enzyme, claimed that it contained magnesium. Vallee discovered that without zinc the enzyme was catalytically inactive. Until then zinc had been known in only one other enzyme, carbonic anhydrase. For some 15 years Vallee and Williams worked together, the former with expertise in cellular medical chemistry and analysis of metal content in enzymes, and the latter with knowledge of the properties of inorganic chemicals (7). They became pioneers of a new subject area. They developed methods of exploring metal binding using spectroscopic methods and binding affinities, by substituting coloured metal ions such as cobalt for colourless zinc, known as isomorphous replacement. Bob spent 1956 at Harvard Medical School devising ways of inhibiting zinc enzymes with standard organic analytical reagents such as *o*-phenanthrolines and 8-hydroxyquinolines (8, 10).

Vallee and Williams put forward, in 1968, a general concept for the reactivity of metalloproteins, proposing that the protein imposes an unusual coordination number and geometry on metal ions to induce enhanced chemical reactivity for catalytic function or rapid electron transfer (23). This was demonstrated, for example, by atypical optical absorption and EPR spectra. They called this an 'entatic state' (figure 5), derived from entasis (from the Greek ἐντείνω), meaning tension, and defined it as 'the existence in the enzyme of an area with energy closer to that of a unimolecular transition state than to that of a conventional stable molecule thereby constituting an energised poised domain'.

For example, in the electron shuttle protein plastocyanin, the copper centre exchanges between Cu(II) and Cu(I) states. Although each Cu oxidation state prefers a distinct coordination geometry—Cu(II) is normally planar, whereas copper(I) is normally tetrahedral—in the protein the Cu site is intermediate between the two, a highly distorted tetrahedron. Because the electron transfer rate depends on the reorganization energy, the fastest rate from a Cu centre occurs at an intermediate geometry that minimizes geometrical reorganization on switching oxidation state. This they considered an entatic state. Others, including H. Eyring, D. Koshland, R. Lumry and B. G. Malmström, had earlier discussed ways in which a substrate might fit into an enzyme's binding pocket, thereby lowering the activation energy of catalysis. This was called an induced fit or the 'rack' mechanism. Vallee and Williams stressed that their view presented a property of the protein or enzyme itself and did not involve a bound substrate. This led to vigorous discussion over priority. In 2000,

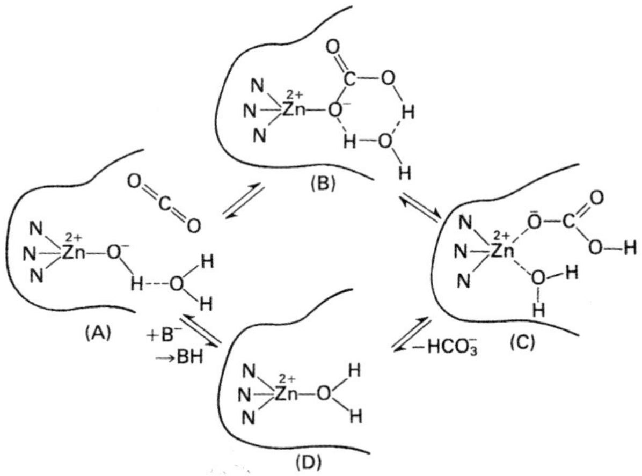

Figure 5. The use of a zinc(II) ion as a Lewis acid in the pathway of hydrolysis of carbon dioxide to give bicarbonate ion by the enzyme carbonic anhydrase. Zinc is held in an ideal coordination site or 'entatic' state. (Taken from p. 241 of (34), by permission of Oxford University Press.)

with Malmström and H. B. Gray, Bob wrote a review about the concept of the entatic state using the example of the coordination of copper in the blue redox proteins to clarify, and dispel, earlier misunderstandings (35).

Protons, ATP and Peter Mitchell

While his own laboratory was investigating electron transfer between transition-metal ions in solid complexes, Bob Williams was attending research conferences on respiration and listening to discussions about the generation of ATP, the universal biological fuel generated in chloroplasts from photons, and in mitochondria from the reduction of oxygen to water concomitant with the oxidation of sugars. The latter process, glycolysis, was known to involve phosphorylated compounds, leading to the formation of ATP. It was thought that the intermediates, precursors of ATP, were energized phosphorylated organic compounds.

Many advocates, including D. E. Green, E. C. Slater (FRS 1975), A. L. Lehninger and E. Racker, argued strongly for the existence of such phosphorylated intermediates although they were unable to identify or isolate any. However, B. Chance (ForMemRS 1981), a physicist by training, rather than searching for such intermediates, studied changes in the spectroscopic properties of mitochondria and chloroplasts during energy transduction. He found three, or possibly four, cross-over points, as he called them, during electron transfer in the spectroscopic analysis of both organelles. This observation seemed to imply that electron transfer was due to three or four chemical changes. However, Bob saw that the generation of a single intermediate, along with electron transfer, was common to all the organelle reactions. He proposed that the intermediate must be the proton and that the formation of ATP in every step entailed the migration of protons back to negative charge on organic molecules. The condensation of ADP and phosphate to ATP is driven by protons. In 1959 Bob gave the first description of this, a completely novel idea, in a chapter of the book called *The enzymes* (edited by P. D. Boyer) (9). In August 1960 he submitted a fuller version of his hypothesis, at the invitation of the editor, Professor J. F. Danielli, to the new *Journal of Theoretical Biology* (11). Williams described the way in which electron flow stimulated by light or chemistry was converted to a proton gradient that was then used to drive ATP formation. He was confident that he had described a fundamental step in biological energetics and that he was the first to have clearly seen that energy could at some point in time and space be accumulated in a gradient of protons. He further stated that this gradient could be across a particle.

Almost immediately Williams received a letter from Dr Peter Mitchell (FRS 1974), a lecturer in Edinburgh, saying he had read Williams's articles back to 1959, and asking for an explanation of his hypothesis. An exchange of letters followed in which Williams explained several times his ideas that Mitchell then interpreted, sometimes incorrectly, and asking for further enlightenment. Only a month or two later Mitchell wrote, suddenly declaring that he had had a similar idea, one of the two forms of Williams's hypothesis. However, during his communications with Williams he did not reveal that he was writing papers or that he had in press a note containing his ideas. This note failed to acknowledge Williams's work or their mutual correspondence. Williams then discovered that Mitchell had included some of his views in an earlier conference report, again without acknowledgement. In 1978 Mitchell was awarded, on his own, the Nobel Prize in Chemistry for his theory of chemiosmosis, published in 1961, defined as ATP synthesis by means of a protein gradient across a membrane driving the condensation of phosphate to form ATP (Mitchell 1961).

These events led to an unusually protracted discussion in the literature, sharpened by the award of the Nobel prize, about the proper attribution of priority of the idea of ATP synthesis by way of proton electrochemical coupling. In the Royal Society Biographical Memoir of Peter Mitchell (Slater 1994), E. C. Slater writes: 'More surprising, however, is the lack of reference in Mitchell's 1961 paper or in subsequent reviews to an earlier proposal by Williams that H^+ ions produced by reduction of ferric iron in the cytochrome system could drive the ATPase in the direction of the synthesis of ATP.' Slater continues:

> The suggestion was first made in a review published in 1959 .... Williams elaborated his ideas in more detail in the *Journal of Theoretical Biology*, submitted on 7 August 1960 and published in January 1961. ... After Williams' paper appeared, Mitchell wrote to him on 24 February asking for clarification, and this letter started an extensive correspondence (six letters from Mitchell, five from Williams, the 11 letters totalling about 7500 words [these are deposited in the Royal Society's archive]. ... the exchange reads as a friendly scientific discussion, mostly concerning Williams' two already published papers, but the opening paragraph of Mitchell's letter of 19 April, written shortly after the meeting of the Biochemical Society in Oxford at which he presented the chemiosmotic theory of oxidative phosphorylation for the first time and just before submitting his article to *Nature*, introduced a new tone.

Slater concludes: 'In view of the extensive correspondence with Williams it is difficult to understand that Mitchell did not refer to his papers in his publications in 1961. Even in his Nobel Lecture, Mitchell gave no reference to Williams' 1959 or 1961 papers.' Slater opines that the 'record shows that Williams was the first to propose that protons produced by the respiratory chain could bring about the synthesis of ATP by reversal of an ATPase, although his concept of the way in which it did so differed from that of Mitchell.'

A lengthy article, published by Weber & Prebble (2006), analyses in detail the hypotheses proposed, their antecedents, and the extensive correspondence between the two parties. It also discusses the development of the dispute between them, examines the cases for priority and explores their motives. They reach the following conclusions:

> Mitchell's proposals were original (a view disputed by Williams) although it is evident that prior to the correspondence Williams had considered and rejected a proposition similar to Mitchell's

theory. However, a major cause of the dispute was the difference in disciplinary backgrounds of Mitchell, a microbial chemist and Williams, a chemist.

Despite the dissension in these lengthy debates, Williams was one of those who supported Mitchell for the 1978 Nobel Prize in Chemistry: footnote 101 in Weber & Prebble (2006) refers to a letter dated 8 January 1978 from R. J. P. Williams to the Secretary, Nobel Committee for Chemistry.

Haemoglobin and Max Perutz

In 1961, a year before receiving the Nobel Prize for solving the crystal structure of haemoglobin, Max Perutz FRS heard Bob Williams give a seminar at a conference in Lucerne, Switzerland. In that talk Bob discussed the possible mechanisms of haem–haem cooperativity in haemoglobin, proposing that when a haem moiety is oxygenated, the spin state of the central Fe(II) ion changes from high to low spin, causing the ionic radius of the Fe(II) ion to decrease. Because the hole in the centre of the haem ring is too small to accommodate the high-spin Fe(II) ion, on oxygenation the decrease in the ionic radius of the Fe(II) ion causes it to move towards the haem plane. Williams pointed out that the iron–histidine bond length would also shorten, thereby triggering protein motion and transmitting the effect to the other haem groups in the protein. In the early 1950s, studying spin-state changes in small iron chelates, Williams had seen that they could entail changes in bond lengths by at least 0.1 Å (0.01 nm) as a result of stronger binding of the low-spin Fe(II) state compared with the high-spin ion (5). This suggested to him that in proteins there would be similar change in bond lengths of Fe(II) and ligating groups on oxidation, or on binding O_2 or CO. Max and Bob met several times in both Cambridge and Oxford, when Bob gave tutorials to Max on crystal field theory and spin states. In 1970 Perutz proposed a detailed mechanism of the stereochemistry of cooperative effects in haemoglobin in which he cited R. J. P. Williams (Perutz 1970). Further details are described in the biography of Max Perutz by Georgina Ferry (Ferry 2007, pp. 219–221).

Iron–sulfur proteins

In the 1960s, with the increasing availability to biologists of EPR spectrometers, plant scientists discovered unique EPR characteristics in a brown protein isolated from spinach. No EPR signal was detectable in the oxidized form, but on addition of strong reductant and at very low sample temperatures, a strong, anisotropic EPR signal was detected centred at $g = 1.98$. Bob asked J. M. H. Thornley, an expert on EPR of metal ions in solid lattices working in the Clarendon Physics Laboratory, Oxford, for his suggestion as to the origin of this signal. Thornley proceeded to show that the signal arose from a mixed valence *pair* of high-spin ions Fe(III) with $S = \frac{5}{2}$ and Fe(II) with $S = \frac{4}{2}$ that interact anti-ferromagnetically, probably via bridging sulfur atoms, to give a resultant spin of $S = \frac{1}{2}$, consistent with the observed g values. This was the first evidence for a dimeric Fe centre in a protein and was the prototype of many family members subsequently discovered (Gibson 1966).

Cisplatin

Bob Williams had an early involvement in the discovery of the anti-tumour platinum compound cisplatin. It began with his meeting Barnett (Barney) Rosenberg, a biophysicist, in March 1963 at a conference at Stanford, California, about the bioelectrochemistry of electrons and protons. The conductivity of biological materials was at that time a means of understanding electron transfer in proteins. Soon afterwards Barney, working at Michigan

State University, East Lansing, passed high-frequency alternating currents between platinum electrodes across liquid cultures of the common gut bacterium *Escherichia coli*, to see whether the electric field would interfere with cell growth. He was inspired by seeing pictures of mitotic spindles in dividing cells that reminded him, as a physicist, of magnetic lines of force that electrical fields might disturb. The fact that the bacteria possessed no such mitotic apparatus did not deter him. The startling outcome was the observation of reversible filamentation of *E. coli* cells—that is, arrest of the cell division process—caused not directly by the electric field but by dissolution by an alternating current of some platinum from the electrodes. Barney, having no understanding of platinum chemistry, asked Bob for help in identifying the chemical state of platinum that was the causative agent of filamentation. Bob drew this intriguing problem to the attention of his student Andrew Thomson (FRS 1993), who was about to complete his DPhil studying the polarized optical spectra of crystals of platinum(II) salts. On completion of his degree in 1965, Thomson went to work with Barney. He discovered that the *cis* stereoisomers of the Pt(IV) and Pt(II) oxidation states, *cis*-[Pt(IV)(NH$_3$)$_4$Cl$_2$] and *cis*-[Pt(II)(NH$_3$)$_2$Cl$_2$], were highly effective at inhibiting cell division of *E. coli*. Barney immediately tested their efficacy on the experimental tumour sarcoma 180 in mice and showed that *cis*-[Pt(II)(NH$_3$)$_2$Cl$_2$] was highly potent in regressing the tumour. This compound, known as cisplatin, has been widely used against human cancers. It has proved particularly effective against testicular cancer, giving a 95% cure rate of a tumour that, with rising incidence, afflicts young men. (A full account of the discovery is given in Christie & Tansey (2007).) Bob Williams continued his interest in this work over several years, writing a seminal review in 1972, with Thomson and Reslova (26), setting out the chemistry significant for activity and the possible modes of binding to biomolecules, including DNA. This period of reading about cancer and chemotherapy was to stand Bob in good stead when he made his successful application in 1974 for the Royal Society Napier Research Professorship that, as part of its responsibilities, was 'to ascertain the cause of cancer, including any corresponding allied disease and the means of prevention, cure and alleviation'.

Teaching and inorganic texts

Over this period Bob Williams had been teaching undergraduate students inorganic chemistry at Wadham in face-to-face tutorials of one or two. The understanding acquired through research enabled him to begin to systematize the subject. Typically, textbooks then were highly descriptive, giving lists of chemical properties element by element. Williams strove always to find the underlying principles. Together with his friend and colleague from Merton College, Courtney Phillips, Bob undertook to write a major textbook to expound a new approach, calling it simply Inorganic Chemistry. The preface states the novel manner of its organization in the following terms: 'Broad general principles and the comparative chemistry of the elements are given pride of place over the detailed descriptive chemistry of individual compounds.' The book was developed over several years and was based on a one-year course of lectures given to Oxford undergraduates. It is said that, unusually, this lecture course retained a very high attendance throughout, and the lecturers, both of whom attended every lecture, one as observer, were rewarded with a round of applause! Two volumes were published, in 1965 and 1966, by Oxford University Press (17, 18). These books have been widely acclaimed as undoubtedly influential not only in the teaching but also in the deeper understanding of the subject. It can be seen, of course, as the exposition of the subject that must underlie the roles of metal ions in biology. This was to be explored explicitly by Bob Williams in a series of books written later, during his retirement.

RESEARCH FROM 1965 ONWARDS

A year in Harvard

The year 1965 marked a watershed in Williams's career. Up to this point he had followed two parallel threads of research. The first had been to acquire a deeper understanding of the chemistry of the metallic elements, enabling him to describe their pathways and functions in biology. Second, through collaboration with biologists he had applied his understanding of metal ion chemistry to several important biological problems. Thus his prescient realization that proton gradients could act as the carrier of free energy in respiration, his tutorials with Max Perutz on the way in which iron spin-state changes underlay haem cooperativity in haemoglobin, and his work with Vallee on zinc enzymes, all gave him the confidence that he could make progress in biology. But this way of working had become frustrating because, *inter alia*, it did not always yield the appropriate credit due to him. He must work with the proteins themselves.

During 1965–66 Bob spent a sabbatical year at Harvard Medical School. Bert Vallee had arranged a one-year Commonwealth of Massachusetts Fellowship to fund a Harvard visit. Bob took lectures in the biochemistry course for graduates reading medicine; he also read widely in the library and began a piece of research with Professor Gene Kennedy. Working with Kennedy's graduate student, Joan Lusk, on the uptake by *E. coli* of magnesium coupled to the generation of an energized proton gradient was for Bob part of his interest in proton-driven events, although the proton dependence was not followed up (19). He also worked with Warren Wacker in Vallee's laboratory. Using literature data on known levels of sodium, potassium, magnesium and calcium in blood, they published a paper in *The New England Journal of Medicine* that began for Bob a deep interest in calcium (20).

During that year at Harvard, Bob wrote to Wadham College resigning his fellowship in chemistry and requesting appointment to a fellowship in biochemistry. Wadham reluctantly agreed, but only on condition that he took a salary drop. Thus in 1966 Bob Williams became a biochemist in both teaching and research.

The Oxford Enzyme Group

From his earlier discussions with Max Perutz about haemoglobin, Bob Williams had realized that proteins must be dynamic and, indeed, might function as molecular machines. However, protein crystallography at that time gave only a static structure in the crystalline phase, not always revealing function. What of the structure in solution? Spectroscopy could provide a comparison between crystalline and solution phases and even allow the dynamics of molecular structures to be observed. The opportunity for Bob to pursue these ideas arose within the Oxford Enzyme Group, which was formally established in October 1969.

In 1966 D. C. (later Lord) Phillips (FRS 1967), who had solved the first three-dimensional structure of an enzyme, lysozyme, at the Royal Institution, London, moved to Oxford. He set up a new Laboratory of Molecular Biophysics, giving impetus to structural enzyme research at Oxford. At fortnightly dinners, Phillips brought together colleagues from several disciplines to form collaborative groups. NMR equipment, X-ray crystallography and high-speed computation, expensive facilities, would be required for such interdisciplinary research. The Science Research Council (SRC) set up a Joint Enzyme Panel in February 1968, drawn from its Biological Sciences, Chemistry, and Chemical Engineering and Technology Committees, to examine where new enzyme research could profitably be undertaken. The panel included Sir Ewart Jones FRS as chair, D. C. Phillips and J. R. Knowles (FRS 1977), all from Oxford University. In February 1969 the panel recommended that support, 'in ways novel to the SRC', should foster research in the enzyme field, 'a highly interdisciplinary, exciting and economically important field'. In Oxford, by 1969, plans for collaborative research were already well advanced, led by R. E. (later Sir Rex) Richards FRS as chair along with D. C. Phillips, J. R. Knowles and Bob Williams, and including some dozen other participants. The three-year programme at Oxford was funded at the first meeting of the Enzyme Chemistry and Technology Committee in April 1969. The subject was the investigation of proteins and enzymes by diffraction methods and by NMR spectroscopy (Oxford Enzyme Group 1968). In the period 1970–85 the Oxford Enzyme Group became a powerful research unit that pioneered many developments in the determination of the molecular structure of proteins, especially in the rapidly developing field of NMR spectroscopy. During this period, under the leadership of Rex Richards, high-resolution Fourier-transform NMR spectroscopy increased in resolving power, with operating frequencies rising from 270 to 600 MHz. This involved collaboration with the Bruker instrument company. It also required the development of powerful magnetic fields of high uniformity generated by superconducting magnets. Oxford Instruments, the first spin-off company from that university, carried out the research and development required. Their expertise in building superconducting magnets was later to allow them to dominate the field of magnetic resonance imaging for medical diagnostics (Oxford Enzyme Group 1968).

Bob Williams applied the NMR technology to study the structures and dynamics of metalloproteins. In 1972 he was elected to the Fellowship of the Royal Society and in 1974 he was awarded the Napier Royal Society Professorship, freeing him from all teaching duties and giving him the research time required. His team developed methods to assign NMR peaks to specific residues, using the paramagnetism of endogenous metal cofactors including haem in cytochrome c and peroxidases and copper in cupredoxins, as well as lanthanide ions as exogenous shift and broadening reagents. Signals from aromatic residues allowed the measurement of degrees of rotational mobility on both protein surfaces and interiors, giving the first evidence of the relative motion of protein α helices. By using lysozyme as a model with pulsed NMR techniques to measure slow exchange rates, the local movements of groups and small segments were demonstrated and shown to allow the fast recognition and binding of substrate. Order–disorder transitions in response to the binding of calcium and zinc ions in calmodulin, osteocalcin and metallothionine were also studied. The motions of protein helices within domains relative to helices or sheets in other domains could act as triggers like mechanical devices. The contributions of the Williams group to our understanding of protein mobility have been summarized (30). By combining NMR and X-ray diffraction methods with theoretical approaches, views of protein structure were changed to one that incorporated dynamics ranging from conventional vibronic–rotational coupling to disordered motions characteristic of random polymers. Only the understanding of dynamics, Bob maintained, could lead to a full appreciation of function.

Over this period Bob had many outstanding collaborators, including the late Iain Campbell (FRS 1995), Raymond Dwek (FRS 1998), Chris Dobson (FRS 1996), Allen Hill (FRS 1990), Peter Sadler (FRS 2005), the late Antonio Xavier, Geoff Moore, Barry Levine, Peter Wright,

Glyn Williams, Rachel Klevit and Nigel Clayden. Early in this period Iain Campbell set about trying to solve complete protein structures in solution by NMR, but with rather limited success. Eventually procedures that allowed the complete determination of protein structures in solution were devised by the group of Kurt Wüthrich (ForMemRS 2010) working at the Eidgenössische Technische Hochschule, Zurich.

Biominerals

In the late 1970s Bob became increasingly fascinated by biological minerals. A medical condition causing him to lose balance had alerted him to the nature of tiny crystalline particles of calcium carbonate, called otoconia, present in the inner ear that sense gravity and acceleration. Bob also met Professor Derek Birchall (FRS 1982) (Kelly 1997), a visiting fellow at Wolfson College, Oxford, between 1977 and 1979. Birchall had spent his career at ICI becoming a distinguished materials scientist, an expert in alumina, silica and their colloidal and hydrated forms, inventing new cements. He drew attention to the remarkable shapes of shells as well as their mechanical properties, including tensile strength. Bob wished to understand the roles of an organic matrix in initiating crystal nucleation and regulating growth within compartments, especially biological cells. Together with two able students, Steve Mann (FRS 2003) and Carole Perry, he began a study of the biological mineralization of calcium carbonate, silica and iron oxides, among many. Initial experiments showed that it was relatively easy to precipitate and grow crystals such as silver salts inside small compartments including liposomes. Jerry Skarnulis modified an electron microscope for these studies. In addition to the spatial resolution, new developments in the technique gave the ability to track metal ions and anions by using their characteristic X-ray fluorescence (28).

Bob came across the beautiful work of the naturalist Ernst Haeckel, who by 1887 had identified and illustrated more than 150 new protozoa, *Radiolaria*, that produce highly symmetrical skeletons 0.1–0.2 mm in diameter. Bob's group investigated *Acantharia*, organisms that produce exoskeletons made of strontium sulfate spicules, and the green algae, desmids, that use barium sulfate. The exoskeleton of *Acantharia* is made of 20 spines, each a single crystal of strontium sulfate, that radiate from a single point towards the surface of a sphere (figure 6). The directions of the spines are true crystallographic planes (31).

Silicon, one of the commonest elements on Earth, is little used in animals or broad-leaved plants, but grasses use silica not only to strengthen structures but also to act as a defence against both biomechanical and biochemical predation. Williams and Perry studied the fine hairs on the leaves of stinging nettle, which are miniature tubes terminated by small balls of amorphous silica. When the hair enters the skin, the ball breaks off and a liquid poison is squirted into the body (29). With typical insight Bob reached the conclusion that plants use silica as a building material to harden their structures because the sap of a plant has an acid pH of about 5 compared with that of circulating fluids in animals, which is about 7.5. At the low pH in sap, calcium carbonates (shell) and phosphates (bone) are too soluble to precipitate, whereas the solubility of silica is independent of pH over this range.

RETIREMENT AND THE WRITING OF BOOKS

Bob retired in 1991, relinquishing his Royal Society Napier Research Professorship and ceasing laboratory-based research. He devoted himself to writing a series of major books

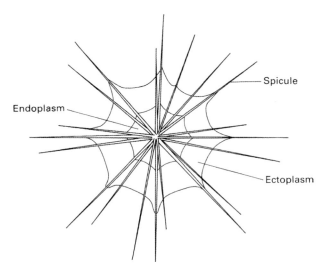

Figure 6. The skeleton of the unicellular, eukaryotic, diatom *Acantharia* consisting of 20 spicules, each a single crystal of strontium sulfate ($SrSO_4$). (Taken from p. 477 of (32), by permission of Oxford University Press.)

setting out the understanding of the roles of metal ions in biology that he had acquired over the preceding 40 years. Five were co-authored with his friend John Fraústo da Silva, who had originally proposed that they should write a book together on biological inorganic chemistry. They had met in 1955 when John studied in Oxford with Irving. John became Professor of Chemistry in Lisbon, later sending some of his finest pupils to Oxford to work with Bob. His contributions to the books were clarification, critical evaluation, and correction. Bob said he could not have written them on his own.

The aims of the first book, *The biological chemistry of the elements* (32), published in 1991, were to

describe the functional value of the chemical elements in living organisms, free or combined with the actual biological molecules *in vivo*, the reasons for the selection of such elements, the processes of their uptake, transport and final localization in cells, the regulation of these processes and the control of their reactions in a very complex holistic system which includes the interactions with their environments.

A second, updated, edition was published in 2001.

This volume, however, did not touch upon the roles of the availability and chemistry of the elements in evolution. Three further books discussed this intriguing aspect. The first, with John Fraústo da Silva in 1996, was called *The natural selection of the chemical elements* (34), and in 2006 appeared *The chemistry of evolution: the development of our ecosystem* (36), again co-authored with John. These dealt with the principles underlying the selection of chemical elements for their functional value to a biological organism and the relationship to Darwinian selection. A discussion of the possible consequences of man's industrial mobilization of elements not hitherto exposed to biology raised the question of whether mankind is entering a new stage of natural selection.

The title of Bob's book published in 2012 with R. E. M. Rickaby, Professor of Biogeochemistry, Department of Earth Sciences, Oxford University, was *Evolution's destiny:*

co-evolving chemistry of the environment and life (37). Only recently has the Earth's geochemical record become detailed enough to be placed alongside the biological trees of evolution. The matching of timescales has led to many new insights into the chemical influences on the course of evolution. Williams and Rickaby examine the development of the chemistry of an ecosystem that took place alongside evolution as set out by Darwin, a random, competitive, selection process. The authors show that a major feature of life and its evolution is a changing availability and utilization of selected inorganic chemical elements from their environment into cells. For example, one particular problem examined is the changing role of inorganic elements in the evolution of an ecosystem. Production of oxygen, a waste product of photosynthesizing cells, relatively rapidly initiated major changes in inorganic chemistry such as the oxidation of water-soluble iron, $Fe(II)$, to insoluble oxides of iron, $Fe(III)$, making this element less available to cells. This contrasts with the increasing biological availability of potentially poisonous copper, as soluble $Cu(II)$, from insoluble $Cu(I)$, copper sulfides. This book, his last major publication, has the broad intellectual sweep typical of Bob's work. It completes his scientific journey seeking to understand questions that had intrigued him as a schoolboy.

LIFE AT WADHAM COLLEGE

Historically, Wadham College, founded in 1614, had not been particularly distinguished except for early meetings of a group that was to lay the foundations of the Royal Society. The group met at Wadham under the leadership of Bishop Wilkins, Warden of Wadham, and sometime later Bishop of Chester, who became Founding Secretary of the Royal Society at Gresham College, London. Bob Williams took up his tutorial fellowship at Wadham in 1954, when the college was led by the highly successful, bluff Warden, Sir Maurice Bowra. The college was determined to improve itself academically. Wadham then, and still today, was different from many Oxford colleges in that it recruited most of its students from grammar schools. This was a policy born of necessity, because the college was not richly endowed and therefore did not have the history of connections with public schools as did some other Oxford colleges. The opportunity for Wadham came at the end of World War II, when the government decided that higher education should be free. Hence students coming from grammar schools as well as those returning from the war provided the opportunity for Wadham to increase student recruitment and expand. Bowra's leadership and forceful personality created among the fellows an *esprit de corps* that rapidly developed the college. Bob firmly believed success to be a matter of selecting young people carefully, guiding them and giving much time and effort to teaching them. Wadham now has some 300 undergraduates, nearly all paid for by the government. The physics fellow, Tom Keeley, a close associate of Lord Lindemann FRS, was the first science fellow of the modern era. Bob initially was the only chemistry fellow. Because more help was needed from fellows capable of tutorial teaching of organic and physical chemistries as well as biochemistry, Bob raised funds, including the Tate & Lyle Bequest. This enabled Jeremy Knowles to be appointed as the first tutor in organic chemistry. Later a fellow in physical chemistry was appointed, and in 1967 Bob himself became tutor in biochemistry. Bob was always a vigorous energizer, persuading the college to expand, to appoint new fellows and research fellows, and to build new buildings. He had no need of formal positions of authority.

Figure 7. Bob making a point, 1985. (Reproduced with kind permission of
the family of R. J. P. Williams.) (Online version in colour.)

THE MAN

Bob Williams was a brilliant scientist who developed considerably our understanding of the chemistry that underlies biology. As a teenager he had read about Darwin's theory of evolution, selection by the survival of the fittest, and realized that the chemistry of the elements themselves must also provide a critical restraint on the evolution of species. He determined to explore how this chemistry might play such a role. His quest for that biological chemistry was to underpin all the science he undertook over 65 years until the day he died. His work, carried out from his base at Oxford University, not only inspired several generations of able research students and fellows, many of whom went on to have successful careers developing the ideas seeded by Bob; he also pioneered the establishment of a new subject known, somewhat paradoxically, as bioinorganic chemistry.

Bob's way of working was unusual. He had little direct involvement in experiments himself. Bob said he actually disliked laboratories, finding them uninspiring places. He preferred to think on his own or with scientists from outside his discipline. Because the research canvas Bob had chosen was wide, he needed to gather knowledge from different areas of chemistry and biological science to find links. His students would jokingly complain about his experimental incompetence. They remarked that 'each day brings a different idea', which had to be converted into an experiment and carried out. A friend once said, 'I have never heard you lecture on the same topic twice.' This was not wholly true but Bob did move quickly from problem to problem. His great strength was to be able to assimilate knowledge widely, thereby gaining deep insights and drawing original conclusions. This method of pursuing science, in multidisciplinary research teams, has become commonplace today.

Bob was vigorous and forthright, but always open and honest, in debating and advocating his ideas (figure 7). He was not slow to challenge when he thought he saw error or

Figure 8. Jim Fraser, Tom Wess, Clive Fell and Bob Williams by Pen-Y-Gwryd, the climber's hotel at the foot of Snowdon. (Reproduced with kind permission of the family of R. J. P. Williams.) (Online version in colour.)

misunderstanding. This strongly competitive spirit sometimes led to friction with other scientists, as has been described earlier. He was often in correspondence with scientists. His ideas and teaching helped many to win accolades, some of whom did not always acknowledge their debt to him. This affronted his strong sense of justice and decent behaviour.

Throughout his career he avoided committee work, claiming he was temperamentally unsuited. He was impatient of such meetings although he did occasionally intervene, usually forcefully, when he foresaw that a bad decision was about to be made. He did make exceptions: he agreed to become President of the Chemistry Section of the British Association for the Advancement of Science in 1985–86 and President of the Dalton Division of the Royal Society of Chemistry between 1991 and 1993.

His mastery of chemistry and deep insights across disciplines made him a charismatic and inspiring teacher of undergraduates and research students. One of Bob's many successful students has said, 'Bob's style of lateral thinking, both as tutor and as research supervisor, profoundly influenced my own approach to looking for novel insights.' Research lectures in many countries never failed to inspire. The books he has left illustrate those qualities.

Bob balanced his vigorous and busy life in science with a happy and supportive family life and a passion for the isolation and beauty of the countryside. Wytham Woods, on a hill just outside Oxford, became a favourite place to escape from Oxford itself. Frequently, from his undergraduate days onwards, Bob went wandering alone on the more remote trails. As a boy he was introduced to walking in north Wales by his parents. His mathematics teacher at school, Mr Eggleshaw, taught him to climb rocks in the mountains of Wales. This remained his favourite landscape for the rest of his life.

Every year in May he visited Snowdonia with three lifelong friends, Jim Fraser, Tom Wess and Clive Fell: a vicar, the export manager of a large company, and a music teacher (figure 8). They always stayed in a climber's hotel, the Pen-Y-Gwryd, at the foot of Snowdon. In the evenings after a long day tramping the hills a few drinks were shared, before putting the world to rights. Bob walked in many mountainous regions of the globe, sometimes as a side trip after attending a conference.

Figure 9. Jelly and Bob with sons, John and Tim in 1958.
(Reproduced with kind permission of the family of R. J. P. Williams)

Bob's strong sense of justice was demonstrated if he felt that a public organization was making bad decisions. He was more than willing to write to the papers to highlight nepotism or official lies. For example, during the miners' strike of the Thatcher era, he wrote to both the Coal Board and the government, trying to persuade them that they were not able to justify their decision to close the pits on logical grounds. He was also strongly committed to the local neighbourhood of north Oxford, where he lived. He cajoled Oxford City Council into converting a large area of derelict land, then used as a rubbish tip, into parkland for all members of the public. For this he received an MBE from The Queen, his proudest achievement of all.

MARRIAGE AND FAMILY

During his stay in Uppsala in 1950 as a Rotary Fellow, Bob met Jelly Büchli, from Groningen, Holland, a vivacious student studying languages. They took long cycle rides together around the countryside of Sweden and even went skiing in the far north. On one occasion when they were cycling home with some eggs in the front basket, some of the eggs fell out and broke on the road. Not wishing to waste money, Jelly leapt off her bike, scooped up the eggs, told him to open his mouth and poured the broken eggs in. Around Easter time they became engaged. Jelly was against rings and 'wasting money on rubbish', so Bob bought her a small brass curtain ring to seal their match. They were married in July 1952. Jelly soon settled into Oxford life. She read English language and literature at St Hilda's College between 1952 and 1955. However, her final exams were interrupted by the birth of their first son, Tim. He was followed two years later by John (figure 9), who became a successful museum designer. Tim qualified as a clinical psychologist and married Nicki, a family doctor. They have three children, Nuala, Kirsten and Jack.

Bob was a devoted family man, taking great pleasure in spending time with his sons and the grandchildren (figure 10). His wife and sons accompanied him to the USA for his sabbatical

Figure 10. Bob with his granddaughters. (Reproduced with kind permission of the family of R. J. P. Williams) (Online version in colour.)

leave at Harvard in 1967. They drove to Montreal to visit Expo 67 that summer. He took them to the mountains of Wales, Cadair Idris being a particular favourite. When the grandchildren arrived, Bob found new roles including, at Christmas, as a designer and constructor of large cardboard structures in which presents were hidden. This included a 6-foot-long Christmas cracker hung over the stairs at home and a 20-foot-long cardboard Eurotunnel, which had to be negotiated to find the presents. He devised a variety of imaginative pursuits to keep them occupied on their frequent babysitting visits.

His family claim that Bob's special gifts have been passed to his descendants. The art of bodging an unattractive but effective repair is known as a 'Williams job', said to be eagerly practised even by the grandchildren. Another is the unerring ability to find boggy or wet ground on any, and every, walk even after months of drought.

When the children had left home, Bob and Jelly travelled widely together (figure 11), sometimes on side trips from a conference. Throughout their long marriage Jelly was a rock of stability for Bob from the vicissitudes of science.

Not only was Bob an inveterate letter writer in his professional life but he also left behind a letter to his family. It was first written before his heart bypass in 1995, but re-dated as each health crisis came and went.

Dearest Jelly and family,

I just want to write a few words in case I do not escape the operation. I have had a wonderful life and nobody gave more to me than you, especially Jelly but I think about Tim and John, Nicki,

Figure 11. Jelly and Bob in Kazakhstan in 1984. (Reproduced with kind permission of the family of R. J. P. Williams.) (Online version in colour.)

Nuala, Kirsten (how do you spell it) and Jack. I have no sense that I have missed out on anything. Thank you.

I leave only one instruction—do not let yourselves do anything but live as you wish for your own fulfilment. I do not want to be a shadow in the background but rather a spirit joining you in the same joys and happiness we have had together.

Bob Williams died in the John Radcliffe hospital in Oxford on 21 March 2015.

Awards, honours and visiting appointments

Civic honour

2010   MBE

Royal Society honours

1974–91   Napier Research Professor
1979   Hughes Medal
1995   Royal Medal

Membership of foreign academies

1981   Lisbon Academy of Science
               Royal Society of Science, Liège
1984   Royal Swedish Academy of Science
1989   Czechoslovakian Academy of Science
1993   Member of Academia Europaea

Academic medals

1970	Tilden Medal, Chemical Society
1972	Keilin Medal, Biochemical Society
1979	Liversidge Medal, Royal Society of Chemistry
1980	Claire Brylants Medal, University of Louvain
1985	Sir Hans Krebs Medal, European Biochemical Society
1986	Linderstrom-Lang Medal, Copenhagen
1987	Sigillum Magnum Medal, University of Bologna
1989	Sir Frederick Gowland Hopkins Medal, Biochemical Society
1998	Heyrovsky Medal, International Union of Biochemistry
2002	Longstaff Medal, Royal Society of Chemistry

Honorary doctorates

1980	University of Liège
1985	University of Leicester
1992	University of East Anglia
1993	University of Keele
1996	University of Lisbon

Appointments

1985–86 President, Chemistry Section of British Association for the Advancement of Science

1991–93 President, Dalton Division of the Royal Society of Chemistry

ACKNOWLEDGEMENTS

The authors would like to thank the members of Bob's family for their help with this memoir, especially Jelly Williams and Bob and Jelly's son, Tim. We have also drawn heavily on two accounts of his life: a lengthy interview with Bob by H.A.O.H. published in (33) and a candid autobiography to which the authors have kindly been given access by the family. We also thank friends, former colleagues, and students for their comments and contributions, particularly Peter Day FRS, Steve Mann FRS, Carole Perry, Robin Perutz FRS and Peter Sadler FRS. Jane Nightingale kindly typed the bibliography.

The frontispiece photograph was taken by Godfrey Argent and is reproduced with permission.

AUTHOR PROFILES

H. A. O. Hill

Photograph by Veronika Vernier

H. Allen O. Hill studied Chemistry at Queen's University Belfast and, after his PhD with Reg Bacon, moved to Oxford, where he worked with Bob Williams. He was appointed a fellow of Queen's College, Oxford, in 1965. Hill and Williams investigated the chemistry of vitamin B_{12}, leading to a study of the enzyme dioldehydrase. Although involved in high-field NMR spectroscopy of biomolecules, Hill initiated attempts to obtain electrochemistry directly between electrodes and redox proteins. While seeking to obtain direct electrochemistry with glucose oxidase, Hill's team discovered that ferrocene was a highly effective mediator. Thus the glucose electrode was born that became the basis of a highly successful sensor that is widely used by diabetic patients. Subsequently he explored the scanning probe microscopy of proteins on surfaces, seeking structure–function relationships. Hill was elected to the Fellowship of the Royal Society in 1990, and was awarded the Mullard Medal in 1993 (with M. J. Green and A. E. G. Cass) and the Royal Medal in 2010.

A. J. Thomson

Between 1959 and 1965 Andrew Thomson was taught chemistry at Wadham College, Oxford, by R. J. P. Williams. After his doctorate he worked with Barnett Rosenberg for two years in the Biophysics Department at Michigan State University, where he discovered a platinum complex that inhibited the cell division of *Escherichia coli*. Known as cisplatin, this compound was the first metal-based anti-tumour agent to be widely deployed; it proved especially effective against testicular cancer. Thomson spent his independent research career at the School of Chemical Sciences, University of East Anglia (UEA), Norwich, where he served as Head of School and then Dean of Science. He developed the application of magnetic circular dichroism spectroscopy, particularly at variable fields and temperatures, to probe the structures of metal centres, such as haem and iron–sulfur clusters, in large multicentred proteins. With the late Colin Greenwood from the School of Biology, UEA, he founded a highly successful inter-disciplinary unit, the Centre for Metalloprotein Spectroscopy and Biology, that attracted many young, and successful, faculty members. He was elected to the Fellowship of the Royal Society in 1993 and awarded the OBE in 2008.

REFERENCES BY OTHER AUTHORS

Christie, D. A. & Tansey, E. M. (eds) 2007 *The discovery and impact of platinum salts as chemotherapy agents for cancer* (Wellcome Witnesses to Twentieth Century Medicine, vol. 30). London: Wellcome Trust Centre for the History of Medicine at UCL (available at http://www.histmodbiomed.org/sites/default/files/44855.pdf).

Dodson, G. 2002 Dorothy Mary Crowfoot Hodgkin OM. *Biogr. Mems Fell. R. Soc.* **48**, 179–219 (http://dx.doi.org/10.1098/rsbm.2002.0011).

Ferry, G. 2007 *Max Perutz and the secret of life*. London: Chatto & Windus.

Gibson, J. F., Hall, D. O., Thornley, J. H. M. & Whatley, F. R. 1966 The iron complex in spinach ferredoxin. *Proc. Natl Acad. Sci. USA* **56**, 987–990 (available at http://www.pnas.org/content/56/3/987.full.pdf).

Jørgensen, C. K., Owen, J., Griffith, J. S., Figgis, B., Williams, R. J. P., Orgel, L. E., Rossotti, F. J. C., Englman, R., Sharp, D. W. A., Magnusson, E. A., Brown, M. G., Chatt, J., Prue, J. E., Staveley, L. A. K. & Sharpe, A. G. 1958 General discussion. In *Ions of the transition elements* (*Discuss. Faraday Soc.* no. 26), 172–192 (http://dx.doi.org/10.1039/DF9582600172).

Kelly, A. 1997 Derek Birchall. *Biogr. Mems Fell. R. Soc.* **43**, 89–104 (http://dx.doi.org/10.1098/rsbm.1997.0006).

Mitchell, P. D. 1961 Coupling of phosphorylation to electron and hydrogen transfer by a chemi-osmotic type of mechanism. *Nature* **191**, 144–148 (http://dx.doi.org/10.1038/191144a0).

Orgel, L. E. 1952 The effects of crystal fields on the properties of transition metal ions. *J. Chem. Soc.*, 4756–4761 (http://dx.doi.org/10.1039/JR9520004756).

Oxford Enzyme Group 1968 Minutes, agendas, circulars, membership records *et al.* for 1968–90. Bodleian Library, Special Collections, Oxford University. Accession codes NCUACS18.3.90 and NRA 33208.

Pauling, L. & Coryell, C. D. 1936 The magnetic properties and structure of haemoglobin, oxyhemoglobin and carbonmonoxyhaemoglobin. *Proc. Natl Acad. Sci. USA* **22**, 210–216 (available at http://www.ncbi.nlm.nih. gov/pmc/articles/PMC1076743/pdf/pnas01768-0018.pdf).

Perutz, M. F. 1970 Stereochemistry of cooperative effects in haemoglobin: haem–haem interaction and the problem of allostery. *Nature* **228**, 726–734 (http://dx.doi.org/10.1038/228726a0).

Pratt, J. M. 1972 *Inorganic chemistry of B$_{12}$*. New York: Academic Press.

Schäffer, C. E. 1994 Jannick Bjerrum (1909–1992): his early years. In *Coordination chemistry: a century of progress* (ACS Symposium Series, no. 565) (ed. G. B. Kauffman), p. 96. Oxford University Press.

Schlapp, R. & Penney, W. G. 1932 The influence of crystalline fields on the susceptibilities of salts of paramagnetic ions. II. The iron group, especially Ni, Cr and Co. *Phys. Rev.* **42**, 666–686 (http://dx.doi.org/10.1103/PhysRev.42.666).

Slater, E. C. 1994 Peter Dennis Mitchell. *Biogr. Mems Fell. R. Soc.* **40**, 282–305 (http://dx.doi.org/10.1098/rsbm.1994.0040).

Weber, B. H. & Prebble, J. N. 2006 An issue of originality and priority: the correspondence and theories of oxidative phosphorylation of Peter Mitchell and Robert J. P. Williams, 1961–1980. *J. Hist. Biol.* **39**, 125–163 (http://dx.doi.org/10.1007/s10739-005-3052-4).

BIBLIOGRAPHY

The following publications are those referred to directly in the text. A full bibliography is available as electronic supplementary material at http://dx.doi.org/10.1098/rsbm.2016.0020 or via http://rsbm.royalsocietypublishing.org.

(1) 1948 (With H. Irving) Order of stability of metal complexes. *Nature* **162**, 746–747 (http://dx.doi. org/10.1038/162746a0).

(2) 1952 Gradient elution analysis. *Analyst* **77**, 905–914 (http://dx.doi.org/10.1039/AN9527700905).

(3) 1953 (With H. Irving) The stability of transition-metal complexes. *J. Chem. Soc.*, 3192–3210 (http://dx.doi. org/10.1039/JR9530003192).

(4)   Metal ions in biological systems. *Biol. Rev.* **28**, 381–412 (http://dx.doi.org/10.1111/j.1469-185X.1953. tb01384.x).

(5) 1956 The properties of metalloporphyrins. *Chem. Rev.* **56**, 299–328 (http://dx.doi.org/10.1021/cr50008a004).

(6) 1958 (With J. C. Tomkinson) Absorption spectra of some ferrous and ferric complexes. *J. Chem. Soc.*, 1153–1158 (http://dx.doi.org/10.1039/JR9580001153).

(7)   (With B. L. Vallee & T. L. Coombs) Spectrophotometric evidence for enzyme inhibitor complexation. *J. Am. Chem. Soc.* **80**, 397–401 (http://dx.doi.org/10.1021/ja01535a038).

(8)   (With F. L. Hoch & B. L. Vallee) The role of zinc in alcohol dehydrogenases. II. The kinetics of the instantaneous reversible inhibition of yeast alcohol dehydrogenase by 1,10-phenanthroline. *J. Biol. Chem.* **232**, 453–464 (available at http://www.jbc.org/content/232/1/453.full.pdf).

(9) 1959 Coordination, chelation and catalysis. In *The enzymes*, 2nd edn (ed. P. D. Boyer, H. Lardy & K. Myrbäck), vol. 1, pp. 391–422. New York: Academic Press.

(10) 1960 Binding of zinc in carboxypeptidase. *Nature* **188**, 322 (http://dx.doi.org/10.1038/188322a0).

(11) 1961 Possible functions of chains of catalysts. *J. Theor. Biol.* **1**, 1–17 (http://dx.doi.org/10.1016/0022-5193(61)90023-6).

(12)   (With B. R. James) The oxidation–reduction potentials of some copper complexes. *J. Chem. Soc.*, 2007–2019 (http://dx.doi.org/10.1039/JR9610002007).

(13)   (With A. S. Brill) The absorption spectra, magnetic moments and the binding of iron in some haemoproteins.. *Biochem. J.* **78**, 246–253 (available at http://www.biochemj.org/content/ppbiochemj/78/2/246.full.pdf).

(14) 1962 (With P. C. H. Mitchell) Some complexes of molybdenum. *J. Chem. Soc.*, 4570–4578 (http://dx.doi. org/10.1039/JR9620004570).

(15) 1963 (With P. S. Braterman & P. B. P. Phipps) Electron transfer in some solids containing complex ions. *Proc. Chem. Soc.*, 12 (http://dx.doi.org/10.1039/PS9630000001).

(16) 1964 (With P. S. Braterman & R. C. Davies) The properties of metal–porphyrin and similar complexes. *Adv. Chem. Phys.* **7**, 360–407.

(17)   1965   (With C. S. G. Phillips) *Inorganic chemistry*, vol. 1 (Principles and non-metals). Oxford University Press.

(18)   1966   (With C. S. G. Phillips) *Inorganic chemistry*, vol. 2 (The chemistry of the metals). Oxford University Press.

(19)   1968   (With J. E. Lusk & E. P. Kennedy) Magnesium and the growth of *Escherichia coli*. *J. Biol. Chem.* **243**, 2618–2624 (available at http://www.jbc.org/content/243/10/2618.full.pdf).

(20)   (With W. E. C. Wacker) Magnesium-calcium balances and steady states of biological systems. *J. Theor. Biol.* **20**, 65–78 (http://dx.doi.org/10.1016/0022-5193(68)90092-1).

(21)   (With D. Culpin, P. Day & P. R. Edwards) Charge transfer in mixed-valence solids. Part III. Spectra and semiconductivity of chlorocuprates(I,II). *J. Chem. Soc.* A, 1838–1842 (http://dx.doi.org/10.1039/J19680001838).

(22)   (With P. K. Das, H. A. O. Hill & J. M. Pratt) The chemistry of vitamin B_{12}. Part VIII. Controlled potential reduction of vitamin B_{12a}. *J. Chem. Soc.*, 1261–1264 (http://dx.doi.org/10.1039/J19680001261).

(23)   (With B. L. Vallee) Metallo-enzymes: the entatic nature of their active sites. *Proc. Natl Acad. Sci. USA* **59**, 498–505 (available at http://www.ncbi.nlm.nih.gov/pmc/articles/PMC224700/pdf/pnas00116-0196.pdf).

(24)   1970   (With S. A. Cockle, H. A. O. Hill, B. E. Mann & J. M. Pratt) The 220 MHz and 60 MHz ^{1}H NMR spectra of 5′-deoxyadenosylcobalamin and cobinamide coenzymes. *Biochim. Biophys. Acta* **215**, 415–418 (http://dx.doi.org/10.1016/0304-4165(70)90043-7).

(25)   1971   (With G. Agnes, H. A. O. Hill, J. M. Pratt, S. C. Ridsdale & F. S. Kennedy) Methyl transfer from methyl vitamin B_{12}. *Biochim. Biophys. Acta* **252**, 207–211 (http://dx.doi.org/10.1016/0304-4165(71)90109-7).

(26)   1972   (With A. J. Thomson & S. Reslova) The chemistry of complexes related to cis-Pt(NH$_3$)$_2$Cl$_2$. An anti-tumour drug. In *Biochemistry* (*Structure and bonding*, vol. 11), pp. 1–46. Berlin: Springer.

(27)   (With S. A. Cockle, H. A. O. Hill, S. P. Davies & M. A. Foster) The detection of intermediates during the conversion of propane-1,2-diol to propionaldehyde by glyceroldehydrase, a coenzyme B_{12} dependent reaction. *J. Am. Chem. Soc.* **94**, 275–277.

(28)   1984   An introduction to biominerals and the role of organic molecules in their formation. *Phil. Trans. R. Soc. Lond.* B **304**, 411–424 (http://dx.doi.org/10.1098/rstb.1984.0035).

(29)   (With C. C. Perry & S. Mann) Structural and analytical studies of the silicified macrohairs from the lemma of the grass *Phalaris canariensis* L. *Proc. R. Soc. Lond.* B **222**, 427–438 (http://dx.doi.org/10.1098/rspb.1984.0074).

(30)   1989   NMR studies of mobility within protein structure. *FEBS J.* **183**, 479–497 (http://dx.doi.org/10.1111/j.1432-1033.1989.tb21076.x).

(31)   (With N. P. Hughes, C. C. Perry & O. R. Anderson) Biological minerals formed from strontium and barium sulphates. III. The morphology and crystallography of strontium sulphate crystals from the colonial radiolarian, *Sphaerozoum punctatum*. *Proc. R. Soc. Lond.* B **238**, 223–233 (http://dx.doi.org/10.1098/rspb.1989.0078).

(32)   1991   (With J. J. R. Fraústo da Silva) *The biological chemistry of the elements: the inorganic chemistry of life*. Oxford: Clarendon Press.

(33)   1993   (With H. A. O. Hill) A celebration of inorganic lives. Interview of R. J. P. Williams (Wadham College, Oxford). *Coord. Chem. Rev.* **122**, 3–39 (http://dx.doi.org/10.1016/0010-8545(93)90002-X).

(34)   1996   (With J. J. R. Fraústo da Silva) *The natural selection of the chemical elements*. Oxford: Clarendon Press.

(35)   2000   (With H. B. Gray & B. G. Malmström) Copper coordination in blue proteins. *J. Biol. Inorg. Chem.* **5**, 551–559 (http://dx.doi.org/10.1007/s007750000146).

(36)   2006   (With J. J. R. Fraústo da Silva) *The chemistry of evolution: the development of our ecosystem*. Amsterdam: Elsevier.

(37)   2012   (With R. E. M. Rickaby) *Evolution's destiny: co-evolving chemistry of the environment and life*. Cambridge: RSC Publishing (http://dx.doi.org/10.1039/9781849735599).